ROMANS

Also by James Montgomery Boice

ROMANS

Volume 3

God and History

Romans 9–11

JAMES MONTGOMERY BOICE

Baker Books

A Division of Baker Book House Co.
Grand Rapids, Michigan 49516

Published by Baker Books
a division of Baker Book House Company
P.O. Box 6287, Grand Rapids, Michigan 49516-6287

Fourth printing, April 2000

Printed in the United States of America

Library of Congress Cataloging-in-Publication Data

Boice, James Montgomery, 1938–
    Romans : An expositional commentary / James Montgomery Boice
        p.   cm.
    Includes bibliographical references and indexes.
    Contents: v. 1. Justification by faith, Romans 1–4 — v. 2. The reign of grace,
Romans 5–8 — v. 3. God and history, Romans 9–11.
    ISBN 0-8010-1002-0 (v. 1)
    ISBN 0-8010-1003-9 (v. 2)
    ISBN 0-8010-1058-6 (v. 3)
    1. Bible. N.T.—Romans—Commentaries. I. Title.
BS2665.3.B58 1991
227′.1077—dc20   91-7204

For current information about academic books, resources for Christian leaders, and all
new releases available from Baker Book House Company, visit our web site:
http://www.bakerbooks.com/

To **HIM**
from whom,
through whom,
and to whom
are all things

Contents

Preface

I am writing the preface to the third volume on my studies of Romans the same week I have finished my studies of the magnificent doxology with which the apostle Paul ends the great eleventh chapter:

> Oh, the depth of the riches of the wisdom and knowledge of God!
>> How unsearchable his judgments,
>> and his paths beyond tracing out!
> "Who has known the mind of the Lord?
>> Or who has been his counselor?"
> "Who has ever given to God,
>> that God should repay him?"
> For from him and through him and to him are all things.
>> To him be the glory forever! Amen.

I have been blessed as I studied this doxology. But I have also realized in a fresh way that it expresses the secret of Paul's extraordinary power as a teacher of the things of God. Paul did not begin with man, as we tend to do in our man-oriented, need-directed churches. Paul began with God! Moreover, he continued with God, knowing that anything of true spiritual value is accomplished only through God and by God's power. And he ended with God, too, in the sense that everything he did was for God's glory.

What a difference it would make if our churches could recapture the apostle's God-centered and God-directed orientation. But, of course, it is not likely to happen, not in the direction we are going. Instead of thinking about God more and coming to know him better, today's Christians spend most of their time thinking about themselves and are therefore bogged down in miserable self-contemplation and analysis, instead of being set free to love and serve God with all their heart, mind, soul, and strength.

This sad prevailing attitude has had its bearing on the study of Romans 9–11, or perhaps I should say on a neglect of a study of these chapters. I do not think it is too much to say that few Christians study them at all, and few preachers preach on them at all. Why? Because they are difficult, perhaps. But most of all because they are focused on the glory and ways of God, more than any other comparable section of the Bible, and because they pull us along in directions we find it uncomfortable to travel.

These themes will stretch our minds—and mind stretching, like any other kind of rigorous exercise, will be painful. But it will be good for us, and it is necessary for us if we are to be strong Christians, equipped by God to challenge the errors and evils of our age with a truly robust Christianity.

In each of my books I like to thank the Session and congregation of Tenth Presbyterian Church in Philadelphia for encouraging me in this kind of careful Bible study and exegetical, doctrinal preaching. I believe they have profited from it over the quarter-century I have been the senior minister of the church, and I know I have. To them and to some others, the material in this book will be somewhat familiar, since the chapters are essentially the sermons I preached to the Tenth Presbyterian congregation from September 1990 to July 1992. They were also aired over the internationally heard "Bible Study Hour" broadcast during 1991 and 1992.

No religion is stronger than its god, and in the case of Christianity, no Christians have ever been stronger than their knowledge of the true God and their desire to obey and glorify him. May God bless these studies to lead many to know more of the character and the greatness of our God, and may many be revitalized as a result. "For from him and through him and to him are all things. To him be the glory forever! Amen."

Philadelphia, Pennsylvania

Part Eleven

Paul and His People

122

What in the World Is God Doing?

Romans 9:1-5

I speak the truth in Christ—I am not lying, my conscience confirms it in the Holy Spirit—I have great sorrow and unceasing anguish in my heart. For I could wish that I myself were cursed and cut off from Christ for the sake of my brothers, those of my own race, the people of Israel. Theirs is the adoption as sons; theirs the divine glory, the covenants, the receiving of the law, the temple worship and the promises. Theirs are the patriarchs, and from them is traced the human ancestry of Christ, who is God over all, forever praised! Amen.

I n the ninth, tenth, and eleventh chapters of Romans, we are dealing with a Christian philosophy of history. It is a philosophy that we can ask as a question, namely: "What in the world is God doing?" Or we can be a bit more precise and ask: "What is God doing in world history?" Or even: "What is he doing with me? Where have I come from? Why am I here? Where am I going when I die?"

There has never been a more important moment in which to ask these questions, because people in our day have lost, not only the Christian answers to them but even the hope of finding them. The great art historian Erwin Panofsky, in a book called *Studies in Iconology*, has pointed out how the figure of Father Time has changed in western art history. In the ancient world, time was pictured positively. It was portrayed by symbols of speed, power, balance, and fertility. In our world, time is pictured as an aged man, accompanied by a scythe, representing death, and an hourglass. In other words, time is pictured negatively. Panofsky terms our view "Time the Destroyer" and traces it to our failure to find any genuine meaning either in world history or in our own personal histories.[1]

Our view is that of the carnival barker's cry as the revolving wheel of fortune turns: "Round and round and round she goes, and where she stops, nobody knows."

Henry Ford said the same thing when, by a different use of language, he called history "bunk."[2]

This is not the Christian view, nor is it the teaching of Romans. The Christian view is not negative, because it sees God at the beginning of history (taking charge of it), the cross of Jesus Christ at the center of history (giving it meaning), and the return of Christ at the end of history (bringing it to a triumphant conclusion). For the Christian, time and history are pregnant with eternal meaning.

The Place and Themes of Romans 9–11

In one sense that is the theme of the next great section of Paul's letter to the Romans, chapters 9 through 11. But these chapters are not introduced into a vacuum. They are linked to what has already been written.

Not every commentator has seen this. C. H. Dodd is impressed with the fact that the opening words of chapter 9 do not have any part of speech deliberately linking them to chapter 8. So he imagines that what we have in chapters 9 through 11 is a separate Pauline composition, a "kind of sermon," that "he kept by him . . . for use as occasion demanded."[3] Well, it is true that Romans 9–11 can stand by itself. Even more significantly, it is easy to see how the last part of Romans, chapters 12 through 16, could follow easily from chapter 8. That would replicate a pattern often found in Paul's letters. But apart from the fact that it is difficult to imagine Paul carrying manuscripts of his sermons around with him and preaching from them, it is really only possible to understand these chapters by seeing their close connection to what has gone before.

For one thing, they are a necessary exposition of Paul's original thesis, stated in Romans 1:16. Paul wrote there that he was "not ashamed of the gospel, because it is the power of God for the salvation of everyone who believes: first for the Jew, then for the Gentile." That is an important state-

---

1. Erwin Panofsky, *Studies in Iconology: Humanistic Themes in the Art of the Renaissance* (New York: Harper Torchbooks, 1962), p. 73.

2. In 1919, during his libel suit against the Chicago Tribune.

3. C. H. Dodd, *The Epistle of Paul to the Romans* (London: Hodder and Stoughton, 1960), pp. 148, 149.

ment, but until this point Paul has not shown how the gospel had been presented first to Judaism. In fact, this priority appears to have been contradicted by the large-scale unbelief of this people.[4]

And that leads to the second matter linking the earlier portions of the letter with these chapters. Paul has completed a chapter in which the eternal security of the believer has been unfolded in glowing and profoundly moving terms. He has declared that "neither death nor life, neither angels nor demons, neither the present nor the future, nor any powers, neither height nor depth, nor anything else in all creation, will be able to separate us from the love of God that is in Christ Jesus our Lord" (Rom. 8:38–39). But can we really believe that if, as an observable fact, those upon whom God had previously set his electing love, the Jewish people, have been cast off? It is all very well to affirm that nothing can separate us from the love of God in Christ. But can we believe that if many Jews, who as a people have preceded us in the long, historical, unfolding plan of salvation, have been abandoned by God and are lost?

Recognizing this progression, one commentator has called chapters 9 through 11 the very "climax of Romans," believing that everything before this is intended to lead to its conclusions.[5] This is probably an overstatement. But it is also equally an understatement to regard these chapters merely as "a kind of postscript," as another writer does.[6]

Robert Haldane (along with others) has a good balance when he writes, "Paul . . . has discoursed largely on the justification and sanctification of believers, and now he proceeds to treat particularly of the doctrine of predestination, and to exhibit the sovereignty of God in his dealings both towards Jews and Gentiles. The way in which, in the ninth, tenth, and eleventh chapters, he so particularly adverts to the present state and future destination of the Jews, in connection with what regards the Gentiles, furnishes the most ample opportunity for the illustration of this highly important subject."[7]

In following through on these themes, Paul introduces some of the most profound and mind-stretching material to be found anywhere in the Bible. We will see, as we study these chapters: (1) the historical advantages of Judaism; (2) the importance and biblical proof of election; (3) the doctrine of reprobation; (4) the justice of God in saving some and passing by others; (5) the glory of God displayed in his judgments; (6) the reason for Jewish failure to believe on Jesus of Nazareth as the Messiah; (7) the place and power

4. See John Murray, *The Epistle to the Romans* (Grand Rapids: Wm. B. Eerdmans, 1968), part 2, p. xiii.

5. Krister Stendahl, *Paul Among Jews and Gentiles* (Philadelphia: The Westminster Press, 1976), pp. 4, 28, 85.

6. D. M. Lloyd-Jones, *Romans, An Exposition of Chapter 8:17–39, The Final Perseverance of the Saints* (Grand Rapids: Zondervan, 1976), p. 367.

7. Robert Haldane, *An Exposition of the Epistle to the Romans* (MacDill AFB: MacDonald Publishing, 1958), p. 438.

of gospel preaching in God's plan; (8) the importance of Christian missions; (9) what God is doing in the present age, and why; (10) the eventual salvation of the Jews as a nation; and (11) the great and indescribable knowledge and wisdom of God that guides it all.

Has the Word of God Failed?

All those themes will occupy us in due course. But, as we begin, it is important to see the overall outline of these chapters as they apply to the central question Paul is raising, namely: Has God's saving purpose toward the Jewish nation failed? It is the question he raises implicitly in verse 6. Paul's answer is a firm "No," for the following seven reasons.

1. God's historical purpose toward the Jewish nation has not failed, because *all whom God has elected to salvation are or will be saved* (Rom. 9:6–24).

The apostle begins his discussion by distinguishing between national, visible Israel and spiritual Israel, consisting of those whom God has chosen to know Christ. He also speaks of Abraham's natural descendants and the children of promise, which makes the same distinction. The point is that membership in the outward, visible Jewish nation did not guarantee salvation, any more than outward, visible membership in a Christian denomination guarantees the salvation of church members today. What determines salvation is the electing grace of God in Christ, and that has always been a separate matter from any national or organizational distinctives.

Paul cites election in the earliest generations of descent from Abraham, showing that Isaac was chosen rather than Ishmael, and that Jacob was chosen rather than Esau. He proves his point by quoting Exodus 33:19:

> I will have mercy on whom I have mercy,
> and I will have compassion on whom I have compassion.

Romans 9:15

2. God's historical purpose toward the Jewish nation has not failed, because *God had previously revealed that not all Israel would be saved and that some Gentiles would be* (Rom. 9:25–29).

If God had promised in advance that all Jews would be saved and had then failed to save some of them, God would indeed have failed. But no one can claim failure on God's part if, as is the case, he foretold in advance that precisely what has happened would happen, namely, that many Jews would not believe and would be scattered and that, in their place, many of the scattered Gentiles would be gathered to Christ. As with the previous point, Paul proves his argument by citing Old Testament texts, in this case Hosea 2:23, Hosea 1:10, Isaiah 10:22–23, and Isaiah 1:9.

> Though the number of the Israelites be
> like the sand by the sea,
> only the remnant will be saved.
>
> Romans 9:27; cf. Isaiah 10:22

Hosea 2:23, which Paul applies to God's calling of the Gentiles to be a new spiritual people, articulates the other half of the argument.

> I will call them "my people" who are not my people;
> and I will call her "my loved one"
> who is not my loved one.
>
> Romans 9:25; cf. Hosea 2:23

3. God's historical purpose toward the Jewish nation has not failed, because *the failure of the Jews to believe was their own fault, not God's* (Rom. 9:30–10:21). Why did the Jews fail to believe in Jesus Christ as their Messiah and Savior? Paul answers that it was because of the way they went about trying to earn their salvation themselves. The way of salvation, as he has shown in Romans 4 from a careful examination of key Old Testament passages, is by faith in God's provision in Christ. Abraham, David, and all the other Old Testament figures who were saved were saved through believing God. But this is precisely what the Jews of Paul's day would not do. They wanted to be approved by God on the basis of their own good deeds and righteousness, and, as a result, they would not submit to the righteousness of God that is received by faith.

Of course, this is also precisely why most Gentiles are not saved. They are self-righteous, which means that they think they deserve salvation and do not need grace. They do not understand the depth or horror of sin, which contaminates even the best of their imagined good works.

4. God's historical purpose toward the Jewish nation has not failed, because *some Jews (Paul himself was an example) have believed and have been saved* (Rom. 11:1).

Paul makes this point in one verse, asking, "Did God reject his people?" He answers, "By no means! I am an Israelite myself, a descendant of Abraham, from the tribe of Benjamin." As long as even one Jewish person has been saved, no one can claim that God has rejected his people utterly. But, in fact, the situation is not as grim as that scenario. On the contrary, as the next section shows, even in the worst times God has preserved a considerable remnant of the Jewish people.

5. God's historical purpose toward the Jewish nation has not failed, because *it has always been the case that not all Jews but only a remnant has been saved* (Rom. 11:2–10).

Paul's proof here is God's speech to Elijah after Elijah had achieved his victory over the priests of Baal at Mount Carmel, had fled exhausted to the wilderness and there, profoundly depressed and discouraged, had pleaded for death on the grounds that of all those who had been faithful to God only he was left, and it would be only a short time before King Ahab and Queen Jezebel discovered his hiding place and killed him, too. God replied that Elijah was only feeling sorry for himself, because, as a matter of fact, God still had seven thousand Israelites who had not abandoned the true faith in order to worship Baal.

The point God was trying to bring out for Elijah's benefit was that there was still a large number of believing Jews in Israel, seven thousand to be exact. Paul's point is that although there were only seven thousand, a small portion of the nation, this was still a sufficiently large number to diffuse the claim of anyone who might suppose that God had failed.

6. God's historical purpose toward the Jewish nation has not failed, because *the salvation of the Gentiles, which is now occurring, is meant to arouse Israel to envy and thus be the means of saving some of them* (Rom. 11:11–24).

The argument Paul develops in these middle verses of the eleventh chapter is one of the most profound in the Bible. This is because in it Paul is trying to explain why God has acted as he has. We can understand that God has a *right* to do anything he wants, particularly with sinners who have only opposed him. He can save whom he wants, since salvation is by grace. He can condemn whom he wants, since this is justice. But, still, rejection seems rather harsh treatment of his ancient and formerly "chosen people." Is God merely writing them off? Paul's answer is that this is not the case. Rather, God is using the day of Gentile salvation for the good of Israel, since it is through God's work among the Gentiles that Israel is being stirred from her self-righteousness, self-complacency, and lethargy, as a result of which some are being saved.

Israel has indeed been rejected for a time, like branches being broken from an olive tree. But Paul turns this back on the Gentiles, warning them that although they have been brought into the covenant people in place of those numerous Jews who have been left out, they are not to think that they are beyond danger nationally. For if God has broken the Jewish branches from their own tree, what is to keep him from cutting off the ingrafted Gentile branches and then bringing the Jewish branches back again?

As a matter of fact, this is exactly what has happened to many Gentile nations. At one time there was a strong Christian church in North Africa, but it has been almost entirely destroyed. Formerly strong churches in Germany, France, England, and other countries have likewise ceased to thrive. No one must ever presume upon the grace of God.

7. Finally, God's historical purpose toward the Jewish nation has not failed, because *in the end all Israel will be saved, and thus God will fulfill his promises to Israel nationally* (Rom. 11:25–32).

This last point has proved extremely controversial in the history of the exposition of Romans 9–11, because there are many who feel that a future day of national blessing for Israel would mean a regression in God's plan of redemption. The argument, a strong one, is theological. It is that the promises to Israel have been fulfilled in Christ and unfolded in the church. Therefore, it is inconceivable that God could again deal nationally with Israel.

I acknowledge that there may be aspects of prophetic interpretation that have over-literalized the day of future Jewish blessing. I am not willing to argue that the fulfillment of this promise necessarily means the reestablishment of a believing Jewish state, the state of Israel, though it seems to me that this is probably the case and may even be in the process of happening. I am not willing to argue for a necessary rebuilding of the temple, particularly if it should become a place where blood sacrifices for sin would be offered. I am willing to discuss many details of the coming endtimes, which seem to include a seven-year period of great suffering and tribulation, a great final worldwide battle known as Armageddon, a literal thousand-year reign of Christ on earth, and other things. I think many of these matters are debatable. But I do not see why a future day of national Jewish blessing is or should be debatable, since that is what Paul clearly says will happen: "And so all Israel will be saved . . ." (v. 26).

To say that this only means true Israel, or the church, seems to me to be an evasion of Paul's obvious teaching. True, this does not mean that every individual Jew who has ever lived will be saved, or even that every Jew living in the final days will be saved necessarily. But it must refer to some great time of national repentance and salvation. For, "as it is written:

> 'The deliverer will come from Zion;
>   he will turn godlessness away from Jacob.
> And this is my covenant with them
>   when I take away their sins.'"

Romans 11:26–27

It is no wonder that at this point, having moved from the distress of the opening of chapter 9—"I have great sorrow and increasing anguish in my heart" for Israel—to the expectation of a glorious future deliverance of that people, Paul should turn to doxology and end the section with a hymn of praise to God for his wisdom.

We are going to be studying all these points in detail as we move through these great but sadly neglected chapters of Romans. Yet even here it is possible to see something of the vast scope of Paul's plan. The apostle is showing what God is doing in the flow of human history from the very earliest moments in which he began to save our fallen race, through the period in which he began to work in a special way through the nation of Israel, to the coming of the Messiah, the rejection of Jesus for the most part by his own people, the offer of the gospel to the Gentiles, and the eventual conversion of the masses of Israel so that the two great religious portions of the human race may be saved and joined together as one people in him. And, in all this, Paul is providing what theologians call a theodicy, a justification of the ways of God to human beings. In other words, he is not only showing what God is doing but also that he is right in so operating.

Fitting In

What I have just talked about is what God is doing in history. And the question before us, as we begin this section, is: "How do we fit in?" What is God doing with your life? If you are a Christian, he is forming Jesus Christ in you so that at the end of time there will be a vast host of believers who will stand before him as sisters and brothers of his beloved Son.

Our problem is that we forget that this is what God is doing. Or we do not think about this enough for it to matter. Instead, we are caught up in our own little plans, most of which have nothing to do with this purpose and will prove meaningless in the end. If you are a believer in Jesus Christ, you must know that you are here to be like Christ and to strive to win others to Christ, so that they as well as yourself might have a share in this great blessing. What is God doing in history? *That* is what he is doing. *That* is a true understanding of historical events.

123

Great Sorrow for a Great People

Romans 9:1–4

I speak the truth in Christ—I am not lying, my conscience confirms it in the Holy Spirit—I have great sorrow and unceasing anguish in my heart. For I could wish that I myself were cursed and cut off from Christ for the sake of my brothers, those of my own race, the people of Israel. . . .

Ⅰt is difficult for any of us to receive a hard truth, however necessary it may be to hear it. But there is always a much better chance of hearing it if it is told to us in love.

In the second volume of his study of Romans, Ray Stedman tells of a congregation that had dismissed its pastor. Someone asked a parishioner why they had done it.

"The pastor kept telling us we were going to hell," the church member answered.

"What does your new pastor say?"

"He keeps saying we're going to hell, too."

"So what's the difference?"

"Well," the churchgoer replied, "when our first pastor said we were going to hell, he sounded like he was glad. But when our new pastor says it, he sounds like it is breaking his heart."[1]

This is what is going on as we begin the ninth chapter of Romans.

We recall that at the end of chapter eight, Paul was riding an emotional high as he declared that there is nothing in all creation that can separate a believer from the love of God in Christ Jesus. We read that, and our souls, too, thrill to the ecstasy. But suddenly we come to chapter 9, and we find Paul exclaiming in a very different mood: "I speak the truth in Christ—I am not lying, my conscience confirms it in the Holy Spirit—I have great sorrow and unceasing anguish in my heart" (vv. 1–2). What has happened? The answer is that he is now suddenly thinking of the members of his own race, the Jewish people, and he is grieving because for the most part they have rejected the gospel of God's grace in Christ that he has been expounding.

Paul is in such anguish for them that he could wish—these are his very words—"that I myself were cursed and cut off from Christ for the sake of my brothers, those of my own race, the people of Israel" (vv. 3–4a).

An Enemy for Christ's Sake

This would be an unacceptable and nearly incomprehensible claim to most Jews who might hear him, for in their sight Paul was the worst of all possible enemies. He was a Jew himself, first of all. But he had become a believer in the one they would have called "that blaspheming imposter," and now he was going about trying to convert both Gentiles and Jews to this religion. From their perspective, Paul was not only dreadfully wrong; he was also a traitor, a man who was trying to destroy the Judaism he had once affirmed.

Paul was not doing that, of course, at least not according to his understanding of the prophets. He was proclaiming Jesus as Israel's true Messiah. But he was aware of the enmity that existed, which is why he is so anxious to declare his love for his people in this chapter.

The important thing in terms of Paul's own statement is not that the Jews perceived him to be their enemy, but that they were enemies of his, having set out to harass, hinder, and defeat him in every way possible. As Paul traveled about the Roman world he had considerable success in gathering congregations of Gentiles to his message. He established churches everywhere. But wherever he did this, Jews stirred up mobs, which frequently drove him from those cities. And sometimes, after Paul had left a particular Gentile area, they sent teachers to subvert the newly established churches.

Later in his life, after he had returned to Jerusalem to try to bridge the widening gulf between the Jewish and Gentile churches and win more of the Jews to Christ, more than forty extremely zealous Jews bound themselves

---

1. Ray C. Stedman, *From Guilt to Glory,* vol. 2, *Reveling in God's Salvation* (Portland: Multnomah Press, 1978), p. 10.

with an oath that they would neither eat nor drink until they had killed him (Acts 23:12–13).

But notice: The truly remarkable thing is *not* that the Jews hated Paul. That was natural, given what each believed and what each was trying to accomplish. The remarkable thing was Paul's overwhelming love for those who were his enemies. He tells us in one place, "Five times I received from the Jews the forty lashes minus one," adding that he was in constant "danger from my own countrymen" (2 Cor. 11:24, 26). Yet nowhere in his writings or anywhere else is there ever found (or is there ever imputed to him) the shadow of personal offense, matching retaliation, or lingering bitterness against the Jews for this abuse. Not once. Nowhere.

On the contrary, Paul's spirit was the spirit of his Master, who wept over the city of Jerusalem even though he knew he was about to be crucified by the nation's hostile leaders.

Jesus said, "If you, even you, had only known on this day what would bring you peace—but now it is hidden from your eyes. The days will come upon you when your enemies will build an embankment against you and encircle you and hem you in on every side. . . . They will not leave one stone on another, because you did not recognize the time of God's coming to you" (Luke 19:41–44).

It was the tragic contrast between the Jews' fierce unbelief and the joys of the gospel that brought tears to the eyes of both Jesus of Nazareth and the apostle Paul.

Cut Off from Christ

But we have not fully sounded the depths of Paul's great love and sorrow for his people even yet. For the fully remarkable thing is not merely his love for those who hated him—remarkable as that is—but what he actually says in this passage. He says that he could wish himself "cut off from Christ" for the sake of his Jewish brothers. Strictly speaking, the words *cut off* are not in the original text, though they convey the right idea. The text actually says that Paul would be willing to be "accursed from Christ" (that is, "damned") for the sake of the Jewish people.

Now that really is remarkable!

"Cut off from Christ"? From the very man who has reveled far beyond any of the other New Testament writers on the glories of being *in Christ* or being *joined to him*?

"Accursed"? From the very teacher who has so passionately affirmed that nothing in all creation can separate us from the love of God in Christ Jesus?

The presence of these astonishing words on Paul's lips has caused more than one commentator to try to understand them in some way other than what is obviously the sense, with a few suggesting that Paul was only speaking of what he had once thought of himself and Christ before becoming a Christian. But that will not do at all, as almost everyone recognizes. It is true that Paul knows he cannot actually be separated from Christ. That is what the previous chapter has proclaimed so forcefully. Paul's words in chapter 9 are only hypothetical. But they are genuine nevertheless. For he is saying that, if it *were* possible, he *could* wish himself accursed from Christ if only his condemnation could achieve the salvation of the people he so fervently loved.

The Example of Moses

Paul was a careful student of the Old Testament, of course. So although he does not say so explicitly, it is hard to imagine that he wrote these words without thinking of a similar statement made by Moses, the great lawgiver of Israel. In fact, Paul is probably deliberately echoing Moses' words in order to identify with Moses and thus add credibility to his own statement.

Moses' words occur in Exodus 32, in the context of one of the greatest stories in the Old Testament.

After their deliverance from Egypt, God had led the people of Israel to Mount Sinai, where Moses was called up into the mountain to receive the law. He was there for forty days. As the days stretched into weeks, the people who were waiting below grew restless and eventually prevailed on Moses' brother, Aaron, to make a substitute god for them. Aaron should have resisted indignantly. But Aaron was weak, as many prominent people are. So he asked for the people's gold, and when he had it he found that he had enough to make a little calf. The people had probably been thinking in terms of Apis, the great bull-god they had known in Egypt. They wanted a bull. But a calf was good enough, so they had a great celebration and orgy to mark their new allegiance to this god. As they danced around the idolatrous golden calf, they exclaimed, "These are your gods, O Israel, who brought you up out of Egypt" (Exod. 32:4).

Moses was up on the mountain and did not know what was going on in the camp. But God did, and God interrupted the giving of the law to tell Moses what was happening.

God said, "Go down, because your people, whom you brought up out of Egypt, have become corrupt. They have been quick to turn away from what I commanded them and have made themselves as idol cast in the shape of a calf. They have bowed down to it and sacrificed to it and have said, 'These are your gods, O Israel, who brought you out of Egypt'" (vv. 7–8).

It was a painfully ironic situation. God had just given the people the Ten Commandments, which begin: "I am the LORD your God, who brought you out of Egypt, out of the land of slavery. You shall have no other gods before me. You shall not make for yourself an idol in the form of anything in heaven above or on the earth beneath or in the waters below. You shall not bow down to them or worship them; for I, the LORD your God, am a jealous God, punishing the children for the sins of the fathers to the third and fourth generation of those who hate me, but showing love to a thousand generations of those who love me and keep my commandments" (Exod. 20:2–6).

But, while God had been giving these commands, the people whom he had freed from slavery were doing precisely what he was prohibiting. They were even ascribing their liberation to the idol. Besides, their idolatrous celebration was undoubtedly leading to transgressions of each of the other commandments, too. They were dishonoring their parents, committing adultery, coveting, and probably doing many other evil things.

God said, "Now leave me alone so that my anger may burn against them and that I may destroy them. Then I will make you into a great nation" (Exod. 32:10).

Instead, Moses interceded for the people, saying, "Why should your anger burn against your people, whom you brought out of Egypt . . . ?" (v. 11). If the situation were not so grim, the words would be funny, because God had just spoken to Moses of "your people" and here Moses was speaking to God of "*your* people." It was as if neither wanted to be identified with the nation in its rebellious state.

Moses pleaded two arguments. First: "What will the Egyptians say if you destroy them? They will say, 'You brought them into the desert with evil intent, only to do them harm.'" Second: "What about your covenant with Abraham, Isaac, and Jacob? You promised to make their descendants numerous and to be their inheritance forever. You cannot break your covenant" (see vv. 12–13).

God heard, and the judgment was at least momentarily restrained.

Now Moses started down the mountain to deal with the people as best he knew how. First, Moses destroyed the golden calf. He burned it in the fire, ground it up, mixed it with water, and made the people drink it. Next, he rebuked Aaron publicly. This was the best he could do in Aaron's case, since Aaron had been anointed to the post of high priest by God. Finally, Moses called any who still remained on God's side to separate themselves from the others and stand by him. The tribe of Levi responded. At Moses' command, these were sent through the camp to execute those who had led the rebellion. About three thousand men died, that is, about one-half of one percent of the 600,000 who had left Egypt at the exodus.

From a human point of view, Moses had dealt with the sin. Aaron was rebuked, the leaders were punished, and the loyalty of the people was at least temporarily reclaimed. All seemed to be well.

But Moses did not only have a leader's relationship to the people. He also represented the people to God, and God still waited in wrath upon the mountain. What was Moses to do? For theologians writing in our day, the wrath of God may be no more than an interesting and (as some assume) outmoded concept. But not for Moses. He had been talking with God. He had received God's commandments. He had heard God say, "You shall have no other gods before me," and "[I will punish] the children for the sin of the fathers to the third and fourth generation of those who hate me." Who was he to think that the merely human measures he had taken would satisfy the righteous demands of such a holy God?

The night passed. The morning came, and Moses was to reascend the mountain. He had been thinking. Sometime during the night, a way that might possibly divert the wrath of God against the people had come to him. He had remembered the sacrifices of the Hebrew patriarchs and the newly instituted sacrifice of the Passover. God had shown by such sacrifices that he was prepared to accept an innocent substitute in place of the just death of the sinner. His wrath could sometimes fall on another.

Moses pondered, "Perhaps. . . ." And then the great man turned to the mountain with determination.

Reaching the top, he began to speak to God. Moses must have been in deep anguish, an anguish almost matched by the apostle Paul's in our Romans passage, for the Hebrew text is uneven, and Moses' second sentence breaks off without ending, indicated by a dash in the middle of Exodus 32:32. It was a strangled cry, a sob welling up from the heart of a man who is asking to be sent to hell if his condemnation could mean the salvation of the people he loved.

The text says, "So Moses went back to the LORD and said 'Oh, what a great sin these people have committed! They have made themselves gods of gold. But now, please forgive their sin—[that is the point at which the sentence abruptly breaks off] but if not, then blot me out of the book you have written.'"

On the preceding day, before Moses had come down from the mountain to the camp, God had said something that could have been a temptation to a lesser man. If Moses would agree, God said, he would destroy the people for their sin and then begin to make a new Jewish nation from Moses (Exod. 32:10). Moses would become a new Abraham. Even then, Moses had rejected the offer, pleading for the people instead. But after he had been with them and had realized again how much he loved them, in spite of their stiff-necked rebellion and sin, his answer, still negative, rises to even greater heights.

God had said, "I will destroy them and made a great nation of you."

Moses replied, "No, rather destroy me and save them."

Moses lived in a relatively early stage of God's dealings with his people and probably did not know, as we know, that what he had prayed for could not be. Moses offered to give himself for his people to save them. But Moses could not save even himself, let alone them. He, too, was a sinner. On one occasion he had even committed murder. He could not be a substitute for his people. He could not die for them.

But there was one who could. Thus, "when the time had fully come, God sent his Son, born of a woman, born under law, to redeem those under law, that we might receive the full rights of sons" (Gal. 4:4–5). This was the only adequate substitute for sinners, the Son of God himself. And Jesus' future, yet foreseen death was the reason God did not destroy the people then and why he does not destroy people who believe on Jesus Christ today. Paul knew this, which is why he speaks hypothetically and not exactly as Moses did, though he echoes his words. He knew that Jesus died to receive the full out-pouring of God's wrath against sin so that those who come to God through faith in him might not experience God's just wrath but rather grace.[2] He knew it was the only way God saves anyone.

Let This Mind Be in You

The spirit that was in Jesus, Paul, and Moses should be in each of us—if we would be soul-winners. No one can die for another person's salvation. Jesus is the only one who could, and he did. But we can love as he loved, and we can point others to him.

Let me close this study with five thought-provoking questions.

1. *Do you anguish over others?* Do you sorrow for those who do not know Jesus Christ and who are therefore perishing without him? I am afraid that most of us do not. Why is that? Is it because we do not believe that they are perishing? Because we do not believe the gospel? Probably it is because we are not very much like Jesus Christ, do not spend much time with him, and do not think of spiritual things much at all.

2. *Do you anguish over those closest to you, the members of your own family?* Paul also grieved over the Gentiles, but the verses we have been studying deal with his own people and with his personal, special sorrow over them. If we were like him, husbands would grieve over unsaved wives, wives over unsaved hus-bands, parents over children, and children over parents. We would grieve for members of our extended families and for our neighborhoods.

Charles Spurgeon knew a story that is like this. A girl who was not in good health approached her pastor with thoughts about her coming funeral. She spoke of her father, who was an unbeliever and who had never accepted an invitation from her to go to church. "Pastor, you will bury me, won't you?" she asked. "My father will have to come to my funeral and hear you speak, and you will speak the gospel. Please speak it clearly. I have prayed for him a long time. I know God will save him." According to Spurgeon, the father came to her funeral and was converted.[3] The girl did not die in her father's place, as Jesus died for us. But she had the spirit of Christ in that she was willing to die if her death might cause the conversion of one close to her whom she very much loved.

---

2. I have told this story elsewhere, particularly in James Montgomery Boice, *Foundations of the Christian Faith* (Leicester, England, and Downers Grove, Ill.: InterVarsity Press, 1986), pp. 252–255. It is told in a similar vein in Donald Grey Barnhouse, *God's Covenants: Exposition of Bible Doctrines, Taking the Epistle to the Romans as a Point of Departure,* vol. 8, *Romans 9:1–11:36* (Grand Rapids: Wm. B. Eerdmans, 1963), pp. 3-7, and is referred to as a parallel to Paul's statement in Romans by many commentators.

3. Charles Haddon Spurgeon, "Concern for Other Men's Souls," *Metropolitan Tabernacle Pulpit,* vol. 24 (Pasadena, Tex.: Pilgrim Publications, 1972), p. 418.

3. *Do you anguish over those who are your enemies?* Paul's sorrow was for those who were his avowed enemies. If you have enemies, you are to love them. In fact, you are to love most those who treat you worst. God loved us while we were "enemies" (Rom. 5:10). How are we to win others unless we love even our enemies in this way?

4. *Do you anguish over those who are great sinners?* The nation for whom Paul grieved was composed of great sinners, for they had rejected the love of God in Christ Jesus. Do you similarly grieve for sinners? If you do not, is it because you do not really consider yourself to be one of them?

5. *Do you anguish over those who have great privileges?* Finally, as the verses we are studying will go on to show, the Jews of Paul's day also possessed great privileges. So we are led to ask ourselves: "Do I anguish over those who are favored spiritually and in other ways, as well as over those who are openly sinners, downtrodden and unfortunate?" Those who are privileged need the gospel, too.

Paul was a great preacher of election. He will preach it again even in these verses. But his knowledge of the need for the electing grace of God in salvation did not prohibit him from sorrowing over those who were lost. I commend the heart of the great apostle to you. Let the sins of others grieve you. Let the fate that hangs over them like the sword of Damocles be often on your mind. For, if it is, you will work for their salvation in exactly the same proportion, and you will speak often of Jesus who actually was accursed for those who should afterward believe on him.

124

Great Advantages for a Great People

Romans 9:4–5

. . . Theirs is the adoption as sons; theirs the divine glory, the covenants, the receiving of the law, the temple worship and the promises. Theirs are the patriarchs, and from them is traced the human ancestry of Christ, who is God over all, forever praised! Amen.

There is little doubt that the opening verses of Romans 9 reveal an intense love on the part of the apostle Paul for those of his own race and nation. He has been eloquent at other places in this letter. But nowhere has he spoken with such depth of feeling as he does here, saying that he would be willing to be "cursed and cut off from Christ" if his damnation could mean the salvation of those of his own race, whom he loves.

This is a wonderful sentiment, of course. But if Paul had said nothing more than this, it might be possible for us to dismiss his words as a mere chauvinistic boast, which might well be very wrong or even sinful. We know of people who have great pride in their nation, even when their nation has not been worthy of that pride or has embarked on some terrible course of action.

"*Gott mit uns,*" said the Germans during World War II.

"My country, right or wrong," say countless others.

This is not what Paul is saying, however. So immediately after having expressed his great love for his people, he writes two sentences that explain the genuine and admirable advantages they possess. "Theirs is the adoption as sons; theirs the divine glory, the covenants, the receiving of the law, the temple worship and the promises. Theirs are the patriarchs, and from them is traced the human ancestry of Christ, who is God over all, forever praised! Amen."

In this chapter Paul is going to say that salvation is of God's grace entirely. But before he does, he reminds us that there are nevertheless very great advantages even to the outward forms of God's revealed religion.

The Advantages of Earthly Israel

There is a well-known story about Benjamin Disraeli, the conservative states-man who served as prime minister of England in 1868 and from 1874 to 1880. He was elected to Parliament at the age of thirty-three and shortly thereafter was attacked by Daniel O'Connell, the Irish Roman Catholic leader. In the course of his unrestrained invective, O'Connell referred to Disraeli's Jewish ancestry. Disraeli replied, "Yes, sir, I am a Jew. And I remind my illustrious oppo-nent that when the ancestors of that right honorable gentleman were brutal savages eating nuts in a German forest, my ancestors were serving as priests in the temple of Solomon and were giving law and religion to the world."[1]

Advantages? Indeed! It is those very real advantages that Paul points out in the verses we are to study. There are eight in all.

1. *The adoption as sons.* This is the only place in the New Testament where adoption is used of Israel. Normally it is used of believers in Jesus Christ, which is how Paul has used it thus far in Romans (Rom. 8:15, 23). When it is used of believers it refers to their new status before God as his spiritual sons and daughters resulting from redemption and the new birth. When it is used of Israel, as here, it refers to God's selection of the Jews as an elect nation through which he would bring salvation to the world.

The following terms spell out what this means. It means that Israel alone received the glory, the covenants, the law, the directions for the temple wor-ship, and the promises. Theirs are the patriarchs, and at the end, it was from this people that the Messiah, the Lord Jesus Christ, came.

2. *The divine glory.* The word *glory* is not explained and could mean several things. It could be an adjective linked to adoption with the sense of "the glo-rious adoption." It could mean the glory of being God's special people. However, most commentators recognize that in the Old Testament "glory"

---

1. *The Little, Brown Book of Anecdotes,* Clifton Fadiman, general editor (Boston and Toronto: Little, Brown, 1985), p. 170. Disraeli's words have been reported in a variety of ways by different writers.

usually refers to the visible symbol of the presence of God described by later Judaism as the Shekinah, and that this is what "glory" probably refers to here.

This visible symbol of God's presence seems to have taken a variety of forms. It appeared first at the time of the exodus from Egypt, when it was a great cloud separating the fleeing nation from the pursuing Egyptians. This cloud guided them during the years of their desert wandering, protecting them from the sun by day and turning into a pillar of fire by night to give both light and warmth to their encampment. Later the glory descended on Mount Sinai as a dark cloud accompanied by thunder and lightning when the law was given to Moses (Exod. 24:16–17). Later it filled the tabernacle (Exod. 40:34–38) and rested over the Ark of the Covenant within the Most Holy Place. Still later it settled down as an intense light above the Mercy Seat of the Ark between the wings of the cherubim (Lev. 16:2). From there, in the time of Ezekiel, it departed and returned to heaven in response to the escalating sins of the people (Ezek. 10; 11).

John Murray wrote, "This glory was the sign of God's presence with Israel and certified to Israel that God dwelt among them and met with them."[2]

3. *The covenants.* Nothing is more characteristic of God's special relationship with the people than the covenants. The word is so rich that it is used in a wide variety of ways. Here it probably refers to the covenants established by God, first with the patriarchs Abraham, Isaac, and Jacob, and then later with Moses and David.

The covenant with Abraham and his immediate descendants, Isaac and Jacob, was made and reinforced on several occasions. The first is in Genesis 12:2–3:

> I will make you into a great nation
> and I will bless you;
> I will make your name great,
> and you will be a blessing.
> I will bless those who bless you,
> and whoever curses you I will curse;
> and all peoples on earth
> will be blessed through you.

The covenant with Abraham is elaborated in Genesis 15, 17, and 22. It was extended to Jacob at the place he called Bethel (Gen. 28; cf. Exod. 2:24; 6:3–5).

The covenant with the patriarchs was confirmed with the nation of Israel by Moses, as told in Exodus 24.

Finally, God elaborated upon it with David, promising him a descendant who would sit upon his throne forever: "When your days are over and you rest with your fathers, I will raise up your offspring to succeed you, who will come

2. John Murray, *The Epistle to the Romans* (Grand Rapids: Wm. B. Eerdmans, 1968), vol. 2, p. 5.

from your own body, and I will establish his kingdom. He is the one who will build a house for my Name, and I will establish the throne of his kingdom forever . . . Your throne will be established forever" (2 Sam. 7:12–13, 16; cf. 23:5).

The idea of the covenant is so important in the Old Testament that the word appears 253 times in its pages.

4. *The receiving of the law.* One of the chief criticisms of Paul by his Jewish countrymen seems to have been his alleged disregard for the law, since he taught that salvation was by grace through the atoning work of Christ and not by law-keeping. But Paul does not discount the law's value. In fact, he has already affirmed its superlative value in Romans 3, where he first raised the matter of Jewish advantages. "What advantage, then, is there in being a Jew?" he asked. The answer: "Much in every way! First of all, they have been entrusted with the very words of God" (vv. 1–2). The phrase "the receiving of the law" means the same thing here.

This extraordinary advantage was possessed by no other nation until the Christian era, when the gospel of God's grace in Christ and the books that taught it were deliberately taken to the entire world by the apostles and early missionaries in obedience to Christ's express command.

5. *The temple worship.* This phrase refers to the extensive set of regulations for the religious rituals to be practiced first at the tabernacle and then at the temple in Jerusalem. It involves the construction of the temple itself, the laws governing the various sacrifices, and the times of the year for and nature of the specified holy days of Israel. The importance of these things is that they were designed to show the way in which a sinful human being could approach the thrice holy God. God must be approached by means of a blood sacrifice, which testified to the gravity of sin ("the wages of sin is death," Rom. 6:23) and to the way in which an innocent substitute could die in the sinner's place. Eventually all such sacrifices, which were only figures of the ultimate and true sacrifice, were brought to completion and fulfilled by Jesus Christ.

6. *The promises.* The Old Testament is filled with many promises of one sort or another, but in this context "promises" refers to the promises of redemption to be fulfilled by the Messiah, who is Jesus Christ. Paul talks about this at length in Galatians 3.

7. *The patriarchs.* The "patriarchs" are the three fathers of the Jewish nation, namely, Abraham, Isaac, and Jacob, though in a looser sense such distinguished ancestors as Moses and David should also be included. These were all illustrious men to whom God revealed himself in special ways and through whom he worked to call out and bless his ancient people. To have such devout, saintly, and influential men in one's past is rightly regarded by Paul as a significant national distinction of which Jewish people could all justly be proud.

8. *The human ancestry of Christ.* Everything Paul has said to this point would have been soundly echoed by his Jewish opponents, for they, too, regarded all these spiritual advantages highly, though they misunderstood and misused some of them. This is not the case with the last item Paul mentions, for they would have understood at once that Paul is referring here to Jesus of Nazareth, and they had no intention of recognizing Jesus as their national Messiah. Yet Paul cannot leave this matter out, if for no other reason than that everything he has mentioned thus far leads up to Jesus.

This is not a random collection of items. There is actually a very close connection between these advantages, according to which each rightly leads to the one following and all lead to Christ. Adoption is the right starting point, for it places the source of salvation in God's electing grace, just as is the case also for believers in Christ. Having chosen to enter into a special relationship with his people, the next step was for God to reveal himself to them in a special way, which is what the word *glory* describes. God has done that for us in Christ, for he is where God's glory must be seen today (John 2:11; 2 Cor. 3:18). When God revealed himself to the people, as he did at Mount Sinai, it was to enter into special covenants or agreements with them, to give them the law by which they were to live, to show the way of salvation through the temple rituals, and to point forward the full realization of their spiritual inheritance when the Messiah should at last be revealed.

The flow of God's actions reaches back to the patriarchs, with which it began, and forward to the coming of Jesus, in whom it culminates (v. 5). These verses are as full and reasoned a statement of the blessings of God to Israel and the spiritual advantages of Old Testament religion as could possibly be given. Israel truly lacked nothing. The nation was enriched with every spiritual blessing and advantage.

Advantages Alone Do Not Save

And yet, the nation as a nation was not saved. It is true that certain Jews were. Paul is going to make that point repeatedly in the following chapters. But nationally—that is, speaking of Israel as a nation—it is nevertheless also true that these great advantages, the greatest spiritual advantages that could possibly be imagined for any people anywhere, did not in themselves guarantee salvation, which is the reason for the great sorrow that Paul has so intensely and poignantly expressed.

In spite of the adoption, in spite of the divine glory, in spite of the covenants, in spite of possessing the law, in spite of the temple worship with its important symbolism, in spite of the promises and the patriarchs—in spite of all these things—no one, not a nation, not an individual, is saved or can be saved apart from Jesus Christ.

This is what Paul himself had experienced. In his letter to the Philippians as well as here in Romans, he reminds us of his experiences in Judaism, saying that he put confidence in these external advantages in his early days. He uses the illustration of an asset and liability statement. On the asset side he had placed seven items (Phil. 3:5–7).

There were four things that Paul had inherited: "circumcised on the eighth day" (which meant that he was a true Jew and not an Ishmaelite, who would have been circumcised later, or a proselyte, who would be circumcised as an adult), "of the people of Israel" (the covenant name of Israel embraces all the items listed at greater length in Romans), "of the tribe of Benjamin" (the only tribe that remained with Judah in the south at the time of the civil war and was later preserved with Judah, after the fall of the northern kingdom), and "a Hebrew of Hebrews" (that is, born of two Jewish parents).

There were three advantages that Paul has earned for himself. He had become "a Pharisee," the strictest sect of the Jews. He was zealous in his faith, which he proved by his persecution of the early Christian church. "As for legalistic righteousness," he was "faultless." That is, he kept the law as perfectly as he knew how.

What a tremendous set of advantages these were! Yet, when Paul met Jesus on the road to Damascus, he discovered at once that they were not enough. He had thought these items added up to salvation, that they made him a righteous person in God's sight. Instead, when he met Jesus and discovered what true righteousness was, he saw that they did not even begin to add up to righteousness, and he realized that, if he was going to be saved, it would have to be by a different means entirely. It would have to be by the righteousness of Jesus Christ imputed to him. It would have to be by grace.

And he also learned that the advantages he had thought were spiritual assets were, in fact, not assets. In reality those items were liabilities, for as long as he was trusting them, they were keeping him from Christ. What he had to do was move that entire list over into the column of liabilities, and in the column of assets write "Jesus Christ alone."

Nominal Christians

We must apply this to those who have been brought up in the Christian church and have benefited from its advantages. That may describe you, and if it does, the application of Romans 9:4 and 5 will be obvious. Here it is: Your spiritual advantages, however great they are or may have been, will not save you. You must be born again.

Some people think they are right with God simply because they have had Christian parents, like the Jews who boasted in the patriarchs or Paul, who took confidence from the fact that he was "a Hebrew of Hebrews." To be born into a Christian family and raised by Christian parents is a good thing, not to be despised. But if this has been your experience, you should realize that you will never be saved simply because you have had a believing father or a godly mother. They have imparted advantages to you. But you will not be saved by their lives or their faith. You must believe yourself. You must be following Jesus Christ. You must be born again.

Some people think they are right with God because they have been blessed by a Christian education, either in their home or in a good evangelical Sunday school or in a Christian high school or college. Their education has given them a great deal of sound theology and right answers to many important questions. But no one has ever been saved by head knowledge alone. The devils know more theology than any of us. They have had thousands of years to learn it. Yet they are not saved.

Perhaps you have been trusting in your membership in a Christian church. If you are a member of a sound, believing church, that is a great advantage, corresponding to Israel's adoption as a nation, her possession of the law, the rituals for the temple worship, and the promises. But membership in a church does not save anyone, any more than being a Jew has saved anyone. Today's churches are filled with people who are Christians in name only. There is nothing in their lives to give any indication that they have been touched by Jesus Christ or been drawn to him.

Even the sacraments will not save you, however valuable they are in pointing to the reality of our new life in Christ and the value of constantly feeding on him by faith.

Not long before I wrote this sermon, I was in Memphis, Tennessee, speaking on Christian discipleship, and I met a man who had corresponded with me some years before. He had sent me a book he had written, entitled *Must Jesus Be Lord to Be Savior?* Now he was reminding me of the testimony of his wife, which he had included in the book as an appendix. I remembered it at once because it was so helpful and vivid.

This woman—her name is Paula Webster—had been raised in a Christian home, had been given a Christian education, and was settled down in what seemed to be a Christian marriage. She was active in church, attended Bible conferences, and even had regular times of personal Bible study. She said that if anyone had asked her if she was a Christian, she would have said yes, immediately and emphatically. Yet something was missing. She knew about God, but she sensed that she did not actually know him. She felt frustrated and unhappy, and as far as her own spiritual life was concerned she knew she was getting nowhere.

As she studied the Bible she was particularly attracted to David and Paul, because each clearly had a heart for God. They knew about God. But in addition they each loved him and wanted to obey him as an expression of that love. As she studied their lives she realized that something was wrong with her own heart and asked God to change her.

God did! He taught her that she had never actually given herself to him and that the surrender of herself was necessary. She needed to become Jesus' genuine disciple.

Here, in her own words, is what happened: "At the moment I surrendered my life entirely to God, I knew that he had heard me and had accepted my surrender. I was conscious immediately that a great burden had been rolled away. I knew that I had been forgiven and cleansed. I knew that I had been changed. Peace, like a great calm following a storm at sea, and joy unspeakable filled my heart. I knew that the great war within had ceased. The sense that all had been made right replaced the agitation and restlessness I had felt only minutes before. I had finally been subdued and conquered by the Lord of Glory before whom I now gladly and gratefully bowed. And he no longer seemed distant or impersonal, nor I unclean and unsure before him. . . . I had been born again."[3]

She confessed that her earlier faith had been a dead faith only, an intellectual acceptance of facts relating to Jesus, and that the advantages she had received in a Christian environment had not changed her heart.

I am sure that describes many hundreds of people who will read this study in book form. How am I sure? It is because there is so much nominal Christianity. You may be such a Christian, and if that is the case, this testimony should move you. Have you had spiritual advantages? If you have had them, thank God. But do not trust in those advantages. Seek God himself, and do not rest until you can say that the burden of your sin has been rolled away and that you are truly a new creature in Jesus Christ.

3. "Personal Testimony" by Paula Webster in William A. Webster, *Must Jesus Be Lord to Be Savior?* (Memphis: Grace Publications, 1986), p. 58.

125

Jesus, Who Is God

Romans 9:5

. . . from them is traced the human ancestry of Christ, who is God over all, forever praised! Amen.

The opening paragraph of Romans 9 lists the extraordinary privileges and advantages of the Jews, God's ancient people. In the words of Paul, they have been given "the adoption as sons . . . the divine glory, the covenants, the receiving of the law, the temple worship . . . the promises [and] . . . the patriarchs." But to this extraordinary list of privileges Paul now adds the greatest privilege of all, namely, that they are those through whom the Redeemer of the human race has come.

". . . from them is traced the human ancestry of Christ, who is God over all, forever praised! Amen."

This is a very striking statement. For Paul is not only saying that the Messiah was born of Israel, that is, that he was a Jew. He is also saying that this Jewish Messiah, born of Israel according to the flesh, is, in fact, God. And he is saying it in stark language. If we substitute the name Jesus for Christ, which we can do, since Paul is obviously writing about Jesus, we have the statement: "Jesus, who is God over all, forever praised!" Or, to simplify it even further, "Jesus . . . is God over all." The sentence means that Jesus is himself the only and most high God.

A Hotly Disputed Text

This is so extreme a statement—and, as some would say, a statement so uncharacteristic of the New Testament writers—that from the time of the Reformation forward numerous commentators and Bible teachers have attempted to understand it differently. This has made Romans 9:5 one of the most hotly disputed texts of the New Testament.

Basically, there are two main interpretations of this verse. The first is what we have in the New International Version: "Christ, who is God over all, forever praised!" This is what most other English versions of the New Testament also say essentially,[1] and it is how nearly all the ancient writers also understood it.[2]

The second interpretation is based on the fact that there are almost no marks of punctuation in the Greek texts of the New Testament and that the phrase may therefore, at least in theory, be broken up. This was proposed first by the Dutch humanist Erasmus of Rotterdam, who was a contemporary of Martin Luther. According to this interpretation, a period should be added to the verse, either after the word *flesh* (which follows "Christ" in the Greek text) or after the words *over all*.

In the first case the sentence would read, ". . . from them is traced the human ancestry of Christ. God who is over all be forever praised!"

In the second case the translation would be: ". . . from them is traced the human ancestry of Christ, who is over all. God be forever praised!" Each of these is essentially one interpretation, since each is designed to avoid calling Jesus "God" explicitly. These alternate translations are indicated in the footnote to the New International Version.

What should we say about this contested passage? The first thing we must say is that almost all arguments, especially grammatical arguments, favor the translation that calls Jesus "God" explicitly.

Here are a few:

1. *The word order favors it.* In the Greek language, as in most other languages, including English, the relative pronoun follows the noun to which it refers. In this text the order of nouns and pronouns is: *Christ, who,* and *God.* "Who" should refer to Christ, which is the noun that comes immediately before, and the meaning should be "Christ, who is . . . God." To make the verse mean "God, who . . ." violates the word order. Of course, the period could be placed after the relative clause, which would solve the word order problem ("Christ, who is over all. God be forever praised!"). But in that case, the translation has the following difficulty.

1. Except the Revised Standard Version and the New English Bible.

2. Godet lists Irenaeus, Tertullian, Origen, Chrysostom, Augustine, Jerome, Theodoret, and later Luther, Calvin, Beza, Tholuck, Usteri, Olshausen, Philippi, Gess, Ritschl, Hofmann, Weiss, Delitzsch, and Schultz (F. Godet, *Commentary on St. Paul's Epistle to the Romans,* trans. A. Cusin [Edinburgh: T. & T. Clark, 1892], vol. 2, p. 139). More recent endorsers of this view are Robert Haldane, Charles Hodge, John Murray, and Leon Morris.

2. *A doxology should begin with the word* blessed. The proper form for a doxology is "Blessed be God [or some person]. . . ." But in order to separate God from Christ, which this interpretation tries to do, the order would be "God," followed by "blessed."

3. *A doxology is out of place in this passage.* It is appropriate to praise God in a passage that speaks of some great spiritual achievement or triumph, as Paul does at the end of Romans 11, for example. But why should God be praised here, in a passage in which Paul has been expressing acute personal sorrow for the Jews' rejection of Jesus? In Romans 11, quite differently, the doxology comes after Paul has explained that in spite of the overall rejection of God by Israel, God is nevertheless going to save the mass of the nation one day.

4. *The reference to Christ being "after the flesh" requires a phrase pointing to his deity.* We have this in Romans 1, where Paul writes of Jesus, "who as to his human nature was a descendant of David, and who through the Spirit of holiness was declared with power to be the Son of God by his resurrection from the dead" (vv. 3–4). If Jesus is not identified as God in Romans 9:5, the antithesis is lacking.[3]

Affirmations of Christ's Deity

The one powerful argument for the interpretation that separates the words *Christ* and *God* by a period is that, according to its proponents, Paul nowhere else explicitly calls Jesus "God." This seems to have carried weight with the translators of the New International Version, since it is the only reason why they would have placed the alternative translations, which I mentioned above, in the footnote.

We have to admit at this point that there is an obvious reticence among the New Testament writers to say starkly that "Jesus is God." And for good reason. Without explanation, a statement like this might be understood as teaching that God left heaven in order to come to earth in the person of the human Jesus, leaving heaven without his presence. Each of the New Testament writers knew that this is not an accurate picture. Each was aware of the doctrine of the Trinity, according to which God is described as being one God but existing in three persons: Father, Son, and Holy Spirit. Since Jesus is the Son of God, it was customary for them to call him that, rather than simply "God," reserving the unembellished word God for *God* the Father.

This is why Jesus is not often called God explicitly.

3. These arguments are developed most succinctly by Leon Morris, *The Epistle to the Romans* (Grand Rapids: Wm. B. Eerdmans, and Leicester, England: Inter-Varsity Press, 1988), p. 350. But they are also found in various forms in other commentators, particularly Charles Hodge, *A Commentary on Romans* (Edinburgh and Carlisle, Pa.: The Banner of Truth Trust, 1972), pp. 300, 301, from which Morris seems to have borrowed.

Yet, although it is unusual to find Jesus called God for the reasons just given, it is not the case that he is never called God.

We think of the Gospel of John, for instance. At the very beginning of that Gospel, John writes: "In the beginning was the Word, and the Word was with God, and *the Word was God*. He was with God in the beginning" (vv. 1–2, emphasis added). A bit later "the Word" is identified as Jesus (v. 14), so the text says that Jesus is God. True, the verses are written so as to distinguish the persons of the Father and Son within the Trinity. But they nevertheless identify Jesus as God explicitly.

Later in John's Gospel we find the same thing in Thomas's great confession, which is the Gospel's spiritual climax. "Thomas said to him, 'My Lord and my God!'" (John 20:28).

Acts 20:28 is another relevant passage. Here Paul is speaking to elders of the church at Ephesus, telling them to, "be shepherds of the church of God, which he bought with his own blood." The blood that was the price of our redemption is the blood of Christ, but here it is called the blood of God. The only way Paul could make this identification is by thinking of Christ as being God so directly and naturally that what he posits of one can without any violence also be said of the other.

Hebrews 1:8 calls Jesus "God" by applying Psalm 45:6–7 to him: "Your throne, O God, will last for ever and ever. . . ."

The best example of an identification of Jesus with God in Paul's writings, apart from our text, is Titus 2:13–14, where Paul writes, "We wait for the blessed hope—the glorious appearing of our great God and Savior, Jesus Christ. . . ." Apart from the context, the words *God and Savior* could mean only "God the Father and God the Son." But since Paul is writing of the second coming and sudden appearance of Jesus, both words must refer to him, for it is not God the Father who is going to appear suddenly but rather "our great God and Savior," who is Jesus.[4]

So it is not true that Paul never identifies Jesus with God explicitly. He does, as do other New Testament writers, in spite of the reticence and care with which they usually write. However, even if it *were* the case that Paul nowhere else explicitly identifies Jesus as God, that fact alone does not prove that he cannot do it here—which, in fact, he does.

I like what John Calvin says of the attempt to separate God from Christ by splitting up the text in the way I have described. He writes wisely, "To separate this clause from the rest of the context for the purpose of depriving Christ of this clear witness to his divinity is an audacious attempt to create darkness where there is full light."[5]

---

4. There is an excellent discussion of each of these texts, and some others, in Oscar Cullmann, *The Christology of the New Testament* (London: SCM Press, 1955), pp. 306–314.

5. John Calvin, *The Epistles of Paul the Apostle to the Romans and to the Thessalonians,* trans. Ross MacKenzie (Grand Rapids: Wm. B. Eerdmans, 1973), p. 196.

Even better is the judgment of Robert Haldane: "The Scriptures have many real difficulties, which are calculated to try or to increase the faith and patience of the Christian, and are evidently designed to enlarge his acquaintance with the Word of God by obliging him more diligently to search into them [sic] and place his dependence on the Spirit of truth. But when language so clear as in the present passage is perverted to avoid recognizing the obvious truth contained in the divine testimony, it more fully manifests the depravity of human nature and the rooted enmity of the carnal mind against God, than the grossest works of the flesh."[6]

Like many other commentators and Bible teachers, I find Romans 9:5 to be one of the most sublime testimonies to the full deity of the Lord Jesus Christ in all the Bible.

The Teaching of the Passage

Yet this is not all the passage teaches. It actually contains four very important teachings, including Jesus' deity.

1. *The humanity of Jesus.* The first heresy in church history was the denial of the true humanity of Christ. It was called docetism, from the Greek word *dokeo,* which means "to seem." It taught that Jesus only *seemed* to be a man. In some forms it taught that the Spirit of Christ came upon the man Jesus at the time of his baptism by John, but that it left him just before the crucifixion, since it was not possible for God to die, according to Greek thinking. There is none of this in the New Testament. For here in Romans 9:5, as in many other passages, the biblical writers are united in their insistence that Jesus was a true human being, a descendant of Abraham according to the flesh.

This has a number of important implications, for it means that God not only fully understands but has also himself likewise experienced all that we experience as human beings.

Do we hunger? Jesus hungered many times, specifically when he was in the wilderness being tempted of the devil.

Do we experience thirst? Jesus thirsted on the cross.

Do we experience rejection and misunderstanding by friends, hostility from enemies, pain, suffering, and even death? So did Jesus, and in a form and with an intensity far greater than anything we might experience.

Even more important perhaps, Jesus experienced temptation just as we do, so that he might be a helper to us when we go through it. The Book of Hebrews says, "For we do not have a high priest who is unable to sympathize with our weaknesses, but we have one who has been tempted in every way, just as we are—yet was without sin" (Heb. 4:15).

6. Robert Haldane, *An Exposition of the Epistle to the Romans* (MacDill AFB: MacDonald Publishing, 1958), p. 445.

The doctrine of Christ's humanity is of great importance for us if we are to live a victorious Christian life.

2. *The deity of Jesus.* As I have said, the earliest heresy in the history of the church was the denial of Christ's humanity. But today the case is the exact opposite. Few would deny his humanity, since to our way of thinking Jesus was obviously a man, even an exemplary man. We do not deny this. Instead there are strong, numerous, and popular attempts to deny his deity. Countless numbers of our contemporaries regard Jesus as having been nothing but a man.

Far more is lost with this denial than in denying Christ's humanity. What is lost is the value of his atonement for sin, for no mere man, however good, would be able to pay the infinite price required for our redemption. In the Middle Ages there was a great English scholar named Anselm who saw this clearly and wrote about it in a book that has become a classic. It is called *Cur Deus Homo?*, which means "Why the God Man?" or, more naturally, "Why Did God Become Man?" Anselm answered that God became man in Christ because only one who was both God and man could achieve our salvation.

Here is his classic statement of this truth: "It would not have been right for the restoration of human nature to be left undone, and . . . it could not have been done unless man paid what was owing to God for sin. But the debt was so great that, while man alone owed it, only God could pay it, so that the same person must be both man and God. Thus it was necessary for God to take manhood into the unity of his Person, so that he who in his own nature ought to pay and could not should be in a person who could. . . . The life of this one man was so sublime, so precious, that it can suffice to pay what is owing for the sins of the whole world, and infinitely more."[7]

This combination of Christ's humanity and deity, and the reason for it, makes Calvary the very center of the Christian faith. It is the reason the Son of God came to earth. There is no gospel without it.

3. *The supremacy of Jesus.* But Jesus did not only die, humbling himself for our salvation. He also rose again and has now ascended to heaven, where he is honored as God, having being given the name that is above every name, even the name of God (Jehovah) himself. This is Paul's teaching in Philippians 2, where he writes of Jesus:

> And being found in appearance as a man,
>   he humbled himself
>   and became obedient to death—
>   even death on a cross!
> Therefore God exalted him to the highest place
>   and gave him the name that is above every name,

---

7. Eugene R. Fairweather, editor and translator, *A Scholastic Miscellany: Anselm to Ockham*, "The Library of Christian Classics," vol. 10 (Philadelphia: The Westminster Press, 1956), p. 176.

> that at the name of Jesus every knee should bow,
>   in heaven and on earth and under the earth,
> and every tongue confess that Jesus Christ is Lord,
>   to the glory of God the Father.

Philippians 2:8–11

If Jesus Christ is Lord, as these passages say he is, the supremacy of Christ described in Romans 9:5 ("who is God over all") includes his rule over us, who are his people, and we are not his people if we fail to submit to that rule.

There is a great deal of bad thinking and even error in this area at the present time. It has become customary in some places to think of Christianity as a two-stage commitment. In the first stage we come to Jesus as Savior, simply believing on him as the one who died for sin. In the second we come to him as Lord, thereby becoming serious about our Christianity and about being Christ's disciples. But nothing like that is found in the New Testament. On the contrary, to become a Christian is to become a disciple and vice versa. In fact, that is the way Jesus himself spoke of evangelism in the Great Commission, since he sent his disciples to "*make disciples* of all nations" (Matt. 28:19, emphasis mine). Submitting to Christ's lordship is the very essence of true faith, or Christianity.

4. *The rightness of praising Jesus.* The fourth doctrine taught in Romans 9:5 is the rightness of praising Jesus, for the text reads, "Christ, who is God over all, forever praised!" It raises two questions: "Do we praise him?" and "Do we praise him as we should?"

The answer to the second question is obviously no, for no mere human or earthly words can be adequate for praising Christ properly. Yet we should do it, knowing that it will be our privilege, joy, and glory to praise Jesus Christ in heaven forever. The angels are doing it. They sing:

> Worthy is the Lamb, who was slain,
> to receive power and wealth and wisdom and strength
> and honor and glory and praise!

Revelation 5:12

According to Revelation, one day we are going to join with them, crying,

> To him who sits on the throne and to the Lamb
> be praise and honor and glory and power,
>   for ever and ever!

Revelation 5:13

So let's do it now! Let us praise our Savior, who is God over all, as best we know how—and live for him until he comes again.

The Greatest Tragedy

I have one last thought as I return to the paragraph in Romans from which our text is taken. We have seen that Paul is expressing sorrow over the fact that the ancient nation of Israel had as a whole rejected Jesus and that, in that context, the ascription of deity to Jesus is appropriate as conveying the full tragedy of the Jews' rejection. It is bad enough that the nation should have missed the full value of the other privileges listed: the adoption, the divine glory, the covenants, the law, the temple worship, the promises, and the patriarchs. But it is a tragedy beyond description that they should have rejected Jesus as the Messiah whom God had promised.

Yet we also need to say more. However tragic the Jews' rejection of Jesus may have been (and is), the rejection of Jesus by others, both Jews and Gentiles, is equally tragic today, perhaps even more so, since the gospel has been so widely proclaimed and been so amply defended in the many centuries of subsequent church history.

It would be especially tragic if you yourself should reject him, either force-fully ("I will not have this man to rule over me") or by neglect ("Speak to me about it again, some other time"). If you are doing either of those two things, how can we who know Jesus have anything other than "great sorrow and unceasing anguish" in our hearts for you? To reject our words is nothing, but to reject *him* is a loss of cosmic proportions. So we say, "Do not reject him. Believe on him."

God is making his appeal through us as we say with Paul, "Be reconciled to God" (2 Cor. 5:20) and remind you that "God made him who had no sin to be sin for us, so that in him we might become the righteousness of God" (v. 21). That is the gospel. Do not allow the opportunity to respond to that wonderful message pass you by.

PART TWELVE

The Justification of God

126

True Israel

Romans 9:6

It is not as though God's word had failed. For not all who are descended from Israel are Israel.

Several years ago I read about a champion woodcarver from Bavaria who found a piece of wood in the mouth of a sack of grain. The wood was the same color as the grains of wheat, so he took it into his head to carve the wood into imitation grains. He carved a handful of them, mixed them with some real wheat, and then invited his friends to tell them apart. The woodcarver had done the work so well that no one could tell the difference. Even he was unable to tell the imitation grains from the true wheat. In the end the only way to distinguish the true from the false kernels was to place the grains in water. After a few days the real grain sprouted, while the imitation grain remained exactly what it was before: dead wood.

There is a parallel here to those who profess to be God's people. To human eyes there may be a time when some of the true children of God are almost indistinguishable from people who are merely behaving as believers or are circulating among believers. But the difference is there nevertheless. It has been put there by God. And in the end, since some of these people have the life of God within them and some do not, these who possess that life will show it by their spiritual growth.

Natural Israel and Spiritual Israel

The distinction between those who seem to be spiritual children and those who actually are is critical to understanding the next section of Romans. But in order to see it we have to step back a bit and review what Paul is saying.

Paul is dealing with a troublesome problem faced by himself and the other early preachers of the gospel. The original Christians were Jews. Thus they very naturally began obeying the Great Commission by witnessing to their Jewish family members, Jewish friends, and Jewish neighbors. Since the promises of the Messiah were to Israel and since Jesus of Nazareth was that Messiah, according to their belief and understanding, Israel should have been willing to embrace him. But Israel as a whole did not, and as time went on the people who were becoming Christians and the largest number of emerging Christian churches were overwhelmingly Gentile.

This was a severe disappointment to the early evangelists, even a great sorrow, as Paul's opening paragraph in Romans 9 makes clear. But even more than this, it was a theological dilemma. The promises of God were to Israel, and yet Israel as a whole was unresponsive. Did this mean that God's promises to Israel had failed, that is, that God had himself failed? That God was impotent in the face of unbelief? Or did it mean that the promises of God could not be trusted? That in the matter of salvation God was simply free to change his mind?

This is the problem Paul wrestles with in the middle section of Romans, chapters 9 through 11. He has a number of arguments, which I summarized in the initial study in this volume. But the first of these, introduced in Romans 9:6, is that the promises of God were not made to all the physical descendants of Abraham, but only to those whom God had elected to salvation and in whom he had therefore implanted or was implanting life.

Paul states this by saying, "It is not as though God's word had failed. For not all who are descended from Israel are Israel." A little later and in a similar way, he contrasts those who are Abraham's "descendants" with those who are his true "children" (v. 7).

At first glance this argument may seem to be merely a novel idea, perhaps even an "argument from desperation," as some would have it. But it is nothing of the sort. That not all Israel was true Israel was already an Old Testament perception. In the following verses, which we will explore in the next study, Paul shows that the distinction goes back to the patriarchs themselves. But even if this original distinction should be discounted, every Jew was aware of the contrast made by the prophets between the nation as a whole and the remnant. In the declining days of ancient Jewish history leading up to the overthrow of the northern kingdom by the Assyrians in 721 B.C. and the destruction of the southern kingdom by the Babylonians in 586 B.C., it was increasingly obvious that the nation as a whole was apostate and that only a few Jews gave any indication of being among God's genuine people.

It was the same at the coming of Christ. The nation as a whole was going about its business with little true faith at all, just as most people, both Jew and Gentile, do today. It was only a few individuals, like Joseph and Mary, Elizabeth and Zechariah, Simeon and Anna, "who were looking forward to the redemption of Jerusalem" (Luke 2:38).

When Jesus appeared on the scene to begin his public ministry, he, too, made the distinction. In fact, this is one of the earliest things recorded of him. In John 1:43–46, we are told how Jesus called Philip to be one of his disciples and how Philip immediately found his friend Nathanael and brought him to Jesus. When Jesus saw Nathanael he said, "Here is a true Israelite . . ." (v. 47). It was the precise distinction Paul is making in this chapter.

Nor should we overlook the fact that Paul has already made this contrast in Romans. In the second chapter he was trying to show that even highly moral and religious Jews need the gospel, like Gentiles, because neither the law, which they fail to keep, nor circumcision, the outward mark of the covenant people, can save them. Circumcision, like other religious ceremonies, has value only if it corresponds to an internal transformation. It is the heart that must be circumcised. Paul's summary says, "A man is not a Jew if he is only one outwardly, nor is circumcision merely outward and physical. No, a man is a Jew if he is one inwardly; and circumcision is circumcision of the heart, by the Spirit, not by the written code" (Rom. 2:28–29a).

How could it be otherwise, so long as we are dealing with spiritual matters and with God, who does not deal only with appearances but with reality? Clearly, God is not deceived by ceremonies.

What Is Required

What is required for one to be a true Israelite? We have already looked at a long list of things that are not required, at least things that do not in themselves make one a true child of God. They are the items Paul lists in verses 2 through 5: "the adoption . . . the divine glory . . . the receiving of the law . . . the temple worship . . . the promises . . . [and] the patriarchs." These are real privileges that impart important spiritual advantages. But they do not bring salvation themselves. Indeed, not even being in the line that produced the Messiah is advantageous for salvation.

What, then, is required?

There is only one answer, and Paul has already developed it fully in the earlier parts of the letter. It is faith, saving faith in Jesus of Nazareth as the Son of God and Savior. It is belief that Jesus died in our place, taking our sins upon himself, and that by faith in him we are delivered from the punishment due us for those transgressions and instead are counted as righteous through the righteousness of Christ. The "true Israel" of the Old Testament looked forward to Jesus' coming and believed on him whom they did not yet know. The "true Israel" of the New Testament looks backward in time, believing on him who has come and whom they do know.

Paul's chief example of such faith is Abraham, whose story is told in summary form in Romans 4. Abraham was not saved by circumcision, because he was declared to be righteous before God in Genesis 15:6, which was years before his later circumcision.[1] Nor was he saved by keeping the law, because no one, not even Abraham, is able to keep the law perfectly. The law only brings wrath and condemnation. Besides, the law was not even given until the time of Moses, which was four hundred years after Abraham's time. How, then, was Abraham saved? It was by faith, which is what made Abraham a true Israelite.

Paul says that "the promise comes by faith, so that it may be by grace and may be guaranteed to all Abraham's offspring—not only to those who are of the law but also to those who are of the faith of Abraham. He is the father of us all. As it is written: 'I have made you a father of many nations.' He is our father in the sight of God, in whom he believed—the God who gives life to the dead and calls things that are not as though they were" (Rom. 4:16–17).

As Paul will show, it is that call of God followed by faith that makes one a true member of God's family.

Cultural Christians and True Christians

This is also true for those who call themselves Christians. That is, not all who call themselves Christians or who are thought of as Christians are true Christians.

Some years ago an English writer named Leslie Stephen said that the name "Christian has become one of the vaguest epithets in the language."[2] This is true, perhaps even more so today than when those words were spoken. To many Jews, the name Christian is nearly synonymous with "goy" or "Gentile," so that for them the world is divided basically into two great parts: Jews and Christians. Other people speak of "Christian nations," by which they usually mean the western nations, those of Europe, the United States, Canada, and some others. They do this even though the cultural life of these nations is inconsistent with Christian teaching and only a small proportion of people in some of those countries ever attend a place of worship on Sunday.

What is happening? Obviously, it is a case of there being many who bear the name "Christian" but who are not actually Christians.

What is a true Christian?

The name itself gives us a clue, since it literally means "a Christ one." Let's approach it by its origins. The first time this name was used was in ancient Antioch of Syria in the early days of the expansion of the gospel beyond Palestine. Antioch was an immoral place. It had several great temples at which

---

1. The giving of the mark of circumcision is recounted in Genesis 17, two chapters later.
2. Cited by Donald Grey Barnhouse, "First Things First" (Philadelphia: The Bible Study Hour, 1961), p. 23.

cultic prostitution was practiced, and the moral tone of the city was so bad that Antioch had become a byword for depravity in the ancient world. The city was on the Orontes River. So, on one occasion, when an orator in Rome wanted to describe the worsening moral conditions of his city, he observed that the Orontes had been diverted so as to flow into the Tiber. It was the equivalent of calling the Orontes a sewer that was carrying the filth of the eastern city into Rome.

In this degenerate city, God planted a body of genuine believers whom the pagans of Antioch began to call Christians. The Christians did not call themselves Christians. They had other names for themselves. They called themselves "people of The Way," "saints" (or separated ones), "disciples," "brothers," and other descriptive titles. Jews did not call them Christians, because Christ means "Messiah," and the Jews would never have called the sect of the Nazarene by that name.

No, the believers were first called Christians by the heathen, and for obvious reasons. The believers were enamored of Christ and followed so closely after Christ that the pagans could hardly think of a believer without thinking of the Jesus he or she was following. They were "Christ's people."

Theologically, this has several parts. It means that:

1. *Christians believe in Christ.* The Christ of the early Christian community, and of all true Christians everywhere, is the Christ of the New Testament, which means that he is the Son of God who became a man for our salvation. This is the one on whom the Christians believed. Moreover, this belief was no mere intellectual conviction. I have often said that faith (or belief) has three elements. The first is its intellectual content: who Jesus is and what he has done for our salvation. The second is the warming of the heart: being moved by Jesus' sacrifice on our behalf. The third is personal commitment, the most important part of all. It means giving oneself to Jesus, becoming his, taking up his cross, being a disciple.

This is what the believers in Antioch had done. They had committed themselves to Jesus so thoroughly that the pagans who looked on said, "They are Christ ones, Christians."

2. *Christians follow Christ.* There was a second characteristic of these first Christians, which is also characteristic of all true Christians at all times. It is wrapped up in the matter of commitment, as I have just indicated: Christians are followers of Jesus. That is, if they have believed on him in a saving way and not merely by some mere abstract intellectual assent to his deity, then they are following after him on the path he sets before them. That path is the path of obedience, and as they walk along it they become increasingly like the one they are following and obeying.

This is an important dimension of what it means to be a Christian. To be a Christian means to believe on Jesus, surely. But it also means to be following

after Jesus and thus becoming increasingly like him. A true Christian is someone who is becoming like Jesus Christ.

3. *Christians witness to Christ.* I think there must have been another reason
why the early Christians were called Christians, and it is that they were apparently always talking about their Savior. The name of Jesus was constantly on
their tongues, his gospel consistently on their hearts, and his glory uppermost
in their minds. They were always looking for others whom they could tell
about him, and they were always praying and working at their witness so that
these others might be saved.

It is significant in this respect that the first great missionary movement of
the church began in Antioch. We are told about it in Acts 13: "While they
were worshiping the Lord and fasting, the Holy Spirit said, 'Set apart for me
Barnabas and Saul for the work to which I have called them.' So after they
had fasted and prayed, they placed their hands on them and sent them off"
(vv. 2–3). Paul undertook three missionary journeys at the direction of this
church and with accountability to it, for at the end of each assignment he
reported back to the congregation what God had done to save other Gentiles
and some Jews through him.

We cannot forget that Jesus himself said that his followers would be witnesses: "You will receive power when the Holy Spirit comes on you; and you
will be my witnesses in Jerusalem, and in all Judea and Samaria, and to the
ends of the earth" (Acts 1:8).

4. *Christians learn more and more about Christ.* Here is a fourth thing that is
characteristic of true Christians. They want to learn more about Jesus. We
are told of the Christians at Antioch that after Barnabas had gone to their
city to encourage the infant church in its faith, he then went to Tarsus in
Turkey to look for Paul, whom he remembered from earlier days (Acts
11:22–25). When he found him, he brought him back to Antioch so that "for
a whole year Barnabas and Saul met with the church and taught great numbers of people" (v. 26a). It is significant that it was immediately after this, after
the Christians at Antioch had been carefully taught about Jesus, that they
"were first called Christians" (v. 26b).

As they learn about Jesus Christ, Christians naturally become more like
him, intensify their love for him, and witness about him to others.

A Time for Self-Examination

The point of all this is that each of us who calls himself or herself a Christian
should be led to self-examination. And what we should ask ourselves is: "Am
I a true Christian, or am I a Christian in name only?" This is a serious question
and a necessary one. For if Israel—with all the spiritual advantages that Paul
mentions in Romans 9—could be composed of thousands or even millions

who were not true Israel, it is certain that the visible church of Jesus Christ in our day is filled with many who are actually unbelievers.

Paul told the Corinthians, "Examine yourselves to see whether you are in the faith; test yourselves" (2 Cor. 13:5a).

Peter told his readers, "Therefore, my brothers, be all the more eager to make your calling and election sure" (2 Peter 1:10a).

How can we test ourselves? How can we be sure we are Christians? There are a number of specific questions to be answered that pertain to the matters I have just been discussing.

1. *Do I believe on Christ?* The first requirement is faith, because faith is our point of contact with the gospel. Paul told the Philippian jailer, "Believe in the Lord Jesus Christ, and you will be saved" (Acts 16:31a). Ask yourself, "Have I believed on Jesus?" Not, "Have I believed on him in broad cultural terms?"—like anyone in the western world might be expected to do, especially if he or she has been raised in a Christian home or has attended a Christian church. But rather, "Have I been touched by knowledge of Jesus' death for me, and have I committed myself to him? Am I serious about following after Christ, obeying his commands, and pleasing him?"

2. *Am I following after Christ?* The first question leads to the next: "Am I actually Jesus' follower?" The way Jesus called his followers was by the words *Follow me.* And when they did follow him, their lives were inevitably redirected. Some had been fishermen, but when they began to follow Jesus they became fishers of men. One had been a tax collector, but after he had followed Jesus, he became concerned with the currency of heaven. Nobody who has begun to follow Jesus Christ has ever been entirely the same or walked in the same paths afterward.

So ask yourself: "Has my life been redirected? Is there anything I am doing now that I did not do before or would not be doing were I not committed to Jesus? And are there things I have stopped doing? Is Jesus my very own Lord and Savior?"

3. *Do I testify to Christ?* This is a harder point for true self-examination, because it is easier for some to talk about Jesus than for others. It is easier for some to talk about nearly anything than for others. Nevertheless, this is an important question and one worth asking. If you never speak to anyone about Jesus, how can you suppose that you really care about him and love him, not to mention caring about and loving the other person, who needs to receive the Savior?

Nominal Christians do not talk about Jesus. They are content to let everyone believe as he or she likes. They wouldn't think of trying to impose their beliefs on others. But not all who are Christians are true Christians, just as "not all who are descended from Israel are Israel."

Examine yourself. Do you testify of Jesus?

4. *Am I learning about Christ?* The last of the four questions I have posed for determining whether or not you are a genuine Christian is: "Am I trying to learn more and more about Jesus Christ? Do I know more about him today than I did at the time of my conversion? Or at this time last year?"

I know people who claim to be Christians who never go to a Bible study, never take notes of a sermon and, as far as I can determine, never seriously study the Bible on their own. If you are one of them how can you think of yourself as a Christian when you have no interest in learning about the one who gave himself for you? How can you consider yourself a believer when you really don't care about Jesus?

Over the last few years I have been talking with diverse Christian leaders, and the one thing most of them say is that they see no hope for the United States or for American Christianity apart from a revival. The drift is so obviously downward. But what is a revival? A revival is the reviving of the alleged people of God, and it is preceded by an awakening in which many who thought themselves to be Christians come to their right senses and recognize that they are not new creatures in Christ and that all is not well with their souls. Revival begins in the church, not in the world. It begins with people like you.

I, too, think we need a revival. But I do not see it happening. I want it to happen. I do not see it. But if it happens, why should it not begin with us? With you? May God grant it for his mercy's sake.

127

Three Generations of Election

Romans 9:7-12

Nor because they are his descendants are they all Abraham's children. On the contrary, "It is through Isaac that your offspring will be reckoned." In other words, it is not the natural children who are God's children, but it is the children of the promise who are regarded as Abraham's offspring. For this is how the promise was stated: "At the appointed time I will return, and Sarah will have a son."

Not only that, but Rebekah's children had one and the same father, our father Isaac. Yet, before the twins were born or had done anything good or bad—in order that God's purpose in election might stand: not by works but by him who calls—she was told, "The older will serve the younger."

I want to begin this study by saying that, in my judgment, we are now entering into the most difficult portion of the entire Bible, more difficult even than those very confusing sections in Daniel, Revelation, and other books that deal with prophecy. Romans 9–11 is concerned with election. But it is not this alone that makes these chapters difficult. What is really difficult is that these chapters, particularly chapter 9, also deal with the negative counterpart to election, the doctrine of reprobation (passing over of those who are not elected to salvation), and that they are written to prove that God is right in doing so.

1051

The proper name for this kind of discussion is "theodicy." A theodicy is an attempt to vindicate the justice of God in his actions.

In this study we begin with the positive side of God's actions: election, which is the easiest place to start. But already we can hear objections. Some objections are pragmatic: "Why are Reformed people always harping on the doctrine of election?" We do not actually do this, of course; usually we speak of other doctrines. But election is so objectionable to most people that it sticks in their memories and makes them think that we are always talking about it.

A second class of objections is theological: "How can election be true? If election is true, free will is impossible, and we all know that we have free will." Or, "If election is true, why should we evangelize?" Election and free will are not incompatible, as we have seen before in these studies and will see again. But an explanation of why they are not incompatible takes time, and most people are not willing to wait for the explanation.

Other objections are belligerent: "If election is true, God is not just. I could never believe in a God like that." That, of course, is the question with which theodicy deals, and we will come to it.

A Basis in Fact

Where do we begin? I suggest that we begin exactly where the apostle begins in Romans, namely, with the fact of election itself. The reasons are obvious. First, there is no sense arguing over the justice of God in electing some to salvation and passing over others unless we are first convinced that he does. If we do not believe this, we will not waste our time puzzling over it. Second, if we are convinced that God elects to salvation, as Paul is going to insist he does, we will approach even the theodicy question differently. We will approach it to find understanding, rather than arrogantly trying to prove that God cannot do what the Bible clearly teaches.

To seek understanding is one thing. God encourages it. But to demand that God conform to our limited insights into what is just or right is another matter entirely.

So let me begin by saying that as long as we believe that God exercises *any* control over history or the lives of his people, then we must come to terms with election one way or another. It is inescapable.

Why? For this reason. When Jesus called his first disciples, he called twelve and not more. Others might very well have profited from having spent the following three years in close association with Jesus. But Jesus chose only twelve for this privilege. Moreover, when he sent his disciples into the world to tell others about him, by necessity each of these early preachers went in one direction rather than another. Philip went to Samaria. Barnabas went to Antioch. Later Paul and Barnabas went north to Asia Minor. Still later Paul and other companions went to Greece, then Italy, and eventually further west. In each case a choice was involved: north rather than south, west rather than east. If God was directing the movement of these servants of his at all, he was choosing that some should hear the gospel of grace rather than others, which is a form of election—even apart from the matter of a choice to call some to active faith by means of an internal call.

The same is true in our experience. If you believe that God is leading you to speak to someone about the gospel, it is an inescapable fact that you are speaking to that person rather than another. And even if a Christian friend should join you and speak to that other person, there are still millions who are inevitably passed by. Election is an inescapable fact of human history.

Abraham, Isaac, and Jacob

This is not the way Paul presents the doctrine, of course, though it is close enough to get us thinking along the right lines. What Paul does do is go back to the earliest moments in the history of the Jewish people, to the stories of the patriarchs—Abraham, Isaac, and Jacob—and show that election operated there. We remember, of course, that the apostle is trying to explain why not all Israel has been saved and why the fact that they have not been saved does not mean that God's purpose or promises have failed. In the case of these three fathers of the nation, he is going to show that Abraham, Isaac, and Jacob became what they were by election and that others were not granted this privilege.

1. *Abraham*. Election is obvious in the case of Abraham, which is one reason why Paul does not discuss his case in detail, though he does mention him. Abraham had a pagan ancestry, having been born in the ancient city of Ur in Mesopotamia. He had no knowledge of the true God, because no one in Ur had knowledge of the true God. In fact, Abraham's family worshiped idols. Joshua said this explicitly in the sermon recorded in the twenty-fourth chapter of the book that bears his name: "This is what the LORD, the God of Israel, says: 'Long ago your forefathers, including Terah the father of Abraham and Nahor, lived beyond the River and worshiped other gods'" (Josh. 24:2). Years later, even after God had called Abraham out of this pagan environment and had taught him and through him had instructed Abraham's son and grandson about himself as the true God, idols were still possessed and cherished in this family, since Rachel, the wife of Jacob, hid them from her father when he came after them in the incident recorded in Genesis 31.

Abraham did not seek God. God sought Abraham.

Since the call of Abraham is recorded in Genesis 12, every Jew would have to confess that Jewish history began with that election.

2. *Isaac*. But those to whom Paul is writing might argue that this is beside the point, which is probably also why Paul does not deal with Abraham's story at great length. They would admit that God had to start somewhere, after all. Besides, they might say, the matter being discussed is not whether God has elected the nation of Israel to some specific destiny apart from other

nations. That much had been conceded by everyone. Paul himself has spoken of the adoption as sons, the divine glory, the covenants, the receiving of the law, and other privileges that were granted to Israel alone. No one disputed the election of the nation. The real issue was whether all the descendants of Abraham, that is, all Jews, were thereby saved, or whether the principle of choice and rejection also applies after the initial choice of Abraham.

In other words, does God continue to choose some but not all, some Jews and some Gentiles but not all from either category?

Since this is the issue, Paul begins his actual argument in verse 7 with the case of Abraham's son Isaac. His argument reads: "Not because they are his descendants are they all Abraham's children. On the contrary, 'It is through Isaac that your offspring will be reckoned.' In other words, it is not the natural children who are God's children, but it is the children of the promise who are regarded as Abraham's offspring. For this was how the promise was stated: 'At the appointed time I will return, and Sarah will have a son'" (vv. 7–9).

The point of this statement is that Abraham had another son. He had begotten Ishmael of Hagar, thirteen years before Isaac was born. Yet Ishmael was not chosen. He was Abraham's physical descendant, but he was not a child of promise as Isaac was.

There is something else in this example: the contrast between "natural" in the phrase "natural children" and "children of the promise" (v. 8). That contrast, plus the quotation from Genesis 18:10, 14 in verse 9, shows that the difference between Isaac and Ishmael was not merely that God elected Isaac and passed over the other son, but also that the choice of God involved a supernatural intervention in the case of Isaac's conception. Ishmael was born of Abraham's *natural* powers. But Isaac was conceived when Abraham was past the age of engendering children and when Sarah was past the age of conceiving and giving birth.

It is the same with our spiritual conception and new birth, which is the inevitable outworking of God's electing choice and is likewise supernatural. We cannot engender spiritual life in ourselves, for, according to Ephesians 2:1, we are spiritually dead. For us to become spiritually alive, God must do a miracle.

3. *Jacob.* Yet there is still an objection. Paul's readers could argue that Ishmael was not a pure-blooded Jew. "It is true," they might say, "that Ishmael was the son of Abraham. Yet he was not the son of Sarah. He was the son of Hagar, and Hagar was only Sarah's servant. That is why Ishmael was not chosen."

In order to answer this point, Paul passes to the third generation of election, to the case of Rebekah's twin children, the sons Jacob and Esau. The words "not only that" in verse 10 show that he is continuing the argument. "Not only that, but Rebekah's children had one and the same father, our father Isaac. Yet, before the twins were born or had done anything good or bad—in order that God's purpose in election might stand: not by works but by him who calls—she was told, 'The older will serve the younger'" (vv. 10–12).

This is a remarkably effective example, since it proves everything that Paul needed or wanted to make his point.

First, Jacob and Esau were born of the same Jewish parents. That is, each was "a Hebrew of the Hebrews," the phrase Paul used to describe his own Jewish ancestry in Philippians 3:5. Each was a pure-blooded Jew. So there is no case of one having been chosen on the basis of a better ancestry and the other having been rejected on the basis of a lesser one. The supposed reason for the choice of Isaac over Ishmael is eliminated in the case of Jacob and Esau.

Second, the choice of Jacob rather than Esau went against the normal standards of primogeniture, according to which the elder should have received the greater blessing. True, the boys were twins. But Esau actually emerged from Rebekah's womb first, though Jacob was chosen. There is nothing to explain this except God's sovereign right to dispose of the destinies of human beings as he pleases, entirely apart from any rights thought to belong to us due to our age or other factors.

Third—and this is the most important point of all—the choice of Jacob instead of Esau was made before either child had opportunity to do either good or evil. It was made while the children were still in the womb. This means—we cannot miss it—that election is not on the basis of anything done by the individual chosen.

Moreover, the choice was made, at least in the case of Jacob, to teach the doctrine of election. That is what verses 11 and 12 say. "Yet, before the twins were born or had done anything good or bad—*in order that God's purpose in election might stand:* not by works but by him who calls . . . " (emphasis added). This means that God made his choice before the birth of Rebekah's sons to show that his choices are unrelated to anything a human being might or might not do. It is a case, as Paul will say just a few verses further on, that "God has mercy on whom he wants to have mercy" (v. 18).

Individuals or Nations?

I am aware that at this point many will already be saying, "But that's not fair. It is wrong for God to choose one and not another. To be fair, God has to give everyone a chance." We are going to come back to that question later and answer it. We are going to show that not only is salvation by election fair, it is the only thing that is fair. Besides, it is the only chance we have. It is election or nothing.

But before we get to that, there is another matter.

I have been writing about three generations of election in the cases of Abraham, Isaac, and Jacob. But there are people who admit Paul's teaching about election in these verses and yet regard it as the election of nations rather than of individuals. They say that it is an election of the Jewish nation only and that, if this is so, these verses have little, if anything, to say about election as it is commonly understood.

Is Romans 9 dealing with the election of Israel only? We need to think through the arguments carefully.

First, there are a few reasons to think that Paul *is* dealing with nations rather than individuals. For one thing, the Bible speaks elsewhere of Israel as an elect nation. So the idea of an election of a specific people to some predetermined destiny is not strange to Scripture.

Again, there is no question that the oracle spoken to Rebekah before the birth of Jacob and Esau did involve more than individuals. The Genesis 25:23 text says—though Paul does not quote this part, and the omission may itself be significant—that "two *nations* are in your womb, and two *peoples* from within you will be separated; one *people* will be stronger than the other . . ." (emphasis added). Later in Genesis a good bit of space is given to the nation that Esau founded, and the remainder is about Israel.

Again, it might be argued that Paul's overall argument in Romans 9–11 concerns the future place of Israel in God's plan. In fact, this is where he ends up: "And so *all Israel* will be saved, as it is written: 'The deliverer will come from Zion; he will turn godlessness away from Jacob. And this is my covenant with them when I take away their sins'" (Rom. 11:26–27, emphasis added).

Good arguments, and yet not sufficient. For, in spite of the fact that Paul's overall argument in these chapters concerns the future of Israel as a nation, that is not the point he is making at the start of chapter 9. At this point he is distinguishing between individual Jews, some of whom have been elected to salvation and are therefore "true Israel," in contrast to others who have not been and are therefore Israel by physical descent alone. These latter may be the natural children of Abraham, but they are not his spiritual children. They are not children of the promise.

Of the more recent commentators, it is John Murray who works through these arguments most carefully, concluding like this: "The thesis that Paul is dealing with the election of Israel collectively and applying the clause in question [that "God's purpose in election might stand"] only to this feature of redemptive history would not meet the precise situation. The question posed for the apostle is: How can the covenant promise of God be regarded as inviolate when the mass of those who belong to Israel, who are comprised in the elect nation in terms of the Old Testament passages cited above (Deut. 4:37 *et al.*), have remained in unbelief and come short of the covenant passages? . . . Paul's answer is not the collective election of Israel but rather 'they are not all Israel, who are of Israel.' And this means, in terms of the stage of discussion at which we have now arrived, 'they are not all elect, who are of elect Israel.' As we found above, there is the distinction between Israel and the *true* Israel, between children and *true* children, between the seed and the *true* seed. In such a distinction resides Paul's answer to Israel's unbelief."[1]

1. John Murray, *The Epistle to the Romans* (Grand Rapids: Wm. B. Eerdmans, 1968), part 2, p. 18.

What does this mean?

It means that although the biblical doctrine of election does not exclude the choice of nations for specific purposes in history, the doctrine does nevertheless also and more fundamentally refer to the choice of individuals—and that it is on this basis alone, not on any supposed right of birth or by the doing of works, that a person is brought into the covenant of salvation.

Radical Depravity and Election

How could it be otherwise, if the condition of fallen humanity is as bad as the Bible declares it to be? When we were studying the third chapter of Romans we saw that Paul's summary of the fall was expressed in these words:

> There is no one righteous, not even one;
> there is no one who understands,
> no one who seeks God.
>
> Romans 3:10–11

This is an expression of what Reformed thinkers refer to as total or radical depravity. It means that there is not a portion of our being that has not been ruined by sin. Sin pervades all our actions and darkens all our natural understanding, with the result that, rather than fleeing to God, who is our only reasonable object of worship and our only hope of blessing, we flee from him.

How could a creature as depraved as that possibly come to God unless God should first set his saving choice upon him, regenerate him, and then call him to faith? How could a sinner like that believe the gospel unless God should first determine that he or she should believe it and then actually enable him or her to believe?

Of course, that is exactly what God does. In fact, we have already seen this action explained at length in Romans 8, where Paul spoke of a five-step process involving foreknowledge (or election), predestination, calling, justification, and glorification. Those five terms describe the very essence of salvation, and the significant thing is that God is the author of each one. It is he who foreknows, he who predestines, he who calls, he who justifies, and he who glorifies.

The only thing Paul is adding in Romans 9 is that this is entirely apart from any supposed right of birth or good works. It is due entirely to the will and mercy of the sovereign God.

Do you still have questions about this? If you do, I am not surprised. I have questions myself. It is why I have called Romans 9–11 the most difficult portion of the Bible. I also have questions about the doctrine of the Trinity and other matters. But although I have questions, I nevertheless believe these doctrines and rejoice in them. I am suggesting that you do, too. Why? Because election means that salvation is of God. It is his idea and his work, and therefore it is as solid as God himself is.

If salvation were up to me, I would blow it. Even if I could choose God savingly, which I cannot, I would soon unchoose him and so fall away and be lost. But because God chooses me, I can know that I am secure because of his eternal and sovereign determination. God began this good work. And "he who began [this] good work . . . will carry it on to completion until the day of Christ Jesus" (Phil. 1:6).

Did you know that the doctrine of election was the chief factor in the conversion of Charles Haddon Spurgeon, the great Baptist preacher of the nineteenth century? Spurgeon believed it and was blessed by it, because he knew his own spiritual inability. Apart from election, he knew he would be lost. Be like him. The more you are, the more you will rejoice in election, however puzzling parts of it may be.

128

Double Predestination

Romans 9:13–18

Just as it is written: "Jacob I loved, but Esau I hated." What then shall we say? Is God unjust? Not at all? For he says to Moses, "I will have mercy on whom I have mercy, and I will have compassion on whom I have compassion." It does not, therefore, depend on man's desire or effort, but on God's mercy. For the Scripture says to Pharaoh: "I raised you up for this very purpose, that I might display my power in you and that my name might be proclaimed in all the earth." Therefore God has mercy on whom he wants to have mercy, and he hardens whom he wants to harden.

When I began the last study I pointed out that, in my judgment, we are examining the most difficult portion of the entire Bible. Not only because it deals with election, which troubles many, but even more because it deals with reprobation, the doctrine that God rejects or repudiates some persons to eternal condemnation in a way parallel but opposite to the way he ordains others to salvation. Reprobation is the teaching we come to specifically in Romans 9:13–18, which makes these verses an excessively difficult passage for many, if not most, people.

The doctrine is brought into our text by two Old Testament quotations: Malachi 1:2–3 ("Jacob I loved, but Esau I hated," cited in v. 13) and Exodus 9:16 ("I raised you [Pharaoh] up for this very purpose, that I might display

1059

my power in you and that my name might be proclaimed in all the earth," cited in v. 17).

Paul summarizes the teaching in these texts by concluding, "Therefore God has mercy on whom he wants to have mercy, and he hardens whom he wants to harden" (v. 18).

In the view of many people, the doctrine these verses express is a "monstrous doctrine" that turns God into an indifferent deity who sits in heaven arbitrarily assigning human destinies, saying, as it were, "This one to heaven, and I don't care. This one to hell, and I don't care."

This is a caricature, of course. But it is something we must deal with, since no one can seriously attempt to study or teach the Bible, as I am doing, without confronting it. More to the point, it is impossible to study election without also dealing with its negative counterpart. Some years ago the theme of the Philadelphia Conference on Reformed Theology, which I began in 1974, was "predestination," and the subject of reprobation was assigned to Dr. W. Robert Godfrey, professor of church history at Westminster Theological Seminary, Escondido, California. He had been talking to his wife about his subject and asked her what she thought he should call it.

She said, "Call it: 'Double or Nothing.'"

That may be a bit frivolous, but it is accurate, since it is impossible to have election, the positive side of predestination, without reprobation, which is the negative side. John Calvin recognized this, as have many others in the course of church history. He wrote, "Election [cannot] stand except as set over against reprobation."[1]

It is easy to distort this doctrine, of course, as the caricature shows. We must proceed slowly and humbly, recognizing our own limited understanding. Still we must try to see what the Bible does teach about reprobation, since the subject cannot be avoided.

Proof from Scripture

The place to begin is with the fact of reprobation, as taught in the Bible, regardless of the questions we may have. In other words, we must follow the same procedure with reprobation as we followed in the last study with its positive counterpart, election.

There are many texts that teach reprobation. Here are a few:

Proverbs 16:4. "The LORD works out everything for his own ends—even the wicked for a day of disaster."

John 12:39–40. "They [the people of Jesus' day] could not believe, because, as Isaiah says elsewhere: 'He has blinded their eyes / and deadened their hearts, / so they can neither see with their eyes, / nor understand with their hearts, / nor turn—and I would heal them.'"

---

1. John Calvin, *Institutes of the Christian Religion*, 2 vols., ed. John T. McNeill, trans. Ford Lewis Battles (Philadelphia: The Westminster Press, 1960), p. 947.

John 13:18. [Jesus said,] ". . . I know those I have chosen. But this [Jesus' betrayal by Judas] is to fulfill the scripture: 'He who shares my bread has lifted up his heel against me.'"

John 17:12. [Jesus prayed,] "While I was with them [the disciples], I protected them and kept them safe by that name you gave me. None has been lost except the one doomed to destruction so that Scripture would be fulfilled."

1 Peter 2:7–8. "Now to you who believe, this stone [Jesus Christ] is precious. But to those who do not believe, 'The stone the builders rejected has become the capstone,' and, 'A stone that causes men to stumble and a rock that makes them fall.' They stumble because they disobey the message—which is also what they were destined for."

Jude 4. "Certain men whose condemnation was written about long ago have secretly slipped in among you. . . ."

There are many other texts along these lines, but the clearest are those in Romans 9, which we are studying, since they use the word *hate* of Esau ("Jacob I loved, but Esau I hated") and "harden" of Pharaoh ("Therefore God has mercy on whom he wants to have mercy, and he hardens whom he wants to harden"). In fact, verses 1–29 are the most forceful statement of double predestination in the Bible.

"Hated" or "Loved Less"?

The language of this chapter is so strong that quite a few writers have tried to soften it.

1. *The word* hate. There are people who, quite understandably, have found themselves unhappy with the word *hate* and who have therefore tried to interpret it in the sense, not of outright hatred but of merely "loving less." The great Charles Hodge has done this, writing, "It is evident that in this case the word *hate* means *to love less, to regard and treat with less favor.*"[2]

Here is where we have to begin to tread very carefully, for there is something to be said for Hodge's view. For one thing, "hate" *is* used this way in Scripture. For example, in Genesis 29:32–33 it is used of Jacob's feelings for Leah, his less-favored wife, where the New International Version rightly has Leah saying, "I am not loved." Or again, in Luke 14:26 Jesus says, "If anyone comes to me and does not hate his father and mother, his wife and children, his brothers and sisters—yes, even his own life—he cannot be my disciple." It is generally felt that Jesus is not speaking of a literal hatred here but of priorities.

Another very telling argument for Hodge's view is that nowhere else in the Bible is God said to hate any specific individual, though he does hate the *deeds* of evildoers and is even said to hate "all who do wrong" in Psalm 5:5. God hates sin.

2. Charles Hodge, *A Commentary on Romans* (Edinburgh and Carlisle, Pa.: The Banner of Truth Trust, 1972), p. 312. Original edition 1935.

What shall we say about this interpretation? Two things. First, even if the word *hate* should be understood to mean "love less," this loving less is nevertheless of a sufficiently negative nature to account for Esau's being rejected by God rather that being chosen, as Jacob was. For that is the point of the citation. Paul is using the example to illustrate how God chooses one and not another, call the rejection what you will.

Second, it is hard to escape seeing that although hatred in God is of a different character than hatred in sinful human beings—his is a holy hatred—hate in God nevertheless does imply disapproval. John Murray is at pains to explain this in his commentary, replying to Hodge, where he concludes rightly that "Esau was not merely excluded from what Jacob enjoyed but was the object of a displeasure which love would have excluded and of which Jacob was not the object because he was loved."[3] Since the selection involved in the words *love* and *hate* was made before either of the children was born, the words must involve a double predestination in which, on the one hand, Jacob was destined to salvation and, on the other hand, Esau was destined to be passed over and thus to perish.

2. *The word* harden. The second term commentators have tried to soften is the word *harden*, usually pointing out that, in Exodus, Pharaoh is also said to have hardened himself (Exod. 8:32; 9:34). The argument is that God hardened Pharaoh's heart only in the sense that he allowed Pharaoh to harden it himself, or hardened him judicially as a punishment for his prior unbelief or self-hardening.

There is no question but that Pharaoh hardened his own heart, of course. The verses say so. But here are a few observations. First, there are many more texts that say that God hardened him than say that he hardened himself. Second, in Exodus, the first references are to God's hardening of Pharaoh (cf. 4:21; 7:3, etc.) and not to Pharaoh's self-hardening. Third, even if Pharaoh's self-hardening is given the strongest possible meaning, it is still in the category of "secondary causes" for which God always assumes primary responsibility. In other words, just as in the case of prayer or witnessing by Christians, what we do matters but is effective only because God has determined beforehand that it should be, so also here. Though human beings have responsibility for what they do or do not do, God nevertheless is in control of his universe. It is he (and not we) who rules history.

Two Important Distinctions

But now it is time to make a few important distinctions between election and reprobation. The question we must ask is: Are the actions involved in these

3. John Murray, *The Epistle to the Romans*, 2 vols. in 1 (Grand Rapids: Wm. B. Eerdmans, 1968), vol. 2, p. 23. See pp. 21–24. Also Robert Haldane, *An Exposition of the Epistle to the Romans* (MacDill AFB: MacDonald Publishing, 1958), pp. 455–467.

two doctrines to be thought of in exactly the same way? Specifically, to use the proper language for this theological differentiation, are they equally ultimate?

What is meant by that question is this: Does God determine the destinies of individuals in exactly the same way so that, without any consideration of what they do or might do, he assigns one to heaven and the other to hell? We know he does that in the case of those who are being saved, because we have been told that election has no basis in any good seen or foreseen in those who are elected. In fact, we are told that in Romans, for Paul's point is that salvation is due entirely to God's mercy and not to any good that could be imagined to reside in us. The question is whether this can be said of the reprobate, too, that God has consigned them to hell apart from anything they have done, apart from their deserving it.

Here, I think, there is an important distinction to be made between election and reprobation. Nor am I the only one who thinks so. This has been the view of the majority of Reformed thinkers and is the teaching embodied in the great Reformed creeds.

Take the Westminster Confession of Faith, for example. Here are the two paragraphs concerning election and reprobation:

> Those of mankind that are predestinated unto life, God, before the foundation of the world was laid, according to his eternal and immutable purpose, and the secret counsel and good pleasure of his will, hath chosen, in Christ, unto everlasting glory, out of his mere free grace and love, without any foresight of faith, or good works, or perseverance in either of them, or any other thing in the creature, as conditions, or causes moving him thereunto: and all to the praise of his glorious grace. (Chap. 3, Sec. 5)

> The rest of mankind God was pleased, according to the unsearchable counsel of his own will, whereby he extendeth or withholdeth mercy as he pleaseth, for the glory of his sovereign power over his creatures, to pass by: and to ordain them to dishonor and wrath for their sin, to the praise of his glorious justice. (Chap. 3, Sec. 7)

Those two statements concerning election and reprobation teach that in some respects they are the same: both flow from the eternal counsels or will of God, rather than the will of man, and both are for the end of making the glory of God known. In that respect we can speak of equal ultimacy.

But there are two important points of difference.

First, the confession speaks of the reprobate being "passed by." Some will argue that in its ultimate effect there is no difference between passing by and actively ordaining an individual to condemnation. But while that is true of the ultimate effect, there is nevertheless a major difference in the cause. The reason why some believe the gospel and are saved by it is that God intervenes in their lives to bring them to faith. He does it by the new birth or regeneration. But those who are lost are not made to disbelieve by God. They do that by themselves. To ordain their end, God needs only to withhold the special grace of regeneration.

Second, the confession speaks of God ordaining the lost "to dishonor and wrath *for their sin*" (emphasis added). That is a very important observation, for it makes reprobation the exact opposite of an arbitrary action. The lost are not lost because God willy-nilly consigns them to it, but rather as a just judgment upon them for their sins.[4]

In these two respects election and reprobation are dissimilar.

Infralapsarian or Supralapsarian?

That leads me to two of the longest theological terms you will ever hear me utter. In fact, with the exception of "antidisestablishmentarianism," which has nothing to do with theology, these are the longest and most confusing words I know: *supralapsarianism* and *infralapsarianism*. I mention them here only because they describe a matter about reprobation that we need to touch on briefly.

Here is why we have to think about it. I have distinguished between election, which is unrelated to anything the elect might do or not do, and reprobation, which is, according to the Westminster Confession of Faith, "for their sin." But the question then is: When does God determine this in the case of the non-elect? If he ordains them to be punished for their sin, does he wait for them to sin before he makes this determination? That can't be right, because we know that election (as well as the passing over of the reprobate) has been determined by God before the foundation of the world. What, then, is the relationship of his preordination of the lost to their sin? Did God foresee their sin and then ordain them to be lost because of it? Or did he first ordain, after which sin inevitably entered into the world, and the lost are punished for it.

That is what these two terms deal with. *Infralapsarianism* means that in the timeless mind of God, this decision was made in view of the fall (the Latin word *lapsus* means "fall"). *Supralapsarianism* means that in the mind of God, this decision was made without any prior reference to it.

I am not sure this matter is of great importance or even if it is a true alternative, since it requires us to think in time categories, and God is clearly above or beyond time. Who are we to force time sequences on God? For what it is worth, however, it should be said that all the Reformed creeds are infralapsarian, simply because they want to keep from suggesting even for a moment that God consigns innocents to hell. They want to insist that God does nothing inconsistent with righteousness when he determines human destinies.[5]

---

4. The same two points are in the Canons of the Synod of Dort: "Not all, but some only, are elected, while others are *passed by* in the eternal decrees" and these are punished "not only on account of their unbelief, but also *for all their other sins*" (Chap. 1, Art. 15).

5. For a fuller discussion of this complex topic, see G. C. Berkouwer, *Divine Election* (Grand Rapids: Wm. B. Eerdmans, 1960), pp. 254–277; Loraine Boettner, *The Reformed Doctrine of*

A Useful Doctrine

I suppose at this point some will be wondering, "If the doctrine of reprobation is as difficult as it seems to be, why should we speak about it at all?" The first answer to that is that the Bible itself does. It is part of the revelation given to us. This is also the primary answer to a person who says, "I could never love a God like that." Fair enough, we may say, but that is nevertheless the God with whom you have to deal. Nothing is to be gained by opposing reprobation.

But this is not a very satisfying answer, and there are satisfying and meaningful things to say about reprobation. It is a doctrine that, like all other parts of Scripture, has its "useful" aspects (cf. 2 Tim. 3:16).

1. *Reprobation assures us that God's purpose has not failed.* The first benefit of this doctrine is the very thing Paul is teaching in Romans 9, namely, that God's word has not failed (v. 6). We might ask the question in a personal way, wondering, "Will God fail me?" But the answer is that God has determined the outcome of all things from the beginning, and his word does not fail either in regard to the elect or to the reprobate. God does not begin a work he does not finish. He does not make promises he does not keep. So if you have heard his promises and believed his word, you can be sure he will be faithful to you. If others are lost, it is because God has determined that they should be. It does not mean that you will follow them.

"But am I one of the elect?" you ask. It is easy to know the answer to that question: Believe on the Lord Jesus Christ and begin to obey him. Those who do are the elect. That is how we determine who those persons are.

2. *Reprobation helps us deal with apostasy.* We all know people who have seemed to believe at one time, but who have then fallen away. Does this mean that God has failed them? No. It means that if they continue in their unbelieving state, they are not among God's elect people. Apostasy does not show that the plan of God has failed. Reprobation helps us understand it.

3. *Reprobation keeps before us the important truth that salvation is entirely of grace and that no works of man contribute to it.* If none were lost, we would assume that all are being saved because somehow God owes us salvation, that he must save us either because of who we are or because of who he is. This is not the situation. All are not saved. Therefore, the salvation of the elect is due to divine mercy only. We must never forget that. Indeed, as we will see over the next few studies, this is the dominant note of these important texts in Romans.

Predestination (Philadelphia: The Presbyterian and Reformed Publishing Company, 1963), pp. 126–130; and Charles Hodge, *Systematic Theology* (London: James Clarke & Co., 1960), vol. 2, pp. 316–321.

4. *Reprobation glorifies God.* As soon as we begin to think that God owes us something or that God *must* do something, we limit him and reduce his glory. Election and its twin, reprobation, glorify God, for they remind us that God is absolutely free and sovereign. We have no power over him. On the contrary, "God has mercy on whom he wants to have mercy, and he hardens whom he wants to harden" (Rom. 9:18). God does as he wants in his universe.

One final question: Is reprobation an evangelical doctrine? That is, Is it part of the gospel? I believe it is, for this reason: Because reprobation stresses the glory of the sovereign God in his election, it inevitably highlights mercy and reduces those who hear and accept the doctrine to a position of suppliancy. It forces us to cry, "Jesus, thou Son of David, have mercy on me." As long as we believe we are in control of our own destinies, we will never assume this posture. But when we understand that we are in the hands of a just and holy God and that we are without any hope of salvation apart from his free and utterly sovereign intervention, we will call out for mercy, which is the only right response.

"I will have mercy on whom I will have mercy," says the Almighty. If we believe that, our cry will be the cry of the tax collector: "God, have mercy on me, a sinner" (Luke 18:13). And who can fault that doctrine?

129

But Is God Just?

Romans 9:14-15

What then shall we say? Is God unjust? Not at all! For he says to Moses, "I will have mercy on whom I have mercy, and I will have compassion on whom I have compassion."

Ever since the fall, human beings have been trying to blame God for his actions or (which is almost the same thing) to call him to account.[1] Adam did it in the Garden of Eden, saying, "The woman you put here with me—she gave me some fruit from the tree, and I ate it" (Gen. 3:12). The people of Malachi's day, at the very end of the Old Testament period, were doing the same thing, asking God: "How have you loved us? . . . How have we shown contempt for your name? . . . How have we defiled you? . . . How do we rob you? . . . What have we said against you?" (Mal. 1:2, 6–7; 3:8, 13). They "wearied the LORD" with their words (2:17), yet were demanding that God give them an explanation for his actions.

1. Calvin says perceptively, "The flesh cannot hear the wisdom of God without being at once disturbed by perplexing questions, and it struggles to call God by some means to account" (John Calvin, *The Epistles of Paul the Apostle to the Romans and to the Thessalonians*, trans. Ross MacKenzie [Grand Rapids: Wm. B. Eerdmans, 1973], p. 202).

It is the same today. In most discussions about spiritual things, our contemporaries are asking God to leave heaven, come down to earth, stand
before the bar of our justice, and give an account of himself according to
our small standards. C. S. Lewis even wrote an article about this characteristic,
which he called "God in the Dock."

"If God is good, how could he let my mother die?"

"What about cancer? Why doesn't God do something about it?"

"It's not my fault. I would have done better if only God had given me a
nicer disposition, more energy, kinder parents, better looks, a more advanced
education, or something else."

We have all heard those accusations. But in no area of theology is the
demand that God justify himself more insistent or accompanied by more shrill
accusations of injustice than in regard to the predestination of some persons
to salvation and the passing by of others. Even if we can be convinced that
God does operate in this way, which most are not, we nevertheless scream
out fiercely that it is not right for him to be selective.

The Second of Two Questions

Well, is it? "What then shall we say? Is God unjust?" That is the way Paul
puts the question in Romans 9:14, as he sets out to answer it.

As we begin, we should remember that this is the second of two important
questions in this chapter. The first question, which we have already studied,
is whether God has broken his word in passing over some Jews, who had not
responded to the gospel, and by saving some Gentiles. The Old Testament
is filled with promises to Israel. Does the fact that not all Jews are being saved
not mean that God has broken those promises? Paul answered the question
by explaining that the promises were never intended for those who are mere
physical descendants of Abraham, that is, all ethnic Jews. Rather, as he says,
the promise is to spiritual Israel, which means those out of ethnic Israel (as
well as from the Gentile nations) whom God had elected to salvation.

Paul proved this by showing how God elected one person rather than
another in the first three generations of Jewish history: Abraham rather than
others who lived in Ur; Isaac rather than Abraham's other son, Ishmael; and
Jacob rather than Esau. The last case was particularly telling, because in this
generation the choice was made between twin boys and was announced to
Rebekah, the mother, even before the sons were born, and thus before either
had had opportunity to do either good or evil.

Clearly, God acts by the principle of election, choosing one and passing
by another—whether or not we like it or agree with the justice of his actions
in doing so.

But that brings us to the second question, the one I described in an earlier
study as the question of theodicy: Is God *just* in his actions? Paul has shown
that God discriminates between one individual and another. Indeed, no one
who thinks deeply at all can readily deny it. All are not equal. Nor do all have

equal opportunities, even in secular matters, not to mention religious ones. But is God just in allowing such situations? That is the question. Is it right for God to operate in this fashion?

Point of Departure

As soon as Paul asks the question, "What then shall we say? Is God unjust?" he answers by an emphatic denial: "Not at all!" It is the strongest denial he can muster. The King James Bible has "God forbid!"[2]

That answer is not calculated to satisfy most people today, of course, and it is true that Paul goes on to give reasons for his answer in the following paragraphs. Nevertheless, the answer even in this form is important and is far more profound than most people might imagine. Besides, it is the only proper starting place.

Why? Because it puts us, fallen human beings, in our proper place, which is the only position from which we can begin to learn about spiritual things. The very nature of sin is wanting to be in God's place. But as long as we are trying to be in God's place, we will never be able to hear what God is saying to us. We will be arguing with him instead. In order to learn, we must begin by confessing that God is God and that he is therefore right and just in his actions, even though we may not understand what he is doing.

That is the only rational thing to do anyway, for two reasons. First, if there were injustice in God, the universe would fly apart. Paul is far more reasonable than our contemporaries when he begins with God's justice, for he knows that the righteous character of God must be the basis of everything that is. It is inconceivable to any right thinking mind that God should act wrongly. As Leon Morris writes, "To say that God is unjust is for Paul self-contradictory."[3]

Second, it is only on the basis of some fundamental awareness of what justice is, an awareness of right and wrong, that we can ask the question we are asking. And where do we get that awareness of right and wrong but from God? In other words, if God were not just, we would not even be able to ask, "Is God just?" We would not be able even to conceive of the question. The fact that we can ask it does not mean that by ourselves we can find the explanation of how God is acting justly. That is why we have Romans 9. But it does mean that even in asking the question we are admitting in advance that God is just, rather than the opposite.

The Justification of God

So how are we to understand God's justice? We can start with the fact that God is just, as well as with the fact that he does elect some persons to salvation

---

2. The Greek (mē genoito) means "let it not be."
3. Leon Morris, *The Epistle to the Romans* (Grand Rapids: Wm. B. Eerdmans, and Leicester, England: Inter-Varsity Press, 1988), p. 359.

and does pass by others. But how are we to think about his justice in doing
so? This is the theodicy question.[4]

Here are the essential elements of the answer.

1. *All human beings deserve hell, not heaven.* No one who has followed Paul's
argument in the earlier chapters of Romans can doubt this, and we do not
need to restate those arguments now. It is enough to say that

> There is no one righteous, not even one
>   there is no one who understands,
>   no one who seeks God.
> All have turned away,
>   they have together become worthless;
> there is no one who does good,
>   not even one.
>
> Romans 3:10–12

But we are talking about the justification of God here, and for that purpose
the key word in what I have just said is "deserve." All human beings *deserve*
hell, not heaven. We are not talking about whether all actually end up in hell
or whether only some end up in hell and some in heaven. We are talking
about what all deserve, and what they deserve is condemnation. That is justice.
The justice of God, if it were to operate without regard to any other factor,
could do nothing other than to send every human being to hell. Apart from
those other factors, namely the electing grace of God and the death of Christ
that makes it possible, this is what happens.

2. *If any individual is to be saved, it must be by mercy only, and mercy is in an
entirely different category from justice.* Just as the key word in my first point was
"deserve," so the key word in this second essential statement is "mercy."

Deserving is based upon what people have done. Mercy has nothing to
do with what people have done but is something that finds its source in the
will of God only. In the text that Paul cites to make his point, the words
"mercy" and "compassion" are used almost synonymously: "I will have mercy
on whom I will have mercy, and I will have compassion on whom I will have
compassion" (Exod. 33:19b). But there is this slight difference. Compassion
has to do with recognizing the poor or helpless state of a person and stooping
to help that person. Mercy does the same, but its unique quality is that it is
shown to people not only who do not deserve it but who in fact deserve the
opposite. In this case, mercy describes the giving of salvation to people who
actually deserve to perish. It is providing heaven for those who merit hell.

---

4. It is discussed in most of the commentaries. For a full treatment of this question, see John
Piper, *The Justification of God: An Exegetical and Theological Study of Romans 9:1-23* (Grand Rapids:
Baker Book House, 1983).

God shows mercy on the basis of Christ's work in taking the punishment due sinners upon himself. Even in this sense, the showing of mercy by God is according to justice. But this is not the theodicy question. The theodicy question has to do only with why God saves some in this way and not others.

3. *Even if God should save people on the basis of something in them—faith, good works, or whatever—this would actually be injustice, since people's backgrounds are unequal.*

Think it through. If God saved some people and not others on the basis of good works, which is what most people would like God to do, there would never be justice, because some inherit kinder or more serving temperaments than others and because environmental factors play a part. It is easy for a person who has been raised by two loving and moral parents to follow in their way and do good. Not all do, of course. But that truth is irrelevant to my argument. My point is only that it is easier for such persons to do good than it is for one who has been neglected by his or her parents or has been raised in a vicious or immoral environment.

Or take faith. Isn't it true that some persons simply are born more trusting than others, and others are instinctively more skeptical? Or, if we think of their environments, isn't it true that some receive the advantages of biblical teaching or moral instruction that others lack? If God's election were based on the ability of some to respond to him, by faith or whatever, God would not be just in his selection. Some would be profoundly disadvantaged, and others inevitably would be privileged.

So election is not only just. It is just, and God is right in choosing some and passing by others. But—and here is the important thing—*election is the only thing that is just.* Election alone starts with all people at the same point and on the same level, all of whom deserve hell. Then it saves some and passes by others, all entirely apart from anything whatever in these elect or reprobate persons.

Two Irrepressible Objections

The answer to the theodicy question is in the points I just made, though we will go into it further as our studies of Romans 9 continue. But I know that it is not as easy as that to satisfy the objections that come to our rebellious (or perhaps merely questioning) minds.

There are two particularly.

1. *Shouldn't God show mercy to everyone?* This is the first question asked by a person who has followed the argument to this point and yet is unsatisfied. The person will agree that all deserve hell and that God does not have to save anyone. He will agree that if any are saved it is by mercy only, apart from anything anyone may have done or may do. "But," he will ask, "shouldn't God show mercy to everyone? Is it right for him to restrict his mercy to one group of people rather than showing it to all?"

If you are asking that question, and I suppose many are, let me say gently that you have still not grasped the situation. The operative word in the question is "should." It means "ought," "must," or "necessary" if justice is to be done. But as soon as we use that word, we are back in the realm of justice, and we are no longer dealing with mercy. "Should" implies obligation, and obligation has to do with justice. If there is any "should" in the matter, the issue is no longer mercy. We are talking about justice, and justice, as we have already seen, can do nothing but send every human being to hell.

It is not justice we need from God. It is grace.

2. *Why doesn't God show mercy to everyone?* The second objection sounds like the first one, but it is really quite different. It is the question raised by a person who understands the difference between justice and mercy but is still wondering why God is selective. "Forget the word 'should,'" this person replies. "My question is simply: Why doesn't God save everyone?"

Let me begin by saying two things. First, this is a proper question to ask, because it is asking for understanding rather than demanding that God come down from heaven and submit to our standards of right and wrong. It is a matter of faith in search of enlightenment. Second, it is more difficult than the questions we have asked so far, because it is asking about God's reasons for doing something, and there is no way we can know what those reasons are unless God reveals them to us. Does he?

Romans 9:15 seems to say merely that this is the way God operates: "I will have mercy on whom I have mercy, and I will have compassion on whom I have compassion." In other words, a perfectly legitimate answer to our question is that the "why" of it is God's business. God does not owe us an answer. What is more, there are undoubtedly parts of the answer, if not all, that are not revealed. God has reasons that may forever be unknown.

Yet there is one revealed answer, though not all persons will like it. A Baptist professor and pastor named John Piper has written a detailed study of Romans 9:1–23 in which he argues that Paul's quotation from Exodus 33:19 in Romans 9:15 has to do with the character of God and with God's proper determination to make his nature known. In a careful study of Exodus 33, which we will also begin to look at carefully in our next study, Piper shows that the verse Paul quotes "is not merely a description of how God acted in any particular instance toward Moses in granting him a theophany or toward Israel in renewing the covenant. Rather it is a solemn declaration of the nature of God, or (which is the same thing) a proclamation of his name and glory."[5]

I admit that Piper's point is not easily seen in verse 15, the quotation from Exodus. It takes some hard technical study of the Old Testament context to realize it. But it is seen in the rest of this chapter.

5. Piper, *The Justification of God*, p. 67.

First, Paul's quotation of Exodus 9:16 in verse 17: "For the Scripture says to Pharaoh: 'I raised you up for this very purpose, that I might display my power in you and that my name might be proclaimed in all the earth.'" This deals with reprobation, the matter we were studying in the last chapter, and it explains at least one purpose of God in passing over some. It is to display his "power" in order that his powerful or sovereign name might be proclaimed throughout the earth. In other words, God thinks it is important that the created order should know that he is all-powerful, especially in overcoming and judging some who stand against him, as Pharaoh did. God shows this by judging them.

Second, Paul argues a few verses further on that God's "wrath," "power," "patience," "glory," and "mercy" are displayed in election, on the one hand, and in reprobation, on the other: "What if God, choosing to show his wrath and make his power known, bore with great patience the objects of his wrath—prepared for destruction? What if he did this to make the riches of his glory known to the objects of his mercy, whom he prepared in advance for glory—even us, whom he also called, not only from the Jews but also from the Gentiles?" (vv. 22–24).

What this means is that God considers the display of his attributes in human history to be worth the whole drama, to be worth the creation, fall, redemption, election, reprobation, and everything else. From God's point of view, the revelation of his glory is the great priority.

Why Is It Necessary?

You will remember that I wrote a bit earlier that I am not at all sure this will satisfy all people. In fact, I know it will not. It may not satisfy you. If you do not find it satisfying, even though it is what we find in Romans 9, you will probably be asking at this point, "But why should it be necessary for God's name to be glorified?"

There is only one answer I know, and it is this: Because it is right that his name be glorified. God is glorious. He should be glorified, and because this is a universe run by God, and not by us, that which is right will in the end be done. God will be honored, and all will bow before him.

But do you see how this is going? We began with the theodicy question: Is God right to act as he does? We were asking it because it did not seem right to us for God to select some for salvation and to pass by and judge others for their sin. But when we examine the question, as we have, we find that the matter is exactly the opposite of what we first imagined it to be. We have found that God acts as he does precisely because he is just. He glorifies his name in displaying wrath toward sinners and the riches of his glory toward those who are being saved because this is the only right thing for God to do. It is his very justice, not his injustice, that causes him to operate in this fashion.

If we object to this, our objection only shows that we are operating by a different and, therefore, a sinful standard. What we mean is that we want to compel God to save everybody, regardless of what they have done or not done or even whether they want his salvation.

The real wonder, of course, is that God displays his mercy. For by its very nature mercy is undeserved and unrequired. Yet God has done so. He has done so in saving sinners like you and me.

I like the way John Piper closes his exegetical study, for it is along the very line I have been following. Piper is aware that many will find these truths unpalatable. But, he says:

> For those who, like myself, confess Romans 9 as Holy Scripture and accord it an authority over our lives, the implications of this exegesis are profound. We will surely not fall prey to the naive and usually polemical suggestions that we cease to pray or that we abandon evangelism. If we did that we would only betray our failure to be grasped by this theology, as Paul was, who "prayed without ceasing" (1 Thess. 5:17) and who labored in evangelism "harder than any of the other apostles" (1 Cor. 15:10).
>
> On the contrary we will be deeply sobered by the awful severity of God, humbled to the dust by the absoluteness of our dependence on his unconditional mercy, and irresistibly allured by the infinite treasury of his glory ready to be revealed to the vessels of glory. Thus we will be moved to forsake all confidence in human distinctives or achievements and we will entrust ourselves to *mercy alone*. In the hope of glory we will extend this mercy to others that they may see our good deeds and give glory to our Father in heaven.[6]

6. Ibid., p. 205.

130

"Mercy" Is His Name

Romans 9:15

For he says to Moses, "I will have mercy on whom I have mercy, and I will have compassion on whom I have compassion."

I hope you have noticed that in the last three of our studies of Romans 9—on election, reprobation, and the justice of God—we have ended by stressing God's "mercy." In the first study we saw that election is grounded in mercy. In the second we discovered that reprobation forces us back upon mercy, rather than causing us to appeal to any supposed rights we may have. In the third study we argued that the justice of God is established precisely upon his right to show and to withhold mercy as he wills.

I suppose there are people who might object to this procedure on the grounds that Christians simply like mercy and so stress it, passing by the much less attractive doctrine of wrath. But that is not the case. We stress mercy because the Bible stresses mercy, and because it is the most remarkable and unexpected of God's attributes.

There is nothing unexpected about condemnation, wrath, or reprobation. We deserve those. But that God should extend mercy to sinners and so save some of them from his wrath is extraordinary.

1075

Mercy is what Paul himself has been emphasizing throughout this section, and it is what he comes to again in verse 15, which we need to study now. The text says, "For he [that is, God] says to Moses, 'I will have mercy on whom I have mercy, and I will have compassion on whom I have compassion.'" In this text the words *hate, harden,* or *pass by* are not even mentioned. Instead, the emphasis is on the word *mercy* and its near equivalent, the word *compassion*.

Mercy in Election

The quotation comes from Exodus 33:19, which means that it has an Old Testament context. So, before we go on with Romans 9, we need to explore the context to better understand this key verse. In fact, from this point on we are going to have to go back into the Old Testament more than once, since Paul gives a number of Old Testament quotations in the latter half of Romans 9, all of which are intended to direct our minds to the ways in which God has operated by mercy in past days. Before we are done we are going to examine the mercy of God as it is revealed in the minor prophets Jonah and Hosea and in the major prophet Isaiah.

We begin by going back to what we have seen earlier in Romans 9. That is, we go back to the mercy of God shown in the choice of Israel to be a special people to whom he would thereafter continue to show grace.

We remember that the history of these people began with God's choice of Abraham, and later of Abraham's son Isaac and Isaac's son Jacob, entirely apart from any good that might be imagined to be in them. Abraham was just like the rest of his contemporaries, a worshiper of false gods. But God set his love upon Abraham and called him out of Ur of the Chaldeans to be the father of a new nation through whom he would eventually send the Savior.

In the second generation God chose Isaac rather than Abraham's other son, Ishmael, and in the third generation he chose Jacob rather than Esau.

Those choices alone demonstrate the truth of the text Paul is quoting, for they prove that God had mercy on whom he would have had mercy and that he had compassion on whom he had compassion.

"Mercy" is God's name.

Mercy in Israel's Deliverance

Coming a bit closer to Exodus 33, we find that the opening chapters of Exodus deal with the deliverance from Egypt, climaxing in the Passover.

Moses had been sent to the powerful Egyptian ruler with the command to let the people go, and Pharaoh had refused, saying, "Who is the LORD, that I should obey him and let Israel go? I do not know the LORD and I will not let Israel go" (Exod. 5:2). As a result, God unleashed a series of plagues on Egypt in which: (1) the waters of the land were turned to blood; (2) frogs were multiplied in huge quantities; (3) gnats infested everyone; (4) flies followed the gnats; (5) the animals were killed; (6) painful boils came upon the Egyptians; (7) hail destroyed the crops; (8) followed by locusts; and (9) darkness blotted out the sun for three days. These were demonstrations of the power of God over the Egyptian gods, who were associated with the water, crops, fields, and sky. The greatest god was Ra, the sun god, who was subdued in judgment number nine. By the time the plagues were over, the country was destroyed, but still Pharaoh would not release the people.

God told Moses that the last plague was to be the death of the firstborn children of the land, as well as the firstborn of the animals, and that after this Pharaoh would let the people go. The plague would be unleashed by an angel of death who would pass through Egypt by night.

The Israelites were to prepare for the Passover by killing a lamb and spreading its blood upon the sides and tops of the door frames of the houses in which they were living, so that when the angel of death came through the land he might see the blood and *pass over* the Israelite houses. This is where the word *Passover* comes from.

The Lord said, "The blood will be a sign for you on the houses where you are; and when I see the blood, I will pass over you. No destructive plague will touch you when I strike Egypt" (Exod. 12:13).

This is what happened. That night the angel of death passed through the land, the firstborn of all the Egyptians were killed, the Jews were spared, and the next morning Pharaoh gave word that the people were to leave the country—though he later reversed his decision, pursued the people to destroy them, and was himself destroyed.

But here is the point of the story.

The people were not very spiritual, as the sequel will show, and there were undoubtedly many among the nation who would have thought for one reason or another that they merited special treatment by God and should therefore have been saved at the time of the exodus simply because they were Jews and deserved saving. Some would have pointed to their ancestry, as Jews did later. "We are Abraham's seed," they might have said. "That is why God delivered us." Many would have thought that they were better or more moral than the oppressive Egyptians. Everyone thinks that he or she is more moral than someone else, particularly someone he or she dislikes. Still others might have pointed to their years of bondage and suffering: "If God is just, surely we should be rewarded for our suffering and the Egyptians should be punished."

The way in which God actually delivered the people dispelled any such mistaken notions. It showed that they were saved by the mercy and grace of God only.

How? In this way. What would have happened if a Jew had decided that his ancestry or morality or suffering or anything else was sufficient to guarantee his deliverance and had therefore refused to spread the blood of the lamb upon the door frame of his or her house? The answer is that the angel of death would have struck down the firstborn in that house just as if it were the house of an Egyptian, for "there is no difference, for all have sinned and fall short of the glory of God" (Rom. 3:23). The Jews were a sinful people, "stiff-necked," as God would later describe them. They, too, deserved to die. But God set his love upon them and saved them for his mercy's sake.

Later Moses would write, "The LORD did not set his affection on you and choose you because you were more numerous than other peoples [or for any other human reason], for you were the fewest of all peoples. But it was because the LORD loved you and kept the oath he swore to your forefathers that he brought you out with a mighty hand and redeemed you from the land of slavery, from the power of Pharaoh king of Egypt" (Deut. 7:7–8).

"Mercy" is God's name.

Mercy at Mount Sinai

We come next to Exodus 32, the chapter immediately preceding the one in which Paul's quotation in Romans 9 is found. In doing so, we come to one of the most moving stories in the Old Testament. (We have already looked at it carefully in study 123 of this series, "Great Sorrow for a Great People.")

The people had left Egypt behind and had now arrived at Mount Sinai, where Moses was called up into the mountain to receive the law from God. While he was there the people whom he had left behind grew tired of waiting (he was there for forty days), and they got Aaron to make a little calf of gold, which they began to worship, calling it the god that had delivered them from Egypt. It was a terrible moment in their history, and God interrupted the giving of the law to Moses to tell Moses what was happening and threaten the destruction of that generation of the people, saying that he would begin again and make a new nation from Moses.

We remember from our earlier study how Moses pleaded for the people and eventually offered himself for judgment in their place, saying, "Oh, what a great sin these people have committed! They have made themselves gods of gold. But now, please forgive their sin—but if not, then blot me out of the book you have written" (Exod. 32:31–32).

Moses did not know that he could not give himself for another. He, too, was a sinner and deserved—there is that word again, "deserved"—to die for his transgressions as much as they deserved to die for theirs. But God was aware that from the beginning he had planned to send his Son, the Lord Jesus Christ, to be a sin offering in their place, to suffer hell for those he had chosen beforehand and would eventually draw to faith, and it was on the basis of that anticipated atonement by Christ that God extended mercy to them. In other words, the mercy shown to the people at Sinai had exactly the same basis as the mercy shown to the people on the night of the Passover, for the blood spread upon the door frames of the houses pointed forward to the coming substitutionary death of Jesus Christ.

"Mercy" is God's name.

The Merciful God

This brings us to Exodus 33 and to the text Paul is quoting, which is a continuation of the story. God had spared the people following their apostasy at Sinai and had promised to send an angel to lead them into the Promised Land. But Moses was not satisfied with this arrangement. In his judgment, to be led by an angel was less than being led by God, and he did not want any lessening of the special relationship between God and the people that he and they had enjoyed previously. They were sinners, and any special relationship between themselves and God would have to be on the basis of the mercy of God and not their deserving. Still, they must be led by God or not at all. Moses did not want to lead the people, even with the help of an angel, unless God himself were with them.

In this moment of acute distress, Moses went out of the camp to the "tent of meeting" to speak with God and present his requests. There were three of them, all closely related.

First, Moses asked to be taught God's ways "so I may know you and continue to find favor with you" (v. 13). This means that he recognized that he was a sinner himself and so needed to be taught and kept by God if he was not to fall into the same sins the people had committed.

God promised to be with him and teach him.

Second, Moses pleaded for God's personal and continued presence: "If your Presence does not go with us, do not send us up from here. How will anyone know that you are pleased with me and with your people unless you go with us? What else will distinguish me and your people from all the other people on the face of the earth?" (vv. 15–16). He meant that the people could never be distinguished from other people by anything in them, but only on the basis of God's undeserved presence with them.

God promised Moses that he would do what he had asked.

Then Moses made the boldest request of all: "Now show me your glory" (v. 18). God replied that he would not be able to show his face to Moses, because no human being can see the face of God and live. But he would reveal his goodness and proclaim his name to Moses, which he did by placing him in the cleft of a rock, covering the opening with his hand, and then causing his goodness to pass before him.

It is in this context, in the midst of God's answer to Moses' third question, that the quotation by Paul in Romans occurs. The text says, "I will cause all my goodness to pass in front of you, and I will proclaim my name, the LORD, in your presence. I will have mercy on whom I will have mercy, and I will have compassion on whom I will have compassion" (v. 19). This verse is the climax of the story, and its point is that the very name or character of God is bound up in his mercy. The display of his name is the proclamation of his compassion.

The record of God's dealings with Israel in her election, deliverance, and preservation, even when the people had sinned against grace, as well as this climactic revelation of glory, show that "mercy" is God's name.

God's Name and God's Glory

When I was writing in the previous study about the justice of God in saving some persons and passing by others, I referred to a study of Romans 9:1–23 by a Baptist professor and pastor whose name is John Piper. Part of his study is an examination of Exodus 33:19 in its context, and his conclusions are what I present here.

Commentators on Romans 9:15 have done all manner of strange things with this verse in an attempt to weaken the doctrine of God's rightful sovereignty in the matters of election and reprobation. Some have referred it only to God's mercy to Moses in granting him a theophany.[1] Others have limited it to God's renewal of the covenant with Israel following the people's sin. But the verse surely means more than this, as Piper and indeed the entire context of God's electing choice, deliverance, and preservation of Israel make clear.

What is involved is no less than the revelation in history of God's true name or character. In other words, election and the corresponding doctrine of reprobation are the means by which God's compassion and mercy (as well as his power and wrath) are made known.

As Piper puts it, "In its Old Testament context, Exodus 33:19 is not merely a description of how God acted in any particular instance toward Moses in granting him a theophany or toward Israel in renewing the covenant. Rather it is a solemn declaration of the nature of God, or (which is the same thing) a proclamation of his name and glory."[2]

Mercy with the Lord

We are going to be coming back to this theme again, as I said when we started, because mercy is the dominant note in this chapter. But we need a few conclusions here before we go on.

1. *We need mercy if we are to be saved.* I have said this before, but it can never be said enough, simply because we do not think this way naturally. We think in terms of justice, because we suppose ourselves to be deserving. But we are not deserving, at least not of anything but eternal punishment. If we are to be saved, we must not come to God pleading our deserts but on the basis of his mercy. We need mercy. Apart from it we will perish.

1. M. L. Legrange, *Saint Paul Epître aux Romains*, p. 233. Cited by John Piper, *The Justification of God: An Exegetical and Theological Study of Romans 9:1–23* (Grand Rapids: Baker Book House, 1983), p. 55.

2. Piper, *The Justification of God*, p. 67.

2. *God is a God of mercy.* Here is the good news. God is a God of mercy. True, he is also God of justice and wrath. Sin will be punished. The wrath of God will be made known along with his other great attributes. But God emphasizes mercy. He offers mercy. To find mercy we must come to God on the basis of the shed blood of his Son, the Lord Jesus Christ, who died to be our Savior. The mercy of God is seen at the cross of the Savior. That is the ultimate expression of mercy and the basis for God's election of some to salvation.

3. *We can appeal to mercy.* We have been speaking about election and therefore of the sovereign right of God to show mercy to whom he will show mercy and compassion to whom he will show compassion. The display of mercy by God is not compelled in any way. Otherwise it is not mercy, as we saw in the previous study. But that does not mean that we cannot appeal to it. We can. Indeed, the Scriptures are full of such appeals. They even tell us that it is through appeals to mercy that mercy may be found.

Remember the tax collector in Jesus' story.

And remember the Pharisee in the same story, the one who was so highly regarded by those who knew him. The Pharisee was moral. He did not steal. He was not an adulterer. He tried to obey the law, even fasting twice a week and tithing all he possessed. But he was not moral enough to please God, and he had no sense of needing God's mercy. His prayer was not heard. He was not justified.

It was altogether different with the tax collector. He was a sinner, but even more important than that, he knew he was a sinner. So he did not come to God to remind God of his ethical attainments. He stood at a distance and would not even look up to heaven. Instead he beat his breast, a sign of genuine remorse or repentance, and prayed, "God, have mercy on me, a sinner." Jesus' judgment was that "this man, rather than the other, went home justified before God. For everyone who exalts himself will be humbled, and he who humbles himself will be exalted" (Luke 18:13–14). It is a judgment each of us needs very much to hear.

Do not try to catch me at this point, saying, "But if mercy has its basis in God's sovereign will, what good does it do to appeal to mercy? Doesn't the text say, 'I will have mercy on whom I have mercy, and I will have compassion on whom I have compassion'?" That is absolutely true. Mercy is God's unique prerogative. But I will tell you who those are upon whom God has set his mercy. They are those who appeal to him on the basis of it. And I will tell you who those are who are elect. They are those who turn from their own self-sufficiency and trust Jesus.

How else can anyone know who God's elect are? In what way other than by faith are the children of God made known?

4. *We can proclaim God's mercy to others.* Can we proclaim him as sovereign? To be sure. As one who passes by those he has not chosen for salvation? That,

too. But also as one who has mercy on whom he wills to have mercy and who has compassion on whom he wills to have compassion. God is a merciful God. There is nothing in the Bible that hinders me from saying that as clearly and as forcefully as I can. His very name is Mercy. And because his name is Mercy, I can assure you that if you will come believing on Jesus Christ, which is how he has made his mercy possible as well as known, you will find it. God has never turned a deaf ear to someone who asked for mercy. He has never rejected any person who has trusted in Christ Jesus.

> Come, every soul by sin oppressed,
>   There's mercy with the Lord,
> And he will surely give you rest,
>   By trusting in his Word.
> Only trust him, only trust him,
>   Only trust him now.
> He will save you, he will save you,
>   He will save you now.

Do you believe that? Will you come? If you believe it and if you will come, you will find God to be exactly what the Bible declares him to be: the merciful God who has reached out to save many through Jesus Christ. And you will be saved.

131

Salvation Is of the Lord

Romans 9:16

It does not, therefore, depend on man's desire or effort, but on God's mercy.

We are in a section of the Bible in which every sentence has exceptional importance. Because of this, we have been moving very slowly. In the last study we looked at Romans 9:15. In this study we look at verse 16.

Verse 16 can be considered an inference drawn from the truth in verse 15, which is a quotation from the Old Testament. If that is the case, the thought would be: If God has mercy on whom he wills to have mercy and shows compassion to whom he wills to show compassion, then salvation is of God who shows mercy and not of man. That is true enough. But it is probably better to see verse 16 as a statement of the truth behind the quotation. If this is the case, it means that salvation is not of man but of God; therefore, God shows mercy on whom he wills to show mercy and has compassion on whom he wills to have compassion.

This is better, because the chief point of verse 16 is the exclusion of any human role in salvation. The verse says, "It does not, therefore, depend on man's desire or effort, but on God's mercy." Or as the King James Version has it, "So then it is not of him that willeth, not of him that runneth, but of God that sheweth mercy."

Today's Evangelism

This text has enormous implications for the way we do evangelism. In fact, it is a rebuke of most popular evangelism in our day.

You may recall from our studies of Romans 6 that when I was writing about sanctification in that context, I said that we tend to approach it in either of two wrong ways. Either we introduce a formula: "Follow these three [or four] steps to sound spiritual growth." Or we recommend an experience: "What you need is the baptism of the Holy Spirit [or meaningful worship or whatever]." I pointed out that neither of these is introduced by Paul. Rather, he bases his approach to sanctification on sound teaching. He tells us that we are to go on in the Christian life for the simple reason that we have become new creatures as the result of God's work in us, and we cannot go back to what we were.[1]

The situation is exactly the same in most of our current approaches to evangelism. We choose either a formula or a feeling.

The formula represents something we must do: "Give your heart to Jesus," "Pray the sinner's prayer," "Hold up your hand and come forward," "Fill out this card." The feeling is something we try to work up in evangelistic services by certain kinds of music, moving stories, and emotional appeals.

Let me say that I do not doubt for a moment that God has sometimes used these methods and that he has sometimes worked through feelings, just as he has also sometimes used quite different things. The problem with these ways of doing evangelism is not that God has not occasionally been gracious enough to use them, but that they distort the truth about salvation by making it something we do or to which we can contribute and thus, to that degree, detract from the glory of God.

Besides, these approaches contradict our text, which says that salvation "does not, therefore, depend on man's desire or effort, but on God's mercy."

These approaches are also ineffective, as we would expect them to be, for they have filled our churches with thousands of people who think they are saved because they have made a profession or come forward at a meeting, but who are not born again. In many cases, those who have done these things are not even any longer present in the churches.

The Negative Teaching

Romans 9:16 contains both negative and positive teaching, each of which is meant to be comprehensive. Negatively, we are told that salvation does not

1. See James Montgomery Boice, "You Can Count on It" (Romans 6:11) and "The Bottom Line" (Romans 6:19–22) in *Romans, Volume 2, The Reign of Grace* (Grand Rapids: Baker Book House, 1991), pp. 673–680 and 697–704.

come by man's desire or effort, that is, neither by his will nor by his personal attainments. Positively, we are told that salvation comes from God.

The words *desire* and *effort* are meant to include everything of which a human being may be capable, and they thus reduce everyone to the position of being saved by the mercy of God or not saved. The first word concerns volition. The second refers to active exertion. Specifically they deny that we are saved by "seeking God" or "wanting to be saved" or, to run with the other term, by "choosing Jesus," "surrendering our lives to Jesus," "taking Jesus into our hearts," or doing anything else of which we may think ourselves to be capable. It is true that there is a faith to be exercised, a choice to be made, a life to be surrendered, and seeking to be done. But those are the result of God's working in us according to his mercy, and not the conditions on which he does.

Robert Haldane wrote rightly, "It is true, indeed, that believers both will and run, but this is the *effect*, not the *cause*, of the grace of God being vouch-safed to them."[2]

I know there are objections, some of them scriptural.

"What about John 1:12?" says someone. "Doesn't that verse say, 'To all who received him, to those who believed in his name, he gave the right to become children of God'?" It does, of course. But the answer to the implied objection—that we become born again as the result of our receiving Jesus—is found in the next verse, which describes those who are saved as "children born not of natural descent, nor of human decision or a husband's will, but born of God" (v. 13). That fixes the sequence rightly, just as Paul has expressed it in Romans 8, Ephesians 1 and 2, and elsewhere: first, election; then, rebirth; third, faith accompanied by repentance; and lastly, adoption into the family of God along with other benefits.

Together, John 1:12 and 13 actually teach that "it does not . . . depend on man's desire or effort, but on God's mercy" (Rom. 9:16).

Another verse that some people will quote is Romans 10:9: "If you confess with your mouth, 'Jesus is Lord,' and believe in your heart that God raised him from the dead, you will be saved." Then they ask, "Doesn't that teach that we have to give our hearts to Jesus and then confess him as Lord to be saved? Doesn't it mean that we are the ones who ultimately determine whether or not we will be saved? If we are saved, isn't it because we want to be saved? If we are lost, isn't it because we choose to be?"

Well, we know the mouth speaks what is in the heart. Jesus said, "For out of the overflow of the heart the mouth speaks" (Matt. 12:34b). So the critical question is: What kind of a heart is it that confesses, "Jesus is Lord"? Is this the new heart, which is given to us by God,—or the old, Adamic heart, which is enmity against God? It cannot be the latter, because the Bible everywhere teaches that the old heart is thoroughly corrupt. Jeremiah wrote, "The heart

---

2. Robert Haldane, *An Exposition of the Epistle to the Romans* (MacDill AFB: MacDonald Publishing, 1958), p. 468.

is deceitful above all things and beyond cure" (Jer. 17:9). Ezekiel called it a "heart of stone" (Ezek. 11:19). Can a stony heart repent of its sin and come to God? Can a heart as wicked as this "choose" Jesus? Impossible! We can no more change our hearts than a leopard can change its spots.

Therefore, if we are to repent and believe the gospel, we must be given a new heart. A "heart of flesh" is Ezekiel's term for it. This heart is given to us by the new birth. It is this heart only that believes on Jesus.

The Positive Teaching

This brings us to the positive teaching of this verse, namely, that salvation is entirely of God. God has mercy on whom he wills to have mercy, and he shows compassion on whom he wills to show compassion.

I have titled this study "Salvation Is of the Lord," which comes, as I am sure you realize, from the Old Testament. It is from the story of Jonah, from chapter 2, and I refer to this now because Jonah is a good illustration of our text in Romans, namely, that salvation "does not . . . depend on man's desire or effort, but on God's mercy." The story of Jonah is a story of God's mercy from beginning to end: mercy to the sailors, mercy to the people of Nineveh, and, above all, mercy to Jonah. Moreover, as far as man's desire or effort is concerned, not only did Jonah not desire God's will or strive to do it, he actually willed and tried to do the opposite. He tried to run away from God as deliberately as he could.

Jonah was a prophet, and God came to him with a command to proclaim a message of judgment on Nineveh, the capital of Assyria: "Go to the great city of Nineveh and preach against it, because its wickedness has come up before me" (Jonah 1:2). We would have expected Jonah to be responsive to such a call at once. Instead, "Jonah ran away from the LORD and headed for Tarshish" (v. 3a). Scholars debate the location of this ancient city, but most believe it was on the far coast of Spain beyond the Rock of Gibraltar. This fits the story, of course, for it means that Jonah was so determined to resist God's sovereign call that he set out in precisely the opposite direction and for a destination as far away as possible. God said, "Go east." Jonah went west, as far west as anyone knew to go. If he went farther than that, he would presumably have fallen off the edge of the world, which is, in a sense, what happened to him.

Why did Jonah disobey God? Strangely, at the end of the story, we find him explaining that it was because he suspected that God was going to be merciful to these people (Jonah 4:2)—and he did not want that, because they were the enemies of his people. No one can successfully run away from God, however. So, although Jonah went west instead of east, God went after him and brought him back. The text says that God hurled a great storm after Jonah.

At this point the mariners come into the story, for the judgment on the disobedient prophet affected them, too, and they were soon in as much danger of drowning from the fierce gale as Jonah was. They were pagans, but they had some spiritual perception and understood that the storm was unusually fierce, supernaturally so, in fact; they reasoned that some powerful god was angry with one or more of them. When they drew straws to find out who it was, the lot fell on Jonah.

Jonah understood that God had found him out and was now exposing his disobedience. He confessed what he was doing. But he was still unrepentant. He had that "heart of stone" Ezekiel had written about. So, when the sailors asked what they should do to him to make the sea calm down for them, Jonah replied, "Pick me up and throw me into the sea, and it will become calm. I know that it is my fault that this great storm has come upon you" (v. 12).

I like to point out that Jonah did not know that God had prepared a great fish to swallow him and eventually return him back to land. So, if he was asking to be thrown overboard in the middle of the Mediterranean Sea, it meant that he was willing to be drowned. It meant that in his heart he was still unrepentant, for he was saying, "I would rather die than submit to God's will."

That is what it means to have a hard heart. It is what every one of us has until God replaces it.

Was Jonah a genuine believer at this point? Good question! I used to say he was. We would expect it of a prophet. If he was, he is an example of how stubbornly disobedient some Christians are with God, at least for a time. Today, however, I am not so sure. It is clear that Jonah was not right with God, and his is more an example of an unregenerate heart than a regenerate one. At any rate, Jonah seems to have experienced what we would call a conversion inside the great fish, which is where the verse "Salvation comes from the LORD" occurs (Jonah 2:9).

What happened inside Jonah while he was inside the fish is the heart of this great story.

Prayer from the Depths

When Jonah was turning his back on God to go to Tarshish, it did not bother him at all that he was abandoning God. But suddenly, when he was thrown overboard to his death and found himself in the position of apparently being abandoned by God, and Jonah actually calls his condition hellish, saying, "From the depths of the grave [that is, from *Sheol*] I called for help" (Jonah 2:2). As the story shows, God had not abandoned Jonah. But Jonah thought he had, and his despair was the very first step in his conversion.

What Jonah did in that great fish was to pray. God brought him to that point. As he prayed, he discovered that God was using the very depths of his misery to show him mercy.

Jonah's prayer has four characteristics of all true prayer, and these have bearing on the question of correct biblical evangelism, which is where we started.

1. *He was honest.* The first thing we notice about Jonah's prayer is that it was honest. That is, his disobedience had gotten him into a mess, and he acknowledged it. Before we get to this point, when God is working in our lives, we tend to explain away the hard hand of God's judgments. We tell ourselves that we are only having a temporary setback, that things will get better, that they are not as bad as they seem. But when God begins to get through to us, the first thing that happens is that we admit our misery and desperate circumstances for what they are. Moreover, we admit that God has caused them. This is what Jonah does. You hear it in his prayer.

> You hurled me into the deep,
>   into the very heart of the seas,
>   and the currents swirled about me;
> all your waves and breakers
>   swept over me.
> I said, "I have been banished
>   from your sight;
> yet I will look again
>   toward your holy temple."
>
> Jonah 2:3–4

To acknowledge that God was behind his misfortune increased his terror, for it was not the sailors or even mere circumstances he was fighting. It was God. God had summoned Jonah to trial, cast a verdict of "guilty" against his sinful prophet, and sentenced him to death. This is a terror almost beyond words! But, in another sense, the acknowledgement of God's hand in his misery also provided comfort. For God is merciful, and it is always better to fall into the hands of God, even the angry God, than of men.

It is often in judgment that mercy may be found.

2. *He repented.* The second characteristic of Jonah's prayer is a spirit of repentance. We see it in two ways. First, he acknowledged that what had happened to him, while caused by God, was nevertheless his own fault. This is the meaning of verse 8, where Jonah says, "Those who cling to worthless idols forfeit the grace that could be theirs." An idol is anything that takes the place of God. So Jonah is confessing that he had rejected God, just as surely as those who literally worship idols. Therefore, he had renounced the source of all mercy.

The second way we know Jonah was genuinely repentant is that he does not ask God for anything. If he had, we might suspect that he was repenting only to get something from God. That is, he would have been treating his repentance as a good work that somehow was supposed to put God in his debt. Salvation does not come that way. Remember: Deserving something and receiving mercy are two entirely different things. Jonah knew now that all he deserved was damnation. Therefore, he was willing to wait upon the mercy of God, if it should come, without demanding anything.

3. *He was thankful.* "Thankful?" we might ask. "From the belly of a fish? Only a few hours or days away from death? What could Jonah possibly be thankful about?" Well, if we continue to think of his plight in physical terms, there probably is no good answer. But it is vastly different if we think spiritually. True, Jonah had no hope of any bodily deliverance. But he had found the grace of God. His entire prayer shows he had. His word for what he had found is "salvation" (v. 9).

This is the greatest miracle of the book. Not the great fish. Not the storm. The greatest miracle is Jonah's salvation.

4. *He was willing to take his position alongside the ungodly, all of whom need salvation by the mercy of God only.* The final characteristic of this prayer is likewise significant. For when Jonah prayed, as he did at the end, "But I, with a song of thanksgiving, will *sacrifice* to you. What I have *vowed* I will make good" (v. 9, emphasis added), he was promising to do exactly what the pagan mariners had been willing to do, and did do, in the previous chapter. When they saw the power and holiness of Jonah's God, "They offered a sacrifice to the LORD and made vows to him" (Jonah 1:16). It was right that they should. But here, in the second chapter, Jonah is taking his place alongside of them.

Earlier he had said, "I don't want to preach to pagans. I am a Jew. I want God to judge the pagans." But now, after he had discovered how much he deserved God's judgment himself, he was willing to come to God as the mariners came—as a suppliant seeking mercy.[3]

"Jesus Saves"

I have two final points. The first is a restatement of the truth that salvation is by the mercy of God and is without conditions.

What conditions could there be? Robert Haldane asks that question and answers with a telling paragraph:

Is it faith? Faith is the *gift* of God. Is it repentance? Christ is exalted as a Prince and a Savior to *give* repentance. Is it love? God promises to circumcise the heart in order to *love* him. Are they good works? His people are the workmanship of God created unto *good works*. Is it perseverance to the end? They are *kept* by the power of God through faith unto salvation. . . . "Thy people," saith Jehovah to the Messiah, "shall be willing in the day of thy power." Thus the believer, in running his race, and working out his salvation, is actuated by God and animated by the consideration of his all-powerful operation in the beginning of

---

3. Some of this material is found in a somewhat different form in James Montgomery Boice, *The Minor Prophets: An Expositional Commentary* (Grand Rapids: Zondervan, 1983), vol. 1, pp. 227–234.

his course, of the continuation of his support during its progress, and by the assurances that it shall be effectual in enabling him to overcome all obstacles and to arrive in safety at the termination.[4]

Second, what does this say about the proper way to do evangelism, the point with which I started?

Well, the weaknesses of our contemporary evangelism have been recognized and critiqued by many, among them Walter J. Chantry, Ernest C. Reisinger, and Gordon H. Clark, all of whom have written things that have been helpful to me.[5] As I have read their books, I have found that there is a common bottom line. Evangelism is to teach the Word of God. Not just a certain evangelistic core, or only certain doctrines, or only truths that will move or motivate the ungodly. It is to teach the Bible and to do this as carefully, consistently, and comprehensively as possible, while looking to God (and praying to God) to give new life. Gordon Clark expressed it by saying quite succinctly, "Evangelism is the exposition of the Scripture. God will do the regenerating."[6]

"Just preach Jesus!" someone says.

Did I hear, "Just preach *Jesus*"?

Let's do it. But remember what Jesus means. Jesus means "Salvation is of the Lord," the very words uttered by Jonah from the belly of the fish. To preach Jesus is to preach a Calvinistic gospel.

---

4. Haldane, *An Exposition of the Epistle to the Romans,* p. 469.

5. Walter J. Chantry, *Today's Gospel: Authentic or Synthetic?* (London and Carlisle, Pa.: The Banner of Truth Trust, 1972); Ernest C. Reisinger, *Today's Evangelism: Its Message and Methods* (Phillipsburg, Pa.: Craig Press, 1982); and Gordon H. Clark, *Today's Evangelism: Counterfeit or Genuine?* (Jefferson, Md.: The Trinity Foundation, 1990).

6. Clark, *Today's Evangelism,* p. 122.

132

God's Power Displayed in Judgment

Romans 9:17–18

For the Scripture says to Pharaoh: "I raised you up for this very purpose, that I might display my power in you and that my name might be proclaimed in all the earth." Therefore God has mercy on whom he wants to have mercy, and he hardens whom he wants to harden.

We have been swimming through some deep doctrinal waters in the last few studies of Romans 9, but we have also had a few mild ripples of application. In the previous study, much of what we examined had bearing on some of the ways we do evangelism.

So, let me pick up at that point and ask a question about evangelism that will be a bridge to what we are to look at now, namely, the display of God's power and justice in his judgments. The question is: What is the ultimate goal of evangelism? We all know what evangelism is. It is telling others about Jesus. Or, if we want to fill that out a bit, evangelism is the proclamation of the good news of salvation in Jesus Christ, through the power of the Holy Spirit, so that those who hear might respond in faith, join with God's other children in the fellowship of the church, and continue growing in Christ as his disciples. But is that the ultimate goal of evangelism? Is it merely to get people saved?

To take another line of thought, at the end of the last study I defined evangelism as the exposition of Scripture. Is that the ultimate goal? Simply to teach the Word of God?

Of course, the important word in my question is the word *ultimate*. For, although the other goals I mentioned are legitimate goals—to teach the Word of God and to see people converted—what I am trying to point out here is that those goals are not ultimate. The ultimate goal is to glorify God, and the reason for that is that the glorification of God is the chief goal of everything, of life, history, creation, and our own existence. The first question of *The Westminster Shorter Catechism* asks, "What is the chief end of man?" It answers, "Man's chief end is to glorify God, and to enjoy him forever." The goal of life is God's glory. So that is evangelism's chief end, too.

Let's ask it as a question: "What is the chief end of evangelism?" The answer would be: "Evangelism's chief end is to glorify God."

But, in the case of evangelism, that happens in two ways: (1) The grace and mercy of God are glorified in the saving of those who will be saved, and (2) The justice and power of God are glorified in the case of those who are not saved, but are instead judged for their sins.

And that is what brings us to our text: "For the Scripture says to Pharaoh: 'I raised you up for this very purpose, that I might display my power in you and that my name might be proclaimed in all the earth.' Therefore God has mercy on whom he wants to have mercy, and he hardens whom he wants to harden" (Rom. 9:17–18). These verses teach that the power of God is made known in his judgments, just as his mercy is made known in saving those to whom he wills to show mercy.

"The Scripture Says"

Before we tackle that, however, we need to look at the unusual way in which Paul's quotation from the Old Testament is introduced. The quotation is from Exodus 9:16, and God is speaking. God tells Moses to tell Pharaoh, "I have raised you up for this very purpose, that I might show you my power and that my name might be proclaimed in all the earth." But Paul did not write, "God said. . . ." He wrote, "The Scripture says to Pharaoh. . . ." This is particularly unusual because the Scriptures did not even exist at that time.

Why did Paul write, "The Scripture says . . ."?

One of the great theological works of this century is a book by former Princeton Theological Seminary Professor of Theology Benjamin B. Warfield (died 1921), titled *The Inspiration and Authority of the Bible*. It contains ten classic studies on the Bible's nature and authority, and one of them is on the phrase "Scripture says" and others like it. The chapter is entitled, "'It says:' 'Scripture says:' 'God says.'" In this chapter Warfield looked at a number of Bible passages in which, on the one hand, the Scriptures are spoken of as if they are God and, on the other hand, God is spoken of as if he is the Scriptures. I quote Warfield:

Examples of the first class of passages are such as these: Galatians 3:8, "The Scripture, foreseeing that God would justify the heathen through faith, preached before the gospel unto Abraham, saying, In thee shall all the nations be blessed" (Gen. 12:1–3); Romans 9:17, "The Scripture saith unto Pharaoh, Even for this same purpose have I raised thee up" (Exod. 9:16). It was not, however, the Scripture (which did not exist at the time) that, foreseeing God's purposes of grace in the future, spoke these precious words to Abraham, but God himself in his own person. It was not the not yet existent Scripture that made this announcement to Pharaoh, but God himself through the mouth of his prophet Moses. These acts could be attributed to "Scripture" only as the result of such a habitual identification, in the mind of the writer, of the text of Scripture with God as speaking, that it became natural to use the term "Scripture says," when what was really intended was "God, as recorded in Scripture, said."

Examples of the other class of passages are such as these: Matthew 19:4, 5, "And he answered and said, Have ye not read that he which made them from the beginning made them male and female, and said, For this cause shall a man leave his father and mother, and shall cleave to his wife, and the twain shall become one flesh?" (Gen. 2:24); Hebrews 3:7, "Wherefore, even as the Holy Ghost saith, Today if ye shall hear his voice," etc. (Ps. 95:7). . . . It is not God, however, in whose mouth these sayings are placed in the text of the Old Testament: they are the words of others, recorded in the text of Scripture as spoken to or of God. They could be attributed to God only through such habitual identification, in the minds of the writers, of the text of Scripture with the utterances of God that it had become natural to use the term "God says" when what was really intended was "Scripture, the Word of God, says."

The two sets of passages, together, thus show an absolute identification, in the minds of these writers, of "Scripture" with the speaking God.[1]

In that volume Warfield was trying to counter modern attempts to lower the authority of Scripture, making it a mere word of man about God rather than God's inerrant word to man. As he showed, the words *Scripture says,* which begin our text, are an important part of the argument leading to a right view. But this is also important for what Paul is saying in Romans. For, in my judgment, this is not just an unconscious way of mixing God and Scripture, though Warfield's handling of the text for his purpose might suggest it. It is actually Paul's way of calling attention to the authority of Scripture on the point he is making.

Robert Haldane says, "By the manner in which the apostle begins this verse, we are taught that whatever the Scriptures declare on any subject is to be considered decisive on the point."[2] And that is important, because what Paul is saying in Romans 9 is authoritative, though it is hard for many people to accept it.

---

1. Benjamin Breckinridge Warfield, *The Inspiration and Authority of the Bible,* ed. Samuel G. Craig (London: Marshall, Morgan & Scott, 1959), pp. 299, 300.

2. Robert Haldane, *An Exposition of the Epistle to the Romans* (MacDill AFB: MacDonald Publishing, 1958), p. 470.

Examination of the Text

This brings us back to the thought of Romans 9:17–18, which we must now examine briefly. We remember that Paul has been arguing the fact of God's election, that he chose some out of Israel to be saved and that he chose some not to be. He proved it in the case of Abraham, Abraham's son Isaac, and Isaac's son Esau. Paul then raised this question: Is God unjust in so operating? He answered: "Not at all!? Then, in verse 15, he proved his denial by quoting from the Old Testament, the acknowledged authority. The quotation is from Exodus 33:19, in which God said, "I will have mercy on whom I will have mercy, and I will have compassion on whom I will have compassion." That led to the conclusion: "It does not, therefore, depend on man's desire or effort, but on God's mercy" (Rom. 9:16).

The verses we are studying are exactly parallel to that first quotation and conclusion, only they are illustrating the negative side of God's action, namely, wrath and judgment, instead of the positive side. Romans 9:15 began with the word *for:* "For he [that is, God] says to Moses. . . ." So also does verse 17: "For the Scripture says. . . ." Then, after the Old Testament proof is cited, our section also gives a conclusion, which is parallel to verse 16: "Therefore God has mercy on whom he wants to have mercy, and he hardens whom he wants to harden" (v. 18).

So, on the one hand, we have God making his mercy known through saving some, like Moses, and, on the other hand, making his power known by judging others. In the latter case, Pharaoh is the Old Testament example.

The exact sense of this emerges when we turn to Exodus. The first six plagues on Egypt have already taken place, and God is now sending Moses back to Pharaoh to say that the seventh, an even more terrible plague, is coming. The first six plagues have been as mild as they have been not because God was unable to deal more harshly. He could have destroyed Pharaoh and all the Egyptians from the start. Rather, God says, he has spared Pharaoh this long so the full range of his power might be known. Here is how it reads: "For by now I could have stretched out my hand and struck you and your people with a plague that would have wiped you off the earth. But I have raised you up for this very purpose, that I might show you my power and that my name might be proclaimed in all the earth" (Exod. 9:15–16).

That is exactly what happened, of course. With each phase of the king's resistance, the force of the judgments increased; and with each raising of the ante, God's power became more visible and his powerful and sovereign name was more widely blazed forth.

The point of these chapters is that God raised Pharaoh to his high position of prominence and sustained him in it through the earlier plagues, so God might be glorified in his power. Paul's point in quoting the text is that God both acts this way and is right in so doing.

We need to remember from our earlier discussion of reprobation that God's raising Pharaoh to this position does not mean that he made him sin.

Pharaoh sinned because he chose to sin, and he resisted God and hardened his heart because it is the nature of sinners to resist God and the nature of sin to harden hearts. But, having noted that, we must not deny that the text also says that God chose to deal with Pharaoh this way because he wished to show his power in judgment to the world through him. God was under no obligation to save Pharaoh, as he saved the Israelites, and he was not unjust in choosing him as the one in whom his justice and power would be known.

I summarize this in three statements:

1. God is not responsible for the sin of men and women, and he passes by those he has chosen not to save, after the fact of their sin rather than before.

2. God retains the freedom to save whom he will and judge whom he will.

3. In both cases his name is glorified.

Jonathan Edwards on Romans 9:18

I know that this does not sound very much like evangelism to most people. In fact, although I have said that evangelism is expounding Scripture, even sections of the Bible like Romans 9, many will wonder how it is possible to find a gospel message in such doctrines. I remind you, however, that the most powerful time of gospel preaching this country has ever seen was during the Great Awakening under such preachers as Jonathan Edwards, and that it was carried forward precisely by such teachings.

As you might expect, Jonathan Edwards himself had a sermon on this text. It was one of his great ones. Would you like to know how he handled it?

Most Puritan sermons were in three parts: (1) exposition, (2) doctrine, and (3) application. Edwards follows this pattern, though here, as in many of his other sermons, he does not spend much time on exposition, treating it rather as his introduction. He simply traces Paul's argument in this chapter, showing that God deals with people in different ways, showing mercy to some and hardening others, and that the basis of this is nothing other than his sovereign will and pleasure.

The doctrine section is much longer. It has four parts:

1. *What is God's sovereignty?* Edwards describes God's sovereignty as "his absolute, independent right of disposing of all creatures according to his own pleasure."[3] His explanation of what this means is that God is under no constraints from any source, under no obligation to conform to another's will, and without any obligation to anyone for anything.

2. *What God's sovereignty in the salvation of men implies.* It implies, Edwards says, that "God can either bestow salvation on any of the children of men,

3. Jonathan Edwards, "Seventeen Occasional Sermons: Sermon IV" in *The Works of Jonathan Edwards* (Edinburgh and Carlisle, Pa.: The Banner of Truth Trust, 1976), vol. 2, p. 850.

or refuse it, without any prejudice to the glory of any of his attributes."[4] In particular, his saving of some does no dishonor to his holiness, majesty, justice, or truth, for he saves them through the work of Christ, whose death for sinners upholds these attributes. God's condemnation of others does no dishonor to his righteousness, goodness, or faithfulness, because he is under no obligation to them.

3. *God actually does exercise his sovereignty in men's salvation.* This is the chief point I have been making in my exposition, but Edwards elaborates by showing the many ways God does this: in choosing one nation or individual rather than another; in giving some great spiritual advantages not given to others; in sometimes saving the low and disadvantaged and denying salvation to the wise and great; in bestowing salvation upon some who have had few advantages; in calling to salvation some who have been particularly wicked and passing by the righteous and moral; in saving some who have sought salvation but not others who also seem to have sought it.

4. *The reason for this exercise.* The reason Edwards gives is the chief point of Romans 9:17–18, namely, to display his glory in each of his many attributes. "It is the will of God to manifest his sovereignty. And his sovereignty, like his other attributes, is manifested in the exercise of it. He glorifies his power in the exercise of his power. He glorifies his mercy in the exercise of his mercy. So he glorifies his sovereignty in the exercise of his sovereignty."[5]

He closes the doctrinal section by quoting verse 18: "Therefore God has mercy on whom he wants to have mercy, and he hardens whom he wants to harden."

The last part of Jonathan Edwards's sermon is the application section, and it is for this that I have chiefly summarized his message. Edwards gives five points of application:

1. *From this we learn how absolutely we are dependent on God in this great matter of the eternal salvation of our souls.* We are not only dependent on God's wisdom and power in being able to devise a way to save us and then actually doing so. We are also dependent on his will to save us, for it is only due to the sheer good pleasure of his will that he saves anyone. Why should he save human beings and not the fallen angels? Why should some people be saved and not others? Why is it that some should have the advantages of possessing the Bible, being exposed to the ordinances of religion and being able to hear fine preaching, while others have none of these things?

4. Ibid.
5. Ibid., p. 853.

2. *We should adore the absolute sovereignty of God with great humility.* This divine freedom to choose some and pass by others is the very essence of the divine glory. So we should give him that glory. "It is impossible that we should go to excess in lowliness and reverence of that Being who may dispose of us to all eternity, as he pleases."[6]

3. *If you are saved, you are to attribute it to sovereign grace alone and give all praise to God who alone makes you differ from another.* When you hear of another's open sin, you should think of how wicked you once were, how you provoked God by your rejection of his grace, and how he saved you in spite of your sin, according to his own good pleasure.

4. *Learn how much cause you have to admire the grace of God, which has stooped to save you.* Specifically, the utterly, unbound, unconstrained, free and sovereign God has stooped to bind himself to you by a covenant, expressed in solemn promises.

God insists that his sovereignty be acknowledged by us. He will not have it any other way. Yet "this is the stumbling-block on which thousands fall and perish; and if we go on contending with God about his sovereignty, it will be our eternal ruin. It is absolutely necessary that we should submit to God, as our absolute sovereign and the sovereign over our souls, as one who may have mercy on whom he will have mercy, and harden whom he will."[7]

5. *We may make use of this doctrine to guard those who seek salvation from two opposing extremes—presumption and discouragement.* Says Edwards:

> Do not presume upon the mercy of God, and so encourage yourself in sin. Many hear that God's mercy is infinite and therefore think that, if they delay seeking salvation for the present and seek it hereafter, that God will bestow his grace upon them. But consider that, though God's grace is sufficient, yet he is sovereign and will use his own pleasure whether to save you or not. If you put off salvation till hereafter [later], salvation will not be in your power. It will be as a sovereign God pleases, whether you shall obtain it or not. Seeing, therefore, that in this affair you are absolutely dependent on God, it is best to follow his direction in seeking it, which is to hear his voice today: "Today if ye will hear his voice, harden not your heart."
>
> Beware also of discouragement. Take heed of despairing thoughts, because you are a great sinner, because you have persevered so long in sin, have back-slidden, and resisted the Holy Ghost. Remember that, let your case be what it may and you ever so great a sinner, . . . God can bestow mercy upon you without the least prejudice to the honor of his holiness, which you have offended, or to the honor of his majesty, which you have insulted, or of his justice, which you have made your enemy, or of his truth, or any of his attri-

6. Ibid., p. 854.
7. Ibid.

butes. Let you be what sinner you may, God can, if he pleases, greatly glorify himself in your salvation.[8]

Brothers and sisters, that is the way to do evangelism. It is not what the hard hearts of sinners want to hear. They want to be told that God owes them something, or at least that their destinies are in their own hands. But even if they hate and heap scorn on these doctrines, that in itself may be a beginning in the matter of their salvation. For it shows that they have at least understood the truth, though they may still be rejecting it. And they cannot accept it until they understand it.

Fight against it as you wish, it is still truth: God will be glorified in your destiny one way or another, in your salvation or in your eternal damnation. But if you have begun to see that, it may be an important first step in the surrender of your own will and great pride, and the discovery of God's mercy in Christ, which is the only thing that has ever saved anyone.

8. Ibid.

133

The Potter and the Clay

Romans 9:19–21

One of you will say to me: "Then why does God still blame us? For who resists his will?" But who are you, O man, to talk back to God? "Shall what is formed say to him who formed it, 'Why did you make me like this?'" Does not the potter have the right to make out of the same lump of clay some pottery for noble purposes and some for common use?

The human heart is a deceitful but very resourceful thing, and two ways it expresses these characteristics are by dismissing God, on the one hand, or blaming him, on the other.

Quite a few years ago, my wife and I had a neighbor who seemed to have no interest in God. She had very little morality, was unfaithful to her husband and often boasted about it, explaining to me on one occasion how she was able to squeeze some of her affairs into her lunch hour. But then one day she discovered that her husband was having an affair, too, and she was devastated. The marriage ended in divorce. This woman came to me when she found out about her husband's affair because I was a pastor, probably the only one she knew. She had not been thinking of God before this, but now she abruptly brought God into the picture.

"Why is God doing this to me?" was her question. She considered God to be terribly unfair.

Who's to Blame?

This is the kind of thinking Paul is dealing with in Romans 9:19–21, as he continues to teach about the sovereignty of God in salvation. In the first half of the chapter, he has been arguing that in the matter of salvation God operates by the principles of election and reprobation, and he has answered the question: Is God just in so operating? He has shown that God is just, since God owes mankind nothing, salvation is by grace, and God rightly demonstrates all aspects of his glory, including his wrath and power as well as his mercy and grace, by so doing. But now the wicked resourcefulness of the human heart, which I mentioned, comes in. For, if a person cannot deny God's sovereignty over human affairs and human destinies or even God's right to save some and pass by others, as God does, the person will at least try to deny his or her own responsibility in the matter.

So a new question arises: "Then why does God still blame us? For who resists his will?" (v. 19).

This, of course, is a major theological question: the relationship between the sovereignty of God and free will. It is a question that can be answered and has been, particularly by Jonathan Edwards in his treatise on "The Freedom of the Will." But Paul does not answer the question here, at least not directly. And the reason he does not answer it is that he already has.

For this objection to have weight, the person making it must assume that God determines to condemn some persons without reference to what they are or do as sinners. It assumes that he creates some people only to damn them, to send them to hell, and that they are passive in the matter. But that is not what Paul has been saying. Nor is it what I have been saying as I have tried to trace out his teaching. Reprobation means "passing by" or "choosing not to save." And those whom God passes by or chooses not to save are not innocent persons but sinners who are in rebellion against him. God does not condemn innocent people. He condemns sinners only. But God does have the right to save or not to save sinners, as he chooses.

So the question is really an objection to God's right to do what he does, which is what has been under consideration all along and which is why I have said that Paul has already answered it.

Not all commentators have seen this. J. C. O'Neill writes that "The objection is entirely warranted, and the reply does nothing to answer it." C. H. Dodd calls this "the weakest point in the whole epistle."[1] But Paul has given answers, and he knows that the objection really rises out of the rebellion of the heart against God's sovereignty. In fact, the very question is rebellion. For the query "Who resists his will?" is itself resistance. Human beings are sinners, are guilty, and they prove it even by the way they ask their questions.

---

1. J. C. O'Neill, *Paul's Letter to the Romans*, and C. H. Dodd, *The Epistle of Paul to the Romans*, cited by Leon Morris, *The Epistle to the Romans* (Grand Rapids: Wm. B. Eerdmans, and Leicester, England: Inter-Varsity Press, 1988), p. 365.

Therefore, Paul answers by reiterating once more that God has a right to do with his (sinful) creatures as he will.

The outline of these three verses is straightforward. Verse 19 states the question. Verse 20 provides the answer. Verse 21 illustrates the answer by a picture drawn from the Old Testament.

Three Humbling Contrasts

We have already looked at the question. The answer (v. 20) and the illustration (v. 21) provide contrasts that are intended to put the question in its proper perspective and ourselves in our proper place. There are three of them.

1. *Man and God.* The first contrast is more apparent in the Greek text than in English, for the verse begins with the words "O man" and ends with the words "the God." Yet it is apparent enough in English. You and I are mere men and women set over against the God who made not only us but all things. It is ludicrous for creatures as small, ignorant, impotent, and sinful as we are to question the propriety of God's moral acts. We may not understand what God is doing in any particular case. In fact, most of the time we will not, because "'my thoughts are not your thoughts, / neither are your ways my ways,' / declares the LORD" (Isa. 55:8). We can ask God to explain what he is doing, if he will. But for us to suggest that he is wrong in what he does is patently absurd.

2. *What is formed and he who formed it.* The contrast between man and God, the first, stresses the insignificance of one and the greatness of the other. This second contrast brings in another matter, namely, that we are mere creatures—God is the Creator—and therefore everything we are and have comes from him, including even our ability to ask such questions.

Robert Haldane is particularly wise in the way he deals with this matter. "Any wisdom the creature possesses must have been received from the Creator; and if the Creator has the power of forming rational beings, must he not himself be infinite in wisdom? And does it not insult the Creator to pretend to find imperfection in his proceedings? . . . The reason and discernment between right and wrong which he [man] possesses is the gift of God; it must, then, be the greatest abuse of these faculties to employ them to question the conduct of him who gave them."[2]

Once again, we must stress that "Paul does not here speak of the right of God over his creatures as creatures, but as sinful creatures, as he himself clearly intimates in the next verses."[3]

2. Robert Haldane, *An Exposition of the Epistle to the Romans* (MacDill AFB: MacDonald Publishing, 1958), p. 481.

3. Charles Hodge, *A Commentary on Romans* (Edinburgh and Carlisle, Pa.: The Banner of Truth Trust, 1972), p. 481. Original edition 1935.

3. *The clay and the potter.* Each of these three contrasts says the same thing. But each also adds a new element, and the new element here is the authority of the Old Testament, since the illustration of the potter and clay is drawn from the Old Testament and shows that the principle involved is a point of revelation. There are four main passages in which the illustration of the potter and the clay is found in the Old Testament, three in Isaiah and one in Jeremiah. It is good to have them before us.

> You turn things upside down,
>> as if the potter were thought to be like the clay!
> Shall what is formed say to him who formed it,
>> "He did not make me"?
> Can the pot say of the potter,
>> "He knows nothing"?
>
>   Isaiah 29:16

> Woe to him who quarrels with his Maker,
>> to him who is but a potsherd
>>> among the potsherds on the ground.
> Does the clay say to the potter,
>> "What are you making?"
>
>   Isaiah 45:9a

> Yet, O LORD, you are our Father.
>> We are the clay, you are the potter;
>> we are all the work of your hand.
>
>   Isaiah 64:8

The best-known passage is in Jeremiah:

This is the word that came to Jeremiah from the LORD: "Go down to the potter's house, and there I will give you my message." So I went down to the potter's house, and I saw him working at the wheel. But the pot he was shaping from the clay was marred in his hands; so the potter formed it into another pot, shaping it as seemed best to him.

Then the word of the LORD came to me: "O house of Israel, can I not do with you as this potter does?" declares the LORD. "Like clay in the hand of the potter, so are you in my hand, O house of Israel. If at any time I announce that a nation or kingdom is to be uprooted, torn down and destroyed, and if that nation I warned repents of its evil, then I will relent and not inflict on it the disaster I had planned. And if at another time I announce that a nation or kingdom is to be built up and planted, and if it does evil in my sight and does not obey me, then I will reconsider the good I had intended to do for it.

"Now therefore say to the people of Judah and those living in Jerusalem, 'This is what the LORD says: Look! I am preparing a disaster for you and devising a plan against you. So turn from your evil ways, each one of you, and reform your ways and your actions.'"

Jeremiah 18:1–11

As far as anyone can tell, Paul does not seem to be quoting specifically from any one of these texts. But the points in Romans are exactly what these verses in the Old Testament also say: (1) It is absurd for a mere man or woman to fault God. (2) God has absolute sovereignty over his creatures, saving whom he will and condemning whom he will. (3) This is not an arbitrary selection, since his judgments are based on his justice in condemning sin. (4) Therefore, "turn from your evil ways . . . and reform your ways and your actions."

What could be more reasonable than that? Thus, instead of objecting to God's actions, we should fear them and allow our fear of judgment to drive us to the repentance we need.

A Plea for Sound Thinking

In the previous study I included a summary of Jonathan Edwards's untitled sermon on Romans 9:18, showing how he preached evangelistically even from such an apparently harsh text. At this point I want to follow the "application" portion of another sermon of Edwards, though in this case the text he is treating is not from Romans 9 but from Romans 3:19: "That every mouth may be stopped" (KJV). I introduce it here, because silencing the objections of sinners to the justice of God in condemning them for their sin is precisely what Paul is getting at in our text. Edwards's sermon is entitled, "The Justice of God in the Damnation of Sinners."[4]

The application is an appeal to right thinking. It asks: If God should reject and destroy you, would that not be appropriate, considering how you have behaved toward both God and others?

1. *"If God should forever cast you off, it would be exactly agreeable to your treatment of him."*

Instead of using the brains God gave you to try to fault God, which is the most foolish of all things to do, you should apply them to right thinking, and the first point of right thinking is to examine how you have treated God. You do not stand up very well under such a direct examination.

To begin with, you have not shown any particular affection or love toward God. When people are in love, they think of the loved one constantly and want to be with that person and are always thinking of what they can do for the object of their love. But you have not done that. You do not think often of God. In fact, you think of him hardly at all, except to blame him when things do not go exactly as you would like. You do not want to be with God.

4. Jonathan Edwards, "The Justice of God in the Damnation of Sinners," *The Works of Jonathan Edwards* (Edinburgh and Carlisle, Pa.: The Banner of Truth Trust, 1976), vol. 1, pp. 668–679.

You do not go to church often or spend much time in prayer or Bible study. You do not try always to be doing something for God. If you have not shown any particular affection or love toward God, why should God be obliged to love you? Why should he be obliged to show you any favor whatsoever?

Again, you have slighted God in thousands of ways throughout your entire life. Everything you are and have comes from God. But you have not been thankful for it. Nor have you made any serious effort to find out why God has given you the abilities, advantages, and opportunities you have been given. You have used these things for yourself, trying to accumulate as much money or pleasure or praise as possible, without any thought of him. Why should God pay attention to you in any saving way when you are negligent of his bountiful gifts and favors?

You have also refused to hear God's calls to you, even though they have come to you many times and in a variety of ways. You have heard the gospel preached. You have read the Good News. You possess a Bible. You have even seen dramatic tellings of the gospel story. Has God never spoken to you, calling you from sin to Christ by these means? Have you never felt your heart moved, your will challenged by these truths? Some in some parts of the world have not received these calls, but you have received them again and again, and still you turn a deaf ear in God's direction. You will not hear him. Why should he hear you, even if you should cry out to him in grief and desperation at the last day?

2. *"If you should forever be cast off by God, it would be agreeable to your treatment of Jesus Christ."*

But it is not only God the Father whom you have rejected. You have also despised the work of the Son of God, the Lord Jesus Christ. It would have been just of God if he had rejected you outright without ever having offered you a Savior. But God has not done that. He has provided a Savior, even Jesus Christ, the most wonderful, the most holy, the most merciful, the most gracious person who has ever walked on the surface of this earth. The Father offered him up to death in the place of sinners such as yourself. But you don't care for that. You care only for your own pleasure. You ignore Jesus completely, at least in all practical ways. If he were here in person to confront you in your sinful behavior and tell you to repent of it, you would, if the truth be told, easily find yourself in a crowd, like that of his own day, crying out to Pilate for his blood.

If God should cast you off forever, wouldn't that be the most just and reasonable thing in the world in light of your treatment of Jesus Christ?

3. *"If God should forever cast you off and destroy you, it would be agreeable to your treatment of others."*

The one thing even sinful human beings find it easy to believe in is fair play, doing to others as they have done to you. And we acknowledge a certain poetic justice when a person who cheats another gets cheated or a bully gets beaten or a thief gets put in jail. You think like that, and you are even so arrogant as to believe that this is how you would like to be treated by Almighty God. But what if he should treat you as you have treated others? You know that sin hurts and destroys, yet you have not been content to sin alone. You have involved others in your sins. And if you have been unable to do that with some particular person—if he or she has resisted your advances or disagreed with your lies or disengaged from your evil schemes—you have been quick to speak against the person for possessing the morality you despise.

And even in that you are harming others. For your example is harmful, even when you do not think about it much, as you probably do not. Fathers, your examples have harmed your children. Mothers, your sins have left their dark stains on your offspring. Young people, your immorality and your lack of any true seeking after God have damaged your friends and peers.

Why does God owe you the favor of salvation when you have been so evil, irresponsible, and harmful in your treatment of other people? If you want justice, would it not be just for God to treat you as you have treated them?

4. *"If God should eternally cast you off, it would but be agreeable to your own behavior toward yourself."*

I will not say that you are able to save yourself. You cannot. But you have failed to do even what you can do. There are many sins from which you could have refrained but have embraced instead. There are many steps toward God that you could have taken, but you have turned away. Indeed, like Jonah, you have run in the opposite direction. You cannot convert yourself, but you can place yourself where a conversion is most likely to happen, if God should be pleased to do it. You can read his Word; you can pursue it diligently. You can seek the company of those who know God and speak often of him.

Is God obliged to take better care of you than you are willing to take of yourself? Neither your responsibility toward God nor your legitimate interest in your eternal welfare has been enough for you to put God and spiritual things before your passing pleasures. Is God obliged to do any differently for you? Why should he seek your welfare, when you yourself will not seek it and, in fact, actually pursue your own destruction willingly?

After presenting a lengthy application of his text along these lines, Edwards concludes, "Thus I have proposed some things to your consideration which, if you are not exceeding blind, senseless, and perverse, will stop your mouth and convince you that you stand justly condemned before God."[5]

The Day of Grace

Yet God's purpose is not solely to condemn. The demonstration of his power and justice in judging sinners is a true part of what God is doing in

---

5. Ibid., p. 678. The previous paragraphs are a contemporary reworking of the arguments Edwards develops on pp. 672–678.

human history, but it is not the whole thing. God is also making known the riches of his glory in the salvation of some, as these verses, particularly the next verses, show. Why should you not be among those who are saved? Particularly since you are hearing these very truths proclaimed?

If all God wanted to do was send people to hell, he would not have needed to tell us these things or anything else. There would have been no need for a Bible, no need for preachers to preach or messengers to explain and teach it, no need for a Savior to be held forth as the heart of the Bible's message. If all God wanted to do was let us go to hell, all he would have needed to have done is nothing. We are capable of rushing off to hell, like lemmings running down a hillside, entirely by ourselves. But God has not done that. He has provided a Savior. He has given us a Bible. He has sent messengers, and their message, like that of all true prophets sent by God is: "Repent, and believe on the Lord Jesus Christ. Turn from your sin now. Today God is setting the way of salvation before you."

You cannot bring God under obligation to save you by anything you might do, and indeed you have not done anything significant. But the way he saves people is by the preaching and teaching of his Word, which is what you have just received, and by the power of his Spirit working through it.

If what you have heard has made sense to you, if you know that God does not owe you anything, that you have actually spurned what good he has shown you, and that all you actually deserve from him is judgment, then God is already using his Word to bring about the needed transformation of your heart. Now, instead of trying to tell him that what he does is unjust, you will wisely and rationally seek his mercy through faith in the Lord Jesus Christ, where alone it may be found.

134

The Patience of God

Romans 9:22–24

What if God, choosing to show his wrath and make his power known, bore with great patience the objects of his wrath—prepared for destruction? What if he did this to make the riches of his glory known to the objects of his mercy, whom he prepared in advance for glory—even us, whom he also called, not only from the Jews but also from the Gentiles?

What is the chief end of man?"

"Man's chief end is to glorify God," answers *The Westminster Shorter Catechism*. But we might also say that the chief end of *God* is to glorify God, that is, to be God. In an earlier chapter we saw that it is right or just for God to do this. In Romans 9:22–24, we are to study how he does it.

These verses speak of five of God's attributes: wrath, power, patience, glory, and mercy (vv. 22–23). Two of these have just been mentioned: power in verse 16 and mercy in verses 15, 16, and 18. Two others, wrath and glory, were introduced earlier in the letter. The new and unexpected attribute in these verses is patience, which Paul declares has been shown to "the objects of his [God's] wrath—prepared for destruction." The verses teach that God's treatment of the wicked is neither arbitrary nor meaningless, but is intended rather to make his wrath, power, and patience known, just as, on the other hand, his treatment of those who are chosen to be saved displays his mercy.

1107

In both cases the glory of God is achieved by God's exercising or making known these attributes.

Some Grammatical Problems

These verses are a bit difficult, however. So we begin by looking at the difficulties. They are grammatical.

The first difficulty is that the passage begins with the word *if.* "If" always introduces a dependent clause, which should be followed by a major or independent clause. But in this case there is none. So the first part of the sentence, which extends as far as verse 24, is left hanging. The technical term for this situation is an anacoluthon. Probably we are to provide an ending mentally. Since the next word is "but," we might be supposed to think of the verse as saying, "But if God, choosing to show his wrath and make his power known, bore with great patience the objects of his wrath, . . . *what objection can you possibly have?*" Or ". . . *why complain about injustice?*"

The New International Version seems to encourage this kind of mental addition by translating the opening words "What if . . . ?" But still, this is a bit conjectural.

The next word is also a problem. It is translated "choosing" by the NIV, but it is the normal word for "willing" *(thelôn).* So the question is: Does the verse mean "although God was willing to reveal his wrath, he nevertheless endured the objects of his wrath with great patience," that is, choosing not to display wrath, at least for a time? Or does it mean "because God wanted to reveal his wrath, he endured the objects of his wrath with patience," that is, in order to have an even greater demonstration of his wrath when at last he did or does show it?[1]

As a follow-up to verses 19–21, the second of these possibilities seems best. That is, the verses seem to be saying again that God is right to show mercy to whom he wills to show mercy and harden whom he wants to harden. And they ask, "Who are we to say we do not like it? Or that God is unjust?"

If this is the meaning of these verses, I would apply them in the following way. God's chief end is to glorify God. Therefore, since God is all-powerful, this end will certainly be achieved. It will be achieved in every detail of history and in the destiny of every individual. Every person who has ever lived or will ever live must glorify God, either actively or passively, either willingly or unwillingly, either in heaven or in hell. You will glorify God. Either you will glorify him as the object of his mercy and glory, which will be seen in you. Or you will glorify him in your rebellion and unbelief by being made the object of his wrath and power at the final judgment. In fact, if you are

---

1. For fuller discussions of these problems of interpretation, see Leon Morris, *The Epistle to the Romans* (Grand Rapids: Wm. B. Eerdmans, and Leicester, England: Inter-Varsity Press, 1988), pp. 366–368; John Murray, *The Epistle to the Romans* (Grand Rapids: Wm. B. Eerdmans, 1968), part 2, pp. 33–37; and others.

rebelling, you are glorifying him even now, because even now his patience is displayed in you by his enduring your sin for a time, rather than sending you to hell immediately, which you deserve.

In my judgment, verses 22–24 are to be interpreted this way and as teaching that the patience of God is seen in his toleration of the wicked for a time.

A Time for Repentance

Yet there is more to the idea of God's patience than this. The word *patience* is not used a great deal in Paul's writings, and most of the time, when it *is* used, it refers to a human virtue that is one of the fruits of the Holy Spirit in our lives (cf. Gal. 5:22). Still, we can hardly overlook the fact that it has already been used of God once in Romans 2.

In that chapter, Paul is writing of God's righteous judgment on those who consider themselves to be better than other people but who actually do the same things and are guilty of the same sins. "Do you think you will escape God's judgment?" Paul asks (v. 3), particularly when you thus "show contempt for the riches of his kindness, tolerance and patience?" (v. 4). At this point Paul adds an interesting phrase: "not realizing that God's kindness leads you toward repentance." This is an indirect purpose clause, showing what God's kindness, tolerance, and patience are for—they are intended to lead sinful men and women to repentance.

This is important, because on the basis of Romans 9:22 alone, we might think that God shows patience to the wicked only to allow the sins of such persons to accumulate so that he might more fully display his wrath and power in judging them at last. True, that is one purpose. It is what has been said of Pharaoh. God raised him up (even hardened his heart) so that the full measure of the divine power might be displayed in him and God's name might be proclaimed in all the earth.

But that is not the only purpose. The patience of God is also displayed so that those whom God is calling to faith might have space to repent. Both purposes are good. The second purpose is gracious.

We also need to look at 2 Peter 3, which is the most important chapter in the Bible for learning about the patience of God. In that chapter Peter is dealing with the problem posed by the delayed return of Jesus Christ. He is warning that it will not be long before scoffers appear, saying, "Where is this 'coming' he promised? Ever since our fathers died, everything goes on as it has since the beginning of creation" (v. 4). Peter then gives the answer to their taunt in three parts.

First, there has already been a judgment of the world by water in the days of Noah. Scoffers willingly forget this, not wanting to be troubled by it, but it is a warning of a greater judgment by fire yet to come (vv. 6–7).

Second, God's sense of time is not like ours. For us a day seems short, and a thousand years seems a long time. But for God "a day is like a thousand years, and a thousand years are like a day" (v. 8).

Then Peter comes to his third and most important argument: "The Lord is not slow in keeping his promise, as some understand slowness. He is *patient* with you, not wanting anyone to perish, but everyone to come to repentance" (v. 9, emphasis added). Some people have understood this in an Arminian or anti-Calvinistic fashion, as if it were denying the doctrine of election. But that is not its meaning at all. Peter is speaking of the elect in this passage—"patient with *you*." So those God is not willing to have perish are the elect, and the reason God seems to be delaying the return of Jesus Christ is to give time for all those whom he has elected to belong to Jesus Christ to be born, to hear the gospel, to repent of sin, and come to faith.

This is what Peter also means later in the chapter where he writes, "Bear in mind that our Lord's patience means salvation, just as our dear brother Paul also wrote you with the wisdom that God gave him" (v. 15). It is because God is patient with us, not hastening to judgment, that we are saved.

I find it interesting, too, that Peter refers to Paul as having written the same thing. Where did Paul do that? Well, there are only two places in his writings where Paul speaks this way of God's patience: Romans 2:4 and Romans 9:22. Since Peter follows this comment with the observation that Paul's "letters contain some things that are hard to understand" and since Romans 9 is a particularly difficult chapter (Romans 2 is not), I would suppose that Peter is referring to the very verses we are studying, that is, Romans 9:22–24. Moreover, he is confessing that he himself found them to be difficult. If Peter, the apostle of the Lord, found them to be difficult, it should not be too disturbing to us if we find them difficult, too.

On the other hand, Peter does tell us what they mean. They teach that "the Lord's patience means salvation." In other words, they reinforce what I have been saying. The verses do not say only that God tolerates the wicked so that he may judge them more severely in the end and thus display both his wrath and power. They also teach that God is patient with sinners so they might repent of their sin and come to faith.

In fact, that is the direction in which Romans 9–11 is moving. The very next verse in Romans 9, verse 25, speaks of God's calling out a new people to himself, and in Romans 11 Paul is going to speak of the final salvation of "all Israel" (v. 26).

A Personal Testimony

There is one more text that needs to be drawn into this composite picture of God's patience as discussed in Paul's writings, and that is 1 Timothy 1:15–16, in which Paul speaks in a very moving way of God's unlimited patience to himself. He calls it a trustworthy saying. "Here is a trustworthy saying that deserves full acceptance: Christ Jesus came into the world to save sinners—of whom I am the worst. But for that very reason I was shown mercy so that in me, the worst of sinners, Christ Jesus might display his unlimited patience as an example for those who would believe on him and receive eternal life."

What Paul is giving in these verses is a personal illustration of what he discusses doctrinally in Romans. Paul was aware that he had been chosen by God in Christ from before the foundation of the world. But he also remembered with sadness how he had been allowed to go his own self-righteous and wicked way for years until God called him. He was a Pharisee who had displayed his religious zeal by persecuting Christians, even hounding them to death. When the first Christian martyr, Stephen, was stoned by the people of Jerusalem with the Sanhedrin's sanction, Paul was holding the garments of those who were throwing stones. Paul hated Christians and the Jesus they worshiped.

Yet God was patient with Paul. Instead of striking him down, God suffered him to march along his own self-righteous path, heaping sin upon sin, until at last God called him to faith in the Jesus he was persecuting. God did it so the horror of Paul's earlier conduct might form a more striking contrast to the grace, mercy, and glory of God that he afterward received.

Every Christian's Story

This is not just Paul's story, of course. It is the story of believers throughout history.

When Adam and Eve rebelled against God in the Garden of Eden, God was not rash in his judgments, hastening to consign them. Even though God had warned them that on the day they ate the forbidden fruit they would die, God did not execute the judgment of physical death upon them. Instead he came to them in the garden, not in wrath but calling quietly, just as he had come to them on earlier occasions. And although he dealt with their sin and pronounced some mild judgments, he also promised a deliverer. He told them of Jesus who would be wounded by Satan but who would one day destroy both Satan and his works.

How patient God was with Adam! How patient with Eve! Surely God was not willing for our first parents to perish but rather that they might come to repentance and find eternal life.

God was patient with Abraham. Abraham was seventy-five years old when he set out from Haran for the land God promised to him. Before this, for many years, he had lived in Ur of the Chaldeans, blinded by the spiritual ignorance and evil of the times, even to the point of bowing down to false gods or idols (cf. Josh. 24:2). God suffered long with Abraham's sin, knowing that the time was coming when he would reveal himself to him and cause him to become the father of a great nation and a believing people.

How patient God was with Abraham!

And with Sarah! When God visited Abraham by the trees of Mamre and renewed the promise of a son, even though Abraham and Sarah were past the age of having children, Sarah laughed, saying, "Will I really have a child, now that I am old?" (Gen. 18:13). But God did not judge Sarah for her unbelief. He was patient with her, and the next year, when Sarah was ninety years old and Abraham was a hundred years old, Isaac was born.

God was patient with Moses, a man who was himself so impatient. When Moses was forty years old he took it into his head that he should be the deliverer of his people from Egypt. So he killed an Egyptian, no doubt hoping to start a rebellion. Instead, he had to flee. He fled to the far side of the great Sinai desert, where God trained him for an additional forty years. When God finally called him to go to Egypt to tell Pharaoh to let the people go, Moses was reluctant and made many excuses. But God was patient with Moses, just as he was patient with the people at the time of the exodus and throughout their forty years of wandering before actually entering Canaan.

How many were the times when Israel blatantly sinned against God! God had delivered the people from Pharaoh. But when they came to Sinai and Moses delayed in coming down from the mountain, they made a golden calf and danced around it saying, "These are your gods, O Israel, who brought you up out of Egypt" (Exod. 32:4).

One writer says, "God might, without any impeachment of his justice, have executed the threatened judgment of destroying instantly that rebellious nation and raising up another from the loins of Moses. But he saw fit to exercise mercy toward them and to impart to them yet more abundant communications of his grace and favor. . . . By his patience and forbearance, his mercy was displayed."[2]

How patient God was with Israel! He was not willing that any of those whom he was calling to faith in Jesus Christ should perish, but that all should come to repentance.

I pass to the New Testament and think of the believing thief who died on a cross at the time of Jesus' crucifixion. The man was a murderer as well as a thief. He deserved to be in hell along with all other sinners. But God was patient with him, sparing him throughout a very long life of sin so that in the very last hours of his life he might demonstrate that grace can come even to the worst of men and in their final moments.

Surely, "our Lord's patience means salvation" (2 Peter 3:15), and "God's kindness leads you toward repentance" (Rom. 2:4).

Patient, But Not Forever

Has it led you toward repentance? Is it doing so now? Let me help you think the matter through by these observations.

1. *God is patient for a reason.* If you are not in hell today, which you are not though you deserve to be, it is because God has been patient with you, and

2. Donald Grey Barnhouse, *God's Covenants: Expositions of Bible Doctrines, Taking the Epistle of Romans as a Point of Departure,* vol. 8, *Romans 9:1–11:36* (Grand Rapids: Wm. B. Eerdmans, 1963), pp. 49, 50.

the purpose of his patience is to lead you to repentance. God's patience is a great thing. We have explored some of its greatness in this study. But you must not abuse it. It is meant to do you good. The day of God's patience is the day of his grace.

Think how patient God has been with you.

You have sinned against knowledge, and he has been exceedingly patient. You are not like the heathen who know nothing of God or his salvation. You live in a country where the Scriptures are known, the doctrines of the Bible are taught, the way of salvation is proclaimed, and the path of godliness is held up for all to see. But you have spurned that knowledge. You are like those described in Romans 1:32 who "know God's righteous decree" but who not only continue to sin but even approve of those who do it.

You may also have sinned against grace, and still God has been patient. You may have been born into a Christian home, belong to a good church, have Christian friends who care for you, witness to you, and pray for you. But you have not profited from those gracious acts and circumstances.

You have even sinned against patience, and yet God has been exceedingly patient with you. You know that "love so amazing, so divine," demands your all. You have refused to give it, and still God has been patient with you.

2. *God will not be patient forever.* Although God's patience is great, it is not eternal. We are warned in Scripture that God's wrath has been withheld by his patience, but that it is building up like waters behind a great dam and that it will one day be poured forth. God was patient with Pharaoh, but God judged him in the end. God was patient with Israel, but many perished in the desert. God was patient with the believing thief, but the other thief died in his sin and was condemned.

God's patience leads to repentance, but you must still repent. You must believe on Jesus. If you do not, you will face God's judgment in the end, however much you may scoff at it now.

Remember the story of the farmer. He was an unbelieving man and his farm was directly across the street from a church. Each Sunday the Christians would worship in church, but the farmer would display his scorn for them by plowing his fields up and down with his tractor during the worship services. Everyone could hear the noise and all were very conscious of what he was doing. He did this all summer. In October, when the crops were harvested, the farmer wrote a letter to the town's newspaper, pointing out that he had worked every Sunday of the summer and that God had not struck him down for it. Instead his crops were in, and he had prospered as well as, if not better than, the Christian farmers. The newspaper printed his letter. But underneath it the editor of the paper added: "The Lord does not settle his accounts in October."

God is patient. His patience means salvation. But God's patience is not unending. One day the accounts will be settled and judgment will come.

3. *Because God is patient, we should be patient.* I mentioned earlier in this study that the word *patience* is not found in Paul with any special frequency. In fact, it is found in reference to God only three times. But here is the interesting thing: It is found as a virtue to be cultivated by Christians six times, that is, twice as often as in reference to God. It is a fruit of the Spirit, as I said earlier (Gal. 5:22; cf. Col. 1:11; 3:12), and it is commended as a virtue in the Christian ministry (cf. 2 Cor. 6:6; 2 Tim. 3:10; 4:2).

If you are a believer in Jesus Christ, perhaps this is the application for you. We tend to be impatient with other people, especially with those we are trying to win to Christ. But God is patient, and we should be also.

There are four other attributes of God in Romans 9:22–24. Wrath is one, but we are not called upon to show wrath. "'It is mine to avenge; I will repay,' says the Lord" (Rom. 12:19). Power is another, but it is God and not ourselves who must show power. Even glory is not for us to demonstrate. But we can show mercy. We are to be merciful people, remembering how God has been merciful to us. And, above all, we can be patient. It is not easy to be patient, but let us try to be. And the God who is himself patient may use our patience to draw many hurting people to the Savior.

135

"Children of the Living God"

Romans 9:25–26

As he says in Hosea:
> *"I will call them 'my people' who are not my people;*
> *and I will call her 'my loved one' who is not my loved one,"*

and,
> *"It will happen that in the very place where it was said to them,*
> *'You are not my people,'*
> *they will be called 'sons of the living God.'"*

There are times in a study of Paul's writings when it seems that the apostle has lost track of his argument. It is because his thought is so rich and because he has the habit of moving on quickly from one connected thought to another. We have found this in chapters 5 through 8 of this letter, and we see it in Paul's other writings too.

That seems to be the case in the verses we have been studying from Romans 9. You will recall from our initial studies that Paul is dealing with the question of Israel's apparent rejection by God and the problem raised by that rejection, namely, that if God has not been faithful to Israel in saving all Jews, but rather has abandoned some to perish in their sins, what is to make us think that he will be faithful to Gentile believers, in spite of the great statements Paul has made to that effect in Romans 8? Paul answered that God never elected all Jews to salvation, any more than he has elected all Gentiles to salvation, but that all those whom he did elect from both Jews and Gentiles will be saved.

That led Paul into a discussion of election and its counterpart, which theologians refer to as reprobation. And this led him into a discussion of theodicy, namely, the justification of the ways of God with men and women. He ended by speaking of the attributes of God displayed in the electing and reprobating process: love, wrath, hatred, power, glory, mercy, and patience. We have been following these digressions and therefore pursued the subject of God's patience in the last study.

Has Paul lost track of his argument? We are wrong if we think so. For at the very end of this section, in verse 24, Paul in a masterful way comes back to the point from which he started out, stating that salvation is for those whom God has chosen and called, "not only from the Jews but also from the Gentiles."

In this verse Paul is showing who the "objects of mercy" are whom he has referred to in the preceding verses. They are the elect from among both Jews and Gentiles. As Robert Haldane says, "They are not only Jews but also Gentiles, and none of either Jews or Gentiles but those who are called by the Spirit and word of God."[1] Among other things, this verse also shows that all along Paul has been speaking about the election of individuals and not merely the election of peoples or nations, as some have argued.

A New Beginning

Verse 24 is not only a return to the point at which Paul began, however. It is also a wrap-up of his first main argument showing why God has not been unfaithful to Israel or, to use the language he himself uses, why the word or purposes of God have not failed. That means that verse 25, to which we come now, is beginning a new section of the argument.

Let me go back to the point at which I started in the first study in this volume. There I asked Paul's question, "Has the word of God failed?" I answered, "No." For seven reasons. The reasons are the outline of Romans 9–11, as I understand them. God's purposes have not failed, because:

1. All whom God has elected to salvation are or will be saved (Rom. 9:6–24).

2. God had previously revealed that not all Israel would be saved and that some Gentiles would be (Rom. 9:25–29).

3. The failure of the Jews to believe was their own fault, not God's (Rom. 9:30–10:21).

1. Robert Haldane, *An Exposition of the Epistle to the Romans* (MacDill AFB: MacDonald Publishing, 1958), p. 489.

4. Some Jews (Paul himself was an example) have believed and have been saved (Rom. 11:1).

5. It has always been the case that not all Jews but only a remnant has been saved (Rom. 11:2–10).

6. The salvation of the Gentiles, which is now occurring, is intended by God to arouse Israel to envy and thus be the means of saving some of them (Rom. 11:11–24).

7. In the end all Israel will be saved, and thus God will fulfill his promises to Israel nationally (Rom. 11:25–32).

That is the overall outline of these chapters, and you will see from this review that we are now at point two, namely, the argument that God's purposes toward the Jews (and Gentiles) have not failed, because God had previously revealed that not all Israel would be saved and that some Gentiles would be.[2] If God had promised in advance that every individual Jew would be saved and then had failed to save all Jews, we could rightly accuse God of having broken his word and complain that his purposes have failed. But that is not the case, as the quotations from the Old Testament found in this next section of Romans 9 prove.

There are four quotations in verses 25–29, two from the minor prophet Hosea and two from the major prophet Isaiah. The passages from Hosea show the acceptability of the Gentiles. The passages from Isaiah show that the call to salvation has never included all Israel.

Jezreel, Lo-Ruhamah, Lo-Ammi

The Hosea quotations occur in the context of a story. So we need to review the story in order to understand them. Hosea had been told to marry a woman who was going to prove unfaithful to him, because God wanted him to provide a visible illustration of how the people of Israel had been unfaithful to God, but how God had remained faithful to them and loved them in spite of their infidelities. Although the woman would eventually leave Hosea in order to go after her lovers, Hosea would continue to love her and in the end would draw her back to himself.

So Hosea married the woman, as the early verses tell us: "When the LORD began to speak through Hosea, the LORD said to him, 'Go, take to yourself an adulterous wife and children of unfaithfulness, because the land is guilty of the vilest adultery in departing from the LORD.' So he married Gomer daughter of Diblaim . . ." (Hos. 1:2–3).

2. Not all commentators outline Romans 9–11 this way, of course. However, both Charles Hodge and F. Godet begin a new section of their commentaries with verse 25, correctly in my judgment.

At this point Gomer began to have children, and God intervened to give the children symbolic names, which is the point of the quotations picked up by Paul in Romans 9.

The first child was a son. God said, "Name the son Jezreel."

Jezreel is a Hebrew word that has to do with the motion of the hand used in scattering something to the winds, or throwing it away. It was a strange name to give a child. But God gave Hosea and Gomer's son this name because the time was coming when God would scatter the people of the northern kingdom among the Gentile nations as punishment for their sins. Hosea prophesied into the reign of Hezekiah, king of Judah (1:1), which was within six years of the fall of Samaria to the Assyrians. So this first prophecy was fulfilled almost immediately following his death.

The second child was a daughter. God said, "Name your daughter Lo-Ruhamah."

Lo-Ruhamah is composed of two Hebrew words, *Lo,* meaning "no" or "not" (the Hebrew negative), and *Ruhamah,* meaning "loved" or "pitied." God called the daughter "Not-Loved" or "Not-Pitied" because during the ages in which the Jews would be scattered among the Gentiles, God would show them no pity and would seem to have ceased loving them at all.

Finally another son was born. God said, "Call this third child Lo-Ammi."

This name also begins with the Hebrew negative "no" or "not," but the rest of it is a word meaning "my people." So Lo-Ammi means "Not-My-People." People who continue to think of the Jews as God's specially chosen people might wonder how this could be, but God was saying that the time would come when the Jews would cease to be his people in any special sense. As we are going to see, today the true people of God are neither the Jews as a nation nor any Gentile nation, but rather the church of Jesus Christ, which is composed of Jews and Gentiles according to the principle of election.

At this point a person might wonder how the story of Hosea can illustrate the unfailing love of God. Clearly, it illustrates the unfaithfulness of mankind and the way God judges sin. But love? Unfailing love? How is the unfailing love of God illustrated by the words *Jezreel, Lo-Ruhamah, Lo-Ammi?*

The answer is in the verses Paul quotes in Romans 9. He quotes two verses. The first is from the second chapter of Hosea, verse 23, though Paul uses only the second half. The full verse says,

> I will plant her for myself in the land;
>   I will show my love to the one I called
>   "Not my loved one."
>   I will say to those called "Not my people,"
>   "You are my people";
>   and they will say, "You are my God."

Each of the children's names is discussed in that verse, and the point is that the names will be changed, thus indicating the outcome of the story.

The first name is changed only in its meaning. It remains Jezreel, but the meaning is no longer "scattered" but "planted," because the same motion that would be used to throw something away was also used by farmers to scatter and thus plant grain. God refers to this change when he says, "I will *plant* her for myself in the land."

The second name is changed by eliminating the negative. Lo-Ruhamah will become Ruhamah, because God is going to love or have pity on the people once again. "I will show my *love* to the one I called 'Not my loved one.'"

In the same way, Lo-Ammi will become Ammi, because, as God says, "I will say to those called 'Not my people,' 'You are *my people*'; and they will say, 'You are my God.'"

The second verse Paul quotes in Romans 9 comes from the end of Hosea 1 and has the same effect as Hosea 2:23, though it deals only with the change in the name Lo-Ammi: "In the place where it was said to them, 'You are not my people,' they will be called 'sons of the living God'" (Hosea 1:10). That is, Lo-Ammi will become Ammi, "My People."

Jews or Gentiles?

There is a difficulty at this point, however, and you may have noticed it if you have been comparing Hosea 1:10 and 2:23 with Romans 9:25–26 closely. In Hosea, the prophet is talking about the rejection and eventual restoration of the Jews of the ten northern tribes, whose capital was Samaria. But, in Romans, Paul is writing about Gentiles.

This problem is sometimes handled by saying that Paul is actually writing about the restoration of the Jews, which he does write about in Romans 11: "And so all Israel will be saved" (v. 26). But this view is clearly out of step with the Romans 9 context. Verse 24 is speaking of a new people, the elect people of God, which is the church of Jesus Christ, composed of Jews and Gentiles. And the verses that follow obviously teach that the Gentiles, which were not a people, have now become the people of God along with believing Jews, and that the Jews as a nation continue to be rejected, although a remnant is saved.

This is also the case in 1 Peter, where Peter uses Hosea 2:23 of Gentiles in exactly this way: "Once you were not a people, but now you are the people of God; once you had not received mercy, but now you have received mercy" (1 Peter 2:10).

Is Paul misusing Scripture, then? There are some who would say so, but this is not actually the case. What Paul's quotation does show is the way he understood the words spoken to Israel when God called the nation Jezreel, Lo-Ruhamah, Lo-Ammi.

Particularly Lo-Ammi, which is the name he focuses on in his quotations. According to Paul's thinking, Lo-Ammi is not to be understood merely in the sense that the people were going to be treated *as if* they were no longer God's people when, in fact, they were. Rather it means that they actually ceased to be God's people in a special sense. That is, they became "Gentiles" so far as their relationship to God was concerned. So it is not actually of Jews that the words "I will call them 'my people' who are not my people" are spoken but of those who have become "Gentiles" by their rejection of God. It is from these Gentiles, both ethnic Gentiles and ethnic Jews who have thus actually become "Gentiles," that the new people of God is formed.

Using other words, Charles Hodge put it like this: "The ten tribes were in a heathenish state, relapsed into idolatry, and, therefore, what was said of them is, of course, applicable to others in like circumstances or of like character."[3]

Likewise Calvin: "When the Jews were banished from the family of God, they were thereby reduced to a common level with the Gentiles. The distinction between Jew and Gentile has been removed, and the mercy of God now extends indiscriminately to all the Gentiles."[4]

Here is another point. You will notice from a careful comparison of Hosea 1:10 and Romans 9:26 that there is an emphasis in Romans on the words "in the very place." In this context the words do not refer to Samaria, which fell to the Assyrians in 721 B.C., or to Jerusalem, which fell in 586 B.C., but to Gentile lands, the very places where it was said of the scattered nation, "You are not my people." So it is among the Gentiles that men and women were to be called to faith and be designated "sons of the living God." You and I are those people, whether Jews or Gentiles, if we have been called to faith in Jesus Christ and trust him as our Savior.

By Grace Alone

All of this makes Paul's chief point, of course, namely, that God's rejection of Israel as Israel and his election of the Gentiles should have taken nobody by surprise, particularly the Jews, since it was prophesied clearly in the Jewish Scriptures. He is going to make the same point by the quotations from Isaiah, which come next. But before we go on to those texts we need to make a few applications from what we have observed so far.

1. *Salvation is of grace.* It seems strange that we should have to make this point again and again, but we do simply because our sinful natures always try to claim some credit with God and put him in our debt. That is exactly what the Jews of Paul's day were attempting to do. They were claiming that they had a special status before God simply because they were Jews and that God was therefore in lasting debt to them. Paul's use of the texts from Hosea shows that this is not the case. God declared the Jews no longer to be "his people." He had no special relationship to them and therefore no obligation to them. So, if they were to be saved, it would only be because God has chosen to be gracious, precisely the way he saves Gentiles.

3. Charles Hodge, *A Commentary on Romans* (Edinburgh and Carlisle, Pa.: The Banner of Truth Trust, 1972), p. 326. Original edition 1935.

4. John Calvin, *The Epistles of Paul the Apostle to the Romans and to the Thessalonians,* trans. Ross MacKenzie (Grand Rapids: Wm. B. Eerdmans, 1973), p. 214.

I need to say that if a Jew thinks differently, supposing himself to have some special relationship to God apart from Jesus Christ, this is at least understandable, since most of the Old Testament does indeed assume a special relationship between God and Israel. The Jew needs to be taught more perfectly from his own Scriptures, as Paul is doing in this chapter. But although a Jew might be excused for his mistake and merely need to be instructed better, there is no excuse for your making this mistake, if you are a Gentile. Why? It is because Gentiles never did have a special relationship to God.

Paul wrote to the Ephesians, saying that before they were called to faith they were "foreigners to the covenants of the promise, without hope and without God in the world" (Eph. 2:12).

If salvation has come to you, it is by grace alone. And if it has not yet come, you should know that it will never be found by any achievement on your part but only by the mercy of God. All you can do is throw yourself and all hope for your salvation on him.

2. *Salvation is all of God.* The first point leads to the second. For if salvation is all of grace, then salvation is all of God. For only God is in a position to be gracious, and only God has power to do what is necessary to save us.

I think this is the reason for the words "sons of the *living* God" in verse 26 (emphasis added). "Living God" does not only refer to the fact that God is real and alive, as opposed to the dead or nonexistent gods of the heathen, but also to the fact that he is the source of life. It was he who gave life to Adam in the Garden of Eden when Adam was only a form shaped out of clay. Likewise, it is he who breathes life into our dead souls today, imparting the Holy Spirit by which alone we live spiritually. No one can save himself. That is what we have been seeing repeatedly in our study of these chapters. So, if salvation is to happen, it must be by God who alone can regenerate the dead soul.

3. *If you are saved, your salvation demands the greatest measure of devotion and love from you to God.* For the last point I go back to the story of Hosea and its ending, which Paul does not mention but which would have been in the minds of everyone who read his words and was also familiar with the Old Testament.

Earlier in this study I took time to explain the symbolism of the names of Hosea and Gomer's children and indicate how the names would be changed, but I did not say much about Gomer. According to the story, the time came when Gomer left Hosea, as God had warned the prophet would happen. She sank lower and lower in the social scale of the times, and the day came when she fell into slavery, probably because of debt, and was sold on an auction block in the city of Samaria. Hosea was told to go and buy her. He bid a high price, fifteen shekels of silver and a homer and a lethek of barley. But at last she was his once more.

If he had hated her, he could have killed her for the pain she had caused him. She was his property. But it was at this point that Hosea's love shone brightest, since it was a reflection of the unfailing love of God, which he was illustrating. Hosea promised to be a faithful husband to Gomer, which he had been, while at the same time demanding faithfulness from her in return.

This is a picture of what Jesus Christ has done for us, for he has purchased us from the slavery of sin by his own blood. It is what the word *redemption* means. Now we belong to him, and we are called on to give him the fullest measure of love of which we are capable. If God did not love us and had not moved to redeem us by the death of Jesus Christ, we might be excused for our failure to love him. But since he has loved us and has saved us, our only proper response is to give him our all. Isaac Watts wrote,

> Love so amazing, so divine,
> demands my soul, my life, my all.

Nothing else is an adequate response to him who died for us.

136

The Testimony of Isaiah

Romans 9:27–29

Isaiah cries out concerning Israel:
"Though the number of the Israelites be like the sand by the sea,
only the remnant will be saved.
For the Lord will carry out
his sentence on earth with speed and finality."
It is just as Isaiah said previously:
"Unless the Lord Almighty
had left us descendants,
we would have become like Sodom,
and we would have been like Gomorrah."

In our study of Romans we have already had several occasions to observe how Paul develops a theological argument, as contrasted to the way Peter does it, for example. In Peter's great sermon on Pentecost, recorded in Acts 2, the pattern Peter used was to quote a text from the Old Testament and then explain it. He did this three times in that one sermon, explaining Joel 2:28–32, Psalm 16:8–11, and Psalm 110:1. Paul's procedure is the opposite. His way is to develop his argument first and then support it in closing by a few choice scriptural citations.

1123

We saw this first in Romans 3:10–18, where Paul introduced a long string of quotations to nail down the argument he had previously unfolded in chapters 1 and 2. We are finding exactly the same thing in Romans 9.

Paul began this chapter by asking whether God's purposes in regard to the Jewish people had failed, which seemed to be the case, since not all Jews—in fact, very few—were believing in Christ. Paul answered that the purposes of God had not failed, because God had never intended to save every individual Jew any more than he intends to save every Gentile. Instead, God has always operated by the principle of election, according to which some out of the great number of both Jews and Gentiles are brought to Christ. This led him to speak also of reprobation and then of the attributes of God displayed in his actions toward the saved and lost. At last Paul returned to the point at which he started out, concluding that God has been calling his elect "not only from the Jews but also from the Gentiles" (v. 24).

At this point the apostle brings in his quotations, two from Hosea and two from Isaiah. The point of the Hosea quotations is that God had announced in advance that he would save Gentiles. The point of the Isaiah quotations is that he had likewise announced that not all Jews, but only a remnant of Israel, would be converted.

The First Quotation: Isaiah 10:22–23

There is an interesting tie-in between Isaiah 10:22–23, the first of Paul's quotations from Isaiah (v. 27), and Hosea 1:10, the second of his two quotations from the lesser prophet, which has just been given (v. 26).

In chapter 1 of Hosea, verse 10 begins with the words "Yet the Israelites will be like the sand of the seashore, which cannot be measured or counted." Paul does not quote those words in Romans 9:26, though he quotes the second half of the verse, because the words are about Israel explicitly and Paul wants to use the verse as a promise of God's future blessing on the Gentiles. I explained how he does this in the previous study. But Paul has not forgotten the words, and it is those words that remind him of the verse from Isaiah, which he cites next, since they begin that verse. It says, "Though the number of the Israelites be like the sand by the sea, only the remnant will be saved."

Do you see what is happening? The first verse is saying that even though the Jewish people of Samaria would be overthrown and scattered, God would bring them back to their land and cause them to grow into a great people once again. But lest someone throw that verse up in Paul's face, saying, "But in Hosea 1:10 God says that he is going to save a vast multitude of Jews," Paul quotes the same words in Isaiah to show that even though there might be a vast number belonging to the reconstituted Jewish nation, only a small portion or remnant of those persons will be saved from sin.

Isn't that exactly what we see? Leaving the unbelief of the Gentiles aside for a moment, isn't it true that Isaiah 10:22 describes the generally poor results and great difficulties of Jewish evangelism?

A Remnant Chosen by Grace

The most important words in verse 27 are "the remnant." This is a very significant term in the Old Testament, and it has importance for the theology of the New Testament, too. Yet, surprisingly, I have not found a great deal written about it even in textbooks of Old Testament theology.

Several Hebrew words are translated "remnant" in our Bibles, but the most significant is the verb *sha'ar* (over 130 occurrences) and the noun forms of the same word, *she'ar* (26 occurrences) and *she'erit* (66 occurrences).[1] Altogether, these words are found hundreds of times in the Old Testament, chiefly in the Prophets. In the New International Bible the English word "remnant" occurs sixty-three times.

Initially the words seem to have had a military meaning.[2] For instance, in Deuteronomy 3 there is a description of a battle between the Israelites, who were passing through the desert after leaving Mount Horeb, and the Rephaites, commanded by King Og of Bashan. The Rephaites were so thoroughly defeated that the text reports, "Only Og king of Bashan was left of the remnant of the Rephaites" (Deut. 3:11a). Similarly, in 2 Kings 19, King Hezekiah, who was besieged and mocked by the Assyrians, sent to Isaiah to ask him to pray for the Jewish "remnant that still survives" (v. 4), and Isaiah responded with an oracle in which God promised that the remnant would not only be spared destruction by Sennacherib but would even prosper for a time like a fruitful tree.[3]

> Once more a remnant of the house of Judah
>   will take root below and bear fruit above.
> For out of Jerusalem will come a remnant,
>   and out of Mount Zion a band of survivors.
>
> 2 Kings 19:30–31

A large number of these passages refer to little more than the physical survival of a small number of Jews following a military catastrophe, such as the fall of Jerusalem to the Babylonians. But, increasingly, particularly in the later Prophets, the remnant becomes, not merely a group of survivors but a chastened, regenerated, and converted people whom we would describe as the elect or "saved" within Israel.

---

1. Other words with virtually the same meanings are *sarid, peleytah, palit, yatar,* and *yeter* (over 200 times alone). See Lawrence O. Richards, *Expository Dictionary of Bible Words* (Grand Rapids: Zondervan, 1985), pp. 521, 522.

2. For a full discussion of this point, see Gerhard von Rad, *Old Testament Theology*, vol. 2, *The Theology of Israel's Prophetic Traditions*, trans. D. M. G. Tasker (Edinburgh and London: Oliver and Boyd, 1965), pp. 21, 22. German edition 1960. Von Rad refers to the remnants of Edom (Amos 9:12), Rephaim (Josh. 13:12), Sihon (Josh. 13:27), Amon (2 Sam. 21:2), and Ashdod (Jer. 25:20).

3. The same story with the same use of the word *remnant* is found in Isaiah 37.

One important example of this is in 1 Kings 19, though the word *remnant* does not occur in that chapter. I refer to it because Paul refers to it himself in Romans 11, applying the word *remnant* to the situation. It is the story of Elijah at Horeb after his great victory over the prophets of Baal on Mount Carmel. Elijah had achieved a stunning victory that resulted in the overthrow and death of the prophets of Baal. The battle had taken an enormous emotional toll on him, so that, when Queen Jezebel threatened to have him killed, Elijah fled to the wilderness discouraged, despondent, and content to die. In fact, that is what he told God.

God asked him, "What are you doing here?" (1 Kings 19:13).

Elijah answered, "I have been very jealous for the LORD God Almighty. The Israelites have rejected your covenant, broken down your altars, and put your prophets to death with the sword. I am the only one left, and now they are trying to kill me too" (v. 14).

God replied that he still had work for Elijah to do, that he would appoint a helper for him in his eventual successor Elisha, and that Elijah was wrong in thinking that he was the only faithful person left in Israel. "Yet I reserve seven thousand in Israel—all whose knees have not bowed down to Baal and all whose mouths have not kissed him" (v. 18). When Paul gets around to referring to this story in Romans 11, he concludes, "So too, at the present time there is a remnant chosen by grace" (v. 5).

This is exactly what we find in Romans 9. And it is the meaning of the bulk of the other Old Testament references. Lawrence O. Richards says that the regenerated remnant referred to in the later Prophets is "made up of those in Israel who will experience conversion and receive the promised covenant blessings."[4] According to my count, the English word *remnant* is used of this new entity six times in Isaiah, three times in Jeremiah, five times in Micah, and three times each in Zephaniah and Zechariah.[5]

This remnant will be saved.

The actual words in Romans 9:27 are "the remnant," that is, the remnant of God's electing choice. As for the rest, "The Lord will carry out his sentence on earth with speed and finality" (v. 28). That is, the rest will perish in God's final judgments.

The Second Quotation: Isaiah 1:9

Verse 29, the second of Paul's two quotations from Isaiah, picks up from the second half of the first quotation, also referring to judgment:

> Unless the Lord Almighty
> had left us descendants,

---

4. Richards, *Expository Dictionary of Bible Words*, p. 521.

5. Isaiah 10:20, 21, 22; 11:11, 16; 28:5; Jeremiah 23:3; 31:7; 50:20; Micah 2:12; 4:7; 5:7, 8; 7:18; Zephaniah 1:4; 2:7; 3:13; Zechariah 8:6, 11, 12.

> we would have become like Sodom,
> 　　and we would have been like Gomorrah.

But this is a different kind of reference. The first Old Testament quotation describes what is surely going to happen: "God will carry out his sentence on earth with speed and finality." This verse describes what is sometimes called "a condition contrary to fact." It teaches that unless the Lord had left a remnant, the people would have been like those of Sodom and Gomorrah, that is, entirely wiped out. They would have ceased to exist. Yet this is not the case. In fact, God has left a remnant, which, as Paul is going to say in Romans 11, he has "chosen by grace" (v. 5).

Apart from the grace of God, destruction! Fire from heaven! The only thing that keeps this from happening to all of us is the mercy and kindness of God. It is only because of the inexplicable grace of God that any of us are spared the fate of Sodom and its sister city.

A Summary

In the next study, beginning with Romans 9:30, we will be going on to the next section of Paul's seven-point argument in Romans 9–11, in which Paul is going to show that God's purposes have not failed, because the failure of the Jews to believe on Christ is their own fault and not God's. Before we do that, however, we need to summarize and apply what we have seen in this section.

1. *God's word can be trusted.* We begin by reminding ourselves that the apostle's main point in this section is that the Bible foretells exactly what has happened through the proclamation of the gospel: (1) Gentiles have been included in what seemed at one time to have been an exclusive privilege of Israel, that is, to be God's elect or saved people, and (2) only a small remnant of Israel has been or is presently being saved. What God foretold has been fulfilled.

We need to learn that truth, and we need to apply it in many areas of our lives. We need it because we all naturally try to outguess or improve on the Bible.

I speak here to professing Christians, who know the Word of God. You know what God says about following him: for example, about seeking "first his kingdom and his righteousness," knowing that "all these things"—food, clothing, the necessities of life, and other good things—"will be given to you" (Matt. 6:33). But you do not do that. You put other things first, leaving God until last, if indeed he gets even that position. You do not think often of him. You do not study his Word. You do not spend time with other Christians. You do not give your money to Christian work or causes. Then you are surprised when life does not go well for you and you run into difficulties. Why should you be surprised? God does not lie, and he has told you in advance how the Christian life is to be lived and what will happen to you if you neglect him.

The Bible says, "Fear the LORD, you his saints, / for those who fear him lack nothing" (Ps. 34:9).

God declares, "Those who honor me I will honor, but those who despise me will be disdained" (1 Sam. 2:30b).

Above all, the Bible says, "God cannot be mocked. A man reaps what he sows. The one who sows to please his sinful nature, from that nature will reap destruction; the one who sows to please the Spirit, from the Spirit will reap eternal life" (Gal. 6:7–8).

I encourage you to learn the important lesson of taking God's Word at face value and not try to explain it away as applying to someone else or to another time or to different circumstances. The Word of God is inerrant, it is everlasting, and it is speaking about you.

The psalmist says,

> Who knows the power of your anger?
> For your wrath is as great as the
> fear that is due you.
> Teach us to number our days aright,
> that we may gain a heart of wisdom.

Psalm 90:11–12

2. *All are not saved.* The second obvious point of these four citations from the Old Testament is that not all people will be saved.

We have a rather fond notion floating around the Christian church today, even in evangelical churches, that this is not true, and that somehow everybody will be brought to heaven because—this is the way it is usually expressed—God is a God of love, and he could not possibly condemn anyone. I do not know anything else to call this notion but the devil's lie. And what a lie it is! If God is so loving that he will never see his way clear to judge me, well then, I can live my life as I please, even doing the worst possible things, and I will still be rewarded for it. I can be an utter scoundrel. I can cheat, rob, lie, and murder, and it will still turn out right. God cannot possibly condemn me. His character forbids it.

What could be more character-destroying than that? What could be more mind-numbing, more soporific? What could be more demonic?

What could be more wrong?

These verses tell us that God is as much a God of justice as he is a God of love, and that he will eventually display the attributes of his justice on the wicked, namely, his wrath and his power. They tell us that God did not save all people in the Old Testament period, not even all the Jewish people, who are called God's "chosen" ones. If God did not do it then, there is no reason to suppose he will do it now or in the future, especially when he has told us the contrary, which he does in these verses. The remnant will be saved, but for the rest "the Lord will carry out his sentence . . . with speed and finality" (v. 28).

With speed! That means before long, with no delays. With finality! That means for good. The judgment will be one from which there will be no appeal and no escape.

So I encourage you to abandon the false notion that God will not condemn you. I can understand why you think that way. No one wants to face hard truths. I do not like them myself. But the fact that judgment will come is nevertheless true, and nothing is to be gained by denying or dodging it. On the contrary, God tells us that judgment is coming so we will flee from sin to Jesus, where alone salvation from God's judgment may be found.

3. *Formal membership in the covenant body does not save anyone.* The third point is that merely formal membership either in the synagogue or in the church does not save anyone. If it could have saved anyone, it would have been the Jews who possessed, according to Romans 9:4–5, "the adoption as sons, . . . the covenants, the receiving of the law, the temple worship and the promises. . . . the patriarchs" and even the "human ancestry" leading to the coming of Jesus Christ. But this did not save them. Only personal faith in Jesus Christ saves anyone. If it did not save them, why should you think that mere membership in a church, even an evangelical church, will save you?

Even less, why should you think that you are on your way to heaven merely because your parents are saved people or other members of your family believe on Christ and take his teaching seriously?

For my part, I cannot understand this delusion. I can understand people rejecting Christianity entirely, believing it simply is not true. I can understand them fighting it, not wanting to surrender to the claims of Jesus Christ on their lives. That does not come easy for anyone. But what I cannot understand is people, particularly young people, believing that everything is well with their souls simply because their parents or friends are Christians, when for their own part they are not following Jesus Christ in any significant way whatsoever.

Is this your delusion? If so, let me ask this—

Can you think of one significant thing in your life, for which you are yourself personally responsible—not something that was decided for you—which is different because of your supposed relationship to Jesus Christ?

One thing?

Is there a sin you have left because you love Christ and know that he would want you to leave it?

Is there a commitment you have made because it is something you know a Christian should do?

Have you ever chosen something that is right simply because it is right and not because it was expedient or because of what someone else might think of you if you had chosen differently?

Think carefully. If you do not have a pattern of life along those lines—rejection of sin, Christian commitments, and righteous choices—how can you possibly suppose you are a Christian? You are merely a member of a Christian family or a member of a Christian church, and that does not make you one of God's true people, any more than mere membership in the nation of Israel made a Jew one of God's elect.

Of course, none of this would matter if all we are speaking about is having a good or slightly better life or avoiding certain temporal problems. But that is not the case. That is "a condition contrary to fact." What we are talking about are issues of life and death, salvation and judgment, faith and rebellion, heaven and hell, truth and falsehood, reality and the bubble of mere human speculation. Judgment is certain. I urge you to turn from your fantasies and surrender your life to Jesus Christ now.

And I emphasize "now." You are moved *now*. You are willing to face the possibility that all this may indeed be true *now*. The Holy Spirit is speaking to you *now*. But you are going to move back into the world, and when you do the devil will be there again with his seductive suggestions. The world will close in upon you with its lies. Will you find it easier to commit yourself to Christ then? You know the answer to that. You will not. The time to settle the matter is right now. Right now is the only proper time to trust your life to Jesus Christ.

PART THIRTEEN

Jewish Unbelief

137

Righteousness Wrongly Sought by Works

Romans 9:30–32

What then shall we say? That the Gentiles, who did not pursue righteousness, have obtained it, a righteousness that is by faith; but Israel, who pursued a law of righteousness, has not attained it. Why not? Because they pursued it not by faith but as if it were by works. . . .

Ⅰf anyone could ever have achieved salvation by his own efforts, it was Martin Luther. In 1505, when he was twenty-one years old, Luther abandoned a promising career in law and entered the monastery of the Augustine hermits at Erfurt. As he later said, this was not to study academic theology but to save his soul.

In those days the monastic orders prescribed ways by which the seeking soul could find God, and Luther, with the determination and strength that characterized his entire life, gave himself rigorously to these tasks. He fasted and prayed. He devoted himself to menial work. Above all, he practiced penance, confessing his sins, even the most trivial, for hours on end until his superiors wearied of his exercise and ordered him to stop until he had

1133

committed some sin worth confessing. Luther's piety gained him a reputation for being the most exemplary of monks.

Later he wrote to the Duke of Saxony, "I was indeed a pious monk and followed the rules of my order more strictly than I can express. If ever a monk could obtain heaven by his monkish works, I should certainly have been entitled to it. Of this all the friars who have known me can testify. If it had continued much longer, I should have carried my mortification even to death, by means of my watchings, prayers, reading and other labors."[1]

Yet Luther found no peace through these exercises.

The monkish wisdom of the day instructed him to satisfy God's demand for righteousness by doing good works. "But what works?" thought Luther. "What works can come from a heart like mine? How can I stand before the holiness of my Judge with works polluted in their very source?"[2]

It was not until John Staupitz, the Vicar-General of the Congregation and Luther's wise spiritual father, set him to studying the Bible that Luther realized what the difficulty was. He was trying to earn salvation by works of human righteousness, when the righteousness we need is not human righteousness at all. It is divine righteousness, and this can become ours only if God gives it to us, which he does in the gospel.

Luther had been seeking righteousness by means of human works, when what he needed was to accept God's righteousness by simple faith and therefore stop trying to work for it.

Election and Human Responsibility

It is not often that I have received objections to a sermon even before I have preached it. But that happened when I was about to preach the sermon that has become this chapter of my studies in Romans. The objection came up because I had already announced the point of this sermon while giving an overall outline of Romans 9–11.

I had said that the third reason why the purposes of God have not failed in regard to Israel, the reason Paul develops in these verses, is that the failure of the Jews to believe the gospel was their fault and not God's. The people who objected felt that, on the one hand, I was unfairly attacking Jewish people and, on the other hand, that I was blaming Israel for unbelief when the Scriptures plainly say that it is God himself who hardened Israel's heart. Paul says this in Romans 11:7–10, quoting several Old Testament texts to prove it.

As far as the first criticism goes, it may be that what I said earlier was not balanced well enough. I have been trying to say that the unbelief of Israel is typical of all human unbelief. I have constantly made links between Jews and

1. J. H. Merle D'Aubigné, *The Life and Times of Martin Luther*, trans. H. White (Chicago: Moody Press, 1958), p. 31.
2. Ibid., p. 32.

Gentiles, stressing that all are equal before God and that all must be saved in precisely the same way, through faith in Jesus Christ, because "God does not show favoritism" (Acts 10:34). Nevertheless, Paul *is* discussing Jewish unbelief particularly, and it is hard to explain Paul's teaching, which I am trying to do, without a great many comments on the Jewish side of the Jewish-Gentile combination.

If I failed to treat that in a clearly evenhanded way, I am sorry.

The second criticism is more substantial and more important, because it suggests that if God hardens hearts, then those he hardens must be excused of the sin of unbelief. That is, the unbelief is not their fault. Or, to put it in the larger categories of election and reprobation that Paul has been treating in these chapters, if God elects some to salvation and passes by others, then those who have been passed by cannot be blamed for failing to have responded to the gospel. At least, that is the argument that was given.

However, anyone who has been closely following these studies of Romans 9 already knows the answer to that objection, because Paul has been dealing with it directly for many verses. The extreme case is that of Pharaoh, whose heart is said many times in Exodus to have been hardened. It is true that God hardened Pharaoh's heart. Exodus says so. But it is also true that Pharaoh had already hardened his own heart. In any case, the hardening of Pharaoh's heart by God was a proper judicial hardening because of Pharaoh's many other sins.

When I discussed this same matter in terms of election and reprobation, I pointed out that the two are alike in some respects but dissimilar in others. They are alike in that both flow from the eternal counsels or will of God and are designed to make the attributes of God known. But they are also different, and one of the ways they are different is that election is due to the special and gracious intervention of God in an individual's life to save that person, while reprobation is merely God's passing by a person, thereby allowing him to continue in his own way and eventually be judged for his sin. That is a very important point.

God never condemns innocent people. Therefore, regardless of what we may or may not understand about the process of election, we can know that if we are judged by God, it must be for the sake of our own sin. And that means that unbelief must be our own fault.

If it is not, whose fault can it be?

You can't blame it on God.

This is the point of Paul's teaching in Romans 9:30–32, because, as I said when providing an overview of chapters 9 through 11, what he is showing is that the unbelief of Israel is not to be blamed on God. And, let me add, the unbelief of the Gentiles is not to be blamed on God either. All human beings instinctively want to do that, both Jews and Gentiles. We do not like the doctrine of election, because it throws us upon the mercy of God. But assuming that we do nevertheless accept the truth of the doctrine, the next evasion is to try to deny our own responsibility.

We are not mere puppets in God's hands. We are responsible human beings, in spite of what we might wrongly deduce from Paul's earlier discussion of election and reprobation.

Romans 9:30–32 could be taken as summing up the preceding verses, which they do in a sense. But they are actually a new section of the argument, as I have been saying.[3] In fact, they introduce a major new portion of the argument, because the matters they raise continue to be discussed throughout the remainder of chapters 9 and 10, and it is not until Romans 11:1 that Paul brings in an entirely new observation.

These verses have a very simple outline. Verse 30 says that the Gentiles as a whole are being saved. Verse 31 says that the Jews as a whole were not being saved. Verse 32 explains why.

Gentile Salvation: By Grace Alone

The critical word in these three verses is "righteousness," which we see at once when we read them. In the New International Version, righteousness is found three times, but it actually occurs four times in the Greek text, one of those instances being translated by the pronoun "it" in our versions. Righteousness is a dominant word in Romans, occurring (in the NIV text) thirty-two times in all. Yet the treatment in these verses and as far as verse 6 in chapter 10, is the first extensive discussion of the idea since chapter 6.[4]

What does righteousness mean? In these verses it is the equivalent of salvation or, to be more precise, justification, which is the same word as righteousness in Greek. Verses 30 and 31 tell us that the Gentiles were not seeking salvation, yet found it, while the Jews, who *were* seeking salvation, did not find it.

And yet, righteousness is the proper word to use, because it more fully describes the kind of salvation being sought. Salvation is a broad term. There can be many kinds of salvation. But righteousness refers to the righteous requirements of the law of God and therefore has to do with a right standing before him. What we are told in verse 30 is that the Gentiles were not seeking this right standing before God by serious attempts to fulfill God's law, and yet they found that right standing anyhow.

How did they do that?

The first part of the verse is not hard to explain. It is a simple observation along the lines of Romans 1. Far from seeking the righteousness of God by

3. See Leon Morris, *The Epistle to the Romans* (Grand Rapids: Wm. B. Eerdmans, and Leicester, England: Inter-Varsity Press, 1988), p. 374.

4. "Righteousness" occurs once in chapter 1, three times in chapter 3, nine times in chapter 4, three times in chapter 5, and five times in chapter 6. It is found only once each in chapters 8 and 14. Besides that, the only other references are in this section of the letter: Romans 9:30 (twice), 31; 10:3 (twice), 4, 5, 6.

obedience to the law of God, the Gentiles had actually rejected God and were in the process of running away from him and his law as rigorously and rapidly as possible. This placed them on that downward slippery path that Paul describes so well. It is a slope on which they began to sin in greater and greater ways until in the end they had lost the ability to distinguish between right and wrong. In fact, they called the wrong, right and the right, wrong—evil, good and good, evil. They had inverted the moral order of God's true righteousness entirely.

The surprising thing is that they were finding righteousness anyhow. Why? Because that righteousness is in Christ, and they were finding it in Christ because they were believing on him as their Savior. If we should ask how this can be, seeing that they were not even seeking it, the answer is that this was due entirely to the seeking grace of God.

Take a moment and circle two words in these verses: "obtained" in verse 30 and "attained" in verse 31. If you have an Authorized or King James Version, you will not be able to do this, because you will find the word *attained* in both places, which is unfortunate, because it suggests that the two situations are alike in nature and differ only in that one was successful and the other was not. Actually, there are two entirely different words in the Greek text, and it is this right and proper distinction that the New International Version and some other versions capture.

Let me illustrate the difference between these words by a cartoon that Donald Grey Barnhouse tells about in his commentary. It showed a boardroom of a large company, with the president standing before his subordinates. Behind him on the wall was a portrait of the company's founder, who was obviously the man's father. The president was scowling at his subordinates, and the caption said, "The trouble with you people is that you have no initiative. Why, by the time I was thirty years old, I had *inherited* my first five million dollars."[5]

There is a big difference between inheriting a million dollars and earning it. So, to use this illustration, what this verse tells us is that the Gentiles, who did not set out to earn their righteousness, nevertheless inherited it or, as the NIV says, "obtained" it as a free gift.

Jewish Failure: A Surprising Fact

Verse 30, then, has introduced us to a surprising situation: the fact that the Gentiles, who had not sought salvation, were nevertheless finding it. The only possible explanation of this mystery is God's grace. But now we come to verse 31, and we find an even greater puzzle. We find that the Jews, who were trying to earn their salvation, did not attain it.

---

5. Donald Grey Barnhouse, *God's Covenants: Exposition of Bible Doctrines, Taking the Epistle to the Romans as a Point of Departure,* vol. 8, *Romans 9:1–11:36* (Grand Rapids: Wm. B. Eerdmans, 1963), p. 56.

We will not appreciate the surprising nature of this situation unless we take Paul's words at full value and acknowledge that the Jews had indeed "pursued a law of righteousness." This takes us back to Romans 2, where Paul described his countrymen as relying on the law, knowing the will of God and then choosing what is superior because of that knowledge (vv. 17–18). He wrote, "You are convinced that you are a guide for the blind, a light for those who are in the dark, an instructor of the foolish, a teacher of infants, because you have in the law the embodiment of knowledge and truth" (vv. 17–20). That was absolutely true. The Jews did have the law, and devout Jews did pursue acceptance before God by that means. Like Paul himself during his years as a Pharisee, they labored earnestly to keep the law in all its many minute particulars, thinking that they would be saved by so doing.

But what those verses from Romans 2 also show is that their trying to keep the law was doomed to failure. What the Jews had not reckoned on was their own sinful natures, which made it as impossible for them to keep the law of God perfectly as it would have been for Gentiles to keep it, had they possessed the law and tried to keep it.

The Jews—Paul himself was one—thought they were closer to salvation than the Gentiles, because they were at least trying to keep God's law. But what they failed to see is that they were still failing. And because they refused to see that, they also failed to see what the law was actually given for: to show that we cannot achieve salvation by our works and to point us to the only way salvation can come, which is through faith in Jesus Christ.

Instead of becoming self-righteous, we should become aware of our radical unrighteousness and turn to Christ. We should see what the hymnwriter Augustus Toplady saw clearly when he wrote:

> Not the labors of my hands
> Can fulfill thy law's demands;
> Could my zeal no respite know,
> Could my tears forever flow,
> All for sin could not atone;
> Thou must save, and thou alone.

Many labor and have zeal, perhaps even tears. But none of this is enough. The hymn rightly says that only God can save us, and—if that is the case—salvation must be received on God's terms, which means through faith in the work of Jesus Christ.

By Works or Through Faith?

What I have just said anticipates the point of verse 32. For, having observed how the Gentiles, who had not sought righteousness, found it and how the Jews, who sought righteousness, had *not* found it, the apostle now adds an explanation of the second case. "Why did the Jews fail to attain salvation?"

he asks. The answer is, "Because they pursued it not by faith but as if it were by works." That is, they sought it in the wrong way.

And so do we all, until God shows us our many stubborn errors and turns our minds and hearts to Jesus Christ.

During the last century, in the worst slum district of London, there was a social worker whose name was Henry Moorehouse. One evening as Moorehouse was walking along the street, he saw a little girl come out of a basement store carrying a pitcher of milk. She was taking it home. When she was a few yards from Moorehouse, she suddenly slipped and fell. Her hands relaxed their grip on the pitcher and it dropped on the sidewalk and broke. The milk ran down into the gutter, and the little girl began to cry as if her heart would break. Moorehouse quickly stepped up to see if she was hurt. He helped her to her feet, saying, "Don't cry, little girl."

But she kept crying, repeating through her tears, "My mommy'll whip me; my mommy'll whip me."

Moorehouse said, "No, little girl, your mother won't whip you. I'll see to that. Look, the pitcher isn't broken in many pieces." As he stooped down beside her, picked up the pieces, and began to work as if he were putting the pitcher back together, the little girl stopped crying. She had hope. She came from a family in which pitchers had been mended before. Maybe this stranger could repair the damage. She watched as Moorehouse fitted several of the pieces together until, working too roughly, he knocked it apart again. Once more she began to cry, and Moorehouse had to repeat, "Don't cry, little girl. I promise you that your mother won't whip you."

Again they began the task of restoration, this time getting it all together except for the handle. Moorehouse gave it to the little girl, and she tried to attach it. But, naturally, all she did was knock it down again. This time there was no stopping her tears. She would not even look at the broken pieces lying on the sidewalk.

Finally Moorehouse picked the little girl up in his arms, carried her down the street to a shop that sold crockery, and bought her a new pitcher. Then, still carrying her, he went back to where the girl had bought the milk and had the new pitcher filled. He asked her where she lived. When he was told, he carried her to the house, set her down on the step, and placed the full pitcher of milk in her hands. Then he opened the door for her. As she stepped in, he asked one more question, "Now, do you think your mother will whip you?"

He was rewarded for his trouble by a bright smile as she said to him, "Oh, no, sir, 'cause it's a lot better pitcher 'an we had before."[6]

---

6. The story of Moorehouse and the little girl is from Donald Grey Barnhouse, *How God Saves Men* (Philadelphia: The Bible Study Hour, 1955), pp. 7–9. I have told it myself in James Montgomery Boice, *Ephesians: An Expositional Commentary* (Grand Rapids: Zondervan, 1988), pp. 62, 63.

That is a wonderful illustration of what we do in trying to earn our salvation, and what God does.

When Adam and Eve fell in the Garden of Eden, it was as if the pitcher of human life and morality fell and was forever broken, while all the goodness it contained began to run out. This is not to say that there is no value at all to the broken pieces. I have seen works of art made from broken pieces of pottery, and archaeologists use pottery shards to date ancient civilizations. In an analogous way, there is some limited value to human character, especially in mere secular affairs. But, as far as establishing a right relationship to God is concerned, human character is as worthless as the broken pitcher.

And it does not matter how much effort we spend trying to fit the pieces back together. "All the king's horses and all the king's men, can never put Humpty Dumpty together again."

In fact, not even God tries to put it back together.

Instead, like Henry Moorehouse, God holds out a new pitcher filled with the new life of Jesus Christ and places it in our empty hands. And he assures us that he won't judge us now, because "it's a much better pitcher than we had before." In fact, it is a perfect one. It is the very righteousness of God's Son.

What do you need to do?

There is only thing you can do, and that is also what you need to do. You can accept it. You need to open up your hands and receive it. You need to wrap your fingers around it and clutch it to your heart. And stop trying to think that you have earned salvation or can earn it, because you cannot. Righteousness is wrongly sought by human works. It is only rightly found by the faith that receives God's gift.

138

Stumbling over Christ

Romans 9:32–33

. . . They stumbled over the "stumbling stone." As it is written:
"See, I lay in Zion a stone that causes men to stumble
and a rock that makes them fall,
and the one who trusts in him will never be put to shame."

One of the most important principles of biblical interpretation is that Scripture interprets Scripture. This means that the best way to discover what a problem passage means is to see what other verses dealing with the same theme say. The related passages may, and usually do, speak more clearly. Scripture always illuminates Scripture, and the comparison of Scripture with Scripture is the only sure way to study the Bible accurately.

This is true of the subject we come to in this study. In the last two verses of Romans 9 the apostle Paul introduces an image to illustrate what he has been saying in the earlier half of the paragraph, namely, that Israel had not obtained salvation because the people as a whole had been offended by Jesus, rather than believing him or placing their faith in him. His image is of a "stumbling stone," which is what he calls Jesus, drawing on two passages in Isaiah for the illustration.

1141

Yet these are not the only places in the Bible where we find this image, and a careful study of the many passages there are shows how rich a theme this was, not only for Paul but for many of the New Testament figures, including Jesus. I want to explore its richness in this study.

The Quotations from Isaiah

The place to begin is with the quotations from Isaiah. There are two of them, Isaiah 8:14 and 28:16, even though Paul has combined them into what seems to be a single quotation in Romans 9:33. Isaiah 28:16 says, "See, I lay a stone in Zion, / a tested stone, / a precious cornerstone for a sure foundation; / the one who trusts will never be dismayed." Isaiah 8:14 says that "for both houses of Israel he [that is, Jehovah] will be / a stone that causes men to stumble / and a rock that makes them fall. . . ." In his citation Paul has used the first and last part of Isaiah 28:16, but has substituted Isaiah 8:14 for what comes between.

Why does he make this alteration? Does this mean that Paul has no real respect for Scripture and therefore quotes it any way he likes, distorting it if necessary?

The answer is exactly the opposite. Instead of distorting Scripture, Paul is doing what I was referring to earlier when I spoke of the manner in which one verse of the Bible interprets another. In Isaiah 8:14, the prophet seems to be saying that Jehovah is the stone that causes people to stumble, the idea that Paul wants to emphasize. But the later verse, Isaiah 28:16, makes clear that the stumbling stone is another individual whom God is going to set "in Zion." This means that the latter passage explains the earlier one, showing that the stumbling stone is actually the Lord Jesus Christ whom the Father sent into the world.

Robert Haldane summarizes many of the implications of this image when he writes:

> The designations of a stone and a rock are given to Jesus Christ, both presenting the idea that the great work of redemption rests solely on him. He is its author, the foundation on which it rests, the center in which all its lines meet, and the origin from which they proceed. He is to that work what the foundation stone and the rock on which it is erected are to the building, sustaining it and imparting to it form and stability. In another sense, he is a stone of stumbling, occasioning his rejection by those who, not believing in him, are cut off from communion with God.[1]

It works the other way, too—for the passages in Isaiah not only identify Jesus as the rock, they also identify him with Jehovah, on the mathematical principle that "things equal to the same thing are equal to each other." By

1. Robert Haldane, *An Exposition of the Epistle to the Romans* (MacDill AFB: MacDonald Publishing, 1958), p. 495.

establishing Jesus as a rock in Zion, God also proclaims him as the divine rock upon which his people are to build. Texts identifying God as "the Rock" or "my rock" are frequent in the Old Testament.[2] So Paul's use of the image is evidence of his belief in the deity of Jesus Christ.

This was an offense to Israel, of course. In fact, it was the root or foundational offense they found in Paul's teaching.

Paul spoke about this in an autobiographical way in 1 Corinthians, saying that the gospel of Jesus and his cross was "weakness" to the Romans, "foolishness" to the Greeks, but a cause of "stumbling" to the Jews:

> Jews demand miraculous signs and Greeks look for wisdom, but we preach Christ crucified, a stumbling block to Jews and foolishness to Gentiles, but to those whom God has called, both Jews and Greeks, Christ the power of God and the wisdom of God. For the foolishness of God is wiser than man's wisdom, and the weakness of God is stronger than man's strength. . . . God chose the foolish things of the world to shame the wise; God chose the weak things of the world to shame the strong. He chose the lowly things of this world and the despised things—and the things that are not—to nullify the things that are, so that no one may boast before him.
>
> 1 Corinthians 1:22–25, 27–29

I find those three problems in preaching the gospel today. I am not dealing with Greeks, Romans, and Jews specifically. But I do find that some people reject Christianity because they consider it a religion for weaklings; they don't need "religion." Others reject it because it seems foolish; it doesn't conform to the "wisdom" of our secular, scientific age. Still others reject it because the idea of a divine Son of God is an offense to them; they do not understand why they cannot "save" themselves.

Three More Causes of Offense

However, it is not only the deity of Jesus Christ that was and is offensive—to Israel and other peoples. There are other matters, too, and the passage in 1 Corinthians suggests at least three more of them.

1. *A stone is a "lowly" thing.* As an illustration, it points to Jesus' humanity and low estate. Most people enjoy getting to know other people they consider important, and they are often delighted to be seen with them or to be a part of their cause. If Jesus had come in the splendor of his divine glory accompanied by legions of angels, the people would have rallied to his side. But this is not how he came. He came as a helpless baby, born of poor parents in a distant region of the Roman Empire, and during his lifetime he moved among the poorest of the poor and was pleased to be one of them. The only

---

2. See Deut. 32:4, 15, 18; 1 Sam. 2:2; 2 Sam. 22:3, 32, 47; 23:3; Pss. 18:2, 31, 46; 42:9; 62:7; 78:35; 89:26; 94:22; Isa. 17:10; 44:8; Hab. 1:12.

"important" people he ever met were Pilate and Herod, and that was only when he was on trial before them. Jesus seemed to be insignificant.

It was as Isaiah said elsewhere: "He had no beauty or majesty to attract us to him, / nothing in his appearance that we should desire him. / He was despised and rejected by men, / a man of sorrows, and familiar with suffering . . ." (Isa. 53:2–3).

A "stone that causes men to stumble" is not one that is placed in some high position in a cathedral tower. It is one that is neglected, one that is lying inconspicuously on the ground.

2. *The gospel must be received by faith.* This is the point Paul makes in the first half of verse 32, in which he introduces the image of the "stumbling stone." He asked why Israel, which was pursuing righteousness, had not attained it, and he answered, "Because they pursued it not by faith but as it were by works." Salvation is God's gift. So salvation must be received as a gift from God or not at all. If we think we can earn it (or if we insist on earning it), it cannot be ours.

Robert Haldane says, "A free salvation becomes an offense to men on account of their pride. They cannot bear the idea of being indebted for it to sovereign grace, which implies that in themselves they are guilty and ruined by sin. They desire to do something, were it ever so little, to merit salvation, at least in part."[3]

3. *God saves whom he will.* The third offense is the one Paul has been elaborating in this chapter as a whole: God's sovereignty in election. God saves whom he will, and he rejects whom he will. Of all the doctrines in the Bible, there is none, in my opinion, so offensive to normal human beings as this, which is probably why even pastors and serious Bible teachers often avoid teaching from this chapter.

I have already quoted Robert Haldane several times, because he is particularly good on this section. Here is a third and final quote:

> There is nothing which more clearly manifests the natural opposition of the mind of man to the ways of God, than the rooted aversion naturally entertained to the obvious view of the doctrine of the sovereignty of God held forth in this ninth chapter of the epistle to the Romans.
>
> Self-righteous people, as is not to be wondered at, hold this doctrine in the utmost abhorrence; and many even of those, who are in some measure taught of God to value [this] great salvation, are reluctant to come to the serious study of this part of his Word. Even when they are not able plausibly to pervert it, and when their consciences will not allow them directly to oppose it, with the Pharisees they say that they do not know what to make of this chapter. But why are they at a loss on this subject? What is the difficulty which they find here? If

3. Haldane, *An Exposition of the Epistle to the Romans,* p. 496.

it be "hard to be understood," does this arise from anything but the innate aversion of the mind to its humbling truths? Can anything be more palpably obvious than the meaning of the apostle? Is there any chapter in the Bible more plain in its grammatical meaning? It is not in this that they find a difficulty. Their great difficulty is that it is too obvious in its import to be perverted. Their conscience will not allow them to do violence to its language, and their own wisdom will not suffer them to submit to its dictation. . . .

. . . ought not believers to renounce their own wisdom and look up to God in the spirit of him who said, "Speak, Lord, for thy servant heareth."[4]

I have spoken thus far of four great offenses of the gospel: (1) the deity of Jesus Christ; (2) his humanity and humble estate; (3) that the gospel must be received by faith rather than being earned by works; and (4) that salvation is according to God's sovereign election and calling.

Four great stones for stumbling!

But now I ask, "Why should God create a gospel that is so offensive?"

This is not the way a modern advertising executive would do it. He would try to make the gospel as attractive as possible. He would try to make it fit "felt needs." That is the way to get a hearing. That is the way to sell a product. Doesn't God understand the techniques of good marketing? The answer, of course, is that God knows exactly what he is doing. And what he is doing is to humble human pride, which is absolutely necessary if you or I or anybody else is to be saved. It is our pride that has gotten us into trouble in the first place. Pride is the very root of sin. There can be no salvation unless our pride is cut down, torn up by the roots, and cast out, which is what the gospel does. When pride is destroyed, then, and only then, are we ready to believe in Jesus and begin to build upon him.

Capstone of Biblical Religion

This leads us to the next step in understanding this important Scripture illustration. According to Scripture, the "stumbling stone" is meant to be the capstone of biblical religion and thus the foundation on which to build any stable life. To see this we need to trace a few other uses of the image of the stone in the Bible.

The starting point is Psalm 118:22, which says, "The stone the builders rejected has become the capstone."

There is a story behind this verse, though it is not in the Bible. It is a two-thousand-year-old tradition that has come down to us from the time of the building of Solomon's temple in Jerusalem. The stones for that temple were quarried away from the temple site, according to detailed plans supplied by the temple architects, and they were transported to the temple site and assembled there without the noise of stonecutting tools. Early in the construction a stone was sent that did not seem to fit the temple. Since the builders did

4. Ibid., p. 497.

not know what to do with it, they laid it aside and forgot it. Later, when they were ready to place a large capstone on the now nearly completed structure and sent to the quarry for it, they were told that it is was not there, that it had already been sent up. The builders searched for it and eventually found the stone that had been laid aside. When they lifted it to its proper place in the building, it fit perfectly.

Thus, "the stone the builders rejected [became] the capstone."

Jesus quoted this verse from Psalm 118 once when he was speaking to the religious leaders who were looking for ways to arrest him. He had told two stories meant to expose their hardhearted rejection of him. In the first they were portrayed as a son who said he would work in the father's vineyard but did not do it. In the second they were portrayed as wicked tenants of a rich man's field, who plotted to steal it and eventually killed the heir. When he had finished these stories, Jesus said, "Have you never read in the Scriptures: / 'The stone the builders rejected / has become the capstone; / the Lord has done this, / and it is marvelous in our eyes'?" (Matt. 21:42; pars. Mark 12:10–11; Luke 20:17).

The disciples seem to have heard this, because later Peter quoted the verse in the same way and with the same application when he and John were put on trial before the Sanhedrin following Jesus' resurrection and ascension. Peter told the religious leaders, "Jesus Christ of Nazareth . . . is 'the stone you builders rejected, which has become the capstone'" (Acts 4:10–11).

The Living Stone and God's Temple

We come now to what I regard as the definitive treatment of this image in the Bible, namely, Peter's handling of it in his first letter. We have seen how Paul quoted Isaiah 8:14 and 28:16 in Romans 9, and how Jesus and Peter himself quoted Psalm 118:22 in Matthew 21:42 (with parallels) and Acts 4:11. In this great passage—1 Peter 2:4–8—Peter draws all three texts together to show how those who believe on Jesus build their lives on him and are made part of a spiritual temple, the church, which God is constructing:

> As you come to him, the living Stone—rejected by men but chosen by God and precious to him—you also, like living stones, are being built into a spiritual house to be a holy priesthood, offering spiritual sacrifices acceptable to God through Jesus Christ. For in Scripture it says:
>
>> "See, I lay a stone in Zion,
>>   a chosen and precious cornerstone,
>> and the one who trusts in him
>>   will never be put to shame."
>
> Now to you who believe, this stone is precious. But to those who do not believe,
>
>> "The stone the builders rejected
>>   has become the capstone,"

and,

> "A stone that causes men to stumble
> and a rock that makes them fall."

They stumble because they disobey the message—which is also what they were destined for.

In view of this passage, I cannot see how anyone can imagine that when Jesus told Peter that "you are Peter, and on this rock I will build my church" (Matt. 16:18), he was teaching that Peter was to be the foundation on which he would build his church. The errors of the supremacy of the Roman pontiff and the infallibility of the pope when speaking *ex cathedra* are constructed on this text. But these are terrible errors, and they are certainly not what Peter himself understood the Lord's words to mean.

In the Greek language in which the New Testament is written, there is a pun on the word *Peter*. The Greek word for Peter is *petros*, which means a piece of rock and can mean something as small as a slingshot stone or pebble. But when Jesus said, "On this *rock* I will build my church," the word he used was *petra* (a feminine form of the same root word), which means "bed rock." It was as if he were saying, "You are a little pebble, *Petros*, but I am going to build my church on myself, because I am the bed rock, *petra*. I am the only foundation on which anyone can securely build."

It was the same thing Jesus was getting at toward the end of the Sermon on the Mount in his illustration of a house built on a solid foundation. He said, "Everyone who hears these words of mine and puts them into practice is like a wise man who built his house on the rock. The rain came down, the streams rose, and the winds blew and beat against that house; yet it did not fall, because it had its foundation on the rock" (Matt. 7:24–25). Those who do not build their lives on Jesus and his teaching are like houses built on sand, which are washed away by any sudden tempest.

I suppose there were people even in Peter's day who imagined that Jesus was going to build his church on Peter, which is why Peter, rather than some other New Testament writer, gives us this definitive explanation of the image of Christ as the rock. I suppose he is saying, "Don't think of me as the rock. I am as unstable as a pebble. Haven't you read my story? Build your life on Jesus Christ."

Building on the Rock

Which is my conclusion, as well as the conclusion of the ninth chapter of Romans. If you will not have Jesus Christ, he will become a stumbling stone to you that will cause you to fall spiritually. That fall will mean your eternal destruction. But if you trust in him, you will find him to be the foundation stone that God has himself established, and you will learn, as you live the Christian life, that "the one who trusts in him will never be put to shame."

Barnhouse sums up the situation wisely:

Men look for something big. God put Christ into this world as a low-lying stone, hid away among the long grass of a distant Roman province. Men held their eyes too high and walked across the world, not seeing Christ as God's only answer to their problems, and they tripped over him and stumbled when they came upon him suddenly. They were offended by a scheme of salvation which brings man to nothingness, and they refused God's way.

But, Barnhouse says, there are some who have accepted God's way:

They have come through the tangled grass of this world with their eyes low upon their own bleeding feet, scarred with their walk on the road of sin. When they have come to this stone, they have been willing to stand on it and ask for nothing further. They have believed God's word about the Lord Jesus Christ as being the only way of salvation. They have abandoned their goal, their road, their strength, their pride, and have taken their stand squarely on the Lord Jesus Christ. To them comes the trumpeted promise from the God of the universe: "Whoever believeth on him shall not be ashamed."[5]

To be "ashamed" means to be utterly confounded in the day of God's final judgment of the world and all persons. It means standing before God with your mouth firmly shut, with nothing to say in your defense as your deeds are read out, their evil judged by the standard of the perfect holiness of God, and your condemnation pronounced in terms so terrible that you will wish to have the mountains fall on you to protect you from the wrath of God or a flood to sweep you from his presence. On that day, your condemnation will be certain unless you are in Jesus Christ. Before it comes, be sure your feet are planted firmly on the Rock.

---

5. Donald Grey Barnhouse, *Epistle to the Romans*, part 58, *Romans 9:19–33* (Philadelphia: The Bible Study Hour, 1955), p. 49. These paragraphs are deleted from the material published later in book form.

139

A Prayer for Israel

Romans 10:1-2

Brothers, my heart's desire and prayer to God for the Israelites is that they might be saved. For I can testify about them that they are zealous for God, but their zeal is not based on knowledge.

Have you ever worked with someone for a long time and been so frustrated with his or her lack of response to your help or teaching that eventually you have just written the person off, saying, "I've done the best I can. He is going to have to learn the hard way." Or perhaps you said, "Whatever she has coming to her is her own fault."

I am sure all of us have reacted that way at some time about someone. So we should not be surprised in our reading of Romans 9–11 if we should find the apostle Paul doing the same thing, due to the unbelief of his countrymen. In fact, far from being surprised, we would be understanding and sympathetic, especially knowing how badly he had been treated by some of them.

But this is not what we find Paul doing.

Instead of dismissing his countrymen and consigning them to some bad end, we find that Paul is praying for them, which is what each of us should do for those who are unbelieving or who try to create problems for Christians who are witnessing to them about Jesus.

The Flow of Paul's Argument

If you have been studying Romans 9–11 closely, you may have noticed something interesting about each of these three chapters. Each one begins with an expression of intense concern by Paul for his own people. In Romans 9 he says that he has "great sorrow and increasing anguish" in his heart for Israel. In Romans 11 he declares that "God did not reject his people," even though, on their part, the rejection of Jesus by the majority might suggest it. In the chapter we are now studying, Romans 10, he protests that his "heart's desire and prayer to God for the Israelites is that they might be saved."

Paul is grieving because of widespread Jewish unbelief, and it is probably because of this feature that the ancient Bible editors divided the chapters as they did.

Yet the first verse of Romans 10 is not actually the beginning of a new section, which you will realize if you remember the outline I gave for these chapters earlier. As I pointed out at the start of this volume, Paul is responding to the erroneous assumption that the promises of God have failed, because the Jews as a whole have not believed on Jesus. He is giving seven reasons why that assumption is wrong, and Romans 10 is part of the third of these responses, which begins with Romans 9:30. The third response is that the promises of God have not failed in regard to Israel, because the failure of the Jews to believe is their own fault, not God's, just as the failure of a Gentile or anybody else to believe is his or her own fault and not God's. The reason people do not believe is that they are trying to earn salvation by their own good works. And they are proud of their efforts, which is why they refuse to receive salvation as God's gift.

This argument continues in one form or another throughout Romans 10, and a new argument does not start until Romans 11.

This means that the first two verses of Romans 10, which we are starting to study now, are linked to the last verses of Romans 9, and it is exactly this that makes the first two verses of Romans 10 so compelling. Paul has just said that the failure of the Jews to believe was due to the mistaken notion that they could earn their own salvation by good works. But, instead of writing them off at this point, as we might have done, Paul immediately goes on to show that he is concerned about them and is continuing to pray for them.

The word translated "desire" by the New International Version is a rare word that actually suggests the idea of "good pleasure" or "delight."[1] So what Paul is saying is that what would really please or delight him would be the salvation of his countrymen.

Therefore, he does what he can, which is to pray for them. His "prayer to God for the Israelites is that they might be saved" (v. 1).

1. See John Murray, *The Epistle to the Romans* (Grand Rapids: Wm. B. Eerdmans, 1968), p. 47.

Praying Always

This is a very simple prayer, but like most Bible prayers it suggests a number of important truths. The first is that prayer is always worthwhile.

The previous chapter of Romans has been on election, and this one is on the fact that the failure of Israel to believe on Jesus is their fault rather than God's, as I have said. Each of these points would seem to be a legitimate reason not to pray. But apparently neither one is a good reason, since Paul is praying. The fact that God elects some to salvation and passes by others does not stop him from praying, and the fact that failure to believe is a human failure rather than a divine failure does not stop him from praying. If he doesn't stop praying because of God and doesn't stop because of man, obviously he doesn't stop at all, which means that he was always accustomed to be praying for the salvation of other people.

He said exactly this when he was writing to the Thessalonians, telling them to "pray continually" (1 Thess. 5:17).

I suppose the problem does not seem to be so great on the human side, since most of us really do believe in prayer. Hudson Taylor, the founder of the China Inland Mission, now the Overseas Missionary Fellowship, said that "it is possible to move men, through God, by prayer alone." We agree on the human side. But what about the divine side? If God has made his decision to save some and pass by others, isn't it useless or even foolish to pray, not to mention presumptuous?

Paul did not seem to think so.

Here is the way John Murray highlights and then resolves the issue:

> In the preceding chapter the emphasis is upon the sovereign and determinative will of God in the differentiation that exists among men. God has mercy on whom he will and whom he wills he hardens. Some are vessels for wrath, others for mercy. And ultimate destiny is envisioned in destruction and glory. But this differentiation is God's action and prerogative, not man's. And, because [it is] so, our attitude to men is not to be governed by God's secret counsel concerning them. It is this lesson and the distinction involved that are so eloquently inscribed on the apostle's passion for the salvation of his kinsmen. We violate the order of human thought and trespass the boundary between God's prerogative and man's when the truth of God's sovereign counsel constrains despair or abandonment of concern for the eternal interests of men.[2]

There is even more that can be said. Murray is saying that we cannot know the mind of God in regard to the salvation of sinners. Therefore, we should always pray for them. But we can also add that one way in which God works to call sinners to repentance is through prayer. So, when we pray, God answers our prayers and saves those for whom he moves us to pray.

2. Ibid.

The theological way of expressing this is to say that God always ordains the means to some goal as well as the ends. So, if he has ordained to save a certain individual through our prayers, it is as necessary that we pray for that individual as it is that the individual be saved. Indeed, we must pray, since the individual will not be saved apart from the ordained intercession.

This should encourage us to pray.

George Müller of Bristol, England, the founder of the great faith orphanages, was a man of outstanding prayer. In his youth he had two friends for whom he began to pray. He kept notes on his prayers, and his notes show that he prayed for them for more than sixty years. One of these men was converted just before Müller's death at one of the last services Müller held. The other became a Christian within a year of Müller's funeral. Toward the end of his life, but before his friends' conversions, someone asked Müller why he was still praying for them after such a long time, since they had shown no response. He answered, "Do you think God would have kept me praying all these years if he did not intend to save them?"[3]

It was a point Paul would easily have understood.

The Greatest Prayer of All

The second truth we can see in Paul's prayer for his countrymen in Romans 10 is that the most important of all prayers are that those for whom we are praying might "be saved."

We are to pray about all sorts of things. Jesus himself said, "My Father will give you whatever you ask in my name" (John 16:23b). He instructed us to ask God for "our daily bread" (Matt. 6:11). He said, "Pray for those who persecute you" (Matt. 5:44). The apostle Paul added, "I urge, then, first of all, that requests, prayers, intercession and thanksgiving be made for everyone—for kings and all those in authority, that we may live peaceful and quiet lives in all godliness and holiness" (1 Tim. 2:1–2). I assume this means that we are to pray for peace, national prosperity, and for wisdom and righteousness on the part of those who rule over us. The items for which we are invited to pray are innumerable.

But Jesus also said something we need to think about carefully. "What good will it be for a man if he gains the whole world, yet forfeits his soul?" (Matt. 16:26a). This means that, however good it is to have peace and enjoy a reasonable measure of prosperity, these and countless other things count as next to nothing (or worse than nothing) if we acquire them and yet fail to receive God's salvation.

Remember that, when you are praying for other people. When you pray for your children, pray that they might do well in school, that they might be kept from sin, that they will develop winsome personalities and make worthwhile contributions in life. But do not fail to entreat God for their salvation.

---

3. J. Oswald Sanders, *Spiritual Leadership* (Chicago: Moody Press, 1967), p. 111.

They can gain all these other things. Yet, if they are not saved, they will lose it all, and these other things by themselves may even be a hindrance to their turning from faith in themselves to trust Jesus. Learn to think biblically, and then pray biblically, too. And do that, not only for your children but for your parents, friends, and whomever else God puts it upon your mind to pray for.

Could My Zeal No Respite Know

The third truth in Paul's prayer for his countrymen is found in the verse that follows it, where he says, "I can testify about them that they are zealous for God, but their zeal is not based on knowledge" (v. 2). This means that zeal is no substitute for conversion. Even the zealous must be saved.

When Paul speaks of Jewish zeal in the matter of religion, he was speaking from experience and of something well known to everyone, which means that this statement was not flattery but an honest admission of a great Jewish strength. No doubt there were numbers of secular-minded Jews in that day, as in ours. But for the most part the Jews took their religion very seriously. Paul had done so himself. He had come to Jerusalem from Tarsus in modern-day Turkey, had studied under the great Jewish rabbi Gamaliel, and had thrown himself into the propagation and defense of Judaism with a zeal few even among the Pharisees could match. Years later, in writing to the Philippians, he claimed that he had proved his zeal for God by persecuting the Christians (Phil. 3:6). As far as zeal went, Paul knew whereof he spoke.

But all of his zeal could not save him. And, in fact, his zeal was so misdirected that for a long time it actually kept him from Christ. It was only when Jesus revealed himself to him on the road to Damascus that Paul realized what he had been doing and committed himself to follow Christ from that time forward. In itself, zeal is a neutral thing. Before this, Paul had used it to attempt to destroy the work of God, though in ignorance. After he had met Jesus, he used it to proclaim the gospel and advance Christ's kingdom.

Paul acknowledged the zeal of his countrymen. Yet he still regarded them as lost, prayed for them fervently, and worked tirelessly for their salvation.

This is extremely relevant in our mindless, pluralistic, all-accepting society. For there is a common error that says that as long as a person is sincere, it does not really matter what he or she believes. In our day we are supposed to be open to everyone's version of the truth. Not long ago I got a letter expressing exactly this view and criticizing me because I had said that unbelieving Jews (as well as unbelieving Gentiles) are lost and need to repent of their sin and believe on Jesus. The writer wondered how anyone could preach such a "narrow, hateful" gospel in this age.

That is quite understandable, given the mind-set of most people today. But it only shows how far our culture has moved from Christianity. Why? Because the religion of Jesus is not "all-accepting," except in the sense that anyone may repent of his sin and come to Jesus. On the contrary, Christianity teaches that all are lost and that even the religiously zealous are not saved by zeal alone.

We are saved by Christ alone, received by faith alone. Anything else is not true Christianity.

The Path to Conversion

The fourth and last truth expressed in Paul's prayer for his countrymen is that the necessary first step to conversion, which all persons need, is knowledge. I say this because of the very last phrase of verse 2, which notes that the problem of the Jews was not their zeal itself. In itself zeal can be a very good thing. It was rather that "their zeal is not based on knowledge."

What was the problem? The next verse, which we will come to in the following study, explains it. It was their ignorance of the righteousness of God. Like Luther, many centuries later, they thought that the righteousness God requires of us is human righteousness, that is, a development of character or a collection of good works of which we ourselves are capable. What they did not understand is that the righteousness God requires is divine righteousness. And since it is divine and not human, the only way it can be obtained is from God himself as a free gift. It is what Paul was writing about earlier in Romans, in the chapters in which he was explaining the gospel.

Which is why he was writing it. If the problem was the Jews' lack of knowledge, the solution was to share or communicate that knowledge. To put it in other language, the task is to teach the Word of God.

This means that Christianity is primarily a teaching religion. It is and always has been. In fact, this was the primary thrust of Jesus' three-year ministry. You say, "But didn't Jesus come to be good to people, to heal them of their diseases?" No. He did that, but his primary ministry was to teach them the way of salvation, and to provide for it by himself dying for sin and then rising from the dead.

There is an excellent example of this in the first two chapters of Mark's Gospel. The first chapter of that Gospel tells us that John the Baptist came preaching a baptism of repentance and that after John was put in prison, Jesus picked up the teaching ministry by "proclaiming the good news of God" (v. 14). This theme carries on throughout the chapter. Verse 21 tells us that Jesus and his disciples went to Capernaum, where "Jesus went into the synagogue and began to teach. The next verse says that "the people were amazed at his teaching because he taught them as one who had authority. . . ." Later we find the people exclaiming, "What is this? A new teaching—and with authority!" (v. 27). Teaching is prominent in the chapter.

Now notice what follows. Verse 29 says that Jesus was brought to the home of Peter, whose mother-in-law was sick, and Jesus healed her. The word of the healing soon spread, and before long a large crowd of diseased people had gathered at the door, and Jesus healed them. Night came. Everyone went to sleep. But early in the morning, while everyone else was sleeping, Jesus got up and went out to a solitary place where he prayed.

Soon the disciples also got up, and by this time the crowd of sick people had regathered at Peter's house. The crowd was probably even larger than the night before. So when his disciples realized that Jesus was not in the house, they went looking for him, and when they found him they protested, "Everyone is looking for you!" (v. 37). They meant, "What are you doing out here? This is your great opportunity. Your healing of the sick has been a huge success."

Jesus didn't return to Capernaum. Instead he replied, "Let us go somewhere else—to the nearby villages—so I can preach there also. That is why I have come" (v. 38).

Wasn't it important to heal the sick? Perhaps. It was certainly a good thing to heal them. But it was not as important to heal as it was to teach, and in this case the pressure to heal the sick was beginning to detract from Jesus' teaching ministry. Jesus abandoned the former in order to pursue the latter. He had come to teach, and he was determined that nothing would keep him from that all-important work.

It was the same with the apostles in the early days of the church. In those days there was a problem with the administration of money for the widows. But rather than dealing with it themselves, the apostles asked the church to elect deacons to oversee the work because, they said, "It would not be right for us to neglect the ministry of the word of God in order to wait on tables" (Acts 6:2).

Paul did miracles. We are told about some of them in Acts. He also spoke in tongues (1 Cor. 14:18). But he said, "In the church I would rather speak five intelligible words to instruct others than ten thousand words in [an unknown] tongue" (v. 19).

Why did Jesus, the apostles, and Paul think along these lines? Why did they concentrate on teaching? Clearly, because Christianity must be according to right knowledge, and they knew that proper teaching was the necessary first step in any individual's conversion.

Prayer and the Ministry of the Word

And yet, proper teaching is not the only step. In the Greek text of these verses it is significant that the word Paul uses for "knowledge" is not the simple Greek word *gnosis*, which gave its name to the Gnostic movement and means "factual knowledge" pure and simple. The word he used is the compound word *epignosis*, which adds the idea of "knowledge that is according to godliness or with understanding."[4] According to Paul, the Jews had *gnosis*. What they lacked was *epignosis*, which is why he was praying for them.

---

4. It is hard to draw a sharp distinction between these words on the basis of their New Testament usage, but they are often used in the ways I have indicated. For a fuller discussion see Murray, *The Epistle to the Romans*, p. 48, including the footnote.

Don't miss the importance of that. Paul dedicated his life to bringing the knowledge of the gospel to both Jews and Gentiles. But he recognized, even as he did so, that no one, either among the Jews or among the Gentiles, would believe on Jesus as his or her Savior unless God opened the person's mind to understand the gospel and regenerated the person's soul to believe and receive salvation. So Paul prayed that God would do the necessary work, even as he did his part preaching and praying for them.

Remember that is what Jesus did, too. He left Capernaum to spend time alone in prayer, and it was after such a time that he determined to keep on teaching, rather than redirecting his ministry to become a miracle worker.

And so did the apostles. They told the early church, "We will turn this responsibility over to [the deacons] and will give our attention to prayer and the ministry of the word" (Acts 6:3–4). Prayer and preaching. The teaching of the Word of God plus intercession for those who are to hear it!

This must be our pattern, too.

140

Two Kinds of Righteousness

Romans 10:3

Since they did not know the righteousness that comes from God and sought to establish their own, they did not submit to God's righteousness.

Most people today are impatient with precise definitions, especially theological definitions or definitions of biblical words, which do not mean much to them in any case. I have had people tell me, "I tune out whenever you start talking about words." This is because they are impatient with precision about almost anything.

Yet some things require precision.

You cannot send a satellite into orbit, wire a house, diagnose an illness, prepare an accurate financial balance sheet, nor do hundreds of other important things without being precise. In the same way, you cannot make much progress in learning about God without precision, since God is himself precise and is the source of all precision. One of the words we have to be precise about is "righteousness," which Paul uses twice in Romans 10:3 and many times more in the verses that come immediately before and after it. This is because, as one writer says, "the issues of life and death, of time and eternity, hang upon a proper understanding of the righteousness of God and our relationship to it."[1]

We have difficulty with this, however, and the biggest difficulty is that our ideas of righteousness are completely different from God's idea of righteousness. This is what Romans 10:3 is saying, of course. It is saying that there are two kinds of righteousness, ours and God's, and that the basic spiritual failure of human beings is that they are so pleased with their own righteousness that they will not have the righteousness of God, which they need if they are to be saved from sin.

The opening word of the text is "since." It introduces the reason for the charge made in the preceding verse, namely, that the zeal of Paul's countrymen was "not based on knowledge." It was a zeal that was ignorant of the precise, accurate meaning of this word.

"Righteousness" in Romans

It would be a fair statement to say that one cannot understand the Bible without understanding what it has to say about righteousness. To be sure, there are books of the Bible that do not use that word. But the pivotal books do, and Romans in particular uses the word a great deal. "Righteousness" is found thirty-three times in Romans, as compared with seven times each in Matthew and 2 Corinthians, which are the books using it most frequently except for Romans. The word occurs eight times alone in Romans 9:30 through 10:6. The longer phrase, "the righteousness of God," is found eight times, one of these also being in our text.

Righteousness is prominent in the Old Testament, too, being linked with the name of God hundreds of times. In a valuable note on "the righteousness of God" in his Romans commentary, the Australian scholar Leon Morris points out how with us righteousness is an ethical virtue, but that with the ancient Hebrews righteousness was first and foremost a legal standing. God is righteous, so righteousness in man is that which enables us to stand before him: "The man who is ultimately righteous is the one who is acquitted when tried at the bar of God's justice."[2]

Yet here is the problem. God is the only righteous one. We are not righteous. So who is able to stand before God or be acquitted in his court? The answer is: No one, unless God provides his own righteousness for us as a free gift.

This is what Paul has been explaining in Romans and will continue to explain in this important tenth chapter.

---

1. Donald Grey Barnhouse, *Epistle to the Romans,* part 59, *Romans 10:1–4* (Philadelphia: The Bible Study Hour, 1956), p. 23. The quotation is missing from the final bound version of the Romans series.

2. Leon Morris, *The Epistle to the Romans* (Grand Rapids: Wm. B. Eerdmans, and Leicester, England: Inter-Varsity Press, 1988), p. 101.

Our Righteousness and God's

A few paragraphs ago I wrote that it is hard for us to understand the meaning of righteousness, because our ideas of it are so completely different from God's. But one thing we should be able to understand clearly is the meaning of our text when it distinguishes sharply between our righteousness (human righteousness) and God's. It is saying that although we use the same word when we are talking about God's righteousness and our righteousness, we are actually speaking about two entirely different things.

God's righteousness is his very nature, for God *is* righteous, just as God *is* love. It is associated with his holiness and is perhaps better discussed as that word. Holiness is what sets God apart. It is what makes him utterly unlike us. Human righteousness is merely a social quality achieved by the avoidance of certain gross forms of depravity and the contrary accumulation of outwardly good deeds. It is what enables people to live with each other in partial peace, when each person actually wants everything in life, as well as all other persons, to focus on himself.

Because they are two different things, the accumulation of human righteousness through avoiding evil and performing good deeds can never add up to the true, divine righteousness that God requires of us if we are to be saved from sin and have fellowship with himself.

Let me give a few illustrations.

When I was thinking about this theme during the week I was preparing this material, I remembered when I was in college and my roommate and I were talking. He was a music major. He had been playing a violin concerto on the stereo, and I was humming along, making a noise to mimic the violin. He found my noise offensive and asked whether that was really the way a violin sounded to me. It was a put-down. I told him I was doing the best I could and asked him to make a noise like he thought a violin should sound. I am not competent to judge whether his noise was more like a violin than my noise. I suppose, because he was the music major, that his noise was closer, though I don't know that for sure. But one thing I do know: No sound that either of us made was anything like a real violin. Our noise and the sound of a violin are in two entirely different categories and will remain so.

Here is an illustration I have used before. I have imagined a situation in which a platoon of American soldiers is captured by soldiers from the north during the Vietnam War and put in a prisoner-of-war camp. The American soldiers have no money and have to barter for whatever one soldier has and another soldier wants, which is a not very satisfactory arrangement. But one day a CARE package arrives, and in it is a game of Monopoly. The soldiers are delighted, not because of the game but because of the money. They divide it up, each man getting an equal number of white, pink, green, blue, beige, and gold bills (except for the sergeant, who gets an extra $500). Now, whenever one soldier has an extra cigarette and a second soldier wants it, the first can sell it to him for $100, or whatever. The money is very useful.

In any group of Americans there is always one who is a born capitalist, and this group is no exception. The capitalistic solider knows how to buy low and sell high, and as a result of his dealing it is not long before he has accumulated nearly all the money in the camp.

About this time there is a prisoner-of-war exchange, and this platoon of soldiers is air-lifted to Danang and then to a base in the Hawaiian Islands. Not long after this, our capitalistic soldier arrives home in San Francisco. The first thing he does after greeting his family is go downtown to the Wells Fargo Bank, make his way to the clerk dealing with new accounts, and tell her that he wants to open an account in the bank. "That's good," the teller says. "We like to see servicemen coming to the Wells Fargo. How much money would you like to start your account with?"

The solider responds by pushing his Monopoly money across the counter. "$1,534,281," he says. The teller takes one look at it and calls the manager, because it is obvious to her that the soldier is suffering brain damage from his confinement.

The Monopoly money might have helped this man get along very well in the prisoner-of-war camp, and even in America it could be used to play games. But it is no use at all in the world of American commerce. In that world you need genuine American greenbacks from the U.S. Treasury.

My third illustration is from Paul's description of his conversion in Philippians 3. He writes there how he had spent the early years of his life trying to accumulate righteousness, which he thought would make him acceptable to God, and he lists the things in which he had confidence: "circumcised on the eighth day, of the people of Israel, of the tribe of Benjamin, a Hebrew of the Hebrews; in regard to the law, a Pharisee; as for zeal, persecuting the church; as for legalistic righteousness, faultless" (Phil. 3:5–6). These items had to do with his birth, religious traditions, affiliations, personal zeal, and outward morality. He thought that was all he needed to attain heaven.

But then Jesus appeared to Paul when he was on his way to Damascus to arrest Christians, and when he saw Jesus in his heavenly glory, a glory that blinded him, all his own righteousness faded away into darkness and seemed to him to be nothing.

I have sometimes said it was as if Paul had been considering himself a 100-watt light bulb, surrounded by people who were only 75-, 60-, and 25-watt light bulbs. But, when Jesus appeared to him, the righteousness of Jesus was like the brightness of the sun. When Paul realized that, he gave up trying to create his own righteousness and instead placed his faith in Jesus, which was the only sensible thing to do.

A Fatal Error

I have used three illustrations of how the righteousness of God and the righteousness of human beings are different things, because this is an important point and I hope to have driven it home by repetition. Yet I admit that

I worry about one thing as I do. Illustrations like this tend to trivialize the issue. They even make the distinction seem fun, when actually the matter is deadly serious, and the failure to distinguish our righteousness from divine righteousness has fatal consequences.

A feeling for the seriousness of the issue can be seen from Charles Hodge's observation on Romans 10:3. He wrote that the Jews' "ignorance on this point implied ignorance of the character of God, of the requirements of the law, and of themselves," obviously three important matters. He added rightly, "Those who err essentially here, err fatally; and those who are right here, cannot be wrong as to other necessary truths."[3]

What Paul actually says is that those who failed to see the distinction I am making sought salvation in the wrong way. But that needs to be spelled out more fully. There are five fatal consequences of this error.

1. *Those who make it are satisfied with their own righteousness.* This is like a woman dying of some disease saying that she is sure everything is all right with her because her face looks good when she puts on her makeup. I have no doubt that a dying woman might look a great deal better with some makeup, particularly if she is very sick. But it is utter folly to trust the makeup and fail to see a doctor, if there is any chance that the doctor can detect the disease and cure it.

Yet this is exactly our folly. Millions of spiritually dying people are willfully ignorant of their true condition and instead trust their efforts to paint over the surface of their lives with human morality. Some do it with sacraments. They suppose that if they have been baptized or take communion regularly, they must be all right with God—since God himself proscribed these things—failing to see that these are meant to be signs of an inward change, not the reality itself, and that in any case they are not something that adds up to God's righteousness. Other people try the same approach by charitable giving, or by giving their time to volunteer causes. They suppose these acts of righteousness add up to God's righteousness. Because they are satisfied with what they have done, they suppose that God must be satisfied, too. They fail to see that they are spiritually dying men and women.

2. *They look down on other people.* People who fail to distinguish between God's righteousness and human righteousness, and who are therefore satisfied with their own righteousness, inevitably look down on other people—whom they suppose to have achieved less. Because they have no high, absolute standard by which to judge themselves, they assume that they are somewhere near the top.

This is one reason why, in our natural sinful condition, we refuse to look up to God and his righteousness. If we were to look up, as Paul was forced

---

3. Charles Hodge, *A Commentary on Romans* (Edinburgh and Carlisle, Pa.: The Banner of Truth Trust, 1972), p. 334. Original edition 1935.

to do on the road to Damascus, what we should be most conscious of is how far short we are of the divine requirements. In fact, we should realize that we are but light bulbs compared with the sun, and it would be foolish to boast of being brighter because we are a few watts above someone else. Seeing the righteousness of God humbles us and takes away all grounds for proud comparison. So we avoid it. We refuse to look up. Instead, we keep our eyes focused on other people and pat ourselves on the back because we imagine ourselves to be superior to them.

3. *They resent Jesus and his gospel.* This explains the next point, too, because when Jesus came to earth it was as if God brought down to our level the righteousness we in our fallen state refused to look up to or acknowledge.

It explains the fierce hatred of the leaders of Israel for Jesus when he was among them. Even people who do not trust Jesus as their own Lord and Savior generally acknowledge that he was a good man. He was gentle, kind, loving, and active in good works. Why is it that such a person should be as hated as Jesus was, hated even to the point of a trial and execution? The only explanation is that he was too good, too kind, too loving, too active in doing good works. In fact, his good was of such a high quality that anyone with any perception at all saw that it was other-worldly. That is, it was a divine righteousness rather than being merely a human righteousness. It was unattainable and—this is the rub—an intolerable offense to people who before Jesus' coming considered themselves to be quite good and clearly better than others.

This is why Jesus had a much better reception among social outcasts than among the model members of the community. The outcasts had no illusions about themselves. They knew they were sinners. They were merely overwhelmed and happy to find that Jesus loved them. But the self-styled righteous people felt offended by Jesus, someone whose true righteousness exposed the limits and falseness of their own.

4. *They misunderstand and mishandle the law.* God gave the law to show that we are sinners, not for us to be saved by it. Paul has already made this point in Romans, and we studied it in some detail earlier.[4] If we reject the revelation of God's true righteousness in Christ and suppose that we are doing well in our efforts to achieve our own righteousness, we will then use the law wrongly, misinterpreting it to require what we feel able to do and then praising ourselves for our achievement.

There is no better illustration of this than how differently the Pharisees and Jesus thought about the law. The Pharisees spent a great deal of effort defining what the particulars of the law meant. When the law said, "Remember the Sabbath day by keeping it holy" (Exod. 20:8), they asked, "What does it mean to keep it holy?" The law said, "On [the Sabbath] you

---

4. In Romans 7:7–12. See "Sin's Sad Use of God's Good Law" in volume 2 of this series, pp. 739–746.

shall not do any work" (v. 10). "But what is work?" they responded. Out of this type of thinking came an elaborate system of rules that proscribed how far you could walk on Saturday, what you could carry with you when you did walk, and the kind of activities you could pursue. It was the same way with each of the other commandments and with the many additional ordinances found in the first five books of the Old Testament. Following these regulations was a daunting task, an enormous burden, but this is precisely what the orthodox set out to do and believed they had accomplished. Paul was one of them himself before his conversion on the road to Damascus. He said of himself, "as for legalistic righteousness, [I was] faultless" (Phil 3:6).

But how did Jesus think about the law? He got to the heart of the law's teaching in Matthew 5, saying, "You have heard that it was said to the people long ago, 'Do not murder, and anyone who murders will be subject to judgment.' But I tell you that anyone who is angry with his brother will be subject to judgment . . ." (vv. 21–22).

Jesus also argued, "You have heard that it was said, 'Do not commit adultery.' But I tell you that anyone who looks at a woman lustfully has already committed adultery with her in his heart" (vv. 27–28).

And Jesus taught, "You have heard that it was said, 'Love your neighbor and hate your enemy.' But I tell you: Love your enemies and pray for those who persecute you" (vv. 43–44).

Jesus understood the law rightly. Therefore, if we, following his example, also use it rightly, which we refuse to do if we are satisfied with our own deficient righteousness, we will see that we can never measure up to this or any right standard and will turn to the mercy of God to save us from our sins, rather than plead our own corrupt morality as grounds for God's approval. If we see this clearly, we will acknowledge that we are condemned by whatever standard we choose, ours or God's, since at the deepest level we have all broken every right standard and will continue to do so.

5. *They will not submit to God's righteousness.* The final consequence of failing to see the difference between the righteousness of God and our own righteousness is that we will not submit to God's righteousness, which means acknowledging that we need it and seeking it in Christ, where alone it may be found. This is the point at which Paul closes his argument (Rom. 10:4), for everything else leads up to it.

Let me summarize. Paul says that the people of his day pursued a law of human righteousness but failed to achieve God's true righteousness because they sought it in the wrong way. They thought they could attain it by works, when it can be received only as a gift of God though faith. The reason they sought it in the wrong way is that they were ignorant of these two types of righteousness. They trusted in their own righteousness and thought that, if they had enough of it, their righteousness would add up to the righteousness of God. Therefore, they did not abandon their own efforts and submit to God's righteousness.

"Cannot" or "Will Not"?

"Abandon" and "submit"!

That is exactly the problem. Although God tells us that our own good works will not save us, we love them too much to abandon faith in them. He tells us that we must submit to the gift of his righteousness in Jesus Christ, but we will not submit to righteousness. We say we cannot do it. We "cannot believe." We "cannot understand." We don't even like the distinctions. But God tells us that it is not a question of "cannot." The real problem is that we *will not*, and the reason we will not submit is our sin. One commentator says, "If we are not to be ignorant of God's righteousness, if we are to turn away from any attempt to establish our own righteousness, we must come to the place where we submit ourselves to the righteousness of God—as it is seen in . . . Jesus Christ."[5]

Won't you do that?

As a minister of the gospel of Jesus Christ, I urge you to bow your proud head and put your whole trust in Christ alone. There is no other way of salvation, not by knowledge, not by sacraments, not even by good works. The Bible says that he, that is, Jesus, "has become for us wisdom from God—that is, our righteousness, holiness and redemption" (1 Cor. 1:30).

---

5. Barnhouse, *Epistle to the Romans,* part 59, *Romans 10:1–4,* p. 31.

141

Christ: The Fulfillment of the Law

Romans 10:4

Christ is the end of the law so that there may be righteousness for everyone who believes.

I have learned many lessons in more than twenty years of Bible study and preaching, and one of the lessons is that things that seem simple often are not. Our text is an example. Romans 10:4 seems to be a very simple verse. After all, what could be more straightforward than the words "Christ is the end of the law so that there may be righteousness for everyone who believes"? The verse has only seventeen words, less in Greek (nine words), and all but three of the English words have only one syllable.

Yet Romans 10:4 is a difficult verse to interpret.

And here is the interesting thing: It is the simple words (not the polysyllabics) that are the problem.

The two most problematic words are "end" and "law."

In his excellent commentary on Romans, the great Princeton Theological Seminary scholar Charles Hodge probably reduced the possible meanings of "end" as much as can reasonably be done, but he still speaks of three possible interpretations: (1) "the object to which any thing leads," (2) the "completion or fulfillment" of something, or (3) an "end or termination."[1] In terms

---

1. Charles Hodge, *A Commentary on Romans* (Edinburgh and Carlisle, Pa.: The Banner of Truth Trust, 1972), pp. 335, 336. Original edition 1935.

of our text, if the first meaning is the right one, the verse means that Jesus is that to which the law points so that, if it is properly used, the law will carry the one using it to him. If the second meaning is correct, the idea is that Jesus has himself perfectly fulfilled the law. If the third meaning is chosen, the verse means that Jesus has brought the dispensation of law to an end by dying for sin, rising again, and inaugurating the Christian Era. Obviously, something can be said for each interpretation.

Then, if you add to these difficulties the possible meanings of "law"—the law of Moses, a principle of conduct, the ceremonial law, or moral law—you can see how the difficulties of interpreting this verse proliferate.

How should we proceed?

I am convinced that in this case the most helpful procedure is not to argue the merits of the various possibilities, but to back off from the text itself and instead ask, "How does Jesus Christ fulfill the law?" He does it in a variety of ways. After we have explored those answers, we can then come back to the text, interpret it, and apply it practically.

To Fulfill All Righteousness

The first way in which Jesus fulfilled the law, and thus became the end of the law, is that he kept it perfectly himself. In books written about Jesus' work, theologians usually distinguish between what they call Christ's "active" and "passive" obedience. Jesus' passive obedience refers to his willingness to accept death in conformity to his Father's will, according to Philippians 2:8:

> And being found in appearance as a man,
>   he humbled himself
>   and became *obedient* to death—
>   even death on a cross!
>   [emphasis added]

Christ's active obedience refers to the way he carefully and deliberately kept the law of Moses in all respects.

This has several dimensions. It is usually said that Jesus fulfilled the *moral law* by obeying it perfectly; he was a perfect man. He fulfilled the *types and ceremonies* of the law by being the reality to which they pointed and by accomplishing in his death what they symbolized; thus, he was himself the perfect sacrifice for sins to which the daily sacrifices and the great sacrifices on the Day of Atonement pointed. Jesus fulfilled the *prophecies* by living them out to the letter.

In the Sermon on the Mount, Jesus referred explicitly to two of these areas (and probably the third) when he said, "Do not think that I have come to abolish the Law or the Prophets; I have not come to abolish them but to fulfill them" (Matt. 5:17).

In the story of Jesus' baptism, according to Matthew, there is a sentence that has bearing on Jesus' fulfillment of the law. John the Baptist had been alerted by God as to who Jesus was. So, when Jesus came to John to be baptized, John demurred, saying, "I need to be baptized by you, and do you come to me?" (Matt. 3:14). John had been teaching about the Messiah's work in baptizing with the Holy Spirit in contrast to his own merely preparatory water baptism. So he meant that he needed to receive a baptism of the Holy Spirit from Jesus, rather than Jesus receiving any benefit from him.

But Jesus responded, "Let it be so now; it is proper for us to do this to fulfill all righteousness" (v. 15).

This has been a puzzling statement to many people, since John's was a baptism for repentance and Jesus had committed no sin for which he needed to repent. But the reason for it seems clear enough.

On the one hand, since baptism signifies identification, it was by his baptism that Jesus willingly identified himself with all the other Israelites who were responding to John's preaching by turning from their sin to faith in the Messiah. That is, it was a symbol of the union of Jesus with the believer, a doctrine basic to Paul's theology. We looked at this earlier in these studies.[2]

On the other hand, since Jesus speaks of fulfilling "*all* righteousness," it is clear that he also considered this act to be part of his conscious obedience to all that God required. Through John, God had commanded his believing people to be baptized. So Jesus was baptized.[3]

However, the word that I think is most important in the exchange between Jesus and John the Baptist is "all." For by it Jesus was declaring his intention to fulfill *all* that God had required. He did this so well that his enemies were unable to accuse him of any wrongdoing, as much as they would have liked to. And God himself affirmed Jesus' perfect obedience to the law by declaring, just two verses later, "This is my Son, whom I love; with him I am well pleased" (Matt. 3:17). This divine evaluation was repeated at the time of the transfiguration (see Matt. 17:5 and parallels).

It was because Jesus fulfilled the law perfectly that he was able to be our substitute in dying for us on the cross, truly "a lamb without blemish or defect" (1 Peter 1:19).

2. See "Union With Jesus Christ" (Romans 5:12) in James Montgomery Boice, *Romans,* vol. 2, *The Reign of Grace* (Grand Rapids: Baker Book House, 1992), pp. 553–560. The following chapters also deal with the subject.

3. H. N. Ridderbos wisely says, "No matter how conscious Jesus was of his exceptional position, up to that time he had no other calling than to comply with the demands that God had imposed on every Israelite. Hence, just as he had once undergone circumcision (Luke 2:21), he now had to be baptized" (H. N. Ridderbos, *Matthew,* trans. Ray Togtman [Grand Rapids: Zondervan, 1987], p. 58). Similarly, John A. Broadus writes, "It was proper for all devout Jews to be baptized; therefore it was proper for Jesus" (John A. Broadus, *Commentary on Matthew* [Grand Rapids: Kregel Publications, 1990], p. 56).

This is the first part of the meaning of Paul's statement in Romans 10:4. It teaches that Christ is "the end of the law" in the sense that he fulfilled or satisfied the demands of the law completely.

Christ Our Righteousness

The second way Jesus became the end of the law is that he fulfilled the law on our behalf, so that now he is not only the source but is himself the righteousness of all who are joined to him by faith. This is what Paul says in 1 Corinthians 1:30 and 2 Corinthians 5:21: "Christ Jesus . . . has become for us wisdom from God—that is, our righteousness, holiness and redemption," and "God made him who had no sin to be sin for us, so that in him we might become the righteousness of God."

This is what justification is about, and it is what Paul seems chiefly to be talking about in this section of Romans 9 and 10.

We know what Paul teaches about righteousness, of course. But if we can lay that knowledge aside for a moment and go back to look at the end of Romans 9 and the verses that come before our text in Romans 10, we can see at a glance that a major question is unanswered. Paul has contrasted a righteousness that is "by works" with a righteousness that is "by faith" (Rom. 9:32). He has defined the righteousness he is talking about as "God's righteousness," showing that it comes "from God" as opposed to righteousness that comes from ourselves (Rom. 10:3). But he has not said in so many words where this righteousness that is "by faith" can be found. Or, to put it in other terms, if righteousness is to be received "by faith" and faith has content, as it must if it is true faith, what is faith's object?

Those questions are answered by verse 4, which introduces the name of Christ for the first time since the opening paragraph of Romans 9.[4] Jesus is faith's object. He is the one in whom is located the righteousness we need to be saved.

This justification, by which we stand or fall in the sight of the holy God, involves two corresponding transactions. On the one hand, if we are believers, our sin has been transferred to Jesus Christ and was punished in him when he died in our place on the cross. That is why we sing:

> My sin—O the bliss of this glorious thought!—
>   My sin, not in part, but the whole,
> Is nailed to the cross and I bear it no more;
>   Praise the Lord, praise the Lord, O my soul!

On the other hand, his righteousness was transferred to us, with the result that we are now counted as being righteous in him.

---

4. Jesus is alluded to as "a stone that causes men to stumble and a rock that makes them fall" in Romans 9:33, but even there Jesus is not named specifically. The questions would be: "Who is this stone?" and "Who is this one in whom we are to trust?"

Jesus, thy blood and righteousness
My beauty are, my glorious dress;
'Midst flaming worlds, in these arrayed,
With joy shall I lift up my head.

Both belong to justification, and both are true for anyone who has turned from sin and committed his or her life to Jesus Christ. It is what Paul has been writing about in much of the earlier portion of Romans and is reiterating in this passage.

So justification is another meaning of our text: "Christ is the end of the law so that there may be righteousness for everyone who believes."

Free at Last

Thus far we have been thinking of the word *end* as "fulfillment," or the "culmination" to which something tends. But "end" also sometimes means "termination," and this, too, is involved in Paul's statement. It teaches that Christ has ended the law as a system by which we are supposed to attain to righteousness. Or, to put it in other language, he has freed us from the law's bondage.

I have to be very careful how I say this, because nothing in this study is more apt to be misunderstood—and that from either of two perspectives.

First, I do not mean, as one commentator has written, that "Christ put a stop to the law as a means of salvation."[5] The reason it cannot mean this is that the law never was a means of salvation. Paul has spoken of the true purpose of the law in Romans 7, showing that the law was given to reveal the nature and extent of our sin and to point us to Jesus Christ as the only place salvation can be found. So, whatever "the end of the law" means, it clearly does not mean that Christ terminated it as a way of getting saved.

But neither does it mean the end of any continuing value for the law, for the law is part of Scripture, and "all Scripture is God-breathed and is useful for teaching, rebuking, correcting and training in righteousness" (2 Tim. 3:16). In fact, in Romans 3 Paul asked, "Do we, then, nullify the law by this faith?" and answered, "Not at all! Rather, we uphold the law" (v. 31). In Romans 7 he said, "So then, the law is holy, and the commandment is holy, righteous and good" (v. 12).

The best way of understanding this point is by something the apostle Peter said at the Council of Jerusalem described in Acts 15. Representatives of the expanding church had gathered in Jerusalem to decide the question of whether or not the Gentiles needed to submit to the law of Moses, which the Jewish church at that time upheld. It involved the ceremonial laws of Israel

---

5. An unfortunate and no doubt uncharacteristic misstatement by A. T. Robertson (cf. Donald Grey Barnhouse, *Epistle to the Romans,* part 59, *Romans 10:1–4* [Philadelphia: The Bible Study Hour, 1956], p. 33).

as well as the moral law, and the focal point of the debate was circumcision. Was it necessary for Gentile males to be circumcised to be Christians?

As you know, the council decided that it was not necessary. But the reason I refer to this debate is for something Peter said in the midst of it. He argued that God had saved the Gentiles without their becoming Jews, giving the Holy Spirit to them just as to Jewish converts. "Now then," he said, "why do you try to test God by putting on the necks of the disciples a yoke that neither we nor our fathers have been able to bear?" (Acts 15:10). The "yoke" was the law. So Peter was admitting that the law had been a burden for the Jews in the past and was arguing that it should not be imposed on the Gentiles, since even the Jews had been unable to sustain that harsh burden.

Does that mean that he was encouraging lawlessness, then? Not at all. He was encouraging righteousness, which is my next point. The council's decree reiterated some of the law's moral absolutes, but Peter was acknowledging that righteousness is not attained by legalism. That is, you do not become a better follower of Jesus Christ or a more holy person by adhering to a list of rules. The moral end of the law is attained by Christians, but it is attained by a different principle. It is by the life of Jesus Christ within the believer.

We need to remember that an entire book of the New Testament, Paul's letter to the Galatians, was written to combat the notion that Christians are to make their lives better or advance their discipleship by legalism. The Galatians were not saved by keeping the law but through faith, as Paul repeatedly points out. Therefore, why should they fall back into legalism? They should continue as they had started out. The main point of Galatians is summarized at the start of chapter 5: "It is for freedom that Christ has set us free. Stand firm, then, and do not let yourselves be burdened again by a yoke of slavery" (Gal. 5:1).

Righteousness in Us

This leads to my final point, because, whenever we speak of Jesus, the law, and righteousness, we need to say that Jesus has as his ultimate goal in saving us that we are to be a holy people. I need to add that I do not believe that is what *this verse* teaches. I think it is primarily teaching about justification—from the context and because Paul says that Jesus is the end of the law "so that there may be righteousness *for* everyone who believes." A righteousness *for* us is a righteousness imparted to us by God for Christ's sake. That is what Paul says.

But Paul also could have said, ". . . so that there may be righteousness *in* [or practiced by] everyone who believes," which would mean an actual righteousness to be attained by us.

How can I say this?

It is because Paul says it himself:

Therefore, there is now no condemnation for those who are in Christ Jesus, because through Christ Jesus the law of the Spirit of life set me free from the law of sin and death. For what the law was powerless to do in that it was weakened by the sinful nature, God did by sending his own Son in the likeness of sinful man to be a sin offering. And so he condemned sin in sinful man, *in order that the righteous requirements of the law might be fully met in us,* who do not live according to the sinful nature but according to the Spirit.

Romans 8:1–4, emphasis added

We are neither justified nor sanctified by the law. But those who are justified will also be progressively sanctified by the Spirit of Christ who lives within them, and this means that they will inevitably and increasingly live righteous lives. If they do not, they are not Christians.

Three Applications

I said at the start of this study that I wanted to return to some practical applications of our text, and I do that now. There are many, but I want to mention three.

1. *Christ is everything.* It is hard for us to imagine how important the law of Moses was for Jewish people living in Paul's day. The law is important for Jews today, of course, even though tradition has tended to replace a thorough knowledge of it. But it was more so then. The law was the very essence of Jewish religion. Yet Paul, who was himself a Jew, is telling us that Christ is the culmination, fulfillment, and (in a sense) termination of the law. For he "is the end of the law." It is a way of saying that everything that matters in salvation and religion is in him.

One commentator writes, "Instead of the temple it is to be Christ; instead of Moses, Christ; instead of Aaron, Christ; instead of the law, Christ; instead of ceremonies, Christ; instead of worship localized in a building, there is to be the eternal, omnipotent Christ."[6] It is impossible to exalt the nature and place of the Lord Jesus Christ too much.

2. *If I am in Christ, I will never be condemned for breaking the law or be rejected by God.* How could I be, since Jesus has fulfilled the law on my behalf and has borne the punishment due to me for breaking it? He has become my righteousness.

3. *To be "in him" I must believe on him.* For the verse also tells me, "Christ is the end of the law . . . for everyone *who believes.*" For everyone? Yes, but for everyone who believes. The promise is universal and specific.

In one of his books, Harry Ironside tells of a young woman he led to the Lord on one occasion. She had received a Christian upbringing, but she had thrown her heritage to the wind and had lived a worldly life. Now she was

6. Barnhouse, *Epistle to the Romans,* part 59, p. 38.

dying of tuberculosis and had sent for Ironside. She had been given three weeks to live. "Do you think there is any hope for a sinner like me?" she asked when she saw Ironside.

Ironside led her through the gospel, coming at last to John 3:16: "For God so loved the world that he gave his one and only Son, that whoever believes in him shall not perish but have eternal life."

"Are you included in that 'whoever'?" he asked the woman.

By this point she was ready to commit herself to Christ and did so, and Ironside assured her that if she was truly in Christ there was no condemnation for her, even though she had lived a sinful life and was coming to Jesus at what was apparently the very end of it. John 3:18 said: "Whoever believes in him is not condemned, but whoever does not believe stands condemned already. . . ."

A month or so later, after Ironside had finished his meetings in that area and had gone elsewhere, he was told of her passing. Her minister had been with her. "Can you hear me?" he had asked.

"Yes," she said.

"Do you believe on the Lord Jesus Christ?" he continued.

"Yes."

"What does he say about you?"

"Not condemned," she replied. And then, uttering her last words, "If you see Mr. Ironside, tell him it's all right."[7]

It is all right, and will be. "For Christ is the end of the law so that there may be righteousness for everyone who believes."

---

7. H. A. Ironside, *Illustrations of Bible Truth* (Chicago: Moody Press, 1945), pp. 56–59.

142

How Faith Speaks

Romans 10:5–9

Moses describes in this way the righteousness that is by the law: "The man who does these things will live by them." But the righteousness that is by faith says: "Do not say in your heart, 'Who will ascend into heaven?'" (that is, to bring Christ down) "or 'Who will descend into the deep?'" (that is, to bring Christ up from the dead). But what does it say? "The word is near you; it is in your mouth and in your heart," that is, the word of faith we are proclaiming: That if you confess with your mouth, "Jesus is Lord," and believe in your heart that God raised him from the dead, you will be saved.

We live in such a mindlessly pluralistic society that it is considered uncouth, if not wickedly immoral, to suggest that some religions may be better than others or, even worse, that some religions may be wrong. But some *are* wrong. In fact, all are wrong that do not call us out of our own inadequate self-righteousness to faith in Jesus Christ.

That is what Paul is saying in the extremely important paragraph to which our study of Romans has now brought us (Rom. 10:5–13). This paragraph is part of a longer section beginning with Romans 9:30 and running to the end of Romans 10, a section in which Paul is explaining that the unbelief of his countrymen is not God's fault but theirs, since the gospel had been communicated to them. The paragraph develops that analysis by contrasting what

1173

Paul calls "a righteousness that is by law" with "a righteousness that is by faith." But the verses we are studying (vv. 5–9) do more than this. They also describe three kinds of religion, pointing us away from the two wrong kinds of religion to the true religion that confesses Jesus Christ as Lord.

These three religions are: (1) the religion of works, (2) the religion of signs, and (3) the religion of faith. Paul develops them by telling us: (1) how legalism speaks, (2) how faith does not speak, and (3) how faith does speak.

How Legalism Speaks

The first religion is the religion of works. We already know a great deal about it because it is what Paul has been chiefly refuting all along. What is different about his treatment of the religion of works in this section is his confirming quotation from the law of Moses.

The quotation is from Leviticus 18:5, in which God is speaking to the Israelites through Moses, saying, "Keep my decrees and laws, for the man who obeys them will live by them. I am the LORD." This verse seems to have meant a great deal to Paul, for in addition to our text he also uses it in the letter to the Galatians. In Romans he says, "Moses describes in this way the righteousness that is by the law: 'The man who does these things will live by them.'" The Galatians passage reads, "The law is not based on faith; on the contrary, 'The man who does these things will live by them'" (Gal. 3:12). In both passages he contrasts the way of works with the way of faith and shows that they are mutually exclusive.

This point is all that is necessary for his argument. We need to keep that in mind, because without it we will get mixed up in our comparison of Moses' words with Paul's use of them.

In Leviticus, Moses seems to be telling the people that they need to keep the law and that, if they keep it, they will enjoy abundant life. That is true, of course. On the simplest level it is true that any person will be blessed to the extent that he or she lives according to the revealed law of God. That is only a way of saying that people who love God, keep the Sabbath, honor their parents, tell the truth, are faithful in their marriages, and do not steal or covet things that are not theirs will be happy. People who dishonor God, break faith, cheat, lie, and live for material possessions are miserable.

In addition, the text can be taken as saying that if the Jews would keep God's law to the extent that people can keep God's law, God would prosper the nation. This is also true. God will do the same at any time with any nation, ours included. He said, "If my people, who are called by my name, will humble themselves and pray and seek my face and turn from their wicked ways, then will I hear from heaven and will forgive their sin and will heal their land" (2 Chron. 7:14).

But Paul is not drawing these points from the quotation, and some who have noticed the difference have supposed that he is misusing it. That is not the case. Paul would readily acknowledge what I just said, namely, that morality is better than immorality and brings blessing. But he would add two important truths:

First, in religion we are talking about more than mere morality. We are talking about how a person can become right with God. If we approach the text at that level, allowing the word *live* to speak not merely of a happy life here but of eternal life, then we need to acknowledge that no one is able to keep the law of God well enough to reap this great benefit. It is true that anyone who is able to keep the law perfectly will be rewarded by God with eternal life. But nobody does keep the law perfectly. Therefore, salvation is beyond the grasp of those who are merely law-keepers. Right standing before God must be sought in a different way entirely, and that is by faith in Jesus Christ as the Savior.

Second, Paul would add that the way of works and the way of faith cannot be mixed, which in my judgment is how he uses the text from Leviticus here. The way of works is the way of law, he says. If you think you are going to be saved by law, it is by keeping the law that you must try to be saved. But you cannot make up for your deficiencies by adding faith to it, just as it is also impossible to begin by faith and then add law.

The Galatians had been trying to add works to faith, which is why Paul cites the same Leviticus passage in his letter to them. He tells them that if they tried to add works to faith as a way of salvation, Christ and his work would be of no value to them (Gal. 5:2).

No one can be saved by a religion of works, however hard he or she tries. Many are trying. Most of the world's religions are works religions. But the Bible says that if you would be saved, you must give up any thought of contributing to your salvation by what you do and instead trust Jesus Christ and his work completely. As one commentator says, Christ "charged himself with the *doing*." He has left us "only the *believing*."[1]

How Faith Does Not Speak

The second religion Paul writes about in these verses is the religion of signs and wonders, which he introduces as a way the religion of faith does *not* speak. The text reads, "But the righteousness that is by faith says: 'Do not say in your heart, "Who will ascend into heaven?"'" (that is, to bring Christ down) 'or "Who will descend into the deep?"'" (that is, to bring Christ up from the dead)" (vv. 6–7).

These verses introduce a second reference to the Old Testament. But they are not an exact quotation, which Paul seems to acknowledge by the way he brings the words in. In the earlier reference (to Leviticus) he said, "Moses describes in this way. . . ." That means "Moses wrote" or even "God, through the hand of Moses, says." In this case, because he is handling the words loosely,

---

1. F. Godet, *Commentary on St. Paul's Epistle to the Romans*, trans. A. Cusin (Edinburgh: T. & T. Clark, 1892), vol. 2, p. 206.

Paul writes instead, "The righteousness that is by faith says. . . ." This looser reference is to Deuteronomy 30:12–14.

In that passage Moses is speaking to the people, assuring them that God will bless the nation if they obey his commands and decrees:

> Now what I am commanding you today is not too difficult for you or beyond your reach. It is not up in heaven, so that you have to ask, "Who will ascend into heaven to get it and proclaim it to us so we may obey it?" Nor is it beyond the sea, so that you have to ask, "Who will cross the sea to get it and proclaim it to us so we may obey it?" No, the word is very near you; it is in your mouth and in your heart so you may obey it.

The point is that Israel had the law and that the law was all they needed. They were not to seek out an additional revelation but rather were to occupy themselves with obeying what they had already been given.

This is the passage Paul refers to, but he throws in an additional twist, explaining Moses' reference to ascending into heaven by adding "that is, to bring Christ down" and his reference to going beyond the sea (or descending into the abyss) by adding "that is, to bring Christ up from the dead." To most people those explanations do not do much to explain anything, not even Deuteronomy, and they even introduce confusion as to what Paul himself is saying.

What is Paul saying? What do those strange explanations mean?

In my opinion, this is not a case in which one explanation rather than others should be chosen, but rather a situation in which there are several overlapping or unfolding meanings. That is, a basic meaning is seen to contain additional meanings, and all are important. Each has bearing on what Paul wants to say in this passage.

Meaning number 1: *Israel did not need an additional word from God.* This is the literal meaning of the words in Deuteronomy, and although Paul adds specifically Christian interpretations to them, this meaning alone is true both for Israel and for the Christian community. As far as Israel is concerned, the people did not need an additional word from God, because, as Paul teaches elsewhere, the law itself contained announcements of the gospel. This was the point of Romans 4, where Paul showed that the doctrine of justification by faith was known to Abraham and David and was taught to Israel through their stories, as well as in other places.

As far as Christians are concerned, the same meaning holds. For neither do Christians need an additional word from God. They have what they need already, and it is the gospel message being proclaimed by the apostles: "That if you confess with your mouth, 'Jesus is Lord,' and believe in your heart that God raised him from the dead, you will be saved" (Rom. 10:9).

Meaning number 2: *Israel did not need to do something in order to bring the Messiah to them.* This is the unique sense of what Moses said to the people. For we notice that he did not speak merely of waiting for a new word from heaven or from beyond the sea but rather of "ascending" into heaven or "crossing" the sea to get it.

In his short but valuable book on Romans 9–11, the Danish Professor of New Testament Johannes Munck argues from rabbinical texts that "the Jews held that it would require an effort to bring the Messiah down from heaven. Israel must repent before the Messianic era can begin."[2] It is hard to say with certainty that this is exactly what Paul is thinking of, but the idea of doing something certainly fits this context. The Jews wanted to do something to earn their salvation. Yet even before the Messiah came they were not expected to do anything, only to believe God's word and look forward to him in faith, as Abraham, David, and the other Old Testament believers had done. Now it is even more apparent that this is the case. The Messiah has come. So there is no need to ascend into heaven to bring him down. He died for sin and has been resurrected. So there is no need to descend into the world of the dead to bring him back. All that is needed is to believe on the Lord Jesus Christ and the gospel.

Meaning number 3: *Neither Israel nor Christians today are to look for miracles.* It is because of this meaning that I have spoken of "the religion of signs." It is part of this passage because, as nearly all commentators recognize, the expressions about ascending into heaven to bring Christ down and descending into the abyss to bring Christ up are proverbial expressions for what is clearly impossible.[3] If someone could produce Christ or his power on demand, bringing him down from above or up from below, that person would be a miracle worker. But we are not to look for that, any more than we are to look for an additional revelation.

This matter is so important that I will return to it in the next study of what I call "The False Religion of Signs and Wonders." I am going to look at its contemporary manifestations.

Here I want to notice the evidence for this same false religion in Israel. Moses had been used by God to do miracles, just as Jesus had done miracles in his lifetime. But at the end of Deuteronomy, which is where these words come from, Moses is about to be taken away from the people, and they were understandably filled with anxiety about this. "Who is going to lead us when Moses, the miracle worker, is gone?" they would have been asking. What Moses tells them is that they do not need another miracle worker, since they have the law of God (which contains the gospel). What they need is very near them; in fact, it is already in their mouths and hearts (Deut. 30:14).

They were not satisfied with this, of course. They wanted miracles, and by the time of Jesus Christ they were actually demanding them. "Teacher, we

---

2. Johannes Munck, *Christ and Israel: An Interpretation of Romans 9–11,* trans. Krister Stendahl (Philadelphia: Fortress Press, 1967), p. 87.

3. Leon Morris notes that they are used this way in the Talmud. See Leon Morris, *The Epistle to the Romans* (Grand Rapids: Wm. B. Eerdmans, and Leicester, England: Inter-Varsity Press, 1988), p. 383, footnote 31.

want to see a miraculous sign from you," the unbelieving Pharisees and hostile teachers of the law brazenly demanded of Jesus (Matt. 12:38).

He replied,

> A wicked and adulterous generation asks for a miraculous sign! But none will be given it except the sign of the prophet Jonah. For as Jonah was three days and three nights in the belly of a huge fish, so the Son of Man will be three days and three nights in the heart of the earth. The men of Nineveh will stand up at the judgment with this generation and condemn it; for they repented at the preaching of Jonah, and now one greater than Jonah is here. The Queen of the South will rise at the judgment with this generation and condemn it; for she came from the ends of the earth to listen to Solomon's wisdom, and now one greater than Solomon is here.
>
> Matthew 12:39–42

Jonah did no miracles in Nineveh, yet Nineveh repented. Solomon did no miracles in Israel, yet the Queen of the South came to hear him speak. So the Jews' demand that Jesus give them a sign was actually an evasion, since their real problem was that they did not like what he was teaching. However, just as the "preaching" of Jonah reached the people of Nineveh and the "wisdom" of Solomon reached the Queen of the South, so the word of the gospel is the means by which God saves sinners today.

Do miracles occur today? There are differences of opinion on this question. I believe they do at times, for God is not bound by anything, and he is obviously as able to do miraculous things today as he ever was. But we are not to seek miracles as part of the gospel presentation. For a religion of signs and wonders is as false a gospel as the religion of works. Both are attempts to do something that God has declared outside true Christian proclamation, and signs, as well as works, detract fatally from the message of Christ's atonement.

Faith's Confession

That brings us to the third of these religious systems, the one Paul has been urging all along. We have seen how faith does not speak. It does not call for signs. How, then, does faith speak? Paul gives the confession of true faith in verses 8 and 9: "But what does [faith] say? 'The word is near you; it is in your mouth and in your heart,' that is, the word of faith we are proclaiming: That if you confess with your mouth, 'Jesus is Lord,' and believe in your heart that God raised him from the dead, you will be saved."

I have said that in the next study we are going to go back and look at verses 6 and 7 for what they have to say about "The False Religion of Signs and Wonders." In the study after that we will come back to verses 8 and 9, studying them for the proper content of genuine "Christian preaching."

But we are studying three kinds of religion in this chapter: the religion of works, the religion of signs, and the religion of faith, and it is important even here to see the essence of this third, true religion.

First, it is a religion based on Jesus and his work alone. When we were looking at verse 4, one of the applications of that study was that "Christ is everything." He is "the end of the law so that there may be righteousness for everyone who believes." It is the same here. For the message that is near us, in our mouths and hearts, is Jesus, and the confession of faith through which we are saved is that "Jesus is Lord" and that God raised him from the dead. Those are not simplistic items, as we will see. They involve a great amount of biblical theology. But they are all about the Savior. That is my point. Christianity *is* Jesus Christ. So anything that detracts from him or his work is a false religion.

Second, faith is essential. We are not saved by works or miracles, but this does not mean that salvation is somehow extraneous to us in the sense that it happens mechanically. On the contrary, it is as intimate and life-transforming as anything could possibly be. It finds us as dead men and women, under the curse of God, and it changes us into spiritually regenerated people who now live under God's protecting love and blessing.

How does that happen? It happens through faith, which is what Paul has been saying all along.

Notice what happens to the language of the passage in verse 9. In verse 5 Paul has been quoting Moses. He tells us what Moses said. Verses 6 through 8 have been quoting "the righteousness that is by faith." They tell us how faith speaks. But what happens in verse 9? For the first time in many verses, the language shifts from the third person to the second person, emphasizing the word *you*. "That if *you* confess with *your* mouth, 'Jesus is Lord,' and believe in *your* heart that God raised him from the dead, *you* will be saved."

Isn't that striking? It is the clearest means Paul could possibly have chosen to use in the context of explaining the nature of true religion and the essence of the true gospel: "*You* must believe it." It is not of works, and it is not in response to miracles. But it is of faith! Therefore, it is only those who believe on the Son of God who are saved.

This kind of religion is not calculated to stroke the fallen, Adamic ego, and it is not "spectacular" in a worldly sense. It will not win the attention of the world as would jumping unharmed from the pinnacle of the temple or casting out demons or predicting the future or healing the sick or turning hurricanes aside. But it is God's true religion. And what is most important, it is the teaching God honors in accomplishing the most important miracle of all, namely, the regeneration of a dead soul, so that one who was formerly bound for hell is thereafter bound for heaven.

Are other things important? Some are, though to different degrees.

Not long ago I was speaking to a group of seminary students, and I was able to point out how a decade or two ago the preaching of biblical theology was pushed aside by psychology and how in our day the preaching of biblical theology is being pushed aside by sociology. Psychology has a place, I said. So does sociology. But what is most important—the one thing we absolutely cannot do without—is an exposition of the Bible that lifts up Jesus Christ as Savior and Lord and calls upon all persons everywhere to turn from their sin and trust this risen Lord for their salvation.

Why? "For it is with your heart that you believe and are justified, and it is with your mouth that you confess and are saved. As the Scripture says, 'Anyone who trusts in him will never be put to shame'" (Rom. 10:10–11).

Have you believed on Christ and confessed him before other people, as he commands you to do? Have you called on his name?

Remember, works will not save you. You cannot keep the law even if you want to, and deep in your heart you do not even want to keep it. And God is not going to give you miracles to titillate your religious appetite. Christ has already descended from heaven. He has already told us who God is and what he requires of us. Jesus has given his life for his people. He has already been raised from the dead. Therefore, the gospel is not far off. It is right here. It is in our mouths and in our hearts. All that remains is for you to embrace it personally and so pass from a false religion to the true one and thus from death to life.

143

The False Religion of Signs and Wonders

Romans 10:6–7

But the righteousness that is by faith says: "Do not say in your heart, 'Who will ascend into heaven?'" (that is, to bring Christ down) "or 'Who will descend into the deep?'" (that is, to bring Christ up from the dead).

We are studying an important paragraph in Romans in which the apostle Paul: (1) compares three types of religion, (2) describes true religion as faith in "Jesus as Lord" and (3) explains how this true religion of faith is to be communicated. In other words, he is talking about the content of the gospel and how to do evangelism.

In our last study we looked at this paragraph in a general way in order to get an overview of the whole. But now, as I indicated then, we need to return to specific parts of it and examine each in detail. In this study we return to the religion of signs and wonders, as suggested by Paul's use of Deuteronomy 30:12–14, which he quotes with his own explanatory additions: "The righteousness that is by faith says: 'Do not say in your heart, "Who will ascend into heaven?"' (that is, to bring Christ down) 'or "Who will descend into the

1181

deep?'" (that is, to bring Christ up from the dead). [It says,] 'The word is near you; it is in your mouth and in your heart. . . .'" (vv. 6–8).

If a person could ascend into heaven to bring Christ and his power down or into the deep to bring him up, that person would be a miracle worker. So Paul is saying, among other things, that miracles are not the way to do evangelism.

The Vineyard Movement

The reason I need to return to this mistaken notion is twofold. First, because people have a fascination with "signs and wonders," it is easy for anyone to get off the right track in this area. Second, there is a powerful movement within so-called evangelical Christianity that embraces and actively promotes this approach. It is called the Vineyard Movement, and it is associated with the name of John Wimber, founder and pastor of the Vineyard Christian Fellowship in Pasadena, California, a church that started in his home in 1977 but has expanded today to more than two hundred congregations scattered throughout the English-speaking world.

For a short time John Wimber taught as an adjunct professor at the School of World Missions at Fuller Theological Seminary, which he refers to often to establish credibility. The course was called MC:510, "The Miraculous and Church Growth." From the material of this course Wimber produced a book, actually written by a man named Kevin Springer, titled *Power Evangelism*. This has been followed by another, titled *Power Healing*.[1]

These books contain endorsements by such evangelical leaders as C. Peter Wagner of the Fuller Seminary School of World Missions, Michael Green of Regent College, and the popular evangelical authors Richard J. Foster and John White. So John Wimber's views are not to be taken lightly.

What, then, does Wimber teach? He has several points of emphasis.

1. *Spiritual warfare.* The starting point of John Wimber's theology is that Christians are involved in a spiritual battle against the devil and demonic forces. This is because the kingdom of God has come into the world as a result of Jesus' coming but is opposed by Satan's kingdom. Christians are Jesus' soldiers in this conflict, and they have been given authority to oppose Satan and cast him out. Wimber calls clashes between the kingdom of God, represented by Christians, and the kingdom of Satan "power encounters." They are tests of strength. Who is stronger? Who will win?

2. *Power evangelism.* It follows from this premise, according to Wimber, that the way to do evangelism is by miraculous demonstrations of the superior power of God, which he calls "signs and wonders." These involve such things

1. John Wimber with Kevin Springer, *Power Evangelism* (San Francisco: Harper & Row, 1986), and *Power Healing* (San Francisco: Harper & Row, 1987).

as casting out demons, healing the sick, and receiving and acting upon special personal revelations from God about what another individual has done or is thinking, facts otherwise unknown to the evangelist. Wimber calls these revelations "words of knowledge."

It is important to realize that Wimber distinguishes at this point between what he is recommending and what he calls "programmatic evangelism." Programmatic evangelism is traditional evangelism. It is "message-oriented" and appeals to "rational arguments." It "attempts to reach the minds and hearts of people without the aid of charismatic gifts." It is evangelism, but because its goal is "decisions for Christ" instead of making disciples, the people reached by it "do not move on to a mature faith. . . . There is something inadequate about their conversion experience."[2]

By contrast, "power evangelism" is dependent upon the moment-by-moment leading of the Holy Spirit and by his revelation of what is going on in other persons' lives. "In power evangelism key obstacles—an adulterous affair, bitterness, a physical ailment, demon possession—are exposed and overcome, striking deeply into the hearts of people. This frees new believers from major obstacles so that they may experience future spiritual growth. Further, power encounters authenticate conversion experiences in a way that mere intellectual assents do not. This gives new Christians confidence about their conversions, a solid foundation for the rest of their lives."[3]

In short, the best and most effective evangelism, strong and rapid growth in the Christian life, and lasting assurance of salvation are attained only by miracles.

This is a long way from what Christians used to believe when they sang, "My hope is built on nothing less / Than Jesus' blood and righteousness" or "How firm a foundation, ye saints of the Lord, / Is laid for your faith in his excellent word!" It is a long way from Romans 10.

John Wimber: An Evaluation

I think this movement is mistaken and dangerous, as anyone can tell from what I have said so far. But before pressing my critique, I want to acknowledge that there are nevertheless points in Wimber's teaching with which all true Christians should agree.

First, we can agree that spiritual warfare is a reality, and a serious matter at that. We cannot forget that Ephesians 6 (and comparable passages) are in the Bible, nor that we are often warned against Satan. However, we will also remember that Ephesians 6 does not promote miracle working as the way to do battle against Satan, but instead admonishes us to be clothed with

2. Wimber with Springer, *Power Evangelism,* pp. 45, 46.
3. Ibid., p. 48.

the armor of Christian character and armed with the "sword of the Spirit, which is the word of God" (v. 17).

Second, we can acknowledge that much traditional Christianity *is* weak, including its evangelism. It often *is* a religion of the intellect only, not a religion of the heart. It *is* frequently formal and even dull. In large sections of the church, very little evangelism takes place.

Third, we can be open to the claim that God can (and does) do miracles. In the last study I acknowledged that there is a difference of opinion on this point. The best and best-known denial of the view that miracles are for today is B. B. Warfield's classic study of the alleged miraculous events in church history titled *Counterfeit Miracles*.[4] It is a devastating exposure of many bogus claims of miracles from the patristic age to the twentieth century. But although Warfield begins from the perspective that miracles were given by God to authenticate the office of the apostles and ceased with them and their immediate successors (those on whom they laid their hands and passed on their gift), this great Princeton theologian nevertheless believes, as do most Christians, that God answers prayer and sometimes heals and does other humanly inexplicable things in answer to it. "We believe in a wonder-working God; but not in a wonder-working church," says Warfield.[5]

Don't you agree with that?

I believe that a Christian can pray for the sick, even, in some cases, praying for the casting out of demons. But this does not mean that we have to believe in the vast majority of alleged miracles or be blinded to the deception of many who pretend to do them. Above all, it does not mean that we should alter Bible-taught ways of doing evangelism by mistakenly claiming special revelations or wrongly aspiring to do miracles.

"Signs and Wonders" in the Bible

The only reliable basis on which to evaluate the views of John Wimber, or anyone else for that matter, is the Bible's teaching, and in this case what we have to ask is: "What does the Bible itself say about 'signs and wonders'?" A "sign," of course, is an event that points to something greater than itself, and a "wonder" is an event that causes wonder or evokes amazement on the part of those who see it. Together, the terms refer to unusual events we might call "significant wonders."

In 1987 John Wimber paid a much-publicized visit to Australia, in response to which pastors in the Evangelical Fellowship in the Anglican Communion (the EFAC of Sydney) prepared a helpful study of Wimber's teaching, which they distributed to their parishes by way of pastoral guidance. The book was titled *Signs & Wonders and Evangelicals: A Response to the Teaching of John Wimber,* and it was written by professors Paul Barnett, Robert Doyle, and John

---

4. Benjamin B. Warfield, *Counterfeit Miracles* (Edinburgh and Carlisle, Pa.: The Banner of Truth Trust, 1986). Original edition 1918.

5. Ibid., p. 58.

Woodhouse and by the Bishop of South Sydney, John Reid.[6] One chapter by John Woodhouse surveys the various ways "signs and wonders" are referred to in the Bible. He observes correctly that the phrase is used in four areas.

1. *Signs accompanying the historical redemptive acts of God.* This is the most common use of the term "signs and wonders," and it is localized at two points of the biblical revelation: the deliverance of the people of Israel from Egypt and the earthly ministry of Jesus Christ.

In the first category are such texts as Exodus 7:3–4 ("I will harden Pharaoh's heart, and though I multiply my miraculous signs and wonders in Egypt, he will not listen to you . . ."), Deuteronomy 26:8 ("The LORD brought us out of Egypt with a mighty hand and an outstretched arm, with great terror and with miraculous signs and wonders"), and Acts 7:36 ("He led them out of Egypt and did wonders and miraculous signs in Egypt, at the Red Sea and for forty years in the desert"). There are also texts saying that God will unleash the same judgment signs against Israel if the people depart from God and do not repent of their sin (cf. Deut. 28:45–46). In the second category are such texts as Acts 2:19, which quotes Joel 2:30 ("I will show wonders in the heaven above and signs on the earth below . . ."), and Acts 2:22 ("Jesus of Nazareth was a man accredited by God to you by miracles, wonders and signs, which God did among you through him . . .").

This comparison suggests that the signs accompanying the redemptive work of Jesus parallel the signs accompanying the redemption of Israel from Egypt. But here is the important thing: Neither the Old Testament signs nor the New Testament signs are put forward as examples of corresponding contemporary miracles but as redemptive events that it is the work of faith to remember.

John Woodhouse writes correctly, "Faith involves remembering the signs and wonders by which God redeemed his people. . . . Unbelief is precisely a failure to remember those wonders. . . . A consequence of this is the fact that a desire for further signs and wonders is sinful and unbelieving."[7]

This is exactly what Jesus said to the Pharisees. "A wicked and adulterous generation asks for a miraculous sign! But none will be given it except the sign of the prophet Jonah" (Matt. 12:39).

We might also note that signs do not in themselves create faith in the hearts of observers and can even harden hearts, as was the case with Pharaoh. In other words, even such spectacular signs as the plagues against Egypt and the miracles of Christ do not in themselves promote faith. Why? Woodhouse answers, "Because the power of God which saves sinners is *not seen* in any contemporary miracle, but only in the death of Christ on the cross."

6. Robert Doyle, ed.; John Woodhouse, Paul Barnett, and John Reid, *Signs & Wonders and Evangelicals: A Response to the Teaching of John Wimber* (Homebush West, Australia: Lancer Books, 1987).

7. Ibid., pp. 21–23.

That is why Paul told the Corinthians, "Jews demand miraculous signs and Greeks look for wisdom, but we preach Christ crucified: a stumbling block to Jews and foolishness to Gentiles, but to those whom God has called, both Jews and Greeks, Christ the power of God and the wisdom of God" (1 Cor. 1:22–24).

2. *Deceptive signs and wonders.* John Wimber does not talk about this second class of miracles, but it, too, is a prominent strain in the Bible. For example, in Deuteronomy the people are warned against prophets who do signs and wonders yet proclaim other gods. "You must not listen to the words of that prophet or dreamer. The LORD your God is testing you to find out whether you love him with all your heart and with all your soul" (Deut. 13:3). In the same way, Jesus warned against "false Christs and false prophets [who] will appear and perform great signs and miracles to deceive even the elect—if that were possible" (Matt. 24:24). In Revelation 13 we have a culmination of these utterly deceptive miracles in "the beast" who serves Satan and Antichrist.

I am not suggesting, by reviewing this evidence, that John Wimber and his followers do miracles by the power of Satan. I am far more inclined to think that they are not real miracles but only self-induced "mind cures." But that is not my point. My point is that miracles alone prove nothing. They may be false and deceptive as well as true and instructive, and we are never told that they are God's means for converting unbelievers.

3. *"Signs" done by God's prophets.* There are a few scattered "signs" done by God's prophets, but these are not usually what we would call miracles. They are usually only symbolic or significant things or actions (cf. Isa. 8:18; 20:3; Ezek. 12:1–11; 24:15–27).

4. *The signs of the apostles.* The final category of biblical signs are those miracles done by the apostles, the effect of which was to authenticate their unique office and ministry. They are referred to in such texts as Acts 2:43 ("Everyone was filled with awe, and many wonders and miraculous signs were done by the apostles"), Acts 5:12 ("The apostles performed many miraculous signs and wonders among the people . . ."), and 2 Corinthians 12:12 ("The things that mark an apostle—signs, wonders and miracles—were done among you with great perseverance").

These, of course, are the miracles that mean so much to the Vineyard congregations. But in their rush to take them over into the present time and perpetuate them, the pastors of the movement make a fundamental error of interpretation. One great principle of hermeneutics (the science of Bible interpretation) is that narrative events are to be interpreted by didactic or teaching events, rather than the other way around. In other words, that something has happened once or even more than once does not mean that it is to be taken as normative for us. What is normative is to be determined by the New Testament's explicit teaching, and, as we have seen, the New Testament does not teach that evangelism is to be done by cultivating miracles.

The bottom line of this investigation is that "signs and wonders" are not to be sought for today and that it is a mistake to understand such phenomena, whether truly miraculous or not, as biblical "signs."

Weakness Rather Than Power

I come now to the last of the arguments I want to develop in this study, which is that the "signs and wonders" movement is not only wrong, according to the Bible's teaching, which any movement that departs from strict biblical teaching must necessarily be, but also that it is harmful. There can be errors that are not harmful—we probably make them all the time—but this is not one of them.

How is it harmful?

First, it cheapens the miraculous. Let me explain by speaking of my own convictions. I believe in miracles. I cannot say that I have ever seen anything I would accurately call a miracle, but I do believe in them. I do not stand with those who say that God does not (still less, cannot) work in miraculous ways today. I believe that God answers prayer in healing the sick. I believe that there are such things as demon possession and exorcisms, particularly in extremely pagan areas of the world, like those targeted by pioneer missionaries.

But if I believed that casting out demons (with healings) was the way to do evangelism, which I do not, what would I do? Well, either I would go around looking for a lot of demons to cast out, or I would begin to interpret demonism as including a lot of other things that I have already encountered.

It is this second approach that describes what Wimber does. It is true that he writes about what seems to be genuine demon possession—people who are taken over by other personalities, speak in other voices, fall down and thrash about, and spew out obscenities and hatred, particularly against Jesus Christ.[8] But these accounts quickly slide over into descriptions of demonization and exorcism of a very different order, descriptions involving demons of bondage, temptation, fear, pain, and even physical ailments like itching.[9] In fact, Wimber explains how he prefers the word "demonized" rather than "demon possession" for the purpose of including these phenomena.[10]

In my opinion, this trivializes Satan and cheapens exorcism. It cheapens what is truly miraculous.

Second, the "signs and wonders" movement cheapens the gospel. It cheapens it by reducing the gospel to shrinking people's goiters, straightening backs, lengthening legs, and other such things, all of which are described in *Power Healing*. In fact, one of the striking things about Wimber's books, espe-

8. Wimber with Springer, *Power Healing*, pp. 97, 98, 113, 114.
9. Ibid., pp. 106–109, 182, 232.
10. Ibid., p. 109.

cially *Power Evangelism,* is that the message of the gospel is virtually unmentioned. There is much about miracles, but we are never told what Jesus accomplished on the cross or by his resurrection.

Indeed, if we are to take Wimber's illustrative material literally, it would seem that it is possible to become converted without hearing the gospel at all. He writes at one point, "One day a group of our young people approached a stranger in a parking lot. Soon they were praying over him, and he fell to the ground. By the time he got up, *the stranger was converted.* He is now a member of our church (emphasis added)."[11]

Third, the "signs and wonders" movement cheapens suffering. Suffering has various causes, some arising within ourselves. But there is suffering that is given to Christians by God that is intended for their growth and God's glory. Such were the trials of Job, the suffering of the man who had been born blind, the thorn in the flesh endured by the apostle Paul, and the hurts, disappointments, and physical anguish endured by countless numbers of God's people today. The religion of signs reduces all these to unnecessary affliction and further burdens us with lacking faith if the demon of suffering cannot be quickly cast out. That is a cruel gospel to impose on God's people. It is, writes Woodhouse, "a version of Christianity in which the gospel is not sufficiently powerful to produce mature Christian faith, the Scriptures are not sufficiently revealing for the life of faithful obedience to God, the finished work of Christ is not sufficiently relevant for effective evangelism, and the hope of Christ's coming is not sufficiently comforting for those who are suffering."[12]

There is a better, *biblical* way to do evangelism. It is indicated in Revelation, where we are told that the saints overcame Satan "by the blood of the Lamb and by the word of their testimony" (Rev. 12:11).

---

11. Wimber with Springer, *Power Evangelism,* p. 26.
12. Doyle, *Signs & Wonders,* pp. 34, 35.

144

Christian Preaching

Romans 10:8–9

But what does it say? "The word is near you; it is in your mouth and in your heart,"
that is, the word of faith we are proclaiming: That if you confess with your mouth, "Jesus
is Lord," and believe in your heart that God raised him from the dead, you will be saved.

In Luke 16:19–31 there is a story that would have been a good addition to the previous study, but which I have held for this one, because it is both a summary of what I wrote about earlier as well as an introduction to the themes I want to develop now.

Jesus was speaking about a rich man, who ate well every day, and a poor beggar named Lazarus. Both men died. Lazarus was carried into the presence of Abraham in paradise, and the rich man went to hell. At first the rich man asked Abraham to send Lazarus to provide him with some comfort. But when that was declared to be impossible, he asked that Lazarus be sent back to earth to warn his five brothers of their impending judgment, since they were as wicked as himself: "I beg you, father, send Lazarus to my father's house, for I have five brothers. Let him warn them, so that they will not also come to this place of torment."

Abraham answered, "They have Moses and the Prophets; let them listen to them."

The rich man persisted, "No, father Abraham, but if someone from the dead goes to them, they will repent."

Abraham's final word and the climactic point of the parable was this: "If they do not listen to Moses and the Prophets, they will not be convinced even if someone rises from the dead" (v. 31).

This is exactly what Paul has been saying in Romans, of course. And it is exactly what Moses was saying before him in the verses from Deuteronomy 30 that Paul is quoting. The people did have "Moses and the Prophets." That is the word that, according to Moses, was "near" them, in their mouths and hearts (Deut. 30:14). That was sufficient for them. If they did not heed that written word and repent of their sin and turn to God in faith on the basis of that revelation, they would not be changed, even by a religion of miracles. No number of "signs and wonders," however great, would save them.

Today, says Paul, in exactly the same way, people have the Christian gospel, which is "the word of faith we are proclaiming: That if you confess with your mouth, 'Jesus is Lord,' and believe in your heart that God raised him from the dead, you will be saved." Because the gospel is here today and because it is being proclaimed, all possible excuses for failing to believe in Christ and be saved from the coming judgment are cut off.

This text leads us into the heart of the content of the gospel and thus of all true Christian proclamation.

The Text Itself

However, at first glance there seems to be a minor problem with the text: the order of the two main items seems to be wrong. The first matter mentioned is mouth confession, followed by heart belief. But, we might ask, isn't it the case that we first believe with our hearts and then, second, confess Jesus Christ as Lord?

This can be explained in a number of ways.

One explanation might be that Paul begins with what can be observed, that is, a person's public confession of Christ, then moves backward to the cause behind it, namely, his belief. Another explanation is that Paul deals first with the content of faith, as expressed by the mouth, then with the assent to it by the heart. However, in my judgment, the best explanation is that Paul is simply following the order found in the text from Deuteronomy, which he is quoting. Deuteronomy says, "The word is very near you; it is in your mouth and in your heart so you may obey it" (Deut. 30:14). Paul repeats that order accurately, adding specific Christian content for each part.

We cannot make too much of the order, of course, because the apostle turns it around again in verse 10, giving what we think of as the correct sequence: "For it is with your heart that you believe and are justified, and it is with your mouth that you confess and are saved."

Yet this leads to an important observation, namely, that Paul is not providing an ordered listing of steps to salvation or contrasting some items of belief that are internal with other items of belief that are external. Those kinds of distinctions are misleading at this point. Rather, taken together, the verses indicate that the items Paul is speaking of are actually all of one package. The confession that "Jesus is Lord" and the belief that God raised him from the dead are both parts of faith's content. That is, they are equally parts of the gospel. They are both truths that we are to believe and then, second, confess to other people.

In other words, preaching should contain both truths, and a Christian is to be defined as one who both believes them and confesses them openly.

"Jesus Is Lord"

The first truth is that "Jesus is Lord." What a tremendous statement! It is impossible to overestimate the significance of these three words (only two in Greek), for this was not only the first essential element of the gospel proclamation as well as of the first Christian confession. It was also a confession of their faith for which believers of the first Christian centuries were willing to die.

How can those three words be that important? The answer, as we know, is that they are literally crammed with meaning. They testify to: (1) the person of Christ, (2) the unique work of Christ, and (3) the ongoing all-embracing rule of Christ over his people and church.

1. *The person of Christ.* The first of these implications is due to the fact that in the Greek version of the Old Testament (the Septuagint), which was well known to the Jewish community of the first century and from which most of the New Testament writers quoted when citing Scripture, the word *kyrios* ("Lord") is used to translate the great Hebrew name for God: Yahweh, or Jehovah. It is used this way over 6,000 times. This is why most of our English Bibles do not use the name *Yahweh* but have the word LORD instead. The disciples of Christ knew that this word was repeatedly used to translate this great name for God. Yet, knowing this, they did not hesitate to transfer the title to Jesus, thereby indicating that in their view Jesus is Jehovah.

This is the meaning of *kyrios* in the great Christological passages of the New Testament. Here are some examples:

1 Corinthians 8:4–6. ". . . We know that an idol is nothing in all the world and that there is no God but one. For even if there are so-called gods, whether in heaven or on earth (as indeed there are many 'gods' and many 'lords'), yet for us there is but one God, the Father, from whom all things came and for whom we live; and there is but one Lord, Jesus Christ, through whom all things came and through whom we live."

Luke 2:11. "Today in the town of David a Savior has been born to you; he is Christ the Lord," that is, Jehovah.

Psalm 110:1. Applied to himself by Jesus in Matthew 22:41–46. "The Lord said to my Lord: 'Sit at my right hand until I put your enemies under your feet'" (v. 44). Peter had this text in mind when he told the Sanhedrin, "God exalted him [Jesus] to his own right hand as Prince and Savior . . ." (Acts 5:31).

Philippians 2:5–11. "Your attitude should be the same as that of Christ Jesus:

> Who, being in very nature God,
> > did not consider equality with God something to be grasped,
> but made himself nothing,
> > taking the very nature of a servant,
> > being made in human likeness.
> And being found in appearance as a man,
> > he humbled himself
> > and became obedient to death—even death on a cross!
> Therefore God exalted him to the highest place
> > and gave him the name that is above every name,
> that at the name of Jesus every knee should bow,
> > in heaven and on earth and under the earth,
> and every tongue confess that Jesus Christ is Lord,
> > to the glory of God the Father.[1]

As far as Romans itself goes, a study of "Lord" shows that Paul uses it forty-four times in this book. In thirty cases it is used of Jesus Christ. In eight cases it is used of God the Father. In the remaining cases it could refer either to the Father or to Jesus referred to as God. In other words, the term is used interchangeably for both Jesus and the Father and is a clear evidence of Paul's belief in Jesus' complete deity.

This first meaning of the title shows why the early Christians would not apply the term "Lord" to any other. They understood that if they had done so, they would have repudiated Christ.

2. *The work of Christ.* The second implication of the title "Lord" is that Jesus is the Savior. This is linked to his lordship, because, as John R. W. Stott writes, "The title 'Lord' is a symbol of Christ's victory over the forces of evil. If Jesus has been exalted over all the principalities and powers of evil, as indeed he has, this is the reason why he has been called Lord. If Jesus has been proclaimed Lord, as he has, it is because these powers are under his feet. He has conquered them on the cross, and therefore our salvation—that is to say, our rescue from sin, Satan, fear and death—is due to that victory."[2]

3. *The rule of Christ over his people and church.* The third important implication of the words "Jesus is Lord" is that Jesus rules over his people and church,

---

1. For a more complete discussion of these texts and their implications see "Jesus Christ Our Lord (Romans 1:4)" in volume 1 of this series (chap. 4). James Montgomery Boice, *Romans: Justification by Faith* (Grand Rapids: Baker Book House, 1991), pp. 45–52.

2. John R. W. Stott, "The Sovereignty of God the Son" in *Our Sovereign God: Addresses Presented to the Philadelphia Conference on Reformed Theology 1974–1976,* ed. James M. Boice (Grand Rapids: Baker Book House, 1977), p. 18.

which he must do if he truly is "the Lord." Does he? That is a personal question. In what areas does Jesus exercise this rule? That is a practical one. In the excellent study of Christ's lordship by John Stott from which I quoted earlier, six areas of Jesus' rule are suggested.

Our minds. If Jesus is our Lord, then one thing he must be Lord of is our thinking. He must be Lord of our minds. On one occasion, when the Lord called disciples, he said, "Take my yoke upon you and learn from me . . ." (Matt. 11:29), meaning that he was to be the disciples' teacher. He is to be our teacher today through the Scriptures, which he caused to be inspired. That is why we must be men and women of the Book, students of the Word, if we really are Christ's followers.

Our ethics. In the study I referred to earlier, Stott points out that Jesus is not just Lord of our minds. He is Lord of our wills and of our moral standards also. "It is not only what we believe that is to come under the lordship of Jesus but also how we behave. Discipleship implies obedience, and obedience implies that there are absolute moral commands that we are required to obey. To refer to Jesus politely as 'our Lord' is not enough. He still says to us, 'Why do you call me Lord and do not the things that I say?'"[3]

Our careers. If Jesus is Lord, then he is not only Lord of our minds, wills, and morals. He is Lord of our time, and this means that he is Lord of our professions, jobs, careers, and ambitions. We cannot plan our lives as if our relationship to Jesus is somehow detached from those plans and irrelevant to them. Like Paul on the road to Damascus, one of our very first questions to Jesus must be, "What shall I do, Lord?" (Acts 22:10).

Our churches. Jesus is also head of the church. This truth delivers us from two banes. One is disorder. It occurs when those who are members of the church pursue their own courses—including what they wish their church to be—without regard to the guidelines for church life laid down in the Bible or without proper consideration for those who are their brothers and sisters in the Lord. The second is clericalism. It occurs when laypeople abandon their God-given responsibilities in the church or when pastors tyrannize the church without acknowledging that they are servants of the people as well as servants of Christ and that they are called to serve the church as Jesus served it.

Our relation to the world. Jesus is not only our own personal Lord and not only Lord of the church, which he founded. He is also Lord of all life, the life of nations included. That is, he is the "King of kings and Lord of lords" (Rev. 19:16). We who are Christians stand as his representatives in the midst of history and cultures to call this world to account. We are here to remind the world that this same Jesus Christ whom we serve has spoken from heaven to reveal what true righteousness is, both for individuals and nations, and that those who disregard him do so at their peril. They will have to give an accounting before him at the final judgment.

3. Ibid., p. 22.

Missions. A final implication flows from the Great Commission by which, on the basis of his own authority, the Lord sent disciples into the world to make disciples everywhere (Matt. 28:18–20). The lordship of Jesus is the most powerful of missionary incentives. It is as Lord of our lives that Jesus tells us to go into the world, and because we acknowledge him as Lord, this is exactly what we do. The Duke of Wellington called the Great Commission Christ's "marching orders" for the church. Because we love him we want everyone to become his disciples.[4]

As soon as we explore these implications of the confession "Jesus is Lord" we see why it was so important to the early Christians and why so many were willing to die rather than renounce it.

A Risen and Living Savior

The second proposition in the summary of the gospel and the confession of faith provided by our text is that "God raised him [that is, Jesus] from the dead." This statement has two great implications.

1. *The resurrection is proof of Christ's claims.* The resurrection proves a great many things. It proves: that there is a God and that the God of the Bible is the true God; that Jesus was a teacher sent from God and that Jesus was inerrant in his teachings and spoke the very words of God; that Jesus is the Son of God; that there is a day of judgment coming; that every believer in Christ is justified from all sin; that all who are united to Christ by faith will live again; and that Christians can have victory over sin.[5]

But chiefly the resurrection proves that every believer in Christ is justified from sin, as Romans 4:25 flatly declares: "He [that is, Jesus] was delivered over to death for our sins and was raised to life for our justification." The resurrection is God's proof that the penalty for our transgressions has been fully paid by Jesus.

When Jesus was on earth, he said that he would die for the sins of others. The time for the crucifixion came, and he did die. But the question remained: Was his death fully adequate for others' sins? Did God accept his atonement? We know that if Jesus had sinned, however slightly, his death could not atone even for his own sin, let alone the sin of others. For three days the question remained unanswered. The body of Jesus lay in the cold Judean tomb. Then the long anticipated hour came. The breath of God swept through the sepulcher, and Jesus rose to appear to his followers and later to ascend to the right hand of the Father. By this means God declared to the entire universe, "I have accepted the atonement Jesus made."

---

4. I have developed these points more fully in the chapter from volume 1 of this series, referred to earlier ("Jesus Christ Our Lord [Romans 1:4]," chap. 4, pp. 45–52).

5. These points are from R. A. Torrey, *The Bible and Its Christ* (New York: Fleming H. Revell, 1904–1906), pp. 101–111.

Reuben A. Torrey writes:

> When Jesus died, he died as my representative, and I died in him; when he arose, he rose as my representative, and I arose in him. . . . I look at the cross of Christ, and I know that atonement has been made for my sins; I look at the open sepulcher and the risen and ascended Lord, and I know that the atonement has been accepted. There no longer remains a single sin on me, no matter how many or how great my sins may have been. My sins may have been as high as the mountains, but in the light of the resurrection the atonement that covers them is as high as heaven. My sins may have been as deep as the ocean, but in the light of the resurrection the atonement that swallows them up is as deep as eternity.[6]

D. Martyn Lloyd-Jones says, "The resurrection is the proclamation of the fact that God is fully and completely satisfied with the work that his Son did upon the Cross."[7]

2. *The resurrection shows we do not serve a dead but rather a living Savior.* Leon Morris writes, "It is at the cross that God did his saving work, but Paul does not believe in a dead martyr but in a living Savior. Not only did Jesus die for our sins but God raised him, triumphant over all the forces of evil. If Christ is not raised, Paul holds, our faith is futile and we are yet in our sins (1 Cor. 15:17)."[8] Jesus was raised and now lives to lead, bless, strengthen, and eventually reward those who love and serve him.

"My King Who Saved Me"

The very last part of Paul's summary of the Christian proclamation is that if we believe these things and confess Jesus as Lord before other people, we will "be saved." That is, we will be saved from the wrath of God about which so much of the Book of Romans has been speaking. That is why the word *saved* is in the future tense. We have been saved. We are being saved. But in this verse Paul teaches that we will also *be saved* from wrath if our faith is truly in Jesus as our Lord and Savior.

What is more, we will stand firm in that confession to the very end, if we are genuinely converted. This is what the aged Bishop of Smyrna, Polycarp, did. He stood firm in his confession even when his life was on the line. He was martyred on February 22, A.D. 156. As Polycarp was being driven to the arena two of the city officials, who had respect for him because of his age and reputation, tried to persuade him to comply with the demand to honor

6. Ibid., pp. 107, 108.
7. D. M. Lloyd-Jones, *Romans: An Exposition of Chapters 3:20–4:25, Atonement and Justification* (Grand Rapids: Zondervan, 1970), p. 244.
8. Leon Morris, *The Epistle to the Romans* (Grand Rapids: Wm. B. Eerdmans, and Leicester, England: Inter-Varsity Press, 1988), p. 386.

Caesar. "What harm is there in saying, 'Caesar is Lord,' and burning incense
. . . and saving yourself?" they asked.

Polycarp refused.

Later, in the arena, he explained his position, saying, "For eighty-six years
I have been [Christ's] slave, and he has done me no wrong; how can I blas-
pheme my king who saved me?" Polycarp refused to call Caesar "Lord,"
because "Lord" meant "God" and there can only be one God. If Polycarp
had called Caesar "Lord," then Jesus could not have been "Lord" for Polycarp,
and Polycarp could not have been a Christian.

Those who recorded Polycarp's story shared his convictions, for they concluded by saying: "He [Polycarp] was arrested by Herod, when Philip of
Tralles was high priest, and Statius Quadratus was governor, *but our Lord Jesus
Christ was reigning forever.* To him be glory, honor, majesty and eternal dominion from generation to generation. Amen."[9]

Polycarp had heard genuine Christian preaching, had believed the gospel
as it had been faithfully proclaimed, had lived for Jesus Christ for eighty-six
years, and he eventually accepted martyrdom rather than retract his confession. He is an example of how one becomes and remains a genuine Christian.

9. "The Martyrdom of Holy Polycarp, Bishop of Smyrna" in *The Apostolic Fathers: An American
Translation*, trans. Edgar J. Goodspeed (New York: Harper & Brothers, 1950), pp. 250, 251, 255.

145

Lordship Salvation

Romans 10:9

If you confess with your mouth, "Jesus is Lord," and believe in your heart that God raised him from the dead, you will be saved.

In the last study I tried to spell out the content of Christian preaching as it is summarized in Romans 10:9. In particular, I tried to show the full meaning of the words that were the first great Christian confession: "Jesus is Lord." I pointed out that those three words, simple as they seem, are actually overflowing with meaning, for they affirm: (1) that Jesus is fully divine, (2) that he is the Savior, and (3) that he rules over his people and church. I elaborated that last point by showing that if we are Christians, Jesus must be Lord of our minds, morals, careers, churches, relation to the secular world without, and missionary outreach.

But there is a segment of the evangelical church that disagrees with all that. It restricts the confession "Jesus is Lord" to the belief that Jesus is a divine Savior and explicitly eliminates any idea that Jesus must be Lord of our lives for us to be Christians.

Even more. It teaches that a person can be a Christian without being a follower of Jesus Christ. It reduces the gospel to the mere fact of Christ's having died for sinners, requires of sinners only that they acknowledge this by the barest intellectual assent, quite apart from any repentance or turning from sin, and then assures them of their eternal security when they may very well not be born again. This view bends faith beyond recognition and promises a false peace to thousands who have given verbal assent to this reductionist Christianity, but who are not in God's family.

Those who take this position call what I have explained as the gospel in the last study "Lordship salvation," and they dismiss it as heresy.

An Old Error in New Wineskins

Few theological positions, orthodox or not, are without precedent. And in this case, the view I am talking about is that of the eighteenth-century Scottish eccentric Robert Sandeman, who taught that everyone who is persuaded that Jesus actually died for sin as testified by the apostles is justified, regardless of any change in his or her life. The view is known by his name, Sandemanianism. However, this old error has appeared in new form in our day, largely through the influence of professors at Dallas Theological Seminary. I do not know anything to call it except "the Dallas doctrine."

The contemporary roots of this teaching lie in the works of Lewis Sperry Chafer, one of the founders of that seminary, who believed that Scripture speaks of two classes of Christians: those that are carnal and those that are spiritual. He wrote, "The 'carnal' Christian is . . . characterized by a 'walk' that is on the same plane as that of the 'natural man.'"[1]

The idea was a novel one when Chafer first expounded it, but it is well known and widely accepted today. It has even been added to and embellished. If a Christian can behave exactly like a natural or unsaved man, then what is it that makes him a Christian? The answer is "simple assent to the fact that Jesus died to be his or her Savior." Nothing else is necessary—in particular: no repentance, no discipleship, no change of behavior, not even any true perseverance in faith. In fact, to insist on any of these additional things is to propound a false gospel. Chafer did not say all this, of course, but since it is a logical extension of the idea of the carnal Christian, his followers eventually did.

One who has done so is Charles Caldwell Ryrie, editor of the popular Ryrie Study Bible.[2] The most extreme proponent of this view is professor Zane C. Hodges, who has defended it in three works titled *The Gospel Under Siege, Dead Faith: What Is It?*, and *Absolutely Free!*

What has made this a major issue today is that the Dallas view has been challenged by pastor John MacArthur in a book called *The Gospel According to Jesus*, to which J. I. Packer and myself provided forewords. It is an attempt by a reformed dispensationalist to turn his fellow dispensationalists from their error.

1. Lewis Sperry Chafer, *He That Is Spiritual*, rev. ed. (Grand Rapids: Zondervan, 1967), p. 21.
2. In a chapter titled "Must Christ Be Lord to Be Savior?" in Charles Caldwell Ryrie, *Balancing the Christian Life* (Chicago: Moody Press, 1969), pp. 169–181.

I want to show why the Dallas doctrine is mistaken at this important point, just as I tried to show the error of the "signs and wonders" approach to evangelism. But, as with the "signs and wonders" movement, I want to state what can be said in favor of this view first.

The chief thing is that Charles Ryrie and Zane Hodges, and those who think as they do, want to preserve the purity of the gospel. That is to their credit. In my opinion, they are actually destroying the true gospel by what they teach, but that is not their intention. They are sons of the Reformation in this respect at least: they believe in justification by faith apart from works and want to guard that gospel from anything that might contaminate its purity. The reason they oppose a demand for repentance, discipleship, or a walk that gives evidence of an inward spiritual change is that they regard this demand as adding works to faith, and that, as we all know, is a false gospel. They want none of it.

Again, they want to affirm the doctrine of eternal security, since that, too, is a Reformation distinctive. They argue that if salvation depends in any way on repenting of sin, commitment, following Jesus as Lord, or a behavioral change, then assurance is destroyed, because we all sin. In fact, one of the reasons the Dallas doctrine eliminates obedience from the essence of saving faith is to include as Christians professing believers whose lives are filled with sin. "If only committed people are saved people," writes Charles Ryrie, "then where is there room for carnal Christians?"[3]

Where indeed?

Clearly there is an error at this point. But seeing the error does not mean that we should miss the rightful concern these men have to uphold and teach the doctrines of grace and eternal security.

Must Jesus Be Lord to Be Savior?

One very lucid statement of the non-lordship position is by Charles Ryrie in the chapter from *Balancing the Christian Life* to which I have already alluded and from which I quoted. Ryrie asks the question: "Must Christ be Lord to be Savior?" He answers negatively for the following three reasons.

1. *There are many examples of Christians who have not surrendered to Jesus Christ as Lord.*

Ryrie cites Peter, who rebuked Jesus on one occasion ("Surely not, Lord!" Acts 10:14); Barnabas and Paul, who quarreled over taking John Mark with them on a second missionary journey (Acts 15:39); and the Ephesian Christians, who did not destroy their magic scrolls and charms until sometime after they had believed on Christ (Acts 19:19). In my opinion, the case of the Ephesians proves the exact opposite of what Ryrie thinks it does. It proves

3. Ibid., p. 170.

that when the Ephesians believed on Christ, the inevitable outcome was the destruction of all rivals to his lordship. But that is not the main point.

The main answer to Ryrie's argument is that he is equating commitment with perfection, which is obviously wrong. Christians sin, but that does not mean that they are not committed to Christ. If they lie down in their sin and do nothing about it, they are indeed uncommitted. They are not Christians. But if they are Christians, the way they show it is by getting up out of the sin—"repenting" is the right word for what they must do—and beginning to follow Christ again.

I have said elsewhere in these studies that there is all the difference in the world between falling down on the path and getting up and going on, and not being on the path at all. It is only those who are on the path who are Christians.

2. *"Jesus is Lord" only means "Jesus is God." Specifically, it does not mean "Jesus is my Master."*

In developing this point, Ryrie rightly states, as I did in the last chapter, that "Lord" means "God" in all the important Christological passages. I said that it is the word used to translate the great name for God, Jehovah, in the Greek Old Testament, so that its application to Jesus by the New Testament writers indicates their belief in Christ's full deity. But Ryrie goes on from that truth to argue wrongly that because "Lord" means "God" it cannot mean anything else. Amazingly, he fails to see that the reason the word *Lord,* which on the human level does mean "master," as he admits, is used of God is that God is the supreme Master over all other masters. It is a case similar to our use of the word *Sovereign* with a capital *S.* There are many sovereigns, but God can be called *the* Sovereign because he is sovereign over all others.

In his zeal to divest "Lord" of all meanings that do not suit his purpose, Ryrie even says, "If the gospel of the Lord Jesus includes lordship over my life, it might as well also include the necessity of believing he is my Creator, Judge, coming King, Example, Teacher, and so forth . . ."[4] But, of course, that is exactly what it *does* include. What is the meaning of "Jesus is divine" if the statement does not mean that Jesus is the Creator, Judge, Example, Teacher, and other obvious functions of divinity? What does the word *God* mean if it does not include these matters?

When you begin to strip away the implications of this word, instead of adding to them and developing them, even the minimum amount you want to affirm becomes meaningless.

3. *To add anything to faith, even commitment, is to turn the gospel of salvation by faith into a gospel of works, which is a false gospel.*

Ryrie says, "The message of faith only and the message of faith plus commitment of life cannot both be the gospel; therefore, one of them is a false

4. Ibid., p. 177.

gospel and comes under the curse of perverting the gospel or preaching another gospel (Gal. 1:6–9)."[5] But this argument fudges on the definition of faith. If true faith includes commitment, as the greatest theologians of the church have always claimed it does, then to insist on commitment is not to add anything to faith but only to insist that faith be true faith.[6] And that is an important point, because a false faith, an imitation faith, or a dead faith saves no one.

Four Costly Errors

It is evident from my response to Ryrie's arguments that I believe the Dallas doctrine goes astray in a number of critical areas. But my remarks have only begun to touch on them. There are four areas in which this faulty understanding of the gospel is mistaken.

1. *The meaning of faith.* This is the chief error, and I have already touched on it in my response to Ryrie's views. According to the Bible, a saving faith is a living faith that inevitably leads to right conduct. It involves substantial content, personal heart response, and commitment to Jesus Christ as Lord. According to the Dallas doctrine, faith is mere intellectual assent to the barest truths of the gospel.

2. *The need for repentance.* The Dallas school speaks of the need for repentance, but because it does not want to acknowledge the corresponding need for behavioral change it redefines repentance to mean only "a change of mind" concerning who Jesus Christ is, irrespective of any reference to sin. G. Michael Cocoris, a Dallas product, writes, "The Bible requires repentance for salvation, but repentance does not mean to turn from sin, nor a change in one's conduct. Those are the fruits of repentance. Biblical repentance is a change of mind or attitude concerning either God, Christ, dead works or sin."[7]

That is not what the Bible means by repentance. The Bible's use of this word always implies a change of life direction, specifically a turning from sin. It is the flip side of faith, its corresponding member. In conversion we turn from sin, which is repentance, on the one hand, and on the other, we turn to Jesus, which is faith.

3. *The demand for discipleship.* The Dallas doctrine divorces salvation from discipleship, thus preserving the school's doctrine of the "carnal Christian." But Jesus defined salvation as discipleship. That is, he did not call people to

5. Ibid., p. 170.

6. In its classic seventeenth-century formulation, faith was defined as possessing three elements: *notitia* (factual knowledge), *assensus* (glad acceptance), and *fiducia* (personal trust in Jesus as Savior). That is far more than a bare intellectual acknowledgement that Jesus died for sin.

7. G. Michael Cocoris, *Lordship Salvation: Is It Biblical?* (Dallas: Redención Viva, 1983), p. 12.

mere intellectual assent to who he was but rather to become his disciples. His call was, "Follow me."

Several years ago I wrote a book to explore the meaning of Christ's call to discipleship, and in it I examined the matter of cost. I found that Jesus always stressed the cost of coming to him. He never said anything to suggest even remotely that a person could come to him as Savior and remain unchanged. That insight changed me. I said in the book that if I had been asked earlier what minimum amount of doctrine a person needed to know in order to become a Christian or what minimum price he would have to pay to follow Jesus, I would probably have replied as many others still do, stressing very little demand. But now I say, "The minimum amount a person must believe to be a Christian is *everything*, and the minimum amount a person must give is *all*. You cannot hold back even a fraction of a percentage of yourself. Every sin must be abandoned. Every false thought must be repudiated. You must be the Lord's entirely."[8]

Students of the Bible can decide for themselves whether this or the minimal demands of the Dallas school come closest to Christ's definition of what it means to be a Christian.

4. *The place of regeneration.* The fourth costly error of the Dallas doctrine is its failure to see the unbreakable link between justification and regeneration. The exponents of the Dallas view speak as if the only thing involved in the salvation of a sinner is justification. But Jesus also said, "You must be born again" (John 3:7). Clearly, there can be no justification without regeneration, just as there is no regeneration without justification. But regeneration means the creation of a new nature by God. Therefore, if one is justified, he is also regenerated; and if he is regenerated, he will have a new nature and will begin to act differently. Indeed, the first evidences of this new nature are the person's turning from sin in repentance and turning to Jesus Christ as Savior in faith.

That is why we say that if there is no evidence of the new life, there is no new life. And if there is no new life, the person is not a true Christian regardless of his or her profession.

Even Worse Errors Than These

I have been speaking of the errors that have been linked to the Dallas doctrine, but at this point I need to say something more. Sometimes an error is not very serious, because it does not touch on matters of great importance. Sometimes an error is serious, but the implications are not worked out and so it does little damage. This is not the case here. As the Dallas school has been challenged in this area, the opponents of "Lordship salvation" have dug in their heels and (in the person of Zane Hodges at least) have affirmed in

8. James M. Boice, *Christ's Call to Discipleship* (Chicago: Moody Press, 1986), p. 114.

their defense that: (1) a person can be saved and eternally secure even though he or she has a dying (or dead) faith, and (2) the person can be saved even if he or she apostatizes, denying Jesus.

The first of these terrible and nearly unbelievable assertions comes as a result of Zane Hodges's attempt to deal with James 2:14–16, which distinguishes between a saving faith and a dead one. In Hodges's handling of this text, the passage is said to have nothing to do with spiritual salvation in the life to come but only with how one can preserve one's life now, here on earth.

According to Hodges, without works faith will wither. In fact, it can even die. "A body dies when it loses the spirit which keeps it alive. In the same way, a person's faith dies when it loses the animating factor of good works."[9] Does that mean that salvation can be lost, then? That we must abandon the doctrine of eternal security? Not at all, according to this writer. The very fact that faith can die means that it was alive once, and on the basis of that once-alive faith we can confidently say, "Once saved, always saved." Writes Hodges, "The dangers of a dying faith are real. But they do not include hell."[10]

That is terrible teaching. But here is a second terrible assertion, based on Hodges's handling of Hebrews 6:4–6. Hodges says that this is a description of real apostasy experienced by real Christians. That is, it is possible for Christians to "fall away." But we do not need to worry, since "we should not construe . . . 'falling away' here as though it meant the loss of eternal life."[11]

The bottom line of this pernicious exegesis is that a person can profess to believe in Christ early in life, live without works and thus see his or her faith wither, and at last die, so that the person no longer professes even the meager intellectual assent possessed at the beginning, and then can even deny Jesus as the divine Savior—that is, be utterly indistinguishable from a pagan, not only in external appearance but in internal conviction as well—*and still be a Christian,* that is, be saved eternally.

It is inconceivable to me how anyone can seriously regard that as the Bible's teaching. Yet it is where the Dallas doctrine leads, even though not all who oppose "Lordship salvation" follow it to Hodges's incredible extremes. That this is the end of the line should be ample warning to anyone that the teaching is unstable at the core.

Historic Christianity

At the end of his critique of these errors in *The Gospel According to Jesus,* John MacArthur has a substantial appendix in which he shows by many quotations from the preachers and theologians of the past that "Lordship salvation" has always been the teaching of the church. In that section he cites thirty-one writers and offers forty-one quotations.

9. Zane C. Hodges, *Dead Faith: What Is It?* (Dallas, Redención Viva, 1981), p. 33.
10. Zane C. Hodges, *The Gospel Under Siege: A Study on Faith and Works* (Dallas: Redención Viva, 1981), p. 33.
11. Ibid., p. 70.

I cannot reproduce them all here, of course. But here is an important one, a series of comments by W. H. Griffith Thomas, one of the founders of Dallas Seminary before its present doctrinal decline. He wrote, "Our relation to Christ is based on his death and resurrection, and this means his Lordship. Indeed, the Lordship of Christ over the lives of his people was the very purpose for which he died and rose again. . . . We have to acknowledge Christ as our Lord. Sin is rebellion, and it is only as we surrender to him as Lord that we receive pardon from him as our Savior."[12]

Here is another. A. W. Tozer wrote:

[Years ago] no one would ever dare to rise in a meeting and say, "I am a Christian" if he had not surrendered his whole being to God and had taken Jesus Christ as his Lord as well as his Savior and had brought himself under obedience to the will of the Lord. It was only then that he could say, "I am saved." Today we let them say they are saved no matter how imperfect and incomplete the transaction, with the proviso that the deeper Christian life can be tacked on at some time in the future. Can it be that we really think that we do not owe Jesus Christ our obedience?

This is bad teaching brethren.[13]

Indeed it is! But unfortunately, it is all too common in our time.

12. W. H. Griffith Thomas, *St. Paul's Epistle to the Romans* (Grand Rapids: Wm. B. Eerdmans, 1950), pp. 370, 371. Quoted by John MacArthur in *The Gospel According to Jesus,* (Grand Rapids: Zondervan, 1988), p. 234.

13. A. W. Tozer, *I Call It Heresy!* (Harrisburg: Christian Publications, 1974), pp. 18, 19. Quoted by MacArthur in *The Gospel According to Jesus,* p. 236.

146

Heart Belief and Mouth Confession

Romans 10:10

For it is with your heart that you believe and are justified, and it is with your mouth that you confess and are saved.

In the last few studies I have been dealing with the nature of Christian preaching and therefore with the nature of the Christian gospel, based on the second paragraph of Romans 10. I want to carry that study further in this chapter, focusing on an important question: Is there such a thing as secret discipleship?

The Dallas doctrine would answer "Yes" since, according to that mistaken view, it is possible to be a Christian without any outward evidence of justification or regeneration at all. If you do not even have to repent of sin to be a Christian, you certainly do not have to confess Christ openly. In fact, you can even deny him. You can turn your back on him altogether. In the previous study I tried to show why that view is wrong, fatally wrong, in fact. Now I want to show that it is not only necessary to repent of sin, trust Jesus Christ as Lord and Savior, and follow him in faithful discipleship throughout life, but that it is also necessary to confess him openly before other men and women.

That is the teaching of our text: "For it is with your heart that you believe and are justified, and it is with your mouth that you confess and are saved" (Rom. 10:10). I want to explore the exact meaning of that clear statement.

Secret Discipleship?

As I prepared this study I remembered doing a sermon on this subject sixteen years earlier in which I asked two questions: "Is it possible for a person to be a secret believer in the Lord Jesus Christ? Is it possible to believe in Jesus with our whole hearts and not confess him openly?"[1] I was asking those questions because I had come to a passage in my study of the Gospel of John in which many of the Jewish leaders are said to have believed on Jesus even though "because of the Pharisees they would not confess their faith for fear they would be put out of the synagogue" (John 12:42).

It was a puzzling text to me, because on the surface it seemed to say that silent belief is possible, while, at the same time, the language was such that I naturally wondered if the belief spoken of in the case of these religious leaders was genuine. After all, the passage goes on to say, "for they loved praise from men more than praise from God" (v. 43)—and that does not sound like genuine Christianity.

I finally concluded that, whatever the case may have been, these men were trying to do something that ultimately is impossible. For this reason: Either the secrecy kills the discipleship, or else the discipleship kills the secrecy. In the end, secret discipleship is a contradiction in terms, and this means that we must confess Jesus openly if we are to be (and remain) true Christians.

Today I am not so hesitant. And one of the reasons I am not so hesitant is our text, which indissolubly links heart belief and mouth confession. You will recall from our earlier studies that we are not to find some prescribed sequence of events in these verses, as if we first believe and then confess, or even some supposed ordering of priorities, as if one item were essential and the other good but not essential. That is not how Paul is speaking. He is describing what it means to be a Christian, and his point is that all must believe the truth about Jesus, receive it into the heart, and then confess him openly before others.

When Paul says we must believe with our hearts and confess with our mouths, he is saying that we must do both and that it is the presence of both together—faith leading to confession and confession proving the reality of faith—that leads to "righteousness" and "salvation."

This is the way all the major commentators handle Romans 10:10. Robert Haldane, the Scottish Bible teacher responsible for the Swiss revival of the early nineteenth century (sometimes called Haldane's Revival), wrote, "Confession of Christ is as necessary as faith in him, but necessary for a dif-

---

1. James Montgomery Boice, "A Silent Majority? (John 12:42–43)" in *The Gospel of John: An Expositional Commentary,* five volumes in one (Grand Rapids: Zondervan, 1985), p. 852.

ferent purpose. Faith is necessary to obtain the gift of righteousness. Confession is necessary to prove that this gift is received. If a man does not confess Christ at the hazard of life, character, property, liberty, and everything dear to him, he has not the faith of Christ."[2]

Charles Haddon Spurgeon, the great Baptist preacher of London who was responsible for a revival of a different sort only a generation later, said, "Faith and confession . . . are joined together; let not man put them asunder."[3]

Leon Morris, a scholar of our own day, writes, "These are but two parts of the same saving experience."[4]

What a great verse this is! It is a preacher's verse. Some verses are for scholars; they are to be probed, analyzed, and fathomed. Some are for devotional reading; our hearts are warmed by them. Others, like this one, are to be declared boldly and joyfully. This is a verse that, together with the one before it, assures us that if we believe in our hearts that Jesus is the Son of God, that he is both Lord and Savior and that God has raised him from the dead, and that if we confess him as Lord before other people, we will be justified by God, being forgiven of all sin, and will be saved, not only now or in future days but at the final judgment.

There is no greater message in all the world than that message. There is nothing so important in life as to believe on and confess Jesus. There is no greater result than the salvation to be gained by receiving and acting upon that gospel.

Heart Belief

The verse is in two parts, of course, and the first of these two parts concerns faith. It is what Paul is talking about when he says, "It is with your heart that you *believe* and are justified."

At this point we do not need to take a great deal of time to speak about the object of faith, for this is what the passage and our study have been exploring all along. The object of faith is "Jesus as Lord." This means, Jesus as: (1) the divine Son of God, (2) the Savior who died to rescue us from sin, and (3) the Lord who rules over his people and church. Some have argued that a person does not have to believe on Jesus as his or her Lord to be a Christian, maintaining that we need only to believe on him as our Savior. But a Savior who is not also Lord is another Jesus, a counterfeit Jesus, and a counterfeit Jesus will save no one. It is only by believing on the *Lord* Jesus Christ that we are saved.

2. Robert Haldane, *An Exposition of the Epistle to the Romans* (MacDill AFB: MacDonald Publishing, 1958), p. 508.

3. Charles Haddon Spurgeon, "Believing with the Heart" in *Metropolitan Tabernacle Pulpit,* vol. 9 (Pasadena, Tex.: Pilgrim Publications, 1969), p. 386.

4. Leon Morris, *The Epistle to the Romans* (Grand Rapids: Wm. B. Eerdmans, and Leicester, England: Inter-Varsity Press, 1988), p. 386.

What is new about this section of the verse is the phrase "with your heart." It is striking because it deals with the nature of true faith or belief. Without these words we might suppose, as the Dallas doctrine teaches, that faith is a matter of the intellect only. But lest we make that mistake, Paul tells us by these words that faith is a matter of the whole being—intellect, will, and emotions—which is what the word *heart* in the Bible signifies. The faith that saves is a faith that takes all we are and commits it to all that Jesus Christ is.

Moreover, "with the heart" implies two other important truths.

1. *It implies sincerity.* In one of her books and in many of her public talks, Corrie ten Boom describes a time in which, years after her deliverance from the Nazi death camps, she was confronted by one of the brutal German guards who had been responsible for the death of her sister Betsie. The guard, who had become a Christian, came forward at one of her meetings and asked her for forgiveness. Corrie described what a struggle it was for her. But at last the Holy Spirit had his way, and she grasped the outstretched hand of her former persecutor, responding, "Yes, I do forgive you—with all my heart."

That is what belief "with the heart" is all about. It means "sincerely" or "wholeheartedly." It is the way the Bible uses the word when it commands us to "love the Lord your God with all your heart and with all your soul and with all your mind" (Matt. 22:37).

Here is what John Calvin said about believing with the heart. "Let us note that the seat of faith is not in the head but in the heart. I am not going to argue about the part of the body in which faith is located, but since the word heart generally means a serious and sincere affection, I maintain that faith is a firm and effectual confidence, and not just a bare idea."[5] It is, in other words, *notitia, assensus,* and *fiducia,* as the theologians of the Reformation and later centuries frequently expressed it.

2. *It implies the Holy Spirit's work.* When we look at what the Bible says about the hearts of men and women, we see, on the one hand, that the heart is "deceitful above all things and beyond cure" (Jer. 17:9) and that, on the other hand, it is the work of the Holy Spirit to renew or regenerate evil hearts ("I will give them an undivided heart and put a new spirit in them . . ." Ezek. 11:19; cf. 18:31; 36:26). Otherwise, we do not get a right spirit, nor do we come to believe on Jesus as our personal Lord and Savior.

God said through the prophet Isaiah, "These people come near to me with their mouth / and honor me with their lips, / but their *hearts* are far from me" (Isa. 29:13, emphasis added). Yet God also spoke through Jeremiah:

> "This is the covenant I will make with the house of Israel
> after that time," declares the LORD.

5. John Calvin, *The Epistles of Paul the Apostle to the Romans and to the Thessalonians,* trans. Ross MacKenzie (Grand Rapids: Wm. B. Eerdmans, 1973), p. 228.

"I will put my law in their minds
   and write it *on their hearts.*
I will be their God,
   and they will be my people.
No longer will a man teach his neighbor,
   or a man his brother, saying, 'Know the LORD,'
because they will all know me,
   from the least of them to the greatest."

Jeremiah 31:33–34, emphasis added

This began to be fulfilled at Pentecost, when the Holy Spirit operated through the preaching of Peter to bring three thousand people to repentance and faith in Jesus Christ. It is being fulfilled in our day whenever people hear the Word of God, turn from sin, believe on Jesus as their personal Lord and Savior, and confess him before others.

Mouth Confession

The second part of this verse is the part with which I actually began, asking, "Is it possible to be a secret believer?" It answers by telling us, "It is with your mouth that you confess and are saved." This second part goes with the first, so that (in one sense) it is as necessary to confess Christ as Lord and Savior as it is to believe on him.

We are to confess him with our mouths, of course, which means openly and audibly. But a simple public testimony in a meeting does not exhaust the ways we can confess Jesus Christ as Lord.

How can we confess him? Let me suggest the following eight ways.

1. *In public worship.* The first and most obvious way in which you can confess Jesus Christ is by assembling with other Christians in public worship. There have been times in history when this has been a mere form for many. It is probably a mere form for many, even today. Yet this is changing. As more and more people are neglecting church, preferring the idle pleasures of the world to the demands of public worship, the mere fact of your joining with other believers to worship God can be a useful and significant confession that you are indeed a Christian.

I am aware of this most Sunday mornings. I live only four blocks from Tenth Presbyterian Church, so I walk to church. As I do this Sunday by Sunday throughout the year, I am aware of those I pass on the streets on those mornings. There are always a number who have been to the convenience store to pick up the Sunday papers and are reading them as they shuffle along sleepily. I also pass joggers. They are working earnestly to preserve their bodies, which will perish anyway in time, while they are indifferent to the condition of their souls. Other people are just walking along, some perhaps returning from an all-night debauch or binge.

But while all this is going on, there is an entirely different group of people, a subculture that is collecting from around the Delaware Valley. These people are alert and expectant. They have their Bibles in hand, and their minds are already attuned to the God they are coming to worship. The mere fact that they are collecting to worship him sets them apart. They are rightly and joyfully confessing Christ by what they do on Sunday mornings.

2. _By the sacraments._ A second way in which we confess Christ openly is by our participation in the sacraments: baptism, the initiatory sacrament of the Christian faith; and the Lord's Supper, the repeatable sacrament. Both are for Christians only, and by both we proclaim before other people that Jesus Christ is our Lord.

Charles Haddon Spurgeon had a wonderful sermon on the second half of this text, the part speaking of confession with our mouths, in which he listed a number of these means of confessing Christ. He spoke of baptism, calling it the crossing of the Rubicon: "If Caesar crossed the Rubicon, there would never be peace between him and the senate again. He draws his sword, and he throws away his scabbard. Such is the act of baptism to the believer. It is the crossing of the Rubicon. It is as much as to say, 'I cannot come back again to you. I am dead to you. And to prove I am, I am absolutely buried to you. I have nothing more to do with the world. I am Christ's and Christ's forever."[6]

So also with the Lord's Supper. As you partake of it you say to the world, "I am not my own. I am Christ's. I am in fellowship with him. Therefore, I cannot indulge in the sins in which you indulge or live for the goals for which you surrender everything."

3. _Through association with God's people._ Not all our associations with other believers are formal, that is, in worship services and sacraments. We also associate with them informally, proving by our identification with these others, of whatever race, nationality, or status in life, that we belong to the same Lord and confess the same gospel. You can do that at work, in weekly Bible studies, or just by your friendships. We remember that in his first letter, the apostle John made our love for other Christians one of the tests by which we can know whether or not we are a Christian (1 John 3:11–13). If this is a way we can know we are Christians and are following Christ, it is obviously also a way by which others can know we are Christians. The pagans said of the early Christians, "Behold, how they love one another."

4. _By how we conduct our business._ How you conduct your business or how you work in someone else's business also testifies to whether or not you belong to Jesus Christ. It is a rare business that is utterly upright and moral. Therefore, there will be many occasions when a person who belongs to Christ will have

---

6. Charles Haddon Spurgeon, "Confession with the Mouth" in _Metropolitan Tabernacle Pulpit_, vol. 9 (Pasadena, Tex.: Pilgrim Publications, 1969), p. 400.

to stand up for him, saying, "I cannot do that, because I am a Christian." Although a stand like that may result in isolation, abuse, ridicule, or persecution, even loss of a job, it is necessary. A faith that is not supported by an upright moral life is not worth having.

5. *In reaching out to others.* A fifth way we confess Christ before others is by reaching out to them in evangelism. Spurgeon said, "I believe, my brethren, that a Christian man can hardly carry out his confession with his mouth, unless he goes a little out of his way at times to bear testimony."[7] Do *you* do that? Do you do anything, even something quite little, merely to be able to speak to others about Jesus? If not, how can you consider yourself to be a Christian? If you are a Christian, Christ is your Lord, and it is he who said, "You will be my witnesses" (Acts 1:8).

6. *In temptation.* There is never a better and more hopeful opportunity to confess Jesus as Lord than in a time of temptation. Remember Joseph. He was pursued by the wife of his Egyptian master, Potiphar. But he refused to sleep with her, proclaiming, ". . . How then could I do such a wicked thing and sin against God?" (Gen. 39:9). The temptation gave him an opportunity to state his true allegiance, and stating it undoubtedly also helped him to resist the sin. You would be wise to do the same.

7. *In severe trials.* The seventh circumstance in which you can confess Christ forcefully is in severe trials. Have you lost your job? Has your wife or husband left you? Have you discovered that you have a serious, perhaps fatal illness? This is your opportunity to show the world that you are not like those who have no knowledge of the true God or of his Son our Savior. It is a time you can say, "I am not afraid of what is coming, for I belong to Jesus Christ. He has shown his love by dying for me, and I know that he will not desert me. Even in the face of a loved one's death, says Paul, though we grieve we do not grieve "like the rest of men, who have no hope" (1 Thess. 4:13).

8. *In the hour of our deaths.* Finally, we sometimes also have the privilege of confessing Jesus as Lord in the hour of our deaths. This is not always possible, given the forms of medical treatment today. But it often is. Some of the greatest testimonies of believers to the grace and power of God have been given on their deathbeds.

When he was dying, William Carey, known as the father of modern missions and a great missionary to India, said to a friend, "When I am gone, say nothing about Dr. Carey; speak about Dr. Carey's Savior."

David Livingstone, the pioneer missionary to Africa, said, "Build me a hut to die in. I am going home."

7. Ibid., p. 404.

John Bunyan, the Bedford tinker who left the world the immortal Christian classic *The Pilgrim's Progress,* said as he died, "Weep not for me, but for yourselves. I go to the Father of our Lord Jesus Christ, who will, no doubt, through the mediation of his blessed Son, receive me, though a sinner. We shall ere long meet to sing the new song, and remain everlastingly happy, world without end. Amen."

Dwight L. Moody, the great evangelist, said, "I see the children's faces. Earth is receding. Heaven is opening. God is calling."[8]

Righteousness and Salvation

Since the end result of heart belief and mouth confession, which we have been studying, is the righteousness and salvation about which the text speaks, and since these are the greatest blessings any human being can receive, let it be your deep desire to believe on Jesus as Savior and Lord wholeheartedly and let it be your earnest endeavor to confess him before others in every possible way. Let's be rid of all "secret discipleship," if such a thing even exists. We do not have long to live. Let us use our time well and wisely, above all by trusting wholly in Jesus Christ and by confessing him boldly with our mouths. Let us stand with him, bearing his reproach, knowing that if we do, one day we will be with him in glory and will reign with him forever.

Jesus himself said, "Whoever acknowledges me before men, I will also acknowledge him before my Father in heaven" (Matt. 10:32).

---

8. The quotations are from Herbert Lockyer, *Last Words of Saints and Sinners* (Grand Rapids: Kregel Publications, 1969), pp. 59, 62, 63.

147

Health, Wealth, and What?

Romans 10:10

For it is with your heart that you believe and are justified, and it is with your mouth that you confess and are saved.

For the last few studies I have been following an alternating procedure in which I have first expounded a text from Romans and then dealt with wrong ways of understanding the gospel or doing evangelism that result from misusing or neglecting what the text teaches. Thus far I have dealt with two wrong approaches: (1) the religion of signs and wonders, and (2) the doctrine that eliminates claims of Christ to lordship from salvation matters.

In this study I want to tackle another serious aberration, namely, the gospel that is often proclaimed on television by the so-called television evangelists. This is sometimes called the "health, wealth, and happiness" gospel.

The reasons I am dealing with this aberration at this point is that it has bearing on the word *saved*, which we came to in the last two verses we were studying. Romans 10:9 says, "If you confess with your mouth, 'Jesus is Lord,' and believe in your heart that God raised him from the dead, *you will be saved*" (emphasis added). The next verse, Romans 10:10, says, "For it is with your heart that you believe and are justified, and it is with your mouth that you confess and *are saved*" (emphasis added). I said in the last study that the future tense of the verb in verse 9 indicates that this is speaking of salvation from the wrath of God against sin at the last judgment. If I had been dealing with this fully, I could have shown that "salvation" is an inclusive term for what the Bible offers. It includes: (1) salvation from the penalty of sin, a past tense; (2) salvation from the power of sin, a present tense; and (3) salvation from the presence of sin, a future tense. Each part has to do with sin.

Most Christians will think this is obvious. What person who claims to be a Christian could deny it? Yet this is precisely what is being lost or even denied by the many popular TV preachers. This is no small matter. The error concerns the very essence of Christianity, and it is unusually harmful if for no other reason than that television is so pervasive and influential. For millions of Americans, the "electronic church" is virtually all they know of Christianity.

The Gospel According to Television

Let me begin by setting some parameters and providing some focus. First, what I am going to say does not apply to all religious television. It does not apply to the broadcasts of the Billy Graham Association, for instance. Billy Graham is an exception in this, as in many other areas of his unique ministry. Joel Nederhood's "Faith 20" program is another exception. So also, though to a lesser degree, is James Kennedy's television program. People who know the television medium well will say rightly that these programs are "bad television." That is, they do not play to television's unique capacities for oversimplification, drama, and entertainment. But that is precisely why they are a *good* exception. I hope they will survive.

What I am referring to are the exceptionally popular (read "financially successful") programs, particularly those that promote what is generally called "positive [or possibility] thinking" and "positive confessionism." These programs are associated with such names as Robert Schuller, Kenneth Copeland, Kenneth Hagin, Oral Roberts, and Robert Tilton. Instead of a traditional gospel of salvation from sin, these TV evangelists preach a man-centered gospel that, in its mildest form, offers self-esteem without repentance and, in its most startling extension, proclaims the deification of man, with its inevitable blasphemous encroachments on God's prerogatives.

This TV gospel promotes self-esteem instead of sin, self-help instead of atonement and redemption, an entertainer instead of Christ, and a lust for power instead of true discipleship.

In 1990, a talented friend of mine named Michael Horton edited a book on the TV evangelists entitled *The Agony of Deceit*. He concluded, after a careful examination of the actual teachings of this influential group of communicators, "All of the televangelists censured in this book tend to trivialize the plan of salvation. There is rarely any serious attempt to explain to the masses such basic redemptive truths as the substitutionary atonement, propitiation, or sacrifice and satisfaction. . . . One thing the viewer comes away with is the sense that the purpose of evangelism is not to satisfy God and his purposes, but to satisfy the consumer with the product."[1]

In the following analysis I am depending in large measure on the material assembled by Horton and his associates.

The Gospel of Self-Esteem

The least objectionable, but still harmful, form of the TV gospel is the message of "self-esteem" associated with the name of Robert Schuller, pastor of the Crystal Cathedral in Garden Grove, California, not far from Disneyland. Schuller's weekly Sunday-morning services are broadcast on more than two hundred television stations worldwide, and he is watched by more than three million people.[2] In an interview feature in late 1984, *Christianity Today* claimed that he is "reaching more non-Christians than any other religious leader in America."[3]

Robert Schuller wants to be orthodox and claims to be. He believes in the inerrancy of the Bible and affirms the Apostles', Nicene, and Athanasian creeds. He even claims to be a Calvinist, professing submission to the Westminster Standards and the Canons of the Synod of Dort, which is the official standard of his denomination. Nevertheless, Schuller's doctrine of sin is deficient, and as a result his doctrine of salvation has shifted away from the message of God's redeeming work in Christ to what is basically a philosophy of positive thinking, at least to the extent that his views are disclosed on television.

In 1982, Schuller wrote a book that was mailed free to every minister in America. It was titled *Self-Esteem: The New Reformation*. In this book Schuller took issue with the ways traditional preaching speaks of sin and proposed a gospel of enlightened "self-esteem" instead. Clearly, Schuller believes that if other ministers follow his approach, most of them will have the same or nearly the same (numerical) success he has had.

What did he say? Schuller wrote, "Reformation theology failed to make clear that the core of sin is a lack of self-esteem." "The most serious sin is the one that causes me to say, 'I am unworthy. I may have no claim to divine sonship if you examine me at my worst.'" "Once a person believes he is an 'unworthy sinner,' it is doubtful if he can really honestly accept the saving grace God offers in Jesus Christ."[4] Writing along the same lines in a paragraph quoted by *Christianity Today* in 1984, Schuller said, "I don't think anything has been done in the name of Christ and under the banner of

---

1. Michael Horton, ed., with R. C. Sproul, Walter Martin, C. Everett Koop, Joel Nederhood, and others, *The Agony of Deceit: What Some TV Preachers Are Really Teaching* (Chicago: Moody Press, 1990), p. 139.

2. *Time*, March 18, 1985, p. 70.

3. *Christianity Today*, August 10, 1985, p. 23.

4. Robert Schuller, *Self-Esteem: The New Reformation* (Waco: Word Books, 1982), p. 98. Cited by Horton, *The Agony of Deceit*, p. 136.

Christianity that has proven more destructive to human personality and, hence, counterproductive to the evangelism enterprise than the often crude, uncouth, and unchristian strategy of attempting to make people aware of their lost and sinful condition."[5]

To be fair to Schuller, he claims that his evangelistic strategy is to get non-Christians in the door, as it were, and then teach them the gospel later. But it is also fair to say that whatever is heard on Schuller's influential television program is not that gospel.

Besides, one cannot help but question whether the true gospel can ever be built on a false foundation. In a helpful analysis of Schuller, authors Dave Hunt and T. A. McMahon write, "One thing is certain . . . : The Bible never urges self-acceptance, self-love, self-assertion, self-confidence, self-esteem, self-forgiveness, nor any of the other selfisms that are so popular today. The answer to depression is not to accept self, but to turn from self to Christ. A preoccupation with self is the very antithesis of what the Bible teaches."[6]

Health, Wealth, and Happiness

The second, and much more harmful brand of the TV gospel is the "health, wealth, and happiness" message of the positive confessionists, men like Kenneth Copeland, Kenneth Hagin, Oral Roberts, and Robert Tilton. These preachers believe that "health, wealth, and happiness" are the birthright of every Christian and that the power to attain them lies within Christians themselves. They affirm the gospel. I know of none who would deny outright that Jesus died for sin and rose again from the dead. But this is not the gospel they preach. In fact, they seem almost intentionally to ignore it.

What these preachers really seem to believe in is the power of the mind to visualize and thus create what one desires. This is New Age thinking. It is not far removed from the fantasies of Shirley MacLaine and may actually have the same origins, as some argue.[7]

A popular slogan for this distortion of the Bible's message is: "Name it and claim it." That is, we have the right to whatever we want because we are God's sons and daughters or even, as we will see, because we are ourselves "little gods." We see this view reflected in book and pamphlet titles such as Kenneth E. Hagin's "How to Write Your Own Ticket with God" and Robert Tilton's magazine, *Signs, Wonders and Miracles of Faith,* which is filled with stories of financial and physical success from his followers. Kenneth Copeland has written "God's Will Is Health" and "God's Will Is Prosperity." Oral Roberts

---

5. *Christianity Today,* October 5, 1984, p. 12. Quoted by Dave Hunt and T. A. McMahon, *The Seduction of Christianity: Spiritual Discernment in the Last Days* (Eugene, Oreg.: Harvest House, 1985), p. 15.

6. Hunt and McMahon, *The Seduction of Christianity,* p. 195.

7. See ibid.

promises people on his mailing list, "prosperity miracles that are within fin-gertip reach of your faith," and one of his most recent books is titled *How I Learned Jesus Was Not Poor.*[8]

Christians who know their Bibles may wonder how the TV evangelists deal with Bible statements to the contrary, statements that say we are called to suffer with Christ or Job's statement that "The LORD gave and the LORD has taken away" (Job 1:21). It is not often that we hear the TV evangelists con-tradict Scripture, but they do at this point. Charles Capps, another "name it and claim it" preacher, said that Job "was sure not under the anointing" when he said, "the Lord gives and the Lord takes away" and called the state-ment a "lie."[9]

Even Pat Robertson, president of the Christian Broadcasting Network and a former candidate for the presidency of the United States in the 1988 elec-tions, said, "I can hardly think that the Bible, which was transmitted through human beings, is totally perfect. I believe it to be the Word of God and a fully inspired book, but not perfection."[10]

The false teaching I have been describing would be serious enough if it stopped here. But, unfortunately, it does not. In an effort to enforce the "authority" the positive confessionists believe to have been given to each Christian, these teachers extend their errors to insist that by their rebirth, Christians have become "little gods" and therefore possess the authority of God himself, not only in "health, wealth, and happiness" matters but in all things. This is either so ignorant or so diabolical that it is hard for most Christians to believe that such "nice Christian men" are teaching this. But they are, as scores of verbatim quotations show. Here are some examples. . . .

Kenneth Copeland, one of the most popular TV evangelists, said, "Every man who has been born again is an incarnation, and Christianity is a miracle. The believer is as much an incarnation as was Jesus of Nazareth."[11] On another occasion he said, "You don't have a god in you. You are one."[12]

Kenneth E. Hagin wrote, "Even many in the great body of Full Gospel people do not know that the new birth is a real incarnation; they do not know that they are as much sons and daughters of God as Jesus."[13]

---

8. Horton, *The Agony of Deceit*, p. 50.

9. Charles Capps, *Can Your Faith Fail?* (Tulsa: Harrison House, n.d.), pp. 27, 28. Quoted by Horton, *The Agony of Deceit*, p. 66.

10. Pat Robertson, *Answers,* Christian Broadcasting Network (CBN) Partner's Edition (Virginia Beach: Christian Broadcasting Network, 1984), p. 71. Cited by Horton, *The Agony of Deceit*, p. 65.

11. Kenneth Copeland, *Word of Faith* (Fort Worth: Kenneth Copeland, 1980), p. 14. Cited by Horton, *The Agony of Deceit*, p. 44.

12. Kenneth Copeland, "The Force of Love," tape BCC-56 (Fort Worth: Kenneth Copeland), on file with the Christian Research Institute. Cited by Horton, *The Agony of Deceit*, p. 92. There is a more extensive treatment of Copeland's views on pp. 113–119.

13. Kenneth E. Hagin, *Zoe: The God-Kind of Life* (Tulsa: Faith Library, 1981), p. 40. Cited by Horton, *The Agony of Deceit*, p. 44.

In a televised interview with Copeland, Trinity Broadcasting Network's Paul Crouch made this statement: "We are gods. I am a little god. I have his name. I am one with him. . . . Critics be gone!"[14]

Here is a particularly offensive example from a tape series called "Believing in Yourself" by Casey Treat.

> The Father, the Son and the Holy Ghost had a conference and they said, "Let's make man an exact duplicate of us." Oh, I don't know about you, but that does turn my crank! An exact duplicate of God! Say it out loud—"I'm an exact duplicate of God!" [The audience repeats it a bit tentatively and uncertainly.]
>
> Come on, say it! [He leads them in unison.] "I'm an exact duplicate of God!" Say it again, "I'm an exact duplicate of God!" [The congregation is getting into it, louder and bolder, with more enthusiasm each time.] Say it like you mean it! [He's yelling now.] "I'm an exact duplicate of God!" Yell it out loud! Shout it! [They follow as he leads.] "I'm an exact duplicate of God!" "I'm an exact duplicate of God!" [Repeatedly] . . . .
>
> When God looks in the mirror, he sees me! When I look in the mirror, I see God! Oh, hallelujah! . . .
>
> You know, sometimes people say to me, when they're mad and want to put me down. . . . "You just think you're a little god." Thank you! Hallelujah! You got that right! "Who d'you think you are, Jesus?" Yep!
>
> Are you listening to me? Are you kids running around here acting like little gods? Why not? God told me to! . . . Since I'm an exact duplicate of God, I'm going to act like God!"[15]

What we see in this teaching is an inevitable multiplication of false doctrines. It began with unlimited faith, but it soon progressed to unlimited health, unlimited wealth, unlimited power, and unlimited divinity. And even that is not the end. The last stage is unlimited dominion, even more dominion or authority than Jesus. Kenneth Hagin tells of a supposed conversation he had with God that was periodically interrupted by Satan. Hagin asked God to silence the devil, but God said he couldn't do it. He was powerless. So Hagin commanded Satan to be quiet. Hagin concluded his story with these words: "Jesus looked at me and said, 'If you hadn't done anything about that, I couldn't have.'"[16]

What is the end purpose of this unlimited, divine authority? I remind you that it is to grow healthy and rich, and to be happy for that reason. That is, it is selfish. Pat Robertson said, "We are to command the money to come to us."[17] Fred Price says, "You, as a Christian, are supposed to be master of your

14. Paul Crouch, "Praise the Lord," Trinity Broadcasting Network, July 7, 1986. Cited by Horton, *The Agony of Deceit*, p. 45.

15. Casey Treat, "Believing in Yourself," tape 2 of a four-tape series (Seattle Christian Center). Cited by Horton, *The Agony of Deceit*, p. 91.

16. Kenneth E. Hagin, *Having Faith in Your Faith* (Tulsa: Faith Library, 1980), Cited by Horton, *The Agony of Deceit*, p. 126.

17. Robertson, *Answers*, p. 76. Cited by Horton, *The Agony of Deceit*, p. 128.

circumstances. . . . There is no way in the world you can reign as a king and be poverty-stricken."[18]

Let me say that I do not know of any teachings anywhere that are a better contemporary illustration of the warning of 2 Timothy 3:1–5, which says that in the last days, "people will be lovers of themselves [the gospel of 'self-esteem'], lovers of money [and] . . . lovers of pleasure rather than lovers of God [the 'health, wealth, and happiness' gospel]."

The Nature of Television

There is one more thing that needs to be said before I drop this topic and go on with our studies of Romans 10. The problems I have been describing result in large measure from the very nature of television, by which I mean that broadcast television is a bad medium for communicating the gospel.

We have been taught to think of television as a powerful educational tool, but education is what television probably does worst. Broadcast television is an entertainment medium, and the result is that it eventually turns everything it touches into entertainment. If entertainment is what it is presenting, that is all right. You may as well watch a movie on television as see it in a theater. But to the degree it tries to be serious, television is harmful, because it trivializes the serious by making news events, politics—yes, even religion itself—entertainment.

Because television creates and thrives on celebrities, when religion goes on television the evangelist inevitably becomes the focus of audience attention, a celebrity. He becomes "a god" and soon begins to think of himself as one, promising the viewers that they can become "gods," too. Again, the program becomes a performance, entertainment, because that is what television is. As a result, religious programs thrive, not by preaching of the gospel but by becoming "holy vaudeville" or talk shows. Above all, television is marketing products. So in the end the gospel (or religion) becomes merely another item to be sold, and success is viewed, not in the number of conversions, still less in the development of Christian character, but in audience share and income.

What I am saying is that television is not a good place to do religion. Those who attempt it do so at their own peril and that of their viewers.

We would be far better off heeding the words of Romans 10, which warn us against ascending into heaven to bring Christ down or descending into the deep to bring him up from the dead—can we say, "trying to be celebrities?"—and instead direct us to the Word of God, which is given to us by revelation, is near us, and is the "word of faith we are proclaiming" (vv. 6–8).

As far as I am concerned, let me say clearly that I have no new word from God, no new revelation. The only word I have is the Word that has been once

18. Fred Price, *How to Obtain Strong Faith* (Tulsa: Harrison House, 1977), p. 104. Cited by Horton, *The Agony of Deceit*, p. 147.

for all delivered to God's saints. I am a teacher. I seek only to point you to those old doctrines and invite you to walk those worn paths. I do not want to entertain. The world will do that. I want to challenge your minds and move your hearts to obey the Bible's teachings. And God forbid that I, or any other preacher, should teach anything contrary to the true gospel doctrine of repentance for sin and corresponding faith in and submission to Jesus Christ.

I echo Michael Horton's own words when he says:

> The biblical gospel offers freedom from sin, not sinlessness; liberation from guilt, not from sin-consciousness; salvation from spiritual, not material, poverty. It offers peace with God won by Christ's bloody sacrifice—not success won by our incessant "decrees." It promises salvation from God's wrath, not freedom from the unhappiness common to all humanity from time to time. And it hides us—in the midst of our pain and grief—in the wounds of Christ, who has made us worthy to share in his suffering.[19]

19. Horton, *The Agony of Deceit*, pp. 149, 150.

148

Freed from Shame or Shameless?

Romans 10:11

As the Scripture says, "Everyone who trusts in him will never be put to shame."

Near the end of the second paragraph of Romans 10, there is a quotation from the Old Testament that Paul has already used once before, at the end of Romans 9.[1] It is from Isaiah 28, and it says, "Anyone who trusts in him will never be put to shame" (Rom. 10:11; cf. 9:23; Isa. 28:16).

This verse teaches two things: (1) the way of salvation is trust or belief in Jesus Christ, a point Paul has made many times earlier, and (2) this way is open to everyone, to the Gentile as well as to the Jew, a point which Paul is now going to stress. At the same time, the verse also paves the way for the invitation to everyone to believe, which is found in verses 12 and 13, and supports the challenge to ministers to preach the gospel to all the world's people, which is in verses 14 and 15.

Like verses 9 and 10 that precede it, this is a tremendous verse for preachers. It speaks of salvation, which is the essential task of preaching, calling on all people everywhere to put their trust in Christ. And it does so powerfully, making an implied contrast between those who do believe in Jesus and are

---

1. It is also used by Peter in 1 Peter 2:6.

saved, and those who do not and are lost. It is a verse from which preachers can bring out many various aspects of the gospel of God's grace.

Whatever Became of Shame?

The new idea in this verse is "shame." I have not discussed it before in this series, so I want to explore it now. But it is hard to talk about shame today, for the reason that very few people in our day are ashamed of anything or even think in such terms.

On the contrary, ours is an exceedingly shameless age.

Nearly twenty years ago, Dr. Karl Menninger of the famous Menninger Clinic in Topeka, Kansas, wrote a book entitled *Whatever Became of Sin?*[2] I thought of that book and its title as I began to work on this subject, because it struck me as I proceeded with my study that in our day "shame" is an even more elusive subject than "sin," and probably for connected reasons. Menninger argued that in recent years "sin" has first been reinterpreted as "crime," which means that it has lost its core definition as being chiefly a violation of the law of God and has become instead only a violation of human law. Then it was changed from being a "crime" into a "symptom," meaning that it is now seen as being no one's fault particularly. At this stage, anything bad that anyone does can be blamed either on one's genes or the environment.

And that is why the sense of shame has gone away, too. Shame implies guilt for wrongdoing. But if none of us ever does anything wrong, there is no need to feel guilty about anything; and if there is no need to feel guilty, there is no need to be ashamed.

People have no sense of shame today. We are a shameless people.

I was surprised to discover this by what is *not* being written today, though I probably should not have been. Let me explain. As I began this study I turned to the many books on pop-psychology, counseling, and self-discovery that find their way to my bookshelves, thinking I would discover lots of interesting material about overcoming or dealing with shame in those books. But I did not. Hardly anything has been written about shame. I couldn't even find it in Menninger's *Whatever Became of Sin?* Apparently, it is not in the category of what are popularly called "felt needs."

Next I looked in my books of anecdotes and quotations. But there were no stories or snappy sayings there.

In the end I turned to the massive *Oxford English Dictionary*, where I found pages of definitions of "shame," supported by scores of quotations from English writers. But here is the interesting thing. The quotations from which the editors of this great dictionary derived their definitions are numerous only from the early centuries of the English language. They become less frequent as the centuries go by and cease somewhere in the last century.

2. Karl Menninger, *Whatever Became of Sin?* (New York: Bantam Books, 1988). Original edition 1973.

Apparently, no one has felt much shame about anything since roughly 1896, the last date for which I could find a quotation.[3]

"Shame" in the Bible

What a difference when we turn to the Bible! I have a computer program that will run through all the occurrences of a word or combination of words in the New International Version text, the one I use. When I ran a check on the words *shame* or *ashamed,* I found that these words occur 181 times: 149 times in the Old Testament and 32 times in the New Testament. So, obviously, shame is an important biblical idea.

What does shame mean?

The Oxford English Dictionary defines shame as a "painful emotion arising from the consciousness of something dishonoring, ridiculous or indecorous in one's own conduct or circumstances . . . or of being in a situation which offends one's sense of modesty or decency." But the Bible carries the meaning further and deeper than that. The Bible definition contains several important elements.

1. *Disappointment.* The first element is best described by the words "acute disappointment," which means being let down by someone or something in which we have believed. Paul has already used the word this way at least twice earlier in Romans, in Romans 1:16 and 5:5. In Romans 1:16 he says, "I am not ashamed of the gospel." He does not mean merely that he is not embarrassed by the gospel, though that is also true, but that he is sure he will never be let down by it, since "it is the power of God for the salvation of everyone who believes." Similarly, in Romans 5:5, where the NIV even translates the word "shame" as "disappointment," the apostle writes, "And hope does not disappoint us." It doesn't let us down.

Therefore, in terms of our text, we can say that "the one who trusts in Jesus Christ will never be disappointed by him," either in this life or the life to come. Jesus will always be found to have fulfilled his promises to us completely.

2. *Being confounded.* The second category of texts carries the idea of shame a bit further, envisioning a situation in which a person is confounded or left speechless. This is the way Job felt in his suffering. He said, "Even if I am innocent, I cannot lift my head, / for I am full of shame / and drowned in my affliction" (Job 10:15). Similarly, God says of those who have done evil, ". . . you will remember and be ashamed and never again open your mouth because of your humiliation" (Ezek. 16:63).

3. A. E. Housman in *A Shropshire Lad:* "Some lads there are, 'tis shame to say, that only court to thieve" (stanza v). But only twenty-four years earlier, Charles Darwin wrote, "Under a keen sense of shame, there is a strong desire for concealment" (*Emotions,* xiii, p. 321), and a century before that, E. B. Pusey in his *Minor Prophets* declared, "Shame at the evil which sin is, works repentance" (p. 240). These and many other quotations indicate a substantial erosion of the idea of shame over the centuries. All quotations are from the *Oxford English Dictionary.*

In my opinion, one of the most offensive things about sin is that it is never silent. Whatever the offense, the one who has committed it will find an excuse, blaming God or others or the environment or his or her genes. But this will cease in the day of God's judgment. In that day all sin and all the circumstances leading up to it will be laid bare, the shame of the wicked will be acute and profound, and they will be utterly speechless, silent, abashed, humiliated, and disgraced. No one whose sin is not covered by the blood of Jesus Christ will have a single thing to say.

3. *Exposure.* Perhaps the most important element in the biblical idea of shame is exposure, particularly exposure of our sins and sinful natures in God's presence. This idea is found in the earliest pages of the Bible in the story of the fall of Adam and Eve.

We are told in Genesis 2:25, which describes the condition of our first parents before the fall, that "the man and his wife were both naked, and they felt no shame." Rightly so, of course. They had nothing to be ashamed about. They had not sinned. So they stood naked before God and felt no shame, and naked before each other and felt no shame. They had no shame in their own eyes either. But when they sinned, which is what Genesis 3 is about, they did feel shame and tried to hide their nakedness by making clothes of fig leaves. Later, when God came to them in the garden, they tried to hide from him by retreating into the shrubbery.

And how about the day of God's final judgment? Jesus said of the wicked in that day, "They will say to the mountains, 'Fall on us!' and to the hills, 'Cover us!'" (Luke 23:30; cf. Hosea 10:8), so great will be their dread of this ultimate exposure.

4. *Disgrace.* The final element in the biblical idea of shame is disgrace or extreme humiliation. It is what Daniel was speaking of when he wrote of God's judgment, "Multitudes who sleep in the dust of the earth will awake: some to everlasting life, others to shame and everlasting contempt" (Dan. 12:2). There are scores of similar texts.

No Shame Now, But Shame Hereafter

We come now to the main point of this study and our text, and it is that those who do not trust Christ, though they may be shameless now, will be overcome with shame in the day of God's judgment, while those who trust Christ here, though they may be made objects of great ridicule, scorn, and shame by unbelievers, will have no shame hereafter.

The first case is that of the unsaved. *The unsaved may have no sense of shame now, but they will have shame hereafter.*

The unsaved sometimes talk about Christians as if they have faith in faith while the worldly build on facts. But everyone has faith in something, even unbelievers. What do the unsaved have faith in? Well, many trust their good reputations. As long as people think well of them, they suppose they will always be able to get by. Some trust their achievements. Certainly they will count for something, they think. Many more trust in their stocks, bonds, property, or bank accounts. Still others place faith in their family, friends, and acquaintances.

But these "good" things do not always last, even here. Reputations fail, achievements are overshadowed or forgotten, wealth is lost, and friends and acquaintances reject us.

And the situation is even worse when we think in terms of heaven. What is a human reputation to count for there? Nothing at all. In fact, it is worse than nothing. We are sinners, according to the Bible's teaching, and the only reputation we have in heaven is for having rejected God, broken his law, and scorned his warnings. Achievements? The only achievement God will recognize is perfection. Jesus said, "Be perfect, therefore, as your heavenly Father is perfect" (Matt. 5:48). None of us have done that. We are all condemned for our willful and sinful imperfections. Wealth? We know that wealth will not help us in God's day of judgment. We even say, "You can't take it with you." Besides, what could our wealth possibly mean to God, who has created and actually owns all things! If God should regard it at all, it would only be to censure us for coveting, hoarding, or misusing the wealth he has entrusted to us. Finally, even friends will fail us in that day, for at the judgment each will be concerned for his or her own standing before God and will not be thinking of us at all.

In an excellent sermon on this text, Charles Haddon Spurgeon wrote, "It will be a sorry business if we have been trusting in our good temper, our charity, our patriotism, our courage or our honesty, and when we come to die shall be made to feel that these cannot satisfy the claims of divine justice or give us a passport to the skies. How sad to see robes turn to rags, and comeliness into corruption!"[4]

In that day the people who have had no shame here, who are like those described by the prophet Jeremiah—"they have no shame at all; they do not even know how to blush" (Jer. 6:15)—these shall be utterly confounded. They will find that the objects of their hopes are empty. They will have nothing to say. Their shame will be exposed, and they will be disgraced in their own eyes and the eyes of others forever.

No Shame (Here or) Hereafter

The second case is that of Christians. *Those who trust Christ here, though they may be made objects of ridicule, scorn, and shame by unbelievers, will have no shame hereafter.*

If the object of their trust, Jesus Christ, were not who he is, I suppose they might know shame hereafter. If they should get to heaven and discover that

4. Charles Haddon Spurgeon, "Scriptural Salvation" in *Metropolitan Tabernacle Pulpit*, vol. 36 (London and Carlisle, Pa.: The Banner of Truth Trust, 1970), p. 282. Original edition 1891.

Jesus is not the Savior they imagined him to be, they would certainly be confounded. If they should find that his death on the cross was not adequate punishment for their sins or that his power to keep them from falling in this life and even after this life was not sufficient, they might be ashamed. They might be ashamed that they confessed him openly before other men and women or that they induced others to turn from their sin and trust him.

They might be disappointed that they had placed him first in their lives, when there were so many other good things to be enjoyed. If Jesus should not be found to be altogether lovely, the treasure above all treasures, they could conclude that they made a bad bargain. They had only Jesus, but they could have had money and land and good times and the pleasures that sin provides.

But how could that be? Jesus is who the Bible declares him to be. He is the very Son of God, our Savior. He is the lily of the valley and the bright morning star. He is the King of kings and Lord of lords. He is Alpha and Omega, the first and the last. He is the Good Shepherd. He is the Light of the World. He is the Bread of Heaven. He is the living water; anyone who drinks of him will never thirst again. Jesus is the resurrection and the life. He is the way, the truth, and the life. He is the Word of God. He is the Lamb of God. He is the faithful and true witness. He is Immanuel, "God with us."

How can anyone be disappointed with Jesus? How can anyone be confounded or disgraced when his or her hope is in the Lord Jesus Christ alone?

But aren't Christians sinners, too? Yes, they are. But they are sinners whose sin has been forgiven and whose nakedness has been covered by the righteousness of Christ.

I go back to the story of Adam and Eve in Eden. Our first parents were made innocent but lost their innocence through their sin of eating the forbidden fruit. Before that, they were naked and felt no shame. Afterwards they knew shame and proved it by trying to hide their nakedness, even when God came to them in the garden. Although that is the place in the story at which we left off earlier, it is not the end of the story. God came to them in the garden to expose their sin and deal with it, for God cannot ignore sin and all sin must (and will) be exposed in his presence. But, having exposed the sin and judged it, God did not stop there. We are told that God killed animals and "made garments of skin for Adam and his wife and clothed them" (Gen. 3:21).

What a wonderful picture that is! There was no way Adam and Eve could go back to the innocence they had enjoyed before the fall. Lost innocence can never be restored. But, although they could never go back, they could go forward, and the way forward was through the clothes of skin that symbolized the righteousness of Jesus Christ, given to all who put their trust in him.

Shame? Yes. But shame recognized, confessed, and dealt with permanently in God's own way. Sin is real. So is the shame that should and eventually will accompany it. But the atonement is also real. Restitution has been made by

Jesus. "Therefore, there is now no condemnation for those who are in Christ Jesus" (Rom. 8:1).

> Jesus, thy blood and righteousness
> My beauty are, my glorious dress;
> 'Midst flaming worlds, in these arrayed,
> With joy shall I lift up my head.
>
> Bold shall I stand in that great day;
> For who aught to my charge shall lay?
> Fully through thee absolved I am,
> From sin and fear, from guilt and shame.

Whoever You Are

I call your attention to one final point. I have pointed out that in Romans 10:11, Paul is quoting from Isaiah 28:16. But to be exact I need to note that at this point he introduces a slight change in the text, a change made readily evident by comparing his first citation of the text in Romans 9:33 and his second citation in Romans 10:11. The first is closer to the Hebrew (and Septuagint, which Paul is actually quoting) when it begins "the one who." Paul broadens the text in his second use of it by substituting "anyone" for the original rendering.

Why does he do this? Doesn't Paul have a proper respect for the biblical text? Doesn't he want to treat the Old Testament carefully?

It is not that at all. What Paul wants to do (and is doing) is to bring out the full meaning of the passage, showing that "the one who" means anybody, Gentiles as well as Jews, Americans as well as Europeans, rich people as well as poor people, the disadvantaged as well as the mighty, and so on. If you do not come to Christ, you will be confounded and ashamed in the day of God's judgment. But you may nevertheless come to Christ, whoever you may be.

Do not delude yourself into thinking that you can do nothing and that everything will nevertheless be all right for you. Apart from Christ you are in deadly peril. The day will come when the Judge of the earth will summon you to his high court, and you will be required to account for your life and explain your wrongdoing. What will you say in that day when the holy God confronts you? What possible excuses can you give? In Romans 3, Paul describes what will happen. He says that in that day "every mouth [will] be silenced and the whole world held accountable to God" (Rom. 3:19).

I tell you as a minister of the Word of God that the day is coming when you will stand in God's court. You will stand there in either one of two ways. Either you will stand clothed in the righteousness of Jesus Christ as one for whom he died, whose sin and shame have been taken away. Or you will stand in the horror of your own spiritual and moral nakedness, in shame, and you will be condemned for your sin.

The Book of Revelation speaks of such people, echoing the words of Jesus himself, which I quoted earlier. "Then the kings of the earth, the princes, the generals, the rich, the mighty, and every slave and every free man hid in caves and among the rocks of the mountains. They called to the mountains and the rocks, 'Fall on us and hide us from the face of him who sits on the throne and from the wrath of the Lamb! For the great day of their wrath has come, and who can stand?'" (Rev. 6:15–17).

But the rocks will not fall. The rocks obey their Master in heaven, and neither they nor anything else will intervene to cover the exposure of those who have rejected Christ and spurned the gospel of God's grace. Their shame and your shame will be profound if you are not in Jesus Christ.

Do not wait until the day of God's judgment overtakes you, when all acts of repentance and faith will be too late. Flee to Christ now! Trust him while there is still an opportunity to do so.

The Bible says that "now is the time of God's favor, now is the day of salvation" (2 Cor. 6:2).

Jesus said, "All that the Father gives me will come to me, and whoever comes to me I will never drive away" (John 6:37).

149

Salvation for All

Romans 10:12-13

For there is no difference between Jew and Gentile—the same Lord is Lord of all and richly blesses all who call on him, for, "Everyone who calls on the name of the Lord will be saved."

One of the delightful things about studying the Bible is that just when we think we have mastered one of its great doctrines, another complementary doctrine comes along to challenge our still-limited understanding of Bible truth and stretch our vision.

We have a case in point in Romans 10. If you can remember back to the beginning of Romans 9, you will recall that this great middle section of the letter began with the doctrine of election. Paul was asking why it is that not all Jews are being saved and whether the fact that they are not means that God has broken his promises to them, promises recorded in the Old Testament. He answered by teaching the doctrine of election, saying that the promises of God are for God's elect people only and that not all Jews, any more than all Gentiles, are elect. He gave three Old Testament examples: Abraham, who was chosen out of a pagan background; Isaac, who was chosen as the son of the promise rather than his half brother, Ishmael; and Jacob, who was chosen by God rather than his twin brother, Esau.

Then, having made his point about election, the apostle went on to teach about divine reprobation, the doctrine that God deliberately passes by some, who are left to perish in their sins, while saving others. He illustrated this by the case of Pharaoh, concluding, "Therefore God has mercy on whom he wants to have mercy, and he hardens whom he wants to harden" (Rom. 9:18; quoting Exod. 9:16).

Most people who first read about or hear of these two doctrines, election and reprobation, do not like them. They seem wrong, which is why Paul takes so much time to explain and defend them. His defense occupies most of the remainder of Romans 9. But here is the amazing thing. After having explained and defended these doctrines, as only Paul can do, and also presumably after having convinced us of their profound truth, the apostle now seems to be saying something utterly contradictory. He says that anyone who wishes can be saved.

At the end of Romans 9 he had quoted Isaiah 28:16, which says that "the one who trusts in him will never be put to shame." So far so good! That form of the verse, the Old Testament form, is not the least bit inconsistent with the doctrine of election, even in appearance. "The one" means "the elect one." But Paul is not content to leave the verse in that form. Instead of leaving it as it is, he alters the subject of the sentence by substituting the word "anyone" for "the one," thereby universalizing it. And lest we miss what he is doing, he makes his point twice, once by requoting Isaiah 28:16 in verse 11 and then by saying the same thing over again in a quotation from Joel 2:32 in verse 13.

We have already studied the first statement, the alteration of the Old Testament quotation in verse 11: "*Anyone* who trusts in him will never be put to shame." The second quotation says, "*Anyone* who calls on the name of the Lord will be saved" (v. 13).

What a stretching of our minds!

On the one hand, "God has mercy on whom he wants to have mercy, and he hardens whom he wants to harden" (Rom. 9:18). That teaches the doctrines of election and reprobation.

But, on the other hand, "Everyone who calls on the name of the Lord will be saved." That is the universal gospel offer.

A Welcome Doctrine

I do not mean to suggest by this introduction to Romans 10:12–13 that there can ever be a contradiction in the Bible, of course, for there cannot. The Bible is God's book, and God does not contradict himself, alter his truth, or lie. In this case, the explanation is that although everyone is free to come to Jesus Christ in salvation and may indeed come if he or she will, the only ones who *do* come are those whom God has chosen and regenerated, because it is only their rebirth that enables them to trust Christ.

But that is not the thrust of these verses. Verses 12 and 13 are not in Romans 10 to give us a theological explanation of election in reference to the parallel truth, which is the gospel offer. They are there to extend the gospel offer, which is clear from what follows, since in the very next section Paul appeals for messengers to take the offer of salvation for all who will trust Jesus Christ as Savior throughout the world.

What a welcome teaching this is—"Everyone who calls on the name of the Lord will be saved." If it were not for this teaching, we might think that the doctrine of election necessarily excludes us or that the gospel is for people other than ourselves. But here we are told that it is for you and me, all of us, if we will trust Jesus. It does not make any difference who you are or what you may or may not have done. You may be rich or poor, educated or uneducated, advantaged or disadvantaged. You may be passive or highly motivated. You may be religious or not religious at all. You may be moral, or you may be very immoral. You may have lived in sin a long time. You may have committed adultery or stolen money. You may even have murdered someone. It does not matter. The text says, "Everyone who calls on the name of the Lord will be saved."

"There Is No Difference"

But perhaps you are still thinking that there is some difference that might exclude you. If so, you need to see that any possible differences are excluded on two counts. Paul expresses them as two reasons why "everyone who calls on the name of the Lord will be saved."[1]

1. *There is no difference between Jew and Gentile.* This means that there is no meaningful difference between any two peoples, of course. Because, if ever there could have been a difference, it would have been the difference between the Jewish people and all others. God had chosen the Jewish people to be a nation through which he would send the Messiah. And not only that, he had given them the law and made special promises to them. Paul knew these advantages and appreciated them, because he had listed them in the ninth chapter of Romans: "Theirs is the adoption as sons; theirs the divine glory, the covenants, the receiving of the law, the temple worship and the promises. Theirs are the patriarchs, and from them is traced the human ancestry of Christ, who is God over all, forever praised!" (Rom. 9:3–5).

If ever any people had the advantage of position and promise, it was the Jewish people. Yet "there is no difference between Jew and Gentile" so far

---

1. The two reasons are not as distinct in the New International Version (v. 12) as they are in the Greek text, which repeats the word *for*, meaning "because." The Greek says, translating literally, "Everyone who trusts in him will never be put to shame, because there is no difference between Jews and Gentile and *because* the same Lord is Lord of all and richly blesses all who call on him." These two "fors" are then followed by another "for" or "because," which introduces the concluding quotation from Joel 2:32: "*Because* everyone who calls on the name of the Lord will be saved."

as the gospel is concerned. Why? Because all are sinners—Paul has made this point in the first two and a half chapters of the letter—and because no sinner, however favored, is able to achieve a right relationship to God by his or her abilities. God has done this himself for sinners through the death of Jesus Christ, and this death is for all who will trust him. In other words, Jesus did not die only for Jews. He died for Gentiles, too. He died to save all who will call on him for salvation.

2. *The same Lord is Lord of all people.* If there were different gods, we might expect that the various peoples of the world who worship these different gods would be treated differently by them. But because there is only one God, it is reasonable to expect that in matters of salvation this one God will treat all his creatures on an equal basis. And he has. We might say that this statement, "the same Lord is Lord of all," is summarized by what Paul wrote to his young protégé Timothy: "There is one God and one mediator between God and men, the man Christ Jesus" (1 Tim. 2:5).

There is a disagreement among commentators whether "Lord" in this verse means Jesus or God the Father, since it could mean either. Charles Hodge presents both sides. The majority of commentators refer the word to Jesus because it is used of him in verse 9, "If you confess with your mouth, 'Jesus is Lord,' and believe in your heart that God raised him from the dead, you will be saved," and because the word is so often used of Jesus in the New Testament. On the other hand, says Hodge, in the next verse "Lord" refers to the Father, since the verse is a quotation from Joel, who uses "Lord" that way. Again, the idea is nearly parallel to Romans 3:29–30, where Paul wrote, "Is God the God of Jews only? Is he not the God of Gentiles too? Yes, of Gentiles too, since there is only one God, who will justify the circumcised by faith and the uncircumcised through that same faith."

There is probably little difference in meaning between these two possibilities, since Jesus is fully God, and God the Father is seen only in Jesus (John 14:9). Nevertheless, as Hodge says, "the analogy of Scripture . . . as well as the context" is in favor of referring it to Christ.[2]

In my judgment, the perfect illustration of these points, embracing the combined truths of "one God and one mediator" is the statement the apostle Peter made when he was brought to the house of the Roman centurion Cornelius, as told in Acts 10. Cornelius was a devout man to whom God had given a vision of an angel who told him to send to Joppa to bring back a man named Simon Peter who would bring him a message from God. Cornelius sent two of his servants and a soldier, and while they were on their way, God gave a corresponding vision to Peter to prepare him for their visit. Peter "saw

2. Charles Hodge, *A Commentary on Romans* (Edinburgh and Carlisle, Pa.: The Banner of Truth Trust, 1972), p. 345. Original edition 1935. Leon Morris has a similar conclusion (see *The Epistle to the Romans* [Grand Rapids: Wm. B. Eerdmans, and Leicester, England: Inter-Varsity Press, 1988], p. 387).

heaven opened and something like a large sheet being let down to earth by its four corners" (v. 11). In it were many animals that were unclean according to Jewish dietary laws. Then Peter heard a voice saying, "Get up, Peter. Kill and eat" (v. 13).

Peter replied as any devout Jew would, "Surely not, Lord! I have never eaten anything impure or unclean" (v. 14).

The voice said, "Do not call anything impure that God has made clean" (v. 15). This happened three times for emphasis.

About this time the men sent by Cornelius arrived, and Peter understood that the vision was in reference to their request. Normally a Jew of Peter's standing would not have entered the house of an "unclean" Gentile. But, being prepared by God, Peter went with them and arrived the following day to find a large gathering of people whom Cornelius had called together. "We are all here in the presence of God to listen to everything the Lord has commanded you to tell us," said Cornelius (v. 33).

Peter began, "I now realize how true it is that God does not show favoritism but accepts men from every nation who fear him and do what is right. [This is] the message God sent to the people of Israel, telling the good news of peace through Jesus Christ, who is Lord of all" (vv. 34–36). These are the exact same points Paul makes in Romans 10:12: that there is no difference between peoples and that the same Lord, in this case, clearly Jesus, is Lord of all. Peter then went on to explain the gospel, beginning with the appearance of John the Baptist to announce Jesus and continuing with the details of Jesus' life, death, and resurrection. Then he said, "All the prophets testify about him that *everyone* who believes in him receives forgiveness of sins through his name" (v. 43, emphasis added). Again, this is the exact point Paul makes in Romans 10:13.

As a result of Peter's explanation, Cornelius and the others believed on Jesus as their Savior, the Holy Spirit came on them in a verifiable way, and they were baptized. The results were proof to Peter, as well as to those Jews who came with him, that, as Paul says, "everyone who calls on the name of the Lord will be saved."

Calling on Christ

Those words are from Joel 2:32, of course, as I pointed out earlier. What is so significant about them is that they conclude that great parenthesis in Joel's prophecy that looks ahead to the pouring out of God's Holy Spirit at Pentecost and to the proclamation of the gospel to all peoples that followed the Spirit's coming. As a matter of fact, Peter quoted these exact words at Pentecost, saying,

This is what was spoken by the prophet Joel:
"In the last days, God says,
    I will pour out my Spirit on all people.

> Your sons and daughters will prophesy,
>> your young men will see visions,
>> your old men will dream dreams.
> Even on my servants, both men and women,
>> I will pour out my Spirit in those days,
>> and they will prophesy.
> I will show wonders in the heavens above
>> and signs on the earth below,
>> blood and fire and billows of smoke.
> The sun will be turned to darkness
>> and the moon to blood
>> before the coming of the great and glorious day
>>> of the Lord.
> *And everyone who calls*
>> *on the name of the Lord will be saved.*"

Acts 2:16–21, emphasis added; cf. Joel 2:28–32

What does it mean to "call on the name of the Lord"? What did Joel mean, and what were Peter and Paul getting at by quoting him?

The words "call on" are simple words that embrace a great deal of truth. Sometimes they are used of *worship*. For example, at the beginning of the Bible, we are told of a time when "men began to call on the name of the LORD" (Gen. 4:26). That is, they acknowledged or worshiped him.

Again, there are times when the words seem to refer explicitly to *prayer*. A clear example is the contest between Elijah and the priests of Baal in which Elijah issued a challenge: "You call on the name of your god, and I will call on the name of the LORD. The god who answers by fire—he is God" (1 Kings 18:24).

A third use of the words is for *praise*. This is a frequent use in the Psalms, as in Psalm 116:12–13:

> How can I repay the LORD
>> for all his goodness to me?
> I will lift up the cup of salvation
>> and call on the name of the LORD.

That is, "I will praise him."

In the New Testament the words often refer to *believing on* God or *trusting* God or Jesus. That is a fourth meaning. For example, in Acts 9 we are told of Paul's attempts to arrest all who "call on [Jesus'] name" (Acts 9:14, 21), that is, the followers of Jesus. The same meaning is present in 1 Corinthians 1:2, where Paul addresses the letter to "all those everywhere who call on the name of our Lord Jesus Christ—their Lord and ours," that is, to those who believe on and are followers of Jesus.

This is what you and I are to do. If you are not a Christian, you have been ignoring the true God. You have not been praying to him, and you are certainly not trusting him. Now you are challenged to reverse that entirely. You are to worship, pray to, and praise God—as he is revealed in Jesus Christ. Above all, you are to believe on Jesus himself and trust in what he has accomplished on the cross by dying for your sin.

The Bible's promise is that you will be saved if you will do this. That is, you will be saved from your sin and from the wrath of God that hangs over you because of it.

I do not care what your condition up to this point may have been. You may have made a shipwreck of your life and be sinking in the waves like Peter was when he started to walk over the Sea of Galilee to Jesus but then took his eyes off Jesus and looked at the churning sea about him. Peter was about to perish, but he called to Jesus, "Lord, save me!" and we are told that "immediately Jesus reached out his hand and caught him" and so rescued Peter (Matt. 14:28–31).

You may have been fighting Jesus like Paul had been trying to do earlier through his attempts to destroy Christianity. But when God stopped him on the way to Damascus, Paul called on the Lord Jesus Christ and was saved.

Perhaps you have been utterly ignorant of the gospel, like the Philippian jailor. But you have been alerted to your need, and you are calling out now as he did, "What must I do to be saved?" The answer is, "Believe in the Lord Jesus, and you will be saved" (Acts 16:30–31). You need to respond, like the jailor did, and commit yourself to Christ.

But don't put it off. You need to call on Jesus today.

Call on Jesus Now

In the summer of 1991, I was in northern Michigan to speak to student leaders of the InterVarsity Christian Fellowship. On the final day of my week there, when I did not have to speak, I drove to Sault Ste. Marie, where the impressive Soo Locks link Lake Superior with Lake Huron. Not far from the locks is a retired Great Lakes freighter, the *Valley Camp,* now turned into a maritime museum, and inside the *Valley Camp* are tragic remains of one of the greatest naval disasters of modern times, two badly mangled lifeboats from the *S.S. Edmund Fitzgerald.* This is her story.

The *Edmund Fitzgerald* was a Great Lakes freighter nearly a thousand feet long, almost as long as the Empire State Building in New York City is high. She had sailed to Duluth, Minnesota, to pick up iron ore, and now, during the first week of November 1975, she was making her way across Lake Superior to the Soo Locks to bring the ore to the industrial cities of the South. The first day out, a terrible storm moved down out of Canada to the lakes. That is common enough on the Great Lakes in the winter months, but this was a particularly bad storm, with waves reaching twenty-five or thirty feet in height.

The captain of a freighter that was following the *Edmund Fitzgerald,* from whom we have sworn testimony to what happened, was worried.

Somewhere along the way, the *Edmund Fitzgerald* began to take on water and developed an increasingly strong list to starboard. She sank low in the water. The captain of the other ship kept in radio and radar contact, but the *Fitzgerald's* captain kept reporting that everything was all right.

The last communication from the doomed freighter was this tragic message: "We are holding our own."

Minutes later the ship headed into a wave that washed over her low-lying decks, and she never came up. In less than ten seconds the *Edmund Fitzgerald* sank, with the loss of all twenty-seven people aboard. The captain of the ship that was following reported that she simply disappeared from his radar screen. One minute she was there. The next she was gone forever, the prop that was still turning driving her directly downward until she broke into pieces on the lake bottom.

If you have not called on the Lord Jesus Christ for salvation, your state is like that of the stricken freighter. You are headed into judgment—and who can say how close you may be to the ultimate disaster?

Do not say, "I am holding my own."

Only a fool would say that when he or she is sinking, and you are sinking. Instead, call on the name of the Lord Jesus Christ for salvation. Do so confidently, because, as our text says, "Everyone who calls on the name of the Lord will be saved."

150

A Plea for Missions

Romans 10:14–15

How, then, can they call on the one they have not believed in? And how can they believe in the one of whom they have not heard? And how can they hear without someone preaching to them? And how can they preach unless they are sent? . . .

When young William Carey, the acknowledged founder of the modern missionary movement, first applied to his church board to be sent to India, he received a classic reply. "Young man," said one of the older church leaders, "when God chooses to save the heathen of India, he will do so without your help." Fortunately, Carey knew better than that. He knew that when God determines that something is to happen he also determines the means to make it happen, and, in this case, the first step to the evangelization of India was the pioneer work of William Carey. Carey persevered, and the rest, as they say, is history.

No Conversions in a Vacuum

I think of that story as I come to Romans 10:14–15, mainly because of the placing of these verses in Romans. The verses themselves are a stirring plea for missions, one of the most important in the Bible. But much of their force comes from their setting in Paul's argument.

Think of the preceding verse: "Everyone who calls on the name of the Lord will be saved" (v. 13). That is a wonderful statement of the universal application of the gospel. It is for everybody. Anyone who calls on Jesus Christ as Savior will be saved. But how can people do that unless they know about him? And how can they know about Jesus unless someone goes to them to teach them about him? Those are precisely the questions Paul has in mind as he begins this new section, asking: "How, then, can they call on the one they have not believed in? And how can they believe in the one of whom they have not heard? And how can they hear without someone preaching to them? And how can they preach unless they are sent?"

The answer is obvious: A person cannot hear the gospel and believe on Christ unless someone takes the gospel to him or her.

However, not only are these verses related to what has gone before, to verse 13. They are also related to what follows, to verses 16–21. For Paul, in this entire section (Romans 9–11), is dealing with Jewish unbelief, and he is going to show in the latter half of chapter 10 that the unbelief of Israel is not God's fault, since God had sent messengers to the Jewish people. Paul himself was one. He had preached the gospel, and he had done so clearly. If the Jews did not believe, it was not because they could not, since they had both heard and understood the message.

While we are at it, we should note that verses 14 and 15 are also related to the letter as a whole. One commentator on Romans, E. F. Scott, remarks, "This passage might seem to be only a digression, but it is central to the whole Epistle. More plainly than anywhere else Paul here discloses his purpose in writing as he does to the Roman church. He is coming to Rome in order to make it his starting-point for a new mission, and he needs the co-operation of the Christians in the capital."[1]

Says John Murray, "The main point is that the saving relation to Christ involved in calling upon his name is not something that can occur in a vacuum; it occurs only in a context created by proclamation of the gospel on the part of those commissioned to proclaim it."[2]

In these verses Paul proves this point by giving us a series of linked statements, leading from an individual's calling on Christ in faith, backward through the mandatory intervening steps of belief in Christ, hearing Christ and preaching about Christ, to a preacher's being sent to proclaim the Lord Jesus Christ to those who need to hear him. In other words, the text is a classic statement of the need for Christian preaching and for the expanding worldwide missionary enterprise.

---

1. Cited by Leon Morris, *The Epistle to the Romans* (Grand Rapids: Wm. B. Eerdmans, and Leicester, England: Inter-Varsity Press, 1988), p. 389.

2. John Murray, *The Epistle to the Romans,* 2 vols. in 1 (Grand Rapids: Wm. B. Eerdmans, 1968), vol. 2, p. 58.

The First Necessity: Calling on Christ

The first thing that is necessary if a person is to be saved, as verse 13 has already said, is that he or she "call on" Christ. This verse alone proves the point, which I have already stressed many times in these studies, that saving faith, a faith that saves, is more than mere intellectual assent to certain truths about Jesus.

This is because the statement in verse 13 flatly distinguishes between "believing" (the Greek word is "faith") in Christ and "calling on" Christ for salvation: "How, then, can they *call on* the one they have not *believed in*?" Many people know about Christ. A significant number of these also probably believe that he is the Son of God and the world's Savior, as the Bible teaches. But they have never called on him in personal trust, and so they are not Christians. They are not saved. Saving faith, as I have said many times, has three elements: (1) intellectual content or knowledge, (2) personal assent to or agreement with that content, and (3) trust or commitment. The Latin words are: *notitia, assensus,* and *fiducia.* In this verse "calling on" Christ means the last of those three elements.

Let me make this personal.

It is not enough for you to sit under the preaching of the Word of God to be a Christian, important as that is. It is not enough for you to know theology or even to be a student of the Bible. I commend all those things to you, but they alone do not make you a Christian. To be a Christian you must call on the Lord Jesus Christ personally, saying, "Lord Jesus Christ, I confess that I am a sinner. I cannot save myself, and I call on you to save me. Help me. Save me from my sin."

If you will do that and really mean it, Jesus will save you. In fact, he already has, because it is his work in you that leads to that confession. But I repeat: Intellectual belief is not enough; you must commit yourself to Jesus as your own personal Lord and Savior to be saved.

The Second Necessity: Belief in Christ

The second step in Paul's linked series of statements is that a person must believe in Christ in order to call upon him. Isn't that interesting? I have just said that mere intellectual belief is not enough. There must be personal trust or commitment to him as Lord and Savior. Yet this does not mean that the other part, intellectual belief or content, is unimportant. On the contrary, it is essential. For how can you call upon one you do not know? How can you ask Jesus to save you from your sin unless you understand and believe that he is the Savior?

Intellectual understanding without commitment is not true faith, but neither is commitment without intellectual understanding. If you must believe on Jesus in order to call on him, then your mind must be engaged in knowing who he is and what he has done for you.

The late Ray Stedman, who was a good friend and former pastor of the Peninsula Bible Church in California, knew Harry A. Ironside when he was pastor of the Moody Church in Chicago. He remembered Ironside describing a visit to Chicago by the flamboyant evangelist Gypsy Smith. Gypsy Smith got his name because he really did have a gypsy background, and he told many fascinating stories about growing up in a gypsy camp. On this occasion the message was made up almost entirely of these stories. At the end of the meeting, Gypsy Smith gave an altar call, and hundreds of people surged forward. Ironside used to say that he wondered what they were coming forward for. "Perhaps," he said, "they wanted to become gypsies."[3]

The point was a good one, since one of the things that sets Christianity off from other world religions is that it deals with objective truth and with the facts of history.

Unless the facts are proclaimed, the message is not Christianity.

Unless the facts are understood and believed, the faith that follows is not true faith, regardless of its intensity.

The Third Necessity: Hearing Christ

The third of Paul's statements is that in order to believe in Christ a person must hear Christ. I repeat the last two words, "hear Christ," because that is what the verse literally says. The New International Version is mistaken when it adds the word "of" so the text reads, "believe in the one *of whom* they have not heard." What it actually says is: "believe in the one *whom* they have not heard."[4]

The point is that it is Christ himself who speaks to the individual, and that it is hearing him that leads first to belief and then to calling on his name in salvation.

This should not surprise us, of course, because this is exactly what Jesus taught. John 10 is a clear example. In that chapter, Jesus was speaking about himself as "the good shepherd," and he was explaining how his sheep know him and respond to his voice:

> The man who enters by the gate is the shepherd of the sheep. The watchman opens the gate for him, and the sheep listen to his voice. He calls his own sheep by name and leads them out. When he has brought out all his own, he goes on ahead of them, and his sheep follow him because they know his voice. But they will never follow a stranger; in fact, they will run away from him because they do not recognize a stranger's voice. . . . I am the good shepherd; I know my sheep and my sheep know me—just as the Father knows me and I know

3. Ray C. Stedman, *From Guilt to Glory,* vol. 2, *Reveling in God's Salvation* (Portland: Multnomah Press, 1978), pp. 50, 51.

4. See Morris, *The Epistle to the Romans,* p. 390. The pronoun *is* in the genitive case, but this is the normal construction after the word *hear* when it refers to hearing persons. It means "whom" and not "about whom." The New American Standard Bible translates correctly.

the Father—and I lay down my life for the sheep. I have other sheep that are not of this sheep pen. I must bring them also. They too will listen to my voice, and there shall be one flock and one shepherd.

John 10:2–5, 14–16

There is a danger that some will use this emphasis on hearing Christ himself as an excuse for subjectivity. This happens when people say, "God told me so-and-so," and then follow it with something entirely unrelated to Scripture. Or when they say, "The Holy Spirit said . . ." and then add some personal desire or utterly unbiblical whim. We all know Christians who have used statements like this to justify behavior that is blatantly contrary to the Word of God.

But our passage provides two entirely adequate safeguards, even while stressing the need for us to "hear" Christ personally. The first safeguard is the step that has gone immediately before this, where Paul stressed the need for intellectual content or belief. This has to do with Bible truths and with the facts of Bible history. There is nothing subjective here. On the contrary, this is soundly objective. By linking the facts of the message to hearing Christ, Paul is saying that although Jesus speaks personally and individually to the one he is calling to faith, he does not do so apart from the truths of Scripture. He speaks to us not by leading us away from Scripture, but by leading us to Scripture and by speaking through Scripture. The subjective word is based on the objective revelation.

The second safeguard is found in the step that follows, namely, the "preaching" of God's Word by God's messengers. This means that the "word" of Christ is not whatever you might choose to make it. Rather it is the content of Christian doctrine as taught by qualified and appointed preachers. "The point," says Morris, "is that Christ is present in the preachers; to hear them is to hear him."[5]

Jesus taught this, too, of course. When he sent seventy-two disciples ahead of him to preach in his name and prepare people for his coming, he encouraged them, saying, "He who listens to you listens to me," and "he who rejects you rejects me" (Luke 10:16). It is the same today. When I (or any other minister) stands up to teach the Bible, if I do it rightly, it is not *my* word you are hearing. It is the Word of God, and the voice you hear in your heart is the voice of Christ. So, if you do not like what I am saying, do not get angry with me. I am only the postman. My job is just to deliver the letters. And when you respond, do not think that you are responding to me. You are responding to Jesus, who is calling you through the appointed channel of sound preaching.

5. Ibid.

The Fourth Necessity: Preaching Christ

In speaking of this passage's second safeguard against subjectivity in hearing the voice of Christ, I have already moved on to the fourth step in Paul's series of linked statements, which are in the last analysis a great plea for missions. It is that for a person to hear Christ, someone must proclaim Christ to him or her. This is a strong statement for the necessity of preaching.

In his excellent commentary, Leon Morris emphasizes that "hearing" is a reflection of first-century life, when few people could read and communication was largely through the spoken word. He suggests that this does not exclude other valid forms of communication today, print media, for instance.[6] That is true enough, of course. The gospel can be taught by qualified and appointed writers—Leon Morris is one—as well as by qualified preachers. But that aside, there is still something special and necessary about verbalized communication, particularly preaching, since it is through such preaching that God most often chooses to make the gospel known.

This was true of apostolic preaching. John Calvin wrote, "By this very statement . . . he [Paul] has made it clear that the apostolic ministry . . . by which the message of eternal life is brought to us, is valued equally with the Word."[7]

It is true of preaching today, too, though in a lesser sense. Today's preaching is not valued equally with the Word, but it is through preaching that the Word is most regularly made known and blessed by God to the saving of men and women. J. I. Packer is right on this point when he says, "A true sermon is an act of God, and not a mere performance by man. In real preaching the speaker is the servant of the Word and God speaks and works by the Word through his servant's lips. . . . The sermon . . . is God's ordained means of speaking and working. The divine commission to ministers is a commission to preach and teach, and the accompanying promise is that, if they preach the word faithfully, they will not preach in vain."[8]

The Fifth Necessity: Sending Christ's Messengers

This brings us to the fifth and last step in Paul's linked statements about the way people are brought to call on Jesus Christ for salvation. It is his bottom line. He has indicated that people must believe in Christ before they can call on him. They must hear Christ before they can believe. There must be preachers of the Word if people are to hear Christ. Now he concludes that for Christ to be proclaimed to such people, preachers must be sent to them.

By whom? By God, of course. This is God's work; no one can take it lightly upon himself. It is why Jesus said, "Ask the Lord of the harvest, therefore, to

---

6. Ibid.

7. John Calvin, *The Epistles of Paul the Apostle to the Romans and to the Thessalonians,* trans. Ross MacKenzie (Grand Rapids: Wm. B. Eerdmans, 1973), p. 231.

8. J. I. Packer, *Beyond the Battle for the Bible* (Westchester, Ill.: Cornerstone Books, 1980), pp. 84, 85.

send out workers into his harvest field" (Matt. 9:38). If God does not send the messenger, the message will not be blessed by him, and those who hear will not be saved. As Leon Morris says, "A self-appointed herald is a contradiction in terms."[9]

But it is also true that messengers must be sent by the churches, just as Paul and Barnabas were sent on their missionary journeys by the Gentile church at Antioch (Acts 13:1–3). In fact, one of the objectives Paul had in writing Romans was to enlist the support of the Roman church in his plan to take the gospel beyond Rome to Spain and other places to the west (Rom. 15:23–29). The application for us is that if people today in unreached areas of the world are to hear the gospel and have the opportunity to believe on Jesus Christ, those who know Christ must pool their resources to send God's messengers to them. We must do it. A strong missions program is mandatory for an obedient church.

Four Applications

This has been a five-point study of Paul's text (one point more than was common even for Charles Haddon Spurgeon, the great "four-point" preacher). Five points is a lot to remember. Nevertheless, here are four more quick points in conclusion. Each is a verse of Scripture.

1. *Matthew 9:37–38. [Jesus said,] "The harvest is plentiful but the workers are few. Ask the Lord of the harvest, therefore, to send out workers into his harvest field."* These are our Lord's own words about praying for Christian missionaries. It is a recognition that God must call and send them. But I ask, "When God calls, will we be prepared to send them, too? Will we give our money to help make the gospel of salvation widely known?"

Let me share some facts with you. According to a recent report by the Foreign Mission Board of the Southern Baptist Convention, the world's population is about 5.3 billion people. Roughly one-third (1.7 billion) are people who would call themselves "Christian." Among the other two-thirds, one-third (1.3 billion) have never heard the gospel, and the other two-thirds (2.3 billion) have heard it but are unconverted. The first group, which includes most of the western nations, accounts for 62% of the world's wealth. It spends 97% of that on itself. The remaining 3% is divided between secular charities, which get 1% of its resources, and Christian causes of all kinds, which get 2%.

Of that 2% allotted to Christian causes, 99.9% is spent in our own countries to provide for our own churches and Christian institutions. *Of the remaining .1%, spent for Christian work abroad, .09% is spent on those who have already heard the gospel but are unconverted, and only .01% on the 1.3 billion persons who have never even heard the name of Jesus Christ.*

9. Morris, *The Epistle to the Romans*, p. 390.

I am sure I do not have to emphasize that this represents a tremendous challenge for Christians who are serious about wanting to take the gospel to the whole world in obedience to the Great Commission.

2. *Second Timothy 4:2.* *"Preach the Word; be prepared in season and out of season; correct, rebuke and encourage—with great patience and careful instruction."* If you are a preacher or Bible teacher, even in a small class, do not be distracted from your primary calling by other useful but secondary things. Many things are important, but nothing is as essential as preaching and teaching God's Word. Be faithful to that task.

3. *Matthew 28:18–20.* *[Jesus said,] "All authority in heaven and on earth has been given to me. Therefore go and make disciples of all nations, baptizing them in the name of the Father and of the Son and of the Holy Spirit, and teaching them to obey everything I have commanded you. . . ."* These are the words of the Great Commission in its best-known form, and they are for all Christians. So I add this reminder: Although not all Christians are called to be preachers or teachers, all are nevertheless called to be agents of Christ's commission. Ask God to give you opportunities to speak to others about Jesus and his death for sinners, and then be sure you actually do it.

4. *Second Corinthians 6:2b.* *"I tell you, now is the time of God's favor, now is the day of salvation."* This is for you, if you have not yet responded to the gospel by believing in and calling on Christ. There are billions of people who have never heard the gospel, but you are not one of them. You have heard it. I have been making it clear to you. What you need to do right now is to turn from your sin and call on Christ.

151

God's Beautiful People

Romans 10:15

. . . As it is written, "How beautiful are the feet of those who bring good news!"

The kind of work I do does not bring me into contact with the world's beautiful people very often. But I have been with them just enough to know that there really are "beautiful people," and my friends in California, who have far more opportunity to mingle with celebrities than I do, confirm it.

Some years ago a friend of mine from Philadelphia was hosting the then well-known singing star and actor, Pat Boone, and his wife. He called our home to ask if he could bring them by, since they were going to be filming something that evening and needed a place to rest for a few hours in the late afternoon. They were with us from about three in the afternoon until six. Mr. and Mrs. Boone really were beautiful. They had flawless features, perfect skin, immaculate grooming, and were meticulously dressed. They were obviously made (or remade) for the camera. And not only that. They smelled good. They seemed to be unlike other people. They were so perfect that I could only relate them to the poem about Richard Cory, who "glittered when he walked."

We are surrounded by a cult of beauty in our day, of course. Ever since the fall of the human race, people have valued beauty too much, usually neglecting the more important inner beauty of the soul. But at no time in history has physical beauty been at a higher premium than today. Movies and television are largely responsible, since they have created an entertainment- and beauty-directed age.

How different when we turn to our text! Though speaking of beauty, it is clearly speaking of a nonphysical kind of beauty when it says, "How beautiful are the feet of those who bring good news!" (Rom. 10:15).

Inner Beauty and Outer Beauty

A good place to start in trying to understand this text is by admitting that it is not a very attractive statement for most of us, and the reason is clear. We usually look at the outward appearance of things, including people, and we make our judgments on that basis. Moreover, we do not think of feet as beautiful. Regardless of what follows, when the text says, "How beautiful are the feet . . ." the idea seems quaint at best and probably even a bit repulsive. It becomes even more so when we remember that the feet of an ancient traveler would be dusty and smelly from the unsurfaced and unsanitary roads.

How strange that we think like this. We should know better. One of the things our grandparents used to say to us was: "Beauty is as beauty does." But instead of thinking about actions, we think of beauty in terms of a perfect figure or a flawless face.

About thirty-five years ago, when I was in high school, I met another "beautiful person," Eddie Fisher, one of the singing idols of the fifties. It happened behind the scenes at Radio City Music Hall in New York City. I suppose it was because of that meeting that I have always had more than a usual interest in Eddie Fisher's life and career. He was married to Debbie Reynolds, dumped her to marry Elizabeth Taylor, and then was dumped by Taylor when she had her affair with Richard Burton on the set of the blockbuster movie *Cleopatra*. That was the way Eddie Fisher's life went, and it was rather sad. Yet I was pleased to read just a year or so ago that in an interview with a reporter, Eddie Fisher summed up his experience of America's cult of beauty by saying rather wisely, "I have learned that a pretty face is just a pretty face." It took him a lifetime to learn it.

What does the Bible say about beauty? You know the answer. In ancient Israel the people favored King Saul because of his large stature and good looks, but God rejected Saul and chose David, explaining, "The LORD does not look at the things man looks at. Man looks at the outward appearance, but the LORD looks at the heart" (1 Sam. 16:7b).

Similarly, the apostle Peter wrote to Christian women, saying, "Your beauty should not come from outward adornment, such as braided hair and the wearing of gold jewelry and fine clothes. Instead, it should be that of your inner self, the unfading beauty of a gentle and quiet spirit, which is of great worth in God's sight. For this is the way the holy women of the past who put their hope in God used to make themselves beautiful . . ." (1 Peter 3:3–5).

The Beauty of God and God's Works

I do not mean to say by this that beauty is undesirable in itself. The Bible says that God is beautiful. In fact, several chapters before the one in Isaiah from which Paul gets the quotation he uses in Romans 10:15, Isaiah tells the people, "Your eyes will see the king in his beauty" (Isa. 33:17), meaning that they would see God.

This was David's great desire, too:

> One thing I ask of the LORD,
>   this is what I seek:
> that I may dwell in the house of the LORD
>   all the days of my life,
> to gaze on the beauty of the Lord
>   and to seek him in his temple.
>
> Psalm 27:4

God's creation is also beautiful, and so are the laws that govern it. In fact, when we conform to those laws, we can end up producing something beautiful ourselves.

There is an illustration of this truth in something Richard Buckminster Fuller (1895–1983), the world-renowned architect and engineer, once said. A student at the Massachusetts Institute of Technology asked Fuller whether he took aesthetic factors into account when he was tackling a technical problem. "No," he replied. "When I am working on a problem, I never think about beauty. I think only of how to solve the problem. But when I have finished, if the solution is not beautiful, I know it is wrong."[1] I doubt Fuller was thinking of God when he said that, but he was nevertheless unwittingly testifying from his own area of expertise that God, God's laws, and God's creation really are beautiful.

Each of the wives of the patriarchs is said to have been beautiful: Sarah (Gen. 12:11, 14), Rebekah (Gen. 24:16; 26:7), and Rachel (Gen. 29:17).

Job's daughters were beautiful (Job 42:15).

In proportion to its length, the book of the Bible that uses the word *beautiful* more than any other is Song of Songs. There the husband rightly expresses delight in the beauty of his bride and the bride in the beauty of her husband. This teaches that there is a place for beauty in our lives and a proper appreciation of beauty among Christians.

1. Clifton Fadiman, ed. *The Little, Brown Book of Anecdotes* (Boston and Toronto: Little, Brown, 1985), p. 226.

Yet that is not the whole story. It is true that Sarah, Rebekah, and Rachel were beautiful, but their beauty was a danger that led to the compromising behavior of at least two of their husbands, Abraham and Isaac. Bathsheba was beautiful, but her beauty contributed to the fall of King David. In the Book of Daniel, Nebuchadnezzar is represented by a beautiful tree, but it was cut down (Dan. 4). Proverbs warns that "beauty is fleeting" (Prov. 31:30), and James says that the beauty of the rich and influential person will inevitably "fade away" (James 1:11).

Most significant of all, we remember Isaiah's description of the earthly appearance of Jesus Christ who, he wrote, "had no beauty or majesty to attract us to him, / nothing in his appearance that we should desire him" (Isa. 53:2). If even Jesus Christ was not physically attractive, we should know that beauty is at best a matter of indifference and at times even a snare.

Beauty Is as Beauty Does

All that prepares us to turn back to our text in Romans. For when we are able to get the idea of mere physical beauty out of our heads, at least for a while, we can begin to understand what the text is saying. The first thing we notice is that the kind of beauty we find here is not descriptive beauty but functional beauty. In other words, it is the kind of definition our grandparents were speaking of when they said, "Beauty is as beauty does." They meant that true beauty is measured by gracious acts or by the gracious and faithful performance of one's duties.

The former Surgeon General of the United States, C. Everett Koop, has published a book of memoirs that contains an illustration of what I am talking about. At one point in his book, Koop expresses appreciation for the outstanding nurses he worked with during his days as Surgeon-in-Chief of the Children's Hospital in Philadelphia. Working with a nurse who knows the way you think and can anticipate your moves and needs is one of the most satisfying things about surgery, according to Koop's testimony. He felt this deeply. So he tells how each Christmas he would hang a long sign over the door to the operating room that said, "Through these portals pass the most beautiful girls in the world." A few years later, when the Intensive Care Unit had developed to a outstanding degree, he did the same thing there. Now there were two signs at Christmas that read: "Through these portals pass the most beautiful girls in the world."

Koop wrote, "The nurses knew I wasn't talking about superficial physical attraction; they knew that I appreciated the beauty of all the things they did to make possible our success in the operating room [and ICU]."[2]

Romans 10:15 is also a functional definition, which means that the beauty it describes is that of someone who is *doing* something. And that is the second

---

2. C. Everett Koop, *Koop: The Memoirs of America's Family Doctor* (New York: Random House, 1991), p. 103.

thing to notice: what the beautiful person is doing is bringing the Good News of the gospel to other people.

I said a few paragraphs back that the quotation is taken from Isaiah—Isaiah 52:7 to be exact, though there is a very similar text in Nahum 1:15. In Isaiah's setting, the passage is speaking of consolation for Israel during the years of Babylonian captivity, picturing a runner appearing on the hills to announce the fall of the people's enemies and the triumph of God's king. The image is the same as that of the well-known story of the Greek runner who made his way from the battlefields of Marathon to Athens to announce the Greek victory over the Persians in 490 B.C. The route was generally uphill for a total distance of more than twenty-six miles, and as soon as he arrived in the city and had gasped the word "Victory!" the runner fell dead from his efforts. It was in honor of this welcome messenger that the marathon race was run in ancient Greece and is still run today in many parts of the world.

But, like many Bible texts, there is even more to it than this. For as even the rabbis recognized, the messenger is the herald of the Messiah, which is appropriate since the next chapter (the continuation of the announcement) introduces us to the Suffering Servant of Isaiah 53. The salvation of the people from earthly enemies was undoubtedly good news, but a message of deliverance from sin is greater still. John Murray says, "As the prophecy found its climactic fulfillment in the Messiah himself, so it continues to be exemplified in the messengers whom he has appointed to be his ambassadors (cf. 2 Cor. 5:20)."[3]

Paul is right on target when he says that the messengers of the cross are beautiful. They are beautiful because they are bearers of the gospel, which is the most beautiful message in the world.

The Elephantiasis Convert

Donald Grey Barnhouse, one of my predecessors at Tenth Presbyterian Church in Philadelphia, heard a story from a missionary in western Africa that is a moving illustration of what I have been writing. It was about a man who had the disease known as elephantiasis. In this disease the skin becomes thick and hard, and the limbs of the victim become enormously enlarged, much like the leg of an elephant, hence the name elephantiasis. The leg from the knee down to the foot can become as large as twelve to fifteen inches in diameter, and of course it is quite restricting and often painful. I have known at least one American who has this affliction.

But here is the story as Barnhouse tells it:

> This poor victim of elephantiasis became a radiant Christian and could do noth-
> ing other than tell people of the grace of God which he had shown in sending

3. John Murray, *The Epistle to the Romans,* 2 vols. in 1 (Grand Rapids: Wm. B. Eerdmans, 1968), vol. 2, p. 59.

his Son Jesus Christ to die for them. He lived in an African village and determined that every soul in the village should hear the good news of salvation. It was extremely difficult for him to walk with the monstrous legs which bore him about, but he thought nothing of the pain and toiled on from hut to hut to tell those who dwelt there about the Savior who had come into his life. Each evening he would return to his own hut where he was maintained by the kindness of his relatives. At the end of several months he was able to tell the missionary that he had visited every hut in the village and that he was now starting to take the gospel message to a village that was about two miles away.

Each morning he would start out painfully, walk the two miles to that village, go from hut to hut with the gospel, and return the two miles before sundown to his own hut. Finally, there came the day when he had visited every hut in the neighboring village. His work being done in these two villages, he remained at home for some weeks but began to be more and more restless.

He spoke to the pastor and to the missionary, who was a medical doctor, about a village that lay ten or twelve miles through the jungle, and asked if the gospel were being taken to that village. As a boy, before he had been afflicted, he had traveled the jungle path to that village, and he remembered that it was a large village and that there were many people there, and he knew that they needed the good tidings of the Savior. He was advised not to think of going to that village, but day after day the burden grew upon him. One day his family came to the missionary and said that the man had disappeared before dawn and they had heard him go but supposed that it was but for a moment. He did not return, and the family was concerned about him.

Afterwards, the full story became known. He had started down the path toward the distant village. Step after weary step he dragged his leathery legs and gigantic feet along the path that led to his goal. The people of the village later told how he had come to them when it was already noon; his feet were further swollen, bruised and bleeding. He had been forced to stop and rest again and again, and it was already past mid-day when he came. They offered him food, but before he would eat he began to tell the people about Jesus. Up and down the village he went, even to the very last hut, telling them that the God of all creation was Love and that he had sent his only Son to die that their sins might be removed. He told how the Lord Jesus had been raised from the dead and had come into his heart, bringing such joy and peace.

There was no shelter for him in that village; and even though the sun was low he started on his way down the jungle path toward home. The darkness of Africa is a terrible darkness, and the night can bring forth many creatures from the jungle. The sun went down and the poor man dragged himself along the path in the darkness guided by some insight which kept him from going astray. He told his pastor later that his fear of the night and the animals which might come upon him was more than balanced by the joy that he had in his heart as he realized that he had told a whole village about the Lord Jesus Christ.

Toward midnight the missionary doctor was awakened by a noise on his front porch. He listened, but all seemed still. Somehow he could not go back to sleep, and he went to the door with a light to see what had caused the noise. He recognized at once that the poor neighbor had returned to the village from his long trip, and had come with his wounded and bleeding leg-stumps to the door of the dispensary. The missionary called his helpers and they lifted the man, almost unconscious, and put him on one of the beds in the little hospital. The doctor said that he had seldom seen such a frightful sight as he looked upon those bleeding feet which had come back from such an errand of love and mercy. Unashamedly the doctor told how he had bent over those feet to minister to them, and as he cleaned and dressed them, he told how his own tears had fallen with the ointment upon them. The doctor ended the story by saying, "In all my life I do not know when my heart was more drawn out to another Christian believer. All I could think of was the verse in the Word of God, 'How beautiful are the feet of them that bring glad tidings, that publish peace.'"

Here was a man who had been sent by God to tell the story of what Christ had done for him, and although he had to do it at the cost of such personal agony, yet he had not flinched but had gone through to the end to tell needy men the good news of salvation for their souls.[4]

Beautiful Bilney

That is a very moving story, of course, as I said when I introduced it. But it is not unusual. For centuries, ever since the days of Jesus Christ, God's beautiful people have strategized and sacrificed and gone out of their way to bring the gospel to those they know need it.

Do you know how the gospel came to Hugh Latimer (1400–1555), that great bishop who became one of the brightest lights of the Protestant Reformation in England? Hugh Latimer was a "beautiful" man, strikingly good-looking and brilliant. But he did not know Christ, and he was using his learning to oppose the teachings of the Reformers, especially that of Melanchthon, Martin Luther's co-worker and friend. Latimer was at Cambridge at this time, and there was at Cambridge a little monk whose name was Thomas Bilney. No one paid much attention to Bilney. But Bilney had discovered the gospel, and he wanted the great Hugh Latimer to come to Christ, too. "What a tremendous influence he would have, if only he would discover the gospel of God's grace in Christ," Bilney thought.

So he hit on a plan. One day after Latimer had been preaching, Bilney caught his arm as he was coming out of the church and asked if he would hear his confession. That was a prescribed duty of a priest. So Hugh Latimer listened to Bilney, and the little monk who had found Christ "confessed" the gospel, sharing how it had changed his life. Latimer later said that he was converted by Bilney's gospel "confession." As for Latimer, he became a great reformer in England and is best known for his encouragement of Nicholas Ridley as they were being led to the stake in Oxford at the height of the English persecutions in 1555: "Be of good comfort, Master Ridley, and play

4. Donald Grey Barnhouse, "Epistle to the Romans," part 62, "Romans 10:14–19" (Philadelphia: The Bible Study Hour, 1956), pp. 7–10. The story is told in a shorter but more polished version in Donald Grey Barnhouse, *Let Me Illustrate: Stories, Anecdotes, Illustrations* (Westwood, N.J.: Fleming H. Revell, 1967), pp. 344–346.

the man; we shall this day light such a candle by God's grace in England as (I trust) shall never be put out."

Bilney was not a beautiful person as we generally think of beauty. But he was the bearer of the gospel to Hugh Latimer, and that means that he was beautiful in the sight of God, just as are all those are who obeying the Lord Jesus Christ in carrying out the Great Commission.

May I suggest that you start thinking of beauty the way God does. What you think is beautiful now is going to be a thing of the past in just a few short years. Those you think beautiful now will no longer be beautiful in physical terms. But the beauty of the bearers of the gospel will last forever. What is more, they will go on getting more and more beautiful, as they use not only this life but eternity to praise the Lord Jesus Christ more fully.

Beauty really is as beauty does.

I invite you to value others not by their outward appearance, but by their service to Jesus Christ and the gospel. And I invite you to become one of God's beautiful people yourself. Our text tells you how.

152

The Sad Reality of Unbelief

Romans 10:16

But not all the Israelites accepted the good news. For Isaiah says, "Lord, who has believed our message?"

Several thousand years ago, there was a man who was chosen to follow a great leader. The leader possessed outstanding religious and moral qualities, and the man I am talking about lived with him and learned from him for three years. He was part of a small group who were privileged to do so. In time this man became disillusioned with his teacher and eventually betrayed him to his enemies when he had an opportunity to profit personally from the betrayal. But then he became disillusioned with himself for what he had done. Disillusionment led to depression, depression to desperation, and desperation to despair. In the end he killed himself by hanging.

That man's name was Judas. His teacher was Jesus Christ.

We All Have "Failures"

In my library at Tenth Presbyterian Church are several dozen books that deal with evangelism, and I have noticed that they rarely speak of failures.

1253

They are filled with stories about people who almost always come to faith as a result of the evangelist's testimony. I understand that, of course. Books rightly try to be positive. Americans are success-oriented. Few people like to discuss their failures, but there are failures for all of us, even as there were for Jesus. (At least they are failures from a human point of view, though not from God's perspective.) My point is that we need to understand "failures."

Paul did. God gave Paul great success in his missionary work, enabling him to plant churches throughout much of the ancient world, particularly in Asia Minor and Greece. But Paul was too honest not to describe his failures, too. One of the places he does so is in Romans 10:16, our text.

I remind you that the apostle has been describing the chain by which the gospel comes to an individual, enabling the person to call on Jesus Christ and be saved. It has five parts: (1) the sending of the messenger, (2) the preaching of the gospel by the messenger, (3) hearing the word of Christ as he speaks through the messenger, (4) the listener's believing the message, and (5) the listener's calling on Jesus Christ for salvation. That had happened many times in Paul's missionary journeys. But the apostle is nevertheless aware that it is possible to fulfill the two human parts of that chain—the sending and the preaching—and still have people fail to believe the good news or call on Jesus.

Isn't that the sad reality in this text?

"But not all the Israelites accepted the good news. For Isaiah says, 'Lord, who has believed our message?'" (Rom. 10:16).

It is as if Paul is saying, "I have preached the gospel in many places and to the best of my ability. God has blessed my efforts. But I want you to know—I am the first to admit it—that not all of my work has been successful. Not everyone to whom I have spoken has believed in Jesus Christ and become a Christian."

As the verse stands in most of our Bibles, Paul seems to be speaking about his efforts among Jewish people, and it is true that he is thinking in Romans 9–11 primarily about Jewish unbelief. That is why the New International Version has added the words "the Israelites" to this verse. But they are not in the Greek text, which means that what Paul actually wrote was: "But not *all* accepted the good news." "All" includes everybody. So what he is acknowledging is that there will always be what we would call failures in our witnessing, regardless of who we may be, where we go, or to whom we may be speaking.

And let me say something else. If Paul is talking about Jews primarily, which the NIV thinks he is doing, then the words "not all" must be what Leon Morris calls "a masterly understatement."[1] Not all? "Hardly any" would be more like it. What is more, those who rejected his message did not merely reject the message. They also rejected Paul, persecuting him so that he was driven from place to place and was often beaten and imprisoned.

---

1. Leon Morris, *The Epistle to the Romans* (Grand Rapids: Wm. B. Eerdmans, and Leicester, England: Inter-Varsity Press, 1988), p. 391.

When we read the account of Paul's missionary journeys in Acts and his personal description of his sufferings, particularly in the Corinthian letters, we expect that Paul might have become embittered. But the opposite was the case. Instead of making him bitter, the unbelief of his countrymen gave him such great sorrow that he was able to cry out at the beginning of this section of the letter, "I speak the truth in Christ—I am not lying, my conscience confirms it in the Holy Spirit—I have great sorrow and unceasing anguish in my heart. For I could wish that I myself were cursed and cut off from Christ for the sake of my brothers, those of my own race, the people of Israel" (Rom. 9:1–4a).

Unbelief is painful to those who know Jesus Christ, which is why I have titled this chapter "The Sad Reality of Unbelief." Unbelief is sad. But it is still a reality, which we must acknowledge if we are not to become discouraged and utterly ineffective in our witnessing.

A Significant Prophecy

"'Not discouraged,' did you say? How does that follow? I would think that acknowledging failure in advance would be the most discouraging thing one could possibly do," a person might be thinking. Although that might seem to be the case, it does not actually work that way. What really happens will become clear in this study.

The first thing we want to notice is that "failure" from a human point of view is something that all God's servants have experienced. Paul reminds us of this (as well as reminding himself) by quoting from Isaiah 53:1, that well-known opening verse of the equally well-known chapter on the Suffering Servant: "Who has believed our message and to whom has the arm of the LORD been revealed?" It is in the form of a question, but in spite of this, Isaiah seems to be saying that the people refused to believe him. He preached, but his message was rejected, just as were the words of Jeremiah and all the other great prophets.

Yet there is more than that to Paul's choice of Isaiah's testimony to the reality of unbelief. I say this because, if we are only trying to think of Old Testament texts to prove that messengers of the gospel have been rejected throughout history, we can probably find better texts than this ourselves. How about, for example, Elijah's complaint from the desert beyond Beersheba? "The Israelites have rejected your covenant, broken down your altars, and put your prophets to death with the sword. I am the only one left, and now they are trying to kill me too" (1 Kings 19:14b). Or how about the many passages in Jeremiah in which the weeping prophet complains that the people would not hear his message? If we were seeking an Old Testament text to show only that others have also had their message rejected, we could find stronger passages than the one Paul actually uses.

But, of course, Paul knew what he was doing. There are at least three reasons why he quotes this verse and not another.

1. *It comes very close to the verse he has just cited about the beauty of those who bring good news.* That verse was taken from Isaiah 52:7, and it was positive and encouraging, which was how I treated it in the last study. But Paul was aware that the prophet who spoke such encouraging words about the reception of the messenger who bore good news to Zion also acknowledged just eight verses later that the ultimate message of good news about the work of the Messiah was not and would not be believed. In other words, the verse is a healthy dose of realism.

2. *It is the introductory verse to the most important chapter in the Old Testament about the Messiah's suffering.* This means there is a link between the unbelief of the hearers and the content or nature of the message. It works two ways. On the one hand, it tells us that the people disbelieved (or would disbelieve) the message. On the other hand, it tells us that the nature of the message was the very reason for their unbelief. It was not the kind of message they wanted.

So what's new? Today, if we preach a message suited to our listeners' wants or felt needs, we can gain a wide hearing. If we tell them that Jesus will give them treasure on earth rather than treasure in heaven, people will line up at the trough. If we tell them that Jesus will make them feel good rather than make them holy, people will clamor for the fix. If we tell them that Jesus died to cure them of their low self-esteem rather than their sins, they will pay for our glass cathedral. Much of the modern church-growth movement is built on exactly such reasoning. And it works! It works well. It builds mega-churches, and it makes the bearers of the "mega-gospel" rich—because it is what sinful people want to hear.

But it is not *the* gospel. The true gospel is a gospel of a crucified Savior, suffering in our place for our sins. That gospel is repugnant to the natural, unsaved man, and because it is, it will be rejected by him unless God first does a work of grace to turn him from his sin and error to the truth.

3. *It is a prophecy about the preaching of the gospel by Christ's messengers.* As I ponder this text, I find myself thinking that it is probably for this reason more than any other that Paul quotes it. In other words, Paul is regarding it as a prophecy of his own days and of precisely what he was experiencing. Isaiah had said that not all would believe the message of Christ's sufferings when it was preached, and that was exactly what was happening. This must have been an important encouragement for Paul, because he has already cited Isaiah to make the same point earlier, writing in Romans 9, "Though the number of the Israelites be like the sand by the sea, / only the remnant will be saved" (v. 27, quoting Isa. 10:22). He is returning to the same theme now.

Unbelief is not a welcome or desired response to our teaching, but it helps to know that this is what God has said will happen in many instances.

Four Kinds of Soil

This was Jesus' teaching, too. In Matthew's Gospel the very first parable Jesus tells is on this theme. It was about a farmer who went out to sow seed:

> As he was scattering the seed, some fell along the path, and the birds came and ate it up. Some fell on rocky places, where it did not have much soil. It sprang up quickly, because the soil was shallow. But when the sun came up, the plants were scorched, and they withered because they had no root. Other seed fell among thorns, which grew up and choked the plants. Still other seed fell on good soil, where it produced a crop—a hundred, sixty or thirty times what was sown.

> Matthew 13:4–8

The disciples did not understand this parable at first, so Jesus explained it to them. The seed that is snatched away by the birds represents the case of those who do not understand the message and from whom Satan comes and snatches away even what they have. The scorched seed represents those who seem to receive the gospel but who are soon turned away by trouble or persecutions. The thorns represent the cares of this world and wealth, for which some barter away their eternal souls. Only a fourth part of the seed lands on good soil, sinks down, grows, and produces a crop.

This is what Jesus had experienced. He was rejected by many. Early in his ministry, most of his supposed disciples turned away. At the end even the Twelve forsook him.

It is also what the early preachers of the gospel experienced, which is why Jesus gave them the story—to prepare them (and us) for what was coming.

Let me be very practical at this point and say that what Isaiah experienced, what Jesus and the early disciples and Paul all experienced, is what you will experience, too—if you are serious about spreading the gospel. You, too, will come up against the sad reality of unbelief.

Think of the kinds of people you will meet who will not believe.

1. *Those who are hard.* I mean by this those who have been hardened by sin, are addicted to vice, and over whom the devil has a very strong control. God is able to break those bands, of course. But it will often be the case that sin remains strong, and the devil snatches away the message even before it is fully understood or is allowed to do its work.

A few years ago I heard two Christian women talking, and one asked the other, "Why is America in such a declining moral state today?"

Her friend answered, "It is because the people love sin."

I suppose that there are other answers that could be given. But it seemed to me when I heard it that it was a perfectly adequate explanation and possibly the best that could be given. People love sin. And they are hardened by it. The problem with American culture is not that people have not heard the gospel. They have heard it. Most have also understood it. The problem is that they love sin rather than God. They do not want the gospel, because they are aware that to receive it they would have to turn from the vices they dearly love.

If you are in that category, the category of the willful and willing sinner, I grieve for you. Your danger is frightful. Here is a true story from the writings of Harry Ironside. There was a young English woman who had been brought up in a Christian home and had often been pressed to come to Christ. But she chose the way of the world instead. In spite of the pain it caused her father and mother, she chose to run with a wild crowd and repeatedly rejected the appeals made to her. One day she was taken with a serious illness. The doctor did all he was able to do in those days. It did not help, and she was expected to die in a short time.

One night this woman awoke out of a fitful sleep with a frightened expression in her eyes, and she asked excitedly, "Mother, what is Ezekiel 7:8 and 9?"

"What do you mean, dear?" her mother asked.

The young woman answered that she had had a dream in which someone seemed to be telling her to read Ezekiel 7:8 and 9. Her mother did not know what those verses were, but she reached for a Bible and began to read them: "I am about to pour out my wrath on you and spend my anger against you; I will judge you according to your conduct and repay you for all your detestable practices. I will not look on you with pity or spare you; I will repay you in accordance with your conduct and the detestable practices among you. Then you will know that it is I the LORD who strikes the blow."

The poor girl sank back onto her pillow with a look of horror on her face, and a few hours later she passed into eternity.[2]

I suppose there are some people who might be able to take that story lightly, especially those who are being hardened by their sin. And I confess that for me it is secondhand. I did not know this family. Still I remind you that even if the story is not true, though I have no reason to doubt it, the verses I just read are in the Bible. It is God himself who has spoken them, and sin will be judged. Sin hardens hearts, and rejected grace only makes judgment more terrible.

2. *Those who are shallow.* The second kind of person who will not believe the gospel is the shallow person, represented by the rocky soil. There are many today. We are surrounded by shallow people, and we are often shallow ourselves—shallow in our thinking, shallow in our passions, shallow in our aspirations, shallow in our deeds. I think T. S. Eliot hit it on the head when he described our empty culture in "The Hollow Men."

> We are the stuffed men
> We are the hollow men

2. H. A. Ironside, *Illustrations of Bible Truth* (Chicago: Moody Press, 1945), pp. 31, 32.

> Leaning together
> Headpiece filled with straw. Alas![3]

Alas, indeed! And that was in 1925, before television! I wonder what Eliot would say now, when television has swept over our culture like a plague, catching everyone in its ever more mindless and ever more embracing web. In Eliot's day, between the two World Wars, people were *refusing* to think. Today, millions no longer know *how* to think. If the message is not mindless, flashy, and entertaining, they will not come to hear it. They cannot even think about their souls.

3. *Those who are choked by wealth.* In Mark 10:17–22, we are told about another of Jesus' "failures." A young man came to him who was spiritually earnest, seeking, and apparently quite moral. Moreover, he came asking the right question: "Good teacher, what must I do to inherit eternal life?" Most of us would have given him a quick presentation of the gospel. But Jesus, who was interested in genuine discipleship rather than in mere numbers of followers, began to probe his understanding of who God is and what God requires of us. Although he reminded the young man of the law, reviewing it with him, the young man imagined he had kept it from his youth. Then Jesus got to the matter that was choking out the new life of the gospel. "One thing you lack," Jesus said. "Go, sell everything you have and give to the poor, and you will have treasure in heaven. Then come, follow me" (v. 21).

The story ends with: "At this the man's face fell. He went away sad, because he had great wealth" (v. 22).

And Jesus was sad, too, because Jesus had loved him. Jesus told the disciples, "How hard it is for the rich to enter the kingdom of God!" (v. 23).

I know many people who are being kept from genuine discipleship because of wealth, and it is not always a case of their having it. In some cases they are merely trying to get it. Their minds are on the high salaries, the company bonuses, and on what those benefits will allow them to do and buy. And for this they perish! Like Esau, they are selling their souls for a bowl of stew. How different are Jesus' teachings! Jesus said, "If anyone would come after me, he must deny himself and take up his cross and follow me. . . . What good will it be for a man if he gains the whole world, yet forfeits his soul?" (Matt. 16:24, 26).

Not Many Perhaps, But Some

But I cannot leave you on this note. The reason is that we have not yet exhausted Paul's statement nor the answer to Isaiah's provocative question.

"Not all . . . accepted the good news," Paul writes. No, but some did and some will. In the very next chapter, after he has explored the subject of

---

3. T. S. Eliot, *The Complete Poems and Plays, 1909–1950* (New York: Harcourt, Brace and Company, 1952), p. 56.

Israel's unbelief a bit further, Paul will insist that *he* at least had believed the gospel and that God has always had a remnant of those who have refused to bow to Baal.

"Lord, who has believed our message?" asks Isaiah. Not many, true. But "not many" is not "no one." Though sparse of results at times, preaching has always been blessed by God to save some. It is not because of anything in them, of course, but because of the power of God in the gospel, which is what we will be talking about in the next study.

In the meantime, let's get on with the task. You are not responsible for the results. God alone is responsible for that. But you *are* responsible for obeying the Lord Jesus Christ in taking the message to others. And if you cannot explain the gospel well—bring them to someone who can. Bring them to where the Bible is taught and Christian theology is explained without compromise. And pray for them. The Bible says, "The prayer of a righteous man [or woman] is powerful and effective" (James 5:16b).

If you are one of the unbelieving ones—unbelieving because of your hard, shallow, or choked heart—know that you do not have to remain in your unbelief, however hard or shallow or entangled you may be. Turn from your sin and call on Jesus Christ now.

Someone has said, "On the great clock of time there is only one word: NOW." It is a throwaway statement, but it is true. *Now* is the time to pass from the sad reality of unbelief to the joyous reality of faith in the Lord Jesus Christ as your Savior.

153

The Bible's Power to Change Lives

Romans 10:17

Consequently, faith comes from hearing the message, and the message is heard through the word of Christ.

During the decade I spent as chairman of the International Council on Biblical Inerrancy (1978–1988), I listened to many sermons on the Bible, as well as preaching quite a few myself. But the best I heard was by Dr. W. A. Criswell, pastor of the First Baptist Church of Dallas. He gave it at ICBI's first "Summit Meeting" in Chicago in the fall of 1978.

At the time, Criswell had been pastor of the First Baptist Church of Dallas for over thirty-five years. He had been in the ministry for more than fifty years, and he had been chosen to address this amazing gathering of 350 pastors, scholars, and leaders of the major para-church organizations on the subject "What Happens When I Preach the Bible as Literally True?" His answer was a *tour de force,* as he explained what had happened to himself, what had happened to his church, and what he believes happens to God when God's Word is thus used and honored.

About a year after Criswell had gone to the Dallas church, he announced to his already well-established congregation that he was going to preach through

1261

the Bible, beginning with Genesis and going right on to the last benedictory prayer in Revelation. "You never heard such lugubrious prognostications," he reported. People said it would kill the church. "Nobody will come to hear someone preach about Habakkuk, Haggai, and Nahum. Most people don't even know who those biblical books or characters are," they said. Criswell did it all the same, however. Much to everyone's astonishment, the problem that developed was not the demise of the church, but where to put all the people who were pressing in weekly to hear such biblical preaching. There were thousands of conversions, and today the First Baptist Church of Dallas is one of the largest, most effective, and most biblically sound churches in the entire country.[1]

Scoffers abound. Critics multiply. But the lesson of history is the unique power of the Bible to change people's lives and build churches.

Hearing What?

This is what Paul is getting at in the verse to which we have come in our study of Romans 10, though there is some question among commentators about how it should be fitted in. Is it a digression? It could be, since Paul has spoken about unbelief in verse 16 and is going to deal with the unbelief of Israel explicitly in verses 18-21. Is it a throwback to what he has already said in verses 13-15? In my judgment, as well as in the judgment of a number of other commentators, the verse is best understood as a succinct summary of what has gone before.[2]

I say "succinct" because the sentence as Paul wrote it has no verbs. The New International Version has added two verbs to make the passage flow better for English readers, "comes" and "is heard." But what Paul actually wrote was: "So, then, faith by hearing, and hearing through the word of Christ." The very tone sounds like a summary of verse 14: "How, then, can they call on the one they have not believed in? And how can they believe in the one of whom they have not heard? And how can they hear without someone preaching to them?"

In our text the idea of "hearing" occurs two times: "faith by *hearing*" and "*heard* through the word of Christ." It makes us ask: "Hearing what?" There are two answers to that question.

1. *The gospel.* The first and most obvious answer is the message of the gospel, that is, the biblical message of salvation from sin through the work of Jesus Christ, as that message is preached by Christ's ambassadors. This is what Paul has been writing about in verses 14 and 15, showing that: (1) for

---

1. W. A. Criswell, "What Happens When I Preach the Bible as Literally True," in Earl D. Radmacher, ed., *Can We Trust the Bible?* (Wheaton, Ill.: Tyndale House, 1979), pp. 91–108.

2. Morris calls it a "summarizing conclusion" to the argument so far, quoting Hendrickson (Leon Morris, *The Epistle to the Romans* [Grand Rapids: Wm. B. Eerdmans, and Leicester, England: Inter-Varsity Press, 1988], p. 391).

people to call on Christ for salvation, they must first believe in Christ; (2) for them to believe in Christ, they must first hear about Christ (or, "hear him," as I said in an earlier study); (3) for them to hear Christ, someone must preach Christ to them; and (4) for someone to preach Christ to them, the messenger must first be sent. Everything Paul says in this section has to do with preaching the gospel. In fact, he will be thinking along these lines in the next verses, too, for his point there will be that his countrymen have had the gospel preached to them and are therefore without excuse in regard to their unbelief.

If we look at the matter in a broader context, we can even say that this is what the entire letter to the Romans is about. It is the gospel. It tells us that when we were hopelessly lost in sin and under the threat of God's judgment, God acted to save us through the work of Christ. He sent Jesus to die for us, taking the punishment of our sins to himself, so that the love of God might go out to save the sinner. What is more, the salvation thus achieved is not only a salvation from the punishment due us for our sins. It is also salvation from the power of sin in our lives and eventually even from the presence of sin. It ends with glorification (Rom. 8:29–30).

This gospel is a glorious message, one the world very much needs to hear. It is why Paul calls it "the good news" in verse 16.

2. *Christ himself.* The large majority of commentators take the phrase "through the word of Christ" as an objective genitive, meaning that the word is the word about Christ or that he is the content of the message.[3] That is a true statement, of course. It is what I have just been saying about the gospel. However, I am convinced that here, rather than being an objective genitive, the phrase "through the word of Christ" is actually a subjective genitive, which means that Jesus is understood to be speaking the gospel message or "word."

I have two reasons for believing this. First, this is the way the word of Christ was referred to in verse 14. In the earlier discussion of that verse I pointed out that the proper translation is not "the one *of whom* they have not heard," as the New International Version has it, but "the one *whom* they have not heard." The point I made there is that Jesus speaks through his messengers, so that those who hear the messenger to the extent of believing on Christ and calling on Christ for salvation have actually heard Jesus as he has spoken his truth to them and called them to faith. Jesus said that this is what he would do (see John 10:3–5, 16). Since this is what "hearing Christ" meant in verse 14, it is right to see that earlier meaning in this verse too.

3. See Morris, *The Epistle to the Romans*, p. 392. Morris sees the phrase as referring either to "the word about Christ" or "the word from Christ," but in each case as the preached gospel, not a word from Christ in and through the preaching. Similarly, Ray Stedman says, "Your faith is aroused by the message. But if it is to be saving faith, it must be a word about Christ" (Ray C. Stedman, *From Guilt to Glory*, vol. 2, *Reveling in God's Salvation* [Portland: Multnomah Press, 1978], p. 56).

Second, if verse 17 only means "the word about Christ," the two parts of the verse are redundant, because this is what the "message" of the first part of the verse means. It would reduce to: "Faith comes from hearing the gospel, and the gospel that is heard is the gospel."

On the other hand, if "hearing Christ" is the meaning, an important truth is added. To paraphrase this a bit, the proper meaning of verse 17 would be: "Faith comes from hearing the gospel preached, and the reason faith comes from hearing the gospel preached is that Jesus himself, the object of the gospel as well as its subject, speaks through the messenger to call the listening one to faith."[4]

Word and Spirit

This is a very important point, as I said. In fact, it was the chief discovery the Reformers made so far as the nature and function of the written Word of God is concerned. The way they talked about it was to stress the mutual working together of the Word of God (the Bible), on the one hand, and the Holy Spirit of God (the Spirit of Christ), on the other.

Martin Luther, John Calvin, and others had a very strong faith in the work of the Holy Spirit to convert, teach, and lead people. They knew verses like John 3:8 ("The wind blows wherever it pleases. You hear its sound, but you cannot tell where it comes from or where it is going. So it is with everyone born of the Spirit"); 1 John 5:6 (". . . And it is the Spirit who testifies, because the Spirit is the truth"); and 1 Corinthians 2:12–14 ("We have not received the spirit of the world but the Spirit who is from God, that we may understand what God has freely given us. This is what we speak, not in words taught us by human wisdom but in words taught by the Spirit, expressing spiritual truths in spiritual words. The man without the Spirit does not accept the things that come from the Spirit of God, for they are foolishness to him, and he cannot understand them, because they are spiritually discerned").

But when the Reformers thought about these verses and others that stress the work of the Holy Spirit, they also remembered verses that taught the importance of the Bible in knowing the mind and will of God. They understood rightly that God speaks only through the written Word.

Without the Holy Spirit, the Bible is a dead book. That is why the man "without the Spirit" cannot understand it. But, on the other hand, without the Word as an objective guide from God, claims to a special leading by the Holy Spirit run to excess, error, or mere foolishness. Knowing the importance of both, the Reformers preached the Word in the power of the Holy Spirit, and the transformation of Europe and the western world was the result.

---

4. The distinction could also be preserved by reversing the ideas, so the text would say, "Faith comes from hearing Christ, and the place where Christ is heard is in the gospel proclamation." But it seems more natural to follow the interpretation I have given.

Let me put the Reformers' doctrine back into the terminology of our text by saying: *When the Bible is preached, Christ speaks.* Isn't that what the verse says? And when Jesus speaks, his voice brings life out of death and his sheep awake from their spiritually lost condition and follow him.

In the sermon I referred to earlier, W. A. Criswell said, "No word spoken for God ever falls to the ground. Somehow, some way, in areas of life that we don't understand and don't know, God blesses it in his good purpose, in his electing choice, and in his heavenly time. That is the basis on which I have tried to build, with God's help, the congregation you call the First Baptist Church of Dallas."[5]

Let me say it again. The reason the Bible is powerful is that it is not the mere words of men, however insightful they may be, or even (do not misunderstand me here) the unique and inerrant Word of God, as important as that is. It is because God speaks to people through the Bible by the Spirit of Christ, and because that Word is life-giving and life-transforming.

"The Book That Set My People Free"

Maybe you are thinking that the Bible only works like that in America or in southern Bible Belt areas of the country, like Texas. If so, let me take you half a world away and tell you the story of Rochunga Pudaite, an Indian national from the people known as the Hmars. He tells his story in a volume titled *The Book That Set My People Free.*[6]

The Hmars were at one time one of the most feared tribes in India. They had descended from Mongols who had come from central China, crossed the lower Himalayas, and settled in northeast India. They were headhunters, and when they fought they took heads that they hung over the doors of their bamboo huts. The British, who ruled India in those days, called them "barbaric tribesmen" and said they were almost like animals. When the British tried to enter the Hmar territory, the Hmars fought back. On one occasion they took five hundred heads in just one raid on a tea plantation. The soldiers pursued them. A few Hmars were killed, but most escaped back into the jungle, which is where they were when a Welsh missionary by the name of Watkin Roberts brought the Bible to their tribe.

Roberts was a chemist who had been converted during one of the great Welsh revivals of the last century, and when he read an account of the pursuit of the Hmar headhunters by British soldiers, he felt that God wanted him to take the Bible to them.

When Roberts arrived at the border of the Hmar territory in India, the British authorities would not let him proceed, declaring the area much too dangerous. So Roberts did the next best thing. He found some Lushais from

---

5. Criswell, "What Happens When I Preach the Bible as Literally True," p. 107.

6. Rochunga Pudaite with James Hefley, *The Book That Set My People Free* (Wheaton, Ill.: Tyndale House, 1982).

a tribe adjoining the Hmars and began to translate the Bible into their related language. When he received a small gift for the work from a lady in England, he printed a few hundred copies of the Gospel of John and sent a copy to each of the tribal villages.

One of these copies came to the village in which Pudaite's father was living. A Lushai tribesman happened to be there and read the book to him. Pudaite's father could not understand what it meant to be "born again," and the neighbor could not explain it to him. He suggested that the chief invite the translator to the village.

When Roberts asked the British agent for permission to go, he was told not to enter the Hmar territory. "When I go in there, I take along a hundred soldiers for protection, and I can't spare a single soldier for you," said the agent. Roberts showed him the tribal chief's invitation but was told it was deceptive. "They only want to chop your head off," he said. Roberts went anyway and was able to explain the gospel to the people. After a week of teaching, the chief and four Hmar men announced that they wanted to make peace with the God of the Bible by believing on Jesus Christ. One of the four men was Pudaite's father.

This man, whose name was Chawanga, became one of the first Hmar preachers. He traveled all over the territory, teaching the Bible, leading people to Christ, and founding churches. These early Hmar preachers founded churches in almost every village. Many people came to Christ. They were tired of their fighting, drinking, and fear. When they became Christians they began living different lives. They began to work harder and built schools for their children.

Strangely enough, the British branded Watkin Roberts a troublemaker for his part in this tribal transformation and ordered him to leave. As a result, he left only a part of the Bible in the Lushai language.

The Hmars chose Rochunga Pudaite to do the Hmar translation. Although none of them had ever been out of their own area of northeast India, they sent Pudaite to a mission school and then to a college in India. The missionary worked with others to see that Pudaite was able to continue his education in Scotland and then in America. Pudaite did the translation and later became the new head of the mission Watkin Roberts had founded, the Indo-Burma Pioneer Mission, which later changed its name to the Partnership Mission.

Today, reports Pudaite:

> The Hmars . . . have become one of the most advanced ethnic groups in all India. At least ninety-five percent are Christians, worshiping in over 200 churches. Except for Mr. [Roberts], the only missionary they have had is the Bible.
>
> Hmar population is now up to about 125,000. Eighty-five percent can read and write, a phenomenal percentage in India [and a higher percentage than the citizens of Philadelphia]. They have eighty-eight church-sponsored elementary schools, seven junior highs, and four high schools—one with an enrollment

of about a thousand. They even have a good hospital, staffed by Hmar doctors and nurses.

One of our Hmars holds the rank of ambassador in the Indian Embassy in Yugoslavia. Another is the Indian *charge d'affaires* in Saudi Arabia. Another is the highest ranking civil servant in India. Another is the administrator of a large state. Every year the government gives tests to select the outstanding young men for government service. Only about twenty are selected in the whole country. For several years one or two Hmars have been in each group of winners. And there is only one Hmar for every 7,000 people in India.[7]

The Hmars have also begun taking the gospel to other tribes, starting hundreds of churches in other territories. They have taken food to tribes that were starving. As for Rochunga Pudaite, he is now head of an organization called Bibles for the World, which has already mailed millions of Bibles to postal addresses in scores of countries and has a vision for mailing in this decade at least one billion Bibles to the more than one billion telephone addresses worldwide.

Pudaite says, "The Bible is the Book that reveals the mind of God, the heart of man, the way of salvation, and the blessedness of believers. It is the Book that tells us where we come from and where we are going. It is the Book that set my people free."[8]

Faith by Hearing

I conclude with two important applications. The first is for believers. The second is for those who have not yet called on Christ.

First, if people can only be converted by hearing the gospel message, which is what Paul says, then believers must make sure they hear it. It is our responsibility to take the gospel to them and to send others to places where we cannot go ourselves. Do not suppose that what you can do is unimportant or that God is going to save people without human messengers, by a direct word from heaven, for example. All who are saved are saved because Christians have done something to bring the gospel to them.

If you object that you were saved while sitting alone in your room, remember that it was by believing the message of the Bible that some Christian communicated to you somehow. It may have been by the direct word of a father or mother, an uncle or grandmother. It may have been years ago, when you were a child. It may have been more recently. But somehow, some Christian brought you the message about Jesus. Perhaps you did not have exposure to Christian teaching in your family. Perhaps you were converted in a distant city in a lonely hotel room through reading a Gideon Bible. Remember that somebody bought that Bible and somebody else put it there. If you were saved by a tract, some Christian wrote it, others published it, and still others

7. Ibid., pp. 14, 15.
8. Ibid., p. 18.

arranged for it to get into your hands. It is the same if you have heard the gospel on the radio or on television or through a book.

The Bible says, "Faith comes from hearing the message, and the message is heard through the word of Christ." That is the way the salvation came to you. It is also the way it must go from you to others.

Second, a word for those who are not yet Christians. If you are not yet a believer in Jesus Christ, you need to understand that our text is true and very accurate when it says that, "faith comes from hearing the message." How do people become believers? It is by hearing the message. And why is that so? It is because the Lord Jesus Christ himself speaks to them through the preacher to call them to faith.

So take advantage of the teaching. Listen to it. Find a faithful pastor who is teaching the Word of God Sunday by Sunday from his pulpit, and learn from him. Open your heart to the words that are being taught. One commentator wrote, "If you will open your heart now, and willingly pay attention to the good news that God has nothing against you, that he loves you, that he sent the Lord Jesus Christ to die for you, that Christ did die for you personally, and that he was buried, and that God raised him from the dead on the third day as the guarantee of your salvation—if you will open your heart to this, you will find faith coming to you."[9]

"Faith comes from hearing." God has planned it that way. The message is being taught. Your part is to open your ears to that truth, trusting that, as you do, God will make the message true for you and that you will find yourself calling on the Lord Jesus Christ to be your Savior.

---

9. Donald Grey Barnhouse, "Faith and the Word" in *Epistle to the Romans*, part 62, *Romans 10:14–19* (Philadelphia: The Bible Study Hour, 1956), p. 32.

154

Excuses

Romans 10:18–20

But I ask, Did they not hear? Of course they did:
 "Their voice has gone out into all the earth,
  their words to the ends of the world."
Again I ask: Did Israel not understand? First, Moses says,
 "I will make you envious by those who are not a nation;
  I will make you angry by a nation that has no understanding."
And Isaiah boldly says,
 "I was found by those who did not seek me;
  I revealed myself to those who did not ask for me."

W̶e are coming to the end of Romans 10. There will only be one more study of this chapter, a study of verse 21 titled "The Outstretched Hands of God." So this is a good point to look back over chapters 9 and 10 to see where Paul's argument has brought us and where we are going.

I pointed out in the introductory study of this third major division of Paul's letter (chaps. 9–11) that Paul is dealing with the meaning of history in these chapters. He is asking in a general way, "Where is history going? What is God doing in history as time goes by and one historical age succeeds another?"

He is also asking, "What is God doing with Israel?"—an important question since the Bible concerns Israel so much. Specifically, Paul is asking, "Have God's purposes in regard to Israel failed?" This seems to be the case, because very few Jews had responded to the gospel.

If you remember that introductory study, you may recall that I outlined chapters 9 through 11 by seven answers Paul gives to that last question. He tells us that God has not failed, because:

1. All whom God has elected to salvation are or will be saved (9:6–24).

2. God had previously revealed that not all Israel would be saved and that some Gentiles would be (9:25–29).

3. The failure of the Jews to believe was their own fault, not God's (9:30–10:21).

4. Some Jews (Paul himself was an example) have believed and have been saved (11:1).

5. It has always been the case that not all Jews but only a remnant has been saved (11:2–10).

6. The salvation of the Gentiles, which is now occurring, is meant to arouse Israel to envy and thus be the means of saving some of them (11:11–24).

7. In the end all Israel will be saved, and thus God will fulfill his promises to Israel nationally (11:25–32).

The entire tenth chapter has developed the third of those seven reasons, which means that we are coming to the end of the argument that the failure of the Jews to believe is not God's fault.

"Keep It Simple, Paul"

But maybe it isn't the Jews' fault either! Have we considered that? This seems to be the question Paul answers in these closing verses. I suppose it came about somewhat like this.

We may imagine Paul teaching these things on some occasion, expounding the details of election, reprobation, free will, human responsibility, grace, and the ways in which the gospel comes to those who need it. But when he pauses for a moment, someone raises his hand and asks a question. "That is all very interesting," this person says. "But is it really necessary to go into all that intricate explanation about words most of us can't even pronounce and can't define? Why do you have to justify the ways of God in that manner? Isn't it just simpler to say that Jews failed to believe because they just haven't heard the gospel? Or, if they have heard it, perhaps they just haven't understood it. You theologians are always making things too complicated."

If something like that happened during one of Paul's teaching sessions—and it probably did happen, not once but scores of times—we can imagine the apostle answering exactly as he does in these verses.

"It might be nice if we could make excuses like that," Paul might have said, "but unfortunately we can't. The Jews have heard the message, just as the Gentiles are now also hearing it. The Bible says, 'Their voice [that is, the voice of the gospel messengers] has gone out into all the earth, their words to the ends of the world.' What is more, the Jews have also understood it. This is proved by Moses, who quoted God as saying, 'I will make you envious by those who are not a nation; I will make you angry by a nation that has no understanding,' and by Isaiah, who told us that God says, 'I was found by those who did not seek me; I revealed myself to those who did not ask for me.'"

The bottom line of Paul's answer is that we cannot blame God for our lack of faith or even for a lack of understanding.

The First "Excuse": They Didn't Hear

Let's look at each of these excuses carefully, especially since they touch on our situation as well as Israel's. The first excuse is that the Jews were not responsible for their unbelief for the reason that they had not heard the message. Paul's answer is that they *have* heard it. He establishes this truth by quoting Psalm 19:4.

There are two problems with this proof. If Paul had merely said, "The Jews have heard the gospel, because I have preached it to them, and so have the other apostles," there would be no problem at all. It would be his testimony. But instead of appealing to what he had done, he quotes from Psalm 19. And as soon as we turn to that psalm, we find that the text deals not with preaching the gospel but with what theologians call the general revelation. It concerns the revelation of God in nature.

Psalm 19 is in two parts. The second part is about the Bible, telling us that the law of God is perfect, trustworthy, right, radiant, pure, and so forth. The first part is about God's creation. It begins,

> The heavens declare the glory of God;
> the skies proclaim the work of his hands.

It is of this natural or general revelation that the verse Paul quotes was written: "There is no speech or language where their voice is not heard" (v. 3). That is, the existence of God is declared by what he has made. It is the point Paul himself developed in Romans 1. This natural revelation is of such quality and extent that all are guilty for their failure to acknowledge God, seek him out, and worship him.

The problem is that this general revelation is not the gospel, and it is the gospel that Paul is talking about in Romans 10.

How are we to explain this?

One way is to say that Paul *is* talking about the general revelation. This was the view of no less weighty a commentator than John Calvin, who held in addition that Paul was writing of the proclamation of the gospel to the Gentiles: "The argument is this—from the very beginning of the world God has displayed his divinity to the Gentiles by the testimony of his creation, if not by the preaching of men."[1] However, despite Calvin's reputation and proven skill as an expositor, most interpreters reject this view, judging, rightly in my opinion, that the passage as a whole is about Jews, rather than Gentiles, and about the Christian gospel of salvation through faith in Jesus Christ, rather than about the general revelation.

A second approach to the problem is to assume that Paul merely borrows the words of Psalm 19 to make his point, but without intending to say that this is what the psalm teaches. Charles Hodge takes this view: "He simply uses scriptural language to express his own ideas, as is done involuntarily almost by every preacher in every sermon."[2] This is a possibility, since Paul does not introduce the quotation by words like "Moses says," "God says" or "the Scripture says." On the other hand, as Leon Morris notes, he does quote the verse exactly, word for word, which suggests that he really is appealing to the specific Old Testament passage for support.

It is probably the case—most writers take this approach—that Paul sees a connection between the first and second parts of Psalm 19, between the general revelation and the specific revelation, and that he does so rightly. In other words, he understands that the two forms of revelation are complementary and that what is said of one can generally be said of the other. Thus, when Psalm 19 insists in its first part, that the revelation of God in nature is continuous ("day after day" and "night after night," v. 2), abundant ("they pour forth speech," v. 2) and universal ("there is no speech or language where their voice is not heard," v. 3), this should be understood of the specific revelation, too. The revelation provided in the Bible is also continuous, abundant, and universal, and what is said of the Bible should be said of the preaching of the Bible's message by the Christian preachers.

John Murray takes this view, arguing, "Since the gospel proclamation is now to all without distinction, it is proper to see the parallel between the universality of general revelation and the universalism of the gospel. The former is the pattern now followed in the sounding forth of the gospel to the uttermost parts of the earth."[3]

The second problem with this quotation follows from what has been said. If Paul means, as I take him to mean, that the gospel has been proclaimed

---

1. John Calvin, *The Epistles of Paul the Apostle to the Romans and to the Thessalonians,* trans. Ross MacKenzie (Grand Rapids: Wm. B. Eerdmans, 1973), p. 234.

2. Charles Hodge, *A Commentary on Romans* (Edinburgh and Carlisle, Pa.: The Banner of Truth Trust, 1972), p. 349. Original edition 1935.

3. John Murray, *The Epistle to the Romans,* 2 vols. in 1 (Grand Rapids: Wm. B. Eerdmans, 1968), vol. 2, p. 61.

to everyone, just as the general revelation is made known to all persons everywhere, how can we believe him? Had all people everywhere really heard the gospel? In Paul's day? In ours? Had even every Jew? The obvious answer to this puzzle is that Paul is speaking representatively, as he does in other places, for example, in Colossians 1:23: ". . . This is the gospel that you heard and that has been proclaimed to every creature under heaven, and of which I, Paul, have become a servant." He does not mean that every creature on earth at that time had literally heard the gospel, but that the gospel had been so widely proclaimed that all types of people—Gentiles as well as Jews, slaves as well as free men—heard it.

Let me say, then, that if this was true in Paul's day, when the gospel was just beginning to be proclaimed throughout the world, it is certainly far more true today. Sometimes we emphasize the roughly one and a half billion people who have not even heard of Christ. It is right that we do. But how about the three and a half billion who have? How about you?

I have traveled over a fairly large portion of the world, and I can testify, as many others also can, that there are Christians nearly everywhere on earth and that Christian churches flourish in nearly every country. There are exceptions, of course. But nearly everywhere you go there is a Christian witness, so that we can say, as Paul does, "Their voice [that is, the voice of the messengers] has gone out into all the earth, their words to the ends of the world." And today, not only have the messengers gone forth, but their voice has gone forth, too, by radio and through the printed word. In some countries, such as the United States, the gospel is proclaimed literally around the clock by radio.

So we cannot object, as this imaginary listener to Paul's teaching might be supposed to object: "But isn't it the case that they have simply not heard?" That is not a way of getting off the hook for most people. The message has been made known, and they have heard it—so they are without excuse. You are without excuse, too, if you have refused to come to Jesus Christ as your rightful Lord and Savior.

The Second "Excuse": They Didn't Understand

Yet the human mind and heart are quite subtle. "True," our imaginary questioner might say, "the Jews as a whole have heard and been acquainted with the gospel. But isn't it true that the problem might lie in another area, not that they have not heard but that they have not understood the message when it has been made known. Wouldn't that explain their unbelief?"

Paul's answer is another quotation, in fact several. He quotes from Deuteronomy 32:21 and Isaiah 65:1 (and, at the very end, from Isaiah 65:2, which we will come to in the next study).

> I will make you envious by those who are not a nation;
> I will make you angry by a nation that has no understanding.

> I was found by those who did not seek me;
>   I revealed myself to those who did not ask for me.

This is generally taken to mean: Didn't the Jews understand that the gospel was to be preached to the Gentiles? They did because the Old Testament (Moses, Isaiah, and other Old Testament writers) prophesied it.[4] I do not agree with this. I think Paul means: Didn't the Jews understand the gospel? They did, because they were provoked to jealousy when the Gentiles, upon whom they had often looked disparagingly, believed it.

Do you see how this works? If Paul's countrymen did not understand the gospel of salvation by grace through the work of Christ—if it was utter foolishness to them—why would they have had such an emotional reaction when it was proclaimed among the Gentiles? It would have been just another example of Gentile foolishness in religious matters. "Who cares what the Gentiles believe?" they would say. "Let them believe anything they like, as long as we have our Judaism, which, as we know, is superior in every way."

But that was not the reaction Paul was seeing. Instead of detached indifference and smug superiority, there was jealousy and anger on the Jews' part. This indicated that they understood very well what was happening. They knew that the message being received by the Gentiles was a message of salvation by the grace of God apart from keeping the law and that it was being taught not as a contradiction of Judaism, but as a fulfillment of it. That is what made it so offensive.

That, and the fact that Christianity was being received by Gentiles of all people, these "no-people," these ignorant and irresponsible people. For that is what the verses from Deuteronomy and Isaiah say about them. Think how offensive each of these items would be, if you considered yourself to be among the privileged people of God, as the Jews did.

1. *"Those who are not a nation."* This does not mean that the Gentiles were not organized into nations. They obviously were. It means that they were not a special people in the sight of God, as the Jews were. The Jews were the nation among whom God had worked exclusively for thousands of years, from the time of Abraham right up to the time of Jesus Christ. Now suddenly, if Christianity were true, their privileged position was being taken away and these "no-people" were replacing them.

2. *Those who have "no understanding."* This was literally true. The Gentiles, for all their vaunted philosophy and secular learning, were ignorant pagans spiritually. They understood nothing about the true God. They did not have the law. They did not know God's ways. So their ways ran to gross pagan vice and depravity. Paul described the Jews' superior self-awareness accurately in Romans 2, when he wrote, "You rely on the law and brag about your relation-

---

4. Godet, Haldane, and Murray take this view.

ship to God. . . . You know his will and approve what is superior" (vv. 17–18). How offensive, then, to have the gospel received by the ignorant Gentiles.

3. *Those who "did not seek" God.* The Jews did seek God. This is how they would have described their religious life and quest. They sought him by trying to obey his revealed law and by keeping his ordinances. The Gentiles did not do any of this. They were happy-go-lucky pagans. Yet they were finding God in spite of themselves, if Christianity were true. You do not have to exercise your mind a great deal to appreciate how this must have worked on Paul's Jewish countrymen and turned them into angry, jealous, and offended opponents of Paul and the early preaching. Pilate they abhorred, but they could live with Pilate. They could endure the Roman occupation, just as they could endure their own corrupt and cynical politicians. But they could not endure Christianity.

Paul was quite right in saying that their anger toward the Gentiles showed that they understood the nature of the gospel very well.

Offended by God's Grace

So do people today understand the gospel, and they oppose it for exactly the same reason. Why do people hate Christianity? Why do they find themselves unable to be utterly indifferent to it? It is because of grace. Grace means that God saves the undeserving. Grace saves "nobodies," those who are "no people" in the judgment of those who are important. Grace saves the ignorant. Grace saves those who are not even seeking God, reaching out to confront them in their lost state and turn them from what is destroying them to the glories of salvation through Jesus Christ.

How the natural man hates that!

If God would only take note of who we are, if he would only pay court to our superior and advanced intelligence, if he would only at least credit us with trying—if he would do that, why, then, we would welcome the gospel and embrace him openly and enthusiastically. Instead, he insists that we come with no claims upon his favor at all. He insists that we accept his judgment when he says of us,

> There is no one righteous, not even one;
> > there is no one who understands,
> > no one who seeks after God.
> All have turned away,
> > they have together become worthless;
> there is no one who does good,
> > not even one.
>
> Romans 3:10–12

What is our problem? Is it that we have not heard the gospel? No, we have heard it—"Their voice has gone out into all the earth, their words to the ends of the world." Is it that we have not understood the gospel? No, we have understood it all too well. That is why we are angry with those who have received it, and with God, who refuses to play by our rules and take note of our accomplishments.

Our problem is not that we have misunderstood grace. It is that we have *rejected* grace. It is because we will not bow our stiff, disobedient, and obstinate necks to God's gospel.

Yet there are those who do. Some are Jews, like the apostle Paul himself. He was a stiff-necked, self-righteous, angry Pharisee at one time. He was trying to stamp out Christianity. But God reached down to him in his sin, showing him how hard and sinful he really was and how desperately he needed a Savior. When Paul finally abandoned his self-righteousness and came to God as he was freely offered in Christ, Paul discovered grace and became the greatest champion of grace the world has yet seen. His letter to the Romans is a lasting testimony to his transformation.

There are also others, not great Pharisees like Paul but merely people who have been a "no-people" up to now, people without any special spiritual understanding, people who have not really been seeking after God, people like you and me. We have found God, too. And the reason is the same: grace. It is because God was pleased to save us. There is no other reason. God has chosen "the foolish things of the world to shame the wise . . . the weak things of the world to shame the strong . . . the lowly things of this world and the despised things—and the things that are not—to nullify the things that are, so that no one may boast before him" (1 Cor. 1:27–29).

If you are making excuses, you are boasting still. Abandon your boasting. Forget your excuses, and come to the one who loved you and died for you in spite of them.

155

The Outstretched Hands of God

Romans 10:21

But concerning Israel he says,
   "All day long I have held out my hands
      to a disobedient and obstinate people."

If we ever need proof that God's ways are not our ways and his thoughts are not our thoughts, we should turn to the ninth and tenth chapters of Romans. Romans 9 is about election, predestination, and reprobation. Romans 10 is about human responsibility.

Many people see these as hopelessly irreconcilable doctrines, supposing that if God elects to salvation, we cannot be responsible for rejecting the offer of salvation or, if we are responsible, salvation must be by works and not by God's grace. This was the argument of Pelagius in the days of Saint Augustine. Augustine answered, showing that these are not irreconcilable doctrines. Predestination and personal responsibility are two mutually supportive truths that need always to be held together, as Paul clearly does in Romans. When we do understand them, we see not only that they must be held together, but that the first is actually the solution to the second.

The progression is like this: first, human responsibility; second, the perverse exercise of human responsibility in rejecting God; and third, salvation by God's sovereign grace. Predestination could be described as "God's secret weapon," because apart from it no one would be saved.

In the last verse of Romans 10, we see what happens when the only working element in man's relationship to God is human responsibility. The result is unbelief. As Robert Haldane says, "We see what is the result, when God employs only outward means to lead men to obedience, and does not accompany them with the influence of his efficacious grace."[1]

The Compassionate God

It is characteristic of Paul's method of teaching that he ends a reasoned argument with quotations from the Old Testament, establishing what he has just said. He did this at the end of Romans 9. He does it here as well. In fact, in Romans 10 he has already given us six quotations from the Old Testament: Joel 2:32 (in v. 13), Isaiah 52:7 (in v. 15), Isaiah 53:1 (in v. 16), Psalm 19:4 (in v. 18), Deuteronomy 32:21 (in v. 19), and Isaiah 65:1 (in v. 20). The seventh quotation is a continuation of the reference to Isaiah 65:1, since with it Paul simply moves on to the next verse (v. 2): "All day long I have held out my hands to a disobedient and obstinate people."

This is a moving statement, because it spells out the nature of God's love in contrast to the disobedient and obstinate rejection of the love of God by human beings. The first part, the part that spells out the nature of God's love, teaches three things about it.

1. *It is continuous.* God pictures himself as holding out his hands toward Israel for an entire day. Have you ever tried to hold out your hands (or arms) for even a few minutes? It is a terribly difficult thing to do. In a short time it becomes excruciatingly painful. Very few persons could hold out their hands for even an hour. No one on earth could do it for a day. Yet God says he has done this continuously: "*All day long* I have held out my hands to a disobedient and obstinate people."

And what a day this has been! With God a thousand years is as a day, and a day is as a thousand years. Thus, the day of God's grace has already lasted over four thousand years, if we begin with Abraham—even longer if we begin with Adam and Eve.

Moreover, it is still continuing. The day of grace has not ended, and it will not end until Jesus returns the final time for judgment.

I want you to think of this personally, especially if you have not yet come to Jesus Christ as your Savior. The day of God's grace has been continuous with you, too. Forget the four thousand years since the time of Abraham. Think only of the years of your life, however long or short they have been. It may be that the time of God's outstretched love began in your childhood when a Christian mother or father told you about Jesus and urged you to

---

1. Robert Haldane, *An Exposition of the Epistle to the Romans* (MacDill AFB: MacDonald Publishing, 1958), p. 516.

commit your life to him. It may have continued into your youth through the godly influence of relatives, Sunday school teachers, or other concerned Christians who explained the gospel to you. It may have been part of your later life, if you are older. Indeed, it is continuing now, if you are not yet a disciple of Jesus Christ.

How many entreaties to believe on Jesus Christ have you heard? How many sermons have you sat through? If you have been attending a good evangelical church for any length of time, I know you have heard the gospel there. Think how continuous and long-suffering the grace of God is. And remember this: If you reject the gospel, each entreaty, each warning, and each sermon will rise up to render you without excuse at the day of God's judgment. If you perish, no one will be responsible for it but yourself.

2. *It is compassionate.* The love of God for sinners is not only a continuing love. It is compassionate, that is, it is filled with passion for you. This is clearly taught in this text, for the picture of the constantly outstretched hands of God is meant to portray compassion. It is the posture of a parent reaching out to a crying child. It is the gesture of a husband to his wife or a wife to her husband. It is the gesture of Jesus, who reached out to us from the cross.

If you want to know what the hands of God are like, I encourage you to think of Jesus and his hands. We see them often in the gospels. One day Jesus was approached by a leper, a man with a loathsome, feared disease, a person no one would touch. "Jesus," we are told, "reached out his hand and touched the man" (Matt. 8:3). On another occasion, two blind men asked for healing. Jesus "touched their eyes . . . and their sight was restored" (Matt. 9:29–30). On still another occasion, Peter was walking to Jesus over the water, as Jesus had invited him to do. But Peter looked around, saw the tumultuous waves, lost faith, and began to sink. "Immediately Jesus reached out his hand and caught him" and so saved Peter from drowning (Matt. 14:31). Jesus "put his hands" on little children and blessed them (Mark 10:16). As he ascended into heaven after his resurrection, he "lifted up his hands and blessed" those who were watching him depart (Luke 24:50). Jesus' hands were always healing, always blessing, always saving. They are compassionate hands.

I am sure also, though the story does not say so explicitly, that the hands of Jesus were stretched out toward Jerusalem when he came to the brow of the hill overlooking that great city and wept over it, saying, "If you, even you, had only known on this day what would bring you peace—but now it is hidden from your eyes" (Luke 19:42).

3. *It is costly.* There is one more important thing to see about the outstretched hands of God. They teach us that the love of God is costly—that is, costly to God. Those hands bear the imprint of the nails brutally pounded through them as Jesus was affixed to the cross to bear the penalty for our sins. Someone has said, "No other god has wounds." Exactly! No other god

has paid the price for redemption because of his continuing and compassionate love for us, except the God/man, who is Jesus Christ.

Disobedience and Passionate Unbelief

What has been the response to God's great love? This is what the second half of the verse is telling us. The response has been rejection. Two words summarize it.

1. *Disobedient.* When we think of the gospel, we usually think of it as an invitation, and it is true that the Good News is sometimes presented in that way. Jesus himself said, "Come to me, all you who are weary and burdened, and I will give you rest" (Matt. 11:28). The Bible ends with an invitation: "Whoever is thirsty, let him come; and whoever wishes, let him take the free gift of the water of life" (Rev. 22:17).

But what most of us forget is that the gospel is also a command. It is a command to turn from sin to faith in Jesus Christ and to follow him in obedient discipleship. Do you remember how Paul preached to the Greeks in Athens? He ended his address on Mars Hill by saying, ". . . we should not think that the divine being is like gold or silver or stone—an image made by man's design and skill. In the past God overlooked such ignorance, but now he *commands* all people everywhere to repent. For he has set a day when he will judge the world with justice by the man he has appointed. He has given proof of this to all men by raising him from the dead" (Acts 17:29–31, emphasis added.)

Similarly, at Pentecost, Peter commanded the people, saying, "Repent and be baptized, every one of you, in the name of Jesus Christ for the forgiveness of your sins" (Acts 2:38).

It is a characteristic of people to labor strenuously to disobey this command. It was that way for Israel, and it is also true for people today. There is nothing we resist so much as a command, no command we resist so much as a command given to us by God, and no command given to us by God that we reject so much as the command to repent and turn to Jesus.

So the first thing set over against the love of God represented by his outstretched hands is disobedience.

2. *Obstinate.* Not only was Israel's response to the gospel one of disobedience; it was an obstinate disobedience. That is, it was hard-nosed, steely-faced, heart-encrusted, and doggedly persistent. So is ours. What was true of Israel is true of all natural human responses to God's love in Christ Jesus.

Jesus described this in a parable (Matt. 21:33–46). He told of a landowner who enclosed a field, planted a vineyard, dug a winepress, and built a watchtower. Then he leased the land to those who were to tend it for him. At harvest time he sent servants to collect his rightful share of the crop, but the renters fell on the servants, beating one, killing another, and stoning a third. The landlord sent other servants, but they were treated the same way. At last he sent his son, thinking, "Surely they will respect my son." But when the wicked tenants saw the son, they said, "This is the heir. Come, let's kill him and take his inheritance" (v. 38). So they threw him out of the vineyard and killed him. When Jesus asked his listeners what the owner would do, they said he would return and destroy the wicked tenants and "rent the vineyard to other tenants who [would] give him his share of the crop at harvest time" (v. 41). Then, anticipating exactly what Paul says in Romans 10, Jesus concluded, "Therefore I tell you that the kingdom of God will be taken away from you and given to a people who will produce its fruit" (v. 43).

The picture is of obstinate resistance to the rights and love of God, and it describes what happened. The prophets were the servants. They had been beaten, killed, and stoned. Jesus was the Son. He was crucified. Therefore, the kingdom was taken from these Jewish tenants, and the door of salvation was thrown open to the entire world.

But even this gospel was resisted. When Jesus was crucified, God did something that should have profoundly shaken every Jew who knew of it. When Jesus died, God tore the great veil of the Jerusalem temple in two. This was the veil separating the Holy Place from the Most Holy Place, and for centuries it had barred the way to God, on the grounds that sinful men and women could not simply barge in upon God's holiness. Now the veil was torn, signifying that the way to God was open. No longer was it necessary to be a Jew to enter the outer temple courts or a priest to enter the temple itself or the high priest to enter the Most Holy Place. Because of Jesus' death, the way was open, and anyone—Gentiles as well as Jews, women as well as men, slaves as well as free-born people—anyone could come to God through him.

But what did the Jews do? They just sewed the torn veil of the temple back together and went on with their exclusively Jewish worship. They rejected the witness of those who had seen the risen Lord, explaining the empty tomb as a theft and deception on the part of the disciples, and perpetuated their sacrificial system, which was now rightly superseded by the perfect sacrifice of himself by Jesus Christ, until the temple was at last destroyed by the Romans. The majority regarded the Christians as renegades and hated every extension of the gospel to the Gentiles, even though passages like those Paul is quoting in Romans foretold that this would happen.

A Terrible Contrast

Most commentators on this passage note the contrast between Isaiah 65:1, quoted in verse 20, and Isaiah 65:2, quoted in verse 21. The first describes how the Gentiles, who had not sought God, found him. The second describes how the Jews, to whom God had specifically and continuously offered a way of salvation, had rejected him. It is a great contrast. But to my way of thinking, the greatest contrast is not this but rather the contrast between the compassionate, loving God, stretching out his hands to save sinners, and the hardness of those who obstinately turn their back upon him. It is this that makes what is being described at the end of Romans 10 so disturbing and so bad.

Once again I need to become personal. In ancient times God could say that he had repeatedly stretched out his hands to Israel. But in that Old Testament period Jesus had not yet come. His coming had been foretold, but he had not come yet, and there was undoubtedly great confusion about what the prophecies of his coming really meant. Besides, the prophets, although numerous over the years, were nevertheless infrequent at any given time in that history, and none of them had access to our amazing "modern" means for proclaiming the gospel.

What a difference today! If God was stretching out his hands toward Israel then, how much more is he stretching out his hands to men and women today. Today Jesus has come. And not only has he come, the meaning of his coming is understood and the messengers of the gospel have literally taken this Good News throughout the world. The gospel has been explained in magazines, tracts, and books. It is heard on radio. It is seen in movies and video tapes. It has been declared dispassionately, as men and women with acute minds and much knowledge have appealed to the reason of their hearers. It has been proclaimed emotionally and fervently, as preachers have pleaded with their congregations to turn from the sin that is destroying them and find salvation in Jesus, where alone it may be found.

What more can be done? Jesus said to those of his day, "We played the flute for you, and you did not dance; we sang a dirge, and you did not mourn" (Matt. 11:17). He was referring to the contrast between the ministry of John the Baptist, which was a serious call to repentance, and his own which was more open, less threatening, and winsome.

Can we not say the same thing today? Preachers of the gospel have reasoned and debated, begged and pleaded, argued and cajoled, coaxed and implored. We have given reasons, argumentation, warnings, and motivations. We have preached and prayed. In the name of God we have stretched out our own hands to sinners, pleading, "Believe in the Lord Jesus Christ, and you will be saved . . ." (Acts 16:31).

But what has been the result? We have found exactly the same thing that both Jesus and Paul found. The unregenerate world is not interested in the gospel. And, if the truth is told, there are a good many apparent Christians who do not seem to be very interested in it either. They treat church attendance lightly, preferring to stay home Sunday evenings and watch television rather than worship God, who saved them, and allow the teaching of his Word to nourish their emaciated souls. They do not study their Bibles. They do not read Christian books. Their minds are flabby, and so are their spiritual muscles. They do not work for Jesus. They do not tell others about him. They do not even give money so that others can do the work in their place. They live for themselves. That is what they are doing. Are they not like those Paul describes? Disobedient?

As for the unsaved world—well, the unregenerate world crucified Jesus when he came the first time. It would lynch him again if it had the opportunity. It is against such hard and rebellious hearts that the love of God, symbolized by his outstretched hands, shines brightly.

But be warned. If what I have said describes you, if you have not yet come to Christ and are resisting him, know that one day those outstretched hands of God will become the hands of his judgment. For Jesus will himself be your judge. The Bible says, "The LORD will judge his people . . ." (Deut. 32:36). When the author of Hebrews comments on that text, he says, "It is a dreadful thing to fall into the hands of the living God" (Heb. 10:31).

What Shall You Do?

Fortunately that end is not yet here. Today is still the day of God's grace. And that is why we are going to find Paul moving back into the reign of grace in Romans 11, where he asks, "Did God then reject his people?" and will answer, "By no means!" citing himself as an example (v. 1).

But what of you? What should you do in this present moment? Some who look at the doctrine of election think it means you should do nothing because you can do nothing. That does not follow. You cannot save yourself. That is certain, which is why the gospel is a gospel of grace. If you could save yourself, it would be a gospel of works. You cannot make God be gracious to you, but you can listen to him as he speaks in the gospel. You can look to him and see his hands outstretched.

"Shouldn't I seek God?" you ask. Not at all! He is already seeking you, and if you think you are seeking him, you will inevitably fall back into trusting in your own efforts. Instead of seeking him, you need merely to be quiet and listen to what he says.

William R. Newell writes,

> Should we not seek God? No! You should sit down and hear what is written in Romans: first, about your guilt, then about your helplessness, and then about the inability of the law to do anything but condemn you; and then believe on Christ whom God hath sent; and then praise God for righteousness apart from works, apart from ordinances! Hear how God laid sin, your sin, on a substitute, his own Son, Jesus Christ our Lord, and that now, sin being put away, God has raised him from the dead. Seek God? No! God is the seeker, and he has sought and is now seeking those that asked not of him, and has been found by those who sought him not!—but simply heard the good news and believed![2]

Let me put it another way. God is calling you, and he is doing it exactly as Paul says he does in Romans 10:14–15. That is the way the gospel comes to everyone. First, the messengers are sent. Second, they preach the Good News. Third, the voice of Jesus is heard in the preaching. Fourth, the sinner

---

2. William R. Newell, *Romans Verse by Verse* (New York: Arno C. Gaebelein, 1938), pp. 406, 407.

believes. Fifth, the person calls on Jesus for salvation. You need to hear the message, because it is in the teaching of the gospel that the voice of God is heard and his outstretched hands are seen.

When Jesus first appeared to the disciples in the upper room following the resurrection, Thomas, one of the disciples, was not present. Although told of the resurrection and that the others had seen Jesus, he was unconvinced. "Unless I see the nail marks in his hands and put my finger where the nails were, and put my hand into his side, I will not believe it," he said (John 20:25).

A week after his first appearance to the disciples, Jesus appeared again. This time Thomas was present. Jesus held out his hands, showing Thomas his wounds, saying, "Put your finger here; see my hands. Reach out your hand and put it into my side. Stop doubting and believe" (v. 27).

Thomas did not even have to do that. Instead, he fell at Christ's feet, confessing, "My Lord and my God!" (v. 28).

That is exactly what happens today as people read the Bible and hear it preached. They see Jesus in the Bible's pages. They hear him speak their name, and they come to him. In that moment the disobedience and unbelief of a lifetime fade away, and they find themselves calling out, "My Lord and my God!" It is a wounded hand that holds out salvation to you and invites you to come. Reach out and touch that hand. Then allow it to enfold you in an embrace that nothing on earth or in heaven will ever diminish or disturb.

PART FOURTEEN

The Times of the Gentiles

156

Has God Rejected Israel?

Romans 11:1

I ask then: Did God reject his people? By no means! I am an Israelite myself, a descendant of Abraham, from the tribe of Benjamin.

Ancient Bibles did not have chapter divisions, as our Bibles have. These were added later, the earliest appearing in Codex Vaticanus in the fourth century. Moreover, the earliest divisions were different from what we have now, and our present chapters came even later, in the Middle Ages. The divisions we have are certainly not from Paul. Still, when we come to the beginning of a new chapter, as we do now in our study of Paul's great letter to the Romans, it is natural to take the division seriously, look back over the distance we have traveled, and try to get a bearing on the matters still to come.

Has God's Word Failed?

The present discussion began in Romans 9, following Paul's magnificent statement about the believer's eternal security in Christ in Romans 8. It began in response to an obvious question: How can we believe in the eternal security of the Christian if, as we can clearly see, Jews as a whole are not responding to

1287

the preaching of the gospel and thus are not being saved? If Christianity is true, doesn't this mean that God has rejected Israel? If God has rejected Israel, how can we suppose that he will avoid rejecting us as well? And if he can or will reject us, isn't it true that we must reject the doctrine of eternal security?

Paul's immediate answer, in Romans 9:6, was that God's plans for Israel have not failed. To prove it he unfolds the seven main arguments found in chapters 9 through 11.

1. God's historical purpose toward the Jewish nation has not failed, because *all whom God has elected to salvation are or will be saved* (Rom. 9:6–24). In this section Paul distinguishes between national Israel and spiritual Israel, which consists of those whom God has chosen to know Christ. His point is that membership in the visible Jewish nation did not guarantee salvation, any more than mere formal membership in a Christian denomination guarantees the salvation of church members today. What determines salvation is the electing · grace of God in Christ, and that has always been a matter separate from any ethnic, national, or organizational distinctives.

2. God's historical purpose toward the Jewish nation has not failed, because *God had previously revealed that not all Israel would be saved and that some Gentiles would be* (Rom. 9:25–29). If God had promised that all Jews would be saved and had then failed to save some of them, God's word would indeed have failed. But this is not the case, since God had foretold in advance that many Jews would not believe and would be scattered and that, in their place, many of the scattered Gentiles would be gathered to Christ.

3. God's historical purpose toward the Jewish nation has not failed, because *the failure of the Jews to believe was their own fault, not God's* (Rom. 9:30–10:21). The Jews refused to believe because they wanted to earn salvation for themselves, even though Abraham, David, and all others who were saved were saved through believing God's promises concerning Jesus Christ. The majority wanted to be approved by God on the basis of their own good works and righteousness, and so would not submit to the righteousness that comes by faith in Christ.

4. God's historical purpose toward the Jewish nation has not failed, because *some Jews (Paul himself was an example) have believed and have been saved* (Rom. 11:1). As long as even one Jewish person has been saved, no one can claim that God has rejected his people utterly. Paul was one, even if there were no others. But, in fact, the situation is not as grim as that. As the next section shows, God has always preserved a considerable remnant of believing Jewish people.

5. God's historical purpose toward the Jewish nation has not failed, because *it has always been the case that even in the worst of times a remnant has been saved* (Rom. 11:2–10). Paul proves this from the days of Elijah, a dark period but

one in which, by God's own count, seven thousand Jews were still faithful to God, having refused to worship Baal. Seven thousand was a small portion of the nation, but it was still a sufficiently large number to derail the claim of anyone who might think that the plan of God had failed.

6. God's historical purpose toward the Jewish nation has not failed, because *the salvation of the Gentiles, which is now occurring, is meant to arouse Israel to envy and thus be the means of saving some of them* (Rom. 11:11–24). God has a right to do anything he wants with sinners. He can save whom he wants. He can condemn whom he wants. Still, condemnation seems rather harsh toward his ancient "chosen" people. "Is God merely writing them off?" we might ask. Paul's answer is that this is not the case. Rather, God is using the day of Gentile salvation for the good of Israel, since it is through God's work among Gentiles that Israel is being stirred from self-complacency and lethargy, and some are being saved.

7. Finally, God's historical purpose toward the Jewish nation has not failed, because *in the end all Israel will be saved, and thus God will fulfill his promises to Israel nationally* (Rom. 11:25–32). This is so gracious and wonderful that Paul concludes with a benediction praising God's great wisdom.

Here is how Leon Morris traces Paul's thought:

> Paul has made it clear that God is working out a great purpose and [has] insisted on divine predestination and election; the will of God is done. He has also insisted that human responsibility is real and important, and he has made it plain that this must be borne in mind when considering the fact that Israel has not entered the blessing as Gentile believers have. What then does it matter to belong to the chosen people? At first sight, it may seem, not very much, for Gentiles may be saved as well as Jews. But it is far from Paul's thought that being a Jew matters little. He goes on to show that, while in the providence of God Israel's sin and unbelief have been used to open up the way for the Gentiles, now the conversion of Gentiles will lead to the conversion of Jews. The Jews still have a place in God's plan.[1]

Charles Hodge looks at the argument of Romans 11 similarly, noting that it has two parts. "In the former [part] the apostle teaches that the rejection of the Jews was not total. There was a remnant, and perhaps a much larger remnant than many might suppose. . . . In the latter [part], he shows that this rejection is not final."[2]

Godet adds, "This partial rejection . . . is not eternal, but temporary (vv. 11–32). For after it has served the various ends which God had in view in

---

1. Leon Morris, *The Epistle to the Romans* (Grand Rapids: Wm. B. Eerdmans, and Leicester, England: Inter-Varsity Press, 1988), p. 397.

2. Charles Hodge, *A Commentary on Romans* (Edinburgh and Carlisle, Pa.: The Banner of Truth Trust, 1972), p. 352. Original edition 1935.

decreeing it, it shall come to an end, and the entire nation shall be restored, and with the Gentiles shall realize the final unity of the kingdom of God."[3] This is an ending worthy of the benediction with which Paul concludes the fourth section of his letter.

Has God Rejected His Ancient People?

At the start of chapter 11, the point to which we have come in our verse-by-verse exposition of Romans, we are at Paul's fourth argument of the seven listed above. It is the shortest of the seven. Question: "I ask then: Did God reject his people?" Answer: "By no means! I am an Israelite myself, a descendant of Abraham, from the tribe of Benjamin" (v. 1).

What Paul says in this terse personal reference has been understood in two ways. One approach is based on the vehemence of his answer and supposes Paul to be denying that any Jew could suppose that God would abandon Israel. "More meaning can be attached to 'of the seed of Abraham, of the tribe of Benjamin' on this interpretation," according to John Murray.[4] The problem with this view is that it turns Paul's reply into a mere emotional response, rather than an argument, and we are in the midst of a very clear set of reasoned arguments in this chapter.

The second view is the one I have assumed from the beginning of these studies, namely, that Paul is using his own case as proof that Israel has not been abandoned. As long as there is only one believing Jew—though, in fact, there are many—no one can affirm that God has rejected Israel utterly. Paul is a remnant by himself, whether or not there are any others. But, in fact, there are and always have been others, as the next section shows.

Why, then, does Paul speak so forcefully of his Jewish ancestry? In my opinion, it was in response to the many unkind things that must have been said to him about it. I have friends who are Jewish believers who report that when they accepted Jesus as the Messiah they were at once rejected as Jews by many of their former friends and family members.

In one case, in a Bar Mitzvah service, the male members of the family were invited to take part in the Torah readings, and a friend of mine who had become a Jewish Christian went forward with them. He was stopped by the rabbi, who claimed that he was no longer a Jew because he believed in Jesus. My friend's instinctive response, which is why I tell this story, was: "Are you telling me that I am not a Jew? How can you say that I am not a Jew? God made me a Jew. My mother and father were Jews. I am descended from Jews. I am a son of Abraham."

It is hard to suppose that Paul did not hear similar accusations many hundreds of times or that his response would not have been precisely what we

3. F. Godet, *Commentary on St. Paul's Epistle to the Romans*, trans. A. Cusin (Edinburgh: T. & T. Clark, 1892), vol. 2, p. 221.

4. John Murray, *The Epistle to the Romans*, 2 vols. in 1 (Grand Rapids: Wm. B. Eerdmans, 1968), vol. 2, p. 67.

find it to be in Romans. "Not a Jew?" he might have objected. "How can you say I am not a Jew? I am an Israelite, a descendant of Abraham, from the tribe of Benjamin."

Each of those terms is worth exploring.

1. *An Israelite.* There are three names used to denote this ancient people: Hebrews (cf. Phil. 3:5), Jews, and Israelites. The origin of "Hebrew" is not known, though it may be derived from the name Eber, found in Genesis 10:21, 25, in which case it denotes a broader grouping of people than ethnic Israel alone. It would be similar to the word *Semite.* "Jew" comes from Judah, the fourth son of Jacob by Leah and (later) the most prominent of the twelve tribes. This name stresses the people's ethnic origins. The distinguishing feature of "Israel" is that it is the people's covenant name. It was the name given to Jacob when he wrestled with the angel at the Jabbok and God blessed him (Gen. 32:28).

As soon as we recognize that "Israel" points to the covenant, we see that Paul's choice is exceedingly appropriate. For the question being raised in Romans is whether or not God can break covenant, and the answer is: Surely not! God never breaks a promise.

2. *A descendant of Abraham.* Nothing designates a Jew so decisively as being "a son of Abraham." Therefore, Paul uses this phrase, too. In his case, of course, being a descendant of Abraham had Christian importance, for he had shown earlier that Abraham is an example of faith and that all who have faith are therefore Abraham's true spiritual children, both Jews and Gentiles (cf. Rom. 4:11–12, 16).

3. *Of the tribe of Benjamin.* Benjamin was small among the tribes of Israel, but it was significant beyond its size for many reasons. First, Benjamin was the only son of Jacob to have been born in Israel. The others were born on the far side of the desert in Paddam Aram. Second, Jerusalem, the capital of Israel, was within its territory. Third, Benjamin was the only tribe that remained with the tribe of Judah in the south at the time of the civil war following the death of Solomon. The northern tribes quickly drifted away from the forms of worship that had been given to Israel, set up apostate altars, became increasingly wicked, and were the first to be carried away into captivity (in 721 B.C.). Benjamin, in the south along with Judah, remained closer to God, preserved a larger measure of righteousness, and thus survived longer, until the conquest by Babylon (in 586 B.C.).

Martin Luther argues at this point that Paul had contended against God "with all this strength" and that "if God had rejected his own people, he surely would have rejected the Apostle Paul."[5] But thoughtful as this may be, it is not the point Paul is making. Paul is not arguing that he has been saved in

---

5. Martin Luther, *Luther's Works,* vol. 25, *Lectures on Romans,* ed. Hilton C. Oswald (St. Louis: Concordia, 1972), p. 421.

spite of his sinful past, which would be an argument for grace, but that he is a Jew and is saved, which is an argument for God's faithfulness to his covenant. In other words, he is saying nothing new, but only what had been stated many times in the Old Testament.

When the people sinned by asking for a king and later confessed it, saying, "We have added to all our other sins the evil of asking for a king" (1 Sam. 12:19), Samuel answered, "Do not be afraid. You have done all this evil; yet do not turn away from the LORD, but serve the LORD with all your heart. . . . For the sake of his great name the LORD will not reject his people, because the LORD was pleased to make you his own" (vv. 20, 22).

Psalm 94 speaks of God's judgment of the wicked and his disciplining of those he loves. Yet it also explains the discipline, saying, "For the LORD will not reject his people; / he will never forsake his inheritance" (v. 14).

Jeremiah quotes God as saying,

> Only if the heavens above can be measured
>   and the foundations of the earth below be searched out
> will I reject all the descendants of Israel
>   because of all they have done.
>
> Jeremiah 31:37

Paul was steeped in the Old Testament. So we can well understand his horrified and extreme reaction to the suggestion that God might somehow break his promises to Israel and cast his people off. Discipline? Yes. A remnant in times like the present? Of course. But cast Israel off? Abandon the covenant? Break the promises? How could God do that and still remain God? If that happened, truth, honor, righteousness, and justice would be torn from the deity, and God would no longer be God.

In view of this argument, we can see why Paul does not only argue that some of Israel are being saved, himself being one example, but also maintains that in the end the fullness of God's blessing will be extended to the Jewish people nationally, and "so all Israel will be saved," as he says in verse 26.

A Few Applications

I realize, as I come to the end of this study, that much of what I have written has been analytical and technical and that its relevance to ourselves and our times is not readily apparent. But it is nevertheless a practical matter, and there are several major points of application.

1. *We should not be discouraged in our evangelism, because all whom God is calling to faith in Jesus Christ will come to him.* If anyone should have been discouraged in his evangelism, it should have been Paul in his attempts to reach the Jewish people. He was God's chosen messenger to the Gentiles (Acts 9:15), but Paul always began his missionary efforts with the Jews and again and again he was

rejected by them. In 2 Corinthians he describes how he had been beaten five times by the Jewish authorities and how he was in constant danger from them, as well as from Gentile rulers (2 Cor. 11:24, 26). Later, when he went to Jerusalem with the offerings from the Gentile churches, he was set upon by a fanatical mob and would have been torn to pieces if the Romans had not intervened to save him. Jewish opposition led to his imprisonment.

Yet Paul was not discouraged by this, because he knew that he had been sent to preach the gospel to all people and that those whom God was calling to faith in Jesus Christ would come to him. In Elijah's day, God had reserved seven thousand faithful Jews. In Paul's day, one by one God was calling out thousands more. So also today. Because God is calling to faith those whom he has chosen to call to faith, we, too, can work on without discouragement and know that our "labor in the Lord is not in vain" (1 Cor. 15:58).

2. *We should be warned against presumption.* It is true that all whom God is calling to faith will be saved, but this does not mean that all of any race, social class, or denomination will be. In the days of Elijah, God had seven thousand believers. But there were other thousands, no doubt hundreds of thousands, who did not obey God, worshiped Baal, and were not saved. They were Jews. Although they were outward, visible members of the covenant community, they were not what Paul earlier termed true "Israel" (Rom. 9:6). They were Abraham's "natural children," but they were not "children of the promise," because they did not follow Abraham's example by believing in the one who was to come.

Being a Jew did not in itself save these people, though there were great advantages to Judaism, as Paul acknowledges. Neither will membership in a Christian denomination save you, though there are also advantages to belonging to a good church. We must not presume on our affiliations. The Bible says to "make your calling and election sure" (2 Peter 1:10). It means, be sure you believe in Jesus Christ as your Savior and that you are actually following him as your Lord.

The five foolish virgins of Jesus' parable thought that they were well off because they had been invited to the wedding banquet, had accepted the invitation, called Jesus "Lord," and were even waiting for his second coming—but they were not "ready" when he came (Matt. 25:1–13). Make sure that you are not among their company.

3. *We should put all our confidence in God, who alone is the source, effector, and sustainer of his people's salvation.* How foolish to put your confidence in anything else, or even in a combination of lesser things. If a person can be a Jew, with all the spiritual blessings attending to that great religious heritage, and yet be lost, certainly you are foolish to trust in your ancestry, nationality, education, good works, or (strange as it may seem) your good intentions. "Salvation comes from the Lord" (Jonah 2:9). It comes from God alone. Make sure that

you are trusting him and what he has done for you in Jesus Christ. Make sure you are able to sing:

> Nothing in my hand I bring,
> Simply to thy cross I cling;
> Naked, come to thee for dress,
> Helpless, look to thee for grace;
> Foul, I to the fountain fly;
> Wash me, Savior, or I die.
>
> Rock of Ages, cleft for me,
> Let me hide myself in thee.

4. *We must never take part in or yield to anti-Semitic attitudes or actions.* If God himself has not rejected the Jews in spite of their long history of willful sin, dogged disobedience, and fierce rejection of him—if he loves them still and has a plan for their eventual salvation as a nation—it is clear that you and I, if we are Gentiles, must not reject them either. We must never yield to or take part in anti-Semitism.

There are many blemishes on the church of Jesus Christ accumulated during the long years of its history, but of all those blemishes one of the most terrible and tragic has been the participation of so-called Christians in the persecution of the Jews. I know that not all, perhaps hardly any, of those actually persecuting Jews were true Christians. But that is another matter. Instead of hatred there should have been love. Instead of prejudice there should have been understanding. Let us determine that regardless of what the past has been, we will think and act like Christians—like Jesus himself, who died with arms outstretched even to those who crucified him.

We must love all men and women and seek to reach all without favoritism until Jesus comes again.

157

God's Remnant

Romans 11:2-5

God did not reject his people, whom he foreknew. Don't you know what the Scripture says in the passage about Elijah—how he appealed to God against Israel: "Lord, they have killed your prophets and torn down your altars; I am the only one left, and they are trying to kill me"? And what was God's answer to him? "I have reserved for myself seven thousand who have not bowed the knee to Baal." So too, at the present time there is a remnant chosen by grace.

Paul's letter to the Romans moves forward by rational arguments and statements, not by stories. But in Romans 11:2-5, the apostle touches on a great Old Testament story as support for his contention that God has not abandoned Israel and that the word of God has not failed. It is the story of Elijah, following his victory over the prophets of Baal on Mount Carmel (1 Kings 18:16–19:18).

The God of Elijah

Elijah had challenged the priests of Baal to a contest in which they were to ask Baal to send fire to consume the sacrifice on their altar, while Elijah would ask God to send fire to consume the sacrifice on his. When Baal failed and

God answered spectacularly, sending fire to consume not only Elijah's sacrifice, but also the wood, stones, soil, and water in the trench, the prophet seized his opportunity and had four hundred prophets and priests of Baal killed.

It was a great victory.

But news of it reached Ahab, the wicked king of Israel, who told his wife, Jezebel, what Elijah had done. She was more wicked even than Ahab, and she swore to have Elijah killed immediately in swift retaliation. Elijah, who was undoubtedly exhausted emotionally by the earlier test of wills, lost confidence in God and fled on a forty-day journey into the remote wilderness of Mount Horeb, which is another name for Sinai.

The next morning God spoke to him. "What are you doing here, Elijah?"

Elijah replied in what is surely one of the most pitiful complaints in all Scripture: "I have been very zealous for the LORD God Almighty. The Israelites have rejected your covenant, broken down your altars, and put your prophets to death with the sword. I am the only one left, and now they are trying to kill me too" (1 Kings 19:10). Never mind that the Israelites had just responded to his challenge to execute the four hundred prophets and priests of Baal.

God did not chide his prophet, as we might have done. Instead, he took care of him, provided what he needed and encouraged him.

First, he gave Elijah a new vision of himself. He placed him on the mountain while a great wind, an earthquake, and a fire passed by. These powerful natural phenomena reflected God's strength and sovereignty, but God was not in them. Instead, after the wind, earthquake, and fire had passed by, God spoke to Elijah in what is described as "a gentle whisper."

God repeated the question: "What are you doing here, Elijah?"

Elijah gave the same answer as before. Then God told him to anoint two new kings: Hazael as king of Aram and Jehu as king of Israel. He was also to anoint Elisha to be his own successor as God's prophet. These three, the two kings and Elisha, would be a strong new team to help him. Finally, God said, "Yet I have seven thousand in Israel—all whose knees have not bowed down to Baal and all whose mouths have not kissed him" (1 Kings 19:18).

This is the story Paul refers to in Romans 11:2–5, quoting verses 10, 14, and 18 of 1 Kings 19 specifically.

The Flow of Paul's Thought

Since this account begins the fifth of Paul's arguments in Romans 9–11—in which he proves that the purposes of God for Israel have not failed and are, in fact, continuing—it will be useful to summarize and review them here, as we have done at each point at which a new argument is introduced.

God's purposes for Israel have not failed because:

1. *All whom God has elected to salvation are or will be saved* (Rom. 9:6–24). What determines salvation is the electing grace of God in Christ, and that has always been separate from any ethnic, national, or organizational distinctives.

2. *God had already revealed that not all Israel would be saved and that some Gentiles would be* (Rom. 9:25–29). This is a proof from prophecy.

3. *The failure of the Jews to believe was their own fault, not God's* (Rom. 9:30–10:21). The Jews refused to believe because they wanted to earn salvation for themselves, just as most people do today.

4. *Some Jews have believed and have been saved* (Rom. 11:1). Paul offers himself as an example.

5. *It has always been the case that even in the worst of times a remnant has been saved* (Rom. 11:2–10). This is the point to which we have come now. It is proved by the fact that even in the dark days of Elijah's ministry, by God's own count and revelation, seven thousand Jews were still faithful to God and had refused to worship Baal.

6. *The salvation of the Gentiles, which is now occurring, is meant to arouse Israel to envy and thus be the means of saving some of them* (Rom. 11:11–24).

7. *In the end all Israel will be saved* (Rom. 11:25–32). Together, these arguments are a powerful case for the irrevocability of God's covenant promises, even in the face of such strong human resistance and rejection as had been shown by Israel.

A Remnant Will Be Saved

The new idea in this argument is the "remnant." This word refers to a small surviving part of something, either an object or a custom or a people. We probably use the word most often to describe a bit of fabric left over from a bolt of cloth after most of it has been sold, or a remnant of carpet after most of the roll has been sold. In the Old Testament the word refers in most cases to the small company of Jews who survived or were to survive the invasions, destructions, and captivities inflicted on them by the Assyrians and Babylonians in the sixth and eighth centuries B.C.

It is an interesting feature of this word that it occurs many times in the Old Testament (sixty-two times in all), but only three times in the New Testament (NIV). In each New Testament occurrence the reference is to an Old Testament text.

The first New Testament reference is in Acts 15, the chapter that describes the Council at Jerusalem. On this occasion the leaders of the church had met to discuss the place of the Gentiles in the expanding church and whether they were to be required to submit to the law of Moses, including circumcision and observance of the Jewish feasts. The decision was to free Gentiles from this Jewish yoke, and it was based in part on a quotation from the Book of Amos, cited by James (emphasis added):

> After this I will return
> and rebuild David's fallen tent.
> Its ruins I will rebuild,
> and I will restore it,
> that *the remnant* of men may seek the Lord,
> and all the Gentiles who bear my name,
> says the Lord, who does these things. . . .

Acts 15:16–17; quoting Amos 9:11–12

In these verses "remnant" refers to the Jews who survived the deportation by the Babylonians, who in the days of the apostles were being given renewed opportunity to seek the Lord and to whom, as the new people of God, believing Gentiles would be added.

The other two New Testament references are in Romans. We have already seen one. It occurred in chapter 9 in a quotation from Isaiah (emphasis added):

> Isaiah cries out concerning Israel:
> "Though the number of the Israelites be like the sand by
> the sea,
> only *the remnant* will be saved.
> For the Lord will carry out
> his sentence on earth with speed and finality."

Romans 9:27; quoting Isaiah 10:22–23

The final New Testament use of the word *remnant* is in the passage we are studying.[1]

We need to ask two questions in order to understand the text well.

1. *What do verses 2–5 add to verse 1?* If you have been following the argument, you will be aware that Paul has already proved God's faithfulness to Israel by showing that, even if no other Jew has been saved, at least he had been. And as long as there is one, nobody can claim that God has utterly abandoned Israel. At first glance, the verses that follow seem to be saying the same thing,

---

1. The earliest Old Testament reference to a "remnant" is in Genesis 45:7, where Joseph explains to his brothers that God sent him to Egypt and raised him to a position of influence in order "to preserve for you a *remnant* on earth and to save your lives by a great deliverance." After that, the word does not occur again in reference to Israel until the later history of the Jewish monarchies, where it suddenly appears in profusion. The majority of texts are in 2 Kings (19:4, 30–31; 21:14), 2 Chronicles (34:9, 21; 36:20), Isaiah (10:20–22; 11:11, 16; 17:3; 28:5; 37:4, 31–32), Jeremiah (6:9; 11:23; 23:3; 31:7; 40:11, 15; 42:2, 15, 19; 43:5; 44:7, 12, 14, 28; 47:4–5; 50:21, 26), and Micah (2:12; 4:7; 5:7–8; 7:18), though references are also scattered throughout the other prophets. The texts usually warn that God will preserve only a remnant or promise that he will indeed preserve a remnant. Many promise blessing on the remnant in the last days.

only by using the story of Elijah and God's revelation of the existence of seven thousand who had not abandoned the true God and bowed to Baal. So do these verses really add anything?

The answer is that they *do* add something. In fact, they add two things.

First, they show that although God could have been faithful to his promises by merely saving *one* of the vast number of the Israelites, his grace extended far beyond that. There were seven thousand in Elijah's time, and by natural implication we are to assume that the same was true in Paul's day and is true in our day, too. Paul is answering the argument that God must have broken his promises since, for the most part, Jews were not receiving Christ and Gentiles were. He is saying that although the number of Jewish believers is proportionately small, there were nevertheless many who had believed. The numbers were not negligible. We remember that three thousand believed in Jerusalem on the day of Pentecost (Acts 2:41) and that from that time on "the Lord added to their number daily those who were being saved" (v. 47). God is doing the same thing today.

Second, the use of Elijah's story shows that God's choice of a believing remnant, far from being an anomaly, has actually always been the case. The story in 1 Kings does not come from the very last days of the monarchies, when destruction by the Assyrians or Babylonians was just around the corner. It occurred somewhat earlier in Israel's history. But even at this earlier time it was the case that only a remnant was being saved.

Paul is grounding his experience and the results of the preaching of the gospel in his time in past Jewish history. He is showing that preaching in the first Christian century perfectly fits the pattern of God's ways.

2. *To whom is Paul referring when he speaks of "his people, whom he foreknew"?* This is an interesting question and one that has divided even the best commentators. I find them almost evenly divided. There are two possibilities. First, the words may refer to the nation as a whole, citing Israel as the "foreknown" or elect people of God. Or, second, they may refer restrictively only to the elect within Israel. F. Godet, John Murray, and Leon Morris hold to the first interpretation.[2] John Calvin, Robert Haldane, and Charles Hodge hold to the second.[3]

It is easy to argue for the second position, because Paul has already distinguished between national Israel and true Israel in Romans 9. Hodge starts

---

2. F. Godet, *Commentary on St. Paul's Epistle to the Romans,* trans. A. Cusin (Edinburgh: T. & T. Clark, 1892), vol. 2, p. 223. John Murray, *The Epistle to the Romans,* 2 vols. in 1 (Grand Rapids: Wm. B. Eerdmans, 1968), vol. 2, pp. 67, 68. Leon Morris, *The Epistle to the Romans* (Grand Rapids: Wm. B. Eerdmans, and Leicester, England: Inter-Varsity Press, 1988), p. 399.

3. John Calvin, *The Epistles of Paul the Apostle to the Romans and to the Thessalonians,* trans. Ross MacKenzie (Grand Rapids: Wm. B. Eerdmans, 1973), pp. 239, 240. Robert Haldane, *An Exposition of the Epistle to the Romans* (MacDill AFB: MacDonald Publishing, 1958), p. 524, 525. Charles Hodge, *A Commentary on Romans* (Edinburgh and Carlisle, Pa.: The Banner of Truth Trust, 1972), p. 354. Original edition 1935.

at this point, arguing that it is the best position because (1) "it is precisely the distinction which Paul had made, and made for the same purpose, in chapter 9:6–8"; (2) "this is apparently Paul's own explanation in the sequel—the mass of the nation were cast away, but 'a remnant, according to the election of grace,' were reserved"; and (3) "the illustration borrowed from the Old Testament best suits this explanation."[4] There is nothing wrong with this, of course. It is based on truth.

On the other hand, there are reasons for thinking that in this chapter Paul is thinking of the nation as a whole and is referring to Israel when he writes "his people, whom he foreknew."

There is no question, of course, but that Paul has been proving God's faithfulness to his people by referring to an elect remnant. Since God has elected some Jews, though a remnant, to be saved along with the believing Gentiles, it is clear that Israel as a nation has not been cast off. But here is the problem. In verse 1 Paul is talking about the nation. His question can be restated as: "Has God cast off the nation of Israel?" The answer is: "No, he has not rejected the nation, because he is saving some of them, and I am one." In other words, "his people" in verse 1 and "his people, whom he foreknew" in verse 2 must refer to the same people, and this people must be the nation as a whole.

Moreover, this is the direction in which the chapter is moving. For, when we get to verses 26–29, we find Paul writing, "And so all Israel will be saved, as it is written:

> The deliverer will come from Zion;
>   he will turn godlessness away from Jacob.
> And this is my covenant with them
>   when I take away their sins.

As far as the gospel is concerned, they are enemies on your account; but as far as election is concerned, they are loved on account of the patriarchs, for God's gifts and his call are irrevocable" (the quotation is a loose rendering of Isaiah 59:20–21 and 27:9).

Here is the way Godet describes what is happening:

Of all the peoples on the earth only one was chosen and known beforehand, by an act of divine foreknowledge and love, as the people whose history would be identified with the realization of salvation. In all others salvation is the affair of *individuals,* but here the notion of salvation is attached to the *nation* itself. . . . The Israelites contemporary with Jesus might reject him; an indefinite series of generations may for ages perpetuate this fact of national unbelief. God is under no pressure; time can stretch out as long as he pleases. He will add, if need be, ages to ages, until there come at length the generation disposed to open their eyes and freely welcome the Messiah. God foreknew

4. Hodge, *A Commentary on Romans*, p. 354.

this *nation* as believing and saved, and sooner or later they cannot fail to be both.[5]

Encouragement for Hard Times

The application of these truths in regard to Israel is what the rest of Romans 11 contains. We will be following it out in detail as we make our way through these verses. But there are also applications for us today, and this is the note on which I want to end this study.

1. *God always has a remnant, and the remnant is often much larger than we might suspect.* I think of Christians who are working in difficult places or under difficult circumstances—in an inner-city mission, for example. Or, as many did for years, behind the Iron Curtain. Or with a class of people who are particularly resistant to the gospel. Or with children who have turned away from God. If you have been called to such a work or been given such a concern, you may be in the depressed state of mind that overcame Elijah. You have worked hard. There have been meager results. What you have done has been misunderstood and rejected, perhaps even violently. You may be inclined to give up, thinking, "Lord, they have killed your prophets and torn down your altars; I am the only one left, and they are trying to kill me" (v. 3).

If you are thinking or feeling that way, you need to know that God still has his seven thousand who have not bowed down to Baal, that you are therefore not alone and that your work will not be without results.

Our problem is a simple lack of faith, which means that we judge by mere outward appearances and not by God's promise. Elijah was a great prophet, yet he made exactly this mistake. He could not see what God was doing, so he assumed that he was the only faithful person left.

Calvin says,

> It follows, therefore, that those who evaluate the church on the basis of their own opinions are in error. And indeed if that distinguished prophet who was so endowed with the light of the Spirit was deceived in this way when he desired to reckon the number of God's people by his own judgment, what will be the case with us, for our highest discernment, when compared with his, is nothing but dullness? Let us, therefore, form no rash decision on this point, but rather let this truth remain fixed in our hearts, that the church, which may not appear as anything to our sight, is nourished by the secret providence of God. . . . for God has a way, accessible to himself but concealed from us, by which he wonderfully preserves his elect, even when all seems lost.[6]

5. Godet, *Commentary on St. Paul's Epistle to the Romans,* vol. 2, 223. Of course, they will be saved not because they become "disposed" to believe by themselves, since they cannot, but rather because God will graciously draw this elect people to himself.

6. Calvin, *The Epistles of Paul the Apostle to the Romans and to the Thessalonians,* p. 240.

If that does not comfort and encourage us, it is hard to know what can.

2. *The remnant of those who are God's people have not bowed to Baal.* Baal was a particularly corrupt god of the ancient Canaanites, whose worship persisted because of the failure of the Jews utterly to exterminate the Canaanites at the time of the conquest under Joshua. It consisted of blatant sex worship, coupled with pure materialism. In fact, the sex was meant to insure the materialism—for the practice of sacred prostitution was supposed to guarantee the recurrence of the seasons, with corresponding blessing on the crops from which came wealth in that society. We have the same thing today. Our western culture, particularly in America, is charging down the twin freeways of sexual promiscuity and blatant materialism. Only with us, the wealth is intended to insure the sex or sexual favors (or perhaps make them more pleasant), rather than the other way around.

What do we say in such times? Many, myself included, are inclined to be pessimistic. "The culture is wicked. Virtue is declining. Only I am left. I might as well give up."

But that is not the true picture. The culture may indeed be rushing down a slippery slope to damnation. But God has his remnant, nevertheless, and this remnant has *not* bowed its knee to the Baal of sex and possessions. There *are* devout people, who are living for God and trying to do the right thing, often in what are terrible circumstances. We should be encouraged to know this, seeking out such persons and encouraging them whenever we can. That is what the church is to be, after all—the company of those who are living for God and are encouraging one another to live for him even in this present evil world.

So let us get on with it. "Let us fix our eyes on Jesus" and so run the race set out for us (Heb. 12:1–2), whatever it may be. Moreover, let us run it, knowing that one day, like ourselves, all God's elect people will stand before him, having conquered this present wicked world. And though we will generally have been despised and persecuted, we will know that God has accomplished his perfect will in us and that nothing we have done for Jesus will have been done in vain.

158

Saved by Grace Alone

Romans 11:6

And if by grace, then it is no longer by works; if it were, grace would no longer be grace.

Two things must characterize any Christian. One is a profound sense of personal sin and unworthiness. The other is an overwhelming awareness of the grace of God. The two go together, of course, for without a proper sense of sin, we will never appreciate grace. We will think that the good we experience from God's hand is merited. On the other hand, the more we appreciate the grace of God, the more aware we will be of our sin and want to be free of it.

A Trophy of God's Grace

The apostle Paul was a trophy of God's grace, and he never forgot it. How could he? He had been raised in Judaism, but his understanding of what that required made him into a self-righteous man who thought that he above all others pleased God. It made him zealous to the point of killing those who disagreed with him. When Stephen was stoned to death, Paul was present to hold the coats of those who threw the stones. In fact, Paul was on his way to

Damascus to arrest more of the followers of Jesus and have them killed when the Lord appeared to him in a bright light, called him to faith, and redirected his energies.

What a miracle of grace Paul was! In spite of his deep self-righteous attitude and vicious acts, God saved him graciously, that is, by grace alone. From that time on Paul preached the grace of God everywhere and to everyone.

Most of the verses in the Bible concerning grace are from Paul. There are only eight occurrences of the word *grace* in the entire Old Testament (NIV), but there are 128 occurrences in the New Testament, and most of them are from Paul's sermons or in his letters. For example,

Acts 20:24. "I consider my life worth nothing to me, if only I may finish the race and complete the task the Lord Jesus has given me—the task of testifying to the gospel of God's grace."

Romans 1:5. "Through him and for his name's sake, we received grace and apostleship to call people from among all the Gentiles to the obedience that comes from faith."

Romans 3:23–24. "All have sinned and fall short of the glory of God, and are justified freely by his grace through the redemption that came by Christ Jesus."

Romans 5:15. "For if the many died by the trespass of the one man, how much more did God's grace and the gift that came by the grace of the one man, Jesus Christ, overflow to the many!"

Romans 5:20–21. "Where sin increased, grace increased all the more, so that, just as sin reigned in death, so also grace might reign through righteousness to bring eternal life through Jesus Christ our Lord."

Romans 6:14. "Sin shall not be your master, because you are not under law, but under grace."

Romans 12:6. "We have different gifts, according to the grace given us."

1 Corinthians 1:4. "I always thank God for you because of his grace given you in Christ Jesus."

1 Corinthians 15:10. "By the grace of God I am what I am, and his grace to me was not without effect. No, I worked harder than all of them—yet not I, but the grace of God that was with me."

2 Corinthians 8:9. "For you know the grace of our Lord Jesus Christ, that though he was rich, yet for your sakes he became poor, so that you through his poverty might become rich."

2 Corinthians 9:8. "God is able to make all grace abound to you, so that in all things at all times, having all that you need, you will abound in every good work."

Galatians 1:6. "I am astonished that you are so quickly deserting the one who called you by the grace of Christ and are turning to a different gospel."

Galatians 5:4. "You who are trying to be justified by law have been alienated from Christ; you have fallen away from grace."

Ephesians 1:5–8. "He predestined us to be adopted as his sons through Jesus Christ, in accordance with his pleasure and will—to the praise of his glorious grace, which he has freely given us in the One he loves. In him we have redemption through his blood, the forgiveness of sins, in accordance with the riches of God's grace that he lavished on us with all wisdom and understanding."

Ephesians 2:4–8. "Because of his great love for us, God, who is rich in mercy, made us alive with Christ even when we were dead in transgressions—it is by grace you have been saved. . . . in order that in the coming ages he might show the incomparable riches of his grace, expressed in his kindness to us in Christ Jesus. For it is by grace you have been saved."

Ephesians 3:7–8. "I became a servant of this gospel by the gift of God's grace given me through the working of his power. Although I am less than the least of all God's people, this grace was given me: to preach to the Gentiles the unsearchable riches of Christ."

2 Timothy 1:9–10. "[God] has saved us and called us to a holy life—not because of anything we have done but because of his own purpose and grace. This grace was given us in Christ Jesus before the beginning of time, but it has now been revealed through the appearing of our Savior."

2 Corinthians 13:14. "May the grace of the Lord Jesus Christ, and the love of God, and the fellowship of the Holy Spirit be with you all."

Colossians 4:18. "Grace be with you."

1 Thessalonians 1:1. "Grace and peace to you."

1 Thessalonians 5:28. "The grace of our Lord Jesus Christ be with you."

1 Timothy 1:2. "Grace, mercy and peace from God the Father and Christ Jesus our Lord."

I count eighty-one verses about grace by Paul, and these are only a few of them. Together they constitute the most profound treatment of this great doctrine in all the world's literature and assure us that the great apostle of grace was himself formed by it.

A Gratuitous Comment

Paul's love of this doctrine is the only reason I can think of for his having included the words about grace that we find in Romans 11:6. I say this because they are really unnecessary at this point of the argument.

Charles Hodge calls this verse an exegetical comment on the last clause of the preceding one."[1] And so it is. But the previous verse has already made the point: "So too, at the present time there is a remnant *chosen by grace*" (v. 5, emphasis added). And so has the one before it: "And what was God's answer to him? 'I have reserved for myself seven thousand who have not bowed the knee to Baal'" (v. 4). The verse does not say merely, "There *are* seven thou-

---

1. Charles Hodge, *A Commentary on Romans* (Edinburgh and Carlisle, Pa.: The Banner of Truth Trust, 1972), p. 356. Original edition 1935.

sand who have not bowed the knee to Baal," but rather, "*I have reserved for myself* seven thousand . . ." (emphasis added). This is the work of God, and it is a gracious work. In the same way, Paul has spoken of the grace of God in salvation in Romans 5 and 6. Romans 5:12–21 is the most extensive treatment of the doctrine of grace in the Bible.

So why does Paul add verse 6 to Romans 11? It is because he loved this doctrine, saw it everywhere, and wanted his readers to see it and love it, too.

And also perhaps because he knew how difficult it is for most people to accept grace and how inclined we are to add works to it. I imagine that as he wrote the preceding verses, referring to the seven thousand faithful Jews from the days of Elijah's ministry, he would have thought that some readers would instinctively give those faithful Jews some credit and by extension give themselves a bit of credit, too. They would be thinking, "Well, it is true that those were dark days. But at least there were seven thousand who did not bow to Baal. Let's give them credit for that, and the Jewish people as well. There have always been Jews who have been faithful. Thank God we have the strong spiritual character we do!"

Because that kind of thinking comes naturally to all of us, and Paul knew it, he interrupts the natural flow of thought that would have led him to the distinctions between the majority of Jews and the remnant, which he develops in verses 7–10, to make sure we all understand that even the remnant exists by God's grace only. It is not that some had it in them to be faithful while others did not. It is rather that God *chose* the remnant to believe.

God's Grace or Man's Works?

The verse itself makes only one point: that grace and works are incompatible opposites. So if a person is to be saved by grace, it cannot be by works; otherwise, grace is not grace. Conversely, if a person is to be saved by works, it cannot be by grace; otherwise, work would not be work. The footnote of the New International Version indicates that some ancient manuscripts include the second part of the contrast.[2]

2. The omission of the second half of verse 6 from the text and the placing of it in the footnotes by the New International Version indicates that in the judgment of the NIV editors it was probably not in the text as originally written. However, the matter is not clear-cut. As far as the manuscripts go, the bulk of the best and earliest manuscripts omit it (including the Chester Beatty papyrus, Sinaiticus, Alexandrinus, and others). But it is in some old manuscripts (including Vaticanus) and is reflected in the ancient Syriac version. As far as non-textual arguments go, some scholars argue for the words on the grounds that it is easier to understand how they might have been dropped out of the original text than how they might have been added, while others reason, conversely, that it is easier to see them as a scribal gloss to an originally shorter verse. Fortunately, the outcome of the debate does not matter, since the second half merely says the same thing as the first, though in an inverted manner. For a discussion of the problem see F. Godet, *Commentary on St. Paul's Epistle to the Romans*, trans. A Cusin (Edinburgh: T & T Clark, 1892), vol. 2, p. 227; Hodge, *A Commentary on Romans*, p. 356; and Leon Morris, *The Epistle to the Romans* (Grand Rapids: Wm. B. Eerdmans, and Leicester, England: Inter-Varsity Press, 1988), p. 402, note 26.

Calvin calls Paul's statement "a comparison of opposites," adding:

> The grace of God and the merit of works are so opposed to one another that if we establish one we destroy the other. If, then, we cannot allow any consideration of works in election without obscuring the unmerited goodness of God, which Paul so greatly desired to commend to us in election, those fanatics, who make the worthiness which God foresees in us the cause of our election, must consider what answer they are to give to Paul. Whether it is past or future works which we are considering, Paul's statement that grace leaves no room for works will always resound in our ears. . . . He states that God was led to make this distinction for no other reason than his own good pleasure, and contends that any concession given to works detracts to that extent from grace.[3]

Today we have many evangelicals who argue for salvation by grace apart from works. But if they are asked why some are saved instead of others, they do not give Paul's answer, which is the electing grace of God, but say rather that it is because of something God sees or foresaw as being in them. Either God foresees their good works, justifying them on that basis. Or else, he foresees their faith. He knows they will believe; therefore, he elects them. The first supposition is a repudiation of the gospel. It means salvation by works instead of faith. The second supposition makes "faith" a work, and thereby excludes grace.

What shall we say about faith, then? Where does it come in? The answer is that faith is a result of regeneration or the new birth and is therefore the product and not the cause of God's election. This is exactly what Paul said in those well-known verses from Ephesians that I quoted in part earlier: "Because of his great love for us, God, who is rich in mercy, made us alive with Christ even when we were dead in transgressions. . . . For it is by grace you have been saved, through faith—and this not from yourselves, it is the gift of God—not by works, so that no one can boast" (Eph. 2:4–5, 8–9).

Isn't it amazing how these great doctrines of grace hang together and reinforce each other! Election, foreknowledge, sin, grace, faith—they are a gallery of doctrines before which any regenerate and understanding mind must marvel, as Paul himself clearly did.

> Amazing grace—how sweet the sound—
> That saved a wretch like me!
> I once was lost, but now am found,
> Was blind, but now I see.

---

3. John Calvin, *The Epistles of Paul the Apostle to the Romans and to the Thessalonians*, trans. Ross MacKenzie (Grand Rapids: Wm. B. Eerdmans, 1973), p. 242.

A Reasonable Doctrine

Amazing Grace! Yes, but also not so amazing, at least when we consider how imperative grace is. We might even call it reasonable, not because we can give a reason why God should be gracious—there is no reason for grace but grace itself—but in the sense that, as Robert Haldane says, it is "necessarily and obviously implied in every other doctrine of the gospel."[4]

1. *"Dead in transgressions."* Sometimes people think they have a problem with grace, even more so with election. But the real problem people have is not with election, grace, or foreknowledge, but with the doctrine of depravity. There are only three possible views of mankind as far as sin is concerned. The first: Some deny it. They say that people are not sinners, at least not in any metaphysical sense. The worst they will say is that we are not perfect. We are evolving beings. We are getting better and better all the time. The second: Some admit the imperfections but argue that it is possible to correct them. We can make ourselves better, if we want to. The third, the biblical view: We are so hopelessly lost in sin that there is nothing we can do to save ourselves or even to make ourselves better. We need outside help, the grace of God.

The first view may be described by saying that human beings are in great moral health. The second view says that we are sick. The third view says that we are dead so far as being able to do anything to help ourselves is concerned. We need a resurrection.

If this is true, how could salvation come in any way other than by the unmerited grace of God without any relationship to anything we might do?

"But surely God foresees which people will have faith," says someone. Really? If we are "dead in [our] transgressions and sins," as Paul writes in Ephesians 2:1, what could God possibly see but an unregenerate and therefore spiritually dead heart, unless he should have determined beforehand to give faith to it? Or again, if as Paul says in Romans 3:10–11, "There is no one righteous, not even one; there is no one who understands, no one who seeks God," what could God possibly see in us but a nature obstinately determined to resist him at every cost? If we are to be saved, clearly it is going to have to be God's work from beginning to end.

2. *"You must be born again."* A second doctrine that is perfectly consistent with grace and makes grace eminently necessary and reasonable is the new birth. When Jesus was talking to Nicodemus, he told him that apart from being born again he could not "see the kingdom of God" (John 3:3) and a little later that he could not "enter the kingdom of God" (v. 5). Nicodemus did not understand very much of that. He began to think in physical terms rather than spiritually, asking, "How can a man be born when he is old? Surely

4. Robert Haldane, *Exposition of the Epistle to the Romans* (MacDill AFB: MacDonald Publishing, 1958), p. 526.

he cannot enter a second time into his mother's womb and be born!" (v. 4). But at least he got the idea that, whatever Jesus was talking about, it was humanly impossible. How, then, can we be born again?

Jesus gave the answer when he said, "Flesh gives birth to flesh, but the Spirit gives birth to spirit. You should not be surprised at my saying, 'You must be born again.' The wind blows wherever it pleases. You hear its sound, but you cannot tell where it comes from or where it is going. So it is with everyone born of the Spirit" (vv. 6–8). If the new birth depends on the sovereign working of God's Spirit, then it does not depend on us, and we can no more control it than we can control the wind. Salvation will have to be of God. It must be of grace from the beginning to the end.

3. *"Through faith."* If salvation is by grace and grace is opposed to works, then to be saved by grace through faith implies that faith is not a work. If it were a work, salvation would be by works; and, as we have already seen, if it were by works, "grace would no longer be grace."

What is faith, then? Faith is receiving what God gives. It is believing him and trusting him. Charles Haddon Spurgeon wrote, "Faith is not a blind thing; for faith begins with knowledge. It is not a speculative thing; for faith believes facts of which it is sure. It is not an unpractical, dreamy thing; for faith trusts, and stakes its destiny upon the truth of revelation. . . . Faith is the eye which looks. . . . Faith is the hand which grasps. . . . Faith is the mouth which feeds upon Christ."[5] It is no credit to us to have an eye that looks or a hand that grasps or a mouth that feeds. These body parts are given to us by God. No more is faith a credit to the one who uses it, for it, too, is given by God and functions rightly only when it rests upon him.

Grace, Mercy, Peace

At the start of the two letters to Timothy, Paul has a greeting that is familiar to us, because it is used so often in benedictions to close a worship service: "Grace, mercy and peace from God the Father and Christ Jesus our Lord" (1 Tim. 1:2; 2 Tim. 1:2; cf. 2 John 3). Those three terms—grace, mercy, and peace—are worth thinking about as I bring this study to a close.

Grace has been the subject of this study. It refers to God's unmerited favor apart from anything seen or foreseen in us. It is utterly contrary to works. For work is something we do, and grace does not look to us but flows from the unfettered will of God.

Mercy is an aspect of grace. Indeed, it is almost the same thing, except that mercy has reference particularly to those who are pitiful. It looks on us and feels sorry for us. It reaches out to save us in Christ.

Peace is the last of these terms. It describes what comes to us as the result of God's grace and mercy. The first result is peace with God. God has made

5. Charles Haddon Spurgeon, *All of Grace* (Chicago: Moody Press, n.d.), pp. 46, 50, 51.

peace between himself and us by the blood of Christ's cross (Col. 1:20). It required an atonement. The second result is peace among human beings. By removing the need for competition, since all Christians have and are is of grace, God makes it possible for them to function peacefully within the church. The third result is personal. It is the peace that comes when we are embraced by the grace of God and know ourselves to be so.

It is for this that I call attention to those three words. As long as you are trusting to your own good works, you will never have personal peace of mind and heart, nor should you. For how can you hope to meet the righteous demands of the holy God? Live by works, and you will perish by works. It is like asking God for justice. Justice is what you will get, and justice will condemn you. But if you throw yourself upon the grace of God, trusting in Christ, then you will have peace, because your peace will depend not on your own imperfect works but upon Jesus' own perfect work for you.

After World War I, President Woodrow Wilson outlined "fourteen points" for a proposed peace settlement between the allied nations and Germany. At the time the French Prime Minister was Georges Clemenceau (1841–1929), who was difficult at the best of times and did not like Wilson's proposals, probably because they came from the United States rather than from France. "Fourteen points?" he objected. "Even God Almighty only has ten."[6]

Actually, God's peace plan has only one point and it is that you give up trying to impress him with your sullied works and instead embrace Jesus Christ as your Savior. If you do, your experience will be like Paul's, who saw the depth of his sin and the glory of God's grace and from that point on was never the same and never stopped talking about it.

6. Clifton Fadiman, ed., *The Little, Brown Book of Anecdotes* (Boston and Toronto: Little, Brown, 1985), p. 130.

159

All of God: A Summary

Romans 11:7–10

What then? What Israel sought so earnestly it did not obtain, but the elect did. The others were hardened, as it is written:

> *"God gave them a spirit of stupor,*
> *eyes so that they could not see*
> *and ears so that they could not hear,*
> *to this very day."*

And David says:

> *"May their table become a snare and a trap,*
> *a stumbling block and a retribution for them.*
> *May their eyes be darkened so they cannot see,*
> *and their backs be bent forever."*

There is a story about a rabbi who was trying to explain a Jew's way of thinking to a Gentile. "I'll show you how a Jew thinks," he said. "Give me the answer to these three questions. Here is the first. Two men fall down a chimney. One comes out clean and the other dirty. Which one washes?"

"That's easy," the Gentile said. "The dirty one, of course."

"Wrong," said the rabbi. "After they fall down the chimney they look at each other. The dirty one sees that his friend is clean and assumes he is clean, too. So he does nothing. The clean one washes because he looks at the other man, sees that he is dirty, and thinks that he is dirty, too."

"Here's the second question. Two men fall down a chimney. One comes out clean and the other dirty. Which one washes?"

"That's the same question," said the Gentile.

"No, it isn't," said the rabbi. "It's quite different."

"Well, then, I suppose it's the one who is clean."

"Wrong again," the rabbi replied. "The dirty one washes because he looks at his hands and sees that they are dirty. He washes. What could be more obvious than that?"

"Here's the third question. Two man fall down a chimney. . . ."

"That's the same question again," said the Gentile.

"No," said the rabbi. "It's entirely different. What's the answer?"

"I don't know," said the Gentile.

"Neither of them washes, because it's a ridiculous story to begin with. How could two men fall down a chimney and one come out clean and the other dirty?"[1]

It is because of this kind of thinking that Jews say that whenever two Jews are together you are always going to find at least three opinions.

I do not know if there is any truth to that story and that saying. But whether or not such things can be said of Jews in general, they were certainly not true of the apostle Paul, who was an ardent Jew and a very careful thinker. Paul never held to two contrary opinions, and the single opinion concerning the gospel he did hold has been pursued in Romans with relentless and irrefutable logic.

It is time to sum up some of that teaching.

A Time to Summarize

A good teacher knows when enough information has been given out and it is time for a summary, and since Paul was a good teacher he seems to have been aware that a summary was needed at precisely this point in his letter. It is what Romans 11:7–10 is about. These verses are a summing up of what Paul has written thus far in Romans 9–11.

What has he written?

First, there is his teaching about *election*. He introduced the subject in Romans 9, showing that God's purposes in salvation have not failed because, even though the great majority of Jews had rejected the gospel, those whom God had elected to salvation beforehand nevertheless were being saved. Later, in Romans 11, he provided examples of what he was talking about, indicating

1. The story is from Ray C. Stedman, *From Guilt to Glory*, vol. 2, *Reveling in God's Salvation* (Portland: Multnomah Press, 1978), pp. 70, 71.

that he was among that elect number himself and that in the days of Elijah there were seven thousand who also fit that category.

Second, there is his teaching about *reprobation*, the doctrine that God passes by the many who are not saved, sovereignly declining to elect them to salvation. In Romans 10 Paul went to great lengths to show that this does not eliminate the guilt of those who are passed by, for we continue to be responsible for our own actions, including our unbelief, and it is for these sinful acts that we are judged.

Third, there is *the reason for man's rejection of the gospel.* The Jews are Paul's prime example, because he is discussing the fate of unbelieving Israel in these chapters. But it is the same for all persons apart from Christ. People reject the gospel because they want to establish their own righteousness and do not want to submit to the righteousness that comes from God. Paul discusses this in chapter 10.

Fourth, there is the teaching that *what has happened historically in the overall rejection of Christ by Israel had been foretold by God* and was therefore no surprise to God, nor did it cause a departure from his plan. In Romans 9, Paul gave four separate Old Testament quotations to make this point (Hos. 2:23; 1:10; Isa. 10:22–23; 1:9). In Romans 11:8–10 he provides two more: verse 8, which combines words from Deuteronomy 29:4 and Isaiah 29:10; and verses 9 and 10, which quote Psalm 69:22–23.

Grace Equals Election

Yet Paul's summaries are never mere summaries. They always seem to carry his argument just a bit further, even in summing up. In this case, Paul's summary has the effect of highlighting the doctrine of election and thus brings him back to the point from which he started out.

Robert Haldane reviews the teaching in verse 7, asking, "What is the result of all that the Apostle has been saying? It is this: Israel as a nation hath not obtained righteousness, of which it was in search (Rom. 9:31), but the election among them—the chosen remnant reserved by God, spoken of above—hath obtained it." He then asks suggestively, "Can anything more expressly affirm the doctrine of election?"[2]

You may have noticed in that quote that, in his summary of verse 7, Haldane used the word "election" rather than "elect" (NIV). Haldane is reflecting the King James Version, rather than the New International Version. The older version says, "the election hath obtained it." But this is not only a matter of translations. The facts are that Paul carefully uses the word "election" rather than "elect" and that this is the only time in the entire New Testament in which he departs from his regular usage.

2. Robert Haldane, *An Exposition of the Epistle to the Romans* (MacDill AFB: MacDonald Publishing, 1958), p. 528.

Is there a reason? There seems to be, for "election" points more strongly than "elect" to the body of the redeemed whom *God has chosen,* which is Paul's chief point. If he had written only that "the *elect* obtained it," the wording might be seen as suggesting that salvation was something the elect were themselves able to achieve. When he says "the *election* obtained it," it is clear they obtained it only because God first gave it to them.

So I repeat again, as I have many times in these studies, salvation is not something any of us are able to earn ourselves. Salvation is entirely of grace (v. 6). In fact, taken together, verses 6 and 7 say that grace is election and that election is grace. Without one you just do not have the other.

Election and Reprobation

There is another thing we have to have in order to have election, and that is reprobation, the passing over of those who are not chosen. These verses are particularly strong in reinforcing this teaching.

But let's do a bit of review ourselves, particularly of the comparison I made between election and reprobation earlier in this volume.[3] I do this here because the matter is disturbing to some people. The question I asked before and now ask again is: Are the actions involved in these two doctrines to be thought of in exactly the same sense? Are they equally ultimate? That is, does God determine the destinies of individuals in exactly the same way so that, without any consideration of what they do or might do, he assigns one to heaven and the other to hell?

We know he does that in the case of those who are being saved, because we have been told that election has no basis in any good seen or foreseen in those who are elected. This is precisely what we saw in Romans 11:6, when we examined it in the previous study. The question is whether this can also be said of the reprobate, that is, that God has consigned them to hell apart from anything they have done, apart from their deserving it.

Here some important distinctions must be made. Election and reprobation are similar in at least two ways: (1) both originate in the eternal counsels or will of God, rather than in the will of man, and (2) both have the glory of God as their objective. But election and reprobation are also dissimilar in important respects.

Here are the two important points of difference.

First, when we refer to reprobation we refer to the reprobate being "passed by" (Westminster Confession of Faith, chap. 3, sec. 7). Some will argue that in its ultimate effect there is no difference between passing by and actively ordaining an individual to condemnation. But while that is true of the ultimate effect, there is nevertheless a major difference in the cause. The reason

---

3. In "Double Predestination" (Romans 9:13–18), chapter 128 of the series.

why some believe the gospel and are saved by it is that God intervenes in their lives to bring them to faith. He does this by the new birth or regeneration. But those who are lost are not made to disbelieve by God. They do that by themselves. To ordain their end, God needs only to withhold the special grace of regeneration.

Second, we speak of God's ordaining the lost "to dishonor and wrath *for their sin*" (Westminster Confession of Faith, chap. 3, sec. 7). That is an important observation, too, for it makes reprobation the opposite of an arbitrary action. The lost are not lost because God merely consigns them to it, but rather as righteous judgment for their wrongdoing.[4]

Of course, the most important thing to say about these doctrines is that they are taught throughout the Bible and are therefore to be believed by all who accept the Bible as God's faithful revelation, whether we understand them well or not. In the earlier study I mentioned:

Proverbs 16:4. "The LORD works out everything for his own ends—even the wicked for a day of disaster."

John 12:39–40. "They [the people of Jesus' day] could not believe, because, as Isaiah says elsewhere: 'He has blinded their eyes and deadened their hearts, / so they can neither see with their eyes, nor understand with their hearts, nor turn—and I would heal them.'"

John 13:18. Jesus said, "I know those I have chosen. But this [his betrayal by Judas] is to fulfill the scripture: 'He who shares my bread has lifted up his heel against me.'"

John 17:12. Jesus prayed, "While I was with them [the disciples], I protected them and kept them safe by that name you gave me. None has been lost except the one doomed to destruction so that the Scripture would be fulfilled."

1 Peter 2:7–8. "Now to you who believe, this stone [Jesus Christ] is precious. But to those who do not believe, 'The stone the builders rejected has become the capstone,' and, 'A stone that causes men to stumble and a rock that makes them fall.' They stumble because they disobey the message—which is also what they were destined for."

Jude 4. "Certain men whose condemnation was written about long ago have secretly slipped in among you."

The clearest texts are in *Romans 9*, where "hate" is used of Esau ("'Jacob I loved, but Esau I hated,'" v. 13) and "harden" of Pharaoh ("Therefore God has mercy on whom he wants to have mercy, and he hardens whom he wants to harden," v. 18). Romans 9 is the most forceful statement of double predestination in the Bible.

---

4. The same two points are in the Canons of the Synod of Dort: "Not all, but some only, are elected, while others are *passed by* in the eternal decrees" and these are punished "not only on account of their unbelief, but also *for all their other sins*" (Chap. 1, Art. 15).

The Hardening of Israel

I said above that Paul's summaries, though summaries, always seem to carry his arguments a bit further. At this point I want you to see another way in which these verses carry the argument further. It comes by comparing Paul's teaching about reprobation in Romans 9 with what we have here.

Who was Paul using as an illustration of reprobation in chapter 9? The answer, as you can tell from the reference to that chapter above, is: Esau, the father of the Edomites, and Pharaoh, the nation's great enemy. Paul wrote that God "hated" Esau and that he "hardened" Pharaoh's heart. And so he did. No Jew would doubt that. Neither Esau nor Pharaoh was among the elect people of God. But here is the striking thing. In Romans 11 Paul is not writing about non-Jews, Edomites, and Egyptians. He is writing about Israel, which means that he is applying the doctrine of reprobation to the allegedly "chosen" people.

What is more, he is saying that even those things that should have been a blessing to them—presumably the very things he lists at the start of Romans 9 ("the adoption as sons; . . . the divine glory, the covenants, the receiving of the law, the temple worship and the promises . . . the patriarchs," vv. 4–5)—have become a "snare," "trap," "stumbling block," and "retribution" for them in their unregenerate state (11:9).

This is a critical point. It means that if the blessings of God are misused—and they always are misused unless we allow them to lead us to faith in Jesus as our Savior—they will inevitably harden our hearts, propel us into further sins, and eventually lead to even greater judgment.

There is a powerful statement of this principle at the very end of the Old Testament, in Malachi. Those were bad days. The people, led by their priests, were far from God. They were so far from God that when he sent Malachi to rebuke them for their sins, their response was one of hostile surprise and confrontation. They retorted, "How have you loved us? . . . How have we shown contempt for your name? . . . How have we defiled you? . . . How have we wearied [God]? . . . How are we to return? . . . How do you rob you? . . . What have we said against you?" when Malachi accused them of those sins (Mal. 1:2, 6–7; 2:17; 3:7–8, 13).

The priests were chiefly to blame for this attitude. So the strongest judgments are pronounced against them: "'If you do not listen, and if you do not set your heart to honor my name,' says the LORD Almighty, 'I will send a curse upon you, and I will curse your blessings. Yes, I have already cursed them, because you have not set your heart to honor me'" (Mal. 2:2). Sober words!

Blessings That Become Curses

Here is where this summary of Paul's teaching comes home forcefully to us. If individual Jews, who were a chosen nation, missed salvation because of their rejection of Christ and if, as a result, the blessings of God that had been given to them became a curse for these people, it is entirely possible (indeed probable) that many sitting in the evangelical churches of America today are also missing salvation because of their failure to trust Jesus in a personal way and that their blessings have become curses, too.

Do you understand that? It means that if you will not allow the good things we enjoy as allegedly Christian people to lead you to Christ, which is what God has given them to us for, they will be worse than worthless to you. They will actually be harmful and propel you inevitably into an even greater spiritual stupor, hardness of heart, and sin.

Here are four examples.

1. *Baptism.* Baptism is an outward sign of an inward, spiritual union with Jesus Christ. It is meant to strengthen our faith by making the inward reality more palpable to us. But countless allegedly Christian people have trusted the outward sign without the inward commitment. They have judged themselves to be saved persons without any true following after Jesus Christ. Therefore, the very thing that should have been an instruction and blessing to them has become a false ground of hope.

2. *Communion.* The same thing is true of communion. Entire branches of the church teach that grace is somehow imparted in the physical partaking of the elements, so that the physical act by itself conveys salvation. But the reality is not physical. The Lord's Supper is meant to show us the broken body and atoning blood of Jesus Christ and lead us to trust him and place our faith in *him,* not in the ceremony. If we do not trust Christ, the sacrament, which is intended to do us good, actually becomes a curse for us, and we become superstitious and even pagan in our practice.

3. *Material possessions.* I do not need to elaborate on this. Money and other material goods are from God. But they are dangerous, particularly when we possess them in abundance. They should lead us to God in gratitude. More often they lead us from him.

4. *The Lord's Day.* My fourth example is particularly timely. A short while ago the United States observed the fiftieth anniversary of the bombing of Pearl Harbor by the Japanese, which brought America into World War II and altered the course of history. It was a terrible disaster for this country, for it crippled the Pacific Fleet and claimed 2,403 young lives.

The bombing took place on Sunday morning, December 7, 1941. What is not so well known is that after the defeat of Japan in 1945, General Douglas MacArthur took control of the archives of the Japanese war department and set translators to work on the enemy's papers. They discovered that in the years prior to the war, the Japanese had sent professors to the United States to study America's national character to determine at what point and in what manner we would be most vulnerable to attack. Their combined reports judged that our guard would be lowest on a Sunday morning following a Friday on which both the Army and the Navy had a payday.

That is precisely what December 7, 1941 was. In earlier years, Sundays were sacred days of rest and worship for the majority of Americans, and even those who were not Christians respected them. But that had changed by the winter of 1941. Our day of national blessing had become a national hangover, and God turned this former blessing into a curse. That weekend at Pearl Harbor was a debauch of vast proportions, and we were unprepared and unable to meet the Japanese attack when it came.[5]

Yet I must say, as terrible as the destruction at Pearl Harbor was, it was only physical and temporal—it is now long past—and it does not begin to compare with the spiritual condemnation of even a single eternal human soul.

Reasonable but Useless

There are probably some people, maybe many, who are taking this in an entirely mistaken fashion. You stopped following me after my review of election and reprobation, and you are now wondering, "What difference does all this make if election is true, as you teach, and I am not among that number?"

That is a reasonable question. But it is a useless one, because we do not know in advance who the elect or reprobate are. It is something hidden in the eternal counsels of God. Yet there is a way to find out if you are among the elect, and that is to turn from your sin and put your trust and confidence in Jesus Christ. That is what the elect do. If you will not have Jesus Christ as your Savior, even this clear summary of his teaching will become a curse for you. You will use it as an excuse to move even farther from Jesus and salvation. But you should not do that. Instead you should allow it to bring you to Christ, and then you will find it to be a blessing.

5. See Donald Grey Barnhouse, *God's Covenants: Exposition of Bible Doctrines, Taking the Epistle to the Romans as a Point of Departure*, vol. 8, *Romans 9:1–11:36* (Grand Rapids: Wm. B. Eerdmans, 1963), pp. 119, 120.

160

Riches for the Gentiles

Romans 11:11–12

Again I ask, Did they stumble so as to fall beyond recovery? Not at all! Rather, because of their transgression, salvation has come to the Gentiles to make Israel envious. But if their transgression means riches for the world, and their loss means riches for the Gentiles, how much greater riches will their fullness bring!

To many people the doctrines of election and reprobation seem wrong because they appear to be arbitrary. "Arbitrary" means that there are no reasons for them. It means that God chooses one and not another as if he were plucking petals from a daisy, saying: "I love you. . . . I love you not. . . . I love you. . . . I love you not."

That is not an accurate picture, of course. True, we dare not think that God owes us an explanation for what he is doing or that we could fully understand it if he should give us a complete one. But even if we do not have an explanation, that does not mean that God does not have his reasons. God is a purposeful God, and we should rightly suppose that everything he does has a purpose, and an infinitely wise one at that.

However, God has given us some explanation of why he chooses some people and passes by others. We saw it when we were studying Romans 9. It is that God might be glorified, that is, that he might be known as he truly is.

In Romans 9, Paul taught that God makes his patience, wrath, and power known in the case of the reprobate, whom he passes by and judges for their sin, and that he reveals his mercy in the case of the elect, whom he saves apart from any supposed worthiness in them.

But there is more. We remember that Paul is dealing with the meaning of history in these chapters, and this means that he is writing on what we might call a down-to-earth level as well as on a theological one. He has been talking about the passing by of the great mass of Israel, which has rejected Jesus as the Messiah. "Does God have a purpose in that?" we might ask.

The verses we come to now teach that God *does* have a purpose. God is using the passing by of Israel to bring salvation riches to the Gentiles.

Four Important Points

We are entering a new section of Paul's overall argument in these verses. They are the start of the sixth of the seven arguments I have outlined and reviewed many times already in this volume.[1] Therefore, this is a good point to look in a comprehensive way at what Paul says. In Romans 11:11–12, Paul makes four points that govern his thought throughout the remainder of the chapter.

1. *Israel has "stumbled," but their stumble is not final.* They fell down, but they will get up again. Earlier, Paul made the point that the unbelief of Israel is not complete; that is, there is and has always been a remnant. In this section he teaches that the unbelief of Israel will not be forever. They stumbled as a nation by their rejection of Jesus as their Savior and Messiah, but they will rise again.

2. *Their "stumble" had a purpose: it would be used by God to bring salvation to the Gentiles.* Later in this chapter, Paul will speak about the opening of salvation to the Gentiles as a "mystery," something that was formerly unknown and hidden but is now revealed (v. 25; cf. Rom. 16:25; Eph. 3:3–4, 6, 9; Col. 1:26). Few would have suspected this from what is taught in the Old Testament, still less that the salvation of the Gentiles would be achieved by the Jewish rejection of Jesus. But such is the case! It is an example of the "riches of the wisdom and knowledge of God" about which Paul will write later (Rom. 11:33).

It is a case of severe judgment resulting in great blessing!

Robert Haldane says of this point, "We ought to remember that the Lord may have infinitely wise and gracious motives for his most severe and terrible judgments."[2]

---

1. The latest was in "God's Remnant" (Romans 11:2–5), but also many times before that.
2. Robert Haldane, *An Exposition of the Epistle to the Romans* (MacDill AFB: MacDonald Publishing, 1958), p. 532.

3. *The salvation of the Gentiles will lead in time to the "fullness" of Israel, that is, to the salvation of the Jews as a nation, and this in turn will lead to even greater Gentile blessing.* If the salvation of the Gentiles was a mystery, this is an apparently greater mystery still. It means that the Jews have not been cast off so that salvation might come to the Gentiles instead, but that through Gentile salvation the Jews themselves might find Jesus as their Savior.

4. *The way this will happen is by the spiritual riches of the Gentiles making Israel envious.* They will see what the Gentiles have, recognize that these spiritual blessings were intended for them, and long to possess them, too. Leon Morris expresses this rightly when he writes, "Paul is saying that the salvation of the Gentiles was intended in the divine providence to arouse in Israel a passionate desire for the same good gift."[3]

Gentile Salvation

The first two of these points are unquestionably true, of course: (1) Israel has rejected Jesus, and (2) their rejection of Jesus has resulted in the spread of the gospel to the Gentiles. The Book of Acts tells the story.

We must remember that nearly all the first Christians were Jews, in spite of the fact that people from scores of nations heard the gospel and believed it as a result of Peter's preaching at Pentecost (Acts 2:15, 40). Acts recounts how in those early days "they continued to meet together in the temple courts" (Acts 2:46), and, as we learn later through the controversy over Gentile circumcision, they all undoubtedly continued to observe the ceremonies, sabbaths, rites, feasts, and holy days of Israel. This would have continued indefinitely, with Christianity becoming only a minority sect of traditional Judaism, were it not for the persecution that broke out as a result of the opposition to the gospel by the Jewish authorities.

Acts 4 tells how Peter and John, the chief leaders, were brought before the Sanhedrin and threatened with harm unless they should cease preaching Jesus. Chapter 5 tells of the arrest and subsequent flogging of all the apostles. Chapter 7 recounts the death of Stephen, the first Christian martyr, which seems to have triggered a general persecution. The text says of that event, "On that day a great persecution broke out against the church at Jerusalem, and all except the apostles were scattered throughout Judea and Samaria" (Acts 8:1).

The scattering caused Philip, one of the newly elected deacons, to go to Samaria, where he preached Christ and many Samaritans believed (Acts 8:4–7). Then God sent him south along the desert road to Gaza, where he explained the gospel to the Ethiopian eunuch (vv. 26–39). Philip led him to Christ, and the eunuch carried the gospel back to his home in Ethiopia. Philip

---

3. Leon Morris, *The Epistle to the Romans* (Grand Rapids: Wm. B. Eerdmans, and Leicester, England: Inter-Varsity Press, 1988), p. 407.

then made his way up the Gentile coast to Caesarea, where he seems to have settled down and carried on a long and effective ministry (Acts 21:8).

Paul's story is similar. Paul was converted on his way to Damascus to arrest Christians there. After his conversion, he might have stayed in that city except for Jewish rejection of Jesus and the consequent persecution. When "the Jews conspired to kill him," the disciples lowered the apostle over the city walls by night in a basket so he could escape (Acts 9:23–25). Paul had been living in Jerusalem before this and would probably have returned and settled there after his escape from Damascus, except for more persecution in the capital. When the Jews of Jerusalem tried to kill him, the disciples "took him down to Caesarea and sent him off to Tarsus" (v. 30).

So also later, during the course of his missionary career. It was Paul's procedure to go to the Jewish synagogues whenever he entered a city. But his message was almost universally rejected, and when that happened he went to the Gentiles. This took him to scores of Gentile cities.

At Pisidian Antioch (Acts 13). "When the Jews saw the crowds, they were filled with jealousy and talked abusively against what Paul was saying. . . . The word of the Lord spread through the whole region. But the Jews incited the God-fearing women of high standing and the leading men of the city. They stirred up persecution against Paul and Barnabas, and expelled them from their region" (vv. 45, 49–50). As a result, the missionary party went to Iconium.

At Iconium (Acts 14). "The Jews who refused to believe stirred up the Gentiles and poisoned their minds against the brothers. . . . There was a plot afoot . . . to mistreat them and stone them" (vv. 2, 5). As a result of this rejection, Paul and Barnabas took the gospel to the Lycaonian cities of Lystra and Derbe.

At Lystra (Acts 14). "Some Jews came from Antioch and Iconium and won the crowd over. They stoned Paul and dragged him outside the city, thinking he was dead" (v. 19). The next day, Paul and Barnabas went to Derbe.

At Thessalonica (Acts 17). On the second missionary journey, Paul and his new missionary companion, Silas, came to Thessalonica. Paul preached in the synagogue, as was his custom. "But the Jews were jealous; so they rounded up some bad characters from the marketplace, formed a mob and started a riot in the city" (v. 5). The trouble caused Paul to move on to Berea.

At Berea (Acts 17). At Berea those who rejected Christ caused trouble (v. 13), and Paul went to Athens.

At Ephesus (Acts 19). On the third missionary journey, Paul came to Ephesus. The riot at Ephesus caused Paul to leave that city and travel again through Macedonia.

In every place it was the same story. It was exactly as Paul later wrote in Romans: "Because of their transgression [he means the rejection of Jesus as Messiah and Savior by the Jews], salvation has come to the Gentiles to make Israel envious." Rejection and persecution have had that effect wherever the messengers of the cross have come. Rejection has always led to the spread of the gospel elsewhere. The great Christian apologist Tertullian said, "The blood of the martyrs is the seed of the church." So it has been.

Jewish Salvation

What about the third of Paul's four points? The first two are obviously true: (1) Israel has rejected Jesus, and (2) the rejection of Jesus by Israel has resulted in the expansion of the gospel to the Gentiles. The third point is that the salvation of the Gentiles would lead in time to the "fullness" of Israel, that is, to the salvation of Israel as a nation, and that this in turn would lead to even greater Gentile blessing. This has not happened yet, but it will happen.

In view of Paul's clear statements here and throughout Romans 11, I cannot see how so many reformed theologians of our day reject the idea of a future time of blessing for Israel.[4] I know *why* they do it. They do not like the details of prophecy that some have worked out, in which Israel seems to have a separate destiny from the church. And they do not like the implied theology. To their way of thinking, any future blessing of Israel as a nation must be a backward step, a regression in God's plan. Spiritual realities in Christ have replaced the Jewish types that pointed to them. The church has replaced Israel. In this view the church becomes the new Israel, and the old Israel is superseded forever.

But how they can affirm that, in view of Paul's teaching here? Paul is not talking about spiritual Israel in these chapters. He is talking about the Jews *as a nation*. And when he asks the question, "Did they stumble so as to fall beyond recovery?" his answer is as emphatic as when he is dealing with antinomianism or with the good purposes of God's law (Rom. 6:2, 15; 7:13). "Not at all!" By no means! God forbid! It was inconceivable to Paul that God would cast Israel off, because to do so would mean that God would be breaking his covenant promises, and he could not do that and remain a truth-keeping, faithful God.

---

4. I say "theologians of our day" because many Reformed writers in the past, though not the sixteenth-century Reformers, have recognized this truth clearly. F. Godet writes forcibly, "It is almost inconceivable how our Reformers could have held out obstinately, as they have done, against a thought so clearly expressed. . . . When Israel shall see the promises of the Old Testament, which ascribe to the Messiah the conversion of the Gentiles to the God of Abraham, fulfilled throughout the whole world by Jesus Christ, and the Gentiles through his mediation loaded with the blessings which they themselves covet, they will be forced to own that Jesus is the Messiah" (*Commentary on St. Paul's Epistle to the Romans*, trans. A. Cusin [Edinburgh: T. & T. Clark, 1892], vol. 2, pp. 254–256). So also Charles Hodge: "Israel . . . must mean the Jewish people, and all Israel the whole nation. The Jews, as a people, are now rejected; as a people, they are to be restored" (*A Commentary on Romans* [Edinburgh and Carlisle, Pa.: The Banner of Truth Trust, 1972], p. 374); and Robert Haldane: "The rejection is to continue till the fullness of the Gentiles shall come in. Then the people of Israel, as a body, shall be brought to the faith of the Gospel" (*An Exposition of the Epistle to the Romans*, p. 541). John Murray and Leon Morris express similar conclusions.

The Problem Is with Us

When we look at these three points, we have to admit that there are no real problems with them: (1) Israel has rejected Christ, (2) their rejection has resulted in an extension of blessings to the Gentiles, and (3) the nation of Israel will yet be saved. The only problem is with *point four.* And it is not God's problem! It is ours. Why has the conversion of Israel as a nation not taken place? If we answer in terms of the mechanism given as an answer in verse 11, the problem is obvious. For the most part, Gentile Christians have not lived in a way that would provoke anyone, let alone the Jews, to envy what they possess.

Does our conduct as Gentiles lead the Jews to desire what we have? Does it lead anybody to desire it? Honesty compels us to admit that our conduct has in general led to exactly the opposite result.

The sin is not entirely on one side, of course. Any Christian who has talked with Jews about Jesus must be amazed at the blindness that seems to have settled over most Jewish people. Even if they know their own Scriptures well, which most do not, they seem to go to incredible lengths to deny their clear teaching. Recently, an intelligent Jewish leader told a member of our staff, "Nowhere in the Scriptures is there a prophecy of an individual Jewish Messiah." This man takes the prophecies to refer to the nation collectively instead. There is much blindness.

But our sin is equal to theirs, or even greater. We know the gospel. We have the power of the Holy Spirit to live like Jesus Christ and show his love to all who are perishing, Jews and Gentiles alike. But instead of showing love to Jews, most Gentiles (even many genuine Christians) have shown the Jews prejudice and hatred. "Instead of showing to God's ancient people the attractiveness of the Christian way, Christians have characteristically treated the Jews with hatred, prejudice, persecution, malice, and all uncharitableness," writes Leon Morris.

He adds in what is surely a major understatement, "Christians should not take this passage calmly."[5]

How Should We Evangelize?

Let us take it seriously. Let us take it seriously enough to ask: "How, then, should we evangelize?" and, "What kind of evangelists should we be?" Here are some suggestions.

1. *We should be friends to those we wish to win.* I do not mean to suggest by this that it is impossible to present the claims of Christ to strangers. It is possible, and we should do it as God gives opportunity. But as striking as stories about speaking to someone on an airplane and having that person make a decision for Christ on the spot may be, most conversions do not happen that

5. Morris, *The Epistle to the Romans,* p. 407.

way. They happen as people who know Jesus as their Savior tell friends about him. The trouble with most of us is that we do not have many non-Christian friends, though we should have.

There is an emphasis today on what is called "friendship evangelism." Joe Aldrich has written books on this subject. It is how the Billy Graham crusades are lifted up and carried forward, and the crusade workers train lay people in this area. I commend it to you.

2. *We should be models of help and service.* We should be models in this area even apart from any evangelistic interest, simply because we should be helpful and serving people. But, in addition to this, there is no doubt that many have been won to Christ by someone who helped them in Christ's name. Aren't you disposed to like and listen to someone who helps you? And aren't you turned off by someone who does not? Or is rude? Why should it be any different with unbelievers?

If you are serious about evangelism, you should seek ways to help others regularly. If you do not know how to do this on your own, find a program that will give you a structure for it.

3. *Let everything you do be characterized by love.* The distinguished missionary statesman E. Stanley Jones once asked the Indian leader Mahatma Gandhi what Christians would have to do to win India for Jesus Christ. Gandhi knew India well, and he knew Christians well, too. He said, "There are four things Christians should do if they want to win India for Christ. First, Christians should act like Jesus Christ. Second, do not compromise your faith. Third, learn all you can about the non-Christian religions. And fourth, let everything you do be characterized by love." Gandhi knew the force of love, and he had seen much of its opposite, particularly from Christians. So he spoke wisely when he reminded the followers of Jesus: "Let everything you do be characterized by love."

4. *We must verbalize the gospel.* We must act out of love, but we must also speak the truth of the gospel in love, because the gospel is truth and it is the truth of his Word that God blesses.

How do we do that in the area of Jewish evangelism? We have to be friends first, of course. We have to be helpful and show love. But, having done that and thus having earned a right to speak, we can begin by reminding the Jews of their own great religious heritage. We can remind them that there were many thousands of years of past history when Israel alone had knowledge of the true God. In the days of Abraham and the patriarchs, Moses, David and the other kings, Isaiah and Jeremiah and the prophets, only the Jews knew God truly. God was the God of Israel. Gentiles were outside of that great national body, and their religions were utter paganism. While the Gentiles lived in their paganism and its resulting moral degeneracy, the Jews were receiving God's moral law and were being taught the way of approach to God by sacrifices.

In that day, the only way a Gentile could be saved was by identifying with the Jewish nation. A few did. Ruth the Moabitess was one. Naaman the Syrian was another. But there were not many. Most Gentiles were cut off from salvation by geography and ethnic origins. Jesus was right when he told the Samaritan woman, "Salvation is from the Jews" (John 4:22).

But when God sent Jesus to be the Savior, he sent him not only to be the Savior of the Jews but as the world's Savior, too. When Jesus died, God showed this by tearing the veil of the temple in two from top to bottom. That act signified that the way to God was now open to anyone who would come through faith in his sacrifice. In one sense that meant the end of Judaism, at least in its ancient form. No Jew today worships at a temple in Jerusalem. No Jew brings the required sacrifices for sin. The end of that system was the opening of salvation to Gentiles.

It is the way I have been saved. Now by the grace of the God of Israel, I, a Gentile "dog," have been brought into the blessings that ancient Israel once enjoyed alone. I have been made a member of the covenant people. I have been brought by faith into the spiritual succession of the patriarchs.

I realize that the very name "Jesus" may be offensive to you if you are a Jew, and I can understand why. Christians, certainly Gentiles, have often behaved horribly toward Jews. But I ask you to recognize this: If Jesus is not the Messiah of Israel, then there is no hope for my salvation. I am a lost pagan, without hope and without God in the world. It is only by the Jewish Messiah and by the grace of the Jews' God that I am saved. That is why I commend Jesus so earnestly to you as your Savior.

161

Life from the Dead

Romans 11:13-15

I am talking to you Gentiles. Inasmuch as I am the apostle to the Gentiles, I make much of my ministry in the hope that I may somehow arouse my own people to envy and save some of them. For if their rejection is the reconciliation of the world, what will their acceptance be but life from the dead?

The title of this study, "Life from the Dead," is taken from the phrase Paul uses for the anticipated salvation of Israel as a nation in the final days of world history: "If their rejection is the reconciliation of the world, what will their acceptance be but life from the dead?" (v. 15). This is a tremendous prediction, a description of what can only rightly be called a national resurrection. But if we are to understand the resurrection part, both for Israel and ourselves, which is our goal in this study, we must begin with the part that speaks about death.

In our day Israel is spiritually dead, though she is to rise again, just as all persons are spiritually dead apart from the life-giving work of God in Jesus Christ. To deal with this important subject, I want to start not with the teaching of Paul in Romans 11, though we will come back to it, but with the teaching of Jesus Christ.

The Death of a Nation

During the last week of our Lord's earthly life, following his entry into Jerusalem on what we call Palm Sunday, Jesus focused nearly all his teaching on events that were to come. John's Gospel has one version of this emphasis; it tells us about Jesus' *private* teaching of the disciples. This instruction had to do largely with the coming of the Holy Spirit, the privilege of prayer, persecution from the world, and Jesus' promise to take care of his disciples and make them fruitful in his service.

The Synoptic Gospels focus on the Lord's *public* teaching.

What did Jesus teach publicly? I ask this question here, because the emphasis was along the lines Paul has been developing in the eleventh chapter of Romans and is the background for it.

Consider the twenty-first chapter of Matthew. The first part of that chapter describes Jesus' triumphal entry into Jerusalem, followed by the cleansing of the temple. This angered the Jewish leaders, with the result that Jesus "left them" figuratively as well as literally (v. 17), returning to Bethany where he and his disciples spent each night of the final week.

The next morning on the way back to the city, Jesus saw a fig tree, which he approached, expecting to find figs. Instead, it was barren; so he cursed it, saying, "May you never bear fruit again!" (v. 19). This was not a rare case of pique on Jesus' part. Everyone can understand that. Rather it was a parable in which the fig tree represented Israel. The tree was supposed to have been fruitful, but it was not. It was judged for its barrenness.

This acted parable is then followed by a pair of spoken parables. The first concerned two sons, each of whom was told by his father to go and work in his vineyard (Matt. 21:28–32). One said he would go, but did not. The other refused, but later went. When Jesus asked which son did what his father wanted, his hearers replied rightly that it was the one who actually went into the vineyard and worked there. Jesus made this application: "I tell you the truth, the tax collectors and the prostitutes are entering the kingdom of God ahead of you. For John came to you to show you the way of righteousness, and you did not believe him, but the tax collectors and the prostitutes did. And even after you saw this, you did not repent and believe him" (vv. 31–32).

The point is obvious. It is not what we say that matters with God, but what we do, and what God requires us to do is to repent of our sin and believe on Jesus. The people as a whole had not done this.

The second parable is even more devastating. It concerned a landowner who planted a vineyard and leased it to tenant farmers (Matt. 21:32–44). He went away on a journey, and when the harvest came, he sent servants to collect his share of the produce. Instead of giving it to him, the tenants seized the servants, beat one, killed another, and stoned a third. At last the owner sent his son, thinking the tenants would respect him. But instead of respecting him and receiving him well, the tenants killed him, too.

"When the owner of the vineyard comes, what will he do to those tenants?" Jesus asked.

The religious leaders answered that he would bring them "to a wretched end," then "rent the vineyard to other tenants," who would "give him his share of the crop at harvest time" (v. 41).

Jesus then made clear that in this parable God is the Father, he himself is the Son, and his hearers are the tenant farmers. He quoted Psalm 118:22, which says, "The stone the builders rejected has become the capstone," concluding, "Therefore I tell you that the kingdom of God will be taken away from you and given to a people who will produce its fruit" (v. 43). This was an unequivocal statement that the kingdom of God would be taken away from the Jewish people and given to the Gentiles, which, of course, is exactly what Paul teaches has happened.

In the verses that are our text (Rom. 11:13–15), Paul speaks of Israel having been rejected (v. 15). In the verses we looked at in the last study, he made the same point by speaking of the people's "fall" and "loss" (vv. 11–12).

A Present Sad Reality

This is an all-too-sad reality, of course. As Paul saw it, the tragedy lay in Israel's rejection of Jesus as the Messiah, with all that entailed. For centuries the Jews had been waiting anxiously for the Messiah's coming, asking themselves whether any leader who emerged above the average might be him. This is what they asked John the Baptist. "Are you the Christ?" "Are you Elijah?" "Are you the Prophet?" (cf. John 1:19–21). If Jesus was the Christ, as Paul firmly preached he was, Israel's rejection of Jesus was a rejection of the very future for which they had been hoping. It was a repudiation of their spiritual destiny. Paul was acutely aware of this and grieved for what his people had lost.

But even that is not the worst that had happened. If Jesus was the Messiah, the kingdom of God was wrapped up in him and to reject him was to reject or lose that kingdom.

This means that by rejecting Jesus, Israel lost all that was truly spiritual in their heritage. They still had their feasts and celebrations, of course, but they lost what those important celebrations stood for. Yom Kippur, the Day of Atonement, is a chief example. On that day the high priest was to perform two important acts. First, he was to sacrifice a goat and then take some of its blood into the Most Holy Place of the temple and sprinkle it on the Mercy Seat of the Ark of the Covenant, thereby making atonement for the people's sins. The blood of the innocent victim thus came between the holy presence of God, understood to be above the Mercy Seat between the outstretched wings of the cherubim, and the broken law of God, which was contained within the Ark. It was a picture of what theologians call substitutionary or vicarious atonement. It is why the day was rightly called the Day of *Atonement*.

The second act involved a live goat. The high priest was to place his hands upon the head of this goat while confessing the sins of the people to God, thereby transferring them to the goat in a symbolic way. Then the goat was to be driven out into the wilderness to die there. This symbolized the bearing away of the nation's sins.

This symbolism was fulfilled by Jesus Christ, who made atonement for our sins by his death and also bore them away from us, which was symbolized by his dying outside the walls of Jerusalem. When Israel rejected Jesus, the people lost what the Day of Atonement stood for. So today, although Jews observe Yom Kippur, it is no longer a true day of atonement, because there is no atonement. There are no sacrifices. Instead, it has become a day merely for confessing one's sin and feeling remorse for it. It has become a ritual rather than a hopeful reality.

Even the Passover has suffered this fate. The central feature of the Passover was the Passover lamb, the blood of which was spread upon the doorposts of the houses of the Jewish people so that the angel of death would pass over them and the firstborn of those homes would not die. The blood of the lamb was an atonement for the people's sin, just as the blood of the goat was an atonement. The Jewish people were as much sinners as the Egyptians. But today, when the Passover is observed by Jews, the day has no atoning significance. Indeed, it has nothing to do with sin or its removal, but only with the memory of the physical deliverance of the people from their earthly bondage.

All this was finalized, as it were, by the destruction of Jerusalem shortly after the time of Jesus and Paul. When the Romans conquered the city in 72 A.D., the temple was destroyed, and it has never been rebuilt. The temple ceremonies ceased with its destruction. In fact, even the nation ceased to exist as a nation, and it is only recently and after nearly two thousand of years of history that a remnant of the people has been regathered in their homeland as the newly reconstructed Israel.

A Resurrected People

That may very well be significant. For although in Paul's day the nation was on the verge of ceasing to be a nation, the regathering of the people in our day may be the beginning of events leading to the resurrection of the people about whom Paul is speaking.

There are three possible ways the phrase "life from the dead" can be taken. It is appropriate to note them here.

1. *A figurative expression.* The words can be no more than a figurative expression, which is how Charles Hodge regards them. "The most common and natural interpretation is that which considers the later clause ['life from the dead'] as merely a figurative expression of a joyful and desirable event."[1] There is noth-

---

1. Charles Hodge, *A Commentary on Romans* (Edinburgh and Carlisle, Pa.: The Banner of Truth Trust, 1972), p. 365. Original edition 1935.

ing wrong with this, of course. The conversion of the masses of Israel, resulting in additional blessing for the Gentile world, can certainly be described by any phrase that is joyful. But "life from the dead" is such a powerful phrase that it is hard to believe that it does not suggest a great deal more than this.

2. *The final resurrection.* A large number of commentators, both ancient and modern, have thought of the phrase "life from the dead" as referring to the final resurrection, on the grounds that only the resurrection of the dead can be the climactic event of world history. The resurrection and the final judgment to follow it are the climax of world history, of course. But it is questionable whether "life from the dead" can mean this. Leon Morris notes that "life from the dead" nowhere else refers to the resurrection, and the closest equivalent phrase ("alive from the dead," Rom. 6:13, Greek text) refers not to the resurrection, but to the spiritual life of Christians through their mystical union with Jesus Christ.

Besides, Paul is speaking of something that is to occur within history, and the resurrection is not to be thought of as being within history so much as being the termination of it.

Paul's use of the illustration of the olive tree in the verses that follow also suggests this, because it places the breaking off of the Jewish branches, the grafting in of the Gentile branches, and the eventual regrafting of the Jewish branches all on the same plane. Since the first two are within history, the last should be also.

3. *The spiritual regeneration of Israel.* The third interpretation does not exclude interpretation number one, but it sees "life from the dead" as referring also to the spiritual regeneration of the Jewish people, which will certainly be necessary if they are to believe on Jesus as their Messiah and be saved by him. It is a necessity for everyone.

Why did the Jews reject Jesus, after all? It is not sufficient to say that they were "a stiff-necked people," extremely stubborn, although many Jews undoubtedly are, just like many Gentiles. The reason people reject Jesus Christ is because they are dead in their sins, and being spiritually dead, they are unable to understand the extent of their need, comprehend the grace of God in the gospel, or yield their hearts to the Savior. This is what Paul was teaching in the earlier chapters of this letter when he pointed out that

> There is no one righteous, not even one;
> there is no one who understands,
> no one who seeks God.
>
> Romans 3:10–11

It is what he teaches in Ephesians when he writes, "As for you, you were dead in your transgressions and sins" (Eph. 2:1). Paul means that apart from a spiritual resurrection, which Jesus called being "born again," no one is able to be good, understand spiritual things, or seek God. On the contrary, we run away from him and make substitute gods to take the true God's place.

"The Resurrection and the Life"

So what is the solution? The solution is obvious. We need to be born again. We need a spiritual resurrection. We need God, because only God is able to give life and provide resurrections. But praise be to God, this is exactly what God does. God is in the resurrection business.

I remind you of the death and resurrection of Lazarus (John 11:1–44). Jesus had been away from Jerusalem and Bethany preaching in the area of the Jordan River when Lazarus got sick, and although the sick man's sisters immediately sent word to Jesus, Lazarus died and had been in his tomb four days before Jesus got back to Bethany where Lazarus's sisters lived. At first Jesus had private conversations with the two sisters, Martha and later Mary. He told Martha, "I am the resurrection and the life. He who believes in me will live, even though he dies, and whoever lives and believes in me will never die" (v. 25). It was a declaration that Jesus is able to bring life out of death, both spiritually and physically, the very thing we are talking about.

When Jesus asked where Lazarus had been buried, the sisters, their friends, and the accompanying mourners led him to the tomb. Jesus asked for the stone to be removed.

"But, Lord," said Martha, "by this time there is a bad odor, for he has been there four days."

Jesus replied that she was going to "see the glory of God." He prayed, thanking God that he had heard him and always heard him. Then he addressed the dead man.

"Lazarus, come out!"

The Bible says, in what is surely a great understatement, "The dead man came out, his hands and feet wrapped with strips of linen, and a cloth around his face" (v. 44).

If this were only the story of a physical resurrection, it would be spectacular enough. We have bodies, and our bodies die. We need physical resurrections if we are to stand before God, see his face, and worship him forever—as we sense we have been destined by God to do. But the deaths of our bodies are not our greatest problem, nor is a physical resurrection our greatest need. We also have dead souls, and we need the resurrection of our souls and spirits if we are to turn to Jesus Christ in living faith and find salvation in him.

Fortunately, the story of Lazarus is also about spiritual resurrections and the promise that spiritual life is to be found in Jesus. He alone can do what needs to be done. He alone can call us from the dark, loathsome charnel house of sin.

And he does. Everyone who has ever come to Christ in saving faith has experienced just such a spiritual resurrection. We were dead in our sins, but we heard Jesus calling, "Lazarus, come out! . . . John, come out! . . . Mary, come out! . . . Robert, come out! . . ." Whatever our name has been! And we responded. All who have ever heard that call have responded and have thereby passed out of spiritual death into spiritual life.

Have you? If you have not, I urge you to pay attention to the Bible, the Word of God, because it is through the Bible and its teaching that Jesus calls men and women today. Read it. Allow yourself to be exposed to sound teaching. Meditate on Bible truths.

I believe that if you do that, you will hear Jesus calling and will find that his call is bringing you to new spiritual life.

Resurrection of a Nation

This brings me back to Israel as a nation, for it is Israel we are talking about primarily, and it is the resurrection of that nation that is our chief concern in this passage. We are studying the teaching that the Jews will have a spiritual rebirth in the final days.

I know there are people who consider that impossible, and for a number of reasons. Some reasons are theological, like those I mentioned in the previous study. Some are practical: "How can such a thing happen, considering the fierce opposition the Jews have shown to the gospel through the centuries?" I grant that these are large obstacles on the human level. I cannot even imagine how my sympathetic Gentile neighbor can come to believe in Christ, considering the effects of sin in blinding the human heart, not to mention Jewish people, who have good historical reasons for resenting Christians and resisting evangelism.

But we are not talking on the human level here. We are speaking about God and about resurrections, of which only he is capable. "With God all things are possible" (Matt. 19:26). Why should the future gathering in of Israel be thought impossible when it is God who is doing the gathering?

New Life Now

Let me add something else as well, even though it is not to be found in our text, strictly speaking. Because God is God of the impossible and of resurrections, God is also more than adequate for your problems in life right now, whatever they might be.

I have had people tell me that their problems are insolvable. They have been trapped in a sinful sexual relationship that they could not break or an addiction from which they could not free themselves. Is that your story? If it is, let me assure you that it is not impossible for God to solve. If Jesus can raise Lazarus from the dead, he can break your destructive habits. He can free you from any sin, however dreadful it may be or however long you may have practiced it. He can release you to serve him.

Other people have told me that a relationship that once meant a great deal to them has died. People often speak this way of a marriage that is going through difficult times. What do you do when love seems to have departed and affection seems to have failed? The world is ready to break off such marriages, of course, claiming that they must have been mistakes. But if this is your situation, I tell you on the authority of the Word of God that this is no course for a Christian. You are to stand against this "easy" escape, and prove by the resurrection of your marriage that God is still the God of miracles.

Do you say it can't happen? Not to you?

Of course, it can happen. Do you think you are a more difficult case than anyone else? You are not. You are like everybody else. And besides, who said it has anything to do with what you are like? We are not talking here about human possibilities. We are speaking about what God can do and will do if you will ask him to do it and determine to obey him, however costly that may be. What is more, if you will do it, you will find that the demonstration of the life-giving power of God in your life will be used by God to draw others to faith, just as many believed on Jesus because of his resurrection of Lazarus.

One of the reasons we have so little true faith today is that we have so few genuine transformations. Let us do what we can to set that straight. Let us have more "life from the dead" Christianity.

162

Holy to the Lord

Romans 11:16

If the part of the dough offered as firstfruits is holy, then the whole batch is holy; if the root is holy, so are the branches.

If I were to ask anyone today what he or she thinks of first when asked to list the characteristics or attributes of God, I am sure that in nearly every case the person I would be speaking to would say "love." Yet that would not have been true for the Old Testament saints. They would have said "holiness." Surprisingly, that is a concept almost never thought about by most people today.

What is more, not only did the Old Testament figures think of holiness when they thought about God. They also thought of holiness in reference to anything or anybody who had contact with God, for they knew that only what is holy can have contact with him. Holiness dominated their religious ideas. We can see this by the variety of ways the word *holy* is used. R. C. Sproul, in his study of *The Holiness of God,* provides a partial list of items to which the word was applied: holy ground, holy Sabbath, holy convocation, holy nation, holy anointing oil, holy linen coat, holy jubilee, holy house, holy field, holy tithe, holy water, holy censers, holy ark, holy bread, holy city, holy seed, holy word, holy covenant, holy ones, the Holy Place, and the Holy of Holies.[1]

1. R. C. Sproul, *The Holiness of God* (Wheaton, Ill.: Tyndale House, 1985), pp. 55, 56.

On top of everything else, God was the thrice-holy God. "Holy, holy, holy is the LORD Almighty," called the angels (Isa. 6:3).

Holy Dough and Holy Branches

We need to remember this when we come to Romans 11:16, for Paul is certainly writing within an Old Testament framework when he says, almost casually, "If the part of the dough offered as firstfruits is holy, then the whole batch is holy; if the root is holy, so are the branches."

That strikes us as very strange.

Holy dough? And holy branches? We can understand how God might be thought of as holy, though we probably do not understand what even that means very well. But to speak of things like dough and branches as "holy" seems almost humorous. It is as though Paul were pulling our leg.

He is not, of course. What he is doing is drawing upon an Old Testament understanding of holiness to carry forward the important point he is making in Romans 11, namely, that God has not given up on Israel. It is true that the mass of Israel has been laid aside temporarily in order that by their rejection, salvation might come to the Gentiles. But even in this period of rejection, Israel has not been rejected *utterly;* a remnant is still being saved. Nor will Israel be rejected *finally;* for at the last the masses of Israel will be brought to faith in Jesus Christ, who died for them that they might have forgiveness for their sins.

We need to look at these two images carefully and then apply them to God and his dealings both with Israel and with us.

1. *The dough.* The translation of the first part of verse 16 given to us by the New International Version is a bit more explicit than Paul himself. Paul does not use the word *dough.* He writes (literally), "If the firstfruit is holy, so also the lump." The emphasis is on "firstfruit," and when we check this concept out in the Old Testament we find it applied to a variety of substances. For example, in Exodus 23:19 it is applied to the first produce of the land, whatever it might be (cf. Deut. 26:1–11). In Exodus 34:22 it is applied to the wheat harvest specifically, and the people are told to present the "firstfruits" in a festival called the Feast of Weeks (cf. Num. 28:26–31) and later at the Feast of Ingathering. Leviticus 2:12, 14 calls the "firstfruits" a grain offering. Leviticus 23 elaborates on the way the offering is to be made. Numbers 15:20–21 describes the offering as a "cake" made from a portion of ground meal. In Numbers 18:12 the "firstfruits" are olive oil and new wine, as well as grain.

Paul does not specify which of these "firstfruit" offerings he has in mind. But since he ends the sentence with the word *lump,* the New International Version translators are probably right to assume that Paul is thinking of Numbers 15 particularly and so offer the interpretive translation, "If the part of the dough offered as firstfruits is holy, then the whole batch is holy."

But we still haven't discovered what this means. We are wondering, "What are the firstfruits? And what does the 'whole batch' represent?"

The only way to understand this image is from the context, of course. But even when we do that there are at least two possibilities. Some writers have identified the "firstfruits" as the first Jewish converts, thus viewing them as a pledge of more converts to come, represented by the "whole batch." That would prepare for the conclusion Paul will reach in verse 26: "And so all Israel will be saved." The trouble is that it would be out of step with the second of the two images Paul uses: that of the root and branches. In that image, the root stands for the patriarchs. It is how Paul himself interprets it in verse 28: "As far as the gospel is concerned, they are enemies on your account; but as far as election is concerned, they are loved on account of the patriarchs."

This parallel suggests that both "firstfruits" in the first illustration and "root" in the second illustration represent Abraham, which is the second of the two possibilities I mentioned. Most commentators hold to this view, among them Charles Hodge, who gives four excellent reasons why the reference must be to Abraham.[2]

2. *The root and the branches.* The second of these two images is not so prominent in the Old Testament, but it is the easier of the two to understand, since Paul develops it himself in this passage. It is what verses 17–24, which follow our text, are all about. In this similitude, the root stands for the patriarchs of Israel (perhaps only Abraham), the natural olive with its many branches stands for the nation of Israel, and the wild olive tree stands for the Gentile peoples. In Paul's development of the idea, the natural branches, representing individual Jews or successive generations of Jews, are broken off in order that branches from the wild tree, representing individual Gentiles or successive generations of Gentiles, are grafted in. The bottom line of the illustration is that in time God is going to graft the original or natural branches back into their own olive tree.

This brings us to the root meaning of verse 16, of course. For Paul is saying that the patriarchs were "set apart" to God and that this has inescapable consequences for their descendants. To put it in the simplest possible terms: The Jews are a special people because of their descent from Abraham, and this is true of them even in their rebellious and unregenerate state. It means that even yet God has not given up on Israel.

A Holy Nation

Here we have to think about the word *holy.* It is one of the hardest words in the Bible to define. There are several reasons for this. One is that it is a chief, if not *the* chief attribute of God, and we can never understand God as

---

2. "1. Because this interpretation alone preserves the propriety of the figure. . . . 2. This interpretation best suits the design of the apostle. . . . 3. This is the apostle's own explanation in verse 28. . . . 4. This interpretation alone can be consistently carried through the following verses" (Charles Hodge, *A Commentary on Romans* [Edinburgh and Carlisle, Pa.: The Banner of Truth Trust, 1972], pp. 366, 367. Original edition 1935).

he is in himself completely. It is also difficult because the word is used of people ("Be holy, because I am holy," Lev. 11:44–45; cf. Lev. 19:2; 20:7; 1 Peter 1:16) and of objects. A few of the objects it is linked to were listed earlier.

The bottom line of these three applications of the word *holy*—(1) to God, (2) to human beings, and (3) to objects—is that holiness has to do with being "set apart." If you can remember that, you will be able to understand the word in each of these rather diverse applications.

1. *A holy God.* When we speak about God being holy, most people think that this means that God does not sin. Everything he does is right. That is involved in the matter of God being holy, but it is not really what holiness is about. Holiness means that God is "set apart" from us. That is, he is not like us. He is over and above and utterly beyond us, so that we cannot even begin to imagine what he is like except to the extent that he stoops to reveal himself to us. Theologians have stretched themselves to find terms to express what this means. Germans speak of God being *ganz anders* or "wholly other." English theologians speak of God being transcendent. Rudolf Otto, a German writer, coined a term in Latin, speaking of God as the *mysterium tremendum,* which means an "awe-inspiring mystery."

Let me express this another way. When we speak of God's attributes, we are inclined to list holiness along with such other things as sovereignty, omnipotence, eternity, grace, mercy, love, and so on. But, strictly speaking, holiness does not belong in this catalogue at all, since it describes all that God is and since it qualifies every other attribute. In other words, God is not just sovereign; his is a holy sovereignty. God is not just love; his is a holy love. And so on.

Holiness is what sets God apart from us and renders him awesome to us, who are both finite and sinful.

2. *Holy objects.* How, then, can objects be called holy? At first glance this seems to be utterly impossible, if holiness refers to what God is wholly in himself. But as soon as we remember that holiness describes what is "set apart," the word begins to make sense. Objects become holy when they are "set apart" to God's service rather than to common uses. It is in this way that the Sabbath becomes holy to the Lord. It is a day set apart to God. We desecrate it when we use it for secular ends. In the same way, water, bread, and the temple become holy water, holy bread, and a holy temple when they are set apart for God's service. Each of them becomes holy because of the use to which it is dedicated. In fact, we can speak of holiness as *dedication,* that is, as something "given to God," or even *consecration,* which means "to render sacred (or holy)."

3. *A holy people.* All this brings us to the main point of our study and to the text. For we are speaking here of a holy people, and in its primary sense a

holy people is a people "set apart" for God. This is what Israel was and is. The Jews were set apart to God by his choice of Abraham. Therefore, because Abraham was set apart, so are his descendants, even to this day. This does not mean that all the descendants of Abraham, all Jews, are saved, of course. Paul has already shown that this is not the case. But it does mean that they remain a people set apart for God's purposes. To put it in other language, God is not finished with Israel yet.

One writer who sees this and develops it well is Robert Haldane. He provides several Old Testament texts to illustrate the principle.

Deuteronomy 7:6. In this chapter, Moses is instructing the people on what they are to do when they enter the Promised Land. They are to destroy the Canaanite peoples and their culture, above all refusing to intermarry with them. Why? "For you are a people holy to the LORD your God. The LORD your God has chosen you out of all the peoples on the face of the earth to be his people, his treasured possession."

Deuteronomy 10:15 (with 4:37; 14:2; 26:19; 32:8–9). Israel had been very rebellious against God. Moses reminds the people of it. Nevertheless, he says, "The LORD set his affection on your forefathers and loved them, and he chose you, their descendants, above all the nations, as it is today."

Exodus 2:24. The people were slaves in Egypt and cried out under their harsh bondage. "God heard their groaning and he remembered his covenant with Abraham, with Isaac and with Jacob."

Deuteronomy 4:31. This chapter foresees a day in which the people would fall into idolatry, forsaking the God who had loved them, delivered them from Egypt, and brought them into their land. It promises that in spite of their sin, if they would call out to God in their distress, God would hear them and deliver them. "For the LORD your God is a merciful God; he will not abandon or destroy you or forget the covenant with your forefathers, which he confirmed to them by oath."

Isaiah 43:21. ". . . my chosen, the people I have formed for myself that they may proclaim my praise."

1 Samuel 12:22. After Israel had asked for an earthly king and was given one, Samuel rebuked them for their sin. Nevertheless, he added, "For the sake of his great name the LORD will not reject his people, because the LORD was pleased to make you his own."

It would be possible to add scores of additional verses like these, all showing that for the sake of the patriarchs the people of Israel had a special relationship to God, even when they sinned, and that God would not abandon them. Did they suffer for their sin? Of course! Were all Jews saved? Of course not! Nevertheless, many were, and down through the course of history the purposes of God for his people continued unchanged and in the end will result in their national conversion. Haldane concludes rightly, "As the lump is holy through the offering of the firstfruit and as the tree derives its character from the root, so the descendants of Abraham, Isaac and Jacob, whom the Lord chose, were set apart by solemn covenant for his service and glory."[3]

Holy "On That Day"

I have spoken several times of the Jews as being holy to God in spite of how they lived, that is, as holy even in Israel's rebellion, since they remain God's special people and fulfill God's purposes even in that state. One of those purposes is the salvation of the Gentiles now being accomplished through their rejection, as we have seen. Yet I recognize that it is possible to gain a wrong impression from what I have said about being holy "even in rebellion" and to assume that God does not care how we live. Or, to put it in other words, to suppose that we can be saved without holiness. I want to correct that now, since we must always remember that "without holiness no one will see the Lord" (Heb. 12:14).

To make this point, let me take you to the end of the Book of Zechariah. I go to Zechariah for three reasons. First, Zechariah is a postexilic prophet. That is, he wrote after the return of the Jews from their exile to Babylon. This is important, because there are people who suppose that all the promises of God to the Jews were fulfilled either in the days of Solomon (when they enjoyed the fullest extent of their territorial possessions), in the days of Ezra and Nehemiah (when they were regathered from many places to which they had been scattered), or by the coming of Jesus Christ (when the types and symbols of their earthly worship were fulfilled spiritually in him). But Zechariah lived after the exile and was looking forward to blessing for Israel in days that were (and are) clearly still to come.

Second, Zechariah envisions a specific great day of national blessing, which he refers to repeatedly in the last chapters of his prophecy by the words "on that day." The phrase occurs sixteen times (Zech. 12:3, 4, 6, 8, 9, 11; 13:1, 2, 4; 14:4, 6, 8, 9, 13, 20, 21), and there are other similar terms in addition. This seems to refer to the day (or days) of the final consummation of all things, for it includes judgment upon the Gentile nations as well as forgiveness, restoration, and spiritual blessing for Israel.

The third reason I refer to Zechariah is that the prophet ends on the exact note we have been studying: holiness. In fact, it is he who uses the phrase "holy to the Lord," which I have taken as the title for this study.

Here is how he writes: "On that day HOLY TO THE LORD will be inscribed on the bells of the horses, and the cooking pots in the LORD's house will be like the sacred bowls in front of the altar. Every pot in Jerusalem and Judah will be holy to the LORD Almighty, and all who come to sacrifice will take some of the pots and cook in them. And on that day there will no longer be a Canaanite in the house of the LORD Almighty" (Zech. 14:20–21).

---

3. Robert Haldane, *An Exposition of the Epistle to the Romans* (MacDill AFB: MacDonald Publishing, 1958), p. 535.

What is Zechariah getting at? Why holy bells? And holy cooking pots? The answer, of course, is that Zechariah is looking ahead to the same day Paul is anticipating in Romans 11, when the Jews as a nation will be brought to God and will be forgiven for their sin and purified from it. In that day there will be no mixture, a remnant saved and the larger portion lost. Nor will the people be saved and yet remain in sin. They will be a thoroughly purified people, so much so that everything associated with them will be holy, even the bells on their horses and the pots on their stoves. They will be set apart to God to such a degree that everything they have or touch will be dedicated to him.

And there is another interesting point. In the paragraph immediately before this, Zechariah describes the revitalized people going to Jerusalem to worship God by celebrating the Feast of Tabernacles (or Ingathering). This was a feast at which the "firstfruits" were offered. But the reason for the reference at this point in Zechariah is that the Feast of Tabernacles was the *final* harvest festival, when the whole year's crop was gathered in. We can hardly miss the symbolism. It is the day when the crop of Israel will be gathered to God, when Israel as a nation will be "holy to the Lord" (Zech. 14:20), when "Israel will be saved" (Rom. 11:26).

Our Common Destiny: Holiness

As I began this study I said that in the end I wanted to apply it to ourselves as well as to Israel as a nation, and I want to do that now in closing. The point is that this is also our destiny as Christians. We, too, are to be "holy to the Lord." And if that is the case, if that is what we will surely be one day—since "without holiness no one will see the Lord"—we must strive to be holy now.

Here is how I applied this in my earlier study of the Minor Prophets.[4] Have you ever thought of your destiny in terms of holiness? If you are a Christian, you have been set apart to God to be wholly his. But you are not holy now. You are sinful now, and the more you live, the more you will be aware of it. Your *destiny* is holiness. That is why we read about this so often in the Bible. God told the people through Moses, "Be holy, because I am holy" (Lev. 11:44–45; cf. 19:2; 20:7). And Peter picks up on the theme, writing, "But just as he who called you is holy, so be holy in all you do; for it is written: 'Be holy, because I am holy'" (1 Peter 1:15–16). This is not only a command. It is our sure end. If we belong to Jesus Christ, God, whose purposes do not change, will make us like him in holiness one day.

We usually think of salvation relationally today. That is why, as I said at the beginning of this study, we think of God's attributes as being, first of all, love, then perhaps mercy, kindness, goodness, and such things. This is not wrong, of course. God is love, and we are being enabled to love him and others because he first loved us and so showed us what love is like.

---

4. James Montgomery Boice, *The Minor Prophets: An Expositional Commentary,* vol. 2, *Micah—Malachi* (Grand Rapids: Zondervan, 1986), p. 225. This final section of the present study is borrowed, with changes, from that volume.

But this is not the way the Bible speaks of our destiny. It is not the love relationship that is emphasized. We are not told that we will spend our time in heaven loving God and others, though we undoubtedly will. The Bible emphasizes holiness. And the reason it does is that a lack of holiness is what accounts for our inability to love rightly and, in fact, to do anything else well. The reason our relationships to God are not all they should be is that we are not holy. The reason why our relationships to others are not all they should be is that we are not holy. We need to be holy.

But, praise God, one day we shall be holy. "We shall be like [Jesus], for we shall see him as he is" (1 John 3:2).

So why not be holy now? That is what John concludes. For immediately after telling us that we will be like Jesus one day, he says, "Everyone who has this hope in him purifies himself, just as he is pure" (v. 3). Do you? You will, if you have your eyes fixed on that great destiny.

163

Root, Shoot, and Branches

Romans 11:17–24

If some of the branches have been broken off, and you, though a wild olive shoot, have been grafted in among the others and now share in the nourishing sap from the olive root, do not boast over those branches. If you do, consider this: You do not support the root, but the root supports you. You will say then, "Branches were broken off so that I could be grafted in." Granted. But they were broken off because of unbelief, and you stand by faith. Do not be arrogant, but be afraid. For if God did not spare the natural branches, he will not spare you either.

Consider therefore the kindness and sternness of God: sternness to those who fell, but kindness to you, provided that you continue in his kindness. Otherwise, you also will be cut off. And if they do not persist in unbelief, they will be grafted in, for God is able to graft them in again. After all, if you were cut out of an olive tree that is wild by nature, and contrary to nature were grafted into a cultivated olive tree, how much more readily will these, the natural branches, be grafted into their own olive tree!

If there is any one thing that illustrations are supposed to accomplish, it is that they are to make what is being taught clear. Charles Spurgeon, the great Baptist preacher who was exceptionally good at illustrations, called them "windows that let in light."

The interesting thing about the Bible's illustrations is that they do not always do that. In fact, they sometimes seem to do the opposite. Think of

Jesus' parable of the sower (Matt. 13:1–23). After Jesus had described to the masses of his listeners the four kinds of soil and the four results of the farmer's sowing, the disciples, who did not understand him, asked what the story meant and why he was speaking in parables. Surprisingly, Jesus replied, "The knowledge of the secrets of the kingdom of heaven has been given to you, but not to them. . . . This is why I speak to them in parables . . ." (vv. 11, 13). He was saying that the purpose of his story was to obscure, rather than make the teaching plain.

A Difficult Illustration

The apostle Paul was *not* trying to be obscure when he introduced in Romans 11 the illustration of the olive tree with its rejected and newly grafted branches. He was trying to be clear. Nevertheless, the illustration seems to have been unusually difficult for subsequent readers of this letter. I gave what I considered to be the obvious meaning of the metaphor in the last study—the "root" is Abraham, the branches that have been "broken off" are subsequent generations of unbelieving Jews, the branches that have been "grafted in" are believing Gentiles. But not everyone thinks it is that clear. One commentator remarked that he uncovered at least a half-dozen different interpretations in the course of his preparation of these verses.[1]

In my opinion these difficulties stem largely from the most common of all errors in studying parables or illustrations. That is, to press them beyond the simple, single point of the illustration. Sometimes people do that by overly stressing the illustration's details. At other times they treat the stories too literally.

Let me show what I think has happened here. I think the chief problems with the treatment of the illustration of the olive tree comes from treating it as concerned with individuals alone, on the one hand, or with nations, on the other. What happens if you think of the broken off branches in terms of individuals? Obviously, you have introduced the thought that a person's salvation can be lost. That allows us to warn against presumption, which we must do in any case. Our next study will do exactly that. But the idea that salvation can be lost runs counter to Paul's explicit teaching in Romans 8, in which he stressed that nothing in all creation will ever "separate us from the love of God that is in Christ Jesus our Lord" (v. 39).

Even worse, if that is the view we take, there is no purpose to Romans 9–11. For the only reason for Paul to be writing these chapters is to answer the objection that we cannot believe in eternal security if Israel is lost, since in that case God would not have been faithful to them.

---

1. Donald Grey Barnhouse, *God's Covenants: Exposition of Bible Doctrines, Taking the Epistle to the Romans as a Point of Departure*, vol. 8, *Romans 9:1–11:36* (Grand Rapids: Wm. B. Eerdmans, 1963), p. 133.

But suppose we treat the illustration as having to do with nations? In that case, the nation of Israel is replaced by Gentile *nations,* and we find ourselves beginning to think about some kind of Gentile supremacy. The commentator I mentioned earlier, the one who discovered at least six different interpretations of the illustration of the olive tree, did just that. For in his detailed treatment of Romans 11, the chapter that follows his study of the olive tree is entitled "Gentile Domination."[2]

These difficulties can be eliminated if we realize that Paul is not talking about either individuals or nations specifically, but only about the masses of Jews and many Gentiles. His point is that most Jews have not believed on Jesus Christ and are therefore cut off from the spiritual blessings that should belong to them because of their being Jews, while many Gentiles, who have no claim upon the spiritual blessings granted Israel, have nevertheless entered into those blessings by faith in the Jews' Messiah.

As far as the covenant of God with Israel is concerned, Paul says that it is being fulfilled, though not with every individual Jewish person. Those whom God has elected to salvation are being saved, both Jews and Gentiles, and in the end there will be a time of repentance and spiritual blessing for Israel nationally.

An "Unnatural" Illustration

In the case of this illustration there is also another problem that we have to deal with, namely, that the grafting process Paul describes seems to be unnatural. Wild shoots are not usually grafted onto cultivated roots, as Paul describes. Rather it is the other way around. William Sanday and Arthur C. Headlam say rightly, in their well-known commentary, "Grafts must necessarily be of branches from a cultivated olive inserted into a wild stock, the reverse process being one which would be valueless and is never performed."[3]

Paul's "error" has led some commentators, like C. H. Dodd, to make smug remarks about the apostle's supposed ignorance. Dodd wrote, "Paul had the limitations of a town-bred man. . . . He had not the curiosity to inquire what went on in the olive-yards which fringed every road he walked."[4]

Well, the process may not have been as impossible as all that, and Paul may not be writing in ignorance. Some years ago, William Ramsay, one of

2. Donald Grey Barnhouse in the original booklet version of the Romans messages, *Epistle to the Romans,* part 64, *Romans 11:11–24* (Philadelphia: The Bible Study Hour, 1956), pp. 32–41.

3. William Sanday and Arthur C. Headlam, *A Critical and Exegetical Commentary on the Epistle to the Romans* (Edinburgh: T. & T. Clark, 1960), p. 328. Original edition 1895.

4. C. H. Dodd, *The Epistle of Paul to the Romans* (London: Hodder and Stoughton, 1960), p. 180. In the article by W. M. Ramsay, mentioned next, another scholar is quoted as saying, "Inspiration did not prevent him [Paul] from bungling in the matter of grafting of an olive tree" (*Pauline and Other Studies in Early Christian History* [New York: Hodder and Stoughton, n.d.], p. 232). C. K. Barrett calls Dodd's objections "absurd" (C. K. Barrett, *A Commentary on the Epistle to the Romans* [London: Adam & Charles Black, 1957], p. 217).

the great students of the apostle Paul's teaching and travels, did a study of "The Olive-Tree and the Wild-Olive," in which he produced what seems to be ancient confirmations of what Paul described. According to Ramsay, the Roman writer Columella said that "when an Olive-tree produces badly, a slip of Wild-Olive is grafted on it, and this gives new vigor to the tree" (*Res Rustica*, V, 9, 16). Similarly, Palladius wrote that "the Wild-Olive graft invigorated the tree on which it was set" (*Opus Agriculturae*, XI, 8, 3). Ramsay referred to the renowned Mediterranean fruit-tree botanist Theobald Fisher as saying that the process described by Paul "is still in use in exceptional circumstances at the present day."[5]

However, there is a problem with Ramsay's solution, too. According to Ramsay, the purpose of grafting in the wild shoot is to invigorate the old tree or root. But, according to Paul's use of the illustration, the Gentiles, who are represented by the wild olive shoots, bring nothing to the fusion. Ramsay's solution, while it may be true horticulturally and may excuse Paul from the charge of ignorance, actually confuses the issue.

In my opinion, the real explanation is in a phrase Paul himself uses in verse 24, when he speaks of the Gentiles being grafted into a cultivated olive tree as "contrary to nature." If this is to be taken at face value, it means that Paul was fully aware that what he was describing—the grafting of a wild shoot into a cultivated stock—was unnatural. But that is precisely his point. It was utterly unnatural that God should work in this manner to save Gentiles. Yet it is what God has done. Salvation is of grace. However, if God did the unnatural thing in saving Gentiles, how much more should we expect him to do the natural thing eventually and thus bring about the future widespread belief of Israel in their own Messiah?

An Instructive Illustration

But enough analysis! What is the point of this substantial biblical illustration (eight verses)? What are its lessons? I see seven of them.

1. *There is only one people of God.* This is an obvious point of the olive-tree illustration, but surprisingly it is often completely overlooked, particularly by those who, like myself, believe that Romans 11 is prophesying a future day of Jewish blessing. A large number of those who do this are dispensationalists who tend to locate the widespread conversion of Israel in a future age and describe it in terms that give the Jews an identity and destiny quite different from the church. I believe in Israel's future conversion, because I believe that Romans 11 and other passages teach it. But the opponents of dispensation-

---

5. Ramsay's article first appeared as an article entitled, "The Olive-Tree and the Wild-Olive" in *The Expositor*, sixth series, XI (1905), pp. 16–34, 152–160. It was later republished as a chapter in Ramsay's *Pauline and Other Studies in Early Christian History*, pp. 219–250. The quotes are from pages 223–225.

alism are right when they insist that there are not two peoples of God with two destinies but one only.

In this letter, Abraham has been presented as the father of all who are saved, since they are saved by faith, as he was. He is the root of the tree. Therefore, all who are saved, whether Jews or Gentiles, are saved only by believing God, as he did, and are thus part of the one olive tree.

Moreover, when Paul speaks of the future day of Jewish conversion, he is not speaking of something outside of or beyond history, nor of a dispensation yet to come. This is within history. It is within the very flow of events that we ourselves know that Gentiles and eventually Jews will all believe in Christ and the entire company of God's elect will be made up.

2. *The people of God must (and will) bear fruit.* Paul does not speak of fruit-bearing specifically in these verses. But that is the whole point of grafting: to produce a more fruitful tree. Besides, although Paul does not speak of fruit by that term, this is certainly what he has in mind when he writes of unbelieving Jews being broken off "because of unbelief" and of believing Gentiles being grafted into the Jewish tree "by faith" (v. 20). Unbelief is the ultimate expression of fruitlessness, and faith is the first of all fruits.

I observed in the previous study that the olive tree is not a prominent image in the Old Testament, especially in regard to Israel. Nevertheless, it is used of Israel in two passages: Jeremiah 11:16 and Hosea 14:6. They have nothing to do with wild branches being grafted into the old stock. But they do have to do with fruitfulness. Jeremiah 11:16 reads:

> The LORD called you a thriving olive tree
>   with fruit beautiful in form.
> But with the roar of a mighty storm
>   he will set it on fire,
>   and its branches will be broken.

Why is the tree to be destroyed by fire and its branches broken? The next verse explains that it is "because the house of Israel and the house of Judah have done evil." That is, they were not fruitful. They were not believing. It is possible that Paul got the idea for his more elaborate illustration in Romans from this passage.

And perhaps from Hosea 14:6, too, the only other verse that applies the olive-tree illustration to the Jewish nation. I say this because, like Romans 11, this verse looks forward to a future day of blessing for Israel, saying, "His [Israel's] splendor will be like an olive tree, / his fragrance like a cedar of Lebanon."

The point, of course, is that God requires fruitfulness in his people. In fact, without fruitfulness they are not his people. This is what Jesus taught in the discourse recorded in John 15, though with the illustration of a vine and its branches rather than an olive tree and its branches. He said, "I am the true vine and my Father is the gardener. He cuts off every branch in me that bears no fruit, while every branch that does bear fruit he prunes [trims clean] so that it will be even more fruitful. . . . I am the vine; you are the branches. If a man remains in me and I in him, he will bear much fruit. . . . This is to my Father's glory, that you bear much fruit, showing yourselves to be my disciples" (John 15:1–2, 5, 8). The vine illustration is prominent in the Old Testament (see Ps. 80:8–16; Isa. 5:1–7).

3. *Gentiles contribute nothing to the salvation process.* This is the point at which I found William Ramsay's material to be unhelpful and even misleading. For although the point of grafting is to bring the strength and fruitfulness of the shoot to enrich the old tree, in Paul's illustration it is entirely the reverse. The engrafted branches are the Gentiles, and the thrust of his words to them is that they are not to boast over the cut-off branches, as if they were valuable themselves. Instead, we who are Gentiles are to bear in mind that we "do not support the root, but the root supports you [us]" (v. 18).

We stand, but our standing is by faith alone, and that means that we stand only by grace. We have no inherent claim to anything.

It follows, too, that there is no "good" in Gentile religion. People today think in terms of all religions bringing their little bit of truth to the whole, each one adding its part, but this is utterly at odds with Paul's illustration. Asians do not contribute their little bit of yin and yang. Africans do not contribute their little bit of superstition from their tribal religions. Indians do not contribute their little bit of folk wisdom or dances. Americans do not contribute their democracy or capitalism. According to Paul's illustration, Gentiles are a "wild olive" (v. 17), one of the most worthless of all trees.

And let's not overlook the word *wild*. Apart from the grace of the gospel in Jesus Christ, all we have are our wild ways. And they are destructive ways, too. The only true way is the way of faith in Christ that has come to us through Judaism.

Do you remember what Jesus told the Samaritan woman? She wanted to engage him in debate over which of the two religious traditions she was acquainted with was best, the religion of the Samaritans or the Jews. "I can see you are a prophet," she said when Christ told her she was living in sin. "Our fathers worshiped on this mountain, but you Jews claim that the place where we must worship is in Jerusalem" (John 4:19–20).

Jesus answered that although a time was coming when the place of worship would be irrelevant ("Believe me, woman, a time is coming when you will worship the Father neither on this mountain nor in Jerusalem"), nevertheless, this did not mean that the religions of the Samaritans and Jews were equal—"You Samaritans worship what you do not know; we worship what we do know, for salvation is from the Jews" (vv. 21–22).

The only true religion is the revealed religion, which God has given to us through the channel of Judaism. Not all Jews are saved, of course. Paul is saying that clearly. Nevertheless, he is also saying clearly that Jews are not saved by becoming Gentiles; rather Gentiles (as well as Jews) are saved by becoming true Jews. That is, all who are saved are and must be the true spiritual children of Abraham.

4. *Neither do Jews.* I have said that Gentiles contribute nothing to the salvation process. But now we have to add that neither do Jews. Is that contradictory? Didn't I just quote Jesus as saying that "salvation is from the Jews"? Yes, but that is quite different from saying "salvation is being Jewish."

The word *from* implies a channel. It means that the way of salvation has been made known through the revelation given to Israel, through its kings and prophets, above all through Jesus Christ. Jews become beneficiaries of that revelation, not by being Jews or by bringing any innate measure of spiritual understanding or intrinsic righteousness to God. They benefit only and in exactly the same way Gentiles do, which is by believing on Jesus. "They were broken off because of unbelief," Paul says—"And if they do not persist in unbelief, they will be grafted in, for God is able to graft them in again" (vv. 20, 23). He could hardly make his point clearer.

Weren't those broken-off branches in the Jewish tree called "holy," in Paul's original use of the root and branches illustration? In what sense, then, were the branches holy? The answer, as we saw in the previous study, is that they were "set apart" to God's purposes. What were those purposes? They were that the Jews might be:

The receivers of the law, the prophets, and the writings. That is, we received our Bibles through Judaism.

The preservers of these for the world. We would not have our Bibles, especially not our Old Testaments, had not Jewish scribes faithfully and meticulously preserved these ancient documents for us.

The earthly line of the Messiah. Jesus was a descendent of Abraham through the tribe of Judah. He was a descendant of King David.

God's witnesses to these truths. All the early preachers, including Paul himself, were Jews. Without their faithful witness to these truths, none of us would have known of Jesus, understood the gospel, or believed.

5. *Do not boast.* The fifth application of the truths embodied in the illustration of the olive tree is the one Paul himself emphasizes. At this point of the letter he is writing to Gentiles specifically, as he says in verse 13, and the burden of his words is that they dare not boast over the Jews because of their present favored position. It is true that Jewish branches were broken off so that, in God's providence, the gospel might come to Gentiles. Their rejection has been a source of Gentile blessing. But Gentiles are not to boast, since they stand only by faith and will themselves be broken off if they do not continue in it.

We must not forget the warnings throughout the Bible about boasting. If we boast, we are not believing. For boasting is being proud of our own (supposed) achievements, and believing is receiving what God in Jesus Christ has done for us.

6. *Do not presume on God's favor.* The sixth application follows closely on the warning not to boast. For when we boast we are presuming on God's favor, and that is fatal. Presuming means assuming that everything is right between ourselves and God, regardless of what we may believe or not believe or of how we may act. The only way we can avoid presumption is to obey God and pursue righteousness diligently. As I have often said, if we are not following after Jesus Christ in faithful discipleship, we are not disciples. And if we are not disciples of Christ, we are not Christians.

7. *Fear (respect) God.* Finally, fear God (vv. 20, 22). This does not mean that we are to cower before God if we are Christians. It has to do with respect. Still it is nevertheless a holy, awesome respect we are to have—awe before both God's kindness and severity. This is reminding us that God is not mocked. Sin will be punished, and unbelief does exclude us from the good tree of salvation, whoever we may be. We need to consider that there is indeed only one people of God and that entry into that one people is by true faith in Jesus in all cases.

164

A Warning to the Gentile Churches

Romans 11:17–22

If some of the branches have been broken off, and you, though a wild olive shoot, have been grafted in among the others and now share in the nourishing sap from the olive root, do not boast over those branches. If you do, consider this: You do not support the root, but the root supports you. You will say then, "Branches were broken off so that I could be grafted in." Granted. But they were broken off because of unbelief, and you stand by faith. Do not be arrogant, but be afraid. For if God did not spare the natural branches, he will not spare you either.

Consider therefore the kindness and sternness of God: sternness to those who fell, but kindness to you, provided that you continue in his kindness. Otherwise, you also will be cut off.

Ín Romans 11, Paul is writing about the future of the Jews as a people. So it is surprising how much of what he says in this chapter is to Gentiles. He began by addressing them directly in verse 13 ("I am talking to you Gentiles"), and he continues speaking to them exclusively until verse 25, where he begins to address a broader group of people again. In verses 17–22, he warns the Gentiles not to boast over Judaism because of the Gentiles' current favored status, saying that if the Jews, who were God's especially chosen people once, have been rejected at least tem-

1351

porarily because of unbelief, the Gentiles also will be rejected if they follow their bad example.

This is a serious warning, one that we must take to heart.

Prosperity seems always to lead to some kind of boasting, and this is true of spiritual prosperity as well as of material prosperity. When we go through hard times, we usually sense our inadequacy and draw close to God, calling on him for help. But as soon as things go well for us, we find it easy to think that it is because of who we are or what we have done and not because of God's unmerited grace and blessing. Then we cease to trust God; we drift away from him and fall into sin. It was an awareness of this ever-present danger that caused Paul to write forcefully to the Christians at Corinth, "If you think you are standing firm, be careful that you don't fall!" (1 Cor. 10:12).

As Paul writes to those of us who are Gentiles, he is aware that our present position might cause us to boast over the Jews who held a privileged position before us. But he warns us not to boast. Rather, fear God, he says. We may be standing now, but we stand only by grace. If we cease to stand in grace by believing God, we, too, will fall.

Does that mean that salvation can be lost? No. Paul has been teaching the doctrine of perseverance. But what he says here is nevertheless a strong warning against spiritual presumption. John Calvin believed in eternal security, but he wrote, "We should never think of the rejection of the Jews without being struck with dread and terror."[1]

The Fall of National Churches

What Paul tells us in these verses is that if the Gentiles fail to stand by faith, they will be cut off, just as the Jews were. So I begin by saying that this has happened to churches in large sectors of the world. At one time these places had thriving churches. But no longer. Today that earlier witness has been radically reduced and in some cases nearly eradicated.

1. *The church in Asia Minor.* I start with Asia Minor, what we today call Turkey. This was the first major area of the ancient Gentile world to be evangelized, largely because of Paul's missionary travels. Thanks to his efforts, churches were planted in Derbe, Iconium, Lystra, and Ephesus, among others, and the gospel spread from Ephesus to such surrounding cities as Smyrna, Pergamum, Thyatira, Sardis, Philadelphia, and Laodicea, which are mentioned in the early chapters of Revelation. By the year 113, about sixty years after Paul's work, Pliny, the Roman governor of Bithynia, complained to the emperor Trajan that the new faith was affecting the older worship patterns. People were neglecting the ancient gods, and the temple revenues had fallen off. Irenaeus, one of the first great Christian writers (*c.* 130–*c.* 200), was from

---

1. John Calvin, *The Epistles of Paul the Apostle to the Romans and to the Thessalonians,* trans. Ross Mackenzie (Grand Rapids: Wm. B. Eerdmans, 1973), p. 251.

Smyrna. The great fourth-century defenders of Nicene orthodoxy, Basil of Caesaria, Gregory of Nazianzus, and Gregory of Nyssa, were from Cappadocia. Yet where is the church of Asia Minor today? Its early vitality faded, its gospel became mere moralism, and the Moslem invasions of the early Middle Ages overwhelmed it and almost entirely snuffed it out. Today Turkey is an almost-virgin mission field for Christianity.

2. *The church in North Africa.* There is an almost identical pattern for North Africa. Tertullian (*c.* 155–*c.* 220), the first great Christian apologist, was from Carthage on the north African coast. Cyprian (*c.* 220–258), who was born about the time Tertullian died, was his predecessor's intellectual heir, and in time he became bishop of the city. There was a major center of the African church at Alexandria, further to the east. It produced such outstanding leaders as Clement (*c.* 150–*c.* 215) and Origen (*c.* 185–*c.* 254). The great defender of Christ's deity during the years of the Arian controversy, Athanasius (*c.* 295–373), was likewise from Alexandria. Most impressive of all, Saint Augustine (354–430), the greatest theologian of the early church, was born in Tagastein, northern Africa and later became the celebrated bishop of Hippo, also on the African continent.

Under such leadership, Christianity thrived in North Africa for several centuries. But, again, it lost its vitality, faded, and was eventually replaced by Islam. Moslems took possession of Jerusalem in 638 and then conquered most of Asia Minor from 1071 onward. In spite of the energetic and repeated efforts of the Crusaders, the last Crusader conquest in Palestine was surrendered in 1291, and Constantinople in Asia Minor fell in 1453.

3. *The church in Italy.* To the north and west, in Italy, the early church was subjected to many years of persecution by the weakened Roman Empire, but it eventually seemed to have triumphed for good as the result of the celebrated conversion of the emperor Constantine on the eve of his battle against the armies of Maxentius on October 28, 312. Constantine claimed to have received a vision the night before the battle in which he saw the Christ symbol (the Greek letter "x" with the character for "r" through the center of it, the first two letters of the Greek word for "Christ") accompanied by the words "In this sign conquer." He had the sign painted on his helmet and the shields of his soldiers, marched into battle, and was victorious.

The final phase of the state's persecution of the church was now ended, and the church was given preferred legal status. Constantine himself presided over the great Council of Nicaea in 325. Ironically, prosperity turned out to be more harmful to the church than persecution. The religious hierarchy became even more corrupt than that of the declining empire. By the late Middle Ages, the western church was selling salvation through the system of indulgences, which appalled Martin Luther, provoked the posting of his Ninety-five Theses in 1517, and sparked the Reformation.

If ever a church had its candlestick removed by Jesus, while nevertheless retaining the outward appearances of influence and prosperity, it was the Roman church of the Middle Ages. The church had apparently triumphed, but wise observers saw it as nothing more than an evil, powerful, and secularized institution.

Calvin must have been thinking of the slide of the early church into the corruption of the Middle Ages when he wrote, referring to our passage in Romans, "The fearful defection of the whole of the world which afterwards took place gives clear evidence of how necessary this admonition was. When God had watered the whole of the world with his grace in but a moment, so that religion flourished universally, the truth of the gospel shortly afterwards vanished, and the treasure of salvation was taken away. The only explanation of so sudden a change is that the Gentiles fell away from their calling."[2]

4. *The church of the Reformation in Europe.* Heirs of the Reformation tend to boast over Roman Catholicism at this point, praising Martin Luther and the other sixteenth-century Reformers. But we must remember that the same decline overtook the Reformation churches. Once a dominant influence in Germany, Switzerland, France, and Holland, the Reformation churches soon forgot the true gospel, grew weak internally, and are now attended by only a small minority of people. Less than 4 percent of Europeans attend church, even on religious holidays.

5. *The church in England and the West.* And what of the church in England and the West? What of the church in the United States? In England attendance at church is only marginally better than on the European continent. England, like Europe, is a great mission field. And who does not sense that churches in the United States, though attended by substantially large numbers of people at the moment, are nevertheless declining? Who would say that the present influence of Christianity on our cultural value system is as great today as it was even a decade ago, not to mention during the early years of our country's history?

The Fall of Particular Churches

What has happened on a national level happens in individual churches too. One of the saddest things I know is the decline of a once-vital church.

I think of the church in which I was ordained. Formerly a bastion of orthodoxy, it has been weakened through a series of ineffective pastorates. Its current pastor, who is neo-orthodox (Barthian) in theology, was not chosen by the pastoral seeking committee for his orthodoxy. Although the members of the pastoral search knew he had departed from a high view of Scripture as God's inerrant Word and from the orthodoxy that had characterized most

2. Ibid., p. 252.

of his predecessors, this man was chosen because the committee felt they needed an "orator" if the church was to survive. It is not surviving, of course. The evening service has gone, and the impact this church once had in the great city in which it is located has evaporated.

What does Paul say in our text? "Do not be arrogant, but be afraid. For if God did not spare the natural branches, he will not spare you either."

It bears repeating that he told the Corinthians, "If you think you are standing firm, be careful that you don't fall" (1 Cor. 10:12). Can such a thing happen to a conservative, Bible-based church? Of course, it can. It will happen if we do not continue strong in the faith once delivered to the saints. We stand by grace through faith. But if we forget that it is by grace that we stand or that we must continue in faith, believing what God teaches in the Bible, then we will fall—as surely as those formerly thriving churches that have preceded us on the stage of world history.

The Fall of Individuals

I intend to turn to what Paul tells us to remember, since it is his solution to the problem I have been describing. Before I do, I will extend the warning one step further by applying it to individuals who suppose they are Christians because they are part of a Christian church and affirm the right things, but who are not actually anchored in the grace of God and are not exercising that true faith in God that comes from the presence of the Holy Spirit within them.

Let me warn you that it is fatally easy to assume that all is well with your soul when actually you are perishing. In fact, in your unbelieving state it is the most natural thing in the world, because you do not perceive what is really spiritual and suppose that the externals of Christianity are what matters.

If you have any sensitivity to spiritual things, you must ask yourself, "Has my commitment to Christ made any discernible difference in my life?" In other words, is there anything you are doing now that you would not be doing if you were not a Christian? Is there anything you are *not* doing because you know it would displease Jesus Christ? Are you obeying his commandments? Do you love to be with other Christians?

Are you studying the Bible? And when you study it can you really say that you hear God speaking to you in its pages? Do you recognize what you read there to be the truth? Do you change what you are doing as a result? Are you trying to order your life according to the Bible's teaching and redirect it according to right Christian priorities?

This is what it means to "make your calling and election sure" (2 Peter 1:10), in sharp contrast to what Jesus was warning of when he described sowing seed on ground where it seemed to grow well but soon dried up for lack of depth, was choked by weeds, or was snatched away by Satan (Matt. 13:1–9).

I have already mentioned John Calvin and the fact that he is strong on the doctrine of eternal security or perseverance. But listen to what he says to individuals who consider themselves Christians but who may nevertheless be presuming on the grace of God: "It is not enough to have embraced only once the grace of God, unless during the whole course of your life you follow his call. Those who have been enlightened by the Lord must always turn their minds to perseverance."[3]

Four Things to Remember

How do we "stand by faith" (Rom. 11:20)? Paul gives the answer in verse 22. According to Robert Haldane, there are four things Paul tells the Gentiles to remember.[4]

1. He urges them to behold *"the severity of God's strict justice in cutting off and casting out the unbelieving Jews."* We tend to treat God as a benevolent old man who will never do anything as harsh as judge anyone. We are especially prone to this if we are only cultural Christians and not truly regenerate. We need to disabuse ourselves of such fantasies. God is love, but he is also a God of strict justice. His rejection of the Jews should be a warning to us never to presume on his goodness but, rather, always to strive to make certain we are truly saved.

2. He reminds them of God's *"goodness in conferring unmerited favor on the Gentiles."* They attained a righteousness they were not even seeking. The emphasis here is on God's unmerited favor, for it takes away all grounds for boasting or presumption. If there is nothing in us that has brought us to Christ, there is obviously nothing in us that keeps us there either. We dare not presume. We stand by grace only.

3. He stresses *"the necessity of [their] continuing in that goodness, by abiding in the faith of the Gospel."* Nothing but faith will enable the believer to stand in grace. Therefore, we must cultivate faith. How? Paul has already given us the answer: "Faith comes from hearing the message, and the message is heard through the word of Christ" (Rom. 10:17). Faith comes by studying the Bible and by hearing it taught and preached. That is why we must continue to go to church to hear sound teaching and why we must study the Bible privately as well. If we do not, we will drift away. And if we drift away without returning eventually—and how can we be sure we will return?—we will perish.

I repeat: Nothing but faith will enable the believer to stand in grace. But I also add now: Nothing but unbelief keeps anyone from grace. No one needs to perish. Paul also wrote, "If you confess with your mouth, 'Jesus is Lord,' and believe in your heart that God raised him from the dead, you will be saved. For it is with your heart that you believe and are justified, and it is with your

---

3. Ibid.
4. Robert Haldane, *An Exposition of the Epistle to the Romans* (MacDill AFB: MacDonald Publishing, 1958), p. 539.

mouth that you confess and are saved. . . . 'Anyone who trust in him will never be put to shame'" (Rom. 10:9–11).

4. He warns them that *"if they abide not in the faith, they should be themselves cut off."* So do not presume! We start with faith, but we must also end with faith. If we do not, we shall be cut off, as Israel was.

"Lest We Forget"

In the summer of 1897, the British Empire held a great celebration to mark the sixtieth anniversary of the accession to the throne of Queen Victoria. She had become the British monarch on June 20, 1837, and there had been a fiftieth-year Jubilee in 1887. This follow-up celebration a decade later was the high point of the Victorian era and the zenith of British power and influence. Prime ministers, judges, statesmen, and other highly placed representatives assembled from every part of the worldwide empire. Hundreds of the great ships of the massed British Navy clogged the Thames. It was unlike anything the world would ever see again.

But at last the festivities were over. The statesmen and the ships departed, and Rudyard Kipling, the outstanding British poet of the Victorian period, had written "Recessional," a reminder of man's impermanent grandeur:

> God of our fathers, known of old,
> 　　Lord of our far-flung battle-line,
> Beneath whose awful hand we hold
> 　　Dominion over palm and pine—
> Lord God of Hosts, be with us yet,
> Lest we forget—lest we forget!
>
> The tumult and the shouting dies;
> 　　The captains and the kings depart:
> Still stands Thine ancient sacrifice,
> 　　An humble and a contrite heart.
> Lord God of Hosts, be with us yet,
> Lest we forget—lest we forget!
>
> Far-called, our navies melt away;
> 　　On dune and headland sinks the fire:
> Lo, all our pomp of yesterday
> 　　Is one with Nineveh and Tyre!
> Judge of the Nations, spare us yet,
> Lest we forget—lest we forget!
>
> If drunk with sight of power, we loose
> 　　Wild tongues that have not Thee in awe,
> Such boastings as the Gentiles use,
> 　　Or lesser breeds without the Law—

> Lord God of Hosts, be with us yet,
> Lest we forget—lest we forget!

> For heathen heart that puts her trust
>   In reeking tube and iron shard,
> All valiant dust that builds on dust,
>   And guarding, calls not Thee to guard,
> For frantic boast and foolish word—
> Thy Mercy on Thy People, Lord!

Kipling was writing of the British Empire, of course. But his words speak equally to churches and to individuals who foolishly boast of their own attainments or coast along in their present favored standing without pausing to remember the grace of God that brought them to that place and the obligation they have to stand together as Christians in grace by faith alone. So do not forget! Stand in your high calling! Stand by faith! Greater individuals than you and I have perished. Nations as powerful as ours have been overthrown. And stronger churches than ours have fallen to the severity of God's just judgments in history.

> Lord God of Hosts, be with us yet,
> Lest we forget—lest we forget!

165

A Future for God's Ancient People

Romans 11:23–24

And if they do not persist in unbelief, they will be grafted in, for God is able to graft them in again. After all, if you were cut out of an olive tree that is wild by nature, and contrary to nature were grafted into a cultivated olive tree, how much more readily will these, the natural branches, be grafted into their own olive tree!

It is not going too far out on a limb to suggest that few of today's Christians have mastered the great prophecy of Ezekiel. Not many could give an outline of that book. Most could not tell even a single thing that is in it. Yet there is a story in Ezekiel 37 that most of us are aware of. It is the story of Ezekiel's preaching in the valley of dry bones, which is acknowledged in the chorus of a Negro spiritual: "Dem bones, dem bones, dem dry bones! / Now hear the word of the Lord."

God brought the prophet to a valley full of dry bones and told him to preach to them. When Ezekiel did as God commanded, the bones began to come together to form complete human skeletons. Tendons, flesh, and skin appeared on them. At last, as Ezekiel continued to preach, breath entered the bones and "they came to life and stood up on their feet—a vast army" (Ezek. 37:10).

God explained the lesson, saying, "These bones are the whole house of Israel. They say, 'Our bones are dried up and our hope is gone; we are cut off.' Therefore prophesy and say to them: 'This is what the Sovereign LORD says: O my people, I am going to open your graves and bring you up from them; I will bring you back to the land of Israel. Then you, my people, will know that I am the LORD, when I open your graves and bring you up from them. I will put my Spirit in you and you will live, and I will settle you in your own land . . .'" (vv. 11–14).

The story is relevant to Paul's teaching in Romans 11, of course. He is writing about Israel, saying that the Jewish people will become believers in Jesus Christ in the last days. Yet, based on our observance, nothing is more improbable than such a conversion, or even the image Paul is using.

He has spoken of a cultivated olive tree whose branches were broken off and of a wild olive tree whose branches were grafted into the cultivated stock. That illustration pictures the inclusion of the Gentiles in Israel's spiritual blessings. But, then, in what is surely an impossible situation in terms of horticulture, Paul begins to speak of the broken and discarded branches being grafted back into *their own* olive tree. Branches once broken off a tree die and cannot be regrafted. True enough. But we are not speaking here about things that are merely possible or impossible in nature. We are speaking of God, and with God all things are possible.

Robert Haldane says wisely, "What is not done in nature, and cannot be effected by the power of man, will be done by God, with whom all things are possible. He is able to make the dry bones live, and to restore the severed branches of the Jewish nation."[1]

In the preceding verses (vv. 20–22), Gentiles are warned that, unless they stand in faith, they will be cut off. Verses 23–24 are the reverse of that, telling the Jews that if they "do not persist in unbelief" but rather believe in Jesus, they will be brought back in.

Two Explanations

Until now, my interpretation of Romans 11 has been following what seems to me to be the general meaning and flow of the chapter. However, most people are aware—you may be one—that there is a sharp debate over the true meaning of these verses, and this is the place both to acknowledge this debate and deal with it. There are two main explanations, though they have numerous modifications.

1. *A present explanation.* The first interpretation rejects any futuristic references in Paul's teaching about the Jews and sees these verses as describing only what we already observe in regard to the general pattern of Jewish unbe-

---

1. Robert Haldane, *An Exposition of the Epistle to the Romans* (MacDill AFB: MacDonald Publishing, 1958), p. 540.

lief coupled with the salvation of some Jews. According to this view, Paul would be teaching that the hardening of the Jews is not so great as to prevent some being converted and entering the Christian church, just as Gentiles do, and that this will continue to the end of the present age of gospel grace.

2. *A future explanation.* The second interpretation sees Paul looking ahead to a future moment in God's dealings with Israel in which there will be a great and general conversion of Jews in fulfillment of ancient but as yet unfulfilled prophecies. This will take place when the salvation of all the Gentiles who are to be saved (but who are not yet saved) shall have been accomplished.

Charles Hodge has a helpful discussion of these two possibilities, showing that the first was developed largely during the Reformation period as the result of two things: first, the extravagant prophetic views of the Millennarians, which the Reformers rejected; and, second, what Hodge freely admits was the Reformers' prejudice against the Jews. Sadly, we must admit that Hodge is right in this. The Jews were the despised people of the late Middle Ages, and the Reformers, Luther especially, did not rise above this unjustified hatred. To illustrate his point, Hodge cites a particularly offensive passage from Luther, which he wisely leaves in German, saying that it "does not admit of translation."[2]

The Present Explanation

Arguments for the first of these explanations can be found in various places, particularly among present-day Reformed people who draw their theology from the sixteenth-century Reformers. I would like to focus on one excellent example. It is a study entitled "A Distinctive Future for Ethnic Israel in Romans Eleven?" by O. Palmer Robertson,[3] who wrote the paper when he was an associate professor of Old Testament theology at Westminster Theological Seminary. He then became pastor of a church north of Washington, D.C. Robertson makes the following points:

1. *Much (if not all) of Romans 11 is dealing with God's purposes for the Jews in the present age.* Robertson discusses verses 1, 5, 13–14, and 30–31 especially, showing rightly that they are speaking about the salvation of some Jews at the present time, a remnant. Paul is an example, and so are those few who responded or will have responded to his teaching and to that of the other ministers of the gospel. Robertson concludes, "These references do not exclude by necessity parallel references to some future purpose of God with

2. Charles Hodge, *A Commentary on Romans* (Edinburgh and Carlisle, Pa.: The Banner of Truth Trust, 1972), p. 371. Original edition 1935.

3. O. Palmer Robertson, "A Distinctive Future for Ethnic Israel in Romans Eleven?" Unpublished paper (Philadelphia: Westminster Theological Seminary Library, dated February 13, 1979).

Israel. They do, however, warn the exegete against assuming too hastily that the entirety of chapter eleven of Romans deals with Israel's distinctive future."[4] There can be no quarrel with this analysis.

2. *Verses assumed to speak of God's distinct dealings with Israel in the future do not necessarily do so.* Here Robertson discusses verses 1, 5, 12, 15, 17–24, and 25–26a, the critical discussion being of verse 25, which speaks of Israel being hardened "*until* the full number of the Gentiles has come in." Robertson concludes that "until" does not refer to a termination of something after which something else will happen, but to a final termination of everything (a *terminus ad quem* rather than a *terminus a quo*). He calls this an eschatological termination. That is, it concerns the return of Christ and the final judgment. Therefore, writes Robertson, the passage means only that "throughout the whole of the present age, until the final return of Christ, hardening will continue among part of Israel."[5]

Here I do find myself disagreeing with the author, for in my judgment that is just not what Romans 11:25 says. There is nothing to indicate that this verse is speaking of the return of Christ, the final judgment, or any such thing, but of the future of the Jews, and it is saying that they will be converted. We will come back to this when we look at the second explanation.

3. *The words "and so all Israel shall be saved" (v. 26a) should read "in this way all Israel shall be saved," meaning that the elect among Israel will be saved by responding to the gospel just as they are currently doing.* This is not foolish reasoning, of course. Robertson is an excellent scholar, and his view is probably the prevailing current view among Reformed Bible students and theologians. But, in my judgment, it overlooks the flow of the chapter. During my student days I was told that the future explanation was a dispensational view only and that no Reformed theologians held to it. Having studied these views carefully, I find instead that the majority of the great commentators on Romans, including Reformed commentators, recognize that the passage is speaking of a future day of Jewish conversion. Moreover, they see a future gathering-in of Israel as the point to which the chapter has been moving. The pattern is:

The *possibility* of a time of future Jewish conversions: "God is able to graft them in again" (v. 23),

The *probability* of a time of future Jewish conversions: "How much more readily will these, the natural branches, be grafted into their own olive tree" (v. 24), and

The *certainty* of a time of future Jewish conversions: "And so all Israel will be saved" (v. 26a).

4. Ibid., p. 6.
5. Ibid., p. 18.

The Future Explanation

Among commentators who defend the second view—the future explanation—none is more thorough than Charles Hodge. He gives eight reasons why the passage is looking forward to a time of future blessing for ethnic Israel.[6] At this point I set his arguments over against Robertson's.

1. *"The whole context and drift of the apostle's discourse is in . . . favor" of the second view.* Hodge discusses the earlier part of the chapter at this point, recalling Paul's statement that the eventual conversion of the Jews is a probable event that would be in the fullest measure beneficial and glorious for the world (v. 12). The only natural extension of that is their actual conversion.

2. *"It is evident that Paul meant to say that the Jews were to be restored in the sense in which they were then rejected."* In the earlier part of the chapter Paul was speaking of the rejection of the Jews not as individuals, but as a nation or community. "Jews" as an ethnic grouping is contrasted with "Gentiles" as an ethnic grouping. Therefore, when Paul speaks of a future time of Jewish conversion he must be thinking of a general conversion of this ethnic body. "How can [verse 15] be understood of the conversion of the small number of Jews which, from age to age, have joined the Christian church?" Hodge asks. "This surely has not been 'life from the dead,' for the whole world."[7]

3. *"It is plain from this and other parts of the discourse that Paul refers to a great event, something which should attract universal attention."* The conversion of a few Jews and their addition to the church from time to time does not fit this expectation.

4. The introduction to verse 25 ("I do not want you to be ignorant of this mystery, brothers") is in words Paul normally uses *"when he wishes to rouse the attention of his readers to something especially important."* The conversion of a few Jews from time to time does not fit this definition. Nor is it something really new, since he has already spoken of the remnant of those who are being converted several times previously.

5. *"The gradual conversion of a few Jews is no 'mystery.'"* In the Bible's language, a mystery is something that at one time was unknown but has now been revealed. Knowledge of the gradual conversion of a few Jews does not require any special revelation. On the contrary, it is a fact of simple observation.

6. *"The words 'all Israel' cannot . . . be understood of 'spiritual' Israel, because the word is just before used in a different sense."* The Israel that has experienced

6. Hodge, *A Commentary on Romans*, pp. 371–373.
7. Ibid., p. 372.

"a hardening in part" (v. 25) is ethnic Israel. It cannot be spiritual Israel, because what distinguishes spiritual Israel from ethnic Israel is that spiritual Israel is not hardened but rather has turned (or will turn) from sin and has embraced (or will embrace) Jesus Christ as Savior. Since ethnic Israel is what is referred to in verse 25, the word cannot be used in an entirely different sense in verse 26, which immediately follows. If it is ethnic Israel which has been hardened, it must be ethnic Israel which will be saved.

7. *"The words . . . correctly rendered in our version 'until' cannot . . . be translated 'as long as' or 'so that,' followed as they are here by the aorist subjunctive."* This is a technical matter that must be argued by experts in the fine points of Greek grammar. It is enough to note here that it is directly opposed to Robertson's interpretation of "until," summarized under point 2 above.

8. *"The following verses seem to require this interpretation."* In these verses the result that is contemplated is a full accomplishment of the ancient prophecies, which predict a general Jewish salvation. What is more, the reason given is the unchangeable nature of God's purposes and covenant, which Paul establishes in verse 26 by combining sentences from Isaiah 59:20–21 and 27:9. His quotation reads:

> The deliverer will come from Zion;
> he will turn godliness away from Jacob.
> And this is my covenant with them
> when I take away their sins.

The rejection of the Jews in Paul's day did not involve every individual of Jewish descent, and the conversion of the Jews in this future day likewise will not necessarily involve every individual Jewish person. But as the masses of Israel are rejected now, so the masses of Israel will be converted then because, having once taken the Jews into a special relationship with himself, God, "whose gifts and . . . call are irrevocable" (v. 29), will not cast them off.

It is hard for me to discover any other valid meaning than this obvious meaning of the passage.

Some Practical Applications

We are not living in the future, however. So although the promise of a day of future blessing for the Jewish people is important for how we are to think of God's promises, gifts, and covenant, I want to end not by thinking ahead to some future day, but rather by applying Paul's teaching to how we should think and act now.

I begin by going back to my opening illustration, which was Ezekiel's experience in the valley of dry bones. This illustration teaches that the salvation of any individual, Jew or Gentile, is a miracle of God and therefore depends on God as much as does the resurrection of a great army of soldiers from mere bones. This is exactly the teaching of Romans 11, of course. For, having spoken of individual Jews as branches that have been broken off from the olive tree that is rooted in the patriarchs, Paul has also spoken of them being grafted back in. That is not humanly possible. Therefore, although it is nevertheless possible, it is so only because "with God all things are possible" (Matt. 19:26).

Leon Morris writes, "If the orchardist wanted certain branches in his tree he would not have cut them off in the first place. But Paul is not talking about orchardists; he is talking about God, and the orchard is no more than an illustration. He is talking about a miracle of grace and assuring his readers that God is able to perform that miracle."[8]

That is what we need, too, of course. We need this supernatural working of God in our minds to give us understanding of the gospel, in our hearts to give us an affection for Jesus Christ, and in our wills to bring us to the point of a personal turning from sin to faith in the Savior.

But we are slow to admit our need of God's gracious working.

What could have caused such blindness? It is a failure to understand four great truths that the meaning of grace presupposes.

1. *The sin of man.* We are complacent about our spiritual condition, so we assume that God is also. The thought that we are fallen creatures who are in rebellion against God's rightful rule seldom enters our heads.

2. *The judgment of God.* Most of us have lost appreciation for all cause-and-effect links, especially in moral areas. So the idea of a final judgment of God at the end of human history, when sin will be punished, seems fantastic to us.

3. *Our spiritual inability.* Our society has taught us that for man "all things are possible." We believe we are the masters of our own fate, the captains of our own ship. So the idea that we need the grace of God in order to get right with God, because we cannot save ourselves, seems—well, it just seems wrong, frankly. We assume that it will always be possible for us to mend our relationships with God.

4. *The sovereign freedom of God.* In this day of so-called human rights, we assume that God owes us something: salvation or at least a chance at salvation. But God does not have to show us favor. He does—that is what the gospel is about—but he does not need to. The freedom of God to give or withhold favor is the very essence of salvation. The Bible teaches that "salvation comes from the LORD" (Jonah 2:9), and the sooner we acknowledge that important truth the better.

8. Leon Morris, *The Epistle to the Romans* (Grand Rapids: Wm. B. Eerdmans, and Leicester, England: Inter-Varsity Press, 1988), p. 417.

Salvation Is from God

Yes, but it is nevertheless also to be received by faith. Salvation depends on God, because only "God is able" to do what is needed. But notice what Paul says: "*If they do not persist in unbelief,* they will be grafted in" (emphasis added). We have seen that because the Jews are God's specifically chosen people it is: (1) possible, (2) probable, and (3) certain that they will be saved as a nation in the final days. But these specifically chosen people must nevertheless also believe on the Lord Jesus Christ to be saved. And if they must have faith, clearly we must also. No one can be saved without faith. I cannot be saved without faith. You cannot be saved without faith. *No one can be saved without faith.*

When Peter preached at Pentecost, he emphasized the electing grace of God in salvation, saying, "The promise is for you and your children and for all who are far off—for all whom the Lord our God will call" (Acts 2:39). But Peter did not understand the sovereignty of God in salvation to eliminate the need for saving faith. His message was: "Repent and be baptized, every one of you, in the name of Jesus Christ for the forgiveness of your sins" (v. 38). The passage concludes, "With many other words he warned them; and he pleaded with them, 'Save yourselves from this corrupt generation'" (v. 40).

My message is exactly the same. Salvation is of the Lord. But it comes by the preaching of the gospel and is something you enter only when you turn from sin and place your trust in Jesus Christ as your Savior. God saves, but he saves by bringing sinners to faith in Jesus Christ. Won't you believe that gospel and trust Jesus, if you have never believed on Jesus before? Today the door of God's grace stands open, and the promise of the Bible is that "everyone who calls on the name of the Lord will be saved" (Acts 2:21).

166

The Mystery of Jewish Hardening

Romans 11:25

I do not want you to be ignorant of this mystery, brothers, so that you may not be conceited; Israel has experienced a hardening in part until the full number of the Gentiles has come in.

In this volume of the *Romans* series, we have been studying Paul's unfolding of the purposes of God in history for more than forty chapters, focusing on the nation of Israel, and we come in Romans 11:25–32 to the last of the seven major points Paul is making. His theme here is the future conversion of the great mass of Israel in the final days.

Most commentators recognize that this is a new section and therefore separate it from the preceding verses by descriptive titles. Leon Morris calls verses 25 through 32 "The Conversion of Israel." John Murray describes this section as "The Fullness of the Gentiles and the Salvation of Israel." C. K. Barrett titles it "God's Plan Complete." Ray Stedman labels it "Our Great and Glorious God." H. C. G. Moule calls these verses "The Restoration of Israel Directly Foretold: All Is of and for God." William Barclay calls them "That All May Be of Mercy."

So also in our Bibles. The New International Version follows this line when it titles Romans 11:25–32 "All Israel Will Be Saved."

Clearly, this section is the culmination of what Paul has been saying in chapters 9 through 11 of this letter. He introduced his line of thought in verse 6 of Romans 9, wondering rhetorically if God's purposes in history may have failed, since so many Jews, God's specially chosen people, have rejected Jesus Christ as their Messiah. Our earlier studies have shown that Paul denied this implication and has been giving reasons for an entirely different view, namely, that God is still in control of history. Therefore, all that has happened both in the rejection of Israel and the conversion of Gentiles has been according to God's wise and perfect plan. You will recall that Paul has seven arguments to show that God's purposes have not been sidetracked by Israel's unbelief:

1. God's historical purposes have not failed, because *all whom God has elected to salvation are or will be saved* (Rom. 9:6–24).

2. God's purposes have not failed, because *God had previously revealed that not all Israel would be saved and that some Gentiles would be* (Rom. 9:25–29).

3. God's purposes have not failed, because *the unbelief of the Jews was their own responsibility, not God's* (Rom. 9:30–10:21).

4. God has not failed, because *some Jews (Paul himself was an example) have believed and have been saved* (Rom. 11:1).

5. God has not failed, because *it has always been the case that not all Jews but only a remnant has been saved* (Rom. 11:2–10).

6. God's plans have not failed, because *the salvation of the Gentiles, which is now occurring, is meant to arouse Israel to envy and thus be the means of saving some of them* (Rom. 11:11–24).

7. Finally, God's historical purposes toward the Jewish nation have not failed, because *in the end all Israel will be saved, and thus God will be seen to have honored his promises toward Israel nationally* (Rom. 11:25–32).

It is this final point, the last of the seven, to which we come now.

The "Mysteries" of God

In the earlier portion of Romans 11, Paul has argued both the possibility and probability of the conversion of the mass of Jewish people. Now he moves from argument to prophecy, stating the certainty of the blessing that shall one day be, and this means that what he has to say now is in the nature of special revelation.

This is the significance of the word *mystery* in verse 25. When we use that word, we have in mind something that is puzzling or unknown. One dictionary calls it "something that has not been, or cannot be, explained; something beyond human comprehension; a profound secret; an enigma." However, that is not the meaning of the word in the New Testament, in Paul's writings specifically, or, for that matter, in the ancient world in general.

In the ancient world a mystery was something unknown to most people but specially revealed to some. This was the meaning of the word as used of the ancient mystery religions, for example. The existence of these religions (Mithras, Isis and Osirus, Dionysus, Attis and Cybele, Eleusis and others) was known to nearly everybody. But the specifics of their religious rites were known only to initiates, much like today's Masons, who also have secret rites, signs, handshakes, and symbols of which most people are unaware.

The apostle Paul uses the word in this way but with specifically biblical elements. He uses "mystery" to refer to something that at one time was not known and could not be arrived at by any amount of human reasoning, but that has now been revealed to us by God through such inspired teachers as himself and the other apostles.

Charles Hodge says, "Any future event . . . which could be known only by divine revelation is a mystery."[1]

This was an important term for Paul, which means that he was aware of being the channel of such divine revelation for our benefit. One proof of this is the number of times he uses the word *mystery* and the variety of ways in which he uses it. Some years ago, H. A. Ironside, a former minister of Moody Memorial Church in Chicago, wrote a book on *The Mysteries of God* in which he explored these formerly hidden but now known doctrines at some length.[2] It is not one of Ironside's best books, in my judgment, since it is poorly written and strongly dispensational. Nevertheless, it has the important virtue of being somewhat comprehensive. In it Ironside explored:

1. "The Mysteries of the Kingdom of Heaven" (Matthew 13:11)
2. "The Mystery of the Olive Tree" (Romans 11:25)
3. "The Great Mystery of Christ and the Church" (Ephesians 5:32)
4. "The Mystery of Piety" (1 Timothy 3:16)
5. "The Mystery of the Rapture of the Saints" (1 Corinthians 15:51)
6. "The Mystery of Lawlessness" (2 Thessalonians 2:7)
7. "The Mystery of God Finished" (Revelation 10:7).

Ironside's main point was that the mysteries of the New Testament are things we should know, yet strangely are largely ignored by masses of today's Christians. We should not be ignorant of these things. It is true that "the secret things belong to the LORD our God," but the mysteries are among those that are revealed and therefore "belong to us and to our children forever" (Deut. 29:29). Ministers are to be faithful stewards of these truths (1 Cor. 4:1).

---

1. Charles Hodge, *A Commentary on Romans* (Edinburgh and Carlisle, Pa.: The Banner of Truth Trust, 1972), p. 372. Original edition 1935.
2. H. A. Ironside, *The Mysteries of God* (New York: Loizeaux Brothers, n.d.).

Israel's Future: A Mystery

This brings us back to the specific mystery Paul is writing about here, namely, that the mass of Israel will be saved. Why is it a mystery? Obviously, because it is not something any of us would ever figure out by mere reason or deduce by observation. As far as we can see, Israel has been rejected permanently. We do not see even a glimmer of national restoration. But what we cannot see or deduce Paul declares by revelation to be a future fact: "Israel has experienced a hardening in part until the full number of the Gentiles has come in," and then "all Israel will be saved" (vv. 25–26).

We have already looked at this statement in some detail, trying to weigh the arguments for and against belief in a time of future Jewish blessing. It is not necessary to argue them again here. Instead, we need only explore the key phrases in the statement more fully.

The "full number" of the Gentiles is actually only "fullness" in the Greek text, but the New International Version is surely right when it amplifies the term by adding the word *number*. Fullness could mean "fullness of blessing," meaning that some Gentiles will receive the full measure of those blessings originally given to the Jews. But Paul has not been dealing with that idea. He has been asking why not many Jews have been saved and why so many Gentiles have been saved instead, and he is prophesying that in the future large numbers of Jews will be converted. In this context the "fullness of the Gentiles" must mean their full number, that is, all the elect to be saved from among the many Gentile nations.

How about the word *until*? We have already seen that this is not a *terminus a quo*, an ending after which nothing else should be expected. Rather, it is a *terminus ad quem*, an ending of one thing, after which something else will happen.

I have not been trying to develop a full treatment of prophecy in our study of Romans 11, because it is not called for. I have merely been trying to explain what Paul is teaching in chapters 9–11. But I should mention that when Paul says "Israel has experienced a hardening in part until the full number of the Gentiles has come in," he is saying almost exactly what Jesus said when he noted that "Jerusalem will be trampled on by the Gentiles until the times of the Gentiles are fulfilled" (Luke 21:24). The context shows that Jesus was thinking of the destruction of Jerusalem by the Romans, which happened under the Roman general Titus in 70 A.D. He was saying that the capital would be in Gentile hands until the end of the "times of the Gentiles," presumably an age of Gentile prominence if not also of widespread Gentile spiritual blessing.

If we think about such things, we can hardly escape noticing that in our lifetimes the city of Jerusalem has once again come under Jewish control, as a result of the reestablishment of the modern state of Israel. This suggests that the Gentile age may be drawing to a close, as Jesus predicted.

The Point of Prophecy

The point of prophecy is never merely to give God's people some special insight into what will one day happen, an insight not possessed by unbelievers. It is always practical; it is revealed for its bearing on how we are to live now. With that in mind we ask: What is the reason for the revelation of this mystery? Why does Paul tell us that "Israel has experienced a hardening in part until the full number of the Gentiles has come in"?

It is not hard to find the answer. He tells us in this very verse. It is "so that you may not be conceited."

What does that mean?

Let me suggest a few answers.

1. *We should not be conceited in thinking that Gentile believers have replaced Jewish believers permanently.*

There are two forms of this error, as I see it. One is a mild form; the other is particularly evil. The mild form is sometimes seen among Reformed theologians and takes the shape of denying that anything spiritual can exist beyond or in addition to the church. I realize there is a valid concern in this. Since the forms and types of the Old Testament have been fulfilled in Jesus Christ, these writers cannot think of going back to anything. It seems to them that if God is thought of as having anything more to do with the Jews as a nation, this must necessarily be a regression. It is to reconstitute a physical people rather than a spiritual people. It is to substitute an earthly kingdom for a heavenly one.

Some others have probably erred in this direction, too. But it seems nevertheless to be a uniquely Gentile form of conceit to suppose that God cannot also begin to work among the Jews after his special saving work among the Gentiles shall have ended. Indeed, how can we presume to limit what God can do historically, even by our Reformed theology? If God says that there will be a day of future Jewish blessing, then there will be one, and we must be humbled by this revelation.

The intense and evil form of this error is anti-Semitism, particularly that which grows out of Gentile Christian arrogance. I am aware that intolerance is not limited to Christians. All over the world, ethnic or racial groups are prejudiced against other groups. A song that I remember from my college days goes:

> The whole world is festering with unhappy souls:
> The French hate the Germans; the Germans hate the Poles;
> Italians hate Yugoslavs; South Africans hate the Dutch,
> And I don't like anybody very much.

A sinful world is like that. But the fact of universal prejudice does not excuse anti-Semitism among Gentile Christians. Unfortunately, we must acknowledge that this has often existed. After all, it is so-called Christians, not Buddhists or Moslems or animists, who have called the Jews "Christ-killers," forgetting that it was a Roman governor named Pilate who actually delivered Jesus to death.

Whenever Gentile Christians start thinking of themselves as having some-how replaced the Jews in God's dealings, they must remember that the Jews are "loved [still] on account of the patriarchs" (Rom. 11:28) and that God says he has a spiritual future for them even yet.

2. *We should not be conceited in thinking that a Gentile church is the culmination of God's dealings in history.*

The fact that there is to be something beyond ourselves and our age in God's historical dealings should humble us in another way also. It should teach us that we are not the "be all" and "end all" of God's plans. Indeed, it should warn us that Christianity will not certainly triumph in our hands. There was a time in the last century and earlier in this one when many Christians in the West thought like this, and their thinking bore fruit in a form of post-millennialism that held that Christianity would inevitably conquer the earth before the return of Jesus Christ.

One who has held this view is Loraine Boettner, who has authored such valuable books as *The Reformed Doctrine of Predestination, Studies in Theology, Immortality,* and *The Millennium.* More than thirty years ago, in an article in *Christianity Today,* Boettner wrote:

> The redemption of the world . . . is a long slow process, extending through the centuries, yet surely approaching an appointed goal. We live in the day of advancing victory and see the conquest taking place. From the human viewpoint there are many apparent setbacks, and it often looks as though the forces of evil are about to gain the upper hand. But as one age succeeds another, there is progress. Looking back across the nearly two thousand years that have elapsed since the coming of Christ, we see that there has been marvelous progress. All over the world, pagan religions have had their day and are disintegrating. None of them can stand the open competition of Christianity. They await only the *coup de grace* of an aroused and energetic Christianity to send them into oblivion. . . . The Church *must* conquer the world, or the world will destroy the church. Christianity is *the* system of truth, the only one that through the ages has had the blessing of God upon it. We shall not expect the final fruition within our lifetime, nor within this century. But the goal is certain and the outcome sure. The future is as bright as the promises of God. The great requirement is faith that the Great Commission of Christ will be fulfilled through the outpouring of the Holy Spirit and preaching of the everlasting Gospel.[3]

That is strong propaganda. And, of course, much of it is true. The work of God *will* triumph. We *are* called to proclaim the gospel worldwide. The

---

3. Loraine Boettner, "Christian Hope and the Millennium," *Christianity Today,* September 29, 1958, p. 14.

gospel *will be* widely known. But this is not the same thing as saying that Christianity, as an historical force, will triumph. Or that Gentile Christianity will one day rule the world.

Moreover, although we can understand how a philosophy like this gained acceptance in a day when the western nations were at the peak of their economic and political power and therefore seemed to dominate the world, we can hardly make such an easy assumption about the flow of history today. The West and western Christianity are surely in decline. And although it is true that Christianity is growing rapidly in the Third World, it is also true that other world religions are also growing. Fueled by oil revenues, the religion of Islam is particularly ascendant.

We must not forget that Jesus once asked pointedly, "When the Son of Man comes [returns], will he find faith on the earth?" (Luke 18:8).

Or that when Peter wrote of the last days, he did not say that Christendom would triumph, but rather that "there will be false teachers among you [who] will secretly introduce destructive heresies, even denying the sovereign Lord who bought them. . . . Many will follow their shameful ways . . ." (2 Peter 2:1–2).

Or that Jude reminded us of the apostles' warning that "in the last times there will be scoffers who will follow their own ungodly desires," adding, "These are the men who divide you, who follow mere natural instincts and do not have the Spirit" (Jude 18–19).

Or that Paul also wrote, ". . . in later times some will abandon the faith and follow deceiving spirits and things taught by demons" (1 Tim. 4:1).

None of these passages encourages us to believe in an inevitable expanding triumph of Gentile Christianity. On the contrary, they warn us of unbelief, apostasy, and false teaching before Christ's return. I do not mean to say that Christianity will perish from the earth, for God will have his remnant among the Gentiles, just as he has had his remnant among the Jews. But I do mean to say that Gentile believers dare not be arrogant but should instead "be afraid," knowing that "if God did not spare the natural branches, he will not spare [us] either" (Rom. 11:20–21).

Knowing that God has a future for the Jews after the Gentile age has drawn to an end should temper and diffuse our nearly insufferable conceit.

3. *We should not be conceited in thinking that in ourselves we are something special.*

Believers in Christ are special to God, of course. But I am not thinking of that. I am thinking of the tendency we have to assume that the reason we are saved and that others are not saved is because we are wiser or more holy or more perceptive or more significant than they are. We are not saved for any of these reasons. We are *not* wiser or more holy or more perceptive or more significant than others. On the contrary, "God [has chosen] the foolish things of the world to shame the wise; God chose the weak things of the world to shame the strong. He chose the lowly things of this world and the despised things—and the things that are not—to nullify the things that are, so that no one may boast before him" (1 Cor. 1:27–29).

If God has chosen the foolish things now and will one day renew a work among his ancient people when the times of the Gentiles shall have been completed, we can never suppose that we are special. Instead, we can only acknowledge that we are saved on account of the mercy of God and by his immeasurable grace.

4. *We should not be conceited in somehow thinking that other people, who are not like us, are hopeless.*

It is easy for us to abandon hope for others. When we see a person who has squandered his or her spiritual opportunities or who has vigorously opposed Christianity or has sinned in some particularly dreadful fashion, we conclude that there is probably no chance for such a person. We write him or her off and say such things as: "The Jews have rejected Jesus, so they are lost," or "My friends will not have Christ, so they are lost." That is the way we think. But we must not think that way, for it is never true. God is the God of all hopeless causes, ourselves included. John Newton was surely close to God's heart when he replied to someone who spoke to him of an acquaintance for whom he despaired, "I have never despaired of any man since God saved me."

What about you? You may be laboring under the thought that you are a hopeless case, because of who you are or because of something you may have done or said or thought. Or you may have a family member whose case seems to you to be hopeless. I assure you on the basis of the Word of God that the case is not hopeless. And you are not hopeless either! Only unbelief keeps a person from salvation, and even today you may still call upon the name of the Lord and be wonderfully saved.

167

"All Israel Will Be Saved"

Romans 11:26–27

And so all Israel will be saved, as it is written:

> *"The deliverer will come from Zion;*
> *he will turn godlessness away from Jacob.*
> *And this is my covenant with them*
> *when I take away their sins."*

About one hundred years ago, Frederick the Great, King of Prussia, was having a discussion with his chaplain about the truth of the Bible. The king had become skeptical about Christianity, largely through the influence of the French atheist Voltaire. So he said to his chaplain, "If your Bible is really true, it ought to be capable of very easy proof. So often, when I have asked for proof of the inspiration of the Bible, I have been given some large tome that I have neither the time nor desire to read. If your Bible is really from God, you should be able to demonstrate the fact simply. Give me proof for the inspiration of the Bible in a word."

The chaplain replied, "Your Majesty, it is possible for me to answer your request literally. I can give you the proof you ask for in one word."

Frederick was amazed at this response. "What is this magic word that carries such a weight of proof?" he asked.

"Israel," said the chaplain.

Frederick was silent.

There are many other proofs for Christianity, of course. But it can hardly be doubted that the continuing existence of Israel as a distinct people throughout the four thousand years of her history is a striking phenomenon. Dispossessed of her homeland and dispersed throughout the world, Israel has nevertheless survived while other peoples in similar situations have not. Coupled with the Bible's identification of the Jews as God's elect people and its many prophecies concerning their unfolding history, the preservation of Israel as a people is strong evidence for the Bible being the inspired and inerrant Word of God.

Even more than that, and much to the purpose for our study, the survival of Israel suggests that God has preserved these people through their many dispersions and persecutions not because he does not care for them, but because he *does*, and because he has a plan for the Jewish people that will unfold in blessing in the last days.

Proof from Isaiah

Romans 11:26 is the conclusion and clearest statement of this argument, the bottom line of Paul's discussion of God's historical purposes with the Jews, namely, that in the last days God will fulfill his promises to the Jews nationally by bringing the mass of Israel to faith in Jesus Christ as the Messiah: "And so all Israel will be saved."

We have already made that point several times over in the studies that have been leading up to this one, but what is unique about verse 26 is the fact that here at last Paul proves his argument from the Old Testament. This has been his pattern before, as I have already pointed out several times. Paul's pattern is to make his argument first and then, when he has completed it, to nail it down with one or more Old Testament citations. He did this in chapter 3, after having argued the case for human depravity. He did it again in chapter 4, after explaining the gospel at the end of the previous chapter. The same pattern was followed in chapters 9 and 10.

This is opposite to the pattern followed by the apostle Peter, to give just one contrary example. In his sermon on Pentecost, Peter first gave his texts and then argued from them, rather than the other way around. He did this three times, expounding Christian truth on the basis of Joel 2:28–32, Psalm 16:8–11, and Psalm 110:1 (cf. Acts 2:14–41).

In Romans 11, Paul proves his argument concerning Israel by a quotation from Isaiah 59:20–21. Isaiah 27:9, Jeremiah 31:33–34, and Psalm 14:7 may have also been in his mind, since he seems to have included wording from those additional verses in his quotation.[1]

However, there are two ways in which this quotation can be taken, and, not surprisingly, they correspond to the two ways of looking at what Paul is saying about Israel, which I have already examined. The text could be saying that the Redeemer will emerge out of Israel in order to take away the people's sins by his death on the cross. In that case, it would be a reference to Jesus' first coming and earthly ministry. Or else it could be saying that Jesus will come out of heaven to Israel in order to turn the hearts of the people from unbelief to faith. In this case, it would (or could) be referring to a time of future blessing. Those who do not believe in a future period of national conversion for Israel naturally incline to the former interpretation. Those who think Paul is prophesying an age of future blessing choose the latter.

I have already indicated my reasons for choosing the second of these views. I add here that in my judgment the emphasis in Paul's quotation of Isaiah 59:20 is on the future tense of the verb "to be," that is, the words "will come." From Isaiah's point in history, to say that the Messiah "will come" could be a reference only to Jesus' first coming. But from Paul's vantage point, which followed that first coming, the verb must be looking to a period still future, and Paul must be thinking of it.

Here are two observations that are very important.

1. Although by itself the passage in Isaiah could refer either to the first coming of Jesus or to a time of future blessing of Israel by God, from the point at which Paul under the guidance of the Holy Spirit has interpreted it as referring to this future blessing, *we have the proper meaning and ought to interpret the verses in this way*. In other words, to go back to the idea of the "mystery" Paul says he is revealing (v. 25), it is as if Paul acknowledges that readers of the Bible could not be sure what Isaiah was referring to before this revelation but that now we can be sure of it because of what he is teaching.

---

1. The text in Romans does not follow any one of the Old Testament texts exactly, either the Hebrew or the Septuagint. However, it is closest to Isaiah 59:20–21, which contains the idea of the Redeemer coming to Zion and the establishment of a covenant with Israel. The chief variation is that where the Hebrew text of verse 20 reads "to Zion" or "for Zion" and the Greek text reads "on behalf of Zion," Paul has "out of Zion," as in Psalm 14:7. On this variation Murray comments rightly that "there should not be any great difficulty. The preposition involved in Hebrew is capable of both renderings and Paul was at liberty to use the one he did. Both significations are true, that the Redeemer came out of Zion and for its deliverance. The accent in Paul's teaching in this passage is on what the Redeemer will do *for* Zion. But in the first clause the thought is focused on the relation of the Redeemer to Zion after the pattern of 9:5. This is germane to the total emphasis of this context and underscores the relevance of the Redeemer's saving work to Israel as a people" (John Murray, *The Epistle to the Romans*, 2 vols. in 1 [Grand Rapids: Wm. B. Eerdmans, 1968], vol. 2, p. 99).

Robert Haldane says, "We may be assured that the Apostle, speaking by the same Spirit as the Prophet, and directed by the Spirit to quote him, has . . . given the meaning of his words."[2]

Following a similar line of thought, Charles Hodge says, "We are, of course, bound to receive the apostle's interpretation as correct."[3]

2. My second observation is that *this positions us to see many passages that might otherwise be construed as referring only to a past blessing as actually referring to a day of future blessing,* or at least possibly referring to it. This is what John Murray is arguing when he says, "This express application is an index to the principle of interpretation which would have to be applied to many other Old Testament passages which are in the same vein as Isaiah 59:20, 21, namely, that they comprise the promise of an expansion of gospel blessing such as Paul enunciates in verses 25, 26."[4]

If that is right, this is the place in our exposition to recognize that there are other Old Testament texts that should be seen as prophesying the future conversion of the mass of Israel and to look at some of them.

Old Testament Texts

There must be hundreds of such passages. An exhaustive study would fill volumes. Yet here are some that are especially significant.

1. *Jeremiah 16:14–16.* "'. . . the days are coming,' declares the LORD, 'when men will no longer say, "As surely as the LORD lives, who brought the Israelites up out of Egypt," but they will say, "As surely as the LORD lives, who brought Israelites up out of the land of the north and out of all the countries where he had banished them." For I will restore them to the land I gave their fore-fathers. But now I will send for many fishermen,' declares the LORD, 'and they will catch them. After that I will send for many hunters, and they will hunt them down on every mountain and hill and from the crevices of the rocks.'"

Since Jeremiah was writing before the fall of Jerusalem to the Babylonian armies under Nebuchadnezzar, this might be taken as a prophecy of the return of the Jews to Judah in the days of Ezra and Nehemiah, and it may even have had a partial fulfillment at that time. However, in view of the apostle Paul's understanding of Isaiah 59:20–21, it may also be referring to a more important return of Israel to her ancient homeland in the last days.

In fact, when we begin to think of the text along these lines, the words "and out of all the countries where he had banished them" take on new meaning. For now the prophecy is seen not merely as foretelling the return of the

2. Robert Haldane, *An Exposition of the Epistle to the Romans* (MacDill AFB: MacDonald Publishing, 1958), p. 542.

3. Charles Hodge, *A Commentary on Romans* (Edinburgh and Carlisle, Pa.: The Banner of Truth Trust, 1972), p. 374. Original edition 1935.

4. Murray, *The Epistle to the Romans,* vol. 2, p. 99.

Jews from one nation alone, that is, from Babylon, but from all the world's nations, where the Jews have indeed been scattered and from which they must come if they are to return to the land of Israel.

2. *Jeremiah 32:36–40.* In Jeremiah 32, the chapter in which God tells Jeremiah to buy a field as a symbol of his lasting commitment to the Jewish homeland, God says, "You are saying about this city, 'By the sword, famine and plague it will be handed over to the king of Babylon'; but this is what the LORD, the God of Israel says: I will surely gather them from all the lands where I banish them in my furious anger and great wrath; I will bring them back to this place and let them live in safety. They will be my people, and I will be their God. I will give them singleness of heart and action, so that they will always fear me for their own good and the good of their children after them. I will make an everlasting covenant with them: I will never stop doing good to them, and I will inspire them to fear me, so that they will never turn away from me."

Like Jeremiah 16:14–16, this passage seems at first to be referring only to the return of the Jews to Jerusalem from Babylon, even though some of the elements in the prophecy do not seem to fit perfectly, for instance, that the people will serve God in "singleness of heart" and "always fear" him, and that God will make "an everlasting covenant with them." Singleness of heart hardly describes the history of the people from the days of Ezra and Nehemiah on. In fact, they were as wayward then as ever, and in the days of Jesus they actually turned against their Messiah.

On the other hand, as soon as we begin to think in terms of a still future blessing, the idea of "singleness of heart" and "always fearing" God and "an everlasting covenant" have an exact meaning and are seen to refer to the same future conversion of the mass of Israel that Paul is prophesying.

3. *Hosea 1:10 and 2:21–23.* A classic and often re-echoed prophecy of this future age is found in Hosea's symbolic naming of his children and God's promise to change their names in that day. Hosea called his children *Jezreel* (meaning "scattered"), *Lo-Ruhamah* (meaning "Not-Loved"), and *Lo-Ammi* (meaning "Not-My-People"). But God said, changing the names to Planted, Loved, and My People, "I will plant her for myself in the land; I will show my love to the one I called 'Not my loved one,' I will say to those called 'Not my people,' 'You are my people'; and they will say, 'You are my God.'" (See study 135, "'Children of the Living God,'" in this volume.)

There are prophecies similar to this toward the end of many of the minor prophets (cf. Joel 3:17–21; Amos 9:11–15; Micah 7:8–20; Zeph. 3:9–20).

4. *Zechariah 12–14.* Special attention should be given to the last three chapters of Zechariah, which are presented as "an oracle" about the final days. The words "on that day," which customarily refer to God's final wrapping-

up of history, including the last judgment, occur sixteen times and tie the chapters together. These chapters describe a time in which:

First, God will deliver Jerusalem from the nations of the earth, which are attacking her (12:1–9),

Second, the people will "look on . . . the one they have pierced" and "mourn for him" (12:10–13),

Third, a "fountain" will be opened to the house of David and the inhabitants of Jerusalem "to cleanse them from sin and impurity" (13:1–3),

Fourth, the people will call on God, causing him to say, as in Hosea 2:23, "They are my people," and the people to say, "The LORD is our God" (13:9),

Fifth, the Lord will descend on the Mount of Olives to save the people in a time of great trouble, deliver Jerusalem, and bring prosperity to the land (14:1–15),

Sixth, Gentiles will go to Jerusalem to worship God (14:16–19), and

Seventh, the people will become holy in all they are and do (14:20–21).

Nothing like this has ever happened; therefore, it must be future. Besides, these things were written after the regathering of the people in the days of Nehemiah and Ezra, which means that they cannot refer to those past days but must refer instead to a time yet future. That is, they must refer to the time of future Jewish belief about which Paul is writing.

Jews for Jesus

At this point the natural reaction is to say that widespread Jewish conversions are unlikely, considering the traditionally strong opposition of Judaism to Jesus and Christianity. But even if we are only looking at this from a human point of view, it may not be as far out as many think, because there seems to be a new interest in Jesus by Jewish thinkers.

Sholem Asch, a Polish Jew who was one of the best-known Jewish writers of his day, said in an interview published in the *Christian Herald* many years ago:

> Since I first met him [Jesus], he has held my mind and heart. . . . I was seeking that something for which so many of us search—that surety, that faith, that spiritual content in my living which would bring me peace and through which I might bring some peace to others. I found it in the Nazarene. . . .
>
> Jesus Christ, to me, is the outstanding personality of all time, of all history, both as Son of God and as Son of Man. . . . No other religious leader . . . has ever become so personal a part of people as The Nazarene. When you understand Jesus, you understand that he came to save you, to come into your personality. It isn't just a case of a misty, uncertain relationship between a worshipper and an unseen God; that is abstract; Jesus is personal."[5]

5. Frank S. Mead, "An Interview with Sholem Asch," *The Christian Herald* (January, 1944). Quoted by Arthur W. Kac, *The Rebirth of the State of Israel—Is It of God or of Man?* (London: Marshall, Morgan & Scott, 1958), p. 227.

Constantine Brunner, the German Jewish philosopher, looked upon Jesus as the great representative of pure Judaism. He wrote:

> Is it only the Jew who is incapable of seeing and hearing all that others see and hear? Are the Jews stricken with blindness and deafness as regards Messiah Jesus, so that to them alone he has nothing to say? . . . Understand, then, what we shall do: We shall bring him back to us. Messiah Jesus is not dead for us—for us he has not yet lived: and he will not slay us, he will make us alive again. His profound and holy words, and all that is true and heart-appealing in the New Testament, must from now on be heard in our synagogues and taught to our children, in order that the wrong we had committed may be made good, the curse turned into a blessing, and that he at last may find us who has always been seeking after us.[6]

Ferdynand Zweig, a contemporary English Jew who has taught at the Hebrew and Tel Aviv universities, says, "The Jewish religion seems to be at present to the large mass of Israeli Jews uninspiring and uninspired. Could it be that Jesus could give it a new lease of life?"[7]

Hans Joachim Schoeps, the Jewish theologian who taught the history of religion at Erlangen University in Germany, wrote:

> The Messianism of Israel aims at that which is to come, the eschatology of the Gentile church at the return of him who has come. Both elective covenants confront the ebb and flow of the finite world in the shared expectation that the decisive event is still to come—the goal of the ways of God that he travels with mankind in Israel and in the Church. The church of Jesus Christ has preserved no portrait of its lord and savior. If Jesus were to come again tomorrow, no Christian would know his face. But it might well be that he who is coming at the end of days, he who is awaited by the synagogue as by the church, is one, with one and the same face.[8]

None of these authors has accepted Jesus as his personal Savior from sin, and no one would say on the basis of these quotations that the Jews as a whole are ready to accept Jesus of Nazareth as their Messiah. But they do indicate what even many Jews are calling a new openness to Jesus and suggest, to Christians at least, that the time of future national conversion that Paul writes of in Romans, may not be far distant.

6. Constantine Brunner, *Der Judenhass und die Juden* (Berlin: Oesterheld, 1918), p. 34. Quoted by Arthur W. Kac, ed., *The Messiahship of Jesus: Are Jews Changing Their Attitude Toward Jesus?* (Grand Rapids: Baker Book House, 1980), p. 26.

7. Ferdynand Zweig, *Israel: The Sword and the Harp* (Cranbury, N.J.: Associated University Press, 1969), p. 229. Quoted by Kac, *The Messiahship of Jesus*, p. 68.

8. Hans Joachim Schoeps, "A Religious Bridge Between Jew and Christian," trans. Ralph Manheim, *Commentary* (February, 1950). Quoted by Kac, *The Messiahship of Jesus*, p. 58.

Jews and the Gentile Church

I close with a few observations on what God's historical dealings with the Jewish people mean for today's largely Gentile church.

First, the experience of Israel through the thousands of years of her history is a demonstration of the biblical principle that where there is obedience there will be blessing, and where there is disobedience there will be judgments. Israel has suffered many judgments during the centuries of her disobedience to God's law and rejection of God's Messiah. But it is the same for Christians. God is not mocked. If we disobey God's Word and persist in going our own way, God will discipline us, gently if he can but also forcefully if he must. Many believers have been so disciplined. You may be one. Learn from it. You cannot fight against God successfully.

Second, God is faithful to his covenant. We are going to pursue this in our next study, because it is the explicit teaching of Romans 11:27 ("And this is my covenant with them when I take away their sins"). This is an encouragement because it tells us that God will not give up on those whom he has chosen, even if our sins cause him to turn away his face for a time.

Third, there is a lesson about grace. For ultimately that is what this discussion is all about. God's relationship to Israel is a tremendous illustration of his grace. Chosen, yet frightfully disobedient, even to the point of rejecting and actually killing the very Son of God sent to them, Israel nevertheless has been loved by God, continues to be loved by him, and will one day be brought back to God—because God is gracious. This is our God, too. The New Testament calls today the day of God's grace.

But this day of grace will not last forever, and the regathering of Israel in her own land may indicate that God's days of grace are fast drawing to a close. Where do you stand in your relationship to Jesus, who came into this world and died on the cross to save you?

He is coming again! Will you be ready for him when he comes?

The Bible says, "We must pay more careful attention, therefore, to what we have heard, so that we do not drift away. For if the message spoken by angels was binding, and every violation and disobedience received its just punishment, how shall we escape if we ignore such a great salvation?" (Heb. 2:1–3a).

168

God's Irrevocable Covenant

Romans 11:27

*And this is my covenant with them
when I take away their sins.*

In the last study I said I would return to the subject of God's covenant in this one, because of verse 27. A covenant is a solemn promise, usually ratified in some formal way. But I begin with a preliminary question: Is the covenant idea important for understanding biblical theology?

Covenant theologians will immediately answer, "Yes, of course." And I must confess that I believe this is right. I will show why as I go along. But the question is still reasonable, if for no other reason than that the idea does not seem to be very important in Romans. Although this is the greatest doctrinal book in the New Testament, as almost everyone will agree, the word *covenant* occurs only twice in the letter: once in Romans 9:4, where it is mentioned as one of the advantages of Judaism ("Theirs is the adoption as sons; theirs the divine glory, *the covenants*") and the second time in our text ("And this is my *covenant* with them when I take away their sins").

The first is a bare mention, with no elaboration at all. The second is a quotation from the Old Testament. In neither case does the apostle develop what is called a covenant theology.

I suppose that is the best defense I have for my personal neglect of the covenant idea in *Foundations of the Christian Faith*.[1] I produced that large volume over five years' time, and it contains over 700 pages of material. Yet although it mentions the word *covenant* in a few places, it does not develop an explicit covenant theology. One of my friends chastised me for that on one occasion, wondering how a "covenant theologian" like myself could write what I call "a comprehensive" theology and ignore this subject.

Many Covenants

In my opinion, the idea does not have quite the prominence in the Bible that many covenant theologians give it. In fact, covenant theology itself was not worked out until late in the Reformation period by two of the followers of John Calvin: Zacharias Ursinus (1534–1583) and Caspar Olevianus (1536–1587). They developed the idea of two main covenants: a covenant of works established between God and Adam, and a covenant of grace established between God the Father and God the Son. Nevertheless, the covenant idea is important, as even a very quick look at the biblical material shows.

In Hebrew the word for "covenant" is *b'rith*. It occurs more than 300 times in the Old Testament and is translated as "covenant" 257 times (NIV). The Greek word is *diathêkê*. It occurs 36 times in the New Testament, more than half of them in the letter to the Hebrews.

We can approach the subject from the number or types of covenants that are mentioned in the Bible. Everyone seems to have a different listing at this point, which complicates matters, but most lists would include:

1. *God's covenant with Adam* (Gen. 1:28–30; 2:16–17). The word *covenant* is not used in the account of God's promises and warnings to Adam, but it is assumed that God established something like a covenant with him. According to the terms of this covenant, Adam was to enjoy the fullness of God's blessing upon the condition of perfect obedience in the matter of the forbidden tree. If he should stand that test, his posterity would stand with him. If he should fail that test, he would bring judgment and death upon the race. Paul seems to be thinking of this covenant in Romans 5:12–19, though the word *covenant* does not occur in that chapter either.

2. *God's covenant with Noah* (Gen. 6:18; 9:9–17). This was a promise never again to destroy the world by flood. It was confirmed by the sign of the rainbow.

---

1. James Montgomery Boice, *Foundations of the Christian Faith: A Comprehensive and Readable Theology*, 4 vols. in 1 (Downers Grove, Ill., and Leicester, England: Inter-Varsity Press, 1986).

3. *God's covenant with Abraham* (Gen. 12:1–3; 13:14–17; 15:1–21; 17:1–22). The first two covenants, those with Adam and Noah, had to do with the human race generally. The covenant with Abraham concerns the nation of Israel and involves the following promises: that Abraham would be the father of a great nation, that God would give this people an extensive land of their own, that the land would be theirs forever, that the Redeemer would come through this line of descent, and that God would bless all the peoples of the world through this Redeemer. This covenant was repeated with Abraham's two immediate descendants: his son Isaac and his grandson Jacob.

4. *God's covenant with the Jews through Moses* (Exod. 19:5–6; 24:7–8; 34:28; Deut. 28:1–30:20). This is sometimes called the Deuteronomic covenant because of its extensive treatment in that book. Like the covenant established with Adam, it is a covenant of blessing contingent upon obedience and of judgment for disobedience.

5. *God's covenant with David* (2 Sam. 7:4–16; 1 Chron. 17:3–14). God promised David that he would establish his throne and kingdom forever, which David recognized to be a promise about the Messiah.

6. *The new covenant* (Jer. 31:31–34; 32:40–41). Jeremiah was the first of the Old Testament writers to use the words "new covenant." He recognized the failure of the people to keep the terms of the old covenant, but he promised a day when God would establish a new covenant in which one of the blessings would be a change of the people's hearts that would enable them to obey God and be holy.

> "The time is coming," declares the Lord,
>   "when I will make a new covenant
> with the house of Israel
>   and with the house of Judah. . . .
>
> "I will put my law in their minds
>   and write it on their hearts.
> I will be their God,
>   and they will be my people."
>
> Jeremiah 31:31–33

7. *The covenant of grace.* This is not a biblical expression, and only one verse in the Bible even puts the words *covenant* and *grace* together in the same sentence (Heb. 10:29). But "covenant of grace" is a phrase that theologians use alongside "covenant of works," which they use to describe the covenant assumed to have been established between God and Adam. Covenant of grace refers to an agreement between God the Father and God the Son according

to which the Father would give a numerous posterity to Jesus contingent upon the accomplishment of his atoning sacrifice on the cross.

We can gain a quick sense of the importance of the covenant idea by remembering: (1) that our Bibles are divided into two covenants: the Old Covenant (or Testament) and the New Covenant (or Testament), and (2) that we speak of a covenant every time we observe the Lord's Supper, remembering how Jesus said, "This cup is the new covenant in my blood . . ." (Luke 22:20; cf. 1 Cor. 11:25).

Unconditional Covenants

We are now ready to look at our text in Romans specifically. When we do, the first thing we notice is that the covenant is described as being God's covenant, that is, a covenant *he* makes: "And this is *my* covenant with them when I take away their sins" (emphasis added). There are covenants in the Bible between human beings, of course, but the significant ones are all between God and man (or men), and *it is God who enacts them.* That is the important thing. Because they are essentially God's promise to do something, they have the character and power of God behind them.

By far the most dramatic example of a covenant is the one established with Abraham, recorded in Genesis 15. The chapter tells how God told Abraham to prepare for a covenant ceremony, just as such ceremonies were apparently enacted in his day. He was to take several animals—a heifer, a goat, a ram, a dove, and a pigeon—cut each into two parts, and lay the parts on the ground in two rows over against each other. (It is helpful to note that the Hebrew word *b'rith* is often accompanied by the verb "to cut," therefore literally "to cut a covenant.") In ancient times the parties would stand in the space between the rows of divided animals and make their vows there. Presumably, the blood of the slain animals, which covered the ground where they stood, made their vows especially solemn and binding.

But here is the interesting thing. After Abraham had prepared the place for the ceremony, God caused Abraham to fall into a deep sleep, and while he was sleeping God appeared to him, symbolized by a smoking cauldron of fire and a blazing torch. These passed between the pieces of the animals, while Abraham watched. God said, "To your descendants I give this land, from the river of Egypt to the great river, the Euphrates" (Gen. 15:18).

This was not a case of covenant making between equals in which, for example, God would promise to do something and Abraham, for his part, also would promise to do something. In this covenant, God made all the promises, and Abraham was not required to do anything. Theologians call such covenants unilateral or unconditional covenants, to distinguish them from those that do involve two parties and are conditional.

The Deuteronomic covenant is the chief example of a conditional covenant, since it promises blessing if the people obey and warns of judgment if they do not. It says:

If you fully obey the LORD your God and carefully follow all his commands I give you today, the LORD your God will set you high above all the nations on earth. All these blessings will come upon you and accompany you if you obey the LORD your God:

> You will be blessed in the city and blessed in the country.
> The fruit of your womb will be blessed, and the crops of your land and the young of your livestock—the calves of your herds and the lambs of your flocks.
> Your basket and your kneading trough will be blessed.
> You will be blessed when you come in and blessed when you go out.

Deuteronomy 28:1–6

However, if you do not obey the LORD your God and do not carefully follow all his commands and decrees I am giving you today, all these curses will come upon you and overtake you:

> You will be cursed in the city and cursed in the country.
> Your basket and your kneading trough will be cursed.
> The fruit of your womb will be cursed, and the crops of your land, and the calves of your herds and the lambs of your flocks.
> You will be cursed when you come in and cursed when you go out."

Deuteronomy 28:15–19

The covenant continues in that vein for several chapters.

Of course, you can see why biblical theologians speak of unconditional covenants, like that established with Abraham, and conditional covenants, like the Deuteronomic covenant. But let me point out that, strictly speaking, all the covenants are unconditional from God's point of view. God sets the terms, and the terms do not alter. They may be without condition: "I will do this, regardless of what you do." They may have multiple responses, depending upon what human beings do: "If you obey, I will bless you; if you do not, I will judge you." But what God promises to do is irrevocable from the start.

Why? It is because God *is* God. He is sovereign in all he does, and he is faithful. He keeps his word. And also because he foresees or, which is a better way of saying it, determines all contingencies. We are not like that. We make promises and then are unable to keep them, because things happen that we could not foresee or because we change. But God does not change, and nothing surprises him. His purposes at the end are exactly what they were at the beginning.

As far as Israel is concerned, this means that God will not forsake the Jews but will continue to work with them as his covenant people, even though they have wandered far from him and for the most part have rejected Jesus Christ. This is why Paul quotes from Isaiah 59 at this point. As John Murray says, "The effect [of this quotation] is that the future restoration of Israel is certified by nothing less than the certainty belonging to [the] covenantal institution."[2]

A Covenant of Grace

There is another thing we need to see about this covenant and text: It is not only a covenant established by God and therefore something that is unilateral and unconditional, it is also a covenant of salvation, which means that it is a covenant of grace. This is because it is a promise to "take away their sins," and we know that the taking away of sin is done only by the death of Jesus Christ.

This is what the Book of Hebrews emphasizes. I wrote earlier that there are thirty-six uses of the word *covenant* in the New Testament and that more than half of them are in Hebrews. The exact number is nineteen. In that book the author is writing to Jews to show that God has replaced the old covenant, which required obedience but did not promise the means to do it, with a new covenant, which is mediated by Jesus and accomplished by his death. He refers to the sacrifices performed by the Old Testament priests and says such things as, "The ministry Jesus has received is as superior to theirs as the covenant of which he is mediator is superior to the old one . . ." (Heb. 8:6). Or again, "Christ is the mediator of a new covenant, that those who are called may receive the promised eternal inheritance . . ." (Heb. 9:15).

The Hebrews writer closes by saying, "May the God of peace, who through the blood of the eternal covenant brought back from the dead our Lord Jesus, that great Shepherd of the sheep, equip you with everything good for doing his will, and may he work in us what is pleasing to him, through Jesus Christ, to whom be glory for ever and ever. Amen" (Heb. 13:20–21).

What Hebrews says is important, for it warns us never to think of Jewish people as somehow enjoying a separate track of salvation, as if they are saved only because they are Jews and by being Jews. Some who have taught that God will save the Jews in the last days have talked like this, leading critics of their view to say that they have created two peoples of God, a heavenly people with a heavenly destiny and an earthly people with an earthly destiny. If they have done that, they are wrong. There is only one people of God, composed both of Jews and Gentiles. The covenant we are considering has nothing to do with a separate people and a separate destiny, only that God will keep his promises to the Jewish people by leading the mass of them to faith in Jesus Christ as their Savior in the final days.

As Paul told Timothy, "For there is one God and one mediator between God and men, the man Christ Jesus" (1 Tim. 2:5).

2. John Murray, *The Epistle to the Romans*, 2 vols. in 1 (Grand Rapids: Wm. B. Eerdmans, 1968), vol. 2, p. 100.

Our Faithful God

My final point is that, therefore, we also are a party to this covenant, if we have believed on Jesus Christ. The Jews are to be brought to faith in the last days. But we stand in that same covenant today, and the attributes of God that have formed the earlier covenants are also for our encouragement. Can't you see that this is how Romans 11 is ending? Paul has been arguing for God's faithfulness to the Jews as being consistent with his faithfulness to us, and now, having shown that "all Israel will be saved," he breaks into praise of God's gracious attributes, since they affect us also.

In these last verses he is going to praise God's mercy, knowledge, wisdom, judgments, and paths, and he will close by saying, "To him be the glory forever! Amen."

When we talk about God's irrevocable covenant, as we have been doing here, and God's irrevocable call, which we will do in our next study, we are speaking about God's immutability. Immutability means that God does not change, and because he does not change he can be counted on.

In what ways does God not change? In his popular book *Knowing God,* English theologian J. I. Packer lists six areas:[3]

1. *God's life does not change.* Created things have a beginning and an end, but God does not. His life is a constant datum. God does not grow old or mature or weaken or grow stronger. God cannot change for the better, because he is already perfect, and he certainly cannot change for the worse.

2. *God's character does not change.* One of the most repeated passages in the Bible is Exodus 34:6–7, in which God reveals himself to Moses, saying, "The LORD, the LORD, the compassionate and gracious God, slow to anger, abounding in love and faithfulness, maintaining love to thousands, and forgiving wickedness, rebellion and sin. Yet he does not leave the guilty unpunished; he punishes the children and their children for the sin of the fathers to the third and fourth generation." That is what God was like in the days of the Jewish exodus, and that is what he is like today. Sickness, old age, or adverse circumstances can destroy our good traits, but nothing like this ever happens to God. He can be counted on to be as kind, gracious, forgiving (and holy) as he always was.

3. *God's truth does not change.* This means that the truths of the Bible do not change. What we read in the pages of Holy Scripture is as right and true today as ever.

4. *God's ways do not change.* Packer writes: "He continues to act towards sinful men in the way that he does in the Bible story. Still he shows his freedom

3. J. I. Packer, *Knowing God* (Downers Grove, Ill.: Inter-Varsity Press, 1973), pp. 68–72.

and lordship by discriminating between sinners, causing some to hear the gospel while others do not hear it, and moving some of those who hear it to repentance while leaving others in their unbelief. . . . Still he blesses those on whom he sets his love in a way that humbles them, so that all the glory may be his alone. Still he hates the sins of his people, and uses all kinds of inward and outward pains and griefs to wean their hearts from compromise and disobedience. . . . Man's ways, we know, are pathetically inconstant—but not God's."[4]

5. *God's purposes do not change.* The ups and downs of history do not frustrate God or cause him to alter what he has determined beforehand to do. Has he planned to bring many sons and daughters into glory through faith in Jesus? Then he will do it. Has he purposed to bless Israel in a special way nationally? Then that will be done. What God does in time he has planned in eternity, and what he has planned in eternity is carried out in time.

6. *God's Son does not change.* Perhaps most blessed of all for Christian people, the Lord Jesus Christ does not change. He is "the same yesterday and today and forever" (Heb. 13:8), and it remains true that "he is able to save completely those who come to God through him . . ." (Heb. 7:25).

When the great protector Oliver Cromwell was dying, he was overcome with spiritual darkness and depression, and in his despair he asked his chaplain, "Tell me, is it possible to fall from grace?"

"No," said his minister. "It is not possible."

"Then I am safe," said Cromwell, "for I know that I was once in grace. I am the poorest wretch that ever lived, but I know that God has loved me."

Do you remember this question from the Heidelberg Catechism?

Question 1: "What is thy only comfort in life and in death?"

Answer: "That I, with body and soul, both in life and in death, am not my own, but belong to my faithful Savior Jesus Christ, who with his precious blood has fully satisfied for all my sins, and redeemed me from all the power of the devil; and so preserves me that without the will of my Father in heaven not a hair can fall from my head; yea, that all things must work together for my salvation. Wherefore, by his Holy Spirit, he also assures me of eternal life, and makes me heartily willing and ready henceforth to live unto him." That is our God forever! Amen.

---

4. Ibid., pp. 70–71.

169

God's Irrevocable Call

Romans 11:28–29

As far as the gospel is concerned, they are enemies on your account; but as far as election is concerned, they are loved on account of the patriarchs, for God's gifts and his call are irrevocable.

Do you remember the Greek philosopher Heraclitus? He lived about 2,600 years ago in Ephesus, and it was he who said, "It is impossible to step into the same river twice." Heraclitus meant that life is in a state of constant change. So, although you can step into a river once, step out, and then step in a second time, by the time you have stepped back in the water has flowed on and the river is no longer the same. It is a different river. To Heraclitus and the Greeks who followed him, all of life seemed to be like that—as if everything is changing and it is changing all the time.

"But if that is so," Heraclitus asked, "how is it that things are not in a state of constant chaos?" He answered that life is not chaos because the change we see is an ordered change, and the reason it is ordered and not random is that the mind, reason, or order of God stands behind it.

To the Greek philosophers, God (or reason) was the only fixed point in an otherwise chaotic universe.

The Character of God

Heraclitus was not a Christian, of course. He lived well before the time of Jesus Christ. But if Heraclitus had lived six or seven hundred years later and had been given an opportunity to read Paul's letter to the Romans, he would have understood our text easily. For what Paul is saying in the closing lines of Romans 11 is that the character and, therefore, also the plans of God do not change, regardless of the way human beings alter or behave.

Anyone who has been studying Romans 11 carefully will be aware that verses 28–32 are a summary of what Paul has been at pains to prove earlier. He has been asking why Jewish people seem to have been rejected by God, why they have turned their backs on the Messiah, and he has answered that it has been for the sake of Gentile conversions. Using the image of a cultivated olive tree and branches from a wild tree, he argued that Jewish branches have been broken off so that wild branches, which represent Gentiles, might be grafted in. Jewish people have been set aside for a time so that salvation might be extended to all the many peoples of the world.

But this setting-aside is only temporary, for once "the full number of the Gentiles has come in . . . all Israel will be saved" (Rom. 11:25–26). That is, there will be a time of widespread Jewish conversions before the final judgment.

This earlier teaching is summarized in our present text: "As far as the gospel is concerned, they are enemies on your account; but as far as election is concerned, they are loved on account of the patriarchs, for God's gift and his call are irrevocable" (Rom. 11:28–29).

But how can Paul say this? Setting aside the matter of special revelation, what could possibly lead Paul to this conclusion? He could conclude on the basis of the widespread Jewish rejection of the gospel, which he had witnessed, that the Jews were being set aside. He could imagine on the basis of the growing Gentile response that Gentiles were being brought into God's salvation plan. But on what possible basis could Paul suppose that one day the Jews as a people would be saved? There is only one answer. It is the character of God. God is unchanging. Therefore, his plans for the Jews are unchanging, and his call, which puts his plans into action, is irrevocable.

To put this in simple language: God chose the Jews to be his special people, and nothing that has happened since, or will happen, can change that choice or relationship.

So these words are not a reflection upon Paul's missionary experience, still less an expression of his fading hope that his own people might nevertheless somehow be saved eventually. It is a deduction from God's character. That is what Leon Morris is getting when he writes at this point, "God had made promises to Israel, and these promises would be kept. Israel's refusal to accept the gospel did not mean either that the gospel was a failure or that God would not perform all he had promised to his ancient people."[1]

God's Gifts and God's Call

In the last study we looked at one expression of God's faithfulness: the covenant. It is because God is faithful to his covenant that I borrowed the word *irrevocable* from verse 29 and linked it to the word *covenant* in verse 27, where it does not actually occur, and I spoke of "God's Irrevocable Covenant." Here two new ideas are introduced to explain the nature of God's faithfulness: God's gifts and God's call.

What do these words refer to?

The Swiss commentator F. Godet thinks that God's gifts are the moral or intellectual aptitudes of a people. He observes that the Greeks, Romans, and Phoenicians each had their own special gifts from God in areas such as science, art, law, politics, industry, and commerce. The Jews received what he called "a higher gift," that is, an aptitude and intuition for holiness.[2] It is doubtful that this is what Paul is thinking of here. In this context, "gifts" is linked to the words call and *covenant,* which means that Paul is thinking of the specific gifts given to the covenant people as part of that relationship.

The true listing of the gifts given to Israel is in Romans 9, which means that the closing verses of this middle section of Romans take us back to the beginning: "Theirs is the adoption as sons; theirs the divine glory, the covenants, the receiving of the law, the temple worship and the promises. Theirs are the patriarchs, and from them is traced the human ancestry of Christ, who is God over all" (Rom. 9:4–5). Paul's mention of the patriarchs in Romans 11:28 itself requires us to think of these verses.

How about the other term, God's call? To what does this refer? Our first instinct is to think of it as God's effectual call, that is, the call of the Holy Spirit that leads the person receiving it to faith. The word was used this way in Romans 8, where Paul wrote, "And those he predestined, he also called" (v. 30).

However, this is probably not the right meaning here. In this verse "call" is virtually synonymous with predestination or election. The meaning is not that God has called or will call the Jews to saving faith, though Paul is teaching that the mass of Israel will come to faith in the final days, but rather that God has chosen the nation to be a special nation for his purposes and that he will not, indeed cannot, abandon that choice because Israel has rejected the Messiah.

1. Leon Morris, *The Epistle to the Romans* (Grand Rapids: Wm. B. Eerdmans, and Leicester, England: Inter-Varsity Press, 1988), p. 423.

2. F. Godet, *Commentary on St. Paul's Epistle to the Romans,* trans. A. Cusin (Edinburgh: T. & T. Clark, 1892), vol. 2, p. 259.

Verse 29 is saying that the adoption, the divine glory, the covenants, the receiving of the law, the temple worship, the promises, and the patriarchs are Israel's still, regardless of her unbelief, and that the people remain God's covenant people.

But God! When you chose Abraham to be the father of a special people, didn't you know that he would be weak in faith himself? Didn't you know that he would step aside from his high calling and go down to Egypt, where he would be willing even to sacrifice the honor of his wife to save his own skin?

"Yes," says God, "I knew that. But I called him anyway, and my gifts to him and my calling of him were irrevocable."

But God! Surely you knew that the people who came along in the line of Abraham would be unfaithful. You gave them the law through Moses. But even Moses, great as he was, dishonored you by taking your glory to himself. He struck the rock contrary to your command, saying, "Must *we* bring you water out of this rock?" (Num. 20:10). You even kept him from entering the Promised Land as a result. Did you really take all that into account when you called the Jews to be a special people?

"Yes," God replies, "I knew what Moses would do. But my gifts and my call are irrevocable."

But God! What about David? David committed adultery with Bathsheba and even had her husband, Uriah, killed to escape detection. Certainly, if you had known what David would be like, you would have done things differently. Did you really consider David's sin when you set your electing love upon this people?

"Yes," God answers, "I did, and my call is irrevocable."

But God! What about the kings who followed David? And the people who copied the debased morality of those kings? How could you have set upon such people an eternal love, expressed in an irrevocable covenant?

"Your ways are not my ways," says God. "I knew the people would be wicked. Everyone is wicked. 'There is no one righteous, not even one; there is no one who understands, no one who seeks God.' I wrote that, remember. Still I have fixed my covenant love upon these people, and my call is irrevocable. My will for them has not changed."

But God! Surely your call must change in light of the way these people treated Jesus Christ. Jesus was loving and compassionate. His greatest offense was to be holy and to speak the truth. Yet they rejected him. They hounded him to death and eventually secured his execution on a cross between two thieves. If you had foreseen that, you would never have made the promises you did. Or now, having seen their treatment of Jesus, surely you will repudiate whatever relationship you did have with them. Surely you are going to cast them off forever!

"No," God replies. "I know the end from the beginning. I knew how it would all turn out. Yet, in spite of what they did, I set an irrevocable love upon them."

Our Faithful God

I am not writing this for Jewish people particularly, of course. I am writing these studies for contemporary Christians, who are largely Gentile. So I am concerned with how this affects them. How *does* it affect them? How does it affect you and me?

If we were only concerned with what is usually called prophecy, that is, with what God will be doing one day, there would be little relevance. But that is not the case. As Leon Morris said, this is not an example of Paul's Jewish patriotism, but rather an outworking of his doctrine of justification. And because he is basing his conclusions on the character of God, everything he emphasizes about God's dealings with the Jews is for us, too. In the previous study we ended by thinking about God's immutability, the fact that God does not change. In this study I want to end by focusing on God's faithfulness. I want to stress that his gifts to you and his calling of you are irrevocable.

A number of years ago, Arthur W. Pink wrote a book in which he discussed seventeen great attributes of God. He expanded that list later, increasing the attributes of God to twenty-five and adding twenty "excellencies" of Jesus Christ.[3] One of the attributes of God he discussed was faithfulness.

In what ways is God faithful? Pink suggested the following:

1. *God is faithful in preserving his people.* We have a phrase for this in theology: the perseverance of the saints. It can be understood in two ways. It can mean that the saints persevere, or it can mean that God perseveres with the saints. Obviously both are true, and the former is true only because the latter also is. That is, the saints persevere only because God perseveres with them. To put it in the language we have been using: The followers of Jesus Christ will be faithful to him because he is faithful to them. God said, "Never will I leave you; never will I forsake you" (Heb. 13:5; cf. Deut. 31:6). Jesus told his disciples, "Surely I will be with you always, to the very end of the age" (Matt. 28:20).

I have often taught that there are four New Testament texts that, more than any others, teach the perseverance of the saints. Two are from the lips of Jesus. Two are from Paul.

The first text is John 6:37–40: "All that the Father gives me will come to me, and whoever comes to me I will never drive away. . . . And this is the will of him who sent me, that I shall lose none of all that he has given me, but raise them up at the last day. For my Father's will is that everyone who looks to the Son and believes in him shall have eternal life, and I will raise him up at the last day."

The second text is John 10:27–30: "My sheep listen to my voice; I know them, and they follow me. I give them eternal life, and they shall never perish;

3. Arthur W. Pink, *The Attributes of God: A Solemn and Blessed Contemplation of Some of the Wondrous and Lovely Perfections of the Divine Character* (Grand Rapids: Baker Book House, n.d.), and *Gleanings in the Godhead* (Chicago: Moody Press, 1975).

no one can snatch them out of my hand. My Father, who has given them to me, is greater than all; no one can snatch them out of my Father's hand. I and the Father are one."

The third text is Romans 8:31–39, which we have already studied in detail: "What, then, shall we say in response to this? If God is for us, who can be against us? He who did not spare his own Son, but gave him up for us all—how will he not also, along with him, graciously give us all things? Who will bring any charge against those whom God has chosen? It is God who justifies. Who is he that condemns? Christ Jesus, who died—more than that, who was raised to life—is at the right hand of God and is also interceding for us. Who shall separate us from the love of Christ? Shall trouble or hardship or persecution or famine or nakedness or danger or sword? As it is written:

> For your sake we face death all day long;
>   we are considered as sheep to be slaughtered.

No, in all these things we are more than conquerors through him who loved us. For I am convinced that neither death nor life, neither angels nor demons, neither the present nor the future, nor any powers, neither height nor depth, nor anything else in all creation, will be able to separate us from the love of God that is in Christ Jesus our Lord."

The final text is Philippians 1:6. "Being confident of this, that he who began a good work in you will carry it on to completion until the day of Christ Jesus."

These texts teach the perseverance of the saints and assure us that the gifts and call of God are irrevocable.

2. God is faithful in disciplining his people. God has called us to be like Jesus Christ, which means that he will do whatever is necessary to conform us to that image. Instruction? Encouragement? Of course. But also discipline. The Bible says, "The Lord disciplines those he loves, and he punishes everyone he accepts as a son" (Heb. 12:6; cf. Prov. 3:11–12).

In one of his later writings, Harry Ironside tells of something that occurred early in his ministry. He had been preaching in Fresno, California, and the day came, surprisingly to him, when he was entirely out of money. He had to check out of his hotel, leaving his suitcase at a drugstore to be picked up later. That evening, hungry, having had no supper, he settled himself under a tree on the lawn of the courthouse for the night. He thought of Philippians 4:19, "My God will meet all your needs according to his glorious riches in Christ Jesus." He complained. Why doesn't God do it, then? Why isn't he faithful to his promise?

As Ironside prayed that night, God brought to his mind things about which he had grown careless, and in his meditation God brought him to a spiritual awakening. And, of course, God did provide for his needs. Old friends appeared to provide housing. The meetings went well, and at the end the people took up a collection that helped him get home.

But here is the interesting thing. As he left Fresno, Ironside stopped by the post office, where he found a letter from his father. He wasn't expecting it, so it surprised him. In it his father had written, "God spoke to me through Philippians 4:19 today. He has promised to supply all our need. Some day he may see I need a starving, and if he does, he will supply that." Ironside saw then that God had been putting him through a time of deprivation for discipline, to bring him closer to himself.[4]

Here is the way Arthur Pink sees it: "God . . . is faithful in what he withholds, no less than in what he gives. He is faithful in sending sorrow as well as in giving joy. The faithfulness of God is a truth to be confessed by us not only when we are at ease, but also when we are smarting under the sharpest rebuke. Nor must this confession be merely of our mouths, but of our hearts also. When God smites us with the rod of chastisement, it is faithfulness which wields it. To acknowledge this means that we humble ourselves before him, own that we fully deserve his correction; and instead of murmuring, thank him for it. God never afflicts without a reason."[5]

3. *God is faithful in glorifying his people.* This truth takes us back to Romans 8, to the chain of saving acts outlined in verses 29 and 30: "For those God foreknew he also predestined to be conformed to the likeness of his Son, that he might be the firstborn among many brothers. And those he predestined, he also called; those he called, he also justified; those he justified, he also glorified."

You may remember from the studies in the second volume of this series that Paul's theme in Romans 5–8 is glorification, and his point is that glorification is certain for those whom God has justified. He introduces this at the beginning of chapter 5, and it is the note on which he ends at the conclusion of chapter 8. What is more, Romans 9–11 are about this truth, too, for Paul's entire discussion of God's dealing with the Jews is to answer the objection that we cannot be sure of our final glorified state, since the Jews, who were once God's chosen people, have been cast off.

Paul says, "Not so!" The Jews are not cast off, because God's covenant, gifts, and calling of them are irrevocable. So also in regard to his calling of us. Having been foreknown by God, predestined, called, and justified, we may know that we shall certainly be glorified as well.

Rock of Ages

"You can't step into the same river twice," said Heraclitus.

True enough. But you can anchor your boat in the faithfulness of God Almighty and plant your feet on the Rock that nothing in heaven or earth

4. H. A. Ironside, *Random Reminiscences from Fifty Years of Ministry* (Neptune, N.J.: Loizeaux Brothers, 1939), pp. 73–85.

5. Pink, *Gleanings in the Godhead*, pp. 49, 50.

will ever shake. If you do, you will find that God is unchanging. You will find him to be exactly as he was to Abraham and Moses and David and all who have gone before or who will come after you. You will not find him withdrawing his gifts because of some failure in you, or repudiating his calling of you, once you have come to Jesus Christ.

"God's gifts and his call are irrevocable."

Arthur Pink wrote, "Unfaithfulness is one of the most outstanding sins of these evil days. In the business world, a man's word is, with rare exceptions, no longer his bond. In the social world, marital infidelity abounds on every hand; the sacred bonds of wedlock are broken with as little regard as discarding an old garment. In the ecclesiastical realm, thousands who have solemnly covenanted to preach the truth have no scruples about attacking and denying it. Nor can reader or writer claim complete immunity from this fearful sin. How many ways have we been unfaithful to Christ, and to the light and privileges which God has entrusted to us!"

The author concludes, "How refreshing, then, and how blessed, to lift our eyes above this scene of ruin, and behold One who is faithful, faithful in all things, at all times."[6]

6. Pink, *Gleanings in the Godhead,* p. 47.

170

Mercy for All

Romans 11:30–32

Just as you who were at one time disobedient to God have now received mercy as a result of their disobedience, so they too have now become disobedient in order that they too may now receive mercy as a result of God's mercy to you. For God has bound all men over to disobedience so that he may have mercy on them all.

The last verses of Romans 11 before the doxology (vv. 33–36) contain an important insight, namely, that all people are on an equal footing before God. For most of us this does not seem particularly perceptive, because we assume it as part of our cultural heritage. The founding document of the American republic says that "all . . . are created equal." But we do not really believe it. We believe in equal rights, perhaps. Or that people deserve equal opportunities. But we do not really believe that all people are equal. What we really believe is that some people—we place ourselves in that number—are better than other people.

Where does belief in equality come from? What produces the insight that all really are equal before God? There is only one answer: awareness that all have sinned and that all stand in need of God's mercy. Sin alone lowers everyone to the same needy level, so that mercy alone can lift us to the heights.

That is why Christianity, with its precise understanding of God's mercy, is the only true hope for brotherhood among human beings.

A Significant Summary

In these verses, Paul is beginning to wrap up the third great section of Romans. Verses 28 and 29 have already done this, repeating in summary what Paul developed in verses 11–24, and reminding us that the rejection of Jesus Christ by Israel worked for Gentile blessing and that the blessing of the Gentiles will in time work for Israel's good. That is the point made by the illustration of the cultivated and wild olive trees and their branches.

In the verses considered in this study (vv. 30–32) that same summation is repeated: (1) the disobedience of Israel had led to the showing of mercy to the Gentiles, and (2) the mercy shown to the Gentiles will in time lead to Israel's blessing.

Yet Paul is never merely repetitious, and what is new in this section is an emphasis on mercy. This means that here Paul's summary is extending further back than over chapter 11 alone. It is going all the way back to chapter 9, where the mercy of God was carefully discussed. In that chapter Paul was explaining God's sovereignty in election, asking: "Is God unjust?" "Not at all!" he answers. "For he says to Moses,

> I will have mercy on whom I have mercy,
> and I will have compassion on whom I have compassion.

It does not, therefore, depend on man's desire or effort, but on God's mercy. . . . God has mercy on whom he wants to have mercy, and he hardens whom he wants to harden" (Rom. 9:14–16, 18).

But we have come a long way since Romans 9, haven't we? There, Paul was explaining how mercy accounts for God's saving some and not others. But here in Romans 11, he is thinking of mercy inclusively rather than exclusively. That is, having pursued to the end his teaching about God's historical dealings with the Jewish people and having prophesied a time of future Jewish blessing, Paul observes that in this way God is showing mercy *to all*. "For God has bound all men over to disobedience so that he may have mercy on them all" (v. 32).

That verse does not teach universal salvation, of course. If it did, it would be contradicting Romans 9. Paul is talking about Jews and Gentiles as groups of people, not as individuals. But he is nevertheless inclusive in his assessment of God's mercy. Although neither Gentiles nor Jews deserve mercy, God is merciful to both. That is the point. And it is this important insight that leads Paul, the formerly self-righteous Jewish patriot and proud Pharisee to regard all human beings as equal before God.

If you are prejudiced against other people in any way, if you think yourself to be superior to them for whatever reason, it is because you do not understand the nature of your sin or God's grace.

The Quality of Mercy

Let's talk about mercy and how it differs from such other qualities of God as goodness and grace. "Goodness" is a general term, involving all that flows from God: his decrees, his creation, his laws, his providences. It extends to the elect and to the non-elect, though in different ways. "Grace" denotes favor, particularly toward the undeserving. "Mercy" is an aspect of grace, but the unique quality of mercy is that it is shown to the pitiful.

Arthur W. Pink says, "Mercy . . . denotes the ready inclination of God to relieve the misery of fallen creatures."[1]

A. W. Tozer says, "Mercy is . . . an infinite and inexhaustible energy within the divine nature which disposes God to be actively compassionate."[2]

Many great Bible texts talk about mercy. When Moses asked to be shown God's glory and God agreed to hide him in a cleft of the rock and cover him with his hand while his glory passed by, God said, "I will cause all my goodness to pass in front of you, and I will proclaim my name, the LORD, in your presence. I will have *mercy* on whom I will have *mercy*, and I will have compassion on whom I will have compassion" (Exod. 33:19–20, emphasis added). The very essence of God is mercy, according to this passage.

When David sinned by counting the fighting men of Israel and God gave him a choice of punishments, one of which was a plague that God himself would send, David chose the plague, saying, "Let us fall into the hands of the LORD, for his *mercy is great;* but do not let me fall into the hands of men" (2 Sam. 24:14, emphasis added). This teaches that God is merciful even in his judgments.

Psalm 51:1 measures God's mercy by his love: "Have *mercy* on me, O God, according to your unfailing love" (emphasis added).

Isaiah 55:6–7 promises mercy to anyone who will seek it:

> Seek the LORD while he may be found;
> call on him while he is near.
> Let the wicked forsake his way
> and the evil man his thoughts.
> Let him turn to the LORD, and *he will have mercy* on him,
> and to our God, for he will freely pardon (emphasis added).

Ephesians 2:4–5 says, "God, who is *rich in mercy,* made us alive with Christ even when we were dead in transgressions—it is by grace you have been saved" (emphasis added). Any one of these texts is more than adequate for this or any number of helpful studies on this subject.

---

1. Arthur W. Pink, *Gleanings in the Godhead* (Chicago: Moody Press, 1975), p. 68.
2. A. W. Tozer, *The Knowledge of the Holy: The Attributes of God, Their Meaning in the Christian Life* (New York, Evanston, and London: Harper & Row, 1961), pp. 96, 97.

Disobedience from All, Mercy to All

But we are now studying Romans 11:30–32, so I want to ask what these verses specifically tell us of God's mercy. I suggest two things.

1. *To appreciate mercy, we must see it against the dark background of sin.* To grasp this point, all we have to do is count words. How many times does the word *mercy* occur in these verses? Answer: It occurs four times, once in verse 30, twice in verse 31, and once in verse 32. Mercy is the dominant idea, which is why we are examining it at this point. But now let's ask: How many times does "disobedient" or "disobedience" occur? The answer is also four times, twice in verse 30 and once each in verses 31 and 32. John Murray says, "The lesson is obvious. It is only in the context of disobedience that mercy has relevance and meaning."[3]

Arthur Pink points out that one way to understand mercy over against grace or even the goodness of God is to think of God's dealings with the unfallen angels:

> He has never exercised mercy toward them, for they have never stood in any need thereof, not having sinned or come beneath the effects of the curse. Yet they certainly are the objects of God's free and sovereign grace. First, because of his election of them from out of the whole angelic race (1 Tim. 5:21). Second, and in consequence of their election, because of his preservation of them from apostasy, when Satan rebelled and dragged down with him one-third of the celestial hosts (Rev. 12:4). Third, in making Christ their Head (Col. 2:10; 1 Pet. 3:22), whereby they are eternally secured in the holy condition in which they were created. Fourth, because of the exalted position which has been assigned them: to live in God's immediate presence (Dan. 7:10), to serve him constantly in his heavenly temple, to receive honorable commissions from him (Heb. 1:4). This is abundant *grace* toward them; but *mercy* it is not.[4]

For God to show mercy, there must first be sin and the misery that attends it. And that is exactly our condition as fallen human beings. Sin abounds! But it is precisely in that context and against that dark and tempestuous background that the mercy of God flashes forth like lightning.

2. *We need mercy if we are to be saved.* This is the second thing that these verses specifically teach. Paul has been writing about the salvation of both Jews and Gentiles, and when he gets to the end of his discussion, as he does here, it is of mercy alone that he is thinking. On what possible grounds could Gentiles hope to be saved apart from God's mercy? There is no other basis. Paul wrote to the Ephesians, who were Gentiles, to remind them that before their con-

---

3. John Murray, *The Epistles to the Romans,* 2 vols. in 1 (Grand Rapids: Wm. B. Eerdmans, 1968), vol. 2, p. 102.
4. Pink, *Gleanings in the Godhead,* pp. 68, 69.

version they "were separate from Christ, excluded from citizenship in Israel and foreigners to the covenants of the promise, without hope and without God in the world" (Eph. 2:12). The Gentiles had nothing going for them. If they were to be saved, it had to be by God's mercy alone.

But mercy is no less necessary for the Jews, according to these verses. Unlike the Gentiles, they did have a great deal going for them. They had the gifts Paul mentions to the Ephesians (Eph. 2:12), plus those he spells out more fully in Romans 9:4–5. Yet these spiritual advantages did not save the Jews. They were unbelieving. Therefore, as Paul says, "God has bound all men over to disobedience so that he may have mercy on them all."

We do not think this way naturally. We think in terms of our own good works and justice. We suppose ourselves to be deserving, which means that we consider ourselves to be better than other people. We are not. Apart from mercy we will perish.

"God Be Merciful"

Earlier in this volume I referred to Jesus' story of the Pharisee and the tax collector as an illustration of how, in order to be saved, we must come to God on the basis of his mercy.[5] I return to the same story now, though at greater length, for exactly the same reason.

The story is based on contrasts, and the first is between the Pharisee and the tax collector themselves. We have a bad mental image of Pharisees because of some of the things Jesus said about them, but the people of that day actually thought very highly of the Pharisees. These men were known for their faithful adherence to the law. Nicodemus was a Pharisee, and so was Paul. They were among the most honored of their contemporaries.

Moreover, that is the way Jesus presented the Pharisee in his story. The Pharisee prayed, thanking God that he was not like other men. He did not steal. He was not an adulterer. He fasted twice a week and tithed what he possessed.

It was altogether different with the tax collector. Nobody had any warm feelings for tax collectors, and not only because paying taxes is an unwelcome duty. Tax collectors were collaborators with the unpopular occupying Roman army, and they were hated for it. Moreover, they were allowed to collect all the money they could, keeping whatever was above what Rome demanded, and that caused resentment.

This tax collector knew he was a sinner: "God, have mercy on me, a sinner." Well, why not? That is exactly what he was. Up to this point everyone who heard Jesus' story would have been right with him. On the one hand, the righteous Pharisee. On the other hand, the sinful tax collector. The first, the center of attention. The other, on the edge of the crowd, where he belonged.

5. The story of the Pharisee and tax collector is told in study 130 in a shortened form (see "'Mercy' Is His Name" [Romans 9:15]). It can also be found in James Montgomery Boice, *The Parables of Jesus* (Chicago: Moody Press, 1983), pp. 83–91.

But then Jesus introduced a second contrast, and it was as unexpected and puzzling as the first was acceptable. Speaking of the tax collector, Jesus said, "I tell you that this man, rather than the other, went home justified before God. For everyone who exalts himself will be humbled, and he who humbles himself will be exalted" (Luke 18:13–14).

What is going on here? Didn't we hear the story right? Or is there perhaps more to the character traits of the Pharisee and the tax collector than we were told. The Pharisee appeared righteous, but perhaps he really was not. Maybe he was a thief on the side or an adulterer or a secret blasphemer of God. And maybe the tax collector was not really so bad. Perhaps we have judged him too harshly. We know at once that this is not the answer. Outwardly and inwardly, the two men were exactly what we know them to be: two sinners, though one was unaware of it. One was a "righteous sinner," the other an "unrighteous sinner." The only difference is that the tax collector *knew* he was a sinner and therefore came to God seeking mercy.

So he found it!

The heart of this story is in the tax collector's prayer. It is one of the shortest prayers in the Bible—only seven words in English, six in Greek—but it is also one of the most profound.

Consider the beginning and the end, eliminating the middle. That is, delete the words "have mercy on" and retain the words "God" and "me, a sinner." These words contain the essential ingredients in all religion—holy God and sinful man—and they express the insight anyone gains when he or she becomes aware of God's presence: God is a holy God. Therefore, to become aware of God in his holiness is to become aware of ourselves in our sin. This is how we know that the tax collector knew God, despite his reputation, and that the Pharisee did not know him. The Pharisee began, "God . . ." but we know that he was not praying to God since he did not see himself to be a sinner. Actually he was praying to himself. The tax collector *was* praying to God, because he did see himself as a sinner. These two always go together.

Now consider the middle section of the prayer: "have mercy on." This shows that the tax collector was pleading for mercy on the basis of what God has done to provide it. The Greek word used is a verb form of the word for "Mercy Seat" *(hilasterion)*, which refers to the covering of the Ark of the Covenant in the Jewish temple. The tax collector's prayer literally means "treat me as a person who comes on the basis of the blood shed on the Mercy Seat as an offering for sins."

Picture the Ark of the Covenant in your mind. It was a wooden box about a yard long, covered with gold and containing the stone tablets of the law of Moses. The lid of this box was the Mercy Seat, constructed of pure gold and with images of cherubim or angels on each end. Their wings went backward and upward, almost meeting over the center of the Ark. God was imagined to dwell symbolically between those outstretched wings. As it stands, it is a picture of judgment. For what does God see as he looks down from between the wings of the cherubim? He sees the law that we have broken. He sees that he must judge sin.

But here is where the Mercy Seat comes in and why it is called the *Mercy* Seat. Upon that covering of the Ark, once a year on the Day of Atonement, the high priest sprinkled the blood of an animal that had been killed just moments before in the courtyard of the temple. The animal was a substitute, an innocent victim dying in place of those who deserved to die. Now, when God looked down from between the outstretched wings of the cherubim, what he saw was not the law that we have broken, but the blood of the innocent victim. He saw that atonement had been made and that his love was now free to reach out to save anyone who would come through faith in that sacrifice.

This is why I say that the prayer of the tax collector is profound. It was an appeal to mercy, and it understood where mercy could be found.

Moreover, its very form expressed the truth taught by the Ark of the Covenant. That is to say, between "God," whom we have offended, and "me, a sinner," which describes us all, the tax collector placed the Mercy Seat and what it symbolized. His prayer puts it on the horizontal level. The Day of Atonement does it vertically. But it is the same thing. Both precisely express the only way of salvation.

Of course, under the Old Testament system, the sacrifices were a picture of the sacrifice of Jesus Christ that was yet to come. They were important. But it was not the death of animals, however many, that actually purged away sin. The true atonement was provided by the Lord Jesus Christ. When the tax collector prayed, "God, have mercy on me, a sinner," he was thinking of the animal sacrifices, because Jesus had not yet died. When *we* pray that prayer, we should be thinking of Jesus and the way God in his mercy has provided for our salvation through him.

Debtor to Mercy Alone

Here are three important things to remember about mercy.

1. *You can appeal to mercy.* The right of God to show mercy to whom he will show mercy, and compassion to whom he will show compassion, cannot be challenged. Mercy cannot be compelled. Otherwise it is not mercy. But that does not mean that you cannot appeal to mercy. You can. The Bible is full of such appeals and says that it is through such appeals that mercy may be found.

2. *If you have received mercy, you must be merciful to others.* Jesus told about a servant who was forgiven a great debt and then prosecuted a man who owed him just a little. The master of the first servant then threw him into jail. The point is that you cannot claim to have been forgiven by God if you are then unforgiving or harsh with other people. The followers of Jesus must be the most merciful of all people.

3. *If you have found mercy, you must make it widely known.* We know that God has mercy on whom he wills to have mercy and compassion on whom he wills to have compassion. God is sovereign. But there is nothing in the Bible that hinders you from saying as clearly and as forcefully as you can that God's very name is Mercy and that he will save all who come to him for it. God has never turned a deaf ear to anyone who asked for mercy. He has never rejected any person who has believed on Christ Jesus.

> Come, every soul by sin oppressed,
>   There's mercy with the Lord,
> And he will surely give you rest,
>   By trusting in his Word.
> Only trust him, only trust him,
>   Only trust him now.
> He will save you, he will save you,
>   He will save you now.

Do you believe that? Will you come? If you do, you will find God to be exactly what Paul declares him to be in this passage: the God of mercy who saves many through faith in Jesus Christ.

PART FIFTEEN

Doxology

171

No One Like God

Romans 11:33–35

Oh, the depth of the riches of the wisdom and knowledge of God!
How unsearchable his judgments,
and his paths beyond tracing out!
"Who has known the mind of the Lord?
Or who has been his counselor?"
"Who has ever given to God,
that God should repay him?"

Several decades ago, when I was growing up, the evangelical church was very much interested in prophecy. Sermons frequently discussed prophecy, books on prophecy circulated widely, and there were scores of prophecy conferences that were well attended. This was not a bad thing, of course. The Bible contains a great deal of prophecy; it should be expounded along with other material in due course. But there was a negative side to this focus that caused many who grew up in evangelical churches during that period to lose substantial interest in the topic. Those who studied prophecy tended to become so proud of being on the inside track of what God was doing that they disengaged from real life.

1409

What happened was summed up for me by a person who reacted to news about any gloomy political situation by being happy about it. "If things are getting worse, the Lord must be about to come back," is how he explained it to me.

The biblical writers did not react this way. Sad current events caused them to grieve. Even when they were discussing future events, as Paul has been doing in the ninth, tenth, and eleventh chapters of Romans, they did not end their discussions by being smug about their superior knowledge but by glorifying and drawing closer to God.

There is no greater example of this than the way in which the apostle Paul ends the third major section of Romans. He has been tracing the ways of God in history and has contributed to our knowledge of those ways by revealing that in the last days God will draw the masses of the Jewish people to faith: "And so all Israel will be saved" (Rom. 11:26). Where does this marvelous discussion of God's ways leave Paul? He is not smug about his knowledge of the future. Instead, he is in awe of God, and his response is to burst forth in the magnificent doxology with which this section ends. Because Paul has been talking about God's mercy, what he does in this section is what Joseph Addison wrote about in his hymn of 1712.

> When all thy mercies, O my God,
>   My rising soul surveys,
> Transported with the view, I'm lost
>   In wonder, love, and praise!

As Paul contemplated the mercies of God, he was so lost in wonder that he composed the doxology similarly, as an outpouring of praise that began:

> Oh, the depth of the riches of the wisdom and knowledge of God!
>   How unsearchable his judgments,
>   and his paths beyond tracing out!
>
>   Romans 11:33

The Problem in the Church

Following this pattern, I want to close our studies of Romans 11 with a careful treatment of the attributes of God that Paul specifically mentions. But I confess that I have a problem doing so. We will sometimes acknowledge that God's thoughts are not our thoughts and that neither are our ways his ways (cf. Isa. 55:8). But we have to acknowledge here that even the thoughts and ways of Paul are not the same as ours. In our day, what we want to do is jump on quickly to Romans 12 and "get practical," rather than taking time to contemplate the perfections of the deity.

When he was only twenty years old, Charles Haddon Spurgeon began his half-century-long career in London with a sermon on knowing God, in which he argued that "the proper study of God's elect is God." Spurgeon said, "The highest science, the loftiest speculation, the mightiest philosophy, which can ever engage the attention of a child of God, is the name, the nature, the person, the work, the doings, and the existence of the great God whom he calls his Father." He argued that thinking about God improves the mind and expands it.[1]

But how many in our day regularly think about God, even in church? It is impossible to know what is going on in another person's mind, of course. But judging by our actions, words, desires, and church programs, I would argue that not one in a hundred churchgoers today actively thinks about God or stands in awe of him as part of an average worship service.

Earlier in this century there was a wonderful Christian and Missionary Alliance pastor in Chicago whose name was A. W. Tozer. He wrote a number of outstanding books that I heartily commend to you, one of which is entitled *The Knowledge of the Holy*. Here is how Tozer saw the situation thirty years ago:

> The church has surrendered her once lofty concept of God and has substituted for it one so low, so ignoble, as to be utterly unworthy of thinking, worshipping men. This she has done not deliberately, but little by little and without her knowledge; and her very unawareness only makes her situation all the more tragic.
>
> This low view of God entertained almost universally among Christians is the cause of a hundred lesser evils everywhere among us. A whole new philosophy of the Christian life has resulted from this one basic error in our religious thinking.
>
> With our loss of the sense of majesty has come the further loss of religious awe and consciousness of the divine Presence. We have lost our spirit of worship and our ability to withdraw inwardly to meet God in adoring silence. Modern Christianity is simply not producing the kind of Christian who can appreciate or experience the life in the Spirit. The words, "Be still, and know that I am God," mean next to nothing to the self-confident, bustling worshiper in this middle period of the twentieth century.
>
> This loss of the concept of majesty has come just when the forces of religion are making dramatic gains and the churches are more prosperous than at any time within the past several hundred years. But the alarming thing is that our gains are mostly external and our losses wholly internal; and since it is the *quality* of our religion that is affected by internal conditions, it may be that our supposed gains are but losses spread over a wider field.[2]

That is how Tozer saw the situation in his day. But who can suppose that the situation has improved over the last three decades? On the contrary, our addiction to television, entertainment, and the me-centered outlooks of our

1. Charles Haddon Spurgeon, "The Immutability of God" (Malachi 3:6) in *The New Park Street Pulpit* (Pasadena, Tex.: Pilgrim Publications, 1975), p. 1. Original edition 1855.

2. A. W. Tozer, *The Knowledge of the Holy: The Attributes of God, Their Meaning in the Christian Life* (New York, Evanston and London: Harper & Row, 1961), pp. 6, 7.

time has made the situation worse. And the really sad thing is that we are largely unaware of what has happened.

No people ever rise higher than their idea of God. Conversely, a loss of the sense of God's high and awesome character always involves a loss of a people's moral values and even what we commonly call "humanity." We are startled by the utter disregard for human life that has overtaken large segments of the United States. But what do we expect to see when a country like ours openly turns its back on God? We deplore the breakdown of moral standards in the church, even among its most visible leaders. But what do we think should happen when we have focused our worship services on ourselves and our own, often trivial, needs rather than on God?

Tozer said, "What comes into our minds when we think about God is the most important thing about us."[3] But if the full truth be told, many of us hardly think about God at all.

The Nature of God

The problem is not merely our preoccupation with ourselves and with material things, of course. Part of the problem lies with the very nature of God. God is not like us. In fact, God is not really like anything else we can actually experience or know. As a result, there is always something about God that is indescribable, and this makes it hard to think about him.

When we begin to talk about God, we use similes. That is, we compare God to someone or something else, saying, "God is like. . . ." But the closer we get to God and the better we understand him, the less those comparisons work for us, and we find ourselves saying, as Paul does, "Oh, the depths. . . ." "How unsearchable. . . ." And "Who has known the mind of the Lord? Or who has been his counselor?"

In the book I have already mentioned, Tozer draws attention to Ezekiel's vision of God recorded in the first chapter of his prophecy and to his increasingly inadequate attempts to describe it.[4] Ezekiel was seeing something he had never seen before. So at first he falls back on the language of resemblance: "I looked, and I saw a windstorm coming out of the north—an immense cloud with flashing lightning and surrounded by brilliant light. The center of the fire *looked like* glowing metal, and in the fire was what *looked like* four living creatures" (Ezek. 1:4–5, emphasis added).

The nearer he approaches to the divine throne, the less sure his words become: "Spread out above the living creatures was what looked like an expanse, sparkling like ice and awesome. . . . When the creatures moved, I heard the sound of their wings, *like* the roar of rushing waters, *like* the voice of the Almighty, *like* the tumult of an army" (vv. 22, 24, emphasis added).

3. Ibid., p. 9.
4. Ibid., p. 15.

Finally, Ezekiel is standing before the throne of God himself, and after a few attempts to describe what he sees, he says only, "This was *the appearance of the likeness* of the glory of the LORD" (v. 28, emphasis added).

This is why God prohibited the worship of himself by images in the second of the Ten Commandments: "You shall not make for yourself an idol in the form of anything in heaven above or on the earth beneath or in the waters below. You shall not bow down to them or worship them; for I, the LORD your God, am a jealous God, punishing the children for the sin of the fathers to the third and fourth generation of those who hate me, but showing love to a thousand generations of those who love me and keep my commandments" (Exod. 20:4–6).

At first glance it seems strange that God should prohibit the worship of himself by images. "What harm can it do?" we might ask. "Don't images merely focus the attention of the worshiper?"

Theologian J. I. Packer says there are two answers to that. First, images dishonor God, for they are always less than he is and therefore obscure rather than reveal his glory. Second, images inevitably mislead the worshiper, for they suggest false ideas by comparison.[5]

Even though God revealed himself to us personally in Jesus Christ, it is surely no accident that Jesus came before the age of photography, movies, or television. So we do not have a picture or electronic image of him. Instead of by pictures, the way God reveals himself—even the way he reveals Jesus to us today—is by the words of Scripture.

The medieval theologians spoke of the *deus absconditus,* meaning "the hidden God." And so God is! God is always partially hidden, and even the parts we see, we see only because God has revealed them to us in the Bible.

The Incommunicable Attributes

One helpful distinction theologians make is between what they call God's communicable attributes and his incommunicable ones.

Communicable attributes refer to characteristics of God that he shares with us in some measure, since we are made in his image—things like knowledge, wisdom, love, and mercy—in fact, the things Paul actually mentions in this doxology in Romans. God is infinitely above us in these things, of course, but we somewhat understand what they are since we share in them on a much lower level. The incommunicable attributes are characteristics of God that he does not share with us, indeed, cannot share, since they are uniquely a part of what it means for God to be God. They involve such things as self-existence, self-sufficiency, and eternality.

We are going to be looking at a few of the communicable attributes as we go on in our study of Paul's doxology, since he specifically mentions God's wisdom, knowledge, judgments, and paths (or ways). Here it is worth looking

---

5. J. I. Packer, *Knowing God* (Downers Grove, Ill.: InterVarsity Press, 1973), pp. 40, 41.

at a few of the attributes that are incommunicable. Let's take the three I just mentioned.

1. *Self-existence.* This means that God has no origins, that he has always been and that he owes his existence to nobody. When you and I speak of our existence, we have to say, "I am what I am by the grace of God." But when God revealed himself to Moses at the burning bush, God said only, "I AM WHO I AM" (Exod. 3:14).

Of course, this is where our problem in knowing God chiefly lies. The way we learn about something is by breaking it down into its constituent parts and then by tracing those parts to their origin. If we can explain how something came to be, we are well on the way to understanding it. God is not subject to that type of analysis. When we analyze things, those things point back to him as their ultimate and only sufficient cause. But God himself points back to nothing. He is existent in himself alone and therefore ultimately is unknowable. God cannot be analyzed and evaluated as created things can be.

2. *Self-sufficiency.* This attribute means that God has no needs and that he therefore depends on no one. Again, we are not like that. We have countless needs—needs for oxygen to breathe, food to eat, clothes to wear, houses in which to live, and other things—and if we are deprived of any one of them, even for a short time, we cease to be. We die. God does not need anything. In himself, he is and has everything he needs.

This runs counter to ideas that many people have about God. Supposing him to be like themselves, they assume that God needs many things, if not to survive, at least to be happy and fulfilled as God. For example, they imagine that at one time God was lonely and that he created men and women to keep him company. They forget that God is a Trinity and that he always had a perfectly fulfilling fellowship in the Godhead.

Other people suppose that God needs worshipers. But if every individual on the face of the earth became an atheist tomorrow, refusing even to acknowledge God's existence, God would be no more deprived by our atheism than the sun would be deprived of light if all of us should become blind.

Still other people suppose that God needs helpers, even suggesting that he created us to help him "get the job done," whatever that is. It is true that God has given us the privilege of doing useful and meaningful work for him. In the Garden of Eden he gave meaningful work to Eve and Adam. In this age of gospel proclamation he has given us the task of being his evangelists and has even called us "fellow-workers" with Jesus Christ. But this does not mean that God needs us. God can manage very well without us and has always done so. That he chooses to use us is due only to his own free and utterly sovereign will.

3. *Eternality.* It is hard to describe in a few word what "eternity" means as an attribute of God, but it has to do with his everlastingness or perpetuity.

In other words, it means that God is, always has been, and always will be, and that he is ever the same in his infinite and eternal being.

This has great practical bearing for us, because it means, among other things, that God can be trusted to remain as he has revealed himself to be. In other words, what we read about him in the Bible remains as true of God today as ever it was, and what others before us have found to be true about God we will find to be true also. Since God has loved us in Christ even before the foundation of the world, we can be sure that he is continuing to love us and will do so forever. Since God has purposed all things from before creation, we can be sure that those purposes will be worked out perfectly. Above all, since God will be present at the end, just as he was at the beginning, we can know that he is inescapable and that one day we will have to give him an accounting for what we have done with our lives.

Right Thoughts about God

How do we form right thoughts about God, if God is so hard to know? We must do so on the basis of the Bible's revelation, of course, thinking and reflecting upon what the Bible tells us propositionally. But here are two additional things that may prove practical. In *Knowing God,* J. I. Packer suggests:[6]

1. *Remove from your thoughts limits that would make God small.* That is what we have been doing in this study. We have been trying to break out of our limited world of cause and effect, dependency and time, and have been trying to think of God as self-existent, self-sufficient, and eternal. It is what the biblical writers do again and again.

2. *Remind yourself of the acts of God that are great.* The biblical writers do this when they remind themselves of God's acts of deliverance on their behalf. They remind themselves of how God created the heavens and the earth, how he intervened in the history of Israel to bring his people out of their Egyptian slavery and establish them in their own land, driving out their enemies. We must remember how he sent the Lord Jesus Christ to die for our sin and rise again as our triumphant Savior.

Who Is Like God?

In the Old Testament there is a book named after its author, whose name means "Who is like God?" The book is Micah. It is a somber book, because Micah lived in evil days, as all the minor prophets did, and his message is one of divine judgment. The people had sinned. They would not repent, and judgment was certain to come upon them. But Micah is not all about judgment, and toward the end of his prophecy Micah asks the question that his

6. Ibid., p. 75.

name conveys: "Who is a God like you?" (Mic. 7:18). He answers exactly as
Paul answers the same implied question toward the end of Romans 11.

> Who is a God like you,
> > who pardons sin and forgives the transgression
> > of the remnant of his inheritance?
>
> You do not stay angry forever
> > but delight to show mercy.
>
> You will again have compassion on us;
> > you will tread our sins underfoot
> > and hurl all our iniquities into the depths of the sea.
>
> You will be true to Jacob,
> > and show mercy to Abraham,
>
> as you pledged on oath to our fathers
> > in days long ago.
>
> Micah 7:18–20

If God were like us, he would never have shown mercy in the first place,
for the people of Micah's day (in fact, of any day) did not deserve it. If he
were like us, even if he showed mercy at one time, he would have ceased to
show mercy later, because the people would have exhausted his patience. But
God is not like us! Thank God for that! God is God, and there is no one like
him. He is "the LORD, the LORD, the compassionate and gracious God, slow
to anger, abounding in love and faithfulness, maintaining love to thousands,
and forgiving wickedness, rebellion and sin. Yet he does not leave the guilty
unpunished . . ." (Exod. 34:6–7).

If God were not like that, there would be no hope for any of us. We would
all perish. But he *is* like that, and there is hope. Think about that, and learn
to praise him for it.

172

The Perfect Knowledge of God

Romans 11:33

Oh, the depth of the riches of the wisdom and knowledge of God!
How unsearchable his judgments,
and his paths beyond tracing out!

A number of years ago at a Bible conference in upstate New York I gave a series of studies on the attributes of God. The series seemed to be a blessing to the people who were there, and afterward one of the men was talking about it to a friend. He remarked that he had been a Christian for nearly forty years, that he had attended church faithfully all that time. "Yet in all those years I have never heard anyone teach about the attributes of God. I have never even thought about them," he said.

His friend asked, "Who did you think you were worshiping all that time?"

Who are *you* worshiping? I do not know what answer the man in my story gave his friend, but if he was like most of us and was honest, he would probably have said, "A god like myself." God is not like us, of course, but we persist in thinking of him as if he were, because we can handle a god who is diminished in that way. We can even dismiss him as irrelevant. The Bible tells us that God rebukes that kind of thinking. God says to those who treat sin lightly, "You

1417

thought I was altogether like you. / But I will rebuke you and accuse you to your face" (Ps. 50:21).

God also says, "My thoughts are not your thoughts, / neither are your ways my ways" (Isa. 55:8). Yet we constantly try to reduce God to our level. And we all do it. It doesn't make any difference how smart we are. Apparently Erasmus, the brilliant Dutch humanist, thought this way, because Martin Luther wrote to him once, saying, "Your thoughts of God are too human."

No One Like God

The very fact that God is not like us is part of the problem, and it would be an insurmountable problem were it not that God has condescended to reveal himself to us.

In the last study we looked at some of God's incommunicable attributes, meaning those characteristics of God that he does not share with us in any way because he cannot: things like self-existence, self-sufficiency, and eternality. Those qualities belong to God alone. Therefore, we can only make the most feeble attempts to understand what they mean, and usually we have to do so by negatives. We have to say things like: God has no origins, God depends on no one, and God had no beginning and will have no end.

On the other hand, there are also what are called God's communicable attributes. These are qualities that God does share with us, and while these, too, are beyond our full understanding, they are nevertheless things we can begin to understand because we possess similar characteristics, though to a lesser degree.

Some of these qualities are found in the doxology that ends Romans 11, particularly verse 33. There Paul writes, "Oh, the depth of the riches of the wisdom and knowledge of God! How unsearchable his judgments, and his paths beyond tracing out!" There are four items in this verse: wisdom, knowledge, judgments, and paths.[1] In this and the following three studies, I propose to look at each of these characteristics, beginning in this chapter with God's perfect knowledge, since it is logically prior to the others. Wisdom flows from knowledge, and God's unsearchable judgments and paths are the outworking of his wisdom.

---

1. The first sentence of verse 33 contains three nouns in the genitive case: riches, wisdom, and knowledge, which means that Paul can be writing of three attributes, rather than two. That is, the verse can mean, "Oh, the depth of the: (1) riches, (2) wisdom, and (3) knowledge of God!" Or it can be translated, "Oh, the rich depth of the: (1) wisdom, and (2) knowledge of God!" In the first case, "riches" would probably refer to the mercy of God mentioned in the immediately preceding verses. The translators and commentators are divided, but the New International Version is probably right to give riches a subordinate meaning, since it is different in nature from the other terms. See John Murray, *The Epistle to the Romans: The English Text with Introduction, Exposition and Notes* (Grand Rapids: Wm. B. Eerdmans, 1968), pp. 105, 106; F. Godet, *Commentary on St. Paul's Epistle to the Romans*, trans. A. Cusin (Edinburgh: T. & T. Clark, 1892), vol. 2, pp. 265, 266; and other commentators.

The Knowledge of God

The unique quality of the knowledge possessed by God is its perfection. That is, God knows all things, and he knows them exhaustively. We also "know" things, but our knowledge is partial and imperfect.

How can we describe God's knowledge? Arthur W. Pink wrote, "God is omniscient. He knows everything; everything possible, everything actual; all events, all creatures, of the past, the present, and the future. He is perfectly acquainted with every detail in the life of every being in heaven, in earth, and in hell. . . . Nothing escapes his notice, nothing can be hidden from him, nothing is forgotten by him. . . . He never errs, never changes, never overlooks anything."[2]

A. W. Tozer expands this description by adding negatives: "God has never learned from anyone." Indeed, says Tozer:

> God cannot learn. Could God at any time or in any manner receive into his mind knowledge that he did not possess and had not possessed from eternity, he would be imperfect and less than himself. To think of a God who must sit at the feet of a teacher, even though that teacher be an archangel or a seraph, is to think of someone other than the Most High God, maker of heaven and earth. . . .
>
> God knows instantly and effortlessly all matter and all matters, all mind and every mind, all spirit and all spirits, all being and every being, all creaturehood and all creatures, every plurality and all pluralities, all law and every law, all relations, all causes, all thoughts, all mysteries, all enigmas, all feeling, all desires, every unuttered secret, all thrones and dominions, all personalities, all things visible and invisible in heaven and in earth, motion, space, time, life, death, good, evil, heaven, and hell. . . .
>
> Because God knows all things perfectly, he knows no thing better than any other thing, but all things equally well. He never discovers anything, he is never surprised, never amazed. He never wonders about anything nor (except when drawing men out for their own good) does he seek information or ask questions.[3]

When we reflect along these lines, we begin to understand why Paul writes naturally but with amazement, "Oh, the depth of the riches of the . . . knowledge of God." He is admitting that God's knowledge is so much greater than ours that we can only stand in awe of it.

The perfection of God's knowledge is also disturbing, however, if we think about it, which is one reason why people try so hard not to think about God. As long as we are merely thinking about God's knowing about things or other people, the idea of his knowledge is only awesome or even amusing, like our reaction to the response of a group of children at school who were asked

2. Arthur W. Pink, *Gleanings in the Godhead* (Chicago: Moody Press, 1975), p. 19.
3. A. W. Tozer, *The Knowledge of the Holy: The Attributes of God, Their Meaning in the Christian Life* (New York, Evanston and London: Harper & Row, 1961), pp. 61, 62.

whether they thought God understood computers. The majority thought he did not. That's amusing. Of course, God understands computers! Although we know that when we think about it, the subject is not so amusing when we consider that God also knows about *us*—all about us. We do not mind an ignorant God, or a God who forgets. But what are we to do with a God "before whom all hearts are open, all desires known"? Such a God is immensely threatening, which is why we try to banish him from our thinking.

God's Knowledge and Believers

Yet we need to know about God's attributes, including his knowledge. Let me first suggest four things that knowledge of the perfect knowledge of God should do for Christians.

1. *It should humble us.* I think here of Job. God allowed Satan to attack righteous Job to demonstrate that a believer is able to love God solely for who he is and not merely for the many blessings he gives. So Satan did attack Job, taking away his possessions, killing his children, and eventually attacking even his health. Job was reduced to abject misery, but even in his most wretched state he did not blame God. "The LORD gave and the LORD has taken away" was his amazing testimony (Job 1:21).

At this point Job's friends came to see him, and most of the rest of the book consists of their long speeches and Job's answers. Job's friends had divergent points of view, but basically they argued that since God is a moral God and this is a moral universe, bad things do not happen without good reasons. Therefore, Job must have sinned in some way and thus have brought his troubles on himself. Job did not consider himself to be innocent of all sin, of course. But he knew that he had done nothing to deserve what was happening to him. He was right. What he did not know was that his suffering was the focal point of an invisible but important cosmic struggle.

All this time—for thirty-seven chapters—God was silent. But at last, at the very end of the book, God speaks. What do we expect God to say? We expect God to explain things to Job or at least offer him some comfort. After all, Job has been through a lot. We expect God to tell him about Satan's accusations and reveal how Job had been singled out as a righteous man who would trust God even in misery. This is not what we find. Instead, we find God rebuking Job for presuming to think that he could understand God's ways, even if they were explained to him. This is in the form of a lengthy interrogation having to do with God's perfect knowledge as contrasted with Job's ignorance. The interrogation begins:

> Who is this who darkens my counsel
>   with words without knowledge?
> Brace yourself like a man;
>   I will question you,
>   and you shall answer me.

Where were you when I laid the earth's foundation?
  Tell me, if you understand.
Who marked off its dimensions? Surely you know!
  Who stretched a measuring line across it?
On what were its footings set,
  or who laid its cornerstone—
while the morning stars sang together
  and all the angels shouted for joy?

Who shut up the sea behind doors
  when it burst forth from the womb,
when I made the clouds its garment
  and wrapped it in thick darkness,
when I fixed limits for it
  and set its doors and bars in place,
when I said, "This far you may come and no farther;
  here is where your proud waves halt"?

Job 38:2–11

These are only the first ten verses of God's questioning. It goes on for four chapters—a total of 129 verses, less the five verses that introduce and then sustain the narrative—and at the end Job is completely humbled. He replies to God,

Surely I spoke things I did not understand,
  things too wonderful for me to know. . . .

Therefore I despise myself
  and repent in dust and ashes.

Job 42:3, 6

If we begin to appreciate the perfect knowledge of God and, by contrast, our own pathetic understanding, the first effect it will have on us will be humility, as in Job's case. We will be embarrassed to think that we ever supposed we could contend with God intellectually.

2. *It should comfort us.* It is not only humility that knowledge of the perfect knowledge of God will work in us. We will also find that our knowledge of God's knowledge brings comfort. This is because God also knows us. He knows the worst about us and loves us anyway. Again, he knows the best about us, even when other people do not and instead blame us for things that are not our fault. Earlier in the story, Job expressed his comfort in God's knowledge of him, saying, "He knows the way that I take; / when he has tested me, I will come forth as gold" (Job 23:10).

Do you remember Hagar, Abraham's concubine who gave birth to Ishmael? Early in the story Hagar was so badly mistreated by Sarah, Abraham's wife, that she decided to run away. God appeared to her to say that he knew what she was suffering but that she should return to Sarah and submit to her. As a result of this revelation Hagar gave a new name to God, which is translated best as "You are the God who sees me" (Gen. 16:13). It was a comfort to Hagar to know that God saw her and knew about her suffering.

The second year he was in London, Charles Haddon Spurgeon preached a sermon on that text in which he told of visiting the cell of a man who had died while imprisoned. The cell was down a long winding stair of a castle, where light never penetrated, and it was only as large as the man himself. "Sometimes they tortured him," said Spurgeon's guide. "But his shrieks never reached through the thickness of these walls and never ascended that winding staircase. Here he died, and there, sir, he was buried," he said, pointing to the ground. Yet, said Spurgeon, there was one who did see him and knew the extent of his suffering, and that was God.[4]

If you are in difficult circumstances and no one on earth either sees or cares, remember that God sees and cares and that, if you are a true Christian, he will make it all up to you one day.

3. *It should encourage us to live for God.* One of the greatest chapters in the Bible having to do with the perfect knowledge of God is Psalm 139, a psalm of David. It begins:

> O LORD, you have searched me
> and you know me.
> You know when I sit and when I rise;
> you perceive my thoughts from afar.
> You discern my going out and my lying down;
> you are familiar with all my ways.
> Before a word is on my tongue
> you know it completely, O LORD.
>
> Psalm 139:1–4

The second stanza remarks that "such knowledge is too wonderful" for David, "too lofty" for him to attain. Then it continues:

> Where can I go from your Spirit?
> Where can I flee from your presence?
> If I go up to the heavens, you are there;
> if I make my bed in the depths, you are there.
> If I rise on the wings of the dawn,
> if I settle on the far side of the sea,
> even there your hand will guide me,
> your right hand will hold me fast.
>
> Psalm 139:7–10

4. Charles Haddon Spurgeon, "Omniscience," *The New Park Street Pulpit*, vol. 2 (Pasadena, Tex.: Pilgrim Publications, 1975), p. 253. Original edition 1856.

The fourth stanza says that God's knowing gaze penetrates the night and deep darkness; the next acknowledges that God knew the writer even before his birth, when he was in his mother's womb. In all the Bible there is no greater tribute to the perfect knowledge of God in respect to an individual.

But where does this great psalm end? Strikingly, it ends on a practical note, like so many of David's psalms. It ends by David asking God to help him lead a godly life, precisely *because* God knows him so well.

> Search me, O God, and know my heart;
> test me and know my anxious thoughts.
> See if there is any offensive way in me,
> and lead me in the way everlasting.
>
> Psalm 139:23–24

Do you see how this works? We know so very little. We do not even know ourselves. But God knows us. He knows our weaknesses and our strengths. He knows our sins and our aspirations toward godliness. He knows when isolation will help us grow strong but also when we need companionship to stand in righteousness. He knows when we need rebuking and correcting but also when we need encouragement and teaching. If anyone can "lead me in the way everlasting" it is God. Moreover, since I know he knows me and wants to help me, I can be encouraged to get on with my Christian living.

4. *It should help us to pray.* Jesus taught this in the Sermon on the Mount when he encouraged his followers to pray to God confidently, expecting answers. "When you pray, do not keep on babbling like pagans, for they think they will be heard because of their many words. Do not be like them, for your Father knows what you need before you ask him" (Matt. 6:7–8). This is then followed by what we call the Lord's Prayer, a model prayer consisting of just fifty-two words.

God's knowledge of what we need is so perfect that he often answers even before we pray to him. "Before they call I will answer; while they are still speaking I will hear," said God through his prophet Isaiah (Isa. 65:24).

God's Knowledge and Unbelievers

Thus far I have been speaking to Christians, whose sins have been judged in Jesus Christ. They can say thankfully, as Paul does in Romans, "Oh, the depth of the riches of the . . . knowledge of God." But I cannot leave this subject without applying it also to those who are not Christians. If you are not yet a believer, let me remind you that you have sinned and that you have sinned in the face of God. You have sinned knowingly, willfully, brazenly, and repeatedly. God is a holy God. How do you suppose you will be able to escape his judgment on the day when you stand before him? "Nothing in all creation is hidden from God's sight. Everything is uncovered and laid bare before the eyes of him to whom we must give account" (Heb. 4:13).

Do not delude yourself on this point. God sees you, and he will punish your sin. After Adam and Eve sinned, they tried to hide in the shrubbery of the Garden of Eden, but the bushes were not dense enough to hide them from the eyes of God. No human eye saw Cain murder his brother, but God saw it and said, "Your brother's blood cries out to me from the ground" (Gen. 4:10). Achan stole a wedge of gold and a beautiful set of Babylonian clothing, but God saw his theft and brought it to light, and Achan's judgment followed (Josh. 7). Ananias and Sapphira lied to the church, but God revealed their deception and they were struck dead (Acts 5:1–13). The Bible says, "You may be sure that your sin will find you out" (Num. 32:23).

What will you do in the day of God's judgment when your sins will be read out? "How does God know *that?*" you will ask. "And *that?* And *that?* I had almost forgotten it myself." On that day you will be abased, confounded, speechless, and overwhelmed, as God unfolds the records of your sinful past life, page after page and paragraph after paragraph.

"Stop!" you will cry. But it will not stop until every sinful thought, every evil deed, every curse, every theft, every lie, every neglect of what you should have done, is read out and justly judged.

I counsel you: Do not wait for that day. Jesus died so that sinners just like you might be saved from judgment. The way to escape God's judgment is to come to Jesus, to believe on him, trust him, follow him. I tell you on the authority of God's Word that if you believe on Jesus Christ and truly trust him, "you will be saved" (Acts 16:31).

173

The Profound Wisdom of God

Romans 11:33

Oh, the depth of the riches of the wisdom and knowledge of God!
How unsearchable his judgments,
and his paths beyond tracing out!

Not long ago I was returning to Philadelphia from a speaking engagement in Toronto, and while I was waiting for the plane to take off so I could put down the tray table and do some work, I picked up the airline's monthly news magazine and read an article on Pinehurst, North Carolina. It seems that Pinehurst is a golfer's paradise. The main country club has seven courses, but there are more than two dozen other courses scattered about. Over the years, Pinehurst has hosted such celebrities as the Rockefellers, Roosevelts, Crosbys, and Swansons, and many golf greats like Sam Snead, Arnold Palmer, and Jack Nicklaus. Pinehurst is also a ninety-seven-year-old village with about five thousand residents.

I was struck by what one resident had said about the place: "People who don't know Pinehurst ask what it's like, and you can't give them an answer. We as human beings like to compare things, but there's no comparison for this place. It's like no other place in the world. That's what makes it special."

But what is *God* like?

You see the problem at once. Unlike Pinehurst—which, in spite of such public-relations statements as the one I just cited, does have places to which it may actually be compared—God is incomparable. That is, he cannot really be compared with anything. This is preeminently true of his incommunicable attributes, things such as God's self-existence, self-sufficiency, and eternality. But it is also true even of his communicable attributes, those qualities that he shares with us in some fashion. One of these is knowledge, which we looked at in the last study. We, too, have knowledge, but because God's knowledge is perfect, it is infinitely greater and infinitely superior to ours. So we speak of him as being omniscient, as knowing all things. God not only knows all things that were or are; he also knows all that could possibly be. That is, he knows possibilities and potentialities as well as actualities.

Another communicable attribute that is also infinitely above and beyond us is God's wisdom.

The Wisdom of God

What do we mean when we say that God is wise or all-wise? We mean that God is omniscient, of course, since God could not be all-wise unless he was all-knowing. But wisdom is more than mere knowledge, more even than total or perfect knowledge. A person can have a great deal of knowledge—we call it "head knowledge"—and not know what to do with it. He can know a great deal about a lot of things and still be a great fool. And there is also the matter of goodness. What about that? Without morality or goodness, wisdom is not wisdom. Instead, it is what we call cunning. Clearly, wisdom consists in knowing what to do with the knowledge one has and in directing that knowledge to the highest and most moral ends.

Charles Hodge says that God's wisdom is seen "in the selection of proper ends and of proper means for the accomplishment of those ends."[1]

A. W. Tozer wrote, "Wisdom, among other things, is the ability to devise perfect ends and to achieve those ends by the most perfect means. It sees the end from the beginning, so that there can be no need to guess or conjecture. Wisdom sees everything in focus, each in proper relation to all, and is thus able to work toward predestined goals with flawless precision."[2]

J. I. Packer says the same thing but wisely emphasizes goodness:

Wisdom is the power to see, and the inclination to choose, the best and highest goal, together with the surest means of attaining it. Wisdom is, in fact, the practical side of moral goodness. As such, it is found in its fullness only in God. He alone is naturally and entirely and invariably wise. "His wisdom ever waketh," says the hymn, and it is true. Wisdom, as the old theologians used to say, is his *essence,* just as power and truth and goodness are his *essence*—integral elements,

1. Charles Hodge, *Systematic Theology,* vol. 1 (London: James Clarke, 1960), p. 401.
2. A. W. Tozer, *The Knowledge of the Holy: The Attributes of God, Their Meaning in the Christian Life* (New York, Evanston and London: Harper & Row, 1961), p. 66.

that is, in his character. . . . Omniscience governing omnipotence, infinite power ruled by infinite wisdom, is a biblical description of the divine character.[3]

As soon as we begin to think along these lines, we see at once why our human wisdom does not begin to compare with God's and why Paul can say, as he does in writing to the Corinthians, "Where is the wise man? Where is the scholar? Where is the philosopher of this age? Has not God made foolish the wisdom of the world? For since in the wisdom of God the world through its wisdom did not know him, God was pleased through the foolishness of what was preached to save those who believe" (1 Cor. 1:20–21).

The Wisdom of God in Our Salvation

Paul's words take us a step further in understanding God's wisdom, however. For as soon as Paul speaks of God's wisdom as exceeding human wisdom, he thinks of the gospel—since it is there above all that God's perfect wisdom is seen. And that is what we have at the end of Romans 11, too. What draws out Paul's awe at the "riches of [God's] wisdom" is not the wisdom God displayed in the ordering of creation, as wonderful as that may be, but rather his wisdom in saving sinners such as you and me.

And I would say this: If at this point you are not standing in awe of the depth of the riches of God's manifold wisdom in salvation, as Paul was, you have not even begun to understand the first eleven chapters of this letter. Let me show you what I mean.

1. *The wisdom of God in justification (Rom. 1–4).* The first main section of Romans includes an introduction to the letter (Rom. 1:1–17), an analysis of man's sin (Rom. 1:18–3:20), a statement of the gospel (Rom. 3:21–31), and a proof of the doctrine of justification by grace through faith from the Old Testament (Rom. 4:1–25). The central portion is Paul's statement of the gospel, and the central passage in that is Romans 3:25–26, where Paul writes, "God presented him [Jesus] as a sacrifice of atonement. . . . to demonstrate his justice, because in his forbearance he had left the sins committed beforehand unpunished—he did it to demonstrate his justice at the present time, so as to be just and the one who justifies those who have faith in Jesus."

Let me illustrate the meaning of these verses by a story. Early in this century, a society for atheism produced a tract in which the life stories of some of the Old Testament heroes were related in lurid detail. One page told the story of Abraham, pointing out that on two occasions he had been willing to sacrifice the honor of his wife to save his own life. Yet the Bible calls Abraham "a friend of God." After pointing this out, the tract asked: What kind of a God is he who can be friends with a cowardly man like Abraham?

The next page told the story of Jacob. Jacob was a cheat. He cheated his brother out of his inheritance. Yet God condescended to refer to himself by

3. J. I. Packer, *Knowing God* (Downers Grove, Ill.: InterVarsity Press, 1973), pp. 80, 81.

the name of Jacob ("the God of Abraham, Isaac, and Jacob"). The tract asked: What kind of God is he who can identify with a scoundrel like Jacob?

Next came Moses. Moses was a great leader and lawgiver, but early in his life Moses had killed a man and buried his body in the sand lest his deed be discovered. Yet God spoke to Moses face to face and called him "my servant." What kind of God could speak face to face with a man who was a murderer?

The last of the atheists' examples was David, their chief witness against God's character. David had committed adultery with Bathsheba, the wife of Uriah the Hittite. Then, when Bathsheba was discovered to be with child by David, David arranged the death of her husband so he could marry Bathsheba and conceal his sin. Yet David is called "a man after God's own heart." The atheists asked: What kind of a heart must God have if David, the adulterer and murderer, was a man who was after it? According to the atheists' reasoning, the mere existence of these stories is sufficient to prove either that God does not exist or that, if he does exist, he does not have a character worth admiring.

The interesting thing about this tract is that the atheists had a good point and that Paul acknowledges its partial validity in Romans 3. They were saying that Abraham, Jacob, Moses, and David were sinners, and they were entirely right to do so. In fact, these men were far greater sinners than the atheists imagined, for their hearts were "deceitful above all things and beyond cure" (Jer. 17:9). It could be said of them, as Paul wrote of the human race in general, that

> There is no one righteous, not even one;
>   there is no one who understands,
>   no one who seeks God. . . .
> there is no one who does good,
>   not even one.
>
> Romans 3:10–12; cf. Psalm 14:1–3

What these men deserved from God was hell. Yet for centuries, instead of sending these depraved and godless characters to hell, God had been saving them, and others like them.

How could God do this? I do not mean: Did God have the power to do it? Of course, he did. God is all-powerful. Nor do I mean: Shouldn't God want to do it? We can understand how God might want to save sinners. After all, we ourselves might choose to be merciful to those who actually deserve condemnation. But that is not the point. My question has to do with God's justice. It means: How could God save such sinners and at the same time remain a just and holy God? To use Paul's language, how could he be both "just and the one who justifies" the ungodly? Since God was justifying the ungodly, it would seem that for centuries there was something like a shadow cast over the good name of God.

Although this puzzle is beyond the wisdom of mere men and women, it was not beyond the wisdom of God. Thus it was that in the fullness of time "God sent his Son, born of a woman, born under law, to redeem those under law, that we might receive the full rights of sons" (Gal. 4:4–5). Or, to go back to the text in Romans, "God presented him as a sacrifice of atonement . . . to demonstrate his justice at the present time." This means that God satisfied the claims of his justice by punishing the innocent Jesus for our sins. Jesus bore the wrath of God in our place. Thus, the demands of God's justice were fully met and, justice being satisfied, the love of God was then free to reach out, embrace, and fully save the sinner.

Who but God could think up such a solution to the sin problem? None of us could have done it. "Oh, the depth of the riches of the wisdom . . . of God!" God suited the most perfect means to the most desirable of ends, and so he saves sinners like ourselves.

2. *The wisdom of God in sanctification (Rom. 5–8).* The next section of Romans discusses the permanent nature of salvation, embracing the sinner's need for sanctification. How is the wisdom of God revealed in this area? We have seen that the justification discussed in Romans 1–4 is provided by the work of Christ, which means that it is not of ourselves. It is of grace. But if that is so, what is to stop a justified person from indulging in his or her sinful nature, since the person's salvation has already been secured by Christ's work? Why should we not continue to sin? In fact, why should we not "go on sinning so that grace may increase?" (Rom. 6:1).

Here we are caught on the horns of a dilemma. Either salvation must be by works, which destroys grace; besides which, no one would be saved, since none can provide sufficient good works. Or else, if salvation is of grace, then we must be free to sin greatly.

God solves this problem by showing us that we are never justified apart from being regenerated or being made alive in Christ. This means that Christians have been given a new nature, and this new nature, being the very life of Jesus Christ within, will inevitably produce good works corresponding to the character of God. In fact, this is the only sure proof of our having been saved by him.

Let's look at this another way. Paul writes of our being joined to Christ in what theologians call "the mystical union." Just as we have been joined to Adam by our natural descent from him, so that when Adam sinned we sinned and when Adam was judged by the penalty of death for sin we, too, were judged, so also, having been joined to Christ, we are now justified by his work and have been made spiritually alive in him. If we have been truly saved, we are different people than we were before. Moreover, since this is the work of God and not our work, it means that we cannot undo it and so somehow go back to being what we were before. Since we cannot go back, the only way we can move is forward. Paul's way of saying this is: "In the same way, count yourselves dead to sin but alive to God in Christ Jesus" (Rom. 6:11).

Here is the way Romans 8:1–4 puts it: "Therefore, there is now no condemnation for those who are in Christ Jesus, because through Christ Jesus the law of the Spirit of life set me free from the law of sin and death. For what the law was powerless to do in that it was weakened by the sinful nature, God did by sending his own Son in the likeness of sinful man to be a sin offering." This means that salvation is utterly of grace. But listen to what follows. "And so he condemned sin in sinful man, *in order that the righteous requirements of the law might be fully met in us, who do not live according to the sinful nature but according to the Spirit*" (emphasis added).

Who but God could think up a gospel like that? We would never do it, because we do not naturally hold grace and works together. If we emphasize morality, as some persons do, we begin to think that we can be saved by our good works and so strive to do it. We repudiate grace. But if, on the other hand, we emphasize grace, knowing that we cannot possibly be saved by our inadequate and polluted works, we have a natural tendency to do away with works entirely and so slide into Antinomianism. If we hold to grace, we repudiate works, and if we hold to works, we repudiate grace. But God has devised a gospel that is entirely and completely of grace and yet produces the most exceptional works in those who are saved.

No wonder Paul stands in awe of "the depth of the riches of the wisdom . . . of God" and calls God's judgments "unsearchable" and "his paths beyond searching out" (Rom. 11:33).

3. *The wisdom of God displayed in human history (Rom. 9–11).* The third main section of Romans is concerned with the acts of God in the flow of historical events. As Paul describes it, the problem is that God made special salvation promises to the Jewish people, and yet, in spite of these promises, the majority of the Jews are not responding to the gospel. Does this indicate that the purposes of God have failed? And what about the Gentiles? There are far less promises for them. Yet in Paul's day the Gentiles seemed to be responding to the apostles' preaching. Does this mean that God has rejected the Jews in favor of the Gentiles? If he has, isn't that wrong? And doesn't it destroy the doctrine of the believer's eternal security? Doesn't it mean that God is fickle?

Paul's answer is a magnificent theodicy in which he justifies the ways of God with men, showing that God has rejected Israel for a time in order that his mercy might be extended to the Gentiles, but adding that Gentile salvation will provoke Israel to jealousy and so in time bring the Jewish people to faith in their Messiah.

Since this is the meaning of history, these chapters are a magnificent exploration of the wisdom of God in the ordering of space/time events. Here is how F. Godet, one of the greatest expositors of Romans, puts it:

Never was survey more vast taken of the divine plan of the world's history. First, the epoch of primitive unity in which the human family forms still only one unbroken whole; then the antagonism between the two religious portions of the race, created by the special call of Abraham: the Jews continuing in the Father's house, but with a legal and servile spirit, the Gentiles walking in their own ways. At the close of this period, the manifestation of Christ determining the return of the latter to the domestic hearth, but at the same time the departure of the former. Finally, the Jews, yielding to the divine solicitations and to the spectacle of salvation enjoyed by the Gentiles as children of grace; and so the final universalism in an infinitely higher form [than] the original unity. . . .

The contrast between the Jews and Gentiles appears therefore as the essential moving spring of history. It is the actions and reactions arising from this primary fact which form its key. This is what no philosophy of history has dreamt of and what makes these chapters . . . the highest theodicy.[4]

Who could devise a plan of that scope for world history? We could not do it: We cannot even understand it apart from the biblical revelation, and even that is difficult for us. But it is not beyond "the depth of the riches of the wisdom . . . of God."

God's Wisdom and Ours

I said at the beginning of this study that the wisdom of God is so much superior to our wisdom that it may hardly be compared to it. Yet I do not want to minimize the need for us on our part to cultivate wisdom. I want to close on that note.

The Bible has much to say about wisdom. The first nine chapters of Proverbs are a sustained exhortation to us to seek this gift. But there is other wisdom literature in the Old Testament (Job, Ecclesiastes), and the New Testament also makes much of wisdom. Ephesians 5:15–17 says, "Be very careful, then, how you live—not as unwise but as wise, making the most of every opportunity, because the days are evil. Therefore, do not be foolish, but understand what the Lord's will is." Colossians 4:5 says, "Be wise in the way you act toward outsiders; make the most of every opportunity." James, the Lord's brother, promises, "If any of you lacks wisdom, he should ask God, who gives generously to all without finding fault, and it will be given to him" (James 1:5).

We are to seek wisdom, then. But where? How may wisdom be found? First, we must begin with reverence for God. Proverbs 9:10 says, "The fear of the Lord is the beginning of wisdom." Second, we must labor to know God's Word, the Bible. The psalmist wrote, "Your commands make me wiser than my enemies" (Ps. 119:98), and Paul urged his young companion Timothy to continue in his study of the God-breathed Scriptures, since they "are able to make you wise for salvation through faith in Christ Jesus" (2 Tim. 3:15).

4. F. Godet, *Commentary on St. Paul's Epistle to the Romans,* trans. A. Cusin (Edinburgh: T. & T. Clark, 1892), pp. 270, 271.

If we really believed that God is all-wise and if we really wanted to be wise ourselves, we would do this. But the problem is that we do not really believe in God's wisdom. Martin Luther once said, "We are accustomed to admit freely that God is more powerful than we are, but not that he is wiser than we are. To be sure, we say that he is; but when it comes to a showdown, we do not want to act on what we say."[5]

From our perspective, the workings of God are irregular, and we like events to run like a train on fixed timetables and along predictable tracks. Because they do not, we are always thinking of how we would be able to do things better. What this means is that in the final analysis we do not trust God to order both the ends and the means to them. How foolish, when in the matter of salvation God has ordered the ends and the means to that end so perfectly! That is a far more complicated matter than the details of our little lives. So we need to repudiate our folly, seek wisdom in the Bible, where alone it may be found, and then seize every opportunity to live for and witness to our all-wise God and heavenly Father.

5. Martin Luther, *What Luther Says: An Anthology*, compiled by Ewald M. Plass (Saint Louis: Concordia, 1959), vol. 3, p. 1453.

174

The Unsearchable Judgments of God

Romans 11:33

Oh, the depth of the riches of the wisdom and knowledge of God!
How unsearchable his judgments,
and his paths beyond tracing out!

Once, when I was reflecting on the purpose of good sermons, I jotted down the following: (1) the chief end of a sermon is to glorify God; (2) it should be faithful to the Bible; (3) it must say something worth saying; (4) it should say it well; and (5) it should be helpful to those who listen to it. Some sermons achieve those objectives better than others, of course, and some subjects lend themselves to one goal better than another. But I do not know of any subject that lends itself to each of those goals better in sermon form than the doctrine of the divine decrees.

The "decrees" have to do with God's ordering of everything that happens, a truth that is clearly of great importance. Yet it is something hardly mentioned by contemporary preachers.

The Westminster divines were aware of this truth and valued it highly. In fact, the Westminster Confession of Faith deals with the subject early in the document, in the third chapter, immediately after the chapters on the Bible and the Trinity. It begins, "God from all eternity, did, by his most wise and holy counsel of his own will, freely, and unchangeably ordain whatsoever comes to pass: yet so, as thereby neither is God the author of sin, nor is violence offered to the will of the creatures; nor is the liberty or contingency of second causes taken away, but rather established" (par. 1).

Judgments and Decrees

The reason I am talking about God's decrees is that this is the probable meaning of the word *judgments* in the second sentence of Romans 11:33. It occurs in the sentence "How unsearchable his judgments, and his paths beyond tracing out!"

The Greek word here is *krimata*. It is generally used in the sense of God's judicial decisions, that is, God's judgments on the wicked. Godet, for one, thinks that this is what it refers to here.[1] But the word is sometimes also used of decisions or determinations, especially in its verbal form (cf. Rom. 14:13; 1 Cor. 2:2; 7:37; 11:13; 2 Cor. 2:1; Titus 3:12), which fits the context better. Charles Hodge explains the broader usage by saying, "As of old, the ruler was also the judge—to judge often means to rule—[therefore] the same word is used for the decisions of the judge and the decrees or ordinances of the ruler."[2]

The fact that "judgments" occurs in parallel with "paths"—or "ways," KJV—also suggests that Paul is thinking of the acts of God generally and not simply of judicial judgments.[3]

Besides, this is the direction of the apostle's thought in these verses. Paul is marveling at the nature of God's ways. He begins with praise of God's knowledge, which is intuitive and infinite. Wisdom is a step beyond knowledge. It is the ability to perceive the proper, best, and most perfect means to achieve God's perfect ends. Still, at this point knowledge and wisdom are only potentialities. It is only when we get to the next step that the potentialities become actualities, as God's wisdom expresses itself in his decrees, and his decrees determine the path his decisions actually take in human history.

---

1. "The word in every case implies the idea of a *judicial* decree; and what Paul has just been referring to, those severe dispensations whereby God has successively chastised the ingratitude of the Gentiles (chap. 1) and the haughty presumption of the Jews (chap. 10), shows clearly that we are to keep to its strict sense" (F. Godet, *Commentary on St. Paul's Epistle to the Romans*, trans. A. Cusin [Edinburgh: T. & T. Clark, 1892], vol. 2, p. 266).

2. Charles Hodge, *A Commentary on Romans* (Edinburgh and Carlisle, Pa.: The Banner of Truth Trust, 1972), p. 378. Original edition 1835.

3. *"Judgments* ('decisions,' GNB) is normally a legal term and is often used of adverse judgments passed on offenders (which would be appropriate in a context dealing with the disobedient). However, it is not confined to the adverse, and in this context where it is in parallel with *paths* or 'ways,' we should not insist on the meaning 'negative judgments.' Paul is simply pronouncing on the impossibility of our ever understanding fully what God is doing" (Leon Morris, *The Epistle to the Romans* [Grand Rapids: Wm. B. Eerdmans, 1988], p. 428).

The Nature of God's Decrees

Let's take a moment to think about the nature of God's decrees. What are they like? How do they differ from decisions *we* might make? And why is it that Paul stands in such awe of them? Here are seven things to bear in mind.

1. *The decrees are for God's glory.* You and I do not usually think this way. We think first of our needs, and even when we are thinking in terms of biblical theology, we think first in terms of our salvation and our happiness rather than of God's glory. The Bible is different at this point. Let me ask three questions:

Why did God create the heavens and the earth? We answer: To give us a beautiful environment in which to live and work. The Bible says, "The heavens declare the glory of God; / the skies proclaim the work of his hands" (Ps. 19:1).

Why did Jesus Christ come into the world? We answer: To save us from our sins. True enough. But the greater answer was given by Jesus himself when he prayed, saying, "I have brought you glory on earth by completing the work you gave me to do" (John 17:4).

What will the saints be saying when they stand before the throne of God in heaven? We suppose that we will be praising God for being so good to us, and we probably will. But the Bible has them saying, "To him who sits on the throne and to the Lamb / be praise and honor and glory and power, for ever and ever!" (Rev. 5:13).

Do you understand what I am saying? Most of us are hopelessly self-centered and subjective. But the universe and all that happens in it is first of all for God's glory, and not primarily for us, though we benefit from it and God does also have our well-being in view. Surely that is why the doxology in Romans 11 ends as it does. It does not end with man. Rather it ends with God: "For from him and through him and to him are all things. / To him be the glory forever! Amen" (v. 36).

2. *The decrees are one.* I have been speaking of the "decrees" (plural) of God, because we live within the flow of historical events and can only think of God's acts in sequence. But the Westminster Confession of Faith is closer to the biblical way of speaking when it titles the chapter to which I referred earlier: "Of God's Eternal Decree" (singular). The word *decree* is singular because God does not see things in sequence, as we do, but rather sees all things as a whole and from the beginning. Besides, what God foresees is only what he has foreordained or planned.

That is why we read in Psalm 2, "I will proclaim the decree [singular] of the Lord" (v. 7). Or in Romans 8, "We know that in all things God works for the good of those who love him, who have been called according to his purpose [singular]" (v. 28). Or in Ephesians 3, "His intent was that now, through the church, the manifold wisdom of God should be made known to the rulers and authorities in the heavenly realms, according to his eternal purpose [singular] which he accomplished in Christ Jesus our Lord" (vv. 10–11). Or in Acts 2, "This man was handed over to you by God's set purpose [singular] and foreknowledge" (v. 23a).

Charles Hodge wrote in his *Systematic Theology*, "It is inconsistent with the idea of absolute perfection, that the purposes of God are successive, or that he ever purposes what he did not originally intend; or that one part of his plan is independent of other parts. It is one scheme, and therefore one purpose."[4]

3. *The decrees are eternal.* To think of any of God's decisions as having been made in time is to suppose that some new circumstance, unforeseen by God, has occurred and that God therefore finds it necessary to accommodate himself to it. This would mean that God does not know everything perfectly, and it would make circumstances more powerful than God, since in some form or another they would be dictating to him. If such were the case, God would not be God, and we would be back in paganism, with its impotent and very human gods and goddesses.

The Bible teaches something very different when it says that believers were chosen in Christ "before the creation of the world" (Eph. 1:4), and speaks of Jesus as the Lamb "chosen before the creation of the world" (1 Peter 1:20). It follows, says Hodge, that "history in all its details, even the most minute, is but the evolution of the eternal purposes of God."[5]

4. *The decrees are wise.* We have already seen how this is so, for we have seen how God's perfect wisdom issues in what he does. This is preeminently the case in salvation matters. It is what I focused on in the last study, following Paul's thought in Romans 1–11. But the wisdom of God's decrees is also evident in every creative act and every historical determination God makes. The psalmist rightly declared, "How many are your works, O LORD! In wisdom you made them all . . ." (Ps. 104:24).

5. *The decrees are free.* Our purposes are also free, even when formed under the influence of other minds or circumstances. It is why we insist on free will. The reason why men and women do not seek God (Rom. 3:11) is because they do not want to, not because they are physically incapable of it. But God's freedom is infinitely above our own. We are free, yet our freedom is within a framework of space/time limitations. In God's case, his will determines the framework. So it is correct to say that he is exalted above all *ab extra* influence, that is, above all influence from without.

4. Charles Hodge, *Systematic Theology* (London: James Clarke, 1960), vol. 1, p. 537. Original edition 1872.
5. Ibid., p. 538.

Arthur W. Pink expressed this when he wrote, "God was alone when he made his decrees. He was free to decree or not to decree, and to decree one thing and not another. This liberty we must ascribe to him who is supreme, independent, and sovereign in all his doings."[6]

This freedom of God in regard to his decrees is taught in the section of Isaiah from which Paul quotes in Romans 11:34. The full passage says,

> Who has understood the mind [Spirit] of the LORD,
>   or instructed him as his counselor?
> Whom did the LORD consult to enlighten him,
>   or who taught him the right way?
> Who was it that taught him knowledge
>   or showed him the path of understanding?
>
> Isaiah 40:13–14

6. *The decrees are absolute and unconditional.* It follows from the fact of God's perfect freedom that his decrees are all also absolute and unconditional. Hodge adds the word *immutable.* This means that what God determines to do is not suspended upon any condition that may or may not come to be, or upon any act that you or I may or may not do. God is infinite in knowledge and perfect in power. Therefore, nothing can arise to cause him to do things differently or thwart his design. The psalmist says, "The plans of the LORD stand firm forever, / the purposes of his heart through all generations" (Ps. 33:11). James tells us that God "does not change like shifting shadows" (James 1:17). God says, "My purpose will stand, / and I will do all that I please" (Isa. 46:10b).

Some complain that if the decrees of God are absolute and unconditional, we cannot speak of free will and responsibility on the part of men and women. But that is not correct. It would be true if (1) God and man were on the same level, operating as equals, and (2) the choices we make were not determined by our sinful natures. Neither is the case. We decide as we do because we are sinners, which means we are responsible. God exercises his will toward us in this area by allowing sin to operate, just as he also exercises his will in other cases by intervening to save us from sin and turn us away from such actions. As to the first condition, we are not on God's level, which means that while our choices embrace only our own choices, God's decrees embrace not only his will but also the contrary wills of sinful and rebellious subjects.

7. *The decrees are effective.* Theologians make a distinction between God's efficient decrees, that is, what he specifically wills, and God's permissive decrees, that is, what he does not specifically will himself but nevertheless permits to come to pass. The entrance of sin into the world and all sinful

---

6. Arthur W. Pink, *Gleanings in the Godhead* (Chicago: Moody Press, 1975), p. 17.

acts are in the latter category. We say that God does good but permits evil. He is the direct author of one, though not the other. This is a valid distinction, but it has nothing to do with the certainty of coming events. Whatever God ordains, whether actively or passively, is certain.

Election and Reprobation

Many years ago, B. B. Warfield, the great Professor of Didactic and Polemic Theology at Princeton Theological Seminary (1887–1921), wrote an article for *The Presbyterian Banner* on the Westminster Confession's chapter on "God's Eternal Decree." Like Paul, Warfield marveled at the doctrine. But he also marveled at the confessional statement, praising the sparse yet precise language with which the authors set forth the doctrine. Religiously, the confession assures us that despite all contrary appearances the arm of God is stretched out beneath us to uphold us and teaches that everything does work for good for those who love God. Philosophically, the confession affirms that the universe has a divine purpose and that nothing will thwart what God is doing.

But what Warfield most marveled at is that the confession does not bog down in fruitless speculation about how God's decree operates in human life, particularly in regard to free will, but instead passes directly to the way the decree operates for our salvation.

This is true if you look at the confession. There are eight paragraphs that deal with God's decree. The first two occupy only ten lines in my edition; they cover the points I have made at greater length in this study. But from that point on, the chapter turns to the matter of election and the accompanying steps that accomplish and then assure our salvation. The confession says:

> Those of mankind that are predestined unto life, God, before the foundation of the world was laid, according to his eternal and immutable purpose, and the secret counsel and good pleasure of his will, hath chosen, in Christ, unto everlasting glory, out of his mere free grace and love, without any foresight of faith, or good works, or perseverance in either of them, or any other thing in the creature, as conditions, or causes moving him thereunto: and all to the praise of his glorious grace.
>
> As God hath appointed the elect unto glory, so hath he, by the eternal and most free purpose of his will, foreordained all the means thereunto. Wherefore, they who are elected, being fallen in Adam, are redeemed by Christ, are effectually called unto faith in Christ by his Spirit working in due season, are justified, adopted, sanctified, and kept by his power, through faith unto salvation. Neither are any other redeemed by Christ, effectually called, justified, adopted, sanctified, and saved, but the elect only. [pars. v, vi]

The final paragraph encourages us to handle the truth of predestination with care, knowing nevertheless that it affords "matter of praise, reverence, and admiration of God; and of humility, diligence, and abundant consolation to all that sincerely obey the gospel" (par. viii).

Two Profitable Questions

I close by asking two questions.

First, isn't this how Paul has himself been handling the doctrine of God's decrees in Romans 9–11? He has handled it with humility, confessing at the end of his discussion the unsearchable nature of God's judgments and the untraceable pattern of his paths. He has also ended with "praise, reverence, and admiration" for God, who has designed and accomplished such a marvelous salvation. It is why Paul is praising him.

We must do the same. We must confess our inability to probe the depths of God's infinitely wise decrees. Like the nineteenth-century hymnwriter Ray Palmer (1858), we may say:

> Lord, my weak thought in vain would climb
> To search the starry vault profound;
> In vain would wing her flight sublime
> To find creation's utmost bound.

> But weaker yet that thought must prove
> To search thy great eternal plan,
> Thy sovereign counsels, born of love,
> Long ages ere the world began.

But we may rejoice in God's decrees, too, as Palmer also did,

> Be this my joy, that evermore
> Thou rulest all things at thy will;
> Thy sovereign wisdom I adore,
> And calmly, sweetly, trust thee still.

No one who knows the reality and joy of salvation can do less.

My second question is this: Despite the way God's eternal decree puzzles us and the little about it we truly understand, would we really wish it to be otherwise? Would we prefer that our salvation depended on something we did or decided, rather than on God's decree and choice?

Here is the way Warfield asked these questions at the end of the essay I referred to earlier:

Do we really wish it to be true that no man in the eternal counsel of God is particularly predestined unto eternal life? That no man who is predestined unto life is unchangeably predestinated unto eternal life? Do we really wish it were dependent on our own strength whether we ourselves enter into life, or having entered, abide in life? Do we really wish that it were only a vague and uncertain number—it may be many, it may be few; experience only can decide—who are predestinated unto eternal life? Do we really care little or nothing whether it be the everlasting arms or merely our own weak arms that we rest on in our Christian life? Do we really care nothing whether we can make our own that

noble paean which the apostle sings at the close of the eighth chapter of
Romans, the keynote of which is the great declaration that if God is for us nothing can be against us? . . . Or do we really fancy that we can believe all these
things are really ours, if we hold it false or doubtful that God's people are particularly and unchangeably designed to glory and their number is certain and
definite and cannot be diminished—in accordance with our Savior's words that
they shall never perish, and no one is able to snatch them out of the Father's
hand—that they have been given him of the Father, and he will lose none of
them, but raise them up at the last day?[7]

I do not think any of us really want that, or would if we stopped to think
about it clearly. So let's rejoice instead, knowing that "God from all eternity,
did, by the most wise and holy counsel of his own will, freely and unchangeably
ordain whatsoever comes to pass."

Even more important, let us say with Paul, "Oh, the depth of the riches
of the wisdom and knowledge of God! How unsearchable his judgments, and
his paths beyond tracing out!"

7. Benjamin B. Warfield, "The Significance of the Confessional Doctrine of the Decree" in
Selected Shorter Writings of Benjamin B. Warfield, ed. John E. Meeter (Nutley, N.J.: Presbyterian and
Reformed Publishing, 1970), vol. 1, pp. 100, 101.

175

The Amazing Ways of God

Romans 11:33

Oh, the depth of the riches of the wisdom and knowledge of God!
How unsearchable his judgments,
and his paths beyond tracing out!

Because God did "unchangeably ordain whatsoever comes to pass," he obviously has ordained a path for us to walk in. But we have trouble with that path because (1) we are not always convinced that it is ordained; (2) we do not know where it is going; and (3) it does not always work out as we believe it should.

God's Painful Paths

Let me tell you about Elisabeth Elliot, who as a young woman went to the jungles of Ecuador to be a missionary. After studying Spanish for a year, she was invited to work with two other lady missionaries who were trying to reduce the language of the Colorado Indians to writing so they could translate the Bible into it. Elisabeth Howard—for that was her name then—prayed for an informant, someone who knew the Colorado language and would help her learn it, and the Lord supplied what seemed to be a perfect individual. His name was Macario. He was bilingual in both Spanish and Colorado, and he was delighted to have the interpreter's job. One day, shortly after they had begun the work, Macario was murdered. It was a pointless, terrible setback to what was apparently a sacrificial and spiritual endeavor. But there it was! No explanation. It was simply something that God, for whatever reason, had allowed to happen.

Elisabeth went on with the work, and at the end of a year she had accumulated thousands of vocabulary cards and done a preliminary analysis of the Colorado language. She had reduced it to a phonemic alphabet and was teaching the other two missionaries to use it. One day when she was away, all her materials were stolen. The women prayed about it, of course, but the materials were never recovered. The year's work was lost, gone. It had been for nothing.

The next stage in this story is better known to us. Elisabeth Howard married Jim Elliot, who in a similar manner had been trying to rebuild a missionary outpost called Shandia station but who had a year's work washed down the river one night by a surprise flood. The couple worked with the Quichua Indians. After only twenty-seven months of marriage, Jim Elliot was speared to death by Auca Indians, whom he and four missionary companions had been trying to reach with the gospel. Again, it was all so pointless and painful. It was "unsearchable . . . beyond tracing out."

And that was not all. After some years Elisabeth married Addison Leitch, a former president of Pittsburgh Theological Seminary. But not long after, he died slowly and painfully from cancer.

What is Elisabeth Elliot's testimony? She says, "The experiences of my life are not such that I could infer from them that God is good, gracious and merciful necessarily. To have one husband murdered and another one disintegrate body, soul and spirit, through cancer, is not what you would call a proof of the love of God. In fact, there are many times when it looks like just the opposite. But my belief in the love of God is not by inference or instinct. It is by faith. To apprehend God's sovereignty working in that love is—we must say it—the last and highest victory of the faith that overcomes the world."[1]

Secret Things and Things Revealed

This is exactly what we are dealing with in Romans 11:33, of course, a text that has already occupied us for three studies. It tells us that God's wisdom and knowledge are perfect and that his decrees and paths, which flow from that wisdom and knowledge, are beyond tracing out.

But this is a truth we find hard to come to grips with, as I said at the beginning. In the last study we were looking at God's judgments or decrees. We explored the meaning of the "eternal decree" together, and at the end we

---

1. Elisabeth Elliot, "Denial, Discipline and Devotion" in *Tenth: An Evangelical Quarterly,* July 1977, p. 64.

were left with two results: (1) *humility* at our inability to comprehend God's decrees, and (2) *awe* of them, coupled with *praise* of God for his greatness. That response carries over into the fourth of the items cited and to which we come now, God's "paths."

"Judgments" refers to God's decrees, flowing from his infinite knowledge and perfect wisdom. "Paths" refers to the course these judgments actually take in human history.

Yet the two terms are closely parallel, and what Paul says of them is exactly parallel. He says that God's judgments "cannot be searched to the bottom" (the Greek word is *anexereunêtos*) and that his paths "cannot be followed to the end" (the Greek is *anexichniastos*).[2]

Paul does not mean that we can never know anything about God's ways, particularly since he has just been explaining some of them. What he means is that God's ways cannot be figured out by us apart from revelation.

Some things God has revealed. That is why we know he has a plan and that events do not happen simply by accident. Paul says, "'No eye has seen, / no ear has heard, / no mind has conceived / what God has prepared for those who love him'—but God has revealed it to us by his Spirit" (1 Cor. 2:9–10). But God does not reveal all things, particularly the detailed circumstances or events of our lives, and in these areas we must live by faith in his sovereign and loving purposes, as Elisabeth Elliot does. The Bible says, "The secret things belong to the LORD our God, but the things revealed belong to us and to our children forever . . ." (Deut. 29:29).

God's Footprints

There is a very interesting image involved in the single Greek word rendered "beyond tracing out." This word, *anexichniastos,* is based on the noun *ichnos*, which means "footprint." It suggests that although we do not know where God is coming from or where he is going, we nevertheless do see his footprints, and it is these that puzzle us.

Let me direct you to the sandy beach of history to show you some of the untraceable footprints of God.

1. *Abraham.* I start with the story of Abraham, because that is where the story of God's preparation of a special people through whom the Messiah should come begins. God called Abraham out of Ur of the Chaldeans to go to Canaan, promising him that he would become the father of a great nation: "I will make you into a great nation and I will bless you; / I will make your

---

2. F. Godet, *Commentary on St. Paul's Epistle to the Romans,* trans. A. Cusin (Edinburgh: T. & T. Clark, 1892), vol. 2, p. 367. "The former of these epithets applies to the supreme principle which the mind seeks to approach, but which it does not reach; the latter to an abundance of ramifications and of details in execution which the understanding cannot follow to the end. These epithets are often quoted with the view of demonstrating the incomprehensibility to man of the divine decrees, and in particular of that of predestination. . . ."

name great, and you will be a blessing" (Gen. 12:2). But Abraham did not become the father of a great nation in his lifetime. In fact, for years he and his wife had no children at all, and it was a source of continual embarrassment to them, particularly in view of God's promise.

Abraham's original name was Abram and it means "father of many." But Abram went through most of his life with no children. It was only when he was a hundred years old and Sarah was ninety years old, that is, when both were past the age at which they might expect to have children, that God intervened and caused Isaac, the son of the promise, to be born.

What was God thinking of? Why the long delay? Why didn't the birth take place sooner and naturally? There is no easy answer. All we can say is that the paths of God are beyond our tracing out.

2. *Moses.* The great emancipator and lawgiver of Israel is my next example. Moses must have understood that God's hand was upon him and that it was time for the deliverance of the people from Egypt, which God had promised many years before (cf. Gen. 15:12–16). But when he started what he thought would be a successful rebellion by killing an Egyptian, the plan backfired and he had to flee Egypt. Moses was forty years old when he left Egypt, and for the next forty years this talented and highly educated man lived on the backside of the desert, working as a shepherd. He must have believed that his life was an utter failure.

At the end of this time, when he was eighty years old, God sent him to Egypt with the command to Pharaoh, "Let my people go." When they were set free, Moses led the people in the wilderness for an additional forty years. Forty years! And what of the earlier eighty years? How wasted they seemed to be! In this case, too, God's decrees were unsearchable, and his paths beyond tracing out!

3. *Israel.* What about God's dealings with Israel, especially during those wilderness years? J. I. Packer writes, "God guided Israel by means of a fiery cloudy pillar that went before them (Exod. 13:21f.); yet the way which he led them involved the nerve-shredding cliff-hanger of the Red Sea crossing, long days without water and meat in 'that great and terrible wilderness' (Deut. 1:19, cf. 31–33), and bloody battles with Amalek, Sihon and Og (Exod. 17:8–13; Numb. 21:21ff.), and we can understand, if not excuse, Israel's constant grumbling (cf. Exod. 14:10ff., 16:3, Numb. 11:4ff., 14:3ff., 20:3ff., 21:4ff.)."[3]

Wasn't there an easier way to do it? What was the point of the many battles, delays, and deprivations? If there was a purpose to this history, surely it is unsearchable to our limited understanding.

4. *David.* I think, too, of David, Israel's great king. God had rejected Saul, David's predecessor, and had sent the prophet Samuel to anoint David to be

3. J. I. Packer, *Knowing God* (Downers Grove, Ill.: InterVarsity Press, 1973), p. 218.

the next king. But years went by in which David first served Saul and then was chased all over the country by him, since Saul saw David as a rival and wanted to put him to death. David did not become king until after Saul's death, when he was thirty-three years old. And even then he did not become king over the entire country. He was king only in Hebron, that is, over the southern territories, where he reigned seven years. He did not become king of the entire land until he was forty.

Whatever could God have had in mind by allowing Saul to reign so long, particularly when a man of David's exceptional character and leadership ability was waiting patiently in the wings? Surely God's ways are not our ways, nor are his thoughts our thoughts. His paths are beyond tracing out.

5. *Paul.* Paul is my next example. We have no difficulty with the story of Paul's remarkable conversion. It is a clear example of God's direct and effective intervention in history. It is what we expect God to be doing always. But think of Paul's career after that. First, three years in the wilderness with no apparent accomplishments during that time, as far as we know (Gal. 1:17–18). Then there were years in Tarsus, his hometown. It is not until mid-life that he is called to active missionary work, and even then it is mostly in the hinterlands of Asia Minor. Paul wanted to get to Rome, which he did eventually. But he arrived in Rome as a prisoner, spent most of his time there in chains and eventually died there by Nero's order.

Here is how Paul described his missionary years:

> Five times I received from the Jews the forty lashes minus one. Three times I was beaten with rods, once I was stoned, three times I was shipwrecked, I spent a night and a day in the open sea, I have been constantly on the move. I have been in danger from rivers, in danger from bandits, in danger from my own countrymen, in danger from Gentiles; in danger in the city, in danger in the country, in danger at sea; and in danger from false brothers. I have labored and toiled and have often gone without sleep; I have known hunger and thirst and have often gone without food; I have been cold and naked. Besides everything else, I face daily the pressure of my concern for all the churches.
>
> 2 Corinthians 11:24–28

"Troubles, hardships and distresses . . . beatings, imprisonments and riots . . . hard work, sleepless nights and hunger" (2 Cor. 6:4–5). Why should that be? Why should the work be so hard? Couldn't God have worked out some of those problems so that Paul would not have had to be beaten, not have had to go hungry, and would have escaped the three shipwrecks and the other dangers? Couldn't God have lessened the burden of Paul's concern for the churches entrusted to him? Or didn't God care?

No, we must not say that. We know that God cares. Yet why should God be planting his steps in history in that precise way? Surely his judgments are unsearchable to us and his paths beyond tracing out.

6. *Jesus.* My last example is Jesus. No individual in all history more evidently had the hand of God upon him. God said of him, "This is my Son, whom I love; with him I am well pleased" (Matt. 3:17). But what a life! J. I. Packer writes:

> No human life has ever been so completely guided by God, and no human life has ever qualified so comprehensively for the description "a man of sorrows." Divine guidance set Jesus at a distance from his family and fellow-townsmen, brought him into conflict with all the nation's leaders, religious and civil, and led finally to betrayal, arrest, and the cross. . . .
>
> By every human standard of reckoning, the cross was a *waste*—the waste of a young life, a prophet's influence, a leader's potential. We know the secret of its meaning and achievement only from God's own statements.[4]

Ah, but we *do* know its meaning and achievement from God's statements. That is, we know that the most miserable of lives was actually the greatest of God's achievements. It was the means by which God accomplished the salvation of our lost race. That "waste," that loss, that suffering, was actually the focal point of history and the highest of achievements. And because we know that, we know that each of the other stories, including our own, is also part of a plan that—though beyond our complete tracing out—is nevertheless a sure and perfect plan, which will have a grand and blessed consummation.

A Crown Beyond the Cross

I am sure you see what I am getting at by this rehearsal of the biblical history. At least I am sure you saw it by the time I reviewed the life of Jesus. Each of these stories involves the incomprehensible. From the perspective of our own wisdom, each is utterly inexplicable. Yet each was part of God's perfect plan. Though beyond our ability to trace out, each was also part of God's unfolding march through history.

Why was the birth of Abraham's son Isaac so long delayed? Abraham could hardly have known the answer, except perhaps dimly and by revelation. But we look back and by that revelation can see how Isaac was a type of Jesus Christ. And we can see how Abraham's steadfast faith in the God who was able to do miracles becomes a model for our faith and an encouragement when we are called to go through difficult times.

Why did Moses have to spend so many years in the wilderness? Why did Israel have such a difficult journey? Why was David's reign so long delayed? As we read these stories, we can see that in each case God was developing character in his people, and that he was showing himself to be more than adequate to their every human need.

As for Paul, he said, "[These things] happened that we might not rely on ourselves but on God, who raises the dead" (2 Cor. 1:9), and "we have this treasure [the gospel] in jars of clay to show that this all-surpassing power is

4. Ibid.

from God and not from us" (2 Cor. 4:7). He added, "Therefore we do not lose heart. Though outwardly we are wasting away, yet inwardly we are being renewed day by day. For our light and momentary troubles are achieving for us an eternal glory that far outweighs them all. So we fix our eyes not on what is seen, but on what is unseen. For what is seen is temporary, but what is unseen is eternal" (2 Cor. 4:16–18).

"Therefore we do not lose heart."

Perhaps you are one who has been losing heart. You began the Christian life with confidence some years ago, but the details of your life have not worked out as you expected. As far as you can tell, you have not become a great saint. You are no great model of what it is to be a prayer warrior, neither have you been terribly effective as an evangelist. Even your personal relationships have not gone as smoothly or as triumphantly as you had hoped. And much of your work, even your Christian work, seems wasted. Don't lose heart! God knows what he is doing with your life. You cannot search out his eternal decrees or judgments or perceive the end of the path on which he has been leading you, but this does not mean that God is confused, the outcome doubtful, or the final achievement vague. Fix your eyes on what is not seen—on God. Trust him and go on.

"Outwardly we are wasting away."

That is literally true for some. Perhaps cancer or some other debilitating disease has invaded your body, and you suspect that you do not have a very long time to live. "What a waste," you are saying. "Why can't I be strong and healthy and live a long, long life?" I do not know the answer to that. What God does with us in detail is not revealed in Scripture. It is one of the secret things that belong to God only. But that does not mean the painful path he calls you to walk has no purpose. It is how you conduct yourself in such "wasting times" that is the stuff of victory.

Set an example for us by lifting your eyes from what is material and tangible and passing away, and point us to him who is invisible and who does everything well. Show us how light and momentary these earthly troubles are. We need to know that. Show us how they are achieving for us an eternal glory that far outweighs them all.

There is a hymn by the English writer W. H. Burleigh that we do not sing much because it is not in most of our hymnbooks. It is one of my favorite hymns. I learned it from that remarkable original hymnbook prepared by InterVarsity. It goes like this.

> Still will we trust, though earth seem dark and dreary,
> And the heart faints beneath his chast'ning rod;
> Though rough and steep our pathway, worn and weary,
>   Still will we trust in God.
>
> Our eyes see dimly 'til by faith anointed,
> And our blind choosing brings us grief and pain;

> Through him alone, who hath our way appointed,
>> We find our peace again.
>
> Choose for us, God, nor let our weak preferring
> Cheat us of good thou hast for us designed;
> Choose for us, God; thy wisdom is unerring,
>> And we are fools and blind.
>
> Let us press on, in patient self-denial,
> Accept the hardship, shrink not from the loss;
> Our portion lies beyond the hour of trial,
>> Our crown beyond the cross.

That is it exactly, isn't it? We have a crown laid up for us in heaven, just as Paul had a crown of righteousness "in store" for him (2 Tim. 4:8). But it is not on this side of suffering. It is beyond it. It is beyond the sickness, beyond the disappointments, beyond the pain. It is beyond the cross.

176

The Inscrutable God

Romans 11:34

Who has known the mind of the Lord?
Or who has been his counselor?

Wiliam Beebe (1877–1962) was a biologist, explorer, and author, and he was also a personal friend of Theodore Roosevelt (1858–1919), the twenty-sixth president of the United States. He used to visit Roosevelt at Sagamore Hill, his home near Oyster Bay, Long Island, and he tells of a little game they used to play together. After an evening of talk, they would go outside onto the lawn surrounding the great house and search the sky until they found the faint spot of light beyond the lower left corner of the great square of Pegasus. One of them would recite: "That is the Spiral Galaxy in Andromeda. It is as large as the Milky Way. It is one of a hundred million galaxies. It consists of one hundred billion suns, each larger than our sun."

Then Roosevelt would grin at Beebe and say, "Now I think we are small enough! Let's go to bed."

Our Smallness before God

I think of that story as we come to the last thoughts of Romans 11, following the apostle Paul's exclamation of wonder at the unsearchable depths of the riches of the wisdom, knowledge, judgments, and paths of God in verse 33. He is still thinking of God and marveling at God. But Paul's glance shifts, as it were, to the man who is doing the thinking and marveling, and he makes a contrast between God's unsearchable grandeur, on the one hand, and the poverty of man's small knowledge, on the other. In verse 34 he queries, "Who has known the mind of the Lord? Or who has been his counselor?" In verse 35 he adds, "Who has ever given to God, that God should repay him?"

Each of these verses is a quotation from the Old Testament, which reminds us that this is Paul's characteristic way of wrapping up an argument. We have already seen several examples of this in the letter, Romans 3:10–18, for example. Those verses contain Old Testament quotations that summarize Paul's arguments for the depravity of the race developed in chapters 1–3. We have the same thing in chapters 4, 9, 10, and earlier in chapter 11. To give a contrary example, the apostle Peter argued by *beginning* with the text, then providing what we would call an exposition (cf. Acts 2).

The quotation we are looking at in this study is from Isaiah 40:13, but it may have elements of several other passages (cf. Job 15:8; Jer. 23:18).

"Who has known the mind of the Lord? Or who has been his counselor?" Although drawn mostly from Isaiah, this was essentially the question put to Job when God interrogated him toward the end of that great Old Testament story. The bottom line is that no human being, however wise, has anything to offer to God in the matters of his knowledge and wisdom. The question fits Paul's context beautifully, for it links up with his earlier reference to "wisdom" and "knowledge" in verse 33, though in reverse order. As F. Godet observed, "The first question contrasts the always limited knowledge of man with the infinite *knowledge* of God. . . . The second goes further, it bears on the relation between human and divine *wisdom*. It is no longer merely the *discovery* of the secrets of God by the study of his works which is in question, but some *good counsel* which man might have been called to give to the Creator in the organizing of his plans."[1]

As I say, Paul is still thinking about God in this verse. But here he also turns our attention from God's attributes—the perfection of his wisdom, knowledge, judgments, and ways—to our limitations as measured by them. He tells us once again that we are not like God.

Isn't it interesting that Paul should have to do this, especially now, at this point in our studies of Romans 11? You may recall the distinction I made earlier between God's incommunicable attributes, those he does not share with us because he cannot, and God's communicable attributes, which he

---

1. F. Godet, *Commentary on St. Paul's Epistle to the Romans*, trans. A. Cusin (Edinburgh: T. & T. Clark, 1892), p. 268.

does share with us. The latter category contains such attributes as we have been studying here: knowledge, wisdom, the ability to make plans and decisions, and the capacity to act. We understand what we are talking about when we say that God has these attributes or possesses these abilities, because we have them ourselves. We, too, know things, possess a measure of wisdom, make decisions or plans, and act on them.

But even in this area we do not measure up to God. In fact, our knowledge, wisdom, planning, and acting are so far from his knowledge, wisdom, planning, and acting that it is even less than the equivalent of comparing ourselves to the billions of suns in the great galaxy of Andromeda or to the many other galaxies. To put it another way, the only things we know, we know because God has known them first and has revealed them to us. Because we are so small, the knowledge we have is itself also pitifully small. Or to put it still another way, we have nothing to contribute to God in any area.

How Little We Know

The way we need to explore this is to look at that part of the biblical writings known as "wisdom literature," particularly Job, Ecclesiastes, and Proverbs. I begin with Job, because that book deals directly with the extreme limitations of our knowledge.

We know Job's story. It is one of the great stories of all time. Job was a fortunate individual in many ways. He was wealthy; he had a wonderful family; he enjoyed good health. Moreover, he was a godly man. Even God called attention to Job's character: "Have you considered my servant Job? There is no one on earth like him; he is blameless and upright, a man who fears God and shuns evil" (Job. 1:8). But within a very short time everything Job had was taken away from him, except his character. His goods were plundered or destroyed; his ten children were killed; and he was afflicted with painful sores that covered him from the soles of his feet to his scalp. He was reduced to abject and utter misery. He sat in ashes, suffering both within (in his soul) and without (in his body).

At this point Job's three close friends, Eliphaz the Temanite, Bildad the Shuhite, and Zophar the Naamathite, came to him to sympathize and offer counsel. The bulk of the book consists of their attempts to explain what had happened, followed by Job's responses to their words.

To put it in our terms, what they were trying to explain is "why bad things happen to good people." And by our standards they did pretty well at it. They rightly assumed that this is a moral universe of cause-and-effect events and that God, who has created the universe and who guides its destiny, is a moral God. Everything has a purpose, they argued, and because this purpose is God's purpose, it must be good. Evil does not triumph. Virtue is rewarded. All this is entirely right, of course. In fact, if you were reading carefully, you will have recognized that these are the exact points I was making when I was speaking about the wisdom, decrees, and paths of God in the preceding studies.

What, then, was wrong with the counsel of Job's friends? And why was God so unhappy with them?—as he reveals himself to be later ("Who is this that darkens my counsel with words without knowledge?" [Job 38:2]).

The problem was not with their starting point or principles, for they were the very things that are revealed about the nature of reality in Scripture. Instead the problem was that these men, wise as they were, lacked sufficient knowledge to discern what God was doing. As the story points out at the beginning, God was waging war against the slanders and lies of Satan. Satan claimed that Job served God only because of what he got out of it, a standard utilitarian argument. God maintained that Job loved God because of who God was, regardless of what it might bring to him personally. Satan said, "Does Job fear God for nothing? . . . Have you not put a hedge around him and his household and everything he has? You have blessed the work of his hands, so that his flocks and herds are spread throughout the land. But stretch out your hand and strike everything he has, and he will surely curse you to your face" (Job. 1:9–11).

God allowed Satan to strike at Job's possessions and family, but though Job was personally crushed by these disasters, Job worshiped God, saying,

> Naked I came from my mother's womb,
>   and naked I will depart.
> The LORD gave and the LORD has taken away;
>   may the name of the LORD be praised.

> Job 1:21

Next Satan wanted to strike at Job's health. "Stretch out your hand and strike his flesh and bones, and he will surely curse you to your face," Satan said to God (Job 2:5). But when God allowed Satan to be the instrument of devastating physical affliction for Job, Job said to his wife, "Shall we accept good from God, and not trouble?"—and the text points out that "in all this Job did not sin in what he said" (v. 10).

Job's friends knew none of this, of course. They had not the faintest idea of what was going on at the cosmic level. Therefore, although they had begun at the right starting place and had the right principles, what they actually had to say to Job turned out to be mere nonsense, which is why God rebuked them.

Moreover, notice the nature of God's rebuke. Their problem was that they were not aware of the invisible, cosmic nature of this struggle. But when God rebuked them (and Job, too) for their ignorance, he rebuked them not because they did not know the invisible dimensions of the struggle—what was going on between himself and Satan—but because they did not understand or know even the things they could see. God chided them for being unable to explain the origins of the earth ("Where were you when I laid the earth's foundation?" [Job. 38:4]). Scientists are not much closer to explaining that today. He chided them for being unable to explain or control the sea ("Who shut up the sea behind doors when it burst forth from the womb?" [v. 8]). Today, with all our scientific advances we cannot even predict the movement of the sea's storms accurately, let alone control either it or them. Chapter after chapter, God chides Job and his friends for their profound and extensive ignorance of all natural forces—light and darkness; rain, snow, wind; the intricacies of the heavens; animal instincts and behavior; the migration patterns of birds and fish; and countless other observable phenomena.

But here is the point: If these people could not explain what they could see, how could they hope to understand and explain what they could not see? Obviously, not at all. They could not contribute to God's perfect knowledge in any respect. The only thing they could possibly do is what Job does at the end of the story—he shuts his mouth and admits his utter ignorance:

> Then Job replied to the Lord:
>
> > "I know that you can do all things;
> > > no plan of yours can be thwarted.
> > You asked, 'Who is this that obscures my counsel
> > > without knowledge?'
> > > Surely I spoke of things I did not understand,
> > > things too wonderful for me to know.
> >
> > You said, 'Listen now, and I will speak;
> > > I will question you,
> > > and you shall answer me.'
> > My ears had heard of you
> > > but now my eyes have seen you.
> > Therefore I despise myself
> > > and repent in dust and ashes.'"
>
> Job 42:1–6

I have previously described the effect of our thinking about God and his "eternal decree" as (1) humility at our incomprehension and (2) awe before God and praise of him. We find both responses in Job's final words, as well as in the closing section of Romans 11.

Fools, and Blind

The second half of verse 34 goes an important step beyond what I have been describing up to this point. I have been writing about our extreme lack of knowledge, which is what "Who has known the mind of the Lord?" refers to. But the next words are also significant, for they add, "Or who has been his counselor?" This part deals with wisdom and how little of it we possess.

I turn here to the Book of Ecclesiastes. This is a short book; it has only twelve chapters. Yet Ecclesiastes is a high point of the wisdom literature in the sense that it shows the limits of man's earthbound wisdom, just as Job shows the limits of man's knowledge. Ecclesiastes is essentially a sermon on one text: "'Meaningless! Meaningless!' says the Teacher. / 'Utterly meaningless! Everything is meaningless'" (Eccles. 1:2). As anyone can tell just by looking at the subheads in the New International Version, the preacher develops the text to make these points: (1) wisdom is meaningless; (2) pleasures are meaningless; (3) wisdom and folly are meaningless; (4) toil is meaningless; (5) advancement is meaningless; and (6) riches are meaningless.

But surely we don't believe that, do we?

Haven't we been saying that God is sovereign over the affairs of his creation, that he has a single supreme purpose in all he does, and that this purpose is a good purpose because he is a good God? Of course, we have. Then how are we to understand Ecclesiastes? Is this merely the last words of an embittered cynic, which we can completely discount? Some Christian leaders have taught that. One of them once told me, "You can never preach a sermon from Ecclesiastes."

We know that is not correct, because "All Scripture is God-breathed and is useful . . ." (2 Tim. 3:16). But how, then, is Ecclesiastes to be taken?

The answer is that this book shows us the limits and hence the folly of human wisdom apart from revelation. Here is the way J. I. Packer, who has done several helpful studies of Ecclesiastes, puts it:

> Look (says the preacher) at the sort of world we live in. Take off your rose-colored spectacles, rub your eyes, and look at it long and hard. What do you see? You see life's background set by aimlessly recurring cycles in nature (1:4ff.). You see its shape fixed by times and circumstances over which we have no control (3:1ff.; 9:11f.). You see death coming to everyone sooner or later, but coming haphazard; its coming bears no relation to good or ill desert (7:15; 8:8). Men die like beasts (3:19f.), good men like bad, wise men like fools (2:14, 17; 9:2f.). You see evil running rampant (3:16; 4:1; 5:8; 8:11; 9:3); rotters get on, good men don't (8:14). Seeing all this, you realize that God's ordering of events is inscrutable; much as you want to make it out, you cannot do so (3:11; 7:13f.; 8:17 RV; 11:5). The harder you try to understand the divine purpose in the ordinary providential course of events, the more obsessed and oppressed you grow with the apparent aimlessness of everything, and the more you are tempted to conclude that life really is as pointless as it looks.
>
> But once you conclude that there really is no rhyme or reason in things, what "profit"—value, gain, point, purpose—can you find henceforth in any sort of constructive endeavor (1:3; 2:11, 22; 3:9; 5:16)? If life is senseless, then it is valueless; and in that case, what use is it working to create things, to build a business, to make money, even to seek wisdom—for none of this can do you any obvious good (2:15f., 22f.; 5:11); it will only make you an object of envy (4:4); you can't take any of it with you (2:18ff.; 4:8; 5:15f.); and what you leave behind will probably be mismanaged after you have gone (2:19). What point

is there, then, in sweating and toiling at anything? Must not all man's work be judged "vanity (emptiness, frustration) and a striving after wind" (1:14 RV)?[2]

That is true, isn't it? Apart from what God is doing in Jesus Christ and in our lives, the last part of which is at best only partially revealed to us, everything is indeed "meaningless." There is more, of course. There *is* what God is doing, what he reveals. But before we can see those things, we need to see that there is no meaning in anything apart from them. One of the great proofs of our lack of wisdom is that we do not see even this fundamental point of earthly wisdom clearly.

Even Christians don't. Otherwise, why would they spend so much of their time and energy working for things that do not satisfy at any significant level and, in fact, will never do so?

Why do they spend their time acquiring houses and cars and television sets and fine furniture, which will eventually depreciate and decay?

Why do they work for increasingly larger paychecks and bank accounts, which they will not be able to take with them to heaven when they die?

Why do they yearn for earthly recognition, which can vanish in a flash?

Why do we do these things? We do them because we have not learned even the rudimentary earthly wisdom of the Book of Ecclesiastes, let alone the infinitely more profound wisdom of the revealed counsels of God. Yet we presume to suppose that we can criticize God for what he is doing in our lives. We think that we could tell him how to do things better, if we only had the chance. What folly! What utter folly! We who think we are teachers need to learn again the first principles of the oracles of God.

Paul asks the Corinthians, "Where is the wise man? Where is the scholar? Where is the philosopher of this age? Has not God made foolish the wisdom of the world?" (1 Cor. 1:20). We need to learn that again. We need to hear again Paul's implied rebuke as he wisely asks the Romans "'Who has known the mind of the Lord? Or who has been his counselor?'"

The answer clearly is "no one." Not you, not me. No one. Not one of us can contribute to the knowledge or wisdom of God in any respect.

Humility and Wisdom

So where does this leave us? Obviously, it is not intended to leave us in our folly. We are not called upon to be either ignorant or foolish. On the contrary, we are to trust God, work to develop our minds, and grow in true spiritual wisdom and understanding. How? Let me suggest these points.

1. *Learn that there is no true wisdom except in God.* That is why Proverbs 9:10 says rightly, "The fear of the LORD is the beginning of wisdom, / and knowledge of the Holy One is understanding." We can know because God is a God

2. J. I. Packer, *Knowing God* (Downers Grove, Ill.: InterVarsity Press, 1973), pp. 94, 95.

who knows, and we can acquire wisdom because God is a God of wisdom. But we will achieve neither unless we begin with him.

2. *Learn that even though you begin with God, you will never fully understand God and therefore you will never fully understand his ways.* God says, "My thoughts are not your thoughts, / neither are your ways my ways" (Isa. 55:8). Moreover, since God's thoughts direct God's actions, clearly it will be his ways rather than yours that will be accomplished, for "Many are the plans in a man's heart, / but it is the LORD's purpose that prevails" (Prov. 19:21).

3. *Finally, learn to trust God and follow hard after him.* This leads me to the wisest saying of all: "Trust in the LORD with all your heart and lean not on your own understanding; / in all your ways acknowledge him, and he will make your paths straight" (Prov. 3:5–6). If you do not do that, your pitifully small knowledge and faulty wisdom will lead you eventually either to arrogance or despair. But if you acknowledge your ignorance and foolishness and learn to trust God, you will find that God will provide all the knowledge you need—you will find it in Scripture—and if you ask him, he will give abundant wisdom, too (James 1:5).

177

The All-Sufficient God

Romans 11:35

Who has ever given to God,
that God should repay him?

One thing most people think about preachers is that they love to take offerings, and I suppose they do, especially if the offerings are for some great cause and the response is generous. I have been part of a few such offerings. My most common examples are the "Easter Sacrificial Offerings" of Tenth Presbyterian Church, which we receive each year for some area of special social need throughout the world. The giving is always generous.

But there was never an offering like the one I am going to discuss now. Israel's great King David was coming to the end of his reign, and his young son Solomon was being left behind to rule the kingdom and build a magnificent temple in Jerusalem. The temple had been David's great dream, what he hoped to leave behind as the capstone of his reign. But God had told David that the task would not be his because he was a man of war and that the temple would be built by Solomon instead. So David contented himself with making preparations for the temple's construction, collecting all the gold, silver, bronze, iron, and precious stones that would be needed.

To do that he took an offering. For his personal share he gave 3,000 talents of gold and 7,000 talents of silver. That converts to 110 metric tons of gold and 260 metric tons of silver. Then the leading families of the nation gave gifts, too. They gave 5,000 talents of gold, 10,000 talents of silver, 18,000 talents of bronze, and 100,000 talents of iron, plus many of the precious stones in their possession. It is difficult to convert these amounts into dollars, and scholars differ on what today's equivalents would be, but the amounts add up to hundreds of millions of dollars at least. So it really was an enormous offering, perhaps the greatest single offering that has ever been taken for a religious work by anyone in any period of history.

For many, the success of a campaign like this would be a cause for self-congratulation. But not for David! Instead of congratulating either himself or the people, David praised God, acknowledging that it was because of him that the people had been able to give as they had given. His prayer of dedication said,

> Praise be to you, O LORD,
>   God of our father Israel,
>   from everlasting to everlasting.
> Yours, O LORD, is the greatness and the power
>   and the glory and the majesty and the splendor,
>   for everything in heaven and earth is yours.
> Yours, O LORD, is the kingdom;
>   you are exalted as head over all.
> Wealth and honor come from you;
>   you are the ruler of all things.
> In your hands are strength and power
>   to exalt and give strength to all.
> Now, our God, we give you thanks,
>   and praise your glorious name.
>
>   1 Chronicles 29:10–13

David continued wisely, "But who am I, and who are my people, that we should be able to give as generously as this? Everything comes from you, and we have given you only what comes from your hand" (v. 14).

This was a very important acknowledgement, meaning, to put it in slightly different language, "The people have given generously, but we have been able to do so only by your grace and by returning to you what you have first seen fit to give us."

Three Rhetorical Questions

I begin our study of Romans 11:35 by referring to this, because the manner in which David responded to the generous offerings of the people for building the Jerusalem temple brilliantly illustrates our text. In this section of

Romans 11, Paul has been praising God for his infinite superiority to his creatures in all areas, and he has made these contrasts graphic by three rhetorical
questions, each of which implies a negative answer.

Question number one: "Who has known the mind of the Lord?" (v. 34a).

Answer: No one! None of us even begins to come close to knowing what
God knows. His knowledge is infinitely beyond ours.

Question number two: "Who has been his counselor?" (v. 34b).

Again, the answer is: No one! No one can possibly advise God so that he
can do the job of governing the world better or more efficiently.

This brings us to question number three, the text for this study: "Who has
ever given to God, that God should repay him?" (v. 35).

Again, the answer is: No one! We may give to God, as the people did when
David appealed to them for offerings for the temple. But what we give is only
what God has first given to us, as David knew and stated. One of our hymns
also states this correctly.

> We give thee but thine own,
> Whate'er the gift may be;
> All that we have is thine alone,
> A trust, O Lord, from thee.

Together these questions remind us of the self-sufficiency, sovereignty, and
independence of God—the attributes of God that Paul has been teaching
us to appreciate—and they show us that we have nothing to contribute. We
have nothing to add either to who God is or to what he does.

And there is this additional point to the third question: We cannot place
God under obligation to ourselves by giving to him. That is so important
that I want to repeat it: *We cannot place God under obligation to ourselves by giving
to him.*

Our Contribution Equals Nothing

That we have nothing to give to God is something Paul has already taught
many times in the earlier parts of this letter. So we should understand it very
well by now. Let me review his teaching briefly.

1. *We are justified by grace apart from human works.* This is the point of the
first four chapters of the letter, in which Paul explains the depth of human
depravity and impotence and shows how God has reached out to save us in
Jesus Christ completely apart from anything in us. In our sin we imagine that
God can be won over by some good work in us, grading us on the curve and
saving us on the basis of some passing moral mark, as it were. Indeed, even
after they have become Christians, there are people who suppose that they
were saved because, although no one can be saved by works, they were nevertheless singled out by God because of something that was found in
them—some aptitude for God, perhaps, or just faith.

Romans teaches that we are saved by none of these things, not even by faith. True, we are saved *through* faith. No one is saved without it. But even faith is God's gift, so that there will be no boasting on the day when the redeemed of the Lord stand before him. We do not contribute to our justification in any way.

2. *We are sanctified by the Holy Spirit apart from works.* This is the point of the second main section of Romans, chapters 5 through 8. It means that just as we have nothing to contribute to our justification, so also do we have nothing to contribute to our sanctification. It is true that there are things we are to do because we have been saved and that we will do them if we truly are. But that does not mean that we give anything to God in this area. What we do is a response to what he has already done. It is because God has taken us out of Adam and placed us in Christ, giving us a new nature that possesses new desires, that we therefore follow after Jesus and grow in the grace God freely supplies.

In fact, when Paul gets to the end of this section, in Romans 8, and reflects on the certainty of our persevering in faith, he is thinking not of anything in us, but of God and what he has done for us. This is why we read, "And we know that in all things *God works* for the good of those who love him, who have been called according to his purpose. For those God foreknew he also predestined to be conformed to the likeness of his Son, that he might be the firstborn among many brothers. And those he predestined, he also called; those he called, he also justified; those he justified, he also glorified" (Rom. 8:28–30, emphasis added).

The next verses tell us that God is for us (v. 31), that he gave his Son for us (v. 32), that he will give us all things (v. 32), that he has justified us (v. 33), that Jesus is interceding for us (v. 34), and that nothing will ever separate us from the love of God that is in Christ Jesus (vv. 35–39). It is all of God from the beginning to the end.

3. *We are chosen apart from works.* The third section of Romans, chapters 9 through 11, teaches that what God is doing in history does not depend on us either, not even in the sense that God is primarily obliged to make us happy. On the contrary, Paul teaches that history unfolds to reveal God's attributes—his love and grace, of course, but also such things as his power, justice, and wrath—and to manifest his glory.

What a transformation that would mean for most of today's Christians, if they could only see it. I have a good friend named Mike Horton, who has written about this well in a book entitled *Made in America: The Shaping of Modern American Evangelicalism.* He says:

> The older theology tended to produce character. . . . By the end of the twentieth century, we have become God's demanding little brats. In church, we must be entertained. Our emotions must be charged. . . . We must be offered amusing

programs—we gave up a lot to become Christians and what little teaching we do get must cater to our pragmatic, self-centered interests. The preaching must be filled with clever anecdotes and colorful illustrations, with nothing more than passing references to doctrine: "I want to know what this means for me and my daily experience!"

We have forgotten that God is a monarch. He is the King by whom and for whom all things were made, and by whose sovereign power they are sustained. We exist for his pleasure, not he for ours; we are on this earth to entertain him, please him, to adore him, to bring him satisfaction, excitement and joy. Any gospel which seeks to answer the question, "What's in it for me?" has it all backwards. The question is, "What's in it for God?"[1]

Of course, that brings us back to our text, where Paul asks, "Who has ever given to God, that God should repay him?" None of us has. Therefore, God is in debt to no one to do what he or she desires.

We Cannot Put God in Debt

Yet we continue to think like this, often even after we have become Christians, even after we have received the kind of teaching we have studied so carefully in Romans. Think with me how we suppose we put God in our debt.

1. *We do so when we think we have caught God in some fault.* Most would not put it this way. But every time we are critical of God or complain to God about something, we are telling him indirectly, and sometimes quite directly, that we believe he has made a mistake and should correct it.

"I think he made me too short. I should be taller."

"Life would be better for me if I were only better-looking."

"God has me stuck in a dead-end job, when I could be accomplishing something important. He should have given me opportunities I did not have or promotions that were given to someone else."

"He made a mistake not giving me a husband."

Or ". . . giving me the one I have."

Whenever we find ourselves thinking along these lines, what we are doing is supplying God with what we suppose is the knowledge or wisdom he lacks and saying that he should acknowledge his mistake and thank us for straightening him out. Moreover, we believe that he is now indebted to us for supplying that particular bit of wisdom and should reciprocate accordingly. Isn't it true that you have often thought like that? Isn't it foolish?

Remember our text the next time you find yourself slipping into such a moronic thought pattern. "Who has ever given to God, that God should repay him?" Job experienced terrible tragedies, but he said, "Surely I spoke of things I did not understand" (Job 42:3).

---

1. Michael Scott Horton, *Made in America: The Shaping of Modern American Evangelicalism* (Grand Rapids: Baker Book House, 1991), pp. 87, 88.

2. *We do so when we think we have caught God in an injustice.* This mistake is closely related to what I just said, but it is a step further along the sad path of human pride and rebellion. The key to this erroneous line of thought is finding ourselves saying that what God is doing is not *right*.

"It's not right that I should be sick when my friends are all well."

"It's not right that she should have gotten the prize rather than myself. I worked harder for it."

"It is not right for God to let me go on like this without answering my prayers as I would like or doing what I have repeatedly asked him to do."

I am sure you get the idea.

When we find ourselves thinking like this, we must remember how Abraham pleaded to God for the cities of Sodom and Gomorrah. He knew that his nephew Lot had gone to live in those cities and that, if God destroyed them, his nephew and his family would also be destroyed. So Abraham pleaded, "Will you sweep away the righteous with the wicked? What if there are fifty righteous people in the city? Will you really sweep it away and not spare the place for the sake of the fifty righteous people in it? Far be it from you to do such a thing—to kill the righteous with the wicked, treating the righteous and the wicked alike. Far be it from you! Will not the Judge of all the earth do right?" (Gen. 18:23–25).

It was basically a good argument, for the Judge of all the earth must do right. The trouble with it is that there were none righteous. So although God did spare Lot and his wife from destruction, the destruction nevertheless did come. The cities were blotted out and their inhabitants were killed. You cannot put God in your debt by crying, "Justice!" Justice condemns! Justice sends people to hell! It is not justice we need from God. It is grace, and grace is the very opposite of debt.

If you think God owes you justice, remember our text: "Who has ever given to God, that God should repay him?" The only thing we have ever earned from God is condemnation.

3. *We do so when we think we have obligated God by some service.* This is a third way Christians sometimes think they have placed God in their debt. They suppose that they have earned credits with him by some acts of self-sacrifice or service. One of my favorite stories along this line was told by R. A. Torrey. He was in Melbourne, Australia, and one afternoon at a meeting for businessmen a note was handed to him. It said,

> Dear Dr. Torrey:
>   I am in great perplexity. I have been praying for a long time for something that I am confident is according to God's will, but I do not get it. I have been a member of the Presbyterian Church for thirty years, and have tried to be a consistent one all that time. I have been Superintendent in the Sunday School for twenty-five years, and an elder in the church for twenty years; and yet God does not answer my prayer and I cannot understand it. Can you explain it to me?

Torrey read the note from the platform and replied, "It is very easy to explain it. This man thinks that because he has been a consistent church member for thirty years, a faithful Sunday School Superintendent for twenty-five years, and an elder in the church for twenty years, that God is under obligation to answer his prayer. He is really praying in his own name, and God will not hear our prayers when we approach him in that way."

After Torrey had finished speaking, a man came up to him and admitted that he had written the note. He said, "You have hit the nail square on the head. I see my mistake."[2]

Many people make that mistake. But even in the area of Christian service we need to see that God cannot be put in our debt by anything you or I do. "Who has ever given to God, that God should repay him?" The answer is: No one, not even the most dedicated, most self-sacrificing, most consistent, most devout, most exemplary Christian. Nothing flows to us from God because of debt. A great deal comes to us, but it is all of grace, and grace is a different category entirely.

Living by Grace

So let's talk about grace again. As soon as we abandon any thought of bringing God down to our level so he becomes answerable to our ideas of what is wise or just, and when we give up thoughts of earning anything from him by our service, we are ready to live the Christian life as he has planned it for us and can discover what living by grace is.

It starts with humility, as we have seen several times already in these studies: humility before God, who is infinitely great, but also humility in terms of our own weak service. We remember that Jesus said, "Suppose one of you had a servant plowing or looking after the sheep. Would he say to the servant when he comes in from the field, 'Come along now and sit down to eat'? Would he not rather say, 'Prepare my supper, get yourself ready and wait on me while I eat and drink; after that you may eat and drink'? Would he thank the servant because he did what he was told to do? So you also, when you have done everything you were told to do, should say, 'We are unworthy servants, we have only done our duty'" (Luke 17:7–10).

We will never get anywhere unless we remember the primary relationships of Creator to creature and Master to servant.

But that is not all that can be said, of course, for we also remember that Jesus told his disciples, "I no longer call you servants, because a servant does not know his master's business. Instead, I have called you friends . . ." (John 15:15). "You are my friends if you do what I command" (v. 14). God owes us nothing. All is of grace. But God, for the sake of his own good pleasure, has rescued us from our sin and has raised us from the status of mere servants

---

2. R. A. Torrey, *The Power of Prayer and the Prayer of Power* (Grand Rapids: Zondervan, 1955), pp. 138, 139.

to being sons and daughters of God, co-workers with Jesus Christ and heirs of all God is and has.

That leads to thanksgiving and also to love for the one who has been so gracious to us.

And one more thing: It leads to service. For although we cannot put God in our debt by our contributions to his knowledge or wisdom or ideas about how things should run or even by our Christian service, as soon as we realize this and understand that we cannot earn God's favor but receive it by grace alone, that truth propels us to service. For what we most want to do when we understand that is to live for God's glory, which is what the start of the next chapter in Romans is about. It is where we will pick up in the next volume of this series: "Therefore, I urge you, brothers, in view of God's mercy, to offer your bodies as living sacrifices, holy and pleasing to God—this is your spiritual act of worship. Do not conform any longer to the pattern of this world, but be transformed by the renewing of your mind. Then you will be able to test and approve what God's will is—his good, pleasing and perfect will" (Rom. 12:1–2).

Let me say it again: God is not obliged to give you anything. Yet he gives you everything, if you will receive it in Christ. The great wonder is that the people who know this, who know they cannot give God anything that he has not first given them, nevertheless give him everything.

178

A Christian World-View

Romans 11:36

For from him and through him and to him are all things.
To him be the glory forever! Amen.

One thing we have a lot of today is buzz words. "Buzz word" is itself a buzz word. But there are also buzz words in psychology (Freudian slip, guilt complex); politics (Reaganomics, sound bytes, a thousand points of light); education (political correctness); computer technology (input, down time); and business (bottom line, bullish or bearish, and market driven). One of my favorites is "paradigm shift." A *paradigm* is a complete model or pattern, originally referring to a list of all the inflectional forms of a verb or noun, showing its complete conjugation or declension. A *paradigm shift* is a total reordering of how one looks at or evaluates something.

If you love someone and then for some reason cease to love that person and begin to hate him or her instead, that is a paradigm shift. If you began as a communist, as the leaders of the Eastern Bloc countries all originally did, and then become a capitalist, that is a paradigm shift of great proportions.

What is the greatest of all paradigm shifts? The greatest paradigm shift is the one that takes place when a person becomes a Christian—or at least that is when it begins to take place. In our unsaved, unregenerate state, everything revolves around ourselves. We are the measure of all things. Everything in the universe is for us and for our glory. When we become Christians, we see that the world and all that is in it is actually from God, is governed by him, and exists for his glory. It is what the last verse of Romans 11 expresses when it says of God, "For from him and through him and to him are all things. To him be the glory forever! Amen."

Let me do something unusual here. Let me give a second introduction to this study. It is in the form of a trivia question: What was the last song recorded by the Beatles before their breakup in the seventies? Answer: "I, Me, Mine." That "last song" is actually the first song as well as the last song of the unregenerate heart. But—in significant and radical contrast—the song of the redeemed is Romans 11:36.

Secular Humanism Is Not New

If we think that the universe revolves around ourselves or that we are the only valid measure of all that is, we are "secular humanists." That is a buzz word, too, of course. It is particularly popular with fundamentalists and television preachers, who speak of secular humanism as if it were the unique and particularly dangerous enemy of our time. But it is not new at all. In fact, it is the ancient, natural inclination of the unsaved mind and heart.

I have always thought that the very best statement of secular humanism is to be found in the Bible, in the Book of Daniel. Nebuchadnezzar was king in Babylon at this time. One day, when he was walking on the roof of his royal palace he looked out over the great capital city of his empire and took unto himself all the glory for its existence. He said—this is the classic statement I referred to—"Is not this the great Babylon I have built as the royal residence, by my mighty power and for the glory of my majesty?" (Dan. 4:30). Nebuchadnezzar was saying that the great city of Babylon and its empire, which he admired (and desired) more than anything else in the world, was *from* him (he "built" it), *through* him ("by my mighty power") and *for* him ("for the glory of my majesty").

God did not look at it that way, of course. So the next paragraph tells how Nebuchadnezzar was judged by God with insanity and was driven away to live with the wild animals, to look like and behave like them. He was insane for seven years, until he came to his senses both mentally and spiritually, which was God's way of saying that secular humanism is a crazy way of looking at the world.

Anyone who thinks he or she is the center of the universe is spiritually insane. A person who thinks like this is out of his or her mind.

The Regenerate Mind

The regenerate mind is a renewed mind, as Paul is going to make clear at the beginning of the next chapter: "Do not conform any longer to the pattern of this world, but be transformed by the renewing of your mind" (Rom.

12:2a). This mind thinks differently about things. But specifically how? What form does a renewed mind take? Or, to express it differently, what is a genuinely Christian world-view?

Here is an initial statement of what is involved, made by A. W. Tozer in a chapter in *The Pursuit of God* called "Restoring the Creator-Creature Relation." Tozer says,

> The moment we make up our minds that we are going on with this determination to exalt God over all we step out of the world's parade. [I think that is a great expression: "out of the world's parade."] We shall find ourselves out of adjustment to the ways of the world, and increasingly so as we make progress in the holy way. We shall acquire a new viewpoint; a new and different psychology will be formed within us; a new power will begin to surprise us by its upsurgings and its outgoings.
>
> Our break with the world will be the direct outcome of our changed relation to God. For the world of fallen men does not honor God. Millions call themselves by his name, it is true, and pay some token respect to him, but a simple test will show how little he is really honored among them. Let the average man be put to the proof on the question of who is *above*, and his true position will be exposed. Let me be forced into making a choice between God and money, between God and men, between God and personal ambition, God and self, God and human love, and God will take second place every time. Those other things will be exalted above. However the man may protest, the proof is in the choices he makes day after day throughout life.
>
> "Be thou exalted" is the language of victorious spiritual experience. It is the little key to unlock the door to great treasures of grace.[1]

A Christian World-View Text

Romans 11:36 is what I call a Christian world-view text. That is, it expresses in classic language this altered understanding of who God is and who we are and what we owe to God.

It is not the only verse in Paul's writings that is along these lines, of course. I think also of 1 Corinthians 8:6 ("Yet for us there is but one God, the Father, from whom all things came and for whom we live; and there is but one Lord, Jesus Christ, through whom all things came and through whom we live") or Ephesians 4:4–6 ("There is . . . one God and Father of all, who is over all and through all and in all") or Colossians 1:16 ("For by him all things were created: things in heaven and on earth, visible and invisible, whether thrones or powers or rulers or authorities; all things were created by him and for him"). Yet Romans 11:36 stands out from these other verses as a particularly succinct statement of the Christian outlook: "For from him and through him and to him are all things. To him be the glory forever! Amen."

1. A. W. Tozer, *The Pursuit of God* (Harrisburg, Pa.: Christian Publications, 1948), pp. 102, 103.

There are two areas in which we specifically need to think through what this means.

1. *God and creation.* We think of the creation first because of the words "all things"—"For from him and through him and to him are *all things.*" "All things" means "all that is," the entire universe. Romans 11:36 teaches that everything in the universe is from God; it has come into existence and is then sustained through God's creative power, and it is for God's glory. John Murray unfolds the meaning of the verse like this: God "is the source of all things in that they have proceeded from him; he is the Creator. He is the agent through whom all things subsist and are directed to their proper end. And he is the last end to whose glory all things will redound."[2]

There was a time when God was alone. In that time before all time, when even space did not exist, God, the great "I AM," existed and was as perfect, glorious, and blessed in his eternal existence as he is now. Before there was a sun, the Triune God—Father, Son, and Holy Spirit—dwelt in light ineffable. Before there was an earth on which to rest it, the throne of God stood firm. If that great God, dwelling in perfect solitude, chose to create anything at all, whether the universe of which we are a part or any other possible universe, it is clear that the conception of it and plans for it must have come from him, since there was no other from whom they could have come.

But it is not only the plan that has come from God. The actualization of the plan was *through* him as well. That is, he is also the Creator and then the Sustainer of the universe. When God set out to create the heavens and earth, he did not call for help, since there were none to help him. He did not even make use of existing matter, for matter itself did not exist. God created everything out of nothing. "In the beginning God created the heavens and the earth" (Gen. 1:1). That means creation *ex nihilo* (out of nothing). It is one of the most profound statements ever written, for it is based on the inescapable assumption that if anything exists, then God, the uncaused First Cause, must exist and be the Creator of it all.

For what were the heavens and earth created? That is, what was the purpose of creation? We think of the universe as being made for us. But since God is a purposeful God and planned the universe for an altogether wise and noble purpose before any of us existed, even in his own mind, it is clear that he could not have taken as his purpose a creature that did not then exist. And that means that his motive must be entirely in himself. Creation must be for his glory.

The text is right when it tells us "to him are all things." And Albert Barnes is right in his *Notes on the New Testament* when he says, "The reason or end for which all things were formed . . . is to promote his honor and glory. . . . It is not to promote his *happiness,* for he was eternally happy; not to *add* anything

---

2. John Murray, *The Epistle to the Romans* (Grand Rapids: Wm. B. Eerdmans, 1968), vol. 2, pp. 107, 108.

to him, for he is infinite; but that he might act as God, and have the honor and praise that is due to God."[3]

This should humble us since, if we understand it, we will understand that even the ability to dispute with God or, for that matter, to deny his existence comes from him. This is a point that got through to that brilliant English professor C. S. Lewis and led in part to his conversion. Lewis wrote, "In the very act of trying to prove that God did not exist—in other words, that the whole of reality was senseless—I found that I was forced to assume that one part of reality—namely my idea of justice—was full of sense. Consequently atheism turns out to be too simple. If the whole universe has no meaning, we should never have found out that it has no meaning: just as, if there were no light in the universe and therefore no creatures with eyes, we should never know it was dark."[4]

We could pursue this at greater length, but it should be clear from what I have said how important Romans 11:36 is, when it teaches that the entire universe is from God, through God, and to God. If you have been thinking differently and come at last to think in this biblical way, it will be a paradigm shift of huge proportions.

2. *God and the gospel.* This is the second area in which we need to think through the meaning of Romans 11:36. Like the first, this is obvious, since it is the gospel of salvation by grace that Paul has been concerned about in this letter, and with this context we cannot miss that the way of salvation is also from God, through God, and for his glory.

It is *from* him, for he has planned it all. Who else could have planned it? No priest. No rabbi. No shaman. No guru. Only God could have planned a way of salvation that meets the austere requirements of his unyielding justice and yet also justifies sinners. Only God could have planned a salvation that is apart from human merit or good works—it is all of grace—and yet be able to transform those who are saved so they achieve a level of righteousness and produce good works that surpass the righteousness and good works of those who are trying to be saved by them.

Even the timing of salvation is of God. He ordained the precise moment in history when the Savior should be born in Bethlehem (Gal. 4:4). He planned the moments of his appearance to the people, his identification by John the Baptist, his years of teaching and healing, his betrayal, trial, and crucifixion. And God ordained the precise time of the resurrection and of Jesus' ascension into heaven.

The accomplishment of our salvation was *through* him, that is, through what Jesus Christ has done. Salvation is not achieved through anything you or I have done or can do. We can do nothing. Jesus did it all. We rightly sing:

---

3. Albert Barnes, *Notes on the New Testament,* vol. 10, *Acts and Romans,* ed. Robert Frew (Grand Rapids: Baker Book House, 1983), pp. 260, 261. Original edition 1884–1885.

4. C. S. Lewis, *Mere Christianity* (New York: The MacMillan Company, 1958), p. 42.

There was no other good enough
To pay the price of sin;
He only could unlock the gate
Of heaven and let us in.

Moreover, that plan of salvation is *to* his glory. To be sure, it also achieves an eternity of blessing for those who are redeemed. We benefit greatly and will praise God forever, thanking him for what he has done for us. But if you understand what Paul has been writing about in Romans 9–11, you will know that our happiness is not God's chief purpose in ordering the plan of salvation as he has. All you have to ask is: "Why are some chosen to be saved while others are passed over? Why are some brought to faith while others are rejected?" The answer is that salvation is for God's glory and that God is glorified in each case. In the case of the elect, the love, mercy, and grace of God are abundantly displayed. In the case of the lost, the patience, power, and wrath of God are equally lifted up.

Give God the Glory

The final thing I want to accomplish in this study is to make Romans 11:36 very personal for you. For it is obvious that if the entire creation is "from him and through him and to him" and if the way of salvation is likewise "from him and through him and to him," then you, as a part of that creation (especially if you are a part of that redeemed creation), are "from him and through him and to him" as well. You also exist for his glory and should give it to him.

Let me start with your natural endowments or talents. Where do they come from? That keen mind, those winsome aspects of personality, that attractive appearance and gracious disposition, that smile that you possess—they all come from God. They have been designed for you by his sovereign decree and imparted to you by his providential working. But they are for *his* glory, not for yours. The Corinthians were a particularly vain people, boasting of their individual superiorities to other people. Paul called them arrogant. But he asked them, "Who makes you different from anyone else? What do you have that you did not receive? And if you did receive it, why do you boast as though you did not?" (1 Cor. 4:7).

You are no different. Therefore, glorify God.

Let's move to salvation. We have seen that the plan of salvation was conceived by God, that it was accomplished through the life and death of Jesus Christ, that its ultimate goal is God's glory. If that is so, and it is, you should abandon the arrogant assumption that getting saved was your idea or that it was accomplished by you, even in part, or that it is meant to honor you. It is not for your honor, but for God's glory.

Do you think God saved you because of any righteousness you possess or might one day acquire by your efforts? The Bible says, "He saved us,

not because of righteous things we had done, but because of his mercy"
(Titus 3:5).

Do you think it was because of some little germ of faith that God was able
to find in you but not in some other less deserving person? The Bible says, "It
is by grace you have been saved, through faith—and this not from yourselves,
it is the gift of God—not by works, so that no one can boast" (Eph. 2:8–9).

Have you had any longings after God? Do you want to pray? Do you find
that you want to read God's Word and come to understand it better? Do you
seek to worship God? Are you attracted to the company of other Christian
people? If those things are true of you, let me ask: Where do you think those
desires came from if not from God? They are not from you. You are sinful.
In yourself you have no aspirations after God. Holy desires come from a holy
God and are present in you through the working of his divine Spirit. They
are for his glory.

Therefore, glorify God. Praise him for them.

What about temptation? We live in a world in which sin and evil bombard
us and in which we are attacked even by the powers of evil themselves. What
keeps you from falling? What is it that enables you to stand your ground
against Satan's forces? It is God, God alone. The Bible says, ". . . God is faithful;
he will not let you be tempted beyond what you can bear. But when you are
tempted, he will also provide a way out so that you can stand up under it" (1
Cor. 10:13).

It is God who keeps you. Therefore, glorify God.

Finally, I ask you to think about your work, particularly your work for God
as a Christian. Perhaps you say, "Surely that at least belongs to me, is achieved
by me, and can be for my honor." Really? If in your unsaved state you had
no righteousness of your own, understood nothing of spiritual things, and
did not seek God (as Romans 3:10–11 tells us), how could you even have had
a desire to work for God unless God himself put it there? Our work for God
flows from our love of God. But "we love because he first loved us" (1 John
4:19). How can anything be achieved except through God? Even the ability
to plan a secular project or the strength to dig a ditch comes from him, since
all is from God. If that is true of even secular efforts, how much more true
must it be of Christian work? Spiritual work must be accomplished through
God's Spirit. So it is not you or I who stir up a revival, build a church, or convert even a single soul. Rather, it is as we work, being led in the work by God,
that God himself by the power of his Holy Spirit converts and sanctifies those
whom he chooses to call to faith.

Do not take the glory of God to yourself. It is fatal to do that in any work,
but especially in Christian work. Instead, glorify God.

I end with these words from Charles Spurgeon:

> "To whom be glory forever." This should be the single desire of the Christian.
> . . . He may desire to see his family well brought up, but only that "To God may

be glory forever." He may wish for prosperity in his business, but only so far as it may help him to promote this—"To whom be glory forever." He may desire to attain more gifts and more graces, but it should only be that "To him may be glory forever."

At my work behind the counter, or in the exchange, let me be looking out to see how I may glorify him. If I be walking in the fields, let my desire be that the trees may clap their hands in his praise. . . . Never be silent when there are opportunities, and you shall never be silent for want of opportunities. At night fall asleep still praising your God; as you close your eyes let your last thought be, "How sweet to rest upon the Savior's bosom!" In afflictions praise him; out of the fires let your song go up; on the sick-bed extol him; dying, let him have your sweetest notes. Let your shouts of victory in the combat with the last great enemy be all for him; and then when you have burst the bondage of mortality, and come into the freedom of immortal spirits, then, in a nobler, sweeter song, you shall sing unto his praise. Be this, then, your constant thought—"To him be glory forever."[5]

What is the chief end of man? The answer comes from *The Westminster Shorter Catechism:* "Man's chief end is to glorify God and to enjoy him forever."

---

5. Charles Haddon Spurgeon, "Laus Deo" in *Metropolitan Tabernacle Pulpit*, vol. 10 (Pasadena, Tex.: Pilgrim Publications, 1973), pp. 310, 311.

179

Soli Deo Gloria

Romans 11:36

To him be the glory forever! Amen.

The title of this study is not an exact translation of the second half of Romans 11:36, but I have selected it because it is the way the Protestant Reformers expressed what this verse is about and because the words, though in Latin, are well known. *Soli Deo Gloria* means "To God alone be the glory." *Soli Deo*—"to God alone." *Gloria*—"the glory." These words stand virtually as a motto of the Reformation.

The Reformers loved the word *solus* ("alone").

They wrote about *sola Scriptura*, which means "Scripture alone." Their concern in using this phrase was with authority, and what they meant to say by it was that the Bible alone is our ultimate authority—not the pope, not the church, not the traditions of the church or church councils, still less personal intimations or subjective feelings, but Scripture only. These other sources of authority are sometimes useful and may at times have a place, but Scripture is ultimate. Therefore, if any of these other authorities differ from Scripture, they are to be judged by the Bible and rejected, rather than the other way around.

The Reformers also talked about *sola fide,* meaning "faith alone." At this point they were concerned with the purity of the gospel, wanting to say that the believer is justified by God through faith entirely apart from any works he or she may have done or might do. Justification by faith alone became the chief doctrine of the Reformation.

The Reformers also spoke of *sola gratia,* which means "grace alone." Here they wanted to insist on the truth that sinners have no claim upon God, that God owes them nothing but punishment for their sins, and that, if he saves them in spite of their sins, which he does in the case of the elect, it is only because it pleases him to do so. They taught that salvation is by grace only.

There is a sense in which each of these phrases is contained in the great Latin motto *Soli Deo Gloria.* In Romans 11:36, it follows the words "for from him and through him and to him are all things," and it is because this is so, because all things really are "from him and through him and to him," that we say, "To God alone be the glory." Do we think about the Scripture? If it is from God, it has come to us through God's agency and it will endure forever to God's glory. Justification by faith? It is from God, through God, and to God's glory. Grace? Grace, too, has its source in God, comes to us through the work of the Son of God, and is to God's glory.

Many Christian organizations have taken these words as their motto or even as their name. I know of at least one publishing company today that is called *Soli Deo Gloria.* It is also an appropriate theme with which to end these studies of the third main (and last doctrinal) section of Paul's letter to the Romans. Indeed, what greater theme could there be? For what is true of all things—that they are "from" God, "through" God, and "to" God—is true also of glory. Glory was God's in the beginning, is God's now, and shall be God's forever. So we sing in what is called the *Gloria Patri.*

> Glory be to the Father, and to the Son
>   and to the Holy Ghost;
> As it was in the beginning, is now
>   and ever shall be:
> World without end. Amen.

Haldane's Revival

At the beginning of this series—in volume 1, chapter 2—177 studies ago, I mentioned a revival that took place in Geneva, Switzerland, under the leadership of a remarkable Scotsman named Robert Haldane (1764–1842). He was one of two brothers who were members of the Scottish aristocracy in the late eighteenth and early-nineteenth centuries. His brother, James Haldane (1768-1851), was a captain with the British East India Company. Robert was the owner of Gleneerie and other estates in Perthshire. When he was converted in the decade before 1800, Robert sold a major part of his lands and applied the proceeds to advancing the cause of Jesus Christ in Europe. James became an evangelist and later an influential pastor in Edinburgh, where he served for fifty-two years.

In the year 1815, Robert Haldane visited Geneva. One day when he was in a park reading his Bible, he got into a discussion with some young men who turned out to be theology students. They had not the faintest understanding of the gospel, so Haldane invited them to come to his rooms twice a week for Bible study. They studied Romans, and the result of those studies was the great *Exposition of Romans* by Haldane from which I so often quote.

All those students were converted and in time became leaders in church circles throughout Europe. One was Merle d'Aubigné, who became famous for his classic *History of the Reformation in the Sixteenth Century.* We know the first part of it as *The Life and Times of Martin Luther.*[1] Another of these men was Louis Gaussen, author of *Theopneustia,* a book on the inspiration of the Scriptures.[2] Others were Frédéric Monod, the chief architect and founder of the Free Churches in France; Bonifas, who became an important theologian; and César Malan, another distinguished leader. These men were so influential that the work of which they became a part was known as Haldane's Revival.

What was it that got through to these young men, lifting them out of the deadly liberalism of their day and transforming them into the powerful force they became? The answer is: the theme and wording of the very verses we have been studying, Romans 11:33–36. In other words, a proper understanding of God's sovereignty.

We know this because of a letter from Haldane to Monsieur Cheneviere, a pastor of the Swiss Reformed Church and Professor of Divinity at the University of Geneva. Cheneviere was an Arminian, as were all the Geneva faculty, but Haldane wrote to him to explain how appreciation of the greatness of God alone produced the changes in these men. Here is his explanation:

> There was nothing brought under the consideration of the students of divinity who attended me at Geneva which appeared to contribute so effectually to overthrow their false system of religion, founded on philosophy and vain deceit, as the sublime view of the majesty of God presented in the four concluding verses of this part of the epistle: Of him, and through him, and to him, are all things. Here God is described as his own last end in everything that he does.
>
> Judging of God as such an one as themselves, they were at first startled at the idea that he must love himself supremely, infinitely more than the whole universe, and consequently must prefer his own glory to everything besides. But when they were reminded that God in reality is infinitely more amiable and more valuable than the whole creation and that consequently, if he views

---

1. J. H. Merle D'Aubigné, *The Life and Times of Martin Luther,* trans. H. White (Chicago: Moody Press, 1958).

2. S. R. L. Gaussen, *Theopneustia: The Plenary Inspiration of the Holy Scripture* (Chicago: Moody Press, n.d.). Original edition 1840.

things as they really are, he must regard himself as infinitely worthy of being more valued and loved, they saw that this truth was incontrovertible.

Their attention was at the same time directed to numerous passages of Scripture, which assert that the manifestation of the glory of God is the great end of creation, that he has himself chiefly in view in all his works and dispensations, and that it is a purpose in which he requires that all his intelligent creatures should acquiesce, and seek and promote it as their first and paramount duty.[3]

A testimony like that leads me to suggest that the reason we do not see great periods of revival today is that the glory of God in all things has been largely forgotten by the contemporary church. It follows that we are not likely to see revival again until the truths that exalt and glorify God in salvation are recovered. Surely we cannot expect God to move among us greatly again until we can again truthfully say, "To him [alone] be the glory forever! Amen."

To Him Be the Glory

Romans 11:36 is the first doxology in the letter. But it is followed by another at the end, which is like it, though more complete: "To the only wise God be glory forever through Jesus Christ! Amen" (Rom. 16:27). It is significant that both doxologies speak of the glory of God, and that forever. Here are two questions to help us understand them.

1. *Who is to be glorified?*
The answer is: the sovereign God. For the most part, we start with man and man's needs. But Paul always started with God, and he ended with him, too. In fact, the letter to the Romans is so clearly focused on God that it can be outlined accurately in these terms. Donald Grey Barnhouse published ten volumes on Romans, and he reflected Paul's focus in the titles for these ten volumes, all but the first of which has God in the title. Volume one was *Man's Ruin*. But then came *God's Wrath, God's Remedy, God's River, God's Grace, God's Freedom, God's Heirs, God's Covenants, God's Discipline,* and *God's Glory*. We say with Paul, "To God be the glory forever! Amen."

2. *Why should God be glorified?*
The answer is that "from him and through him and to him are all things," particularly the work of salvation. *Why is man saved?* It is not because of anything in men and women themselves but because of God's grace. It is because God has elected us to it. God has predestinated his elect people to salvation from before the foundation of the world. *How is man saved?* The answer is by the redeeming work of the Lord Jesus, the very Son of God. We could not save ourselves, but God saved us through the vicarious, atoning death of Jesus

---

3. Robert Haldane, *An Exposition of the Epistle to the Romans* (MacDill AFB: MacDonald Publishing, 1958), p. 552.

Christ. *By what power are we brought to faith in Jesus?* The answer is by the power of the Holy Spirit through what theologians call effectual calling. God's call quickens us to new life. *How can we become holy?* Holiness is not something that originates in us, is achieved by us, or is sustained by us. It is due to God's joining us to Jesus so that we have become different persons than we were before he did it. We have died to sin and been made alive to righteousness. Now there is no direction for us to go in the Christian life but forward. *Where are we headed?* Answer: to heaven, because Jesus is preparing a place in heaven for us. *How can we be sure of arriving there?* It is because God, who began the work of our salvation, will continue it until we do. God never begins a work that he does not eventually bring to a happy and complete conclusion.

"To him be the glory forever! Amen."

The great Charles Hodge says of the verse we are studying;

> Such is the appropriate conclusion of the doctrinal portion of this wonderful epistle, in which more fully and clearly than in any other portion of the Word of God, the plan of salvation is presented and defended. Here are the doctrines of grace, doctrines on which the pious in all ages and nations have rested their hopes of heaven, though they may have had comparatively obscure intimations of their nature. The leading principle of all is that God is the source of all good, that in fallen man there is neither merit nor ability, that salvation, consequently, is all of grace, as well satisfaction as pardon, as well election as eternal glory. For of him, and through him, and to him, are all things; to whom be glory forever. Amen.[4]

So let us give God the glory, remembering that God himself says:

> I am the LORD; that is my name!
> I will not give my glory to another
> or my praise to idols.
>
> Isaiah 42:8

and

> For my own sake, for my own sake, I do this.
> How can I let myself be defamed?
> I will not yield my glory to another.
>
> Isaiah 48:11

People Who Give God Glory

What of the objections? What of those who object to the many imagined bad results of such God-directed teaching? Won't people become immoral,

---

4. Charles Hodge, *A Commentary on Romans* (Edinburgh and Carlisle, Pa.: The Banner of Truth Trust, 1972), pp. 379, 380. Original edition 1835.

since salvation, by this theory, is by grace rather than by works? Won't they lose the power of making choices and abandon all sense of responsibility before God and other people? Won't people cease to work for worthwhile goals and quit all useful activity? Isn't a philosophy that tries to glorify God in all things a catastrophe?

A number of years ago, Roger R. Nicole, professor of systematic theology at Gordon-Conwell Divinity School in South Hamilton, Massachusetts, and now at Reformed Theological Seminary in Orlando, Florida, answered such objections in a classic address for the Philadelphia Conference on Reformed Theology (1976), basing his words on an earlier remarkable address by Emile Doumergue, a pastor who for many years was dean of an evangelical seminary in southern France. Nicole's address was likewise titled "Soli Deo Gloria." The quotations below are from his answers to three important questions.[5]

1. *Doesn't belief in the sovereignty of God encourage evil by setting people free from restraints? Doesn't it make morality impossible?*

"I suppose one could proceed to discuss this in a theological manner—to examine arguments, consider objections, and line up points in an orderly disposition. I would like, however, instead of going into a theological discussion, to challenge you in terms of an historical consideration. In the Reformation, there was a group of men who made precisely these assertions. Over against the prevailing current, they said that man is radically corrupt and is therefore totally unable by himself to please God. He is incapable of gathering any merits, let alone merit for others. But did these assertions damage morality? Were these people a group of scoundrels who satisfied their own sinful cravings under the pretense of giving glory to God? One does not need to be very versed in church history to know that this was not so. There were at that time thefts, murders, unjust wars. Even within the church there was a heinous and shameful trafficking of sacred positions.

"But what happened?

"These people, who believed that man is corrupt and that only God can help him, came forward like a breath of fresh air. They brought in a new recognition of the rights of God and of his claim upon the lives of men. They brought in new chastity, new honesty, new unselfishness, new humbleness, and a new concern for others. "Honest like the Huguenots," they used to say. . . . Immorality was not promoted; it was checked by the recognition of the sovereignty of God.

"'That is impossible,' some say. Yet it happened."

2. *Doesn't belief in the sovereignty of God eliminate man's sense of responsibility and destroy human freedom? Doesn't it destroy potential?*

5. Roger R. Nicole, "Soli Deo Gloria" in James M. Boice, ed., *Our Sovereign God: Addresses Presented to the Philadelphia Conference on Reformed Theology, 1974–1976* (Grand Rapids: Baker Book House, 1977), pp. 171–175.

"Again, rather than going into the arguments of the matter, let us merely examine what happened in the sixteenth century when the sovereignty of God was asserted. Did the people involved allow themselves to be robbed of all initiative? Were they reduced to slavery under the power of God? Not at all! On the contrary, they were keenly aware of their responsibility. They had the sense that for everything they were doing, saying and thinking they were accountable to God. They lived their lives in the presence of God, and in the process they were pioneers in establishing and safe-guarding precious liberties—liberty of speech, religion and expression—all of which are at the foundation of the liberties we cherish in the democratic world.

"Far from eclipsing their sense of freedom, the true proclamation of the sovereignty of God moved them toward the recognition and expression of all kinds of human freedoms which God has himself provided for those whom he has created and redeemed.

"'It is impossible that this should happen,' we are told. Perhaps! But it happened."

3. *Doesn't commitment to God's sovereignty undercut strenuous human activity? Doesn't it make people passive?*

"We may make an appeal to history. What did these people—Calvin, Farel, Knox, Luther—what did they do? Were they people who reclined on a soft couch, saying, 'If God is pleased to do something in Geneva, let him do it. I will not get in his way'? Or, 'If God wants to have some theses nailed to the door of the chapel of Wittenberg Castle, let him take the hammer. I will not interfere'? You know very well that this is not so. These were not people lax in activity. They were not lazy. Calvin may be accused of many things, but one thing he has seldom been accused of is laziness. No, when the sovereignty of God is recognized, meaningfulness comes to human activity. Then, instead of seeing our efforts as the puny movements of insignificant people unable to resist the enormous momentum of a universe so much larger than ourselves, we see our activity in the perspective of a sovereign plan in which even small and insignificant details may be very important. Far from undermining activity, the doctrine of the sovereignty of God has been a strong incentive for labor, devotion, evangelism and missions.

"'Impossible!' Yet it happened."

God's Blessings for Our World

Nicole continues: "In the first century the world was in a frightful condition. One does not need to be a great authority on Roman history to know that. There were signs of the breakdown of the Roman Empire—rampant hedonism and a dissolution of morals. But at that point God was pleased to send into the world that great preacher of the sovereignty of God, the apostle Paul, and this introduced a brand new principle into the total structure. The preaching of Paul did not avert the collapse of the Roman Empire, but it postponed it. Moreover, it permitted the creation of a body of believers that persisted through the terrible invasions of the barbarian hordes, and even through the Dark Ages. . . .

"In the sixteenth century . . . the church had succumbed to deep corruption. It was corrupt 'in its head and members.' In many ways it was a cesspool of iniquity. People did not know how to remedy the situation. They tried councils, internal purges, monastic orders. None of these things seemed to work. But God again raised up to his glory men who proclaimed the truth of his sovereignty, the truth of God's grace. In proclaiming this truth they brought a multitude of the children of God into a new sense of their dependence upon and relationship to Christ. In proclaiming this truth they benefited even the very people who opposed them in the tradition of the church. They are small, these men of the Reformation. They had little money, little power and little influence. One was a portly little monk in Germany. Another was a frail little professor in Geneva. A third was a ruddy but lowly little man in Scotland. What could they do? In themselves, nothing. But by the power of God they shook the world.

> Radically corrupted, but sovereignly purified!
> Radically enslaved, but sovereignly emancipated!
> Radically unable, but sovereignly empowered!

"These men were the blessing of God for our world."

"To God alone be glory!" To those who do not know God that is perhaps the most foolish of all statements. But to those who do know God, to those who are being saved, it is not only a right statement, it is a happy, wise, true, inescapable, and highly desirable confession. It is our glory to make it. "To him be the glory forever! Amen."

Subject Index

Scripture Index